EPIC COLLEC

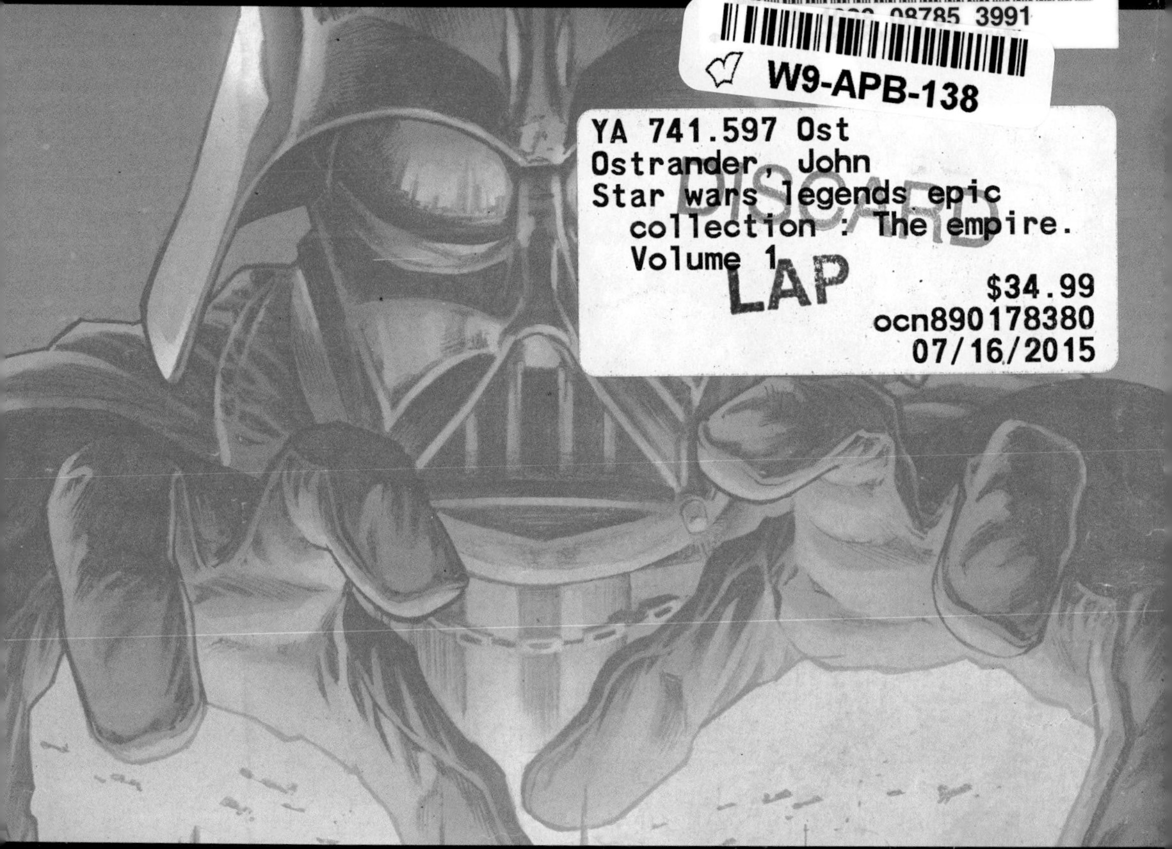

STAR WARS®

THE EMPIRE

VOLUME 1

STAR WARS: REPUBLIC #78-80, STAR WARS: PURGE, STAR WARS: PURGE — SECONDS TO DIE, STAR WARS: PURGE — THE HIDDEN BLADE, STAR WARS: PURGE — THE TYRANT'S FIST #1-2, STAR WARS: DARTH VADER AND THE LOST COMMAND #1-5 & STAR WARS: DARK TIMES #1-5

WRITERS:
JOHN OSTRANDER, RANDY STRADLEY, HADEN BLACKMAN & ALEXANDER FREED

PENCILERS:
LUKE ROSS, DOUGLAS WHEATLEY, JIM HALL, CHRIS SCALF, MARCO CASTIELLO, ANDREA CHELLA & RICK LEONARDI

INKERS:
LUKE ROSS, DOUGLAS WHEATLEY, CHRIS SCALF, MARCO CASTIELLO, ANDREA CHELLA & DAN GREEN WITH **ALEX LEI & MARK MCKENNA**

COLORISTS:
JASON KEITH, CHRIS CHUCKRY, RONDA PATTISON, CHRIS SCALF, MICHAEL ATIYEH & WES DZIOBA

LETTERERS:
MICHAEL DAVID THOMAS & MICHAEL HEISLER WITH **DAN JACKSON**

ASSISTANT EDITORS:
DAVE MARSHALL & FREDDYE LINS

ASSOCIATE EDITOR:
JEREMY BARLOW

EDITORS:
RANDY STRADLEY & DAVE MARSHALL

FRONT COVER ARTISTS:
LUKE ROSS & JASON KEITH

BACK COVER ARTISTS:
DOUGLAS WHEATLEY

COLLECTION EDITOR: MARK D. BEAZLEY
ASSISTANT MANAGING EDITOR: JOE HOCHSTEIN
ASSOCIATE MANAGING EDITOR: ALEX STARBUCK
EDITOR, SPECIAL PROJECTS: JENNIFER GRÜNWALD
SENIOR EDITOR, SPECIAL PROJECTS: JEFF YOUNGQUIST
RESEARCH: MIKE HANSEN
LAYOUT: JEPH YORK
PRODUCTION: RYAN DEVALL
BOOK DESIGNER: RODOLFO MURAGUCHI
SVP PRINT, SALES & MARKETING: DAVID GABRIEL

EDITOR IN CHIEF: AXEL ALONSO
CHIEF CREATIVE OFFICER: JOE QUESADA
PUBLISHER: DAN BUCKLEY
EXECUTIVE PRODUCER: ALAN FINE

SPECIAL THANKS TO JENNIFER HEDDLE & LUCASFILM, ANDY GROSSBERG, DEIDRE HANSEN, GREGORY HECHT, LANCE KREITER, SUSIE LEE, STUART MANN, STUART VANDAL & JEFF WATKINS OF CLOUD CITY COMICS

STAR WARS LEGENDS EPIC COLLECTION: THE EMPIRE VOL. 1. Contains material originally published in magazine form as STAR WARS: REPUBLIC #78-80, STAR WARS: PURGE, STAR WARS: PURGE — SECOND TO DIE, STAR WARS: PURGE — THE HIDDEN BLADE, STAR WARS: PURGE — THE TYRANT'S FIST #1-2, STAR WARS: DARTH VADER AND THE LOST COMMAND #1-5 and STAR WARS: DARK TIMES #1-5. Fir printing 2015. ISBN# 978-0-7851-9398-2. Published by MARVEL WORLDWIDE, INC., a subsidiary of MARVEL ENTERTAINMENT, LLC. OFFICE OF PUBLICATION: 135 West 50th Street, New York, NY 1002

Printed in the U.S.A. ALAN FINE, EVP - Office of the President, Marvel Worldwide, Inc. and EVP & CMO Marvel Characters B.V.; DAN BUCKLEY, Publisher President - Print, Animation & Digital Divisions; JOE QUESADA, Chief Creative Officer; TOM BREVOORT, SVP of Publishing; DAVID BOGART, SVP of Operations & Procurement, Publishing; C.B. CEBULSKI, SVP Creator & Content Development; DAVID GABRIEL, SVP Print, Sales & Marketing; JIM O'KEEFE, VP of Operations & Logistics; DAN CARR, Executive Director of Publishing Technology; SUSAN CRESPI, Editor Operations Manager; ALEX MORALES, Publishing Operations Manager; STAN LEE, Chairman Emeritus. For information regarding advertising in Marvel Comics or on Marvel.com, please contact Niza Disla, Direct of Marvel Partnerships, at ndisla@marvel.com. For Marvel subscription inquiries, please call 800-217-9158. **Manufactured between 2/18/2015 and 3/23/2015 by R.R. DONNELLEY, INC., SALEM, VA, US**

10 9 8 7 5 5 4 3 2 1

STAR WARS: REPUBLIC #78, SEPTEMBER 2005
"LOYALTIES"

8 *STAR WARS: REPUBLIC #79,* OCTOBER 2005
**"INTO THE UNKNOWN,
PART ONE OF TWO"**

1 *STAR WARS: REPUBLIC #80,* NOVEMBER 2005
**"INTO THE UNKNOWN,
PART TWO OF TWO"**

4 *STAR WARS: PURGE,* DECEMBER 2005

7 *STAR WARS: PURGE —
SECONDS TO DIE,* NOVEMBER 2009

20 *STAR WARS: PURGE —
THE HIDDEN BLADE,* APRIL 2010

43 *STAR WARS: PURGE —
THE TYRANT'S FIST #1,* DECEMBER 2012

66 *STAR WARS: PURGE —
THE TYRANT'S FIST #2,* JANUARY 2013

39 *STAR WARS: DARTH VADER AND THE
LOST COMMAND #1,* JANUARY 2011

13 *STAR WARS: DARTH VADER AND THE
LOST COMMAND #2,* FEBRUARY 2011

236 *STAR WARS: DARTH VADER AND THE
LOST COMMAND #3,* MARCH 2011

259 *STAR WARS: DARTH VADER AND THE
LOST COMMAND #4,* APRIL 2011

282 *STAR WARS: DARTH VADER AND
THE LOST COMMAND #5,* MAY 2011

305 *STAR WARS: DARK TIMES #1,* OCTOBER 2006
**"THE PATH TO NOWHERE,
PART 1 (OF FIVE)"**

328 *STAR WARS: DARK TIMES #2,* NOVEMBER 2006
**"THE PATH TO NOWHERE,
PART 2 (OF FIVE)"**

351 *STAR WARS: DARK TIMES #3,* MAY 2007
**"THE PATH TO NOWHERE,
PART 3 (OF FIVE)"**

374 *STAR WARS: DARK TIMES #4,* JULY 2007
**"THE PATH TO NOWHERE,
PART 4 (OF FIVE)"**

397 *STAR WARS: DARK TIMES #5,* OCTOBER 2007
**"THE PATH TO NOWHERE,
PART 5 (OF FIVE)"**

THE EMPIRE
Volume 1

Darkness has fallen on the galaxy. After a thousand generations, the Galactic Republic is no more, the culmination of a plan masterminded by the evil Dark Lords of the Sith. In its place stands the Galactic Empire, ruled by the fearsome Emperor Palpatine.

As a member of the Republic's Senate, Palpatine secretly orchestrated the Sith Order's plan to crush its hated enemies, the guardians of peace known as the Jedi. Elected Supreme Chancellor, Palpatine ensured that war throughout the galaxy would lead the Senate to declare him head of a new Empire to replace the corrupted Republic.

With the galaxy now ripe for conquest, the Emperor has become the most powerful Sith Lord of all and a master of the Dark Side of the Force, ordering the extermination of the Jedi Order with the aid of his apprentice, the deadly Darth Vader.

Vader was once a young Jedi named Anakin Skywalker, a hero of the Clone Wars convinced that he was destined for greatness. Anakin was manipulated by Palpatine into embracing his anger and fear and betraying the Jedi, in the process losing his limbs and his love, Padmé Amidala. His fall to the Dark Side complete, Anakin has become more machine than man, reborn as Darth Vader.

As Emperor Palpatine continues to increase his power and hold over the galaxy through his ever-growing armies of stormtroopers and the building of massive weapons of war, Darth Vader embraces the only purpose left to his existence: serving the will of the Emperor, his master. But his hatred of the Jedi remains strong....

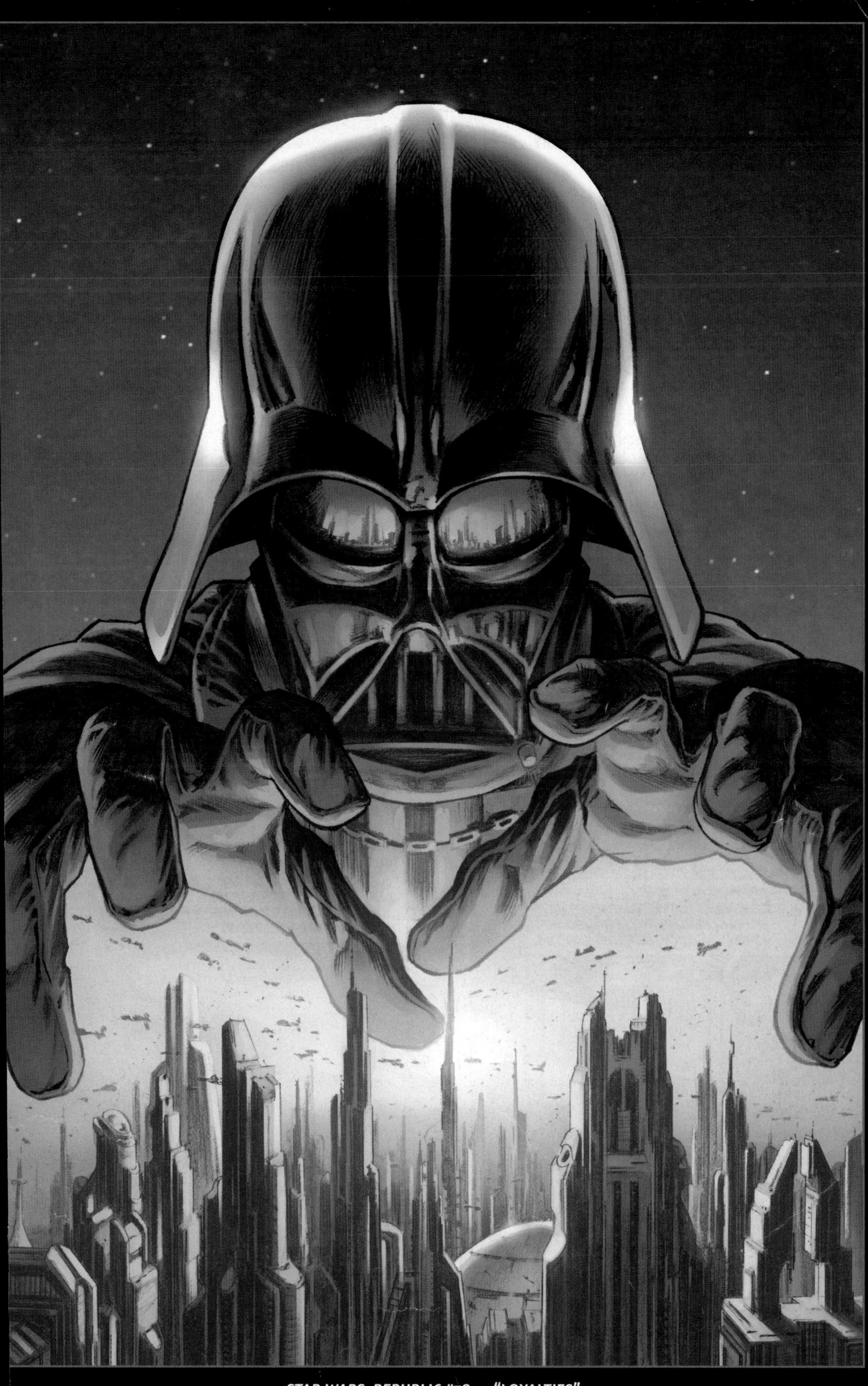

STAR WARS: REPUBLIC #78 — "LOYALTIES"

WRITER: JOHN OSTRANDER • ARTIST: LUKE ROSS • COLORIST: JASON KEITH • LETTERER: MICHAEL DAVID THOMAS • DESIGNER: DAVID NESTELLE
ASSISTANT EDITOR: DAVE MARSHALL • ASSOCIATE EDITOR: JEREMY BARLOW • EDITOR: RANDY STRADLEY • COVER ARTISTS: LUKE ROSS & JASON KEITH

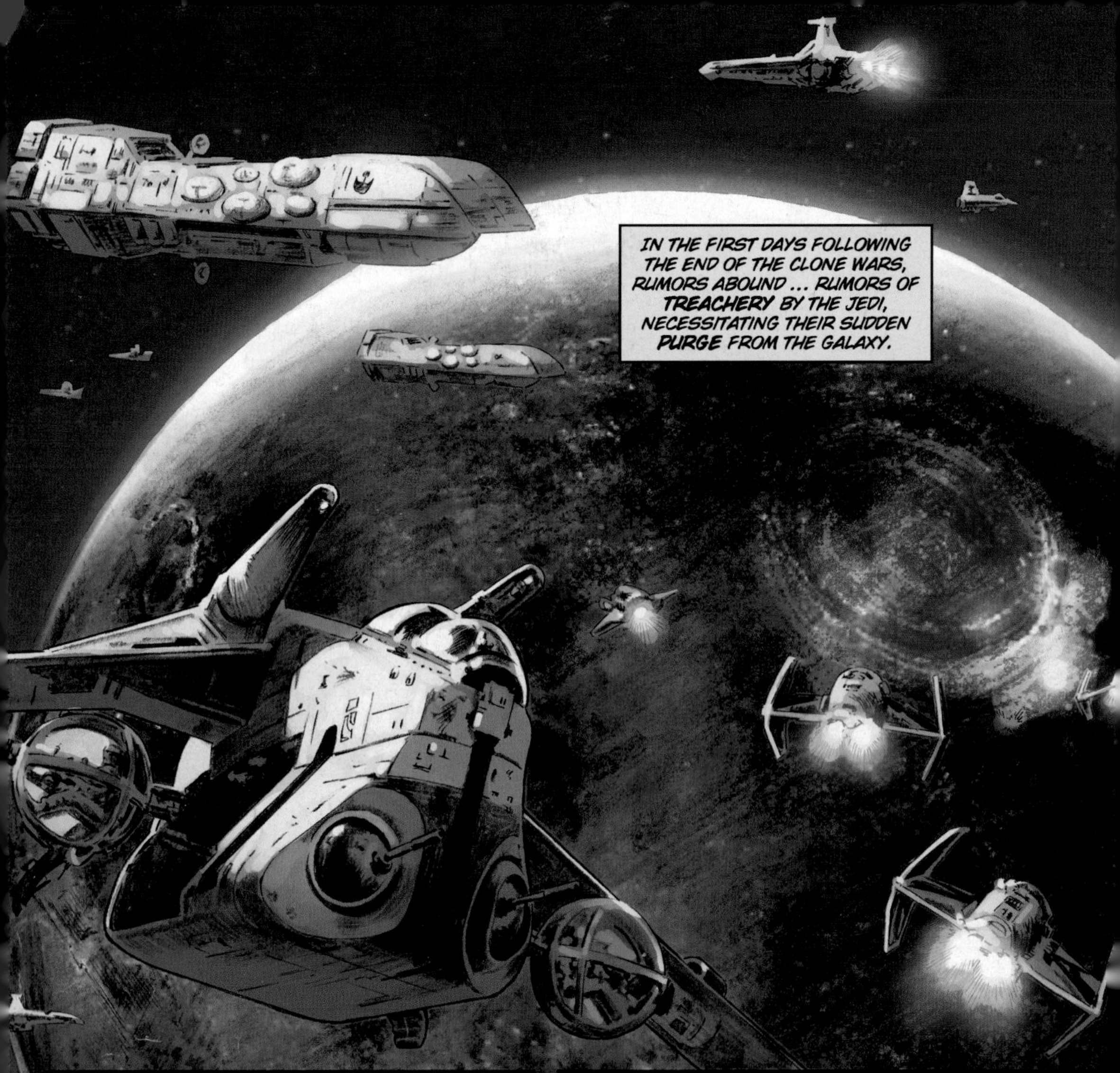
IN THE FIRST DAYS FOLLOWING THE END OF THE CLONE WARS, RUMORS ABOUND ... RUMORS OF TREACHERY BY THE JEDI, NECESSITATING THEIR SUDDEN PURGE FROM THE GALAXY.

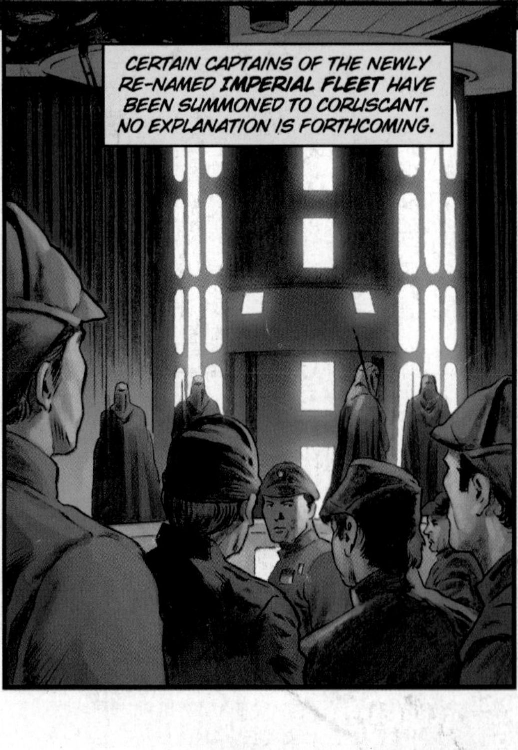
CERTAIN CAPTAINS OF THE NEWLY RE-NAMED IMPERIAL FLEET HAVE BEEN SUMMONED TO CORUSCANT. NO EXPLANATION IS FORTHCOMING.

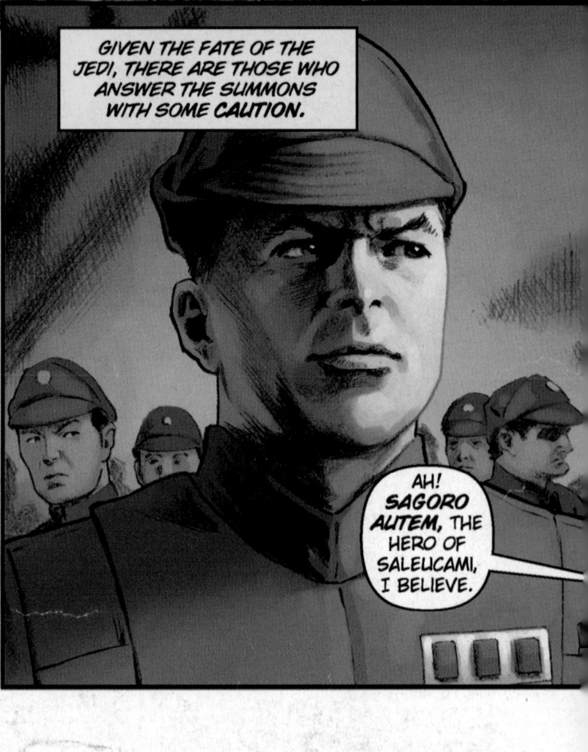
GIVEN THE FATE OF THE JEDI, THERE ARE THOSE WHO ANSWER THE SUMMONS WITH SOME CAUTION.
AH! SAGORO AUTEM, THE HERO OF SALEUCAMI, I BELIEVE.

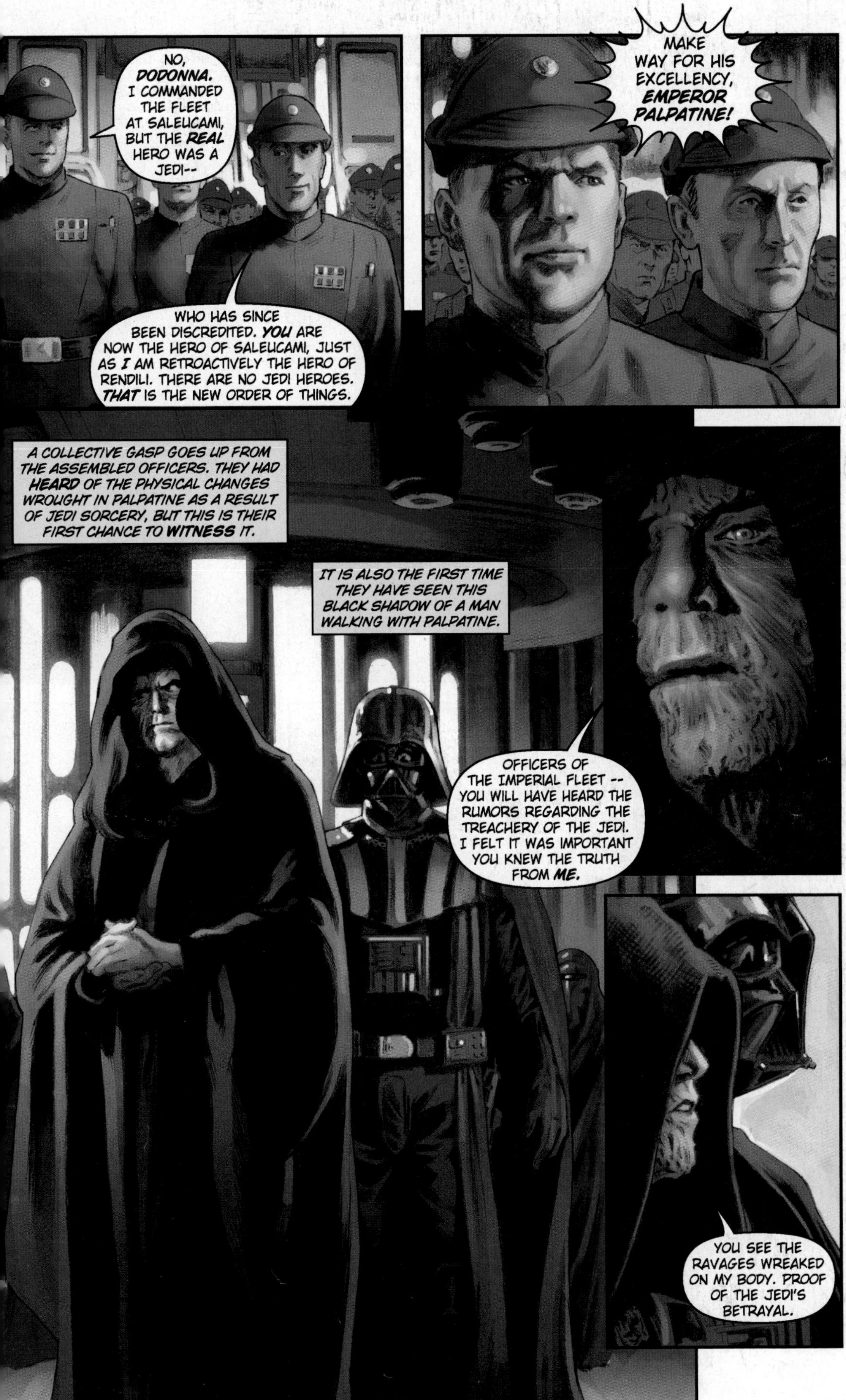

NO, DODONNA. I COMMANDED THE FLEET AT SALEUCAMI, BUT THE REAL HERO WAS A JEDI--
WHO HAS SINCE BEEN DISCREDITED. YOU ARE NOW THE HERO OF SALEUCAMI, JUST AS I AM RETROACTIVELY THE HERO OF RENDILI. THERE ARE NO JEDI HEROES. THAT IS THE NEW ORDER OF THINGS.
MAKE WAY FOR HIS EXCELLENCY, EMPEROR PALPATINE!
A COLLECTIVE GASP GOES UP FROM THE ASSEMBLED OFFICERS. THEY HAD HEARD OF THE PHYSICAL CHANGES WROUGHT IN PALPATINE AS A RESULT OF JEDI SORCERY, BUT THIS IS THEIR FIRST CHANCE TO WITNESS IT.
IT IS ALSO THE FIRST TIME THEY HAVE SEEN THIS BLACK SHADOW OF A MAN WALKING WITH PALPATINE.
OFFICERS OF THE IMPERIAL FLEET -- YOU WILL HAVE HEARD THE RUMORS REGARDING THE TREACHERY OF THE JEDI. I FELT IT WAS IMPORTANT YOU KNEW THE TRUTH FROM ME.
YOU SEE THE RAVAGES WREAKED ON MY BODY. PROOF OF THE JEDI'S BETRAYAL.

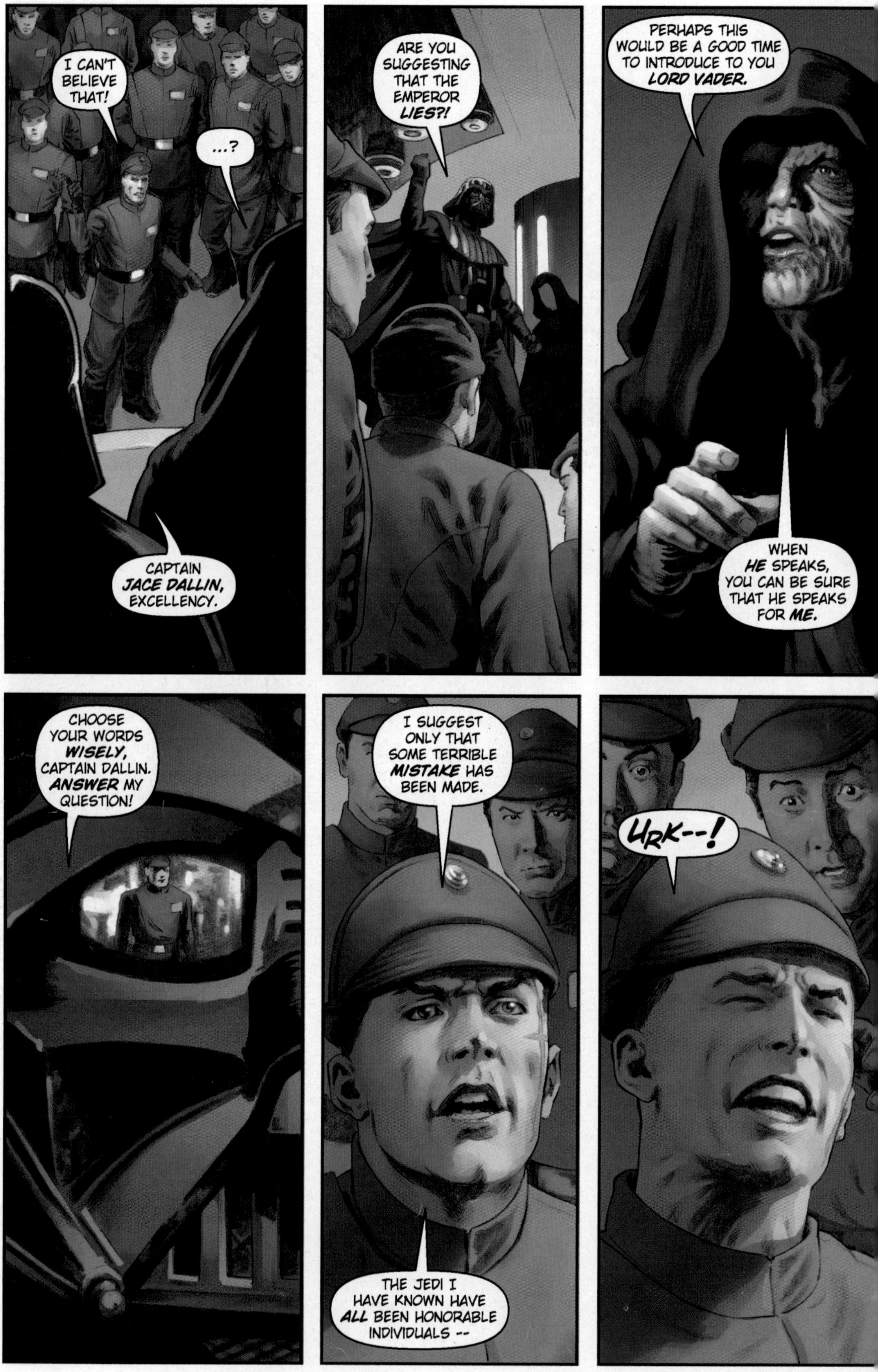
I CAN'T BELIEVE THAT!
...?
CAPTAIN JACE DALLIN, EXCELLENCY.
ARE YOU SUGGESTING THAT THE EMPEROR LIES?!
PERHAPS THIS WOULD BE A GOOD TIME TO INTRODUCE TO YOU LORD VADER.
WHEN HE SPEAKS, YOU CAN BE SURE THAT HE SPEAKS FOR ME.
CHOOSE YOUR WORDS WISELY, CAPTAIN DALLIN. ANSWER MY QUESTION!
I SUGGEST ONLY THAT SOME TERRIBLE MISTAKE HAS BEEN MADE.
THE JEDI I HAVE KNOWN HAVE ALL BEEN HONORABLE INDIVIDUALS --
URK--!

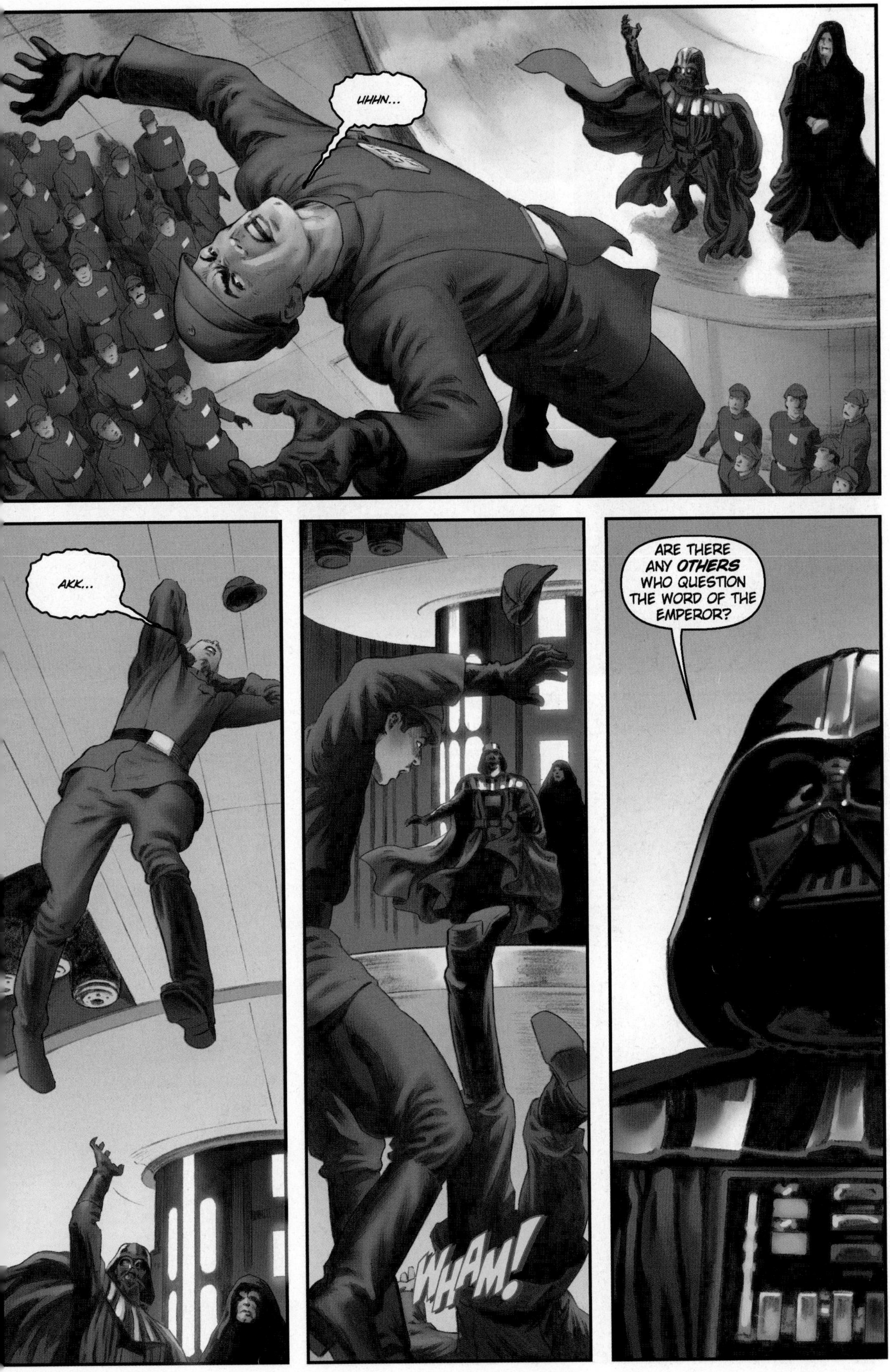
UHHN...
AKK...
WHAM!
ARE THERE ANY OTHERS WHO QUESTION THE WORD OF THE EMPEROR?

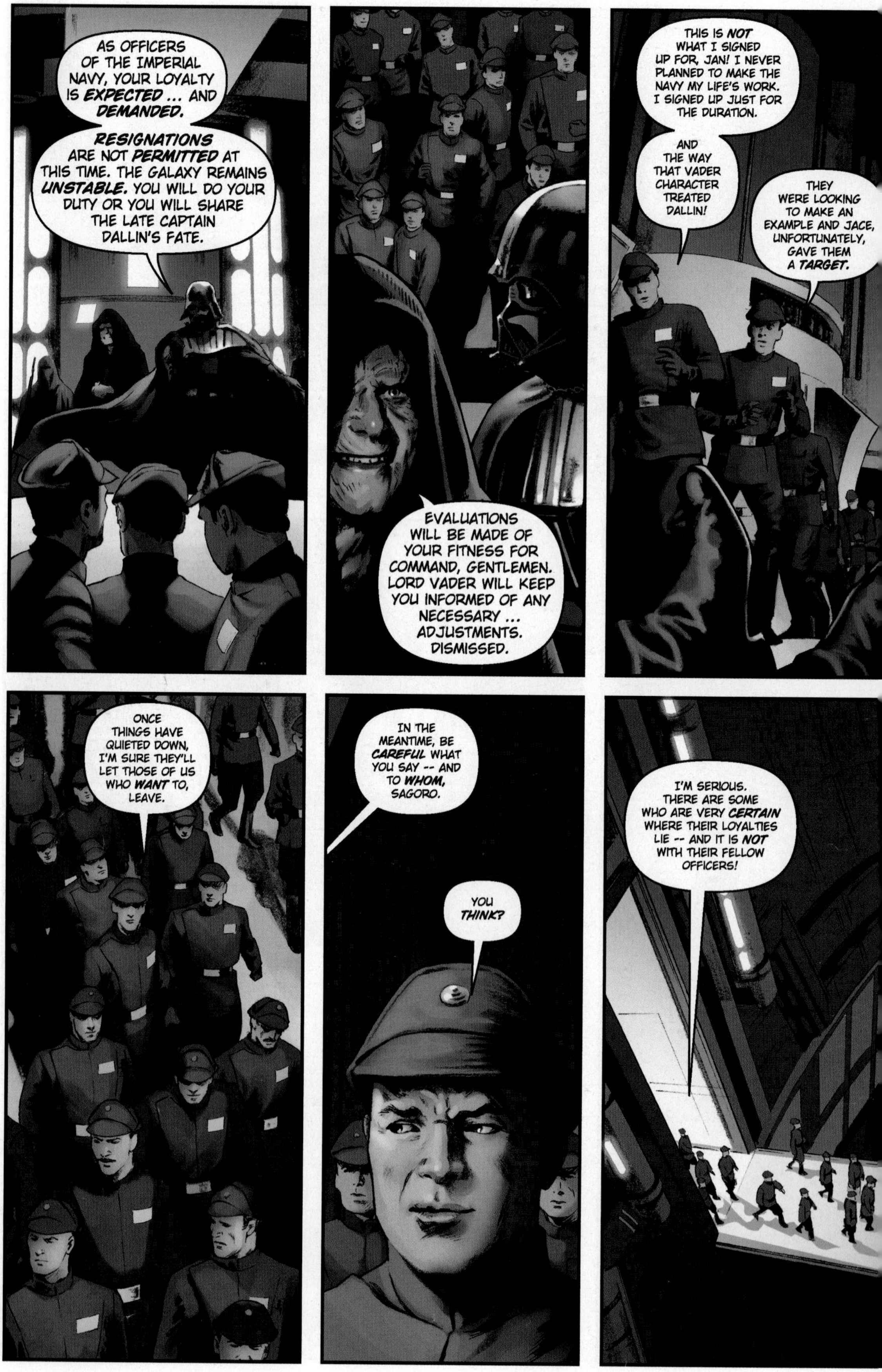
AS OFFICERS OF THE IMPERIAL NAVY, YOUR LOYALTY IS EXPECTED ... AND DEMANDED.
RESIGNATIONS ARE NOT PERMITTED AT THIS TIME. THE GALAXY REMAINS UNSTABLE. YOU WILL DO YOUR DUTY OR YOU WILL SHARE THE LATE CAPTAIN DALLIN'S FATE.
EVALUATIONS WILL BE MADE OF YOUR FITNESS FOR COMMAND, GENTLEMEN. LORD VADER WILL KEEP YOU INFORMED OF ANY NECESSARY ... ADJUSTMENTS. DISMISSED.
THIS IS NOT WHAT I SIGNED UP FOR, JAN! I NEVER PLANNED TO MAKE THE NAVY MY LIFE'S WORK. I SIGNED UP JUST FOR THE DURATION.
AND THE WAY THAT VADER CHARACTER TREATED DALLIN!
THEY WERE LOOKING TO MAKE AN EXAMPLE AND JACE, UNFORTUNATELY, GAVE THEM A TARGET.
ONCE THINGS HAVE QUIETED DOWN, I'M SURE THEY'LL LET THOSE OF US WHO WANT TO, LEAVE.
IN THE MEANTIME, BE CAREFUL WHAT YOU SAY -- AND TO WHOM, SAGORO.
YOU THINK?
I'M SERIOUS. THERE ARE SOME WHO ARE VERY CERTAIN WHERE THEIR LOYALTIES LIE -- AND IT IS NOT WITH THEIR FELLOW OFFICERS!

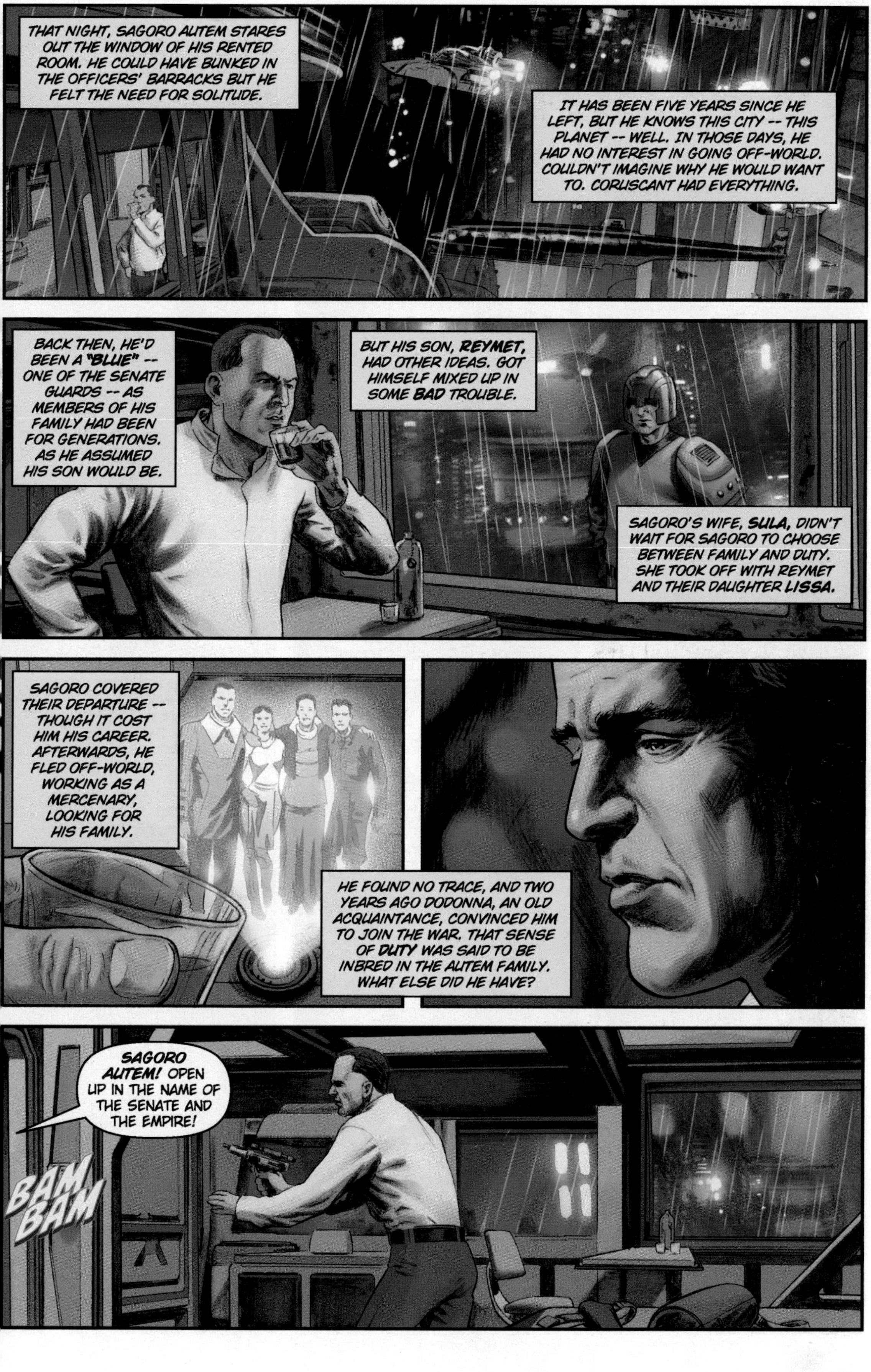

THAT NIGHT, SAGORO AUTEM STARES OUT THE WINDOW OF HIS RENTED ROOM. HE COULD HAVE BUNKED IN THE OFFICERS' BARRACKS BUT HE FELT THE NEED FOR SOLITUDE.
IT HAS BEEN FIVE YEARS SINCE HE LEFT, BUT HE KNOWS THIS CITY -- THIS PLANET -- WELL. IN THOSE DAYS, HE HAD NO INTEREST IN GOING OFF-WORLD. COULDN'T IMAGINE WHY HE WOULD WANT TO. CORUSCANT HAD EVERYTHING.
BACK THEN, HE'D BEEN A "BLUE" -- ONE OF THE SENATE GUARDS -- AS MEMBERS OF HIS FAMILY HAD BEEN FOR GENERATIONS. AS HE ASSUMED HIS SON WOULD BE.
BUT HIS SON, REYMET, HAD OTHER IDEAS. GOT HIMSELF MIXED UP IN SOME BAD TROUBLE.
SAGORO'S WIFE, SULA, DIDN'T WAIT FOR SAGORO TO CHOOSE BETWEEN FAMILY AND DUTY. SHE TOOK OFF WITH REYMET AND THEIR DAUGHTER LISSA.
SAGORO COVERED THEIR DEPARTURE -- THOUGH IT COST HIM HIS CAREER. AFTERWARDS, HE FLED OFF-WORLD, WORKING AS A MERCENARY, LOOKING FOR HIS FAMILY.
HE FOUND NO TRACE, AND TWO YEARS AGO DODONNA, AN OLD ACQUAINTANCE, CONVINCED HIM TO JOIN THE WAR. THAT SENSE OF DUTY WAS SAID TO BE INBRED IN THE AUTEM FAMILY. WHAT ELSE DID HE HAVE?
SAGORO AUTEM! OPEN UP IN THE NAME OF THE SENATE AND THE EMPIRE!
BAM BAM

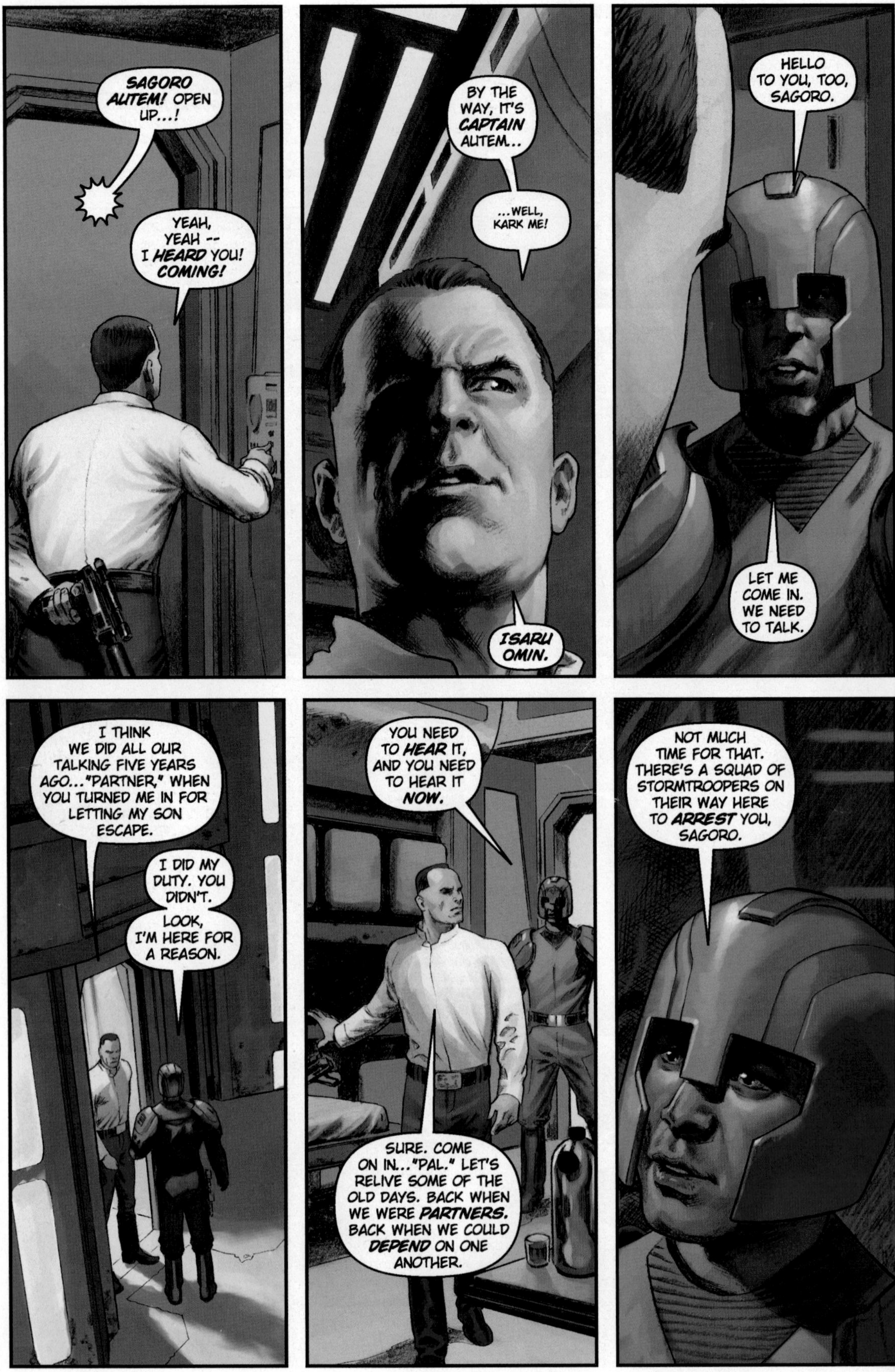
SAGORO AUTEM! OPEN UP...!
YEAH, YEAH -- I HEARD YOU! COMING!
BY THE WAY, IT'S CAPTAIN AUTEM...
...WELL, KARK ME!
ISARU OMIN.
HELLO TO YOU, TOO, SAGORO.
LET ME COME IN. WE NEED TO TALK.
I THINK WE DID ALL OUR TALKING FIVE YEARS AGO..."PARTNER," WHEN YOU TURNED ME IN FOR LETTING MY SON ESCAPE.
I DID MY DUTY. YOU DIDN'T.
LOOK, I'M HERE FOR A REASON.
YOU NEED TO HEAR IT, AND YOU NEED TO HEAR IT NOW.
SURE. COME ON IN..."PAL." LET'S RELIVE SOME OF THE OLD DAYS. BACK WHEN WE WERE PARTNERS. BACK WHEN WE COULD DEPEND ON ONE ANOTHER.
NOT MUCH TIME FOR THAT. THERE'S A SQUAD OF STORMTROOPERS ON THEIR WAY HERE TO ARREST YOU, SAGORO.

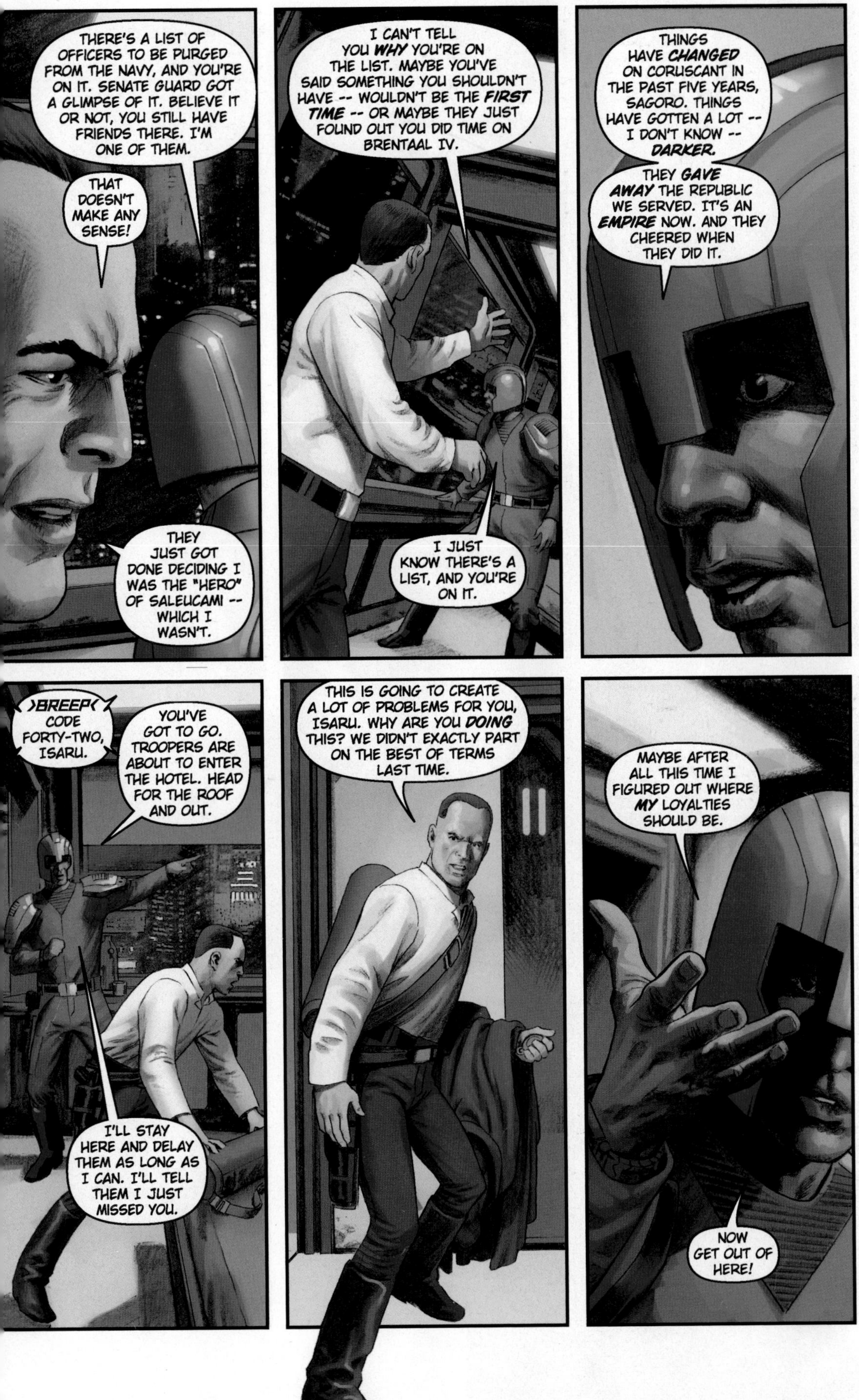
THERE'S A LIST OF OFFICERS TO BE PURGED FROM THE NAVY, AND YOU'RE ON IT. SENATE GUARD GOT A GLIMPSE OF IT. BELIEVE IT OR NOT, YOU STILL HAVE FRIENDS THERE. I'M ONE OF THEM.
THAT DOESN'T MAKE ANY SENSE!
THEY JUST GOT DONE DECIDING I WAS THE "HERO" OF SALEUCAMI -- WHICH I WASN'T.
I CAN'T TELL YOU WHY YOU'RE ON THE LIST. MAYBE YOU'VE SAID SOMETHING YOU SHOULDN'T HAVE -- WOULDN'T BE THE FIRST TIME -- OR MAYBE THEY JUST FOUND OUT YOU DID TIME ON BRENTAAL IV.
I JUST KNOW THERE'S A LIST, AND YOU'RE ON IT.
THINGS HAVE CHANGED ON CORUSCANT IN THE PAST FIVE YEARS, SAGORO. THINGS HAVE GOTTEN A LOT -- I DON'T KNOW -- DARKER.
THEY GAVE AWAY THE REPUBLIC WE SERVED. IT'S AN EMPIRE NOW. AND THEY CHEERED WHEN THEY DID IT.
>BREEP< CODE FORTY-TWO, ISARU.
YOU'VE GOT TO GO. TROOPERS ARE ABOUT TO ENTER THE HOTEL. HEAD FOR THE ROOF AND OUT.
I'LL STAY HERE AND DELAY THEM AS LONG AS I CAN. I'LL TELL THEM I JUST MISSED YOU.
THIS IS GOING TO CREATE A LOT OF PROBLEMS FOR YOU, ISARU. WHY ARE YOU DOING THIS? WE DIDN'T EXACTLY PART ON THE BEST OF TERMS LAST TIME.
MAYBE AFTER ALL THIS TIME I FIGURED OUT WHERE MY LOYALTIES SHOULD BE.
NOW GET OUT OF HERE!

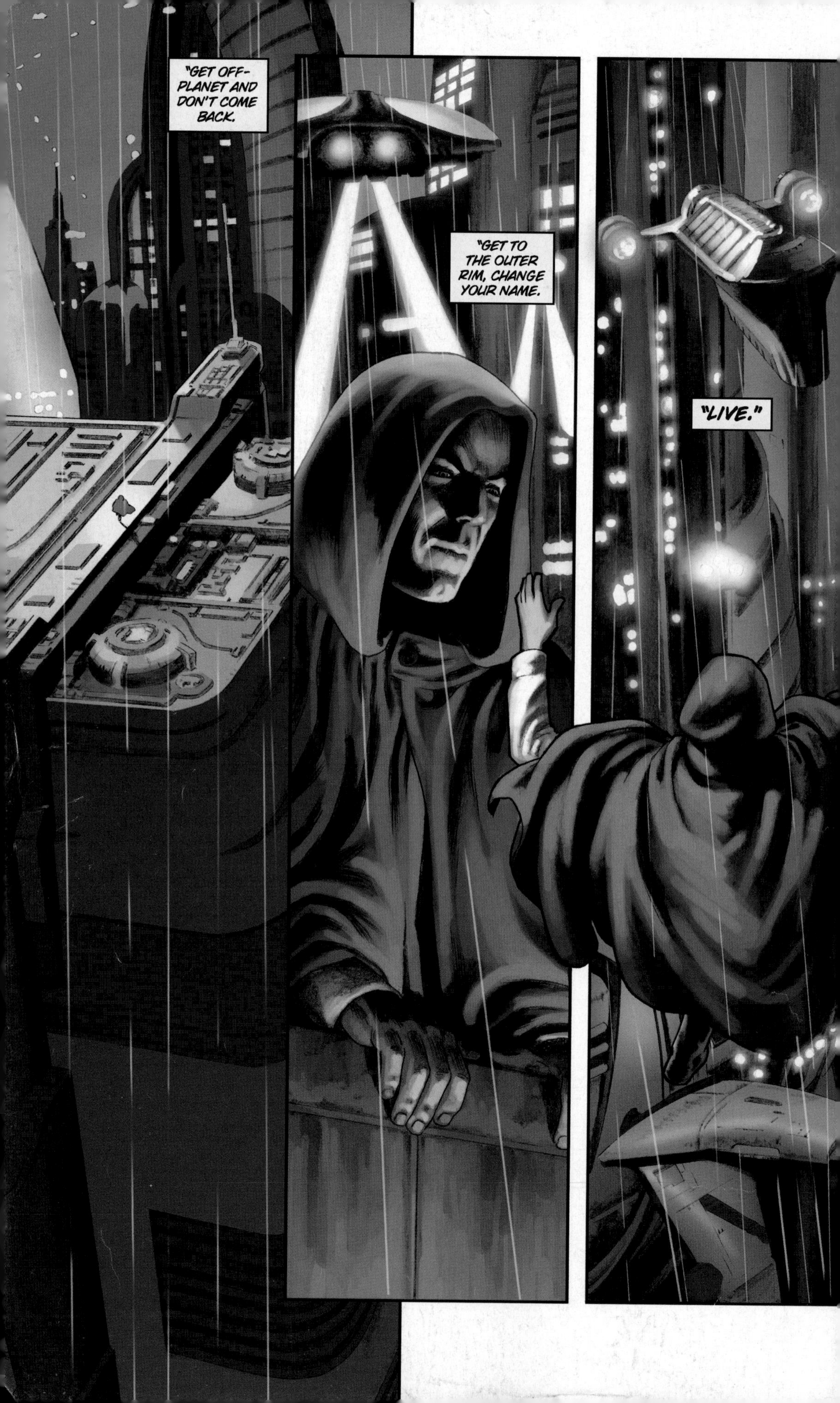
"GET OFF-PLANET AND DON'T COME BACK.
"GET TO THE OUTER RIM, CHANGE YOUR NAME.
"LIVE."

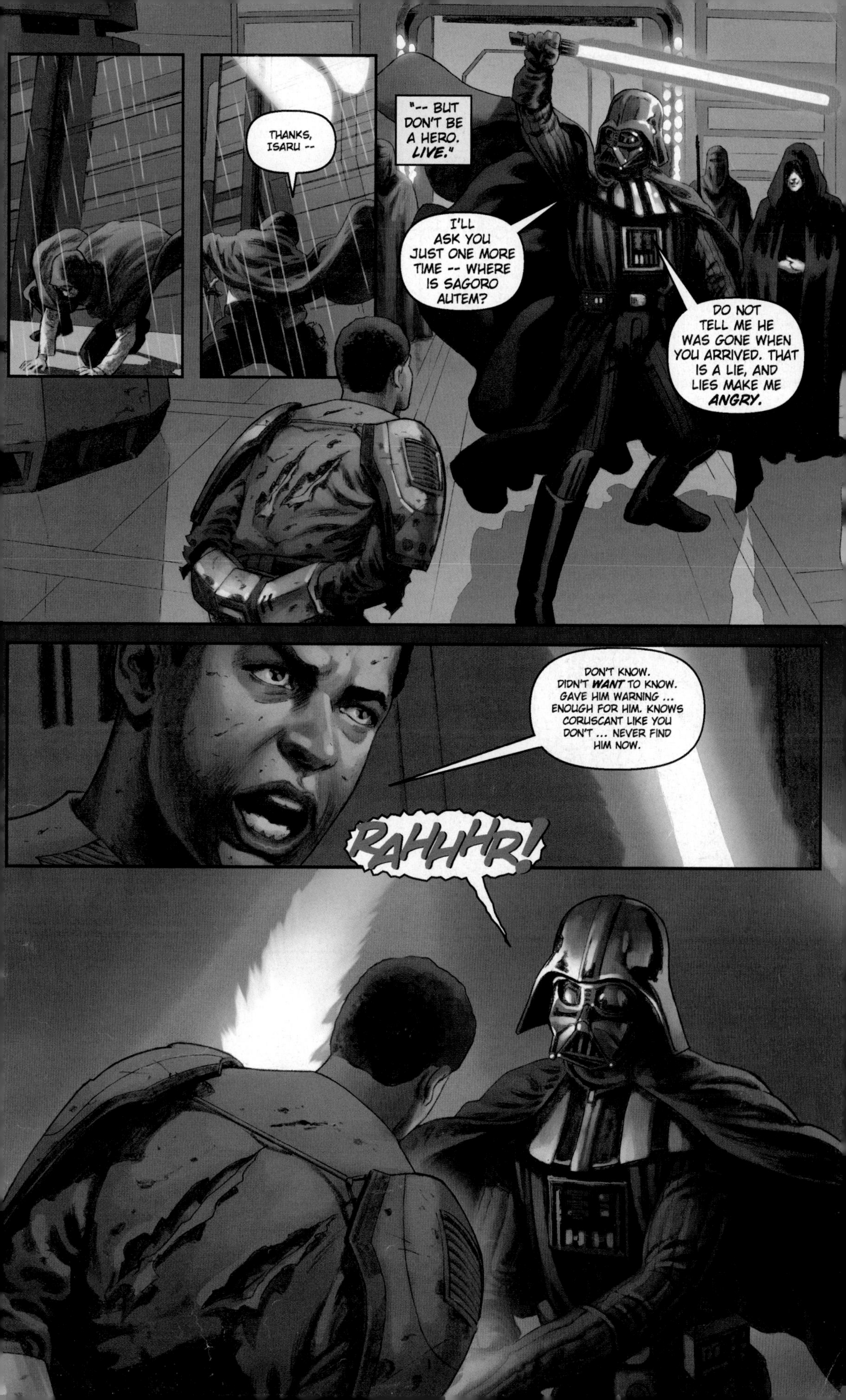
THANKS, ISARU --
"-- BUT DON'T BE A HERO. *LIVE.*"
I'LL ASK YOU JUST ONE MORE TIME -- WHERE IS SAGORO AUTEM?
DO NOT TELL ME HE WAS GONE WHEN YOU ARRIVED. THAT IS A LIE, AND LIES MAKE ME *ANGRY.*
DON'T KNOW. DIDN'T *WANT* TO KNOW. GAVE HIM WARNING ... ENOUGH FOR HIM. KNOWS CORUSCANT LIKE YOU DON'T ... NEVER FIND HIM NOW.
RAHHHR!

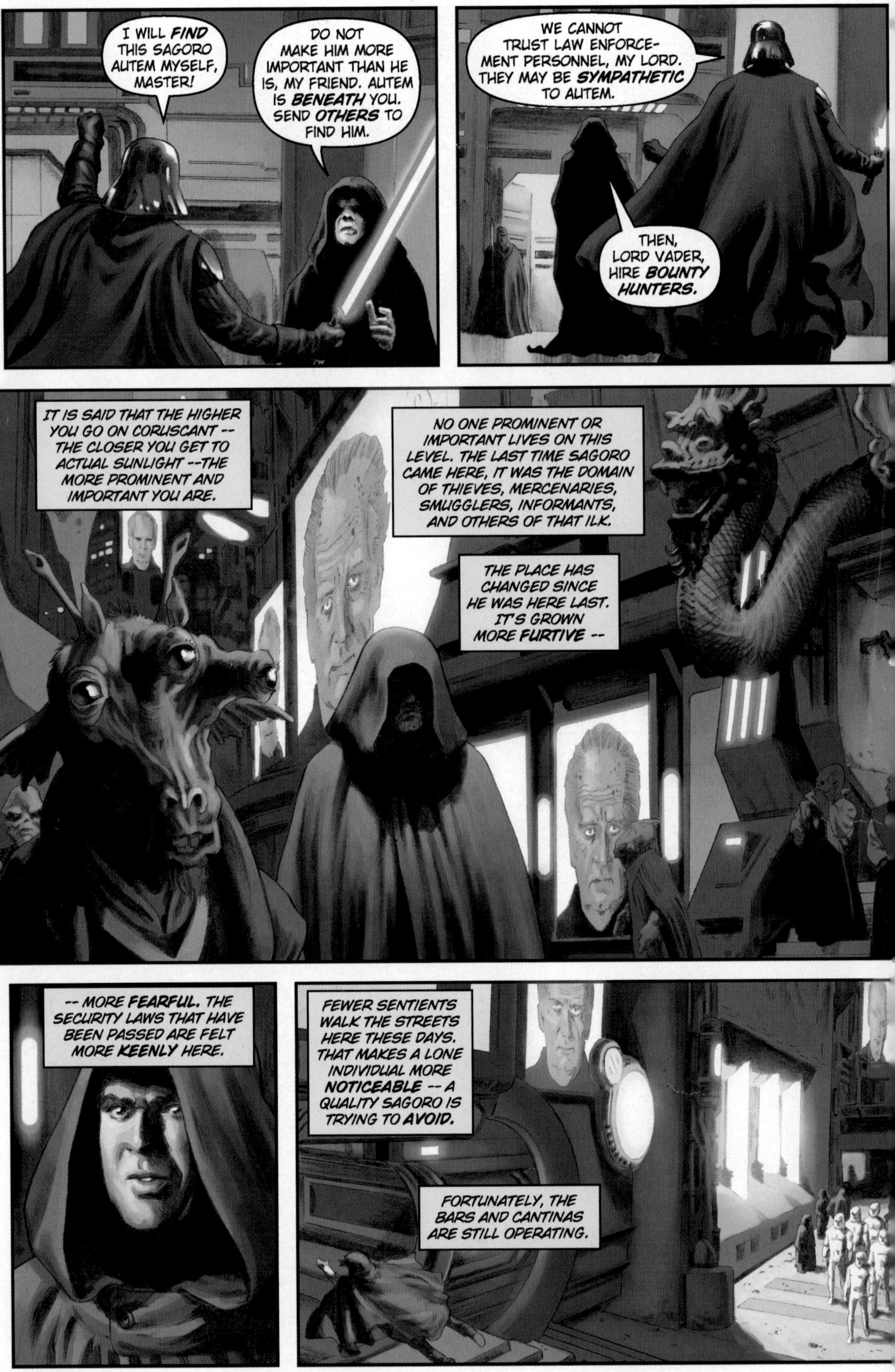
I WILL FIND THIS SAGORO AUTEM MYSELF, MASTER!
DO NOT MAKE HIM MORE IMPORTANT THAN HE IS, MY FRIEND. AUTEM IS BENEATH YOU. SEND OTHERS TO FIND HIM.
WE CANNOT TRUST LAW ENFORCEMENT PERSONNEL, MY LORD. THEY MAY BE SYMPATHETIC TO AUTEM.
THEN, LORD VADER, HIRE BOUNTY HUNTERS.
IT IS SAID THAT THE HIGHER YOU GO ON CORUSCANT -- THE CLOSER YOU GET TO ACTUAL SUNLIGHT --THE MORE PROMINENT AND IMPORTANT YOU ARE.
NO ONE PROMINENT OR IMPORTANT LIVES ON THIS LEVEL. THE LAST TIME SAGORO CAME HERE, IT WAS THE DOMAIN OF THIEVES, MERCENARIES, SMUGGLERS, INFORMANTS, AND OTHERS OF THAT ILK.
THE PLACE HAS CHANGED SINCE HE WAS HERE LAST. IT'S GROWN MORE FURTIVE --
-- MORE FEARFUL. THE SECURITY LAWS THAT HAVE BEEN PASSED ARE FELT MORE KEENLY HERE.
FEWER SENTIENTS WALK THE STREETS HERE THESE DAYS. THAT MAKES A LONE INDIVIDUAL MORE NOTICEABLE -- A QUALITY SAGORO IS TRYING TO AVOID.
FORTUNATELY, THE BARS AND CANTINAS ARE STILL OPERATING.

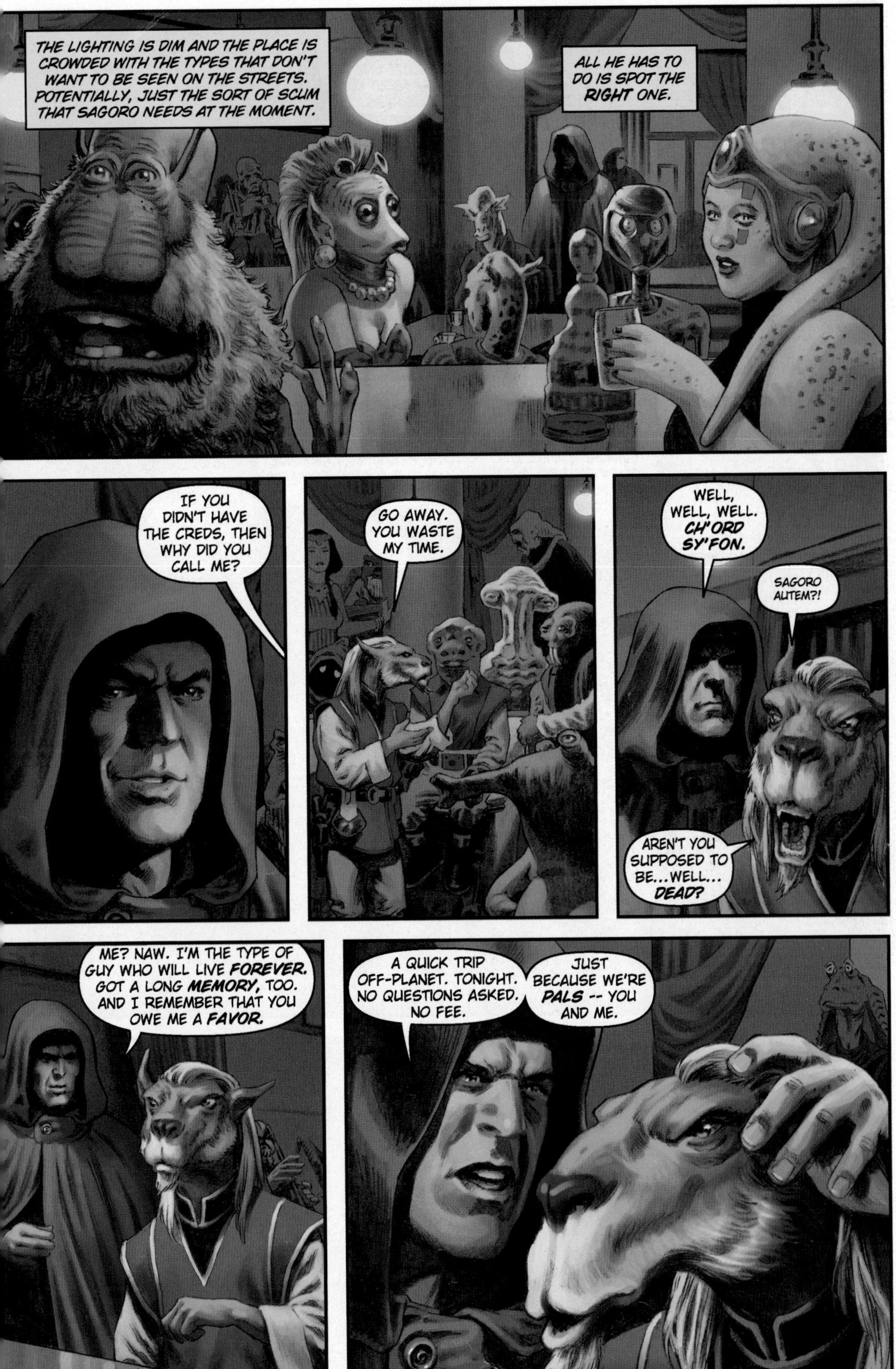
THE LIGHTING IS DIM AND THE PLACE IS CROWDED WITH THE TYPES THAT DON'T WANT TO BE SEEN ON THE STREETS. POTENTIALLY, JUST THE SORT OF SCUM THAT SAGORO NEEDS AT THE MOMENT.
ALL HE HAS TO DO IS SPOT THE RIGHT ONE.
IF YOU DIDN'T HAVE THE CREDS, THEN WHY DID YOU CALL ME?
GO AWAY. YOU WASTE MY TIME.
WELL, WELL, WELL. CH'ORD SY'FON.
SAGORO AUTEM?!
AREN'T YOU SUPPOSED TO BE...WELL... DEAD?
ME? NAW. I'M THE TYPE OF GUY WHO WILL LIVE FOREVER. GOT A LONG MEMORY, TOO. AND I REMEMBER THAT YOU OWE ME A FAVOR.
A QUICK TRIP OFF-PLANET. TONIGHT. NO QUESTIONS ASKED. NO FEE.
JUST BECAUSE WE'RE PALS -- YOU AND ME.

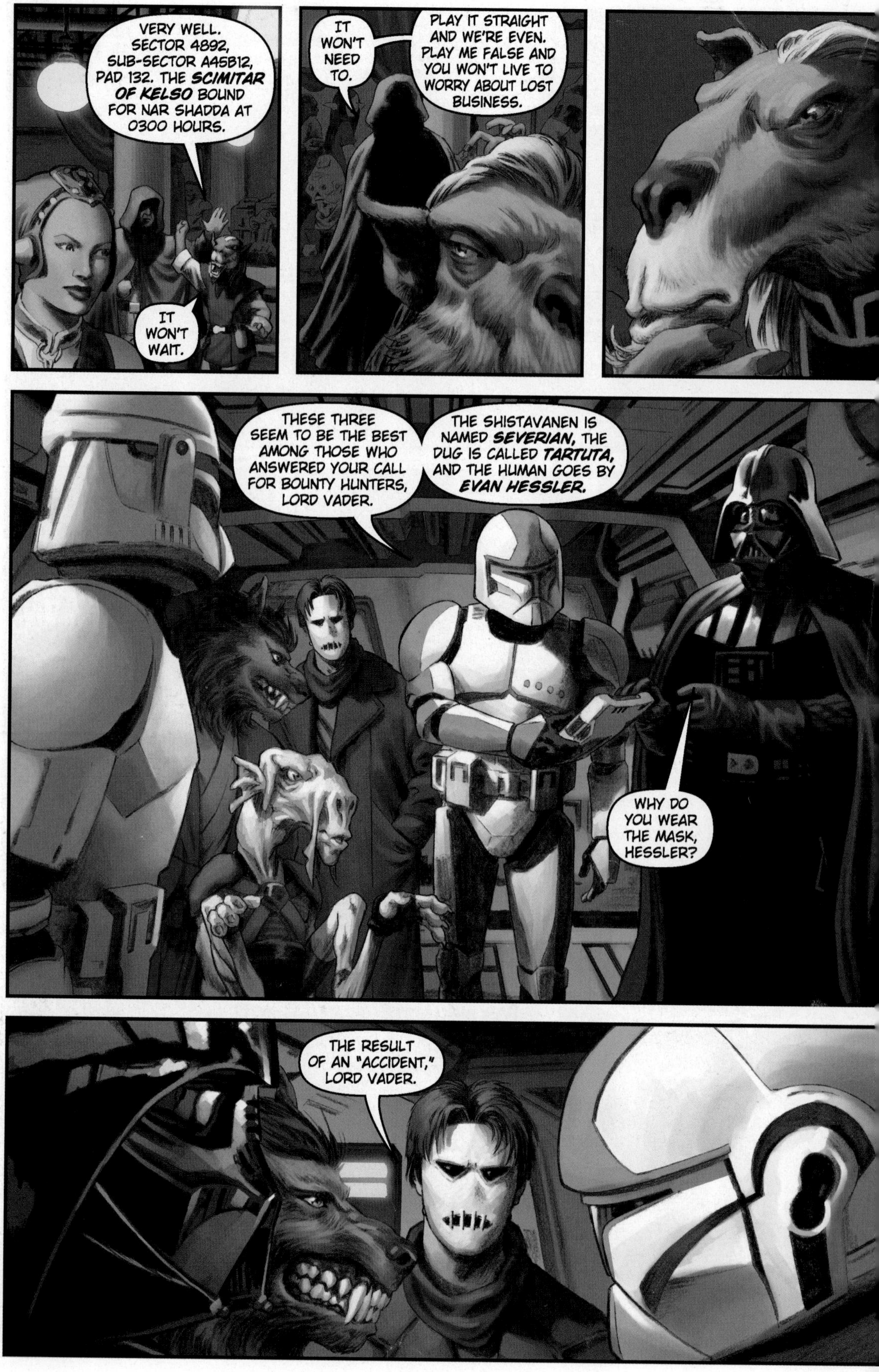
VERY WELL. SECTOR 4892, SUB-SECTOR A45B12, PAD 132. THE SCIMITAR OF KELSO BOUND FOR NAR SHADDA AT 0300 HOURS.
IT WON'T WAIT.
IT WON'T NEED TO.
PLAY IT STRAIGHT AND WE'RE EVEN. PLAY ME FALSE AND YOU WON'T LIVE TO WORRY ABOUT LOST BUSINESS.
THESE THREE SEEM TO BE THE BEST AMONG THOSE WHO ANSWERED YOUR CALL FOR BOUNTY HUNTERS, LORD VADER.
THE SHISTAVANEN IS NAMED SEVERIAN, THE DUG IS CALLED TARTUTA, AND THE HUMAN GOES BY EVAN HESSLER.
WHY DO YOU WEAR THE MASK, HESSLER?
THE RESULT OF AN "ACCIDENT," LORD VADER.

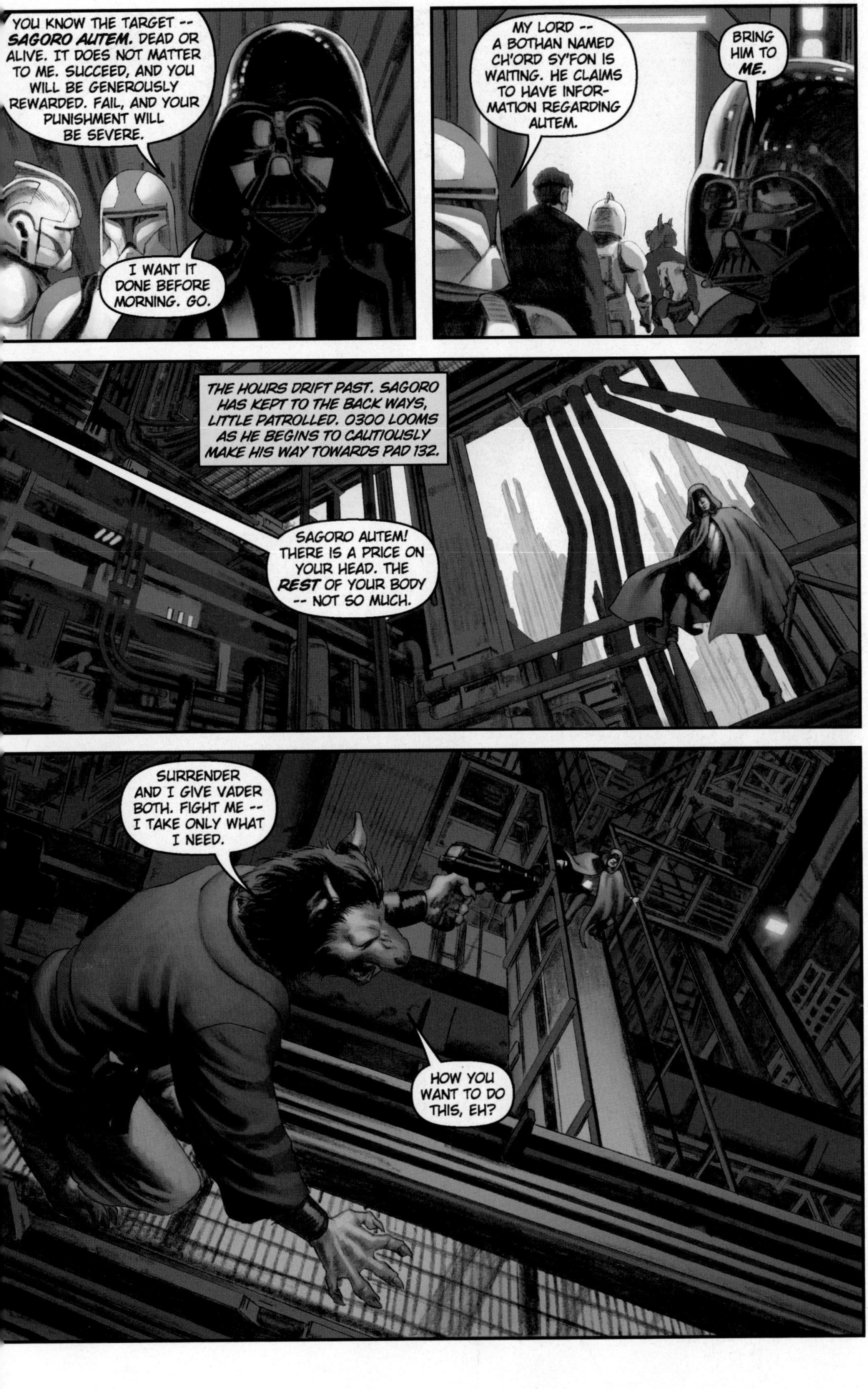
YOU KNOW THE TARGET -- SAGORO AUTEM. DEAD OR ALIVE. IT DOES NOT MATTER TO ME. SUCCEED, AND YOU WILL BE GENEROUSLY REWARDED. FAIL, AND YOUR PUNISHMENT WILL BE SEVERE.
I WANT IT DONE BEFORE MORNING. GO.
MY LORD -- A BOTHAN NAMED CH'ORD SY'FON IS WAITING. HE CLAIMS TO HAVE INFORMATION REGARDING AUTEM.
BRING HIM TO ME.
THE HOURS DRIFT PAST. SAGORO HAS KEPT TO THE BACK WAYS, LITTLE PATROLLED. 0300 LOOMS AS HE BEGINS TO CAUTIOUSLY MAKE HIS WAY TOWARDS PAD 132.
SAGORO AUTEM! THERE IS A PRICE ON YOUR HEAD. THE REST OF YOUR BODY -- NOT SO MUCH.
SURRENDER AND I GIVE VADER BOTH. FIGHT ME -- I TAKE ONLY WHAT I NEED.
HOW YOU WANT TO DO THIS, EH?

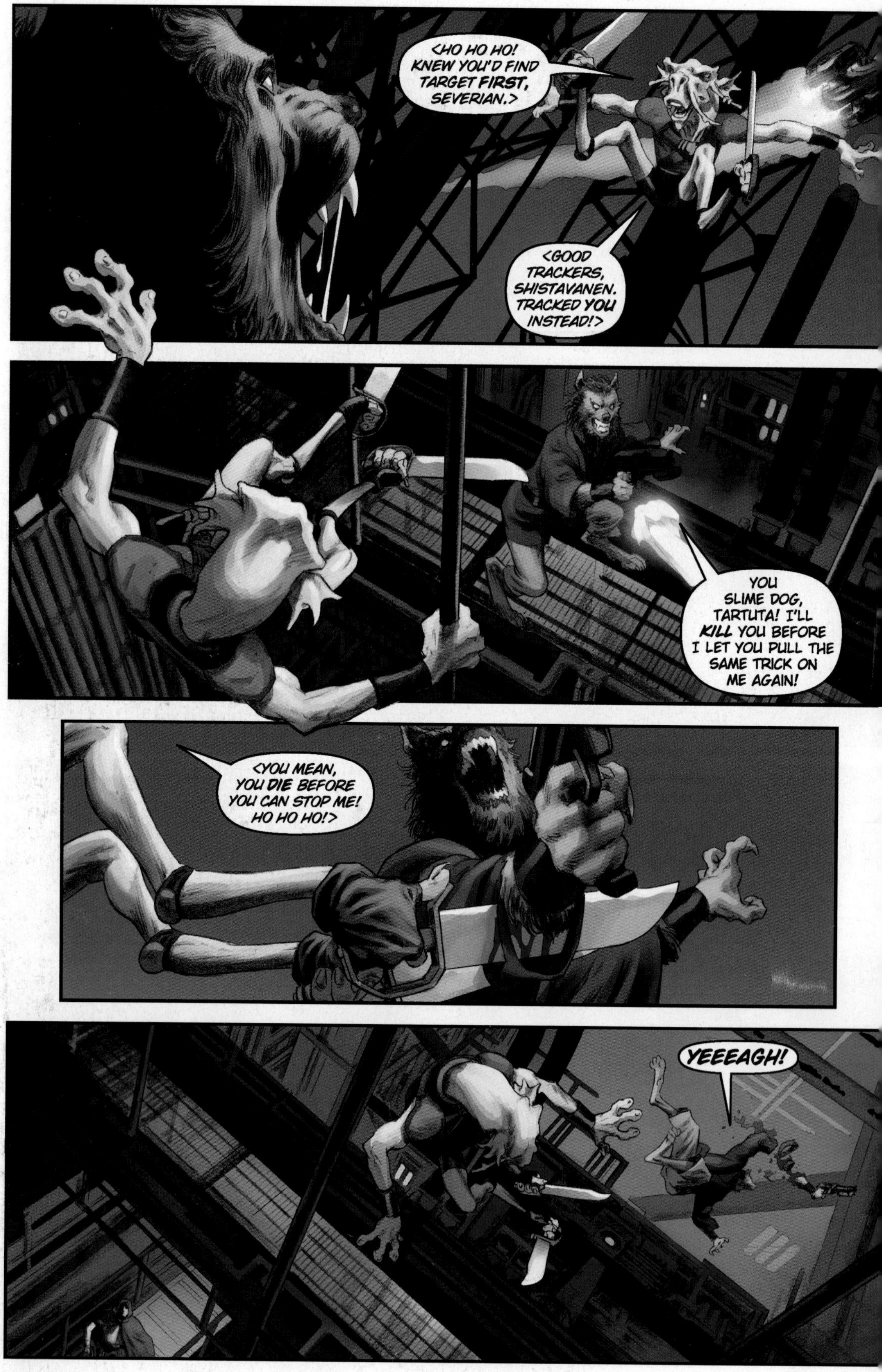

<HO HO HO! KNEW YOU'D FIND TARGET FIRST, SEVERIAN.>
<GOOD TRACKERS, SHISTAVANEN. TRACKED YOU INSTEAD!>
YOU SLIME DOG, TARTUTA! I'LL KILL YOU BEFORE I LET YOU PULL THE SAME TRICK ON ME AGAIN!
<YOU MEAN, YOU DIE BEFORE YOU CAN STOP ME! HO HO HO!>
YEEEAGH!

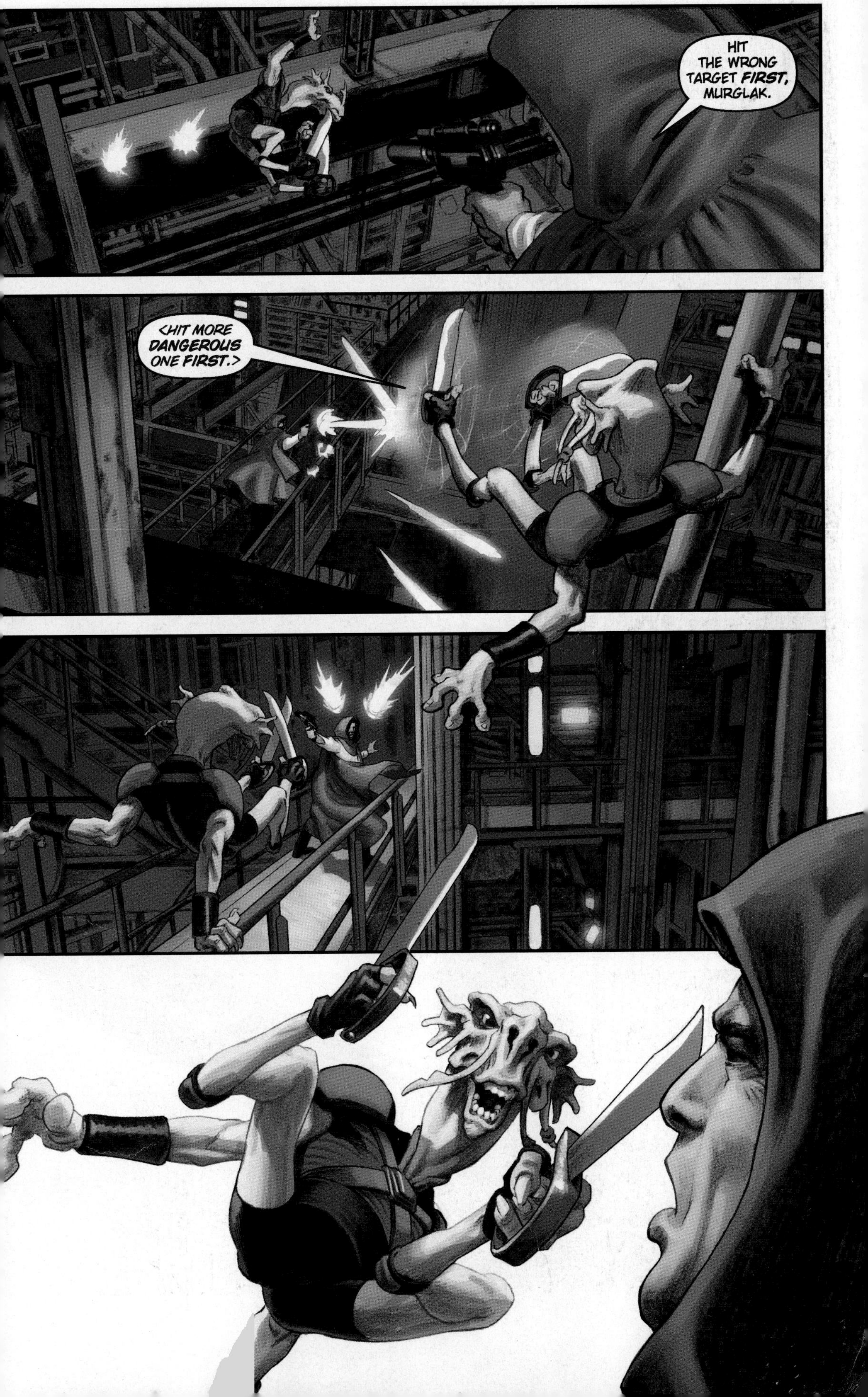
HIT THE WRONG TARGET FIRST, MURGLAK.
<HIT MORE DANGEROUS ONE FIRST.>

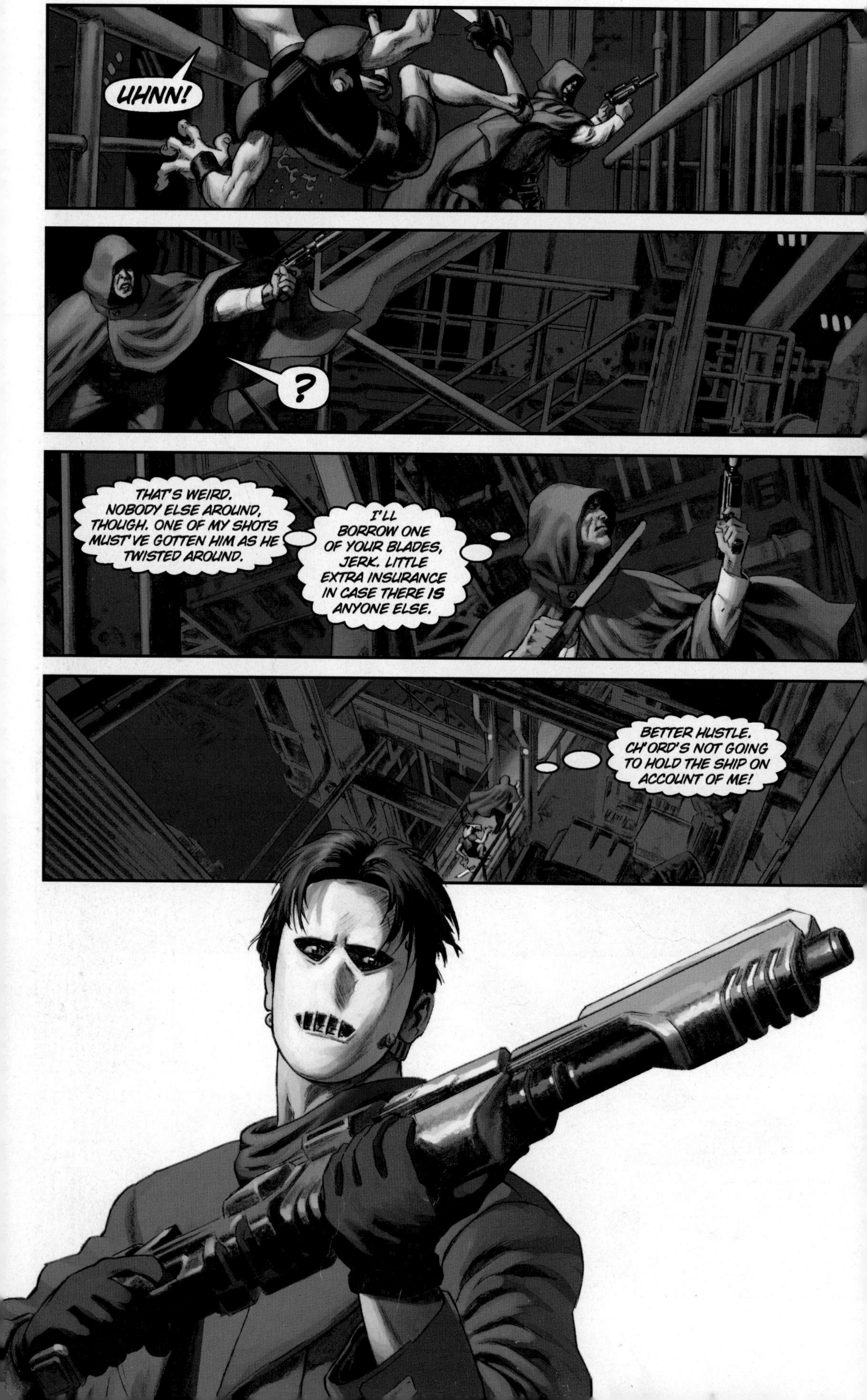
UHNN!
?
THAT'S WEIRD. NOBODY ELSE AROUND, THOUGH. ONE OF MY SHOTS MUST'VE GOTTEN HIM AS HE TWISTED AROUND.
I'LL BORROW ONE OF YOUR BLADES, JERK. LITTLE EXTRA INSURANCE IN CASE THERE IS ANYONE ELSE.
BETTER HUSTLE. CH'ORD'S NOT GOING TO HOLD THE SHIP ON ACCOUNT OF ME!

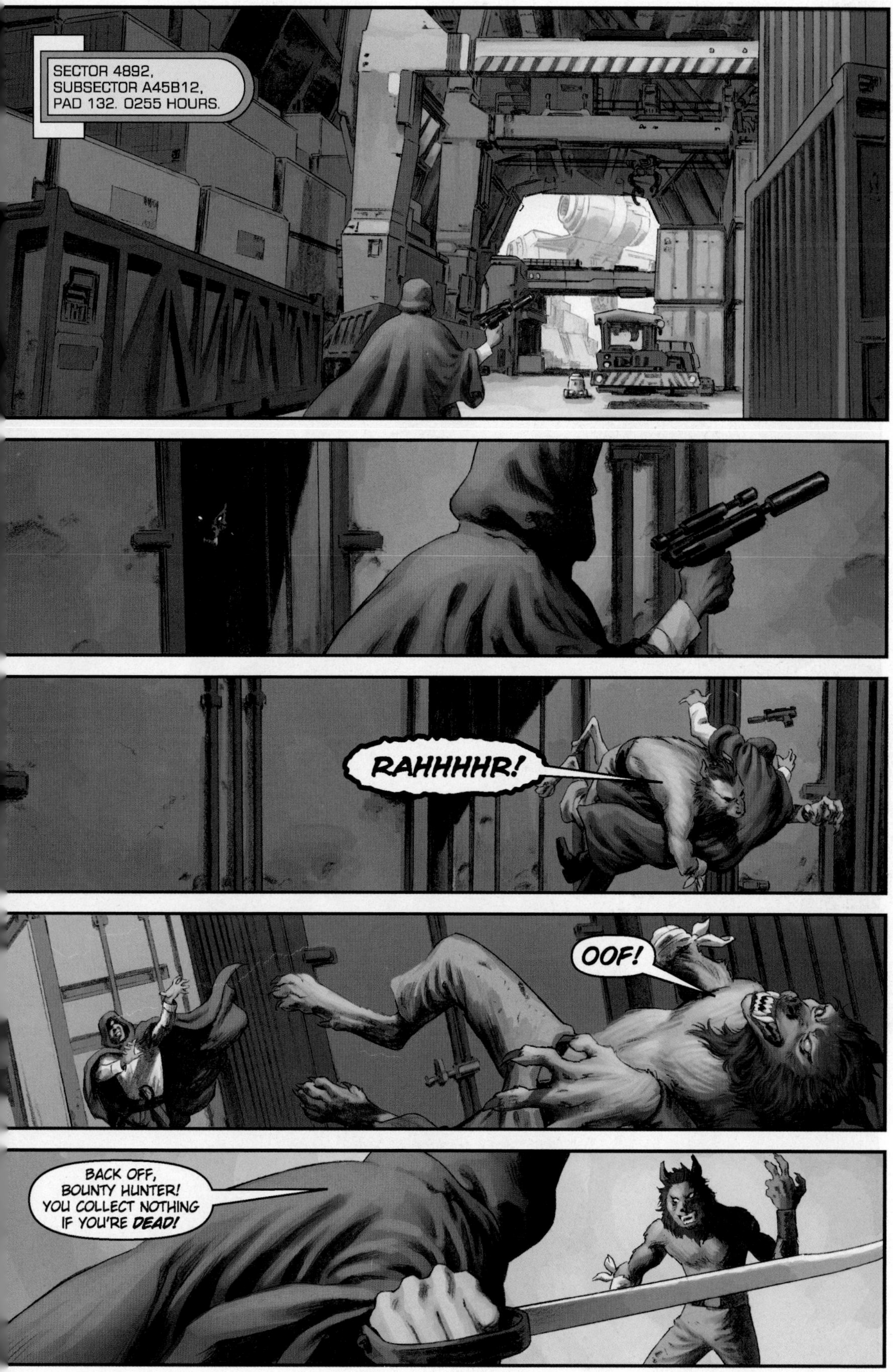
SECTOR 4892,
SUBSECTOR A45B12,
PAD 132. 0255 HOURS.
RAHHHHR!
OOF!
BACK OFF, BOUNTY HUNTER! YOU COLLECT NOTHING IF YOU'RE DEAD!

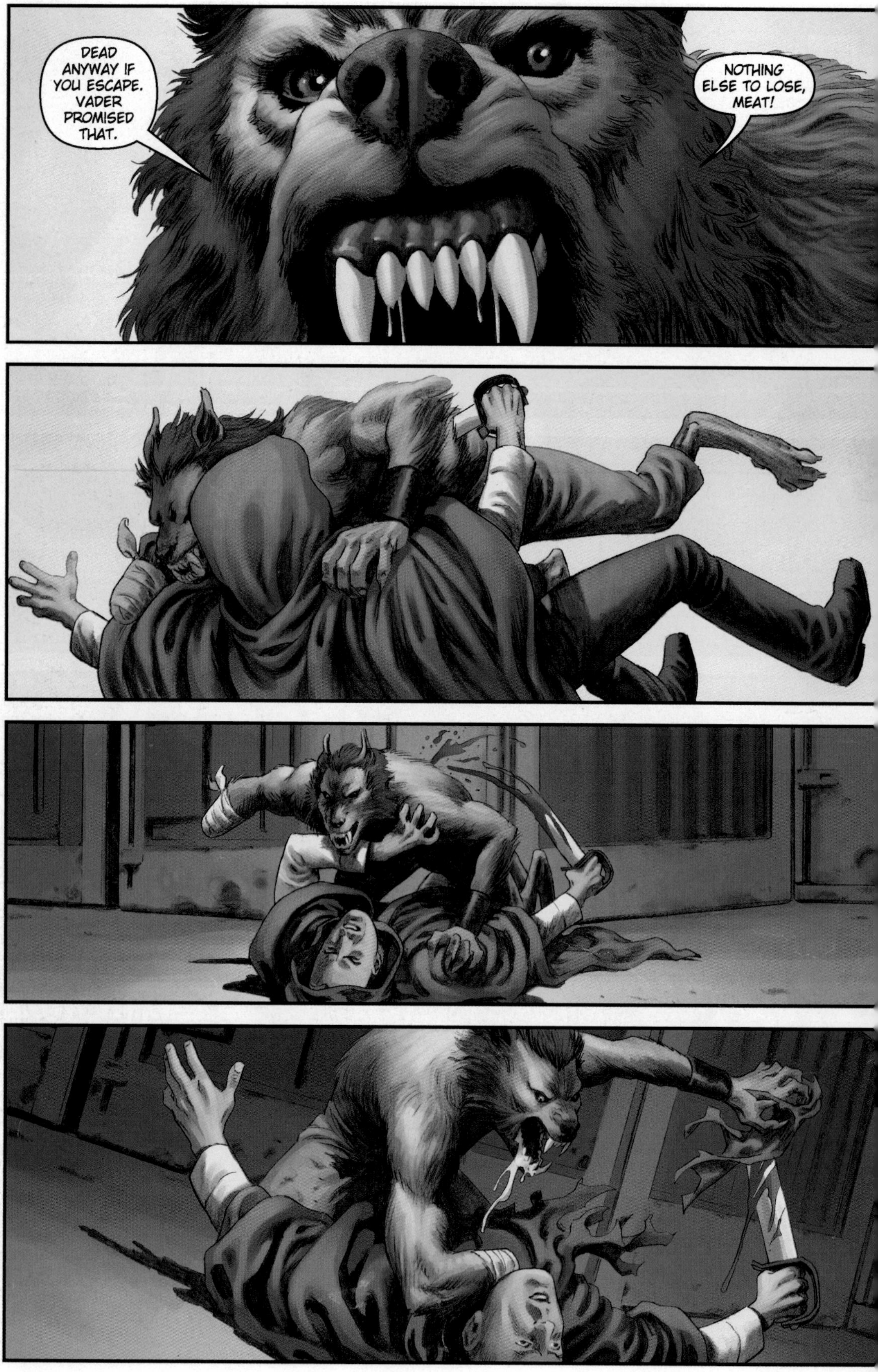
DEAD ANYWAY IF YOU ESCAPE. VADER PROMISED THAT.
NOTHING ELSE TO LOSE, MEAT!

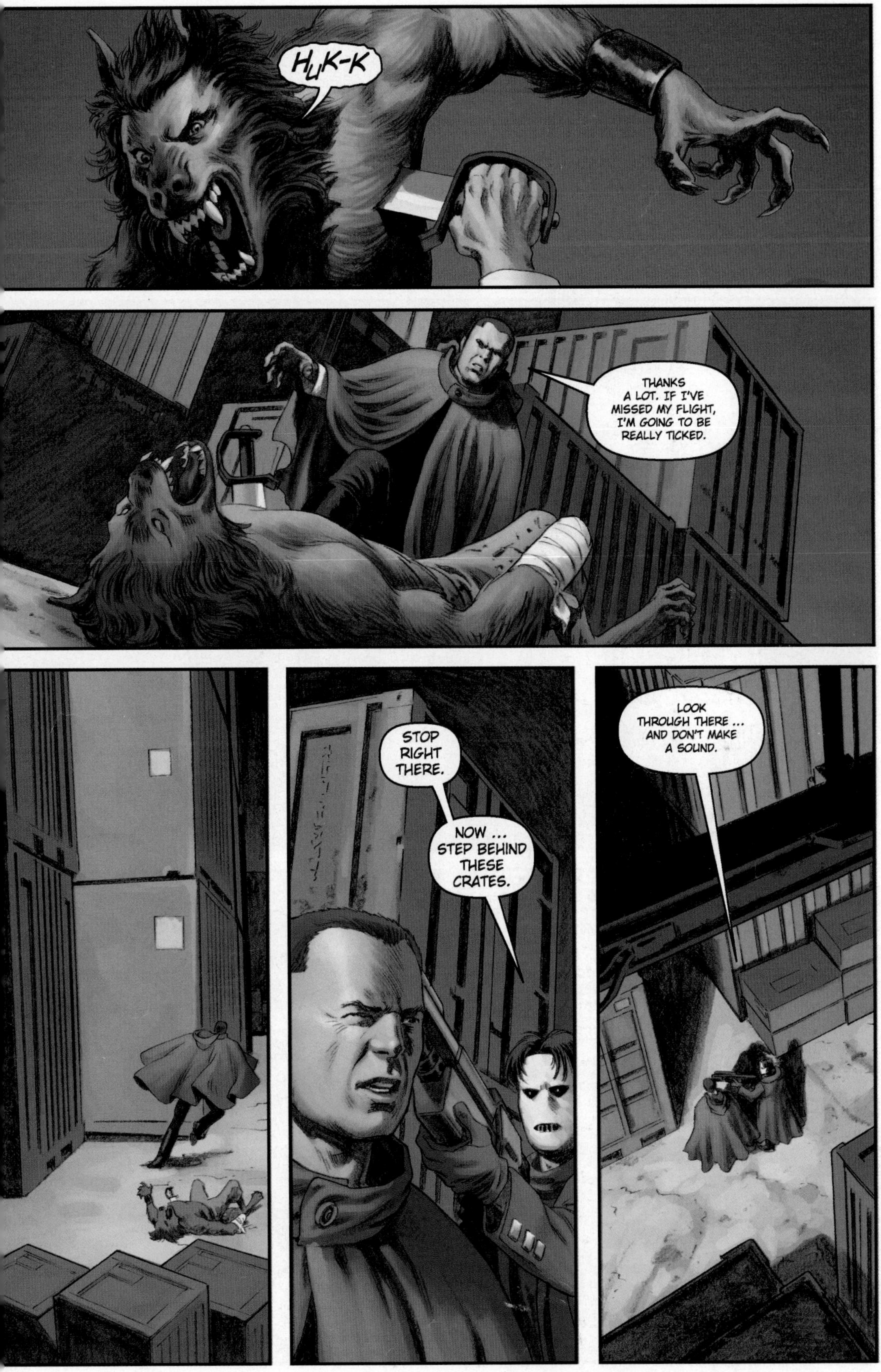

HUK-K
THANKS A LOT. IF I'VE MISSED MY FLIGHT, I'M GOING TO BE REALLY TICKED.
STOP RIGHT THERE.
NOW ... STEP BEHIND THESE CRATES.
LOOK THROUGH THERE ... AND DON'T MAKE A SOUND.

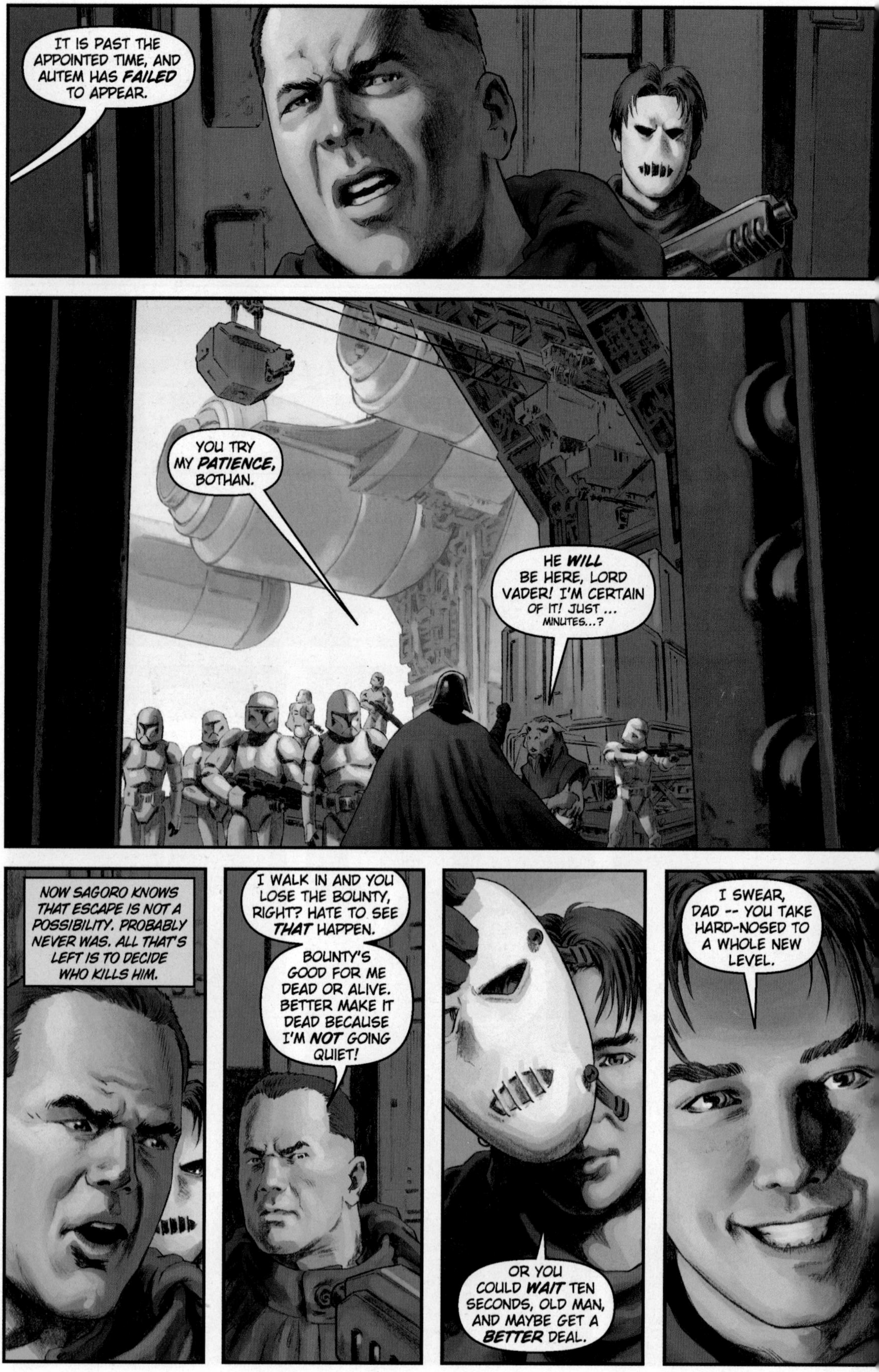
IT IS PAST THE APPOINTED TIME, AND AUTEM HAS *FAILED* TO APPEAR.
YOU TRY MY *PATIENCE,* BOTHAN.
HE *WILL* BE HERE, LORD VADER! I'M CERTAIN OF IT! JUST ... MINUTES...?
NOW SAGORO KNOWS THAT ESCAPE IS NOT A POSSIBILITY. PROBABLY NEVER WAS. ALL THAT'S LEFT IS TO DECIDE WHO KILLS HIM.
I WALK IN AND YOU LOSE THE BOUNTY, RIGHT? HATE TO SEE *THAT* HAPPEN.
BOUNTY'S GOOD FOR ME DEAD OR ALIVE. BETTER MAKE IT DEAD BECAUSE I'M *NOT* GOING QUIET!
OR YOU COULD *WAIT* TEN SECONDS, OLD MAN, AND MAYBE GET A *BETTER* DEAL.
I SWEAR, DAD -- YOU TAKE HARD-NOSED TO A WHOLE NEW LEVEL.

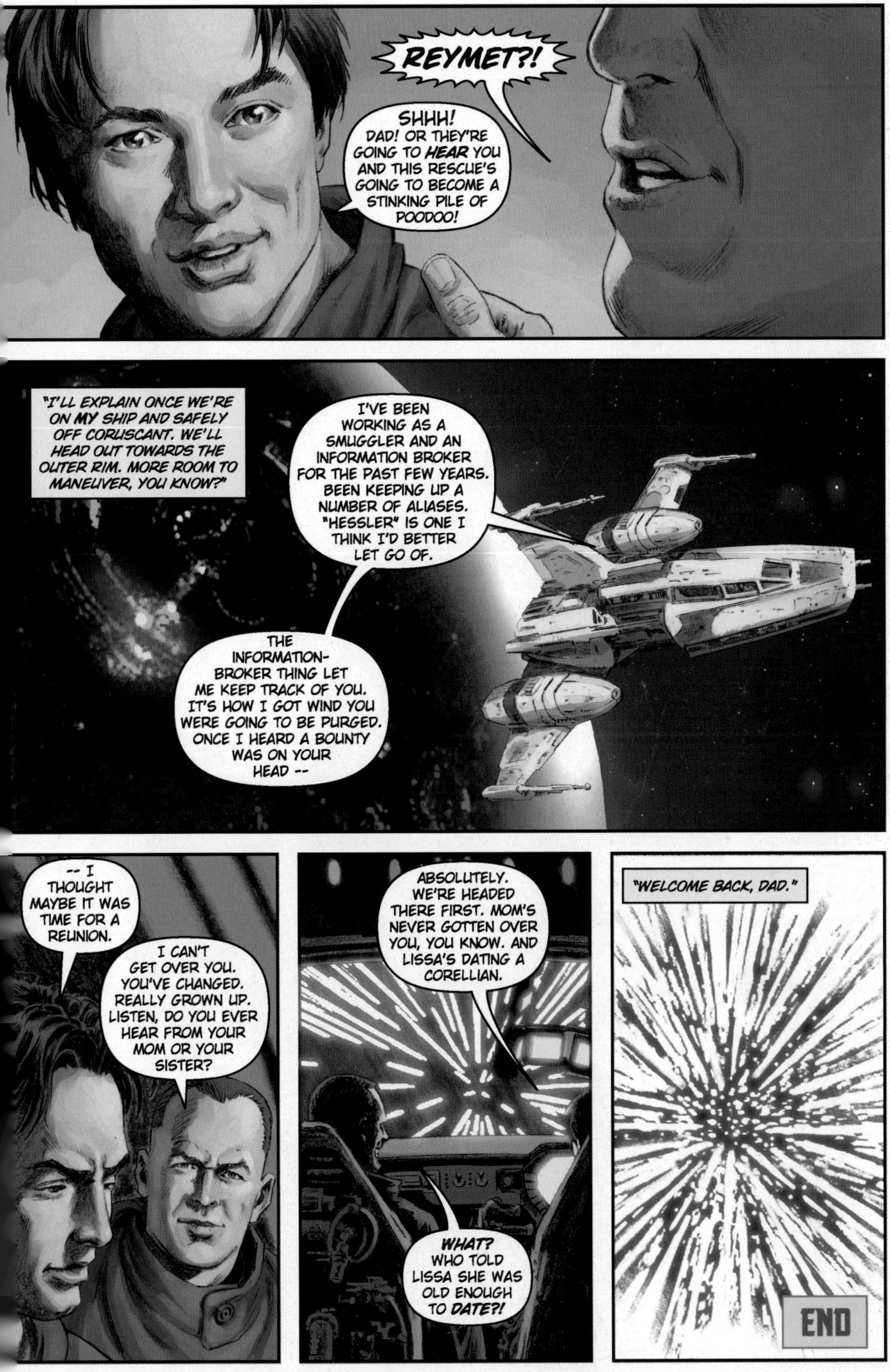
REYMET?!
SHHH! DAD! OR THEY'RE GOING TO HEAR YOU AND THIS RESCUE'S GOING TO BECOME A STINKING PILE OF POODOO!
"I'LL EXPLAIN ONCE WE'RE ON MY SHIP AND SAFELY OFF CORUSCANT. WE'LL HEAD OUT TOWARDS THE OUTER RIM. MORE ROOM TO MANEUVER, YOU KNOW?"
I'VE BEEN WORKING AS A SMUGGLER AND AN INFORMATION BROKER FOR THE PAST FEW YEARS. BEEN KEEPING UP A NUMBER OF ALIASES. "HESSLER" IS ONE I THINK I'D BETTER LET GO OF.
THE INFORMATION-BROKER THING LET ME KEEP TRACK OF YOU. IT'S HOW I GOT WIND YOU WERE GOING TO BE PURGED. ONCE I HEARD A BOUNTY WAS ON YOUR HEAD --
-- I THOUGHT MAYBE IT WAS TIME FOR A REUNION.
I CAN'T GET OVER YOU. YOU'VE CHANGED. REALLY GROWN UP. LISTEN, DO YOU EVER HEAR FROM YOUR MOM OR YOUR SISTER?
ABSOLUTELY. WE'RE HEADED THERE FIRST. MOM'S NEVER GOTTEN OVER YOU, YOU KNOW. AND LISSA'S DATING A CORELLIAN.
WHAT? WHO TOLD LISSA SHE WAS OLD ENOUGH TO DATE?!
"WELCOME BACK, DAD."
END

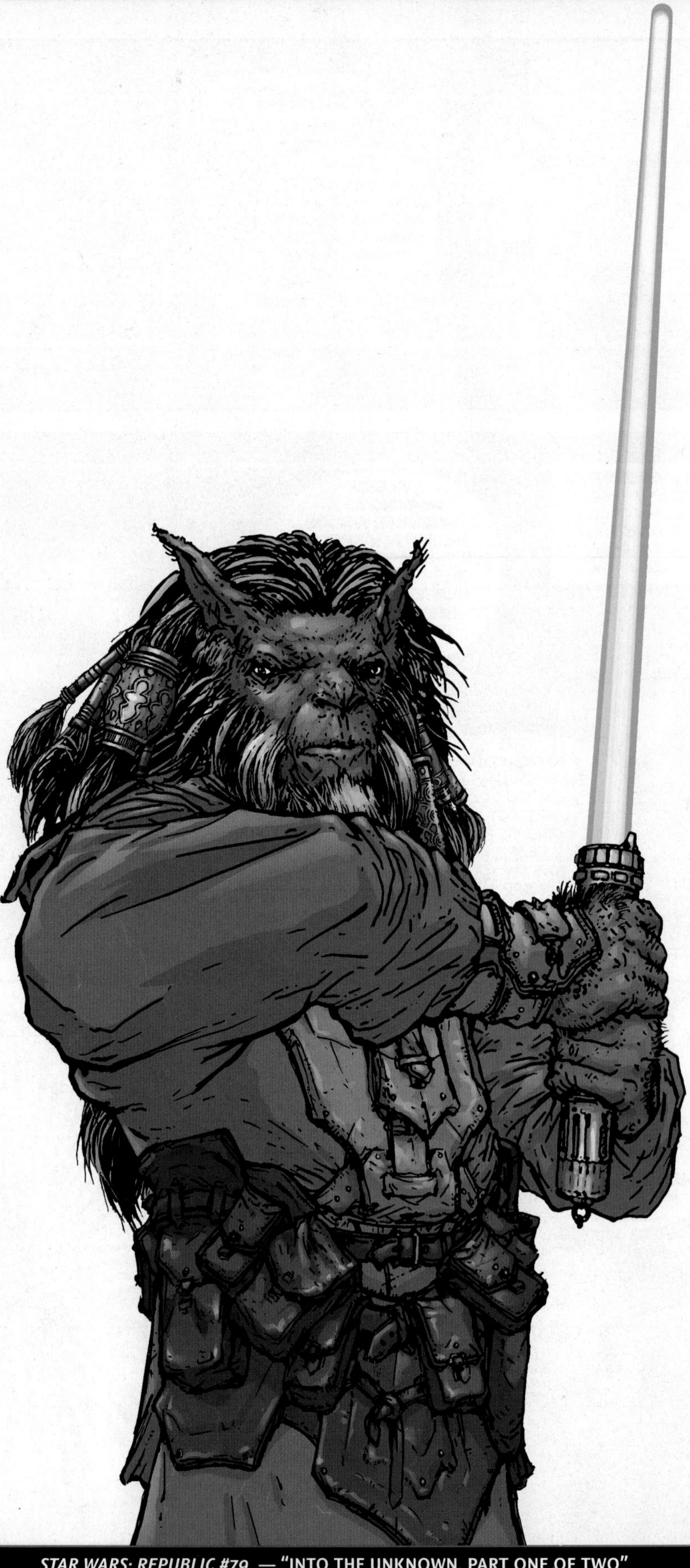

STAR WARS: REPUBLIC #79 — "INTO THE UNKNOWN, PART ONE OF TWO"

WRITER: RANDY STRADLEY (AS WELLES HARTLEY) • ARTIST: DOUGLAS WHEATLEY • COLORIST: CHRIS CHUCKRY • LETTERER: MICHAEL DAVID THOMAS
DESIGNER: DAVID NESTELLE • ASSISTANT EDITOR: DAVE MARSHALL • ASSOCIATE EDITOR: JEREMY BARLOW • EDITOR: RANDY STRADLEY
COVER ARTISTS: JOHN GALLAGHER & CHRIS CHUCKRY

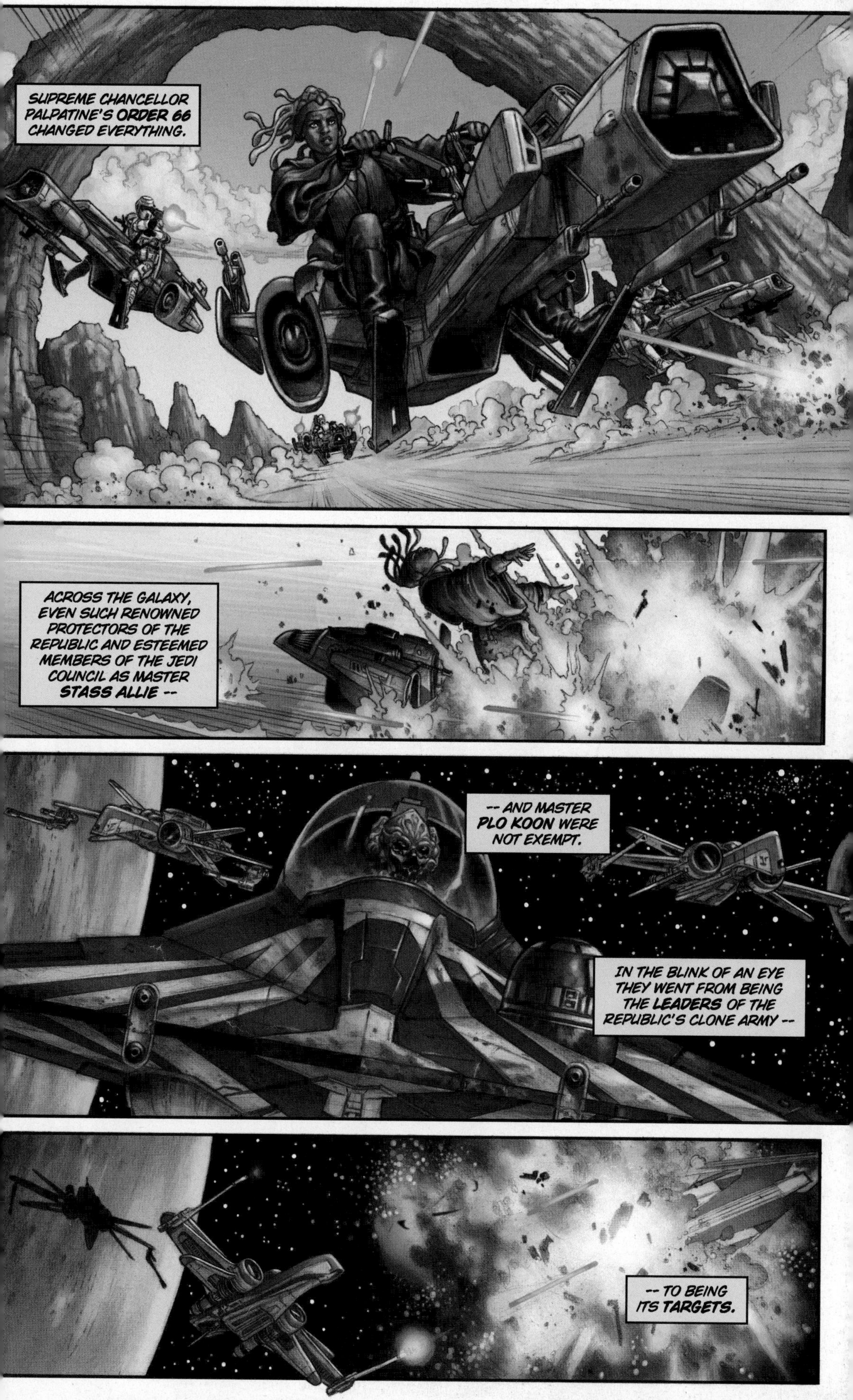
SUPREME CHANCELLOR PALPATINE'S ORDER 66 CHANGED EVERYTHING.
ACROSS THE GALAXY, EVEN SUCH RENOWNED PROTECTORS OF THE REPUBLIC AND ESTEEMED MEMBERS OF THE JEDI COUNCIL AS MASTER STASS ALLIE --
-- AND MASTER PLO KOON WERE NOT EXEMPT.
IN THE BLINK OF AN EYE THEY WENT FROM BEING THE LEADERS OF THE REPUBLIC'S CLONE ARMY --
-- TO BEING ITS TARGETS.

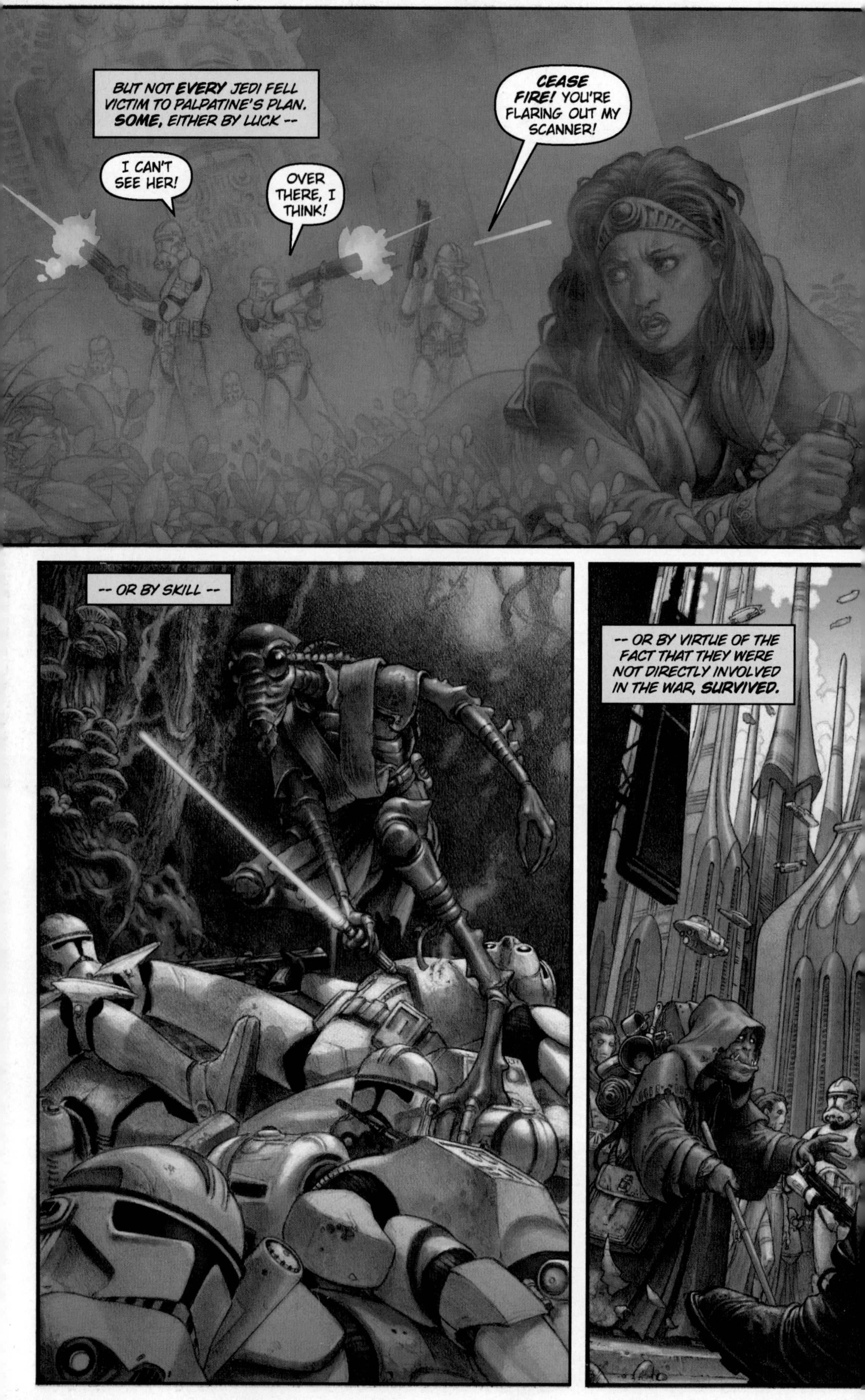

BUT NOT EVERY JEDI FELL VICTIM TO PALPATINE'S PLAN. SOME, EITHER BY LUCK --
I CAN'T SEE HER!
OVER THERE, I THINK!
CEASE FIRE! YOU'RE FLARING OUT MY SCANNER!
-- OR BY SKILL --
-- OR BY VIRTUE OF THE FACT THAT THEY WERE NOT DIRECTLY INVOLVED IN THE WAR, SURVIVED.

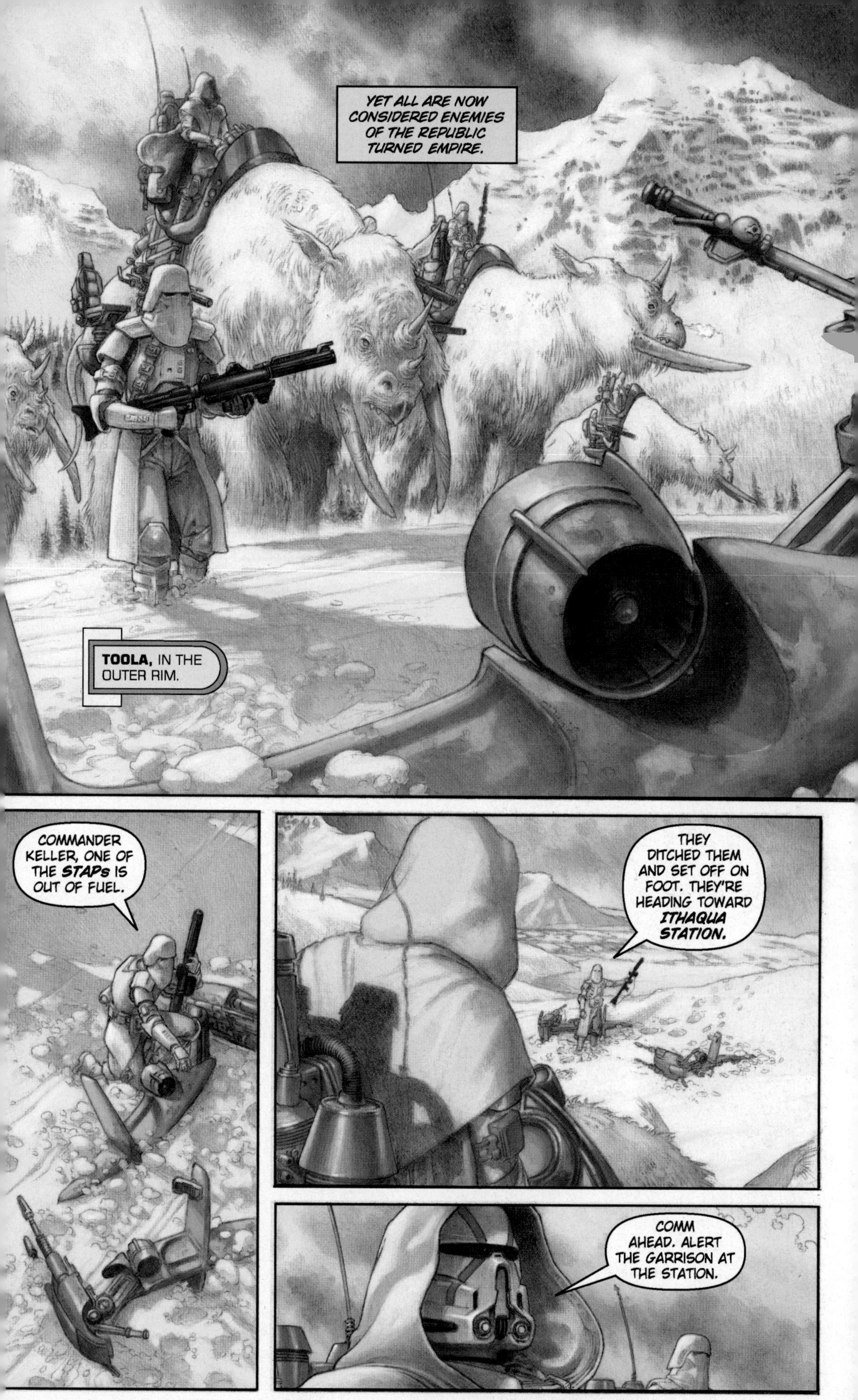
YET ALL ARE NOW CONSIDERED ENEMIES OF THE REPUBLIC TURNED EMPIRE.
TOOLA, IN THE OUTER RIM.
COMMANDER KELLER, ONE OF THE STAPs IS OUT OF FUEL.
THEY DITCHED THEM AND SET OFF ON FOOT. THEY'RE HEADING TOWARD ITHAQUA STATION.
COMM AHEAD. ALERT THE GARRISON AT THE STATION.

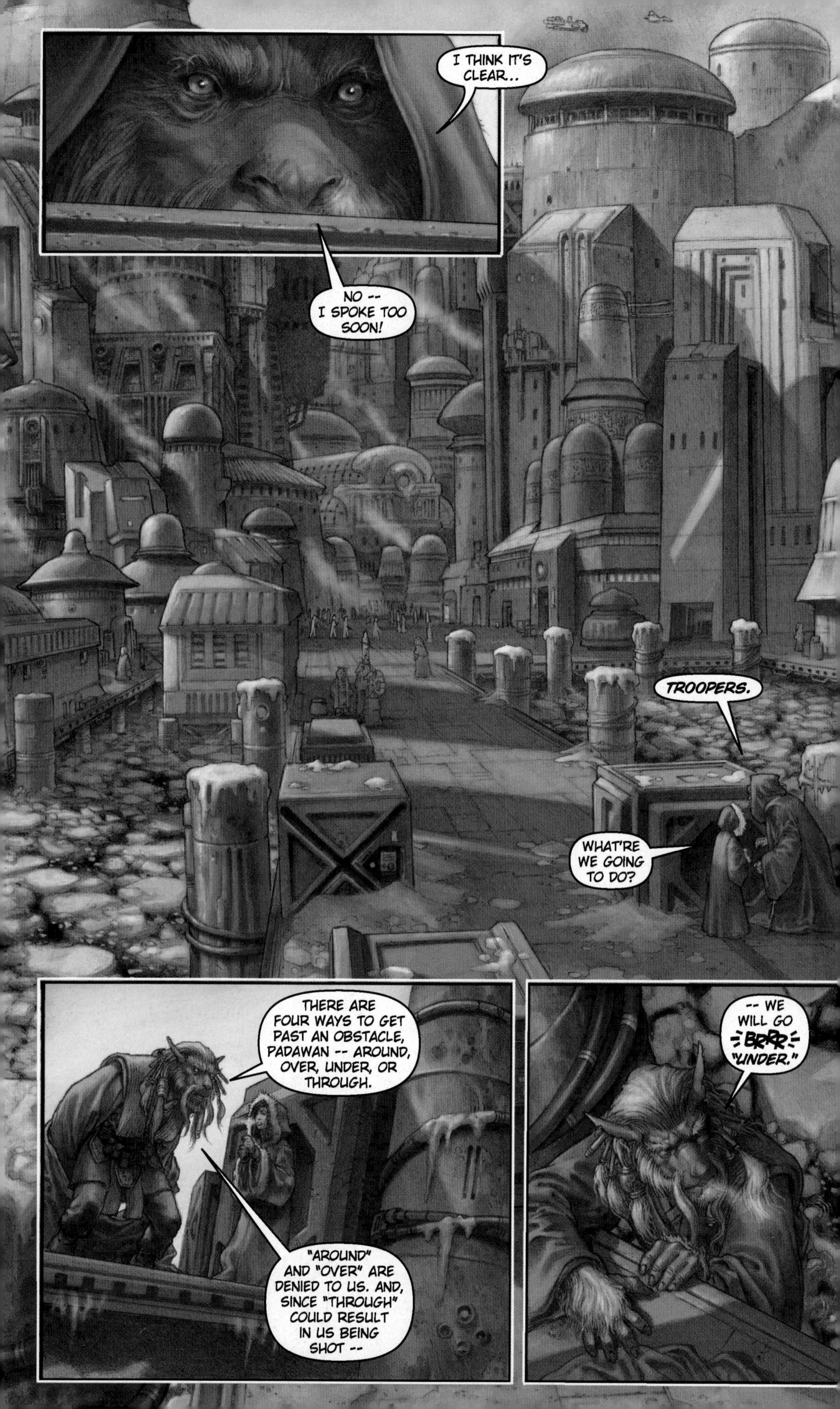
I THINK IT'S CLEAR...
NO -- I SPOKE TOO SOON!
TROOPERS.
WHAT'RE WE GOING TO DO?
THERE ARE FOUR WAYS TO GET PAST AN OBSTACLE, PADAWAN -- AROUND, OVER, UNDER, OR THROUGH.
"AROUND" AND "OVER" ARE DENIED TO US. AND, SINCE "THROUGH" COULD RESULT IN US BEING SHOT --
-- WE WILL GO
BRRR
"UNDER."

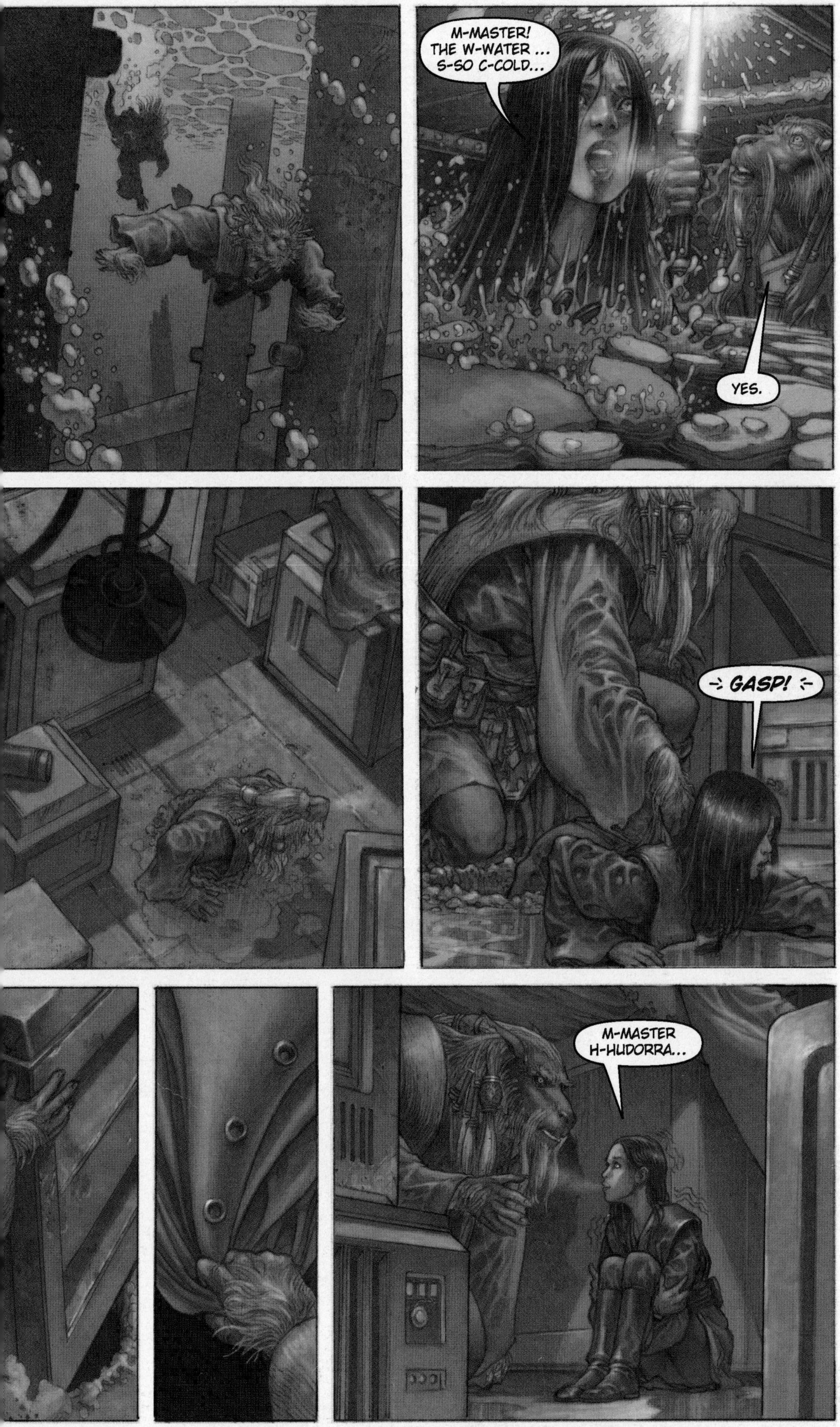
M-MASTER! THE W-WATER ... S-SO C-COLD...
YES.
GASP!
M-MASTER H-HUDORRA...

...THE CL-CLONES ARE EVERYWHERE. W-WHY ARE TH-THEY TRYING TO K-KILL US? WHY D-DID THEY K-KILL M-MASTER SIMMS?

W-WHAT ARE W-WE G-GOING TO D-DO?

MASTER KAI HUDORRA HAS BEEN ASKING HIMSELF THOSE SAME QUESTIONS FOR THE PAST THIRTY-SIX HOURS...

AFTER WEEKS OF STALEMATE AGAINST SEPARATIST FORCES, HE, MASTER SIMMS, AND HER PADAWAN NOIRAH NA LED AN ASSAULT TEAM AGAINST THE DROIDS' MAIN GENERATORS--

--WHILE REST OF T TROOPS ST A DIVERSIO ATTACK

THEIR PLOY WAS SUCCESSFUL. BUT SHORTLY AFTER THEIR VICTORY, THEIR OWN CLONE TROOPS INEXPLICABLY TURNED AGAINST THEM.

MASTER!

VASTLY OUTNUMBER HUDORRA AND NA HAD CHOICE BUT TO FLEE

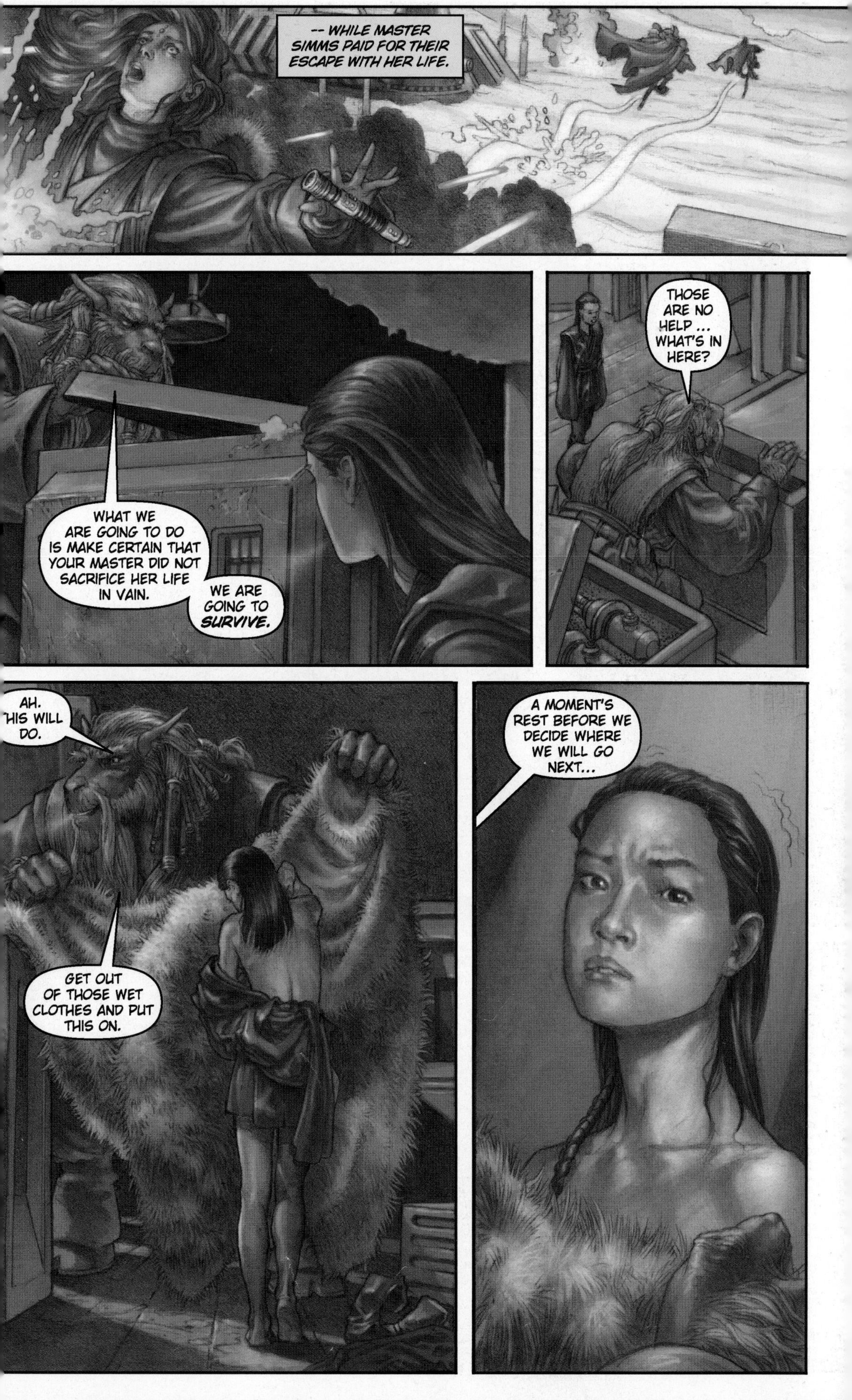
-- WHILE MASTER SIMMS PAID FOR THEIR ESCAPE WITH HER LIFE.
WHAT WE ARE GOING TO DO IS MAKE CERTAIN THAT YOUR MASTER DID NOT SACRIFICE HER LIFE IN VAIN.
WE ARE GOING TO SURVIVE.
THOSE ARE NO HELP ... WHAT'S IN HERE?
AH. THIS WILL DO.
GET OUT OF THOSE WET CLOTHES AND PUT THIS ON.
A MOMENT'S REST BEFORE WE DECIDE WHERE WE WILL GO NEXT...

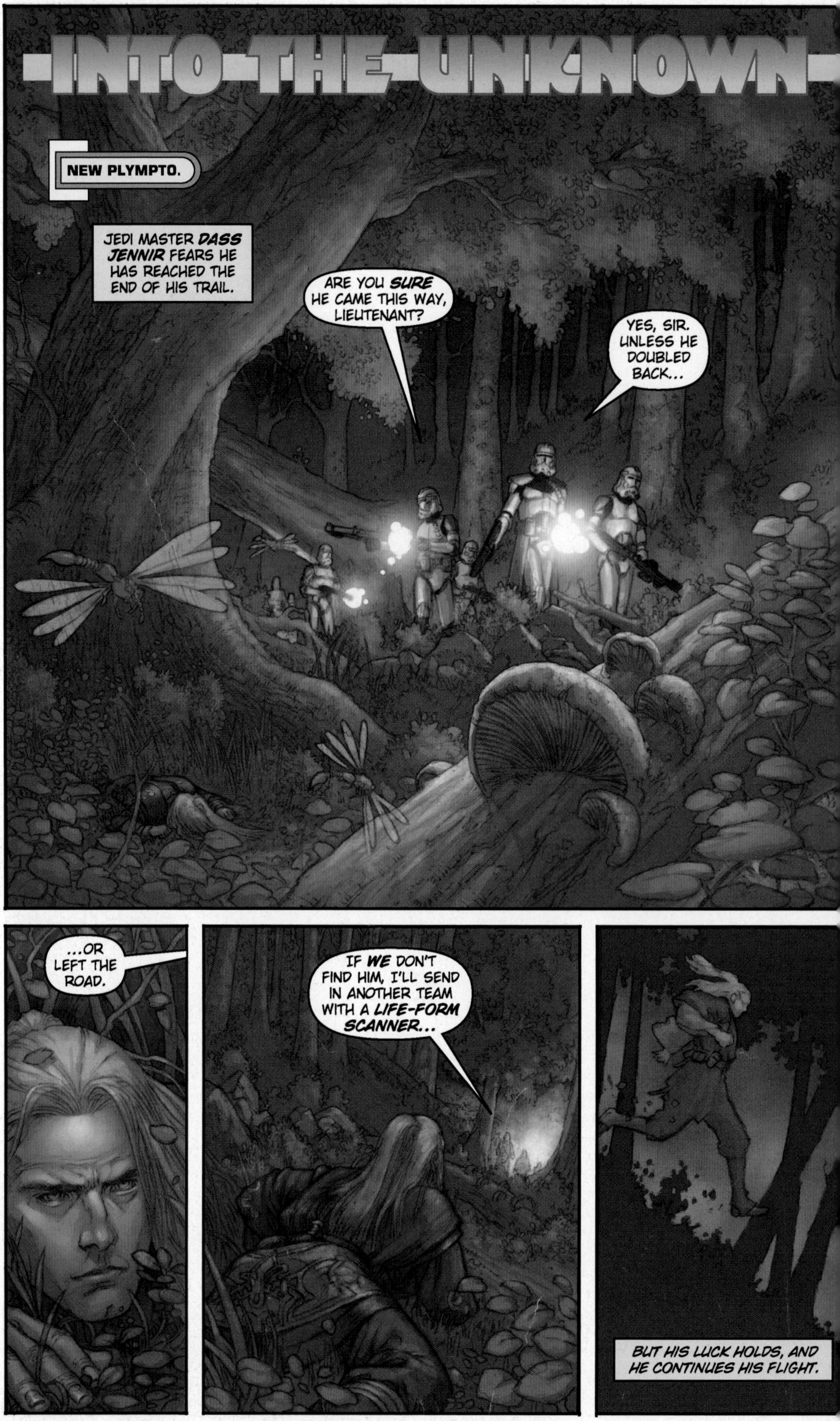

INTO THE UNKNOWN
NEW PLYMPTO.
JEDI MASTER DASS JENNIR FEARS HE HAS REACHED THE END OF HIS TRAIL.
ARE YOU SURE HE CAME THIS WAY, LIEUTENANT?
YES, SIR. UNLESS HE DOUBLED BACK...
...OR LEFT THE ROAD.
IF WE DON'T FIND HIM, I'LL SEND IN ANOTHER TEAM WITH A LIFE-FORM SCANNER...
BUT HIS LUCK HOLDS, AND HE CONTINUES HIS FLIGHT.

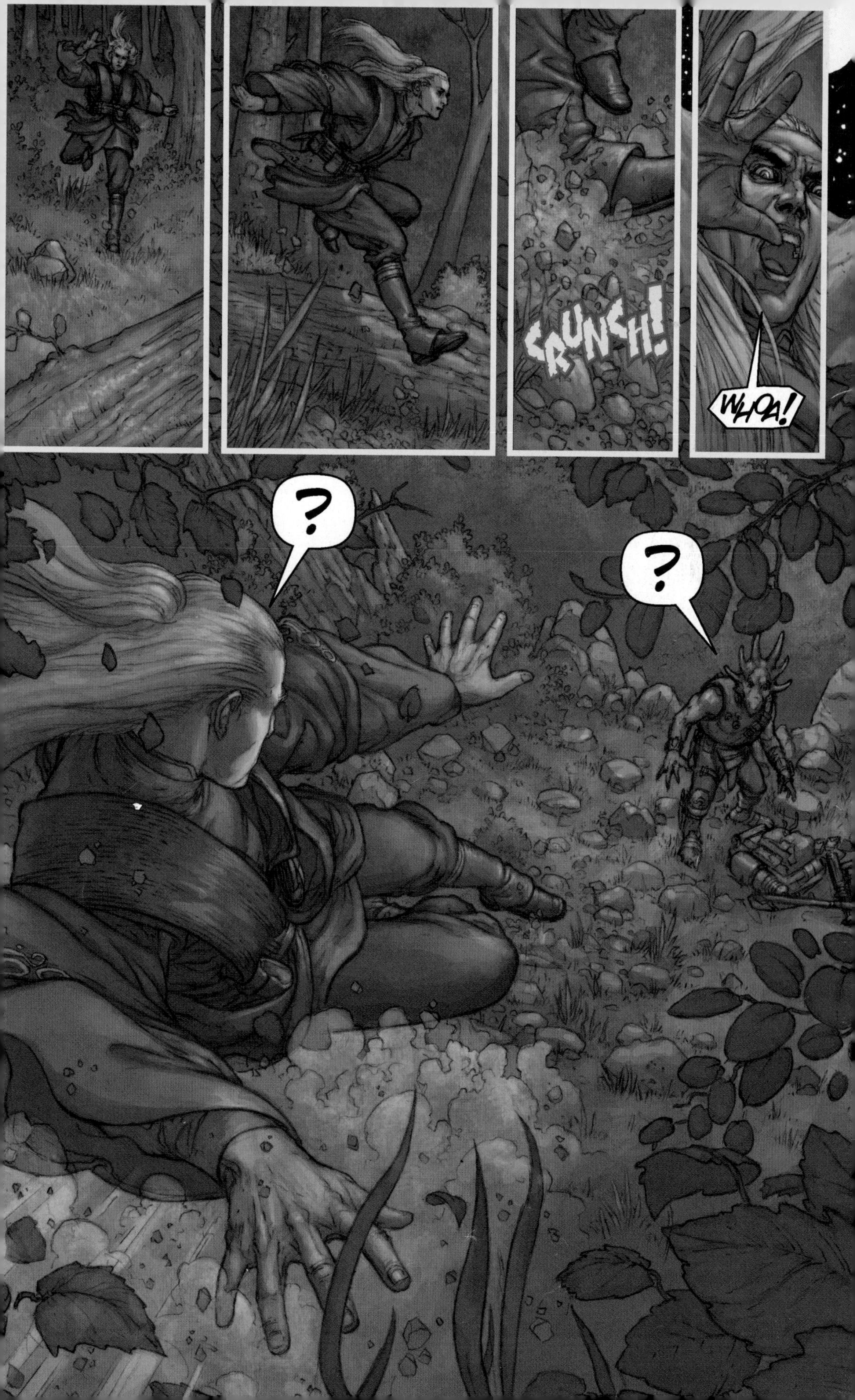
CRUNCH!
WHOA!
?
?

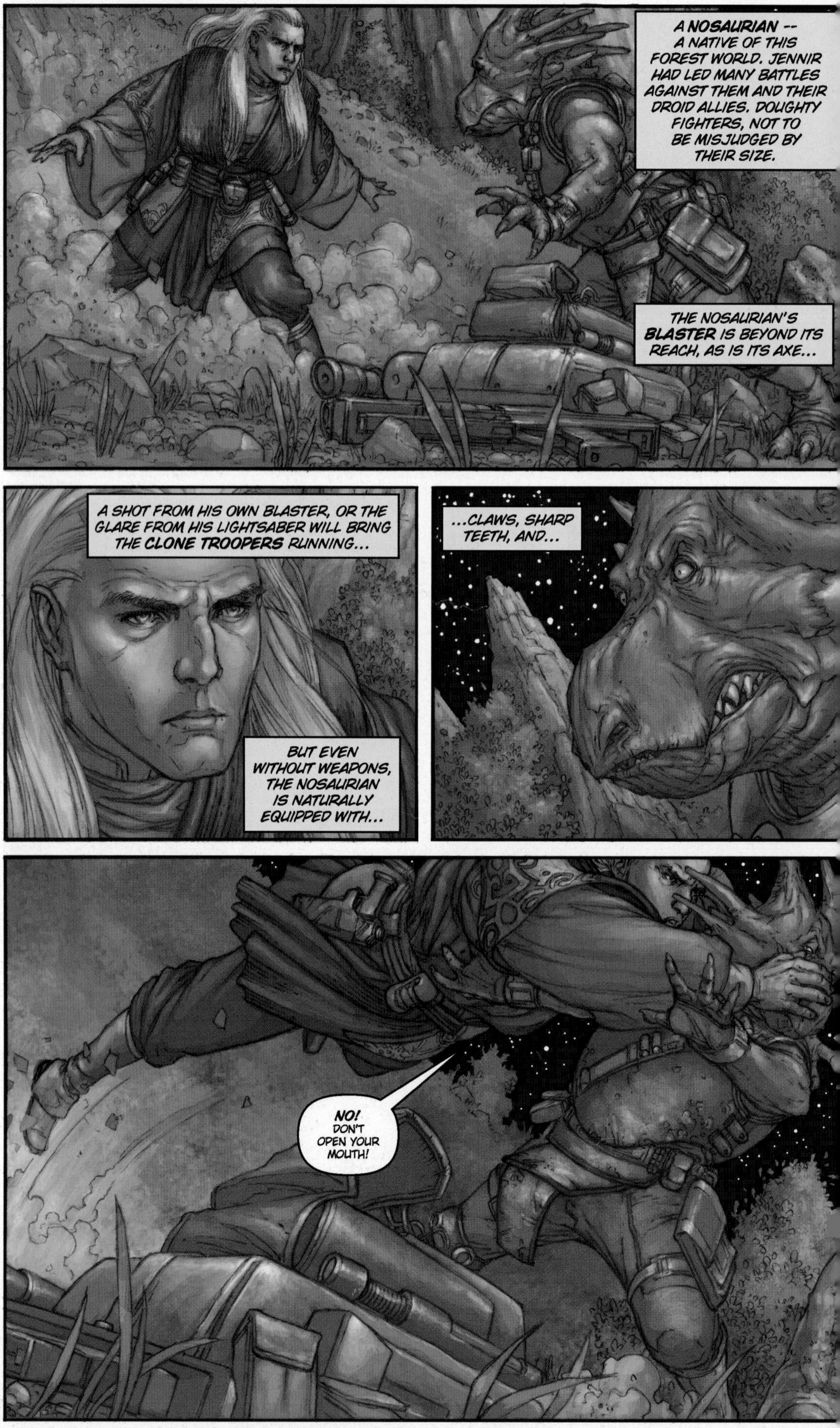
A NOSAURIAN -- A NATIVE OF THIS FOREST WORLD. JENNIR HAD LED MANY BATTLES AGAINST THEM AND THEIR DROID ALLIES. DOUGHTY FIGHTERS, NOT TO BE MISJUDGED BY THEIR SIZE.
THE NOSAURIAN'S BLASTER IS BEYOND ITS REACH, AS IS ITS AXE...
A SHOT FROM HIS OWN BLASTER, OR THE GLARE FROM HIS LIGHTSABER WILL BRING THE CLONE TROOPERS RUNNING...
BUT EVEN WITHOUT WEAPONS, THE NOSAURIAN IS NATURALLY EQUIPPED WITH...
...CLAWS, SHARP TEETH, AND...
NO! DON'T OPEN YOUR MOUTH!

NOSAURIANS HAVE THE ABILITY TO MAKE THE LININGS OF THEIR MOUTHS *PHOSPHORESCE* AT WILL. USEFUL FOR FLASHING *SIGNALS* TO ONE ANOTHER ACROSS LONG DISTANCES --

-- SOMETHING JENNIR CANNOT ALLOW.

LOOK, I MEAN YOU NO HARM.

I'LL LET YOU GO, BUT YOU MUST PROMISE NOT TO FLASH YOUR GUMS -- THERE ARE CLONE TROOPERS IN THE WOODS ABOVE US.

BLINK YOUR EYES IF YOU AGREE.

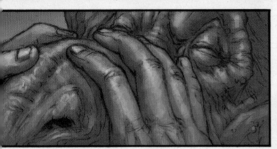

-÷ SPUTTER ÷- MANY THANKS FOR NOT *KILLING* ME, *HUMAN.*

QUIET!

BUT YOU'RE RIGHT TO THANK ME. I *COULD* HAVE KILLED YOU.

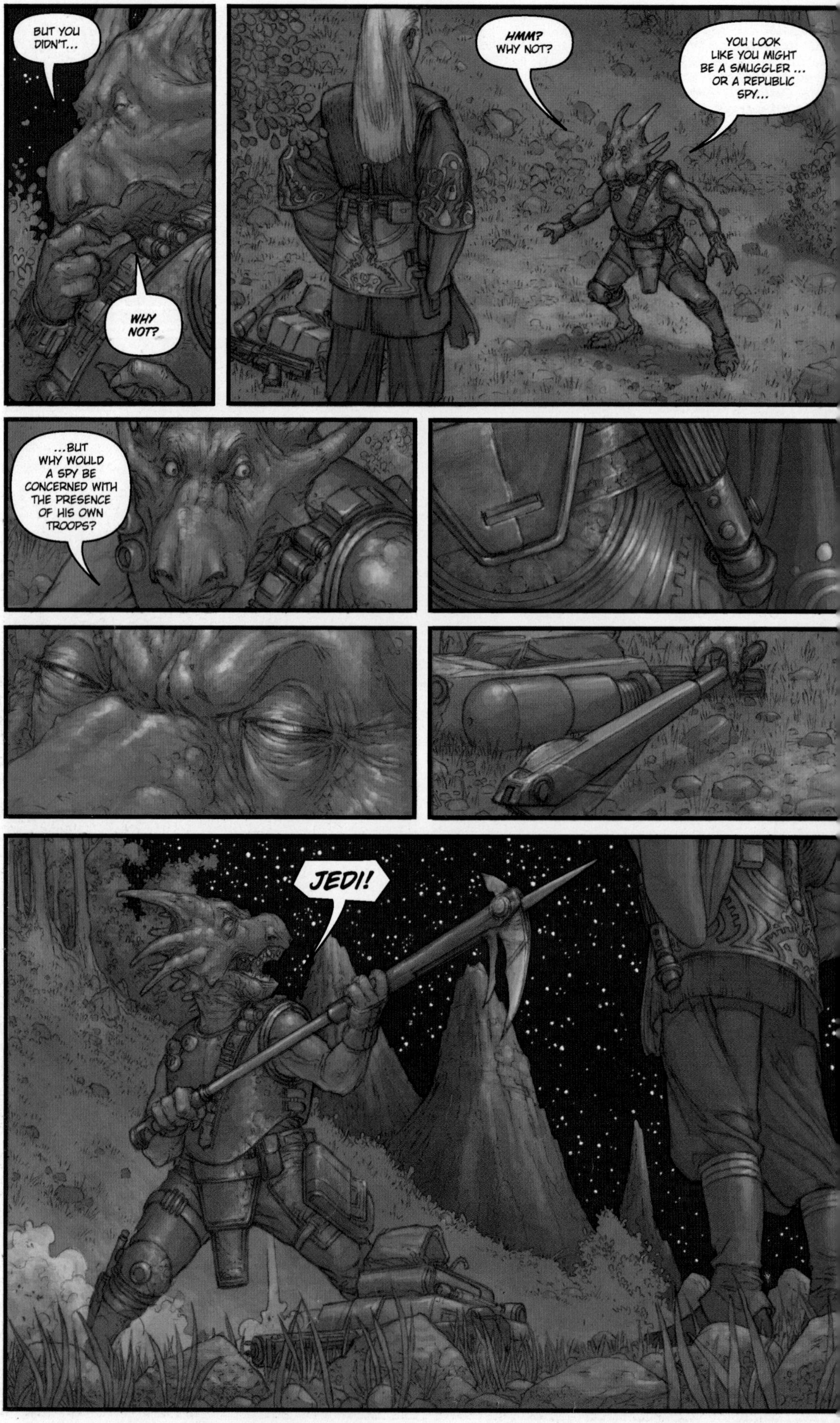

BUT YOU DIDN'T...
WHY NOT?
HMM? WHY NOT?
YOU LOOK LIKE YOU MIGHT BE A SMUGGLER ... OR A REPUBLIC SPY...
...BUT WHY WOULD A SPY BE CONCERNED WITH THE PRESENCE OF HIS OWN TROOPS?
JEDI!

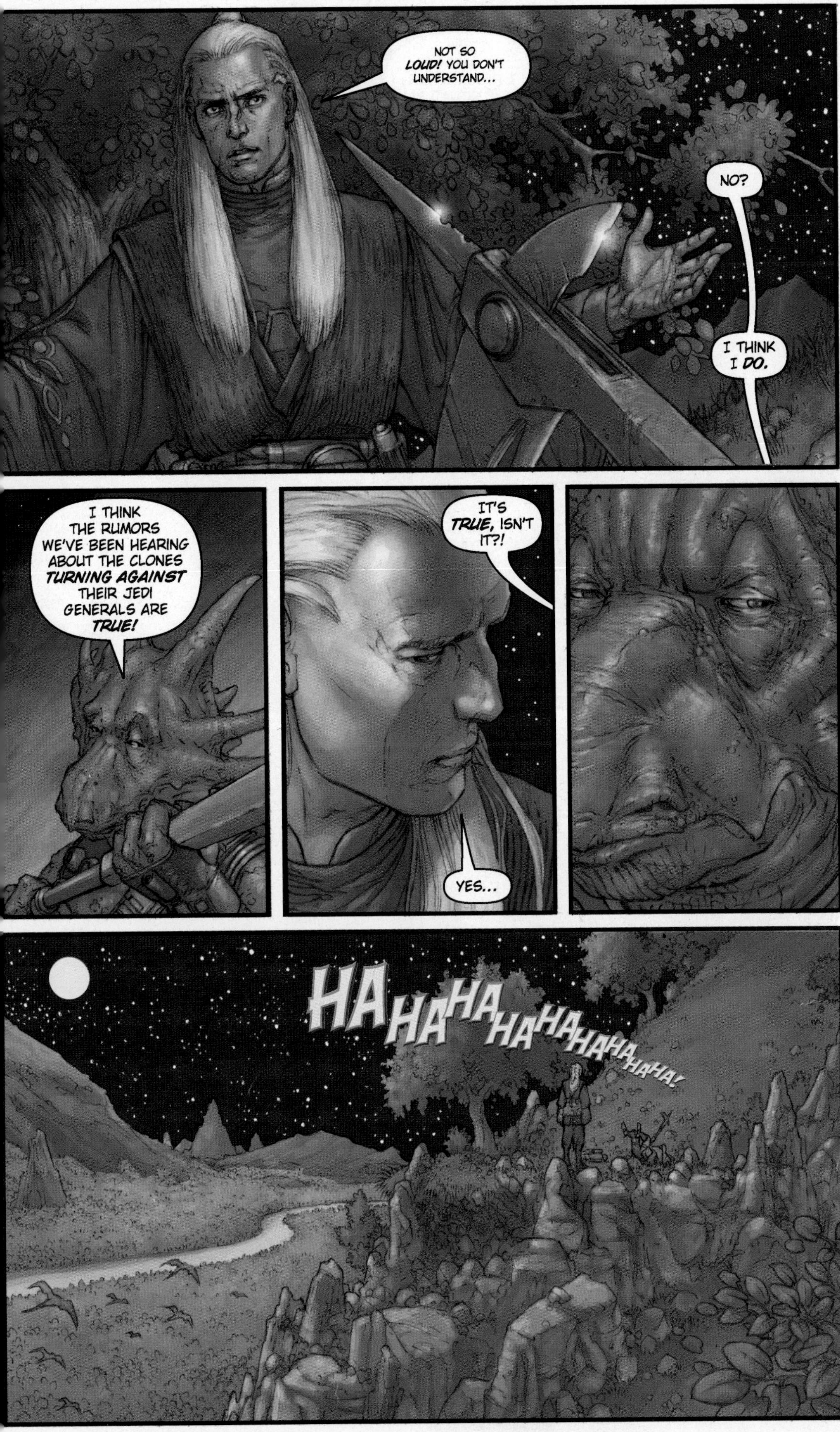
NOT SO LOUD! YOU DON'T UNDERSTAND...
NO?
I THINK I DO.
I THINK THE RUMORS WE'VE BEEN HEARING ABOUT THE CLONES TURNING AGAINST THEIR JEDI GENERALS ARE TRUE!
IT'S TRUE, ISN'T IT?!
YES...
HAHAHAHAHAHAHAHAHAHA!

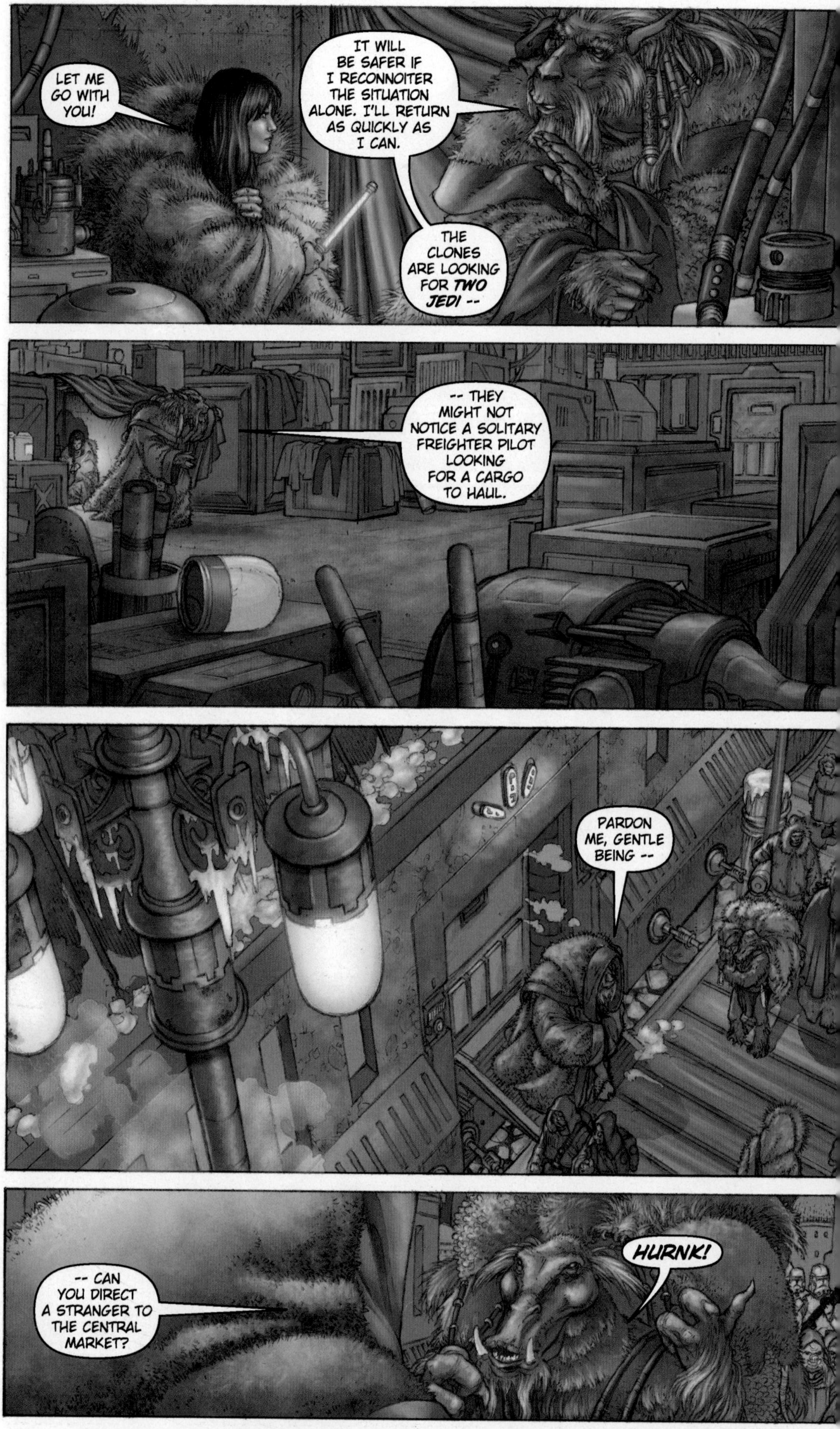
LET ME GO WITH YOU!
IT WILL BE SAFER IF I RECONNOITER THE SITUATION ALONE. I'LL RETURN AS QUICKLY AS I CAN.
THE CLONES ARE LOOKING FOR TWO JEDI --
-- THEY MIGHT NOT NOTICE A SOLITARY FREIGHTER PILOT LOOKING FOR A CARGO TO HAUL.
PARDON ME, GENTLE BEING --
-- CAN YOU DIRECT A STRANGER TO THE CENTRAL MARKET?
HURNK!

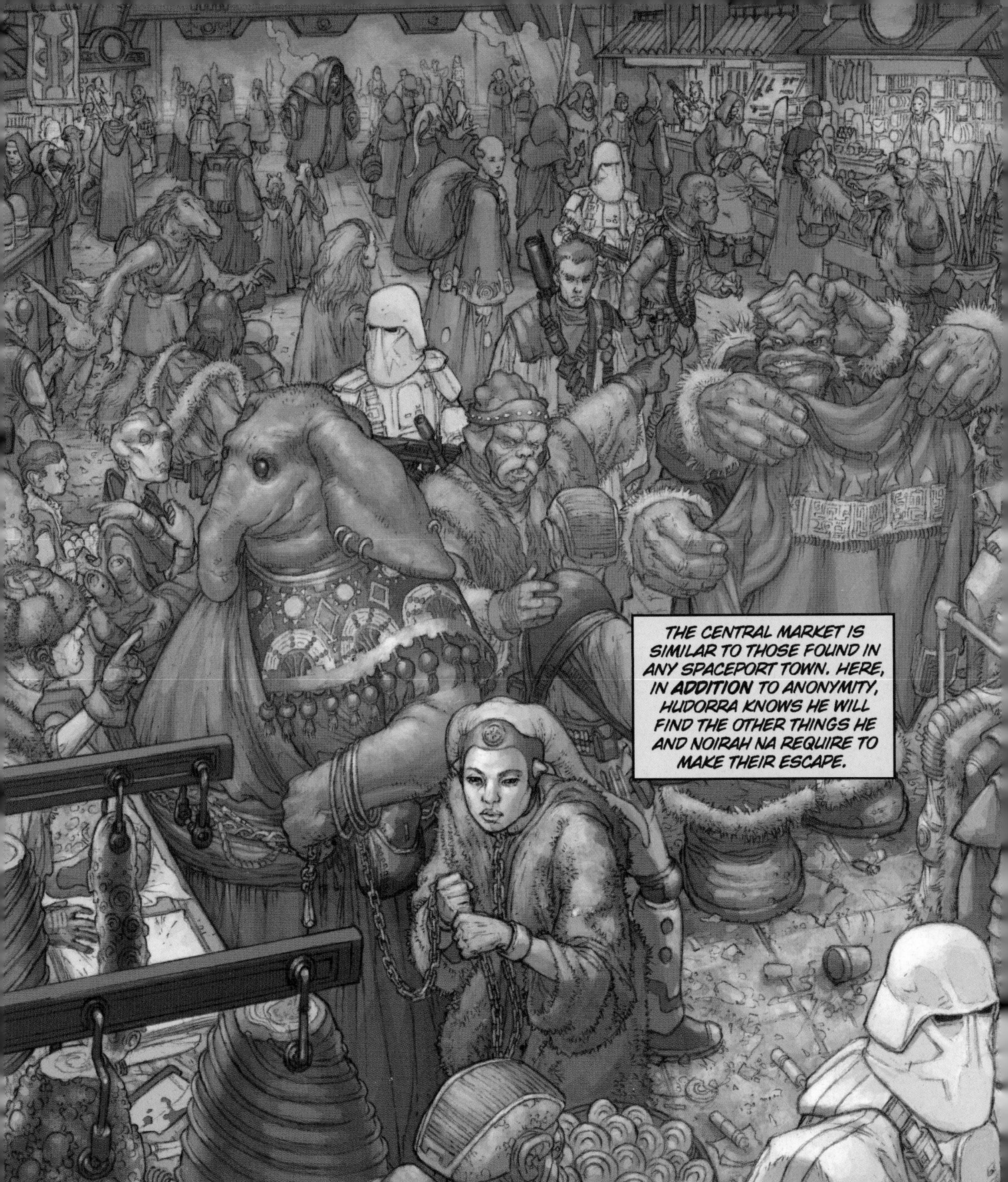
THE CENTRAL MARKET IS SIMILAR TO THOSE FOUND IN ANY SPACEPORT TOWN. HERE, IN ADDITION TO ANONYMITY, HUDORRA KNOWS HE WILL FIND THE OTHER THINGS HE AND NOIRAH NA REQUIRE TO MAKE THEIR ESCAPE.

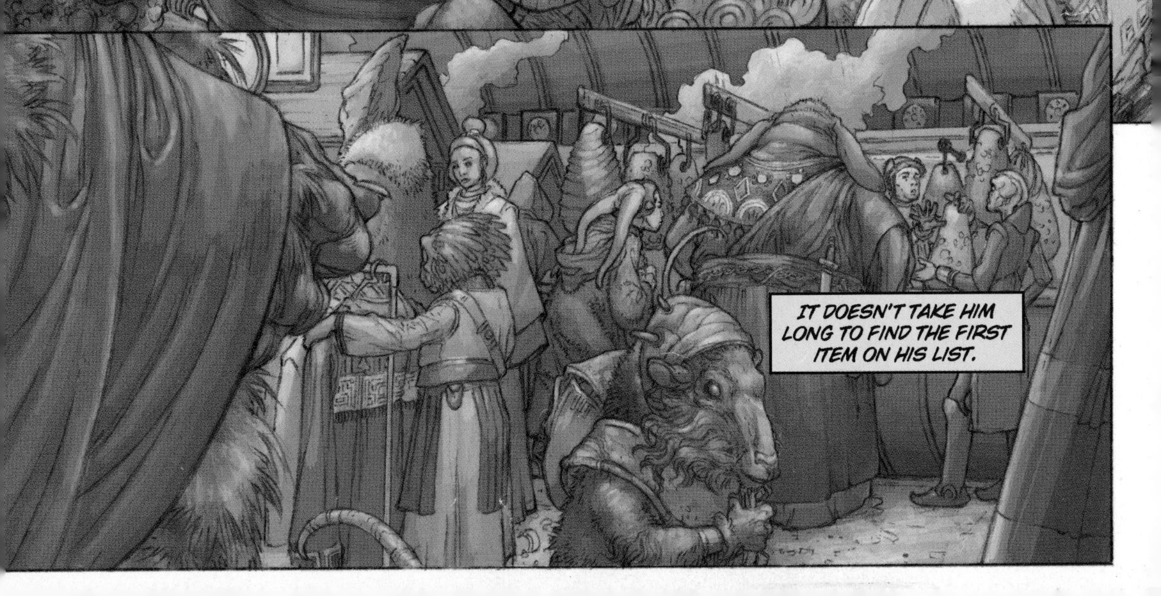
IT DOESN'T TAKE HIM LONG TO FIND THE FIRST ITEM ON HIS LIST.

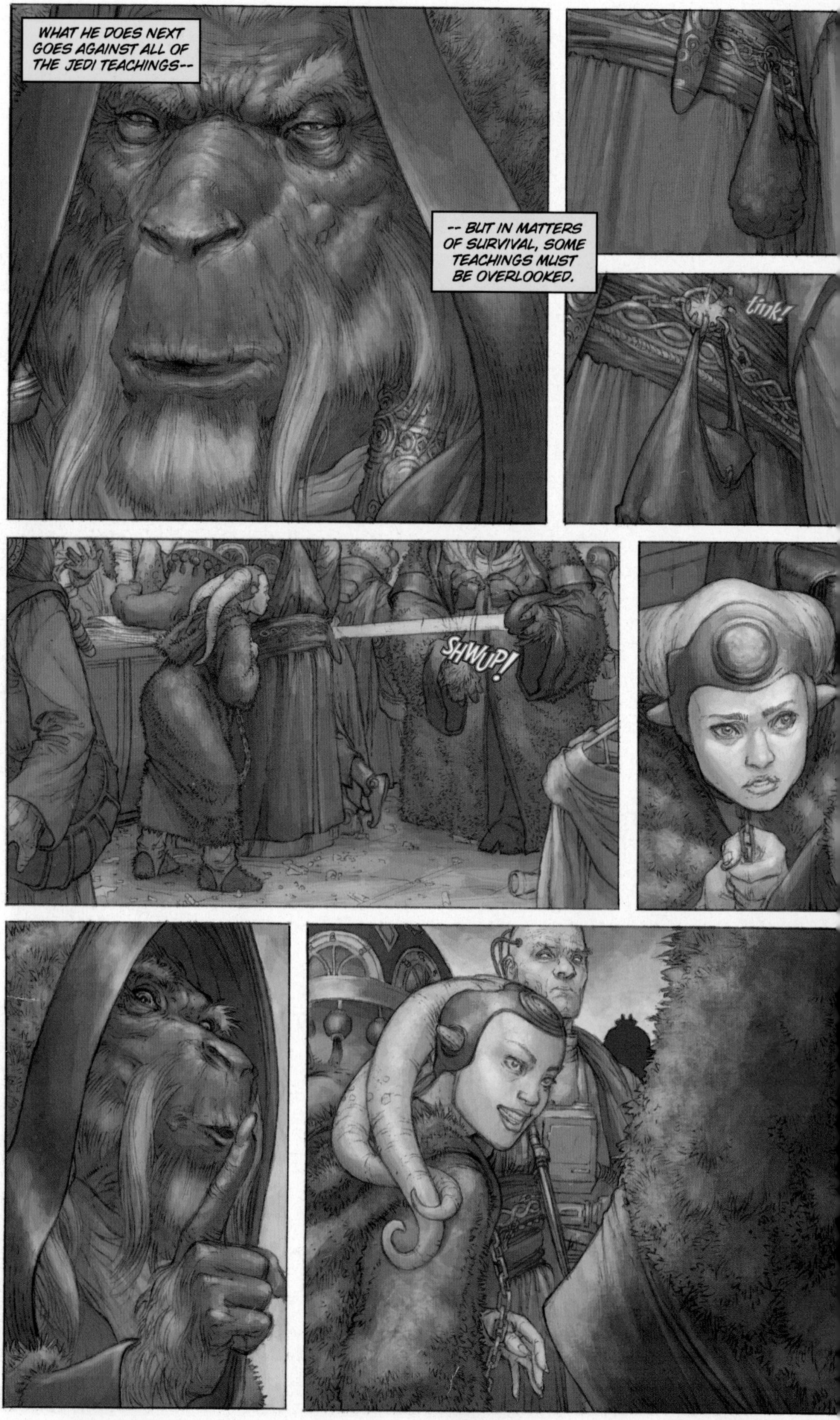
WHAT HE DOES NEXT GOES AGAINST ALL OF THE JEDI TEACHINGS--
-- BUT IN MATTERS OF SURVIVAL, SOME TEACHINGS MUST BE OVERLOOKED.
tink!
SHWUP!

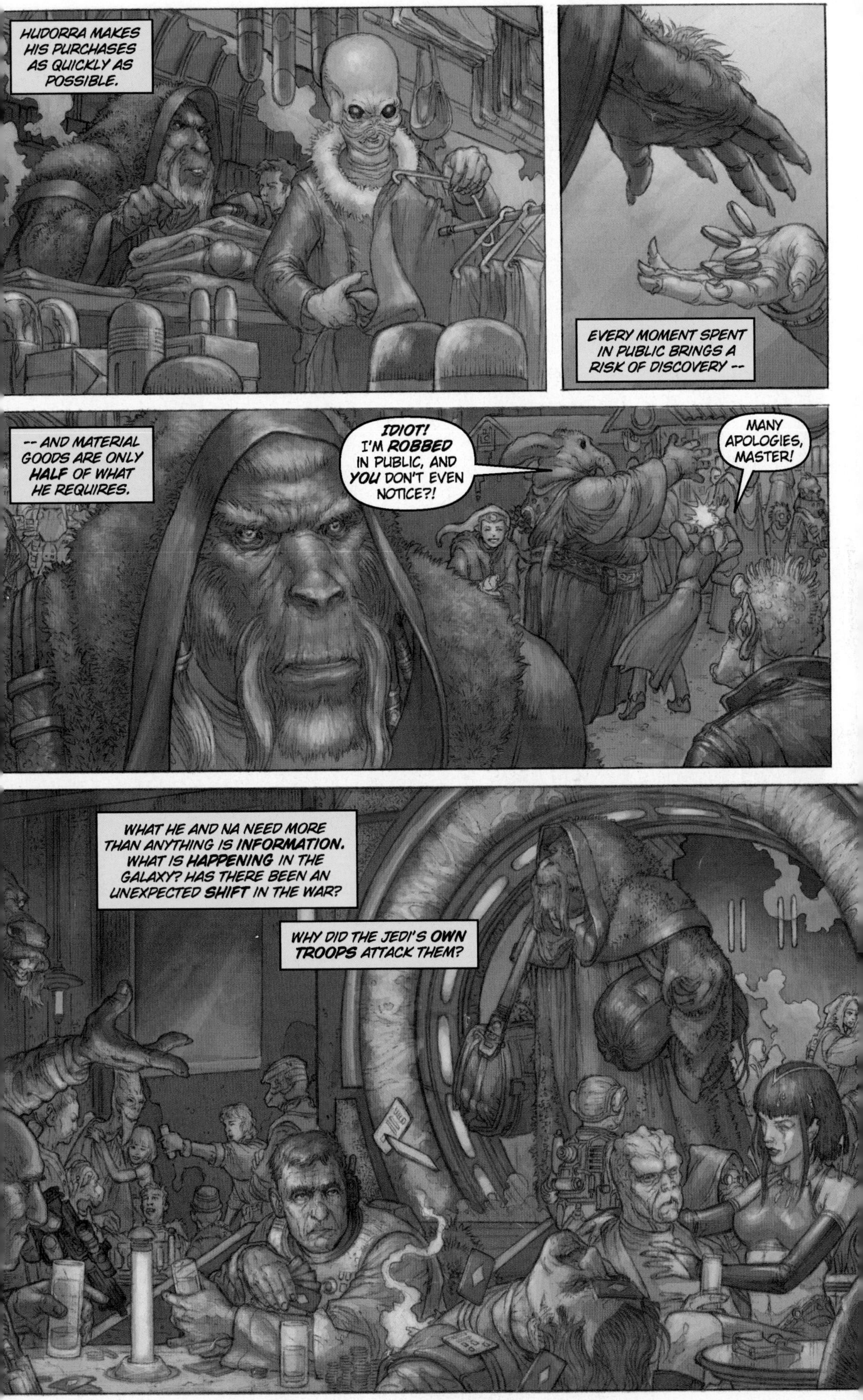
HUDORRA MAKES HIS PURCHASES AS QUICKLY AS POSSIBLE.
EVERY MOMENT SPENT IN PUBLIC BRINGS A RISK OF DISCOVERY --
-- AND MATERIAL GOODS ARE ONLY HALF OF WHAT HE REQUIRES.
IDIOT! I'M ROBBED IN PUBLIC, AND YOU DON'T EVEN NOTICE?!
MANY APOLOGIES, MASTER!
WHAT HE AND NA NEED MORE THAN ANYTHING IS INFORMATION. WHAT IS HAPPENING IN THE GALAXY? HAS THERE BEEN AN UNEXPECTED SHIFT IN THE WAR?
WHY DID THE JEDI'S OWN TROOPS ATTACK THEM?

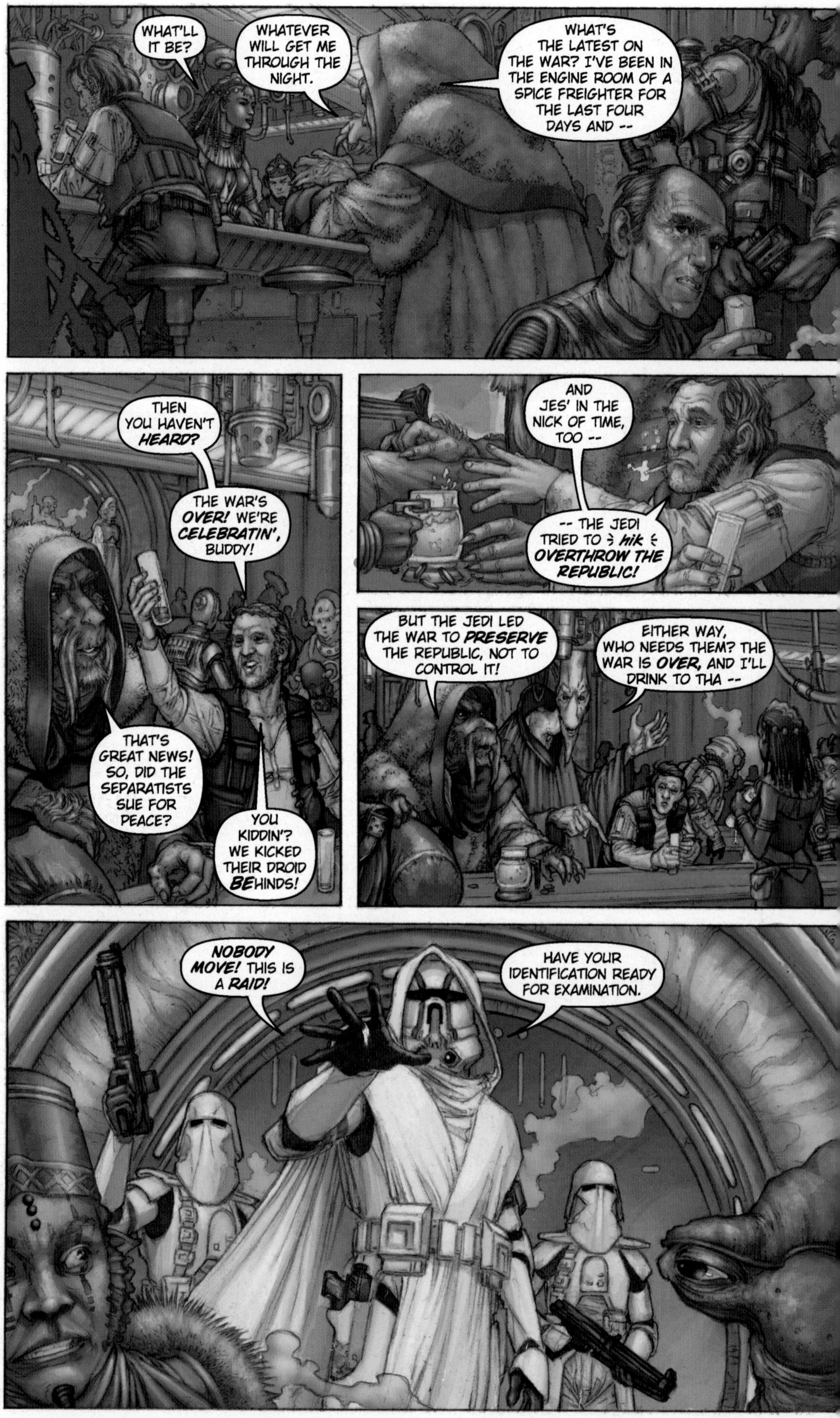
WHAT'LL IT BE?
WHATEVER WILL GET ME THROUGH THE NIGHT.
WHAT'S THE LATEST ON THE WAR? I'VE BEEN IN THE ENGINE ROOM OF A SPICE FREIGHTER FOR THE LAST FOUR DAYS AND --
THEN YOU HAVEN'T **HEARD?**
THE WAR'S **OVER!** WE'RE **CELEBRATIN'**, BUDDY!
THAT'S GREAT NEWS! SO, DID THE SEPARATISTS SUE FOR PEACE?
YOU KIDDIN'? WE KICKED THEIR DROID **BE**HINDS!
AND JES' IN THE NICK OF TIME, TOO --
-- THE JEDI TRIED TO *hik* **OVERTHROW THE REPUBLIC!**
BUT THE JEDI LED THE WAR TO **PRESERVE** THE REPUBLIC, NOT TO CONTROL IT!
EITHER WAY, WHO NEEDS THEM? THE WAR IS **OVER**, AND I'LL DRINK TO THA --
NOBODY MOVE! THIS IS A **RAID!**
HAVE YOUR IDENTIFICATION READY FOR EXAMINATION.

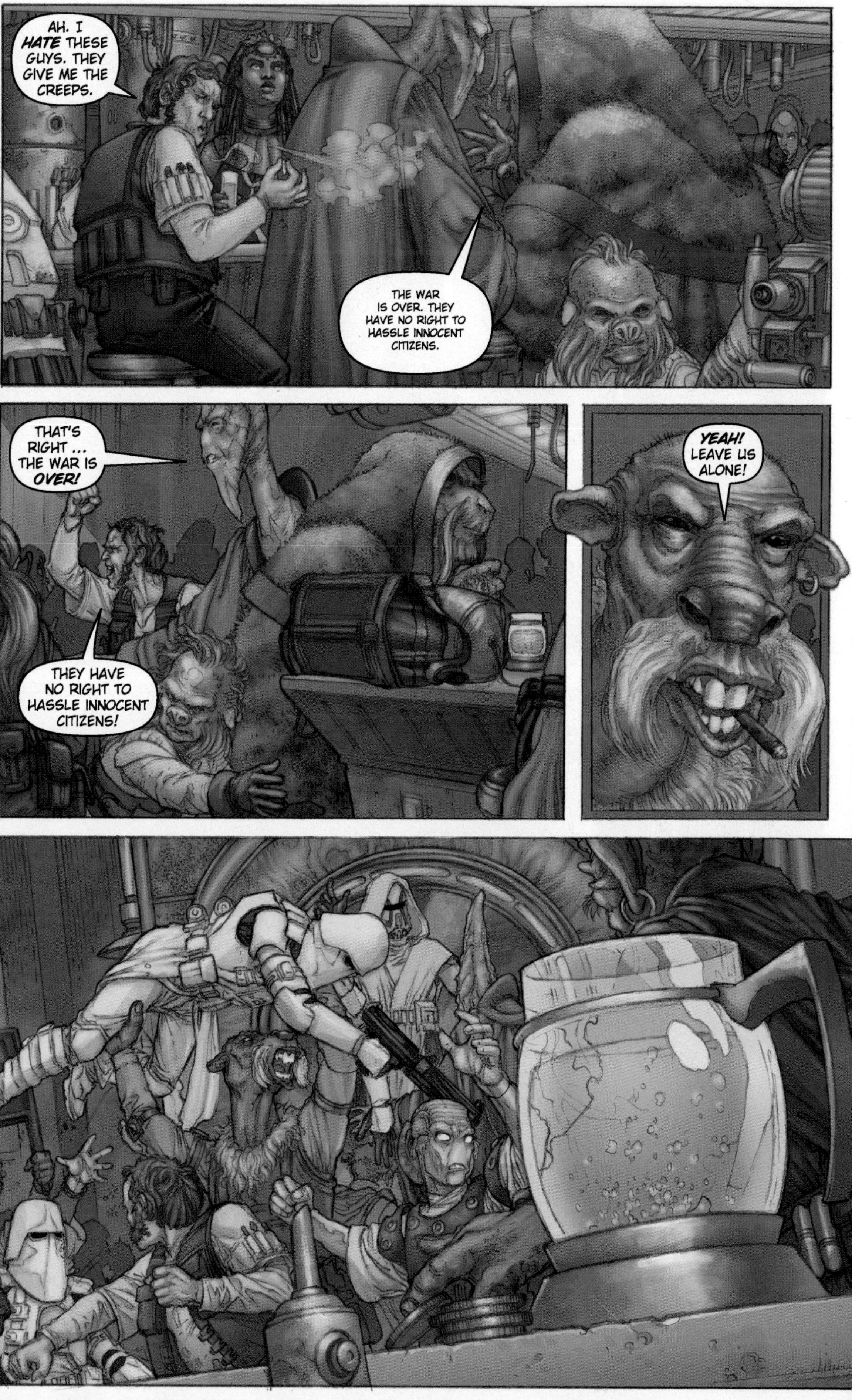
AH. I *HATE* THESE GUYS. THEY GIVE ME THE CREEPS.
THE WAR IS OVER. THEY HAVE NO RIGHT TO HASSLE INNOCENT CITIZENS.
THAT'S RIGHT ... THE WAR IS *OVER!*
THEY HAVE NO RIGHT TO HASSLE INNOCENT CITIZENS!
YEAH! LEAVE US ALONE!

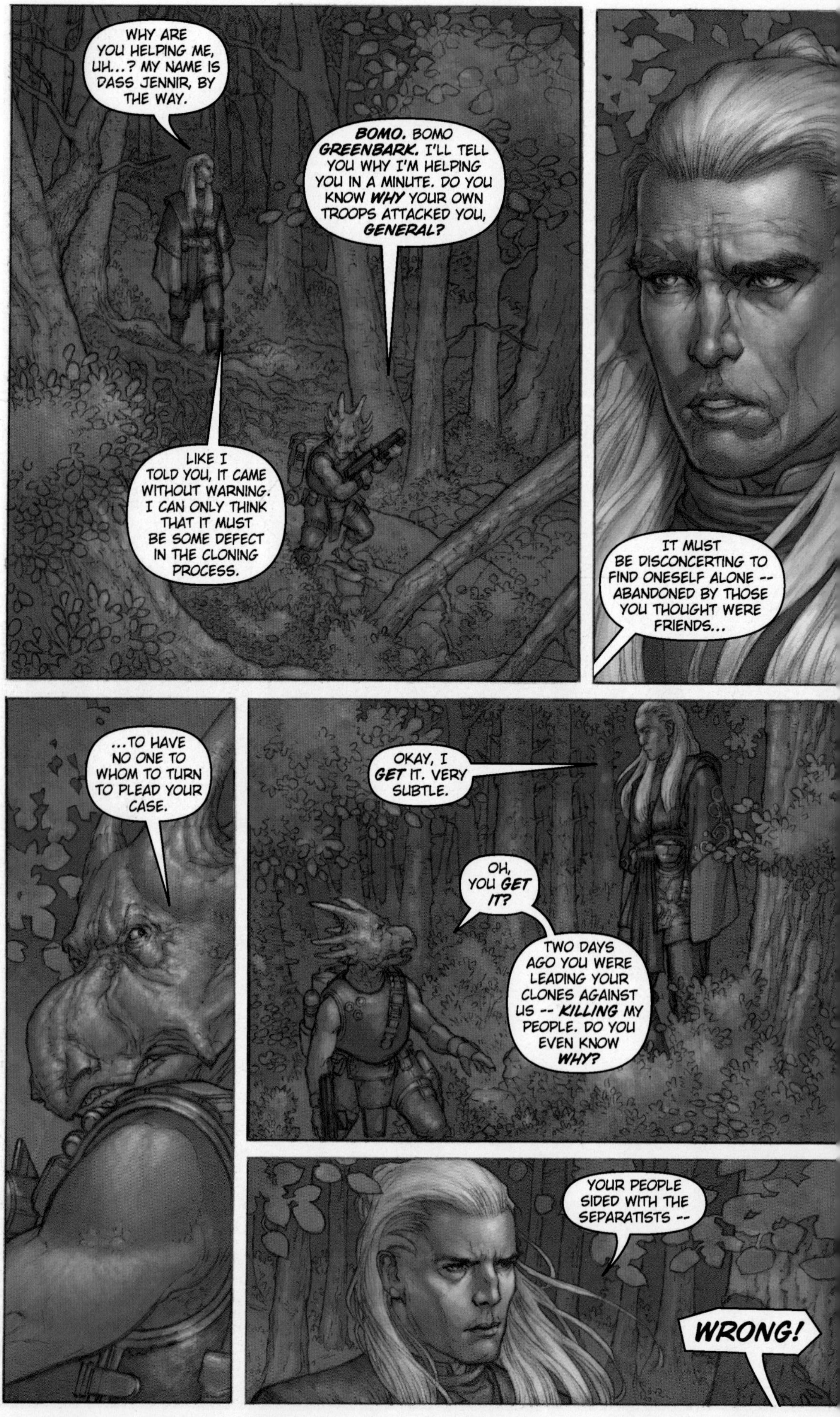
WHY ARE YOU HELPING ME, UH...? MY NAME IS DASS JENNIR, BY THE WAY.
BOMO. BOMO GREENBARK. I'LL TELL YOU WHY I'M HELPING YOU IN A MINUTE. DO YOU KNOW WHY YOUR OWN TROOPS ATTACKED YOU, GENERAL?
LIKE I TOLD YOU, IT CAME WITHOUT WARNING. I CAN ONLY THINK THAT IT MUST BE SOME DEFECT IN THE CLONING PROCESS.
IT MUST BE DISCONCERTING TO FIND ONESELF ALONE -- ABANDONED BY THOSE YOU THOUGHT WERE FRIENDS...
...TO HAVE NO ONE TO WHOM TO TURN TO PLEAD YOUR CASE.
OKAY, I GET IT. VERY SUBTLE.
OH, YOU GET IT?
TWO DAYS AGO YOU WERE LEADING YOUR CLONES AGAINST US -- KILLING MY PEOPLE. DO YOU EVEN KNOW WHY?
YOUR PEOPLE SIDED WITH THE SEPARATISTS --
WRONG!

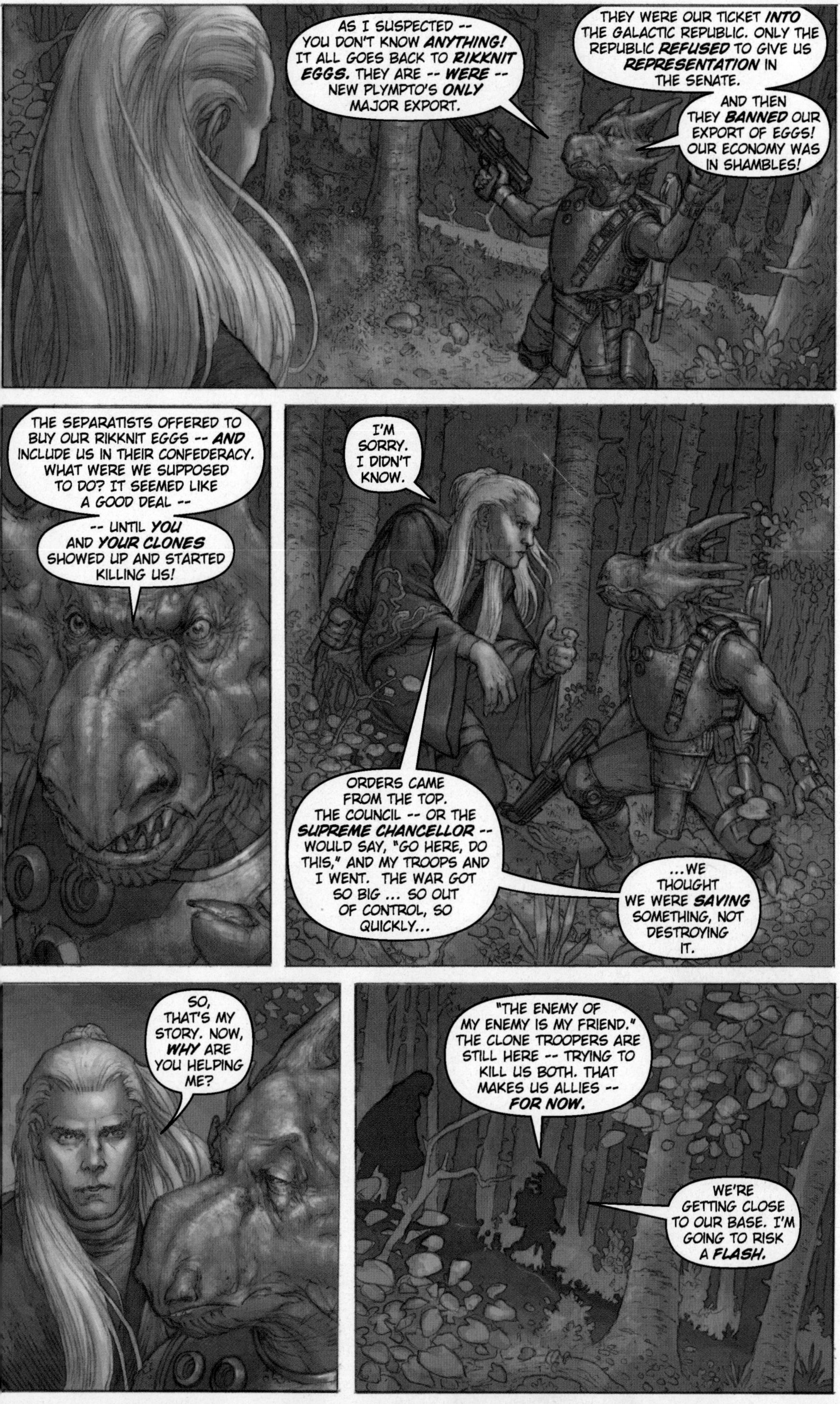
AS I SUSPECTED -- YOU DON'T KNOW ANYTHING! IT ALL GOES BACK TO RIKKNIT EGGS. THEY ARE -- WERE -- NEW PLYMPTO'S ONLY MAJOR EXPORT.
THEY WERE OUR TICKET INTO THE GALACTIC REPUBLIC. ONLY THE REPUBLIC REFUSED TO GIVE US REPRESENTATION IN THE SENATE.
AND THEN THEY BANNED OUR EXPORT OF EGGS! OUR ECONOMY WAS IN SHAMBLES!
THE SEPARATISTS OFFERED TO BUY OUR RIKKNIT EGGS -- AND INCLUDE US IN THEIR CONFEDERACY. WHAT WERE WE SUPPOSED TO DO? IT SEEMED LIKE A GOOD DEAL --
-- UNTIL YOU AND YOUR CLONES SHOWED UP AND STARTED KILLING US!
I'M SORRY. I DIDN'T KNOW.
ORDERS CAME FROM THE TOP. THE COUNCIL -- OR THE SUPREME CHANCELLOR -- WOULD SAY, "GO HERE, DO THIS," AND MY TROOPS AND I WENT. THE WAR GOT SO BIG ... SO OUT OF CONTROL, SO QUICKLY...
...WE THOUGHT WE WERE SAVING SOMETHING, NOT DESTROYING IT.
SO, THAT'S MY STORY. NOW, WHY ARE YOU HELPING ME?
"THE ENEMY OF MY ENEMY IS MY FRIEND." THE CLONE TROOPERS ARE STILL HERE -- TRYING TO KILL US BOTH. THAT MAKES US ALLIES -- FOR NOW.
WE'RE GETTING CLOSE TO OUR BASE. I'M GOING TO RISK A FLASH.

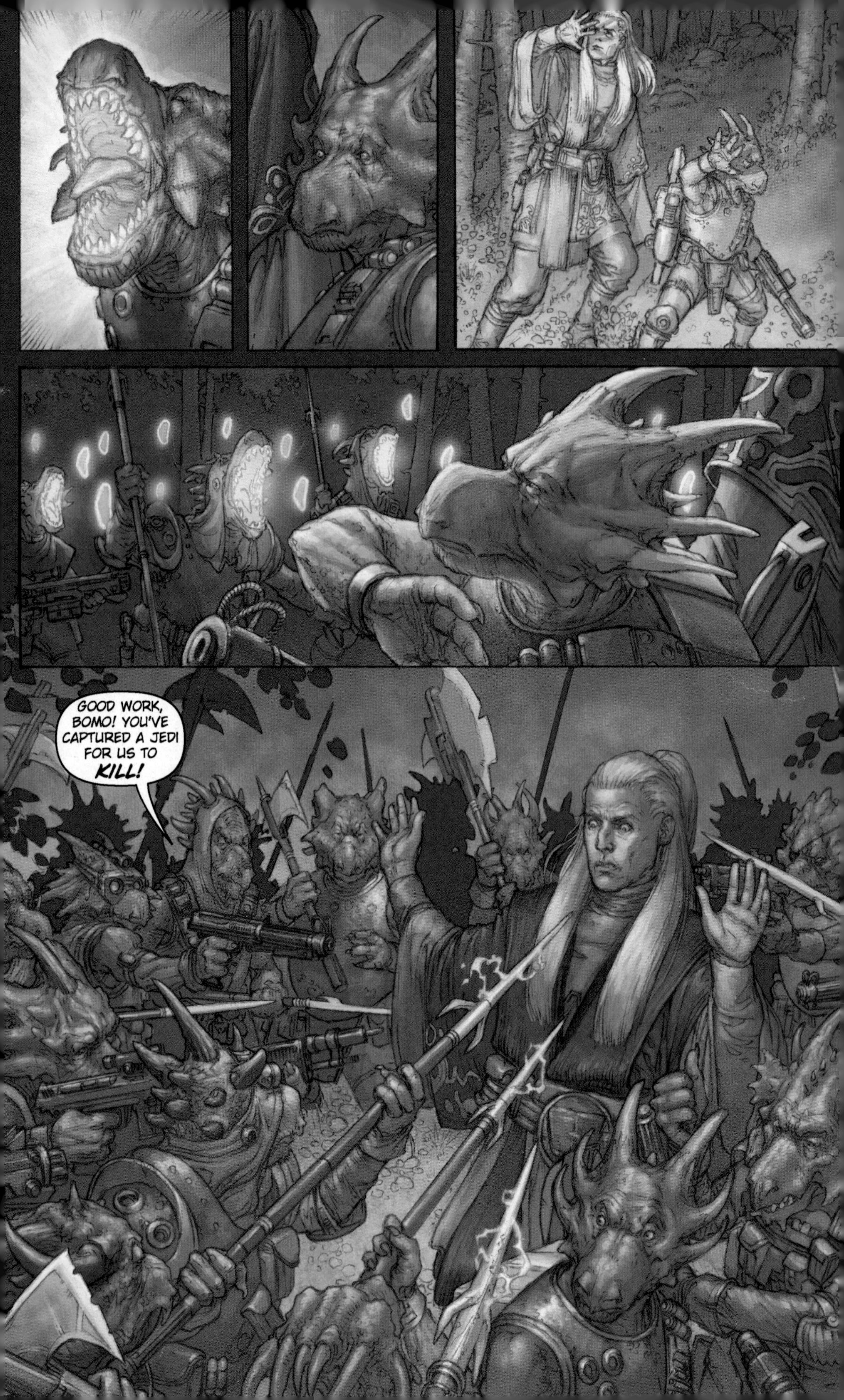
GOOD WORK, BOMO! YOU'VE CAPTURED A JEDI FOR US TO KILL!

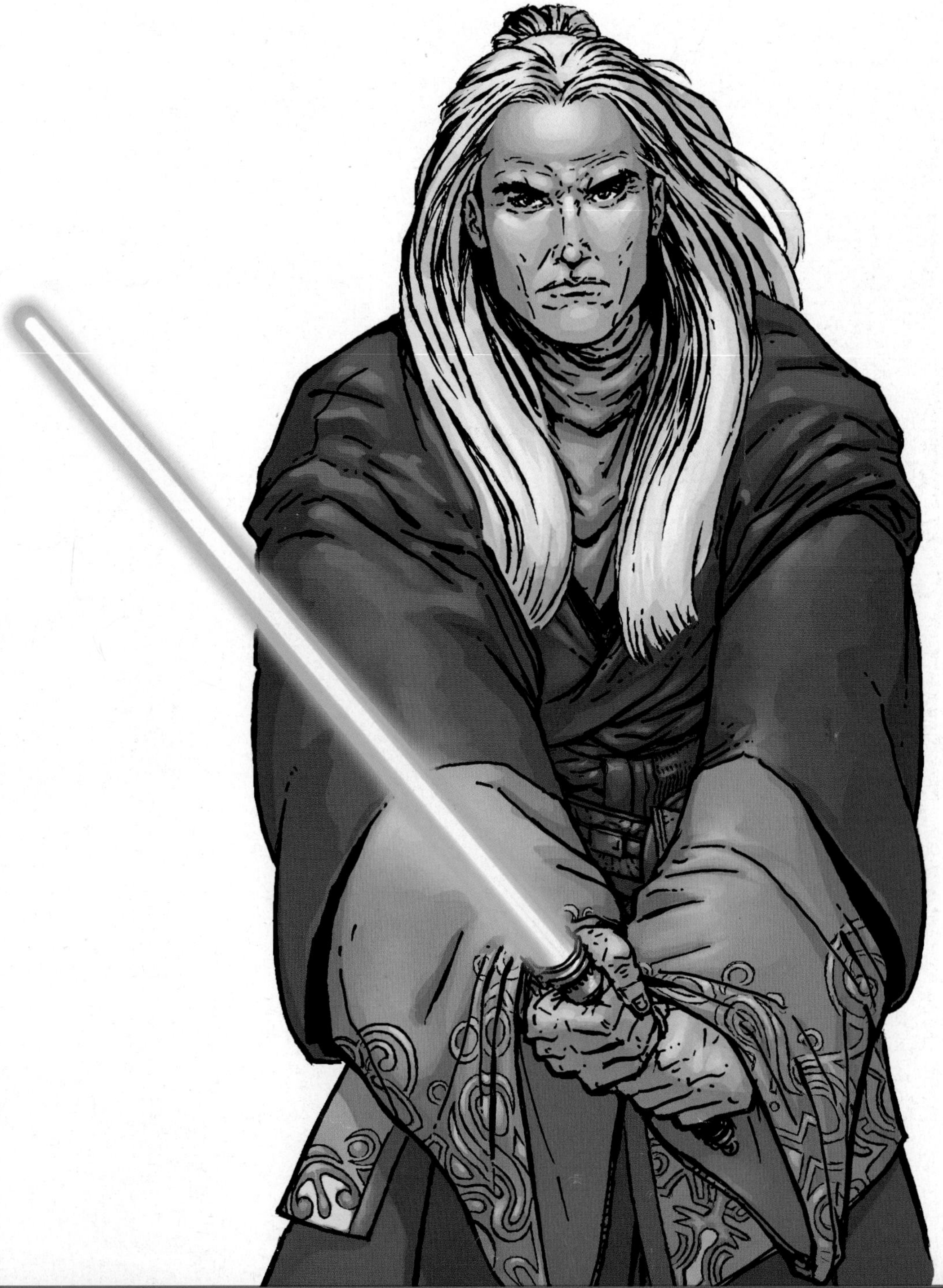

STAR WARS: REPUBLIC #80 — "INTO THE UNKNOWN, PART TWO OF TWO"

WRITER: RANDY STRADLEY (AS WELLES HARTLEY) • ARTIST: DOUGLAS WHEATLEY • COLORIST: CHRIS CHUCKRY • LETTERER: MICHAEL DAVID THOMAS
DESIGNER: DAVID NESTELLE • ASSISTANT EDITOR: DAVE MARSHALL • ASSOCIATE EDITOR: JEREMY BARLOW • EDITOR: RANDY STRADLEY

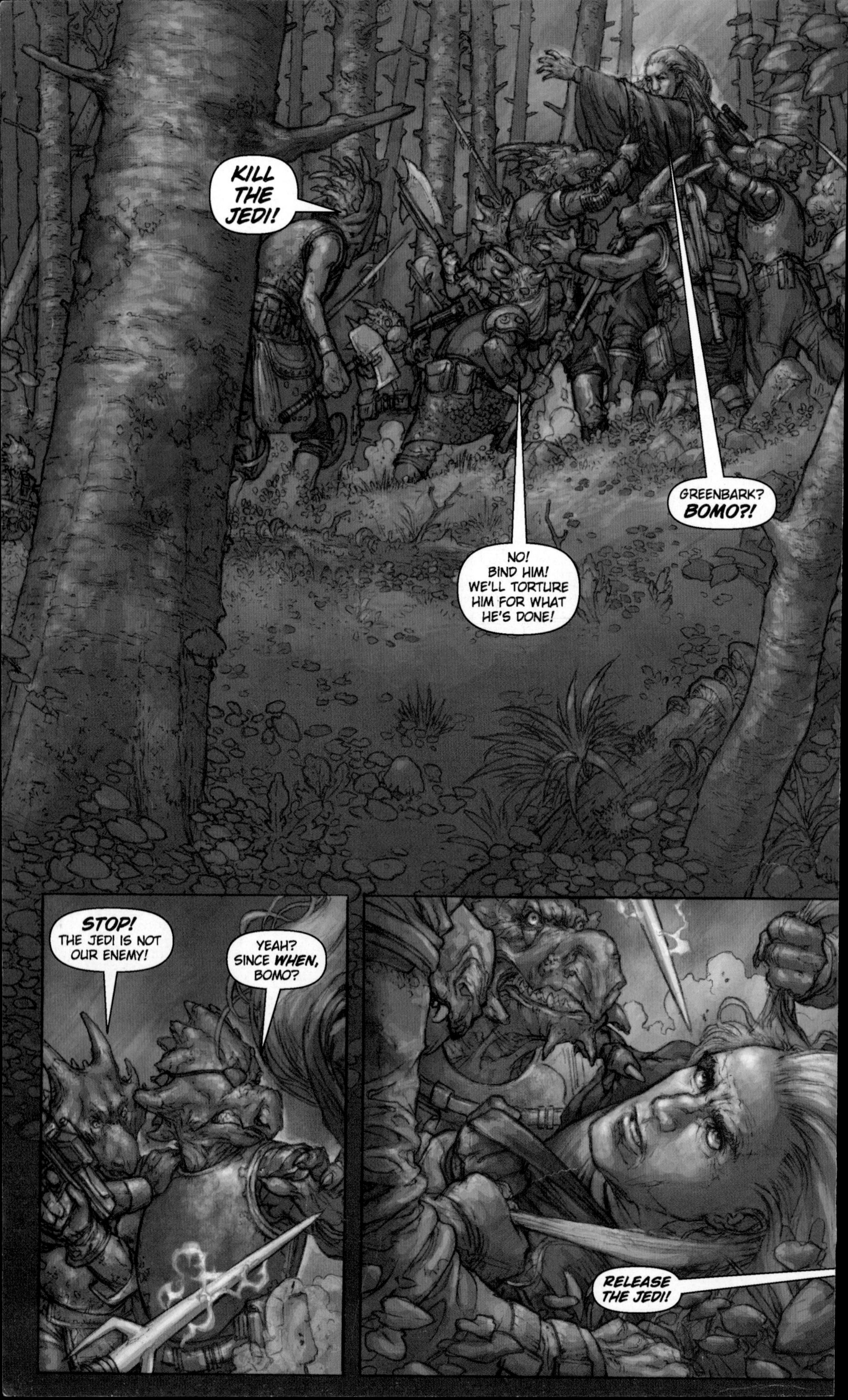
KILL THE JEDI!
GREENBARK? BOMO?!
NO! BIND HIM! WE'LL TORTURE HIM FOR WHAT HE'S DONE!
STOP! THE JEDI IS NOT OUR ENEMY!
YEAH? SINCE WHEN, BOMO?
RELEASE THE JEDI!

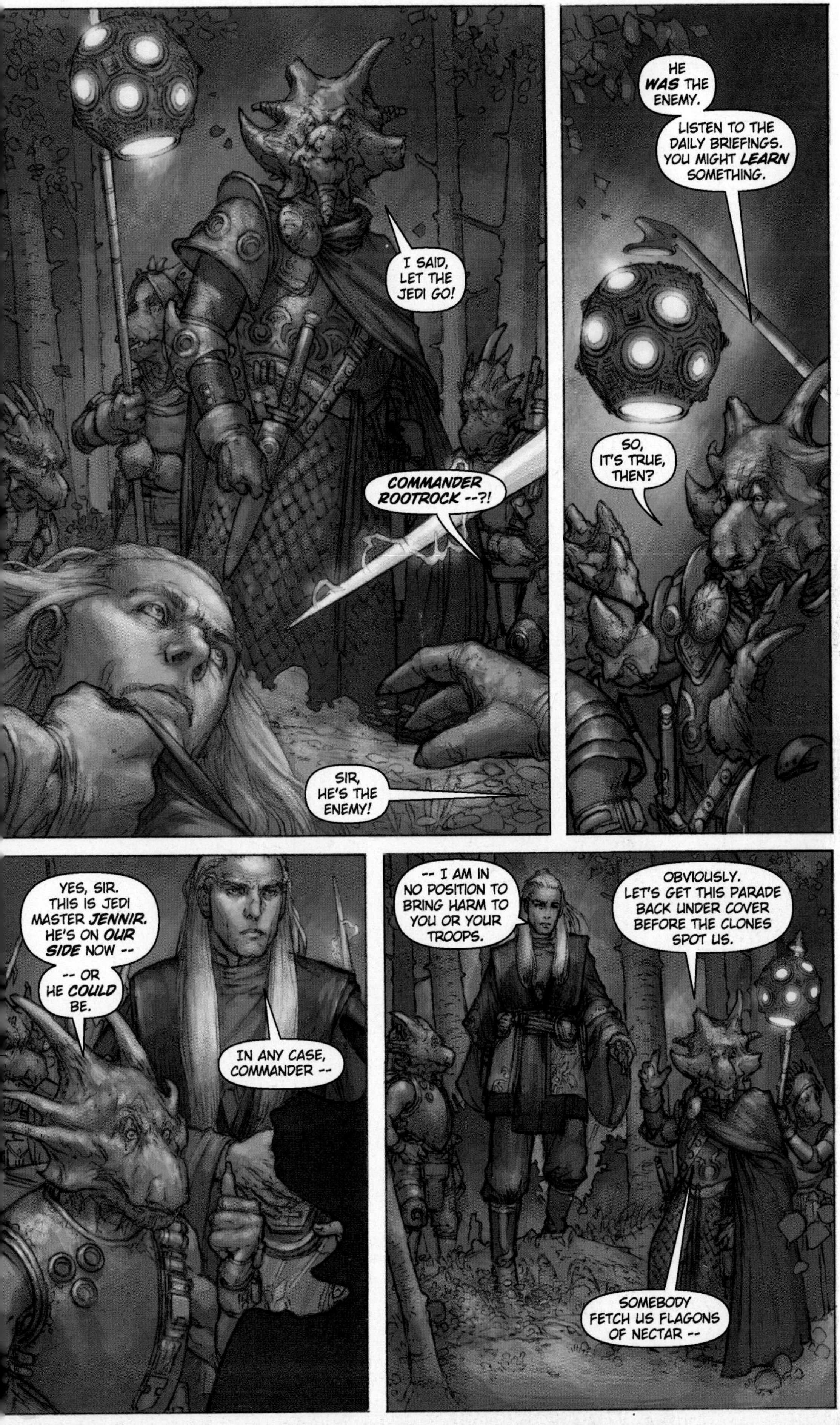
I SAID, LET THE JEDI GO!
COMMANDER ROOTROCK --?!
SIR, HE'S THE ENEMY!
HE WAS THE ENEMY.
LISTEN TO THE DAILY BRIEFINGS. YOU MIGHT LEARN SOMETHING.
SO, IT'S TRUE, THEN?
YES, SIR. THIS IS JEDI MASTER JENNIR. HE'S ON OUR SIDE NOW --
-- OR HE COULD BE.
IN ANY CASE, COMMANDER --
-- I AM IN NO POSITION TO BRING HARM TO YOU OR YOUR TROOPS.
OBVIOUSLY. LET'S GET THIS PARADE BACK UNDER COVER BEFORE THE CLONES SPOT US.
SOMEBODY FETCH US FLAGONS OF NECTAR --

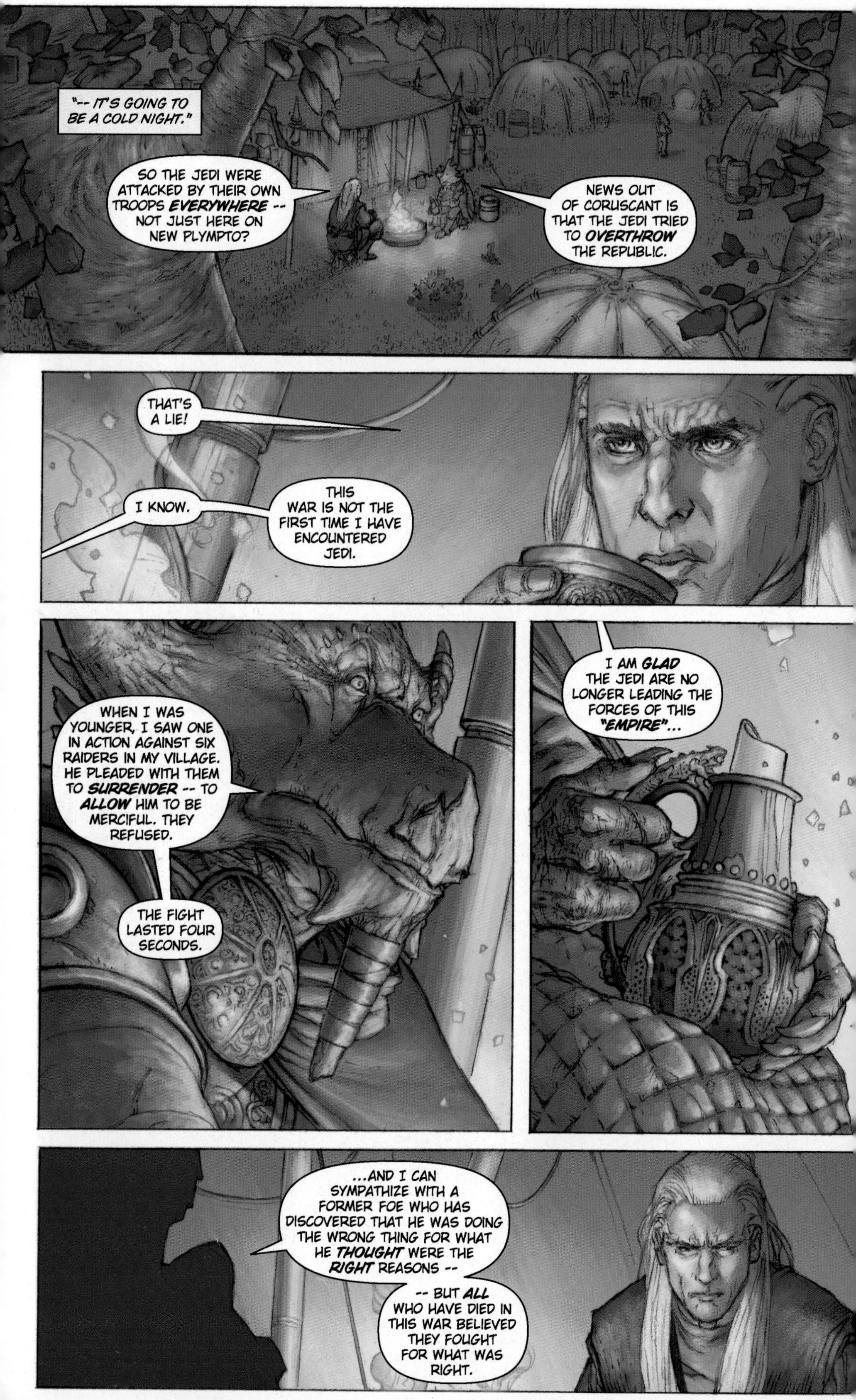
"-- IT'S GOING TO BE A COLD NIGHT."
SO THE JEDI WERE ATTACKED BY THEIR OWN TROOPS EVERYWHERE -- NOT JUST HERE ON NEW PLYMPTO?
NEWS OUT OF CORUSCANT IS THAT THE JEDI TRIED TO OVERTHROW THE REPUBLIC.
THAT'S A LIE!
I KNOW.
THIS WAR IS NOT THE FIRST TIME I HAVE ENCOUNTERED JEDI.
WHEN I WAS YOUNGER, I SAW ONE IN ACTION AGAINST SIX RAIDERS IN MY VILLAGE. HE PLEADED WITH THEM TO SURRENDER -- TO ALLOW HIM TO BE MERCIFUL. THEY REFUSED.
THE FIGHT LASTED FOUR SECONDS.
I AM GLAD THE JEDI ARE NO LONGER LEADING THE FORCES OF THIS "EMPIRE"...
...AND I CAN SYMPATHIZE WITH A FORMER FOE WHO HAS DISCOVERED THAT HE WAS DOING THE WRONG THING FOR WHAT HE THOUGHT WERE THE RIGHT REASONS --
-- BUT ALL WHO HAVE DIED IN THIS WAR BELIEVED THEY FOUGHT FOR WHAT WAS RIGHT.

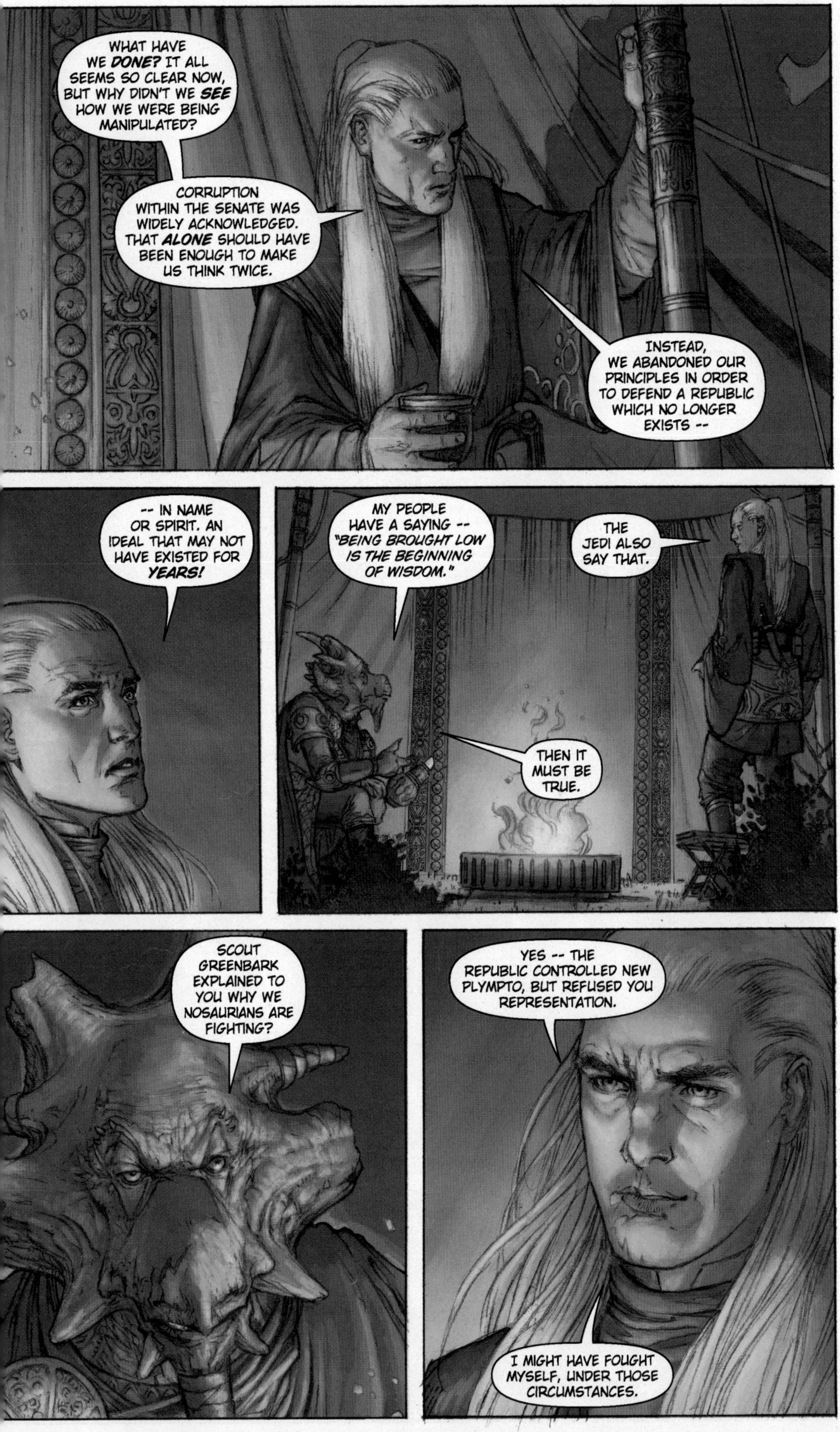
WHAT HAVE WE *DONE?* IT ALL SEEMS SO CLEAR NOW, BUT WHY DIDN'T WE *SEE* HOW WE WERE BEING MANIPULATED?
CORRUPTION WITHIN THE SENATE WAS WIDELY ACKNOWLEDGED. THAT *ALONE* SHOULD HAVE BEEN ENOUGH TO MAKE US THINK TWICE.
INSTEAD, WE ABANDONED OUR PRINCIPLES IN ORDER TO DEFEND A REPUBLIC WHICH NO LONGER EXISTS --
-- IN NAME OR SPIRIT. AN IDEAL THAT MAY NOT HAVE EXISTED FOR *YEARS!*
MY PEOPLE HAVE A SAYING -- *"BEING BROUGHT LOW IS THE BEGINNING OF WISDOM."*
THE JEDI ALSO SAY THAT.
THEN IT MUST BE TRUE.
SCOUT GREENBARK EXPLAINED TO YOU WHY WE NOSAURIANS ARE FIGHTING?
YES -- THE REPUBLIC CONTROLLED NEW PLYMPTO, BUT REFUSED YOU REPRESENTATION.
I MIGHT HAVE FOUGHT MYSELF, UNDER THOSE CIRCUMSTANCES.

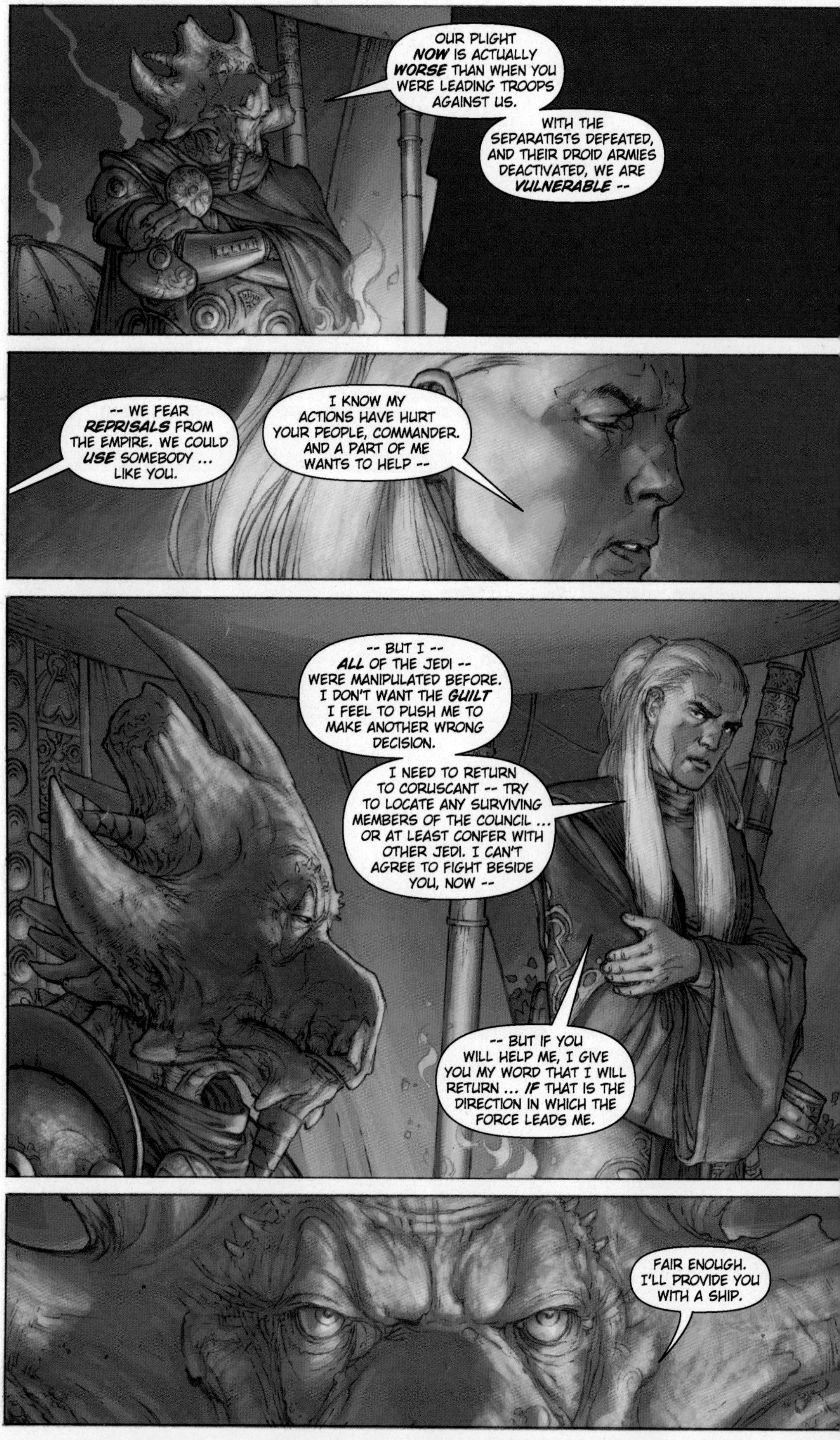

OUR PLIGHT NOW IS ACTUALLY WORSE THAN WHEN YOU WERE LEADING TROOPS AGAINST US.
WITH THE SEPARATISTS DEFEATED, AND THEIR DROID ARMIES DEACTIVATED, WE ARE VULNERABLE --
-- WE FEAR REPRISALS FROM THE EMPIRE. WE COULD USE SOMEBODY ... LIKE YOU.
I KNOW MY ACTIONS HAVE HURT YOUR PEOPLE, COMMANDER. AND A PART OF ME WANTS TO HELP --
-- BUT I -- ALL OF THE JEDI -- WERE MANIPULATED BEFORE. I DON'T WANT THE GUILT I FEEL TO PUSH ME TO MAKE ANOTHER WRONG DECISION.
I NEED TO RETURN TO CORUSCANT -- TRY TO LOCATE ANY SURVIVING MEMBERS OF THE COUNCIL ... OR AT LEAST CONFER WITH OTHER JEDI. I CAN'T AGREE TO FIGHT BESIDE YOU, NOW --
-- BUT IF YOU WILL HELP ME, I GIVE YOU MY WORD THAT I WILL RETURN ... IF THAT IS THE DIRECTION IN WHICH THE FORCE LEADS ME.
FAIR ENOUGH. I'LL PROVIDE YOU WITH A SHIP.

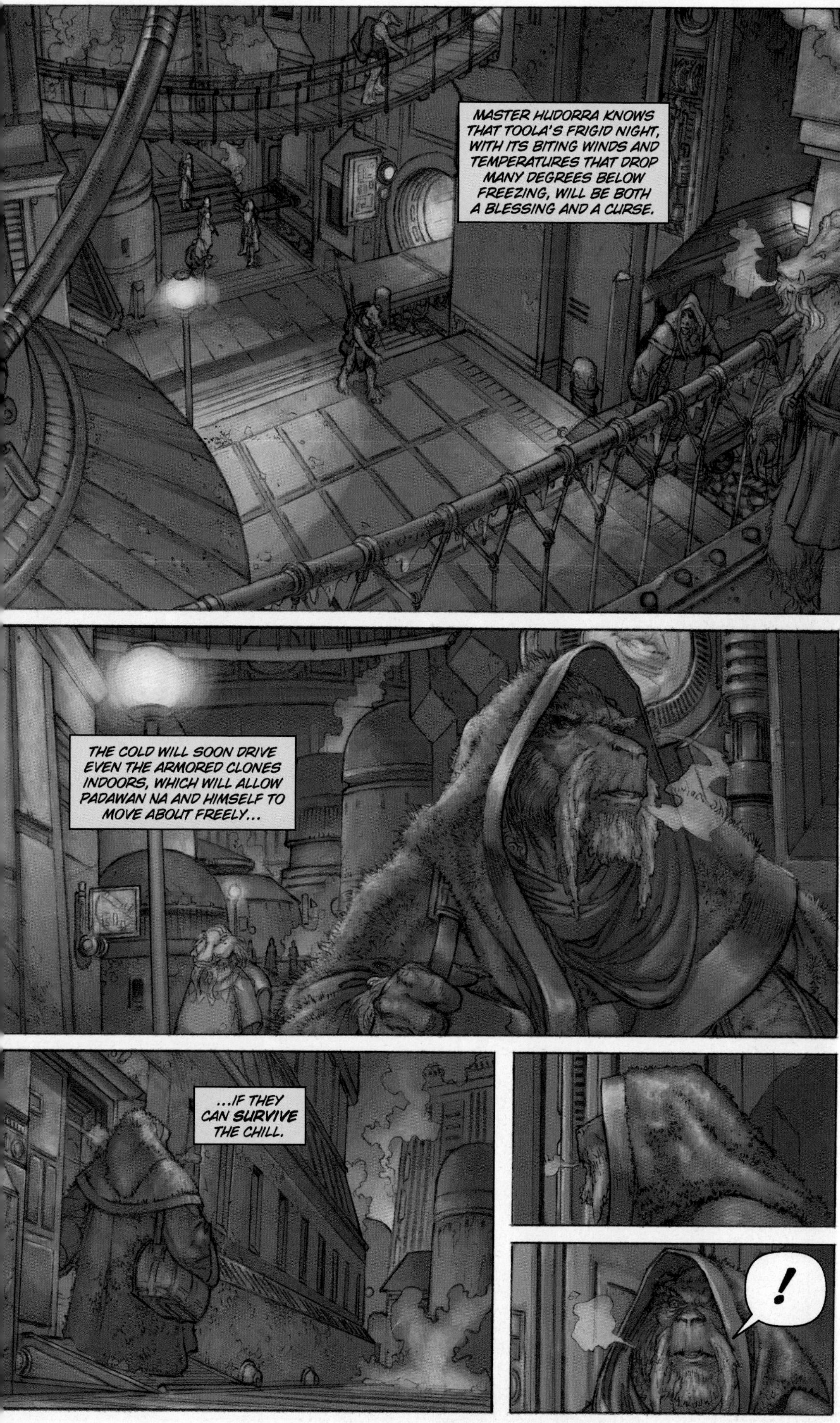
MASTER HUDORRA KNOWS THAT TOOLA'S FRIGID NIGHT, WITH ITS BITING WINDS AND TEMPERATURES THAT DROP MANY DEGREES BELOW FREEZING, WILL BE BOTH A BLESSING AND A CURSE.
THE COLD WILL SOON DRIVE EVEN THE ARMORED CLONES INDOORS, WHICH WILL ALLOW PADAWAN NA AND HIMSELF TO MOVE ABOUT FREELY...
...IF THEY CAN **SURVIVE** THE CHILL.
!

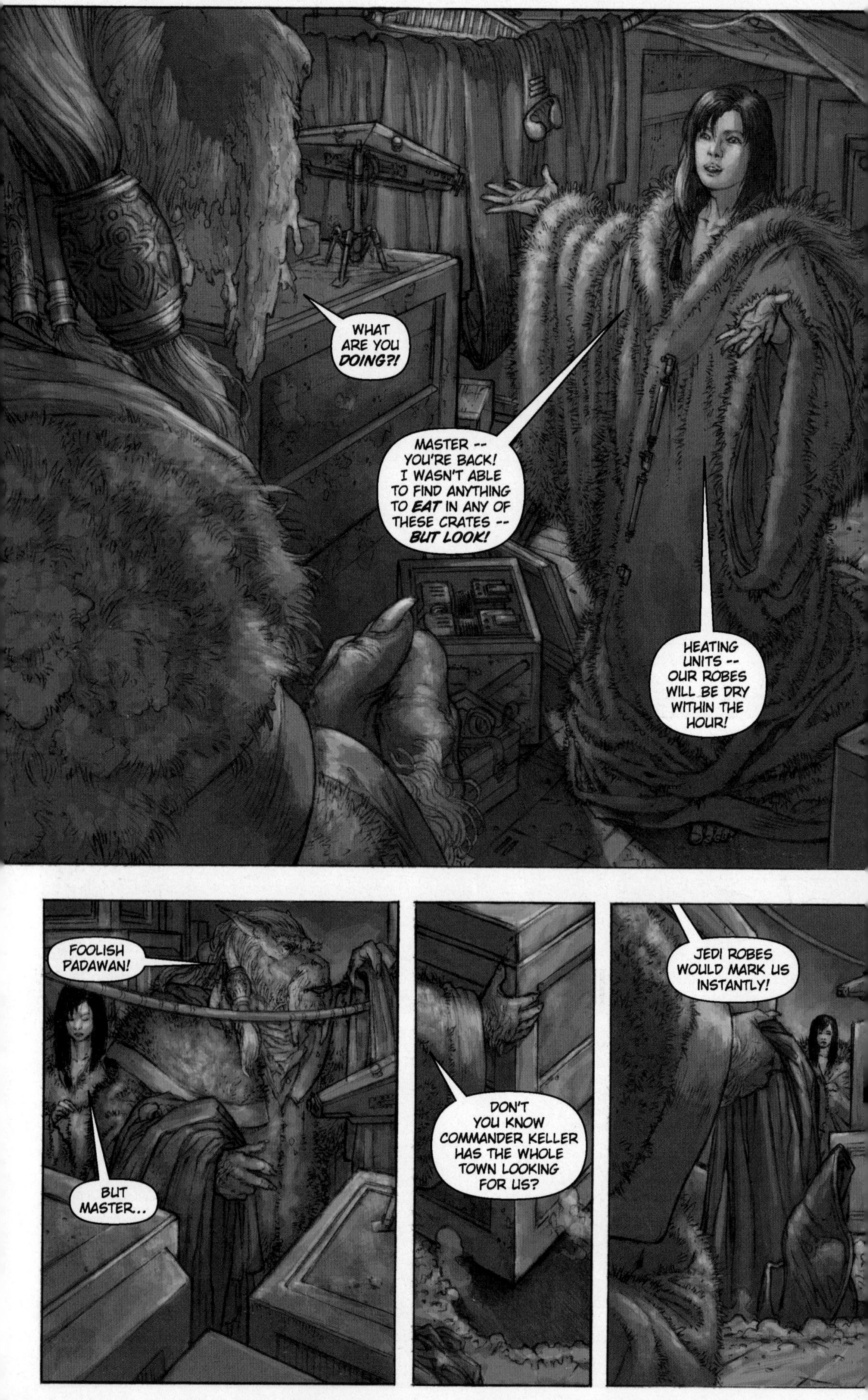
WHAT ARE YOU DOING?!
MASTER -- YOU'RE BACK! I WASN'T ABLE TO FIND ANYTHING TO EAT IN ANY OF THESE CRATES -- BUT LOOK!
HEATING UNITS -- OUR ROBES WILL BE DRY WITHIN THE HOUR!
FOOLISH PADAWAN!
BUT MASTER...
DON'T YOU KNOW COMMANDER KELLER HAS THE WHOLE TOWN LOOKING FOR US?
JEDI ROBES WOULD MARK US INSTANTLY!

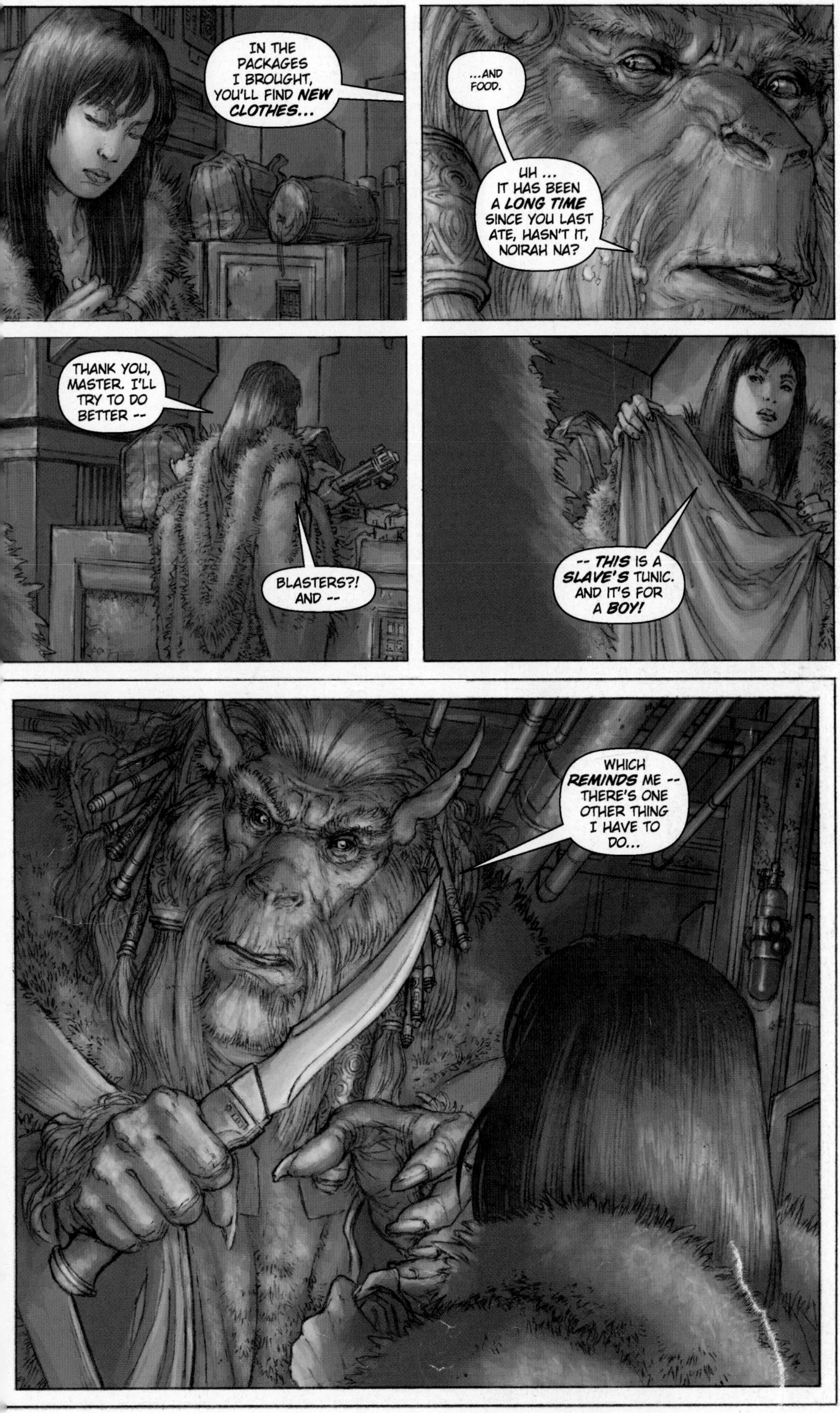

IN THE PACKAGES I BROUGHT, YOU'LL FIND **NEW CLOTHES...**
...AND FOOD.
UH ... IT HAS BEEN A **LONG TIME** SINCE YOU LAST ATE, HASN'T IT, NOIRAH NA?
THANK YOU, MASTER. I'LL TRY TO DO BETTER --
BLASTERS?! AND --
-- **THIS** IS A **SLAVE'S** TUNIC. AND IT'S FOR A **BOY!**
WHICH **REMINDS** ME -- THERE'S ONE OTHER THING I HAVE TO DO...

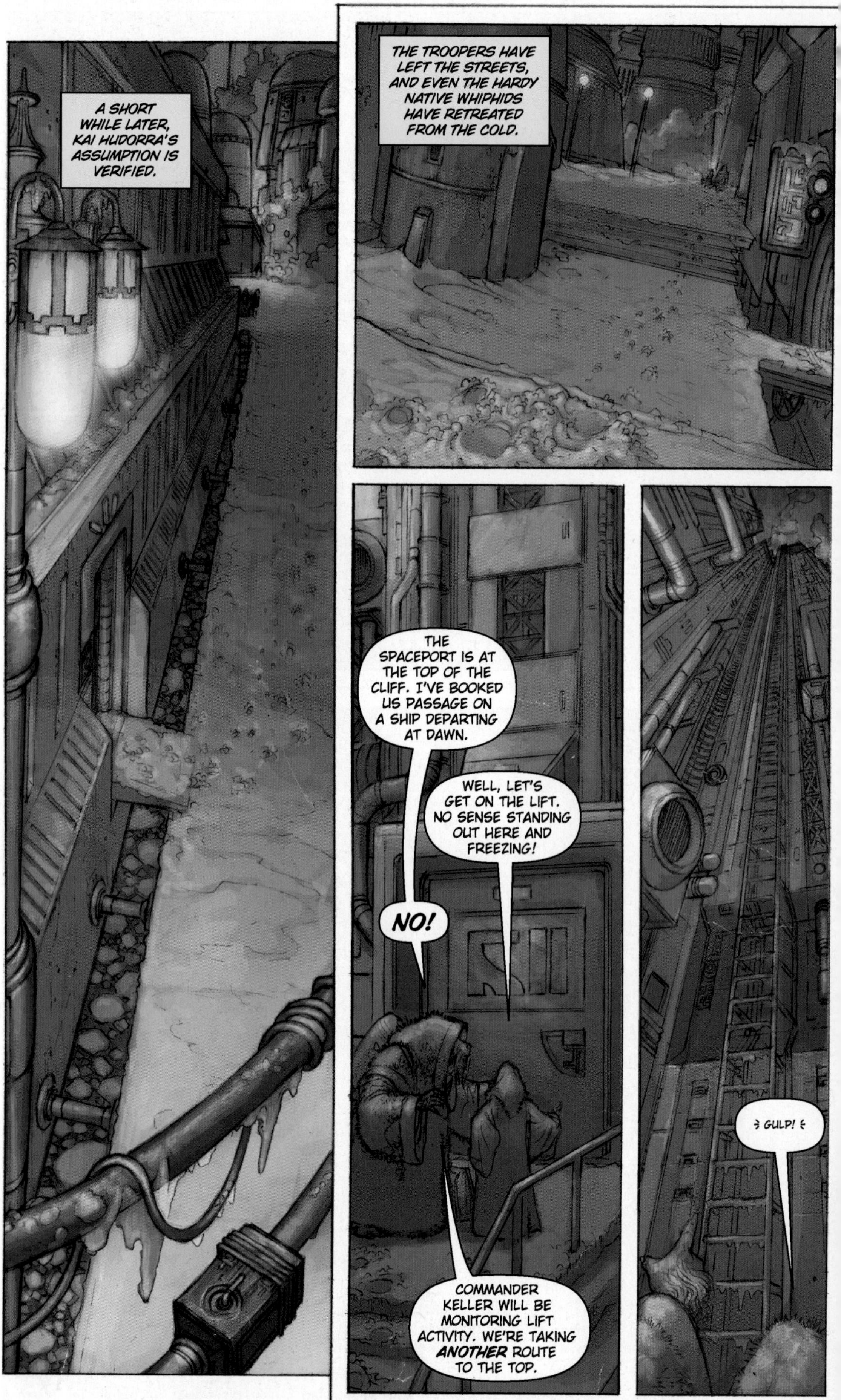
A SHORT WHILE LATER, KAI HUDORRA'S ASSUMPTION IS VERIFIED.
THE TROOPERS HAVE LEFT THE STREETS, AND EVEN THE HARDY NATIVE WHIPHIDS HAVE RETREATED FROM THE COLD.
THE SPACEPORT IS AT THE TOP OF THE CLIFF. I'VE BOOKED US PASSAGE ON A SHIP DEPARTING AT DAWN.
WELL, LET'S GET ON THE LIFT. NO SENSE STANDING OUT HERE AND FREEZING!
NO!
COMMANDER KELLER WILL BE MONITORING LIFT ACTIVITY. WE'RE TAKING ANOTHER ROUTE TO THE TOP.
GULP!

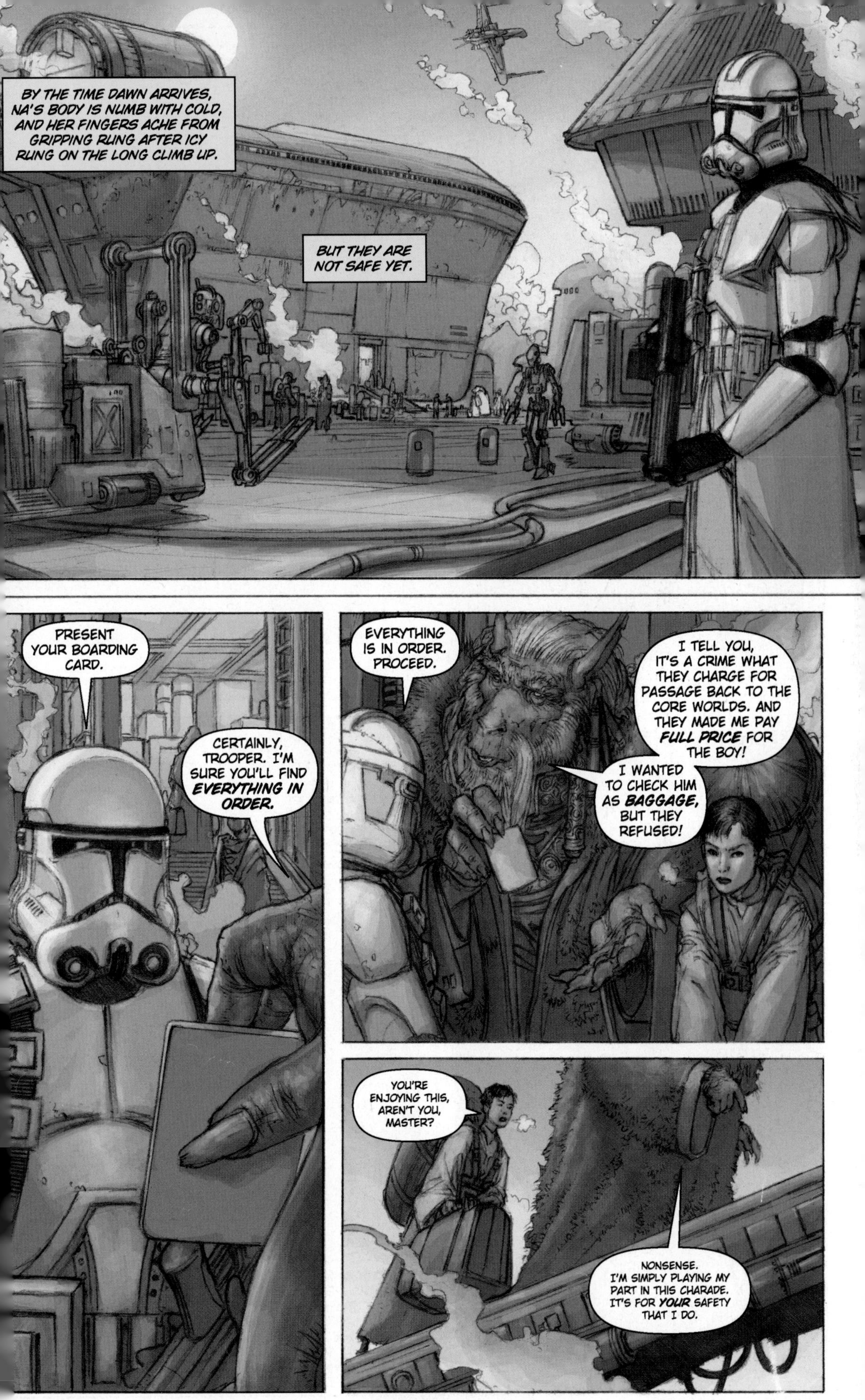
BY THE TIME DAWN ARRIVES, NA'S BODY IS NUMB WITH COLD, AND HER FINGERS ACHE FROM GRIPPING RUNG AFTER ICY RUNG ON THE LONG CLIMB UP.
BUT THEY ARE NOT SAFE YET.
PRESENT YOUR BOARDING CARD.
CERTAINLY, TROOPER. I'M SURE YOU'LL FIND *EVERYTHING IN ORDER.*
EVERYTHING IS IN ORDER. PROCEED.
I TELL YOU, IT'S A CRIME WHAT THEY CHARGE FOR PASSAGE BACK TO THE CORE WORLDS. AND THEY MADE ME PAY *FULL PRICE* FOR THE BOY!
I WANTED TO CHECK HIM AS *BAGGAGE,* BUT THEY REFUSED!
YOU'RE ENJOYING THIS, AREN'T YOU, MASTER?
NONSENSE. I'M SIMPLY PLAYING MY PART IN THIS CHARADE. IT'S FOR *YOUR* SAFETY THAT I DO.

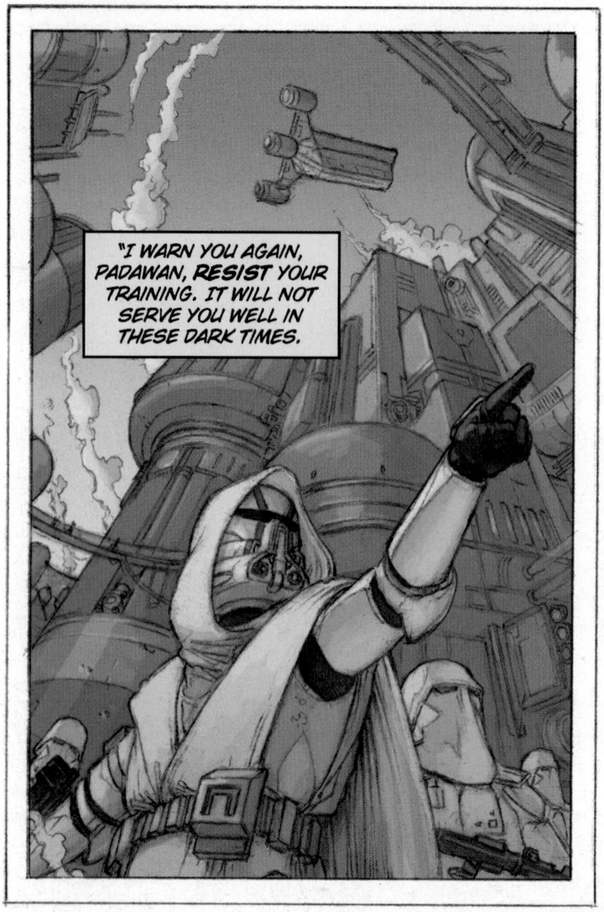
"I WARN YOU AGAIN, PADAWAN, RESIST YOUR TRAINING. IT WILL NOT SERVE YOU WELL IN THESE DARK TIMES.

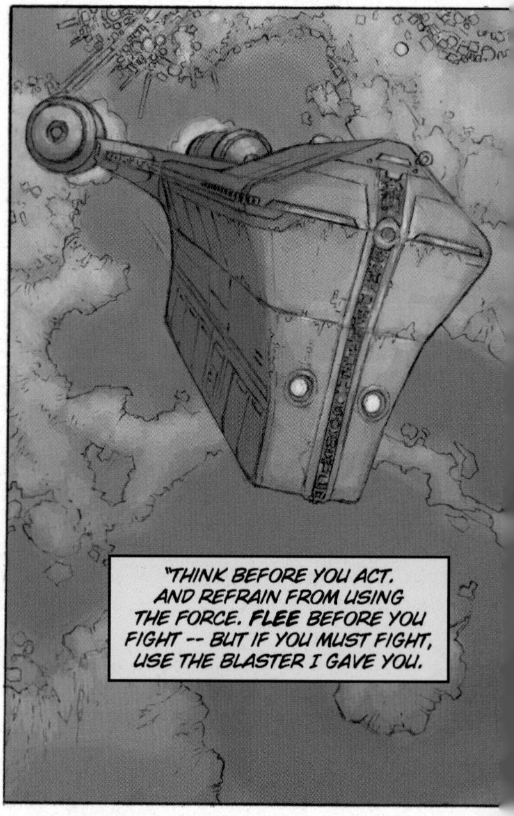
"THINK BEFORE YOU ACT. AND REFRAIN FROM USING THE FORCE. FLEE BEFORE YOU FIGHT -- BUT IF YOU MUST FIGHT, USE THE BLASTER I GAVE YOU.

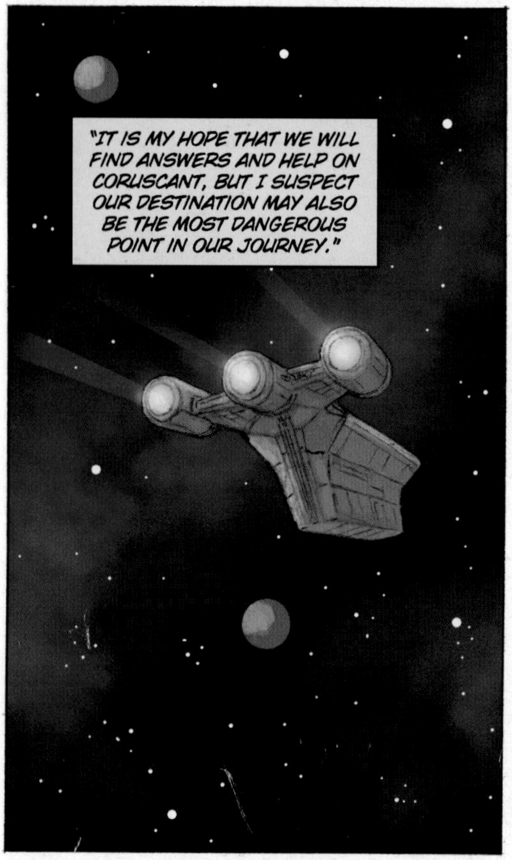
"IT IS MY HOPE THAT WE WILL FIND ANSWERS AND HELP ON CORUSCANT, BUT I SUSPECT OUR DESTINATION MAY ALSO BE THE MOST DANGEROUS POINT IN OUR JOURNEY."

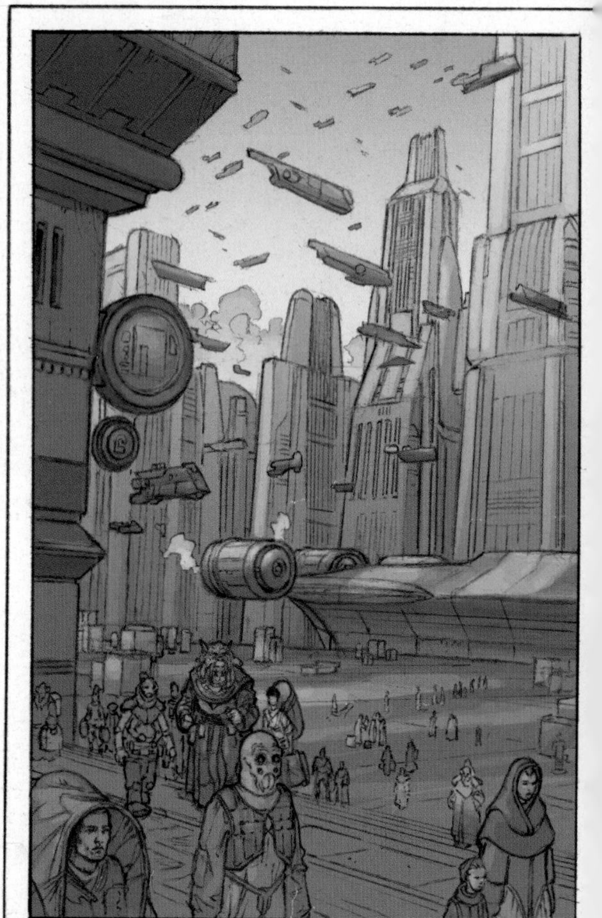

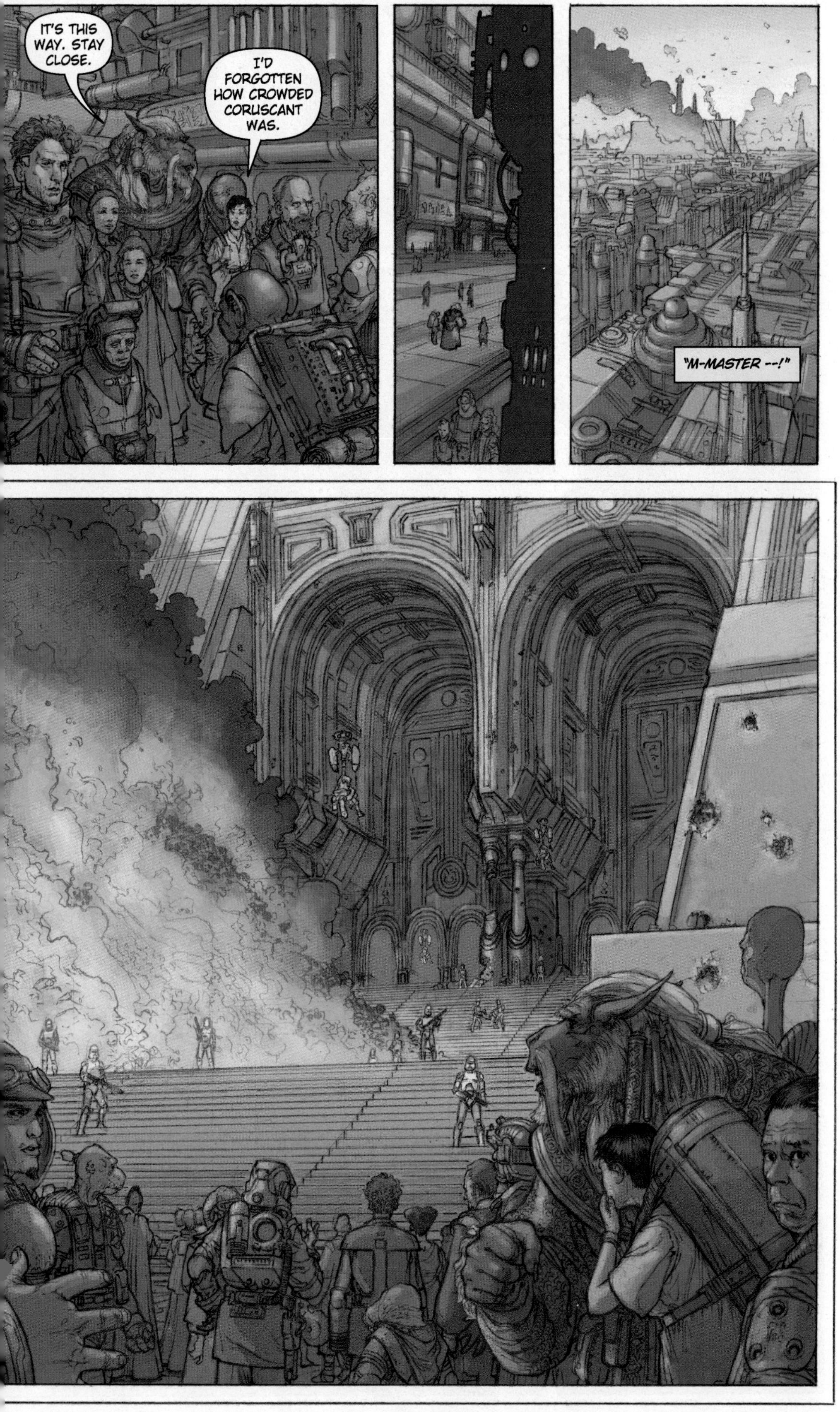
IT'S THIS WAY. STAY CLOSE.
I'D FORGOTTEN HOW CROWDED CORUSCANT WAS.
"M-MASTER --!"

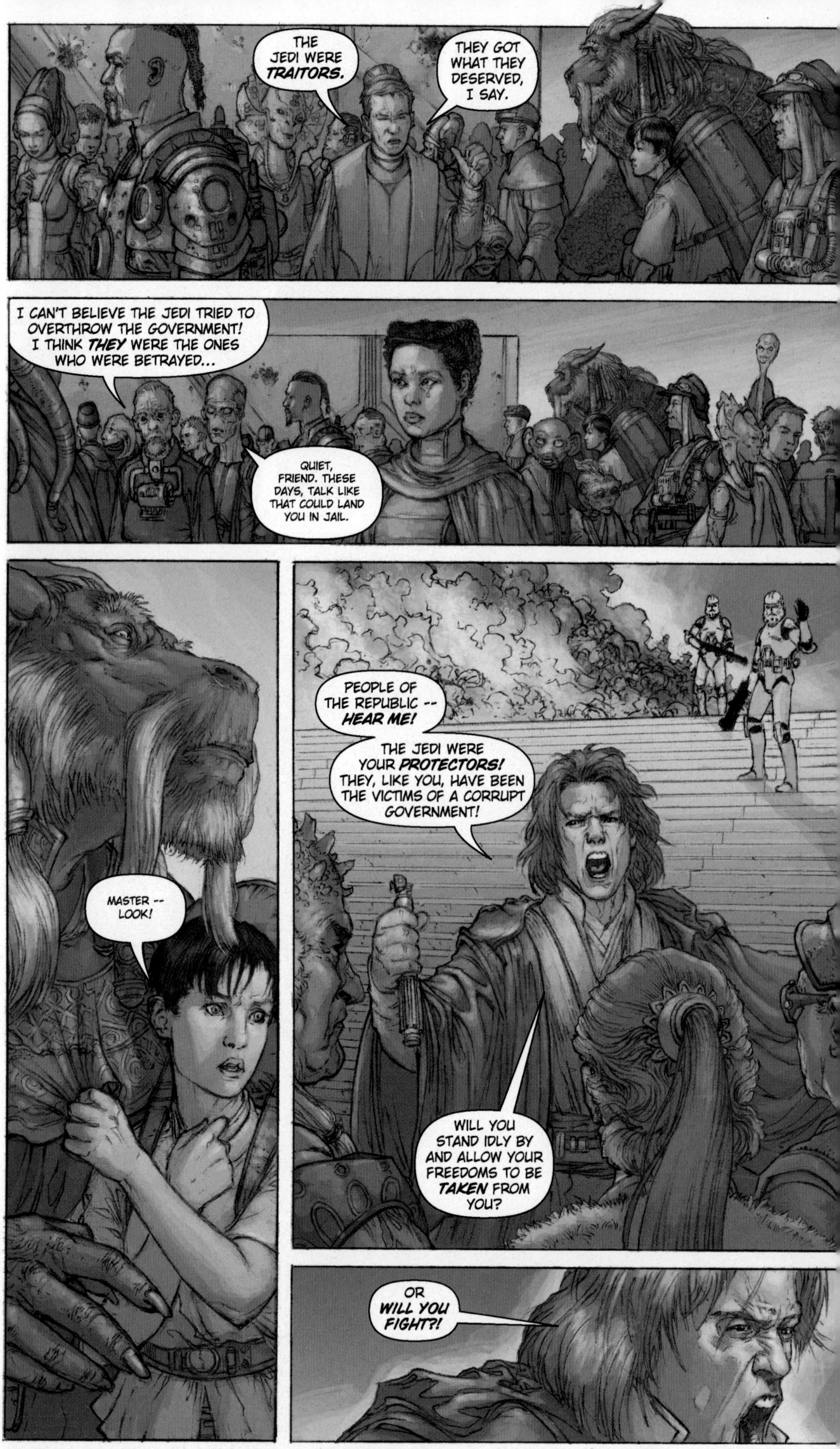

THE JEDI WERE *TRAITORS.*
THEY GOT WHAT THEY DESERVED, I SAY.
I CAN'T BELIEVE THE JEDI TRIED TO OVERTHROW THE GOVERNMENT! I THINK *THEY* WERE THE ONES WHO WERE BETRAYED...
QUIET, FRIEND. THESE DAYS, TALK LIKE THAT COULD LAND YOU IN JAIL.
MASTER -- LOOK!
PEOPLE OF THE REPUBLIC -- ***HEAR ME!***
THE JEDI WERE YOUR ***PROTECTORS!*** THEY, LIKE YOU, HAVE BEEN THE VICTIMS OF A CORRUPT GOVERNMENT!
WILL YOU STAND IDLY BY AND ALLOW YOUR FREEDOMS TO BE ***TAKEN*** FROM YOU?
OR ***WILL YOU FIGHT?!***

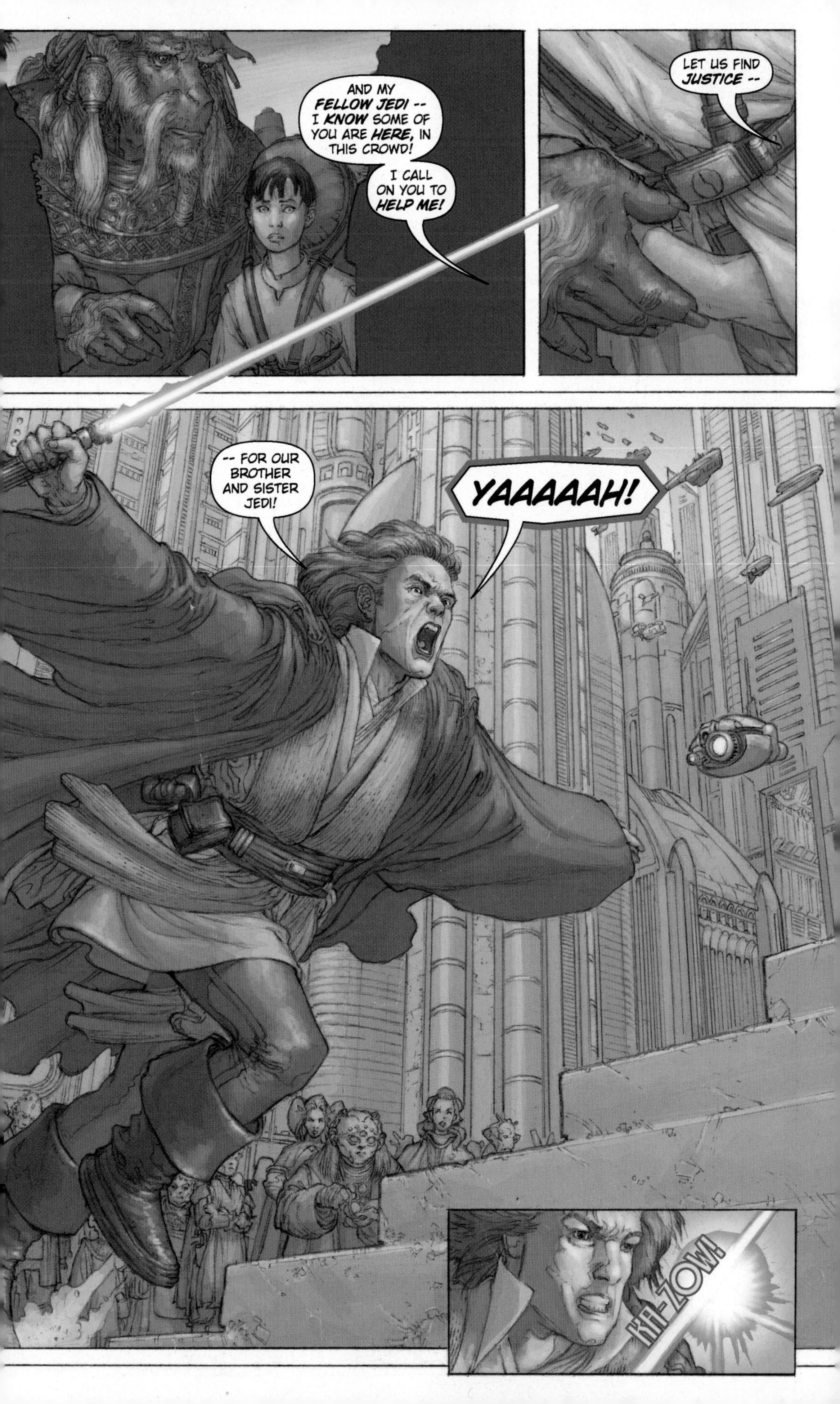
AND MY FELLOW JEDI -- I KNOW SOME OF YOU ARE HERE, IN THIS CROWD!
I CALL ON YOU TO HELP ME!
LET US FIND JUSTICE --
-- FOR OUR BROTHER AND SISTER JEDI!
YAAAAAH!
KH-ZOW!

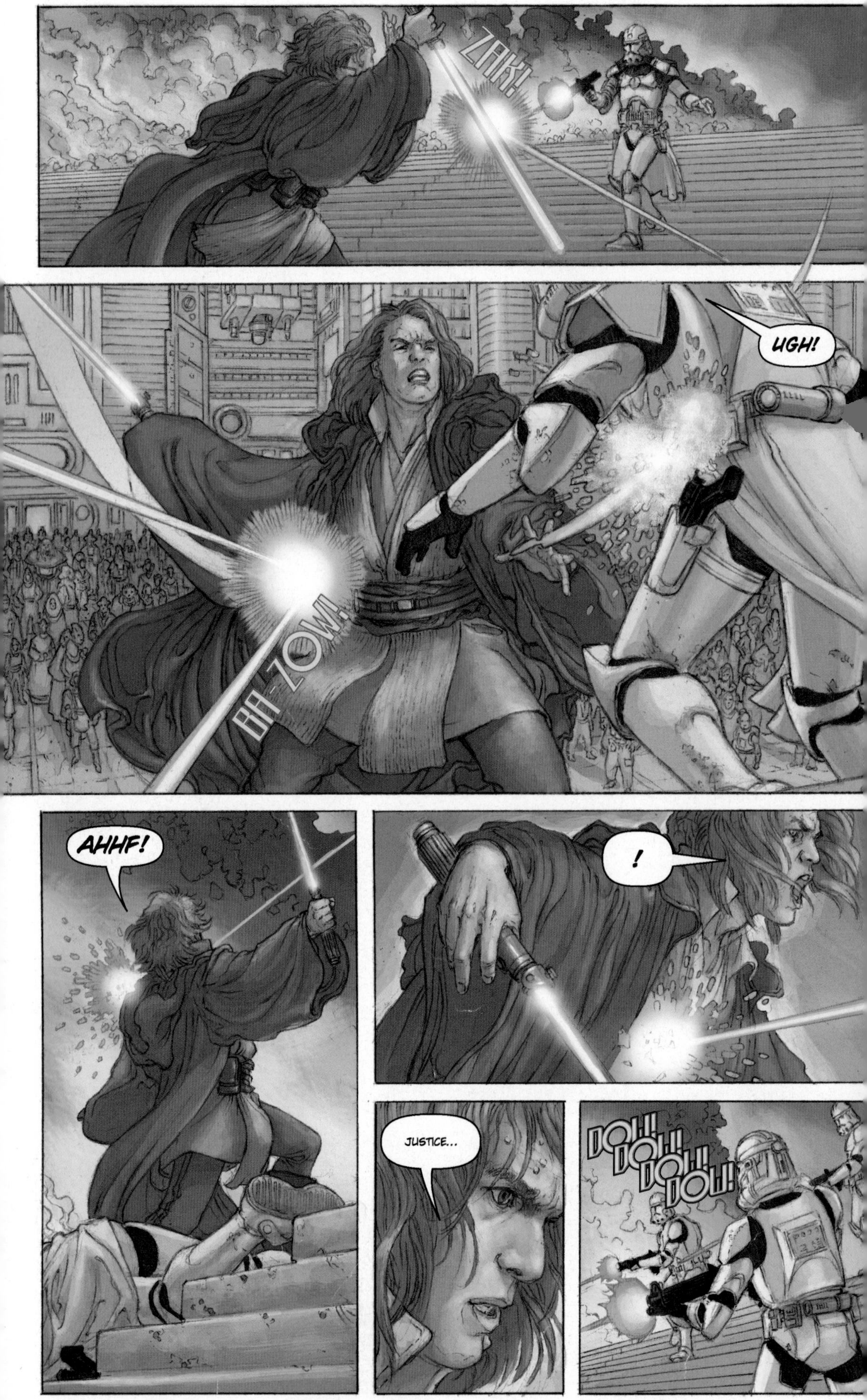

ZAK!
UGH!
BA-ZOW!
AHHF!
!
JUSTICE...
DOW! DOW! DOW! DOW!

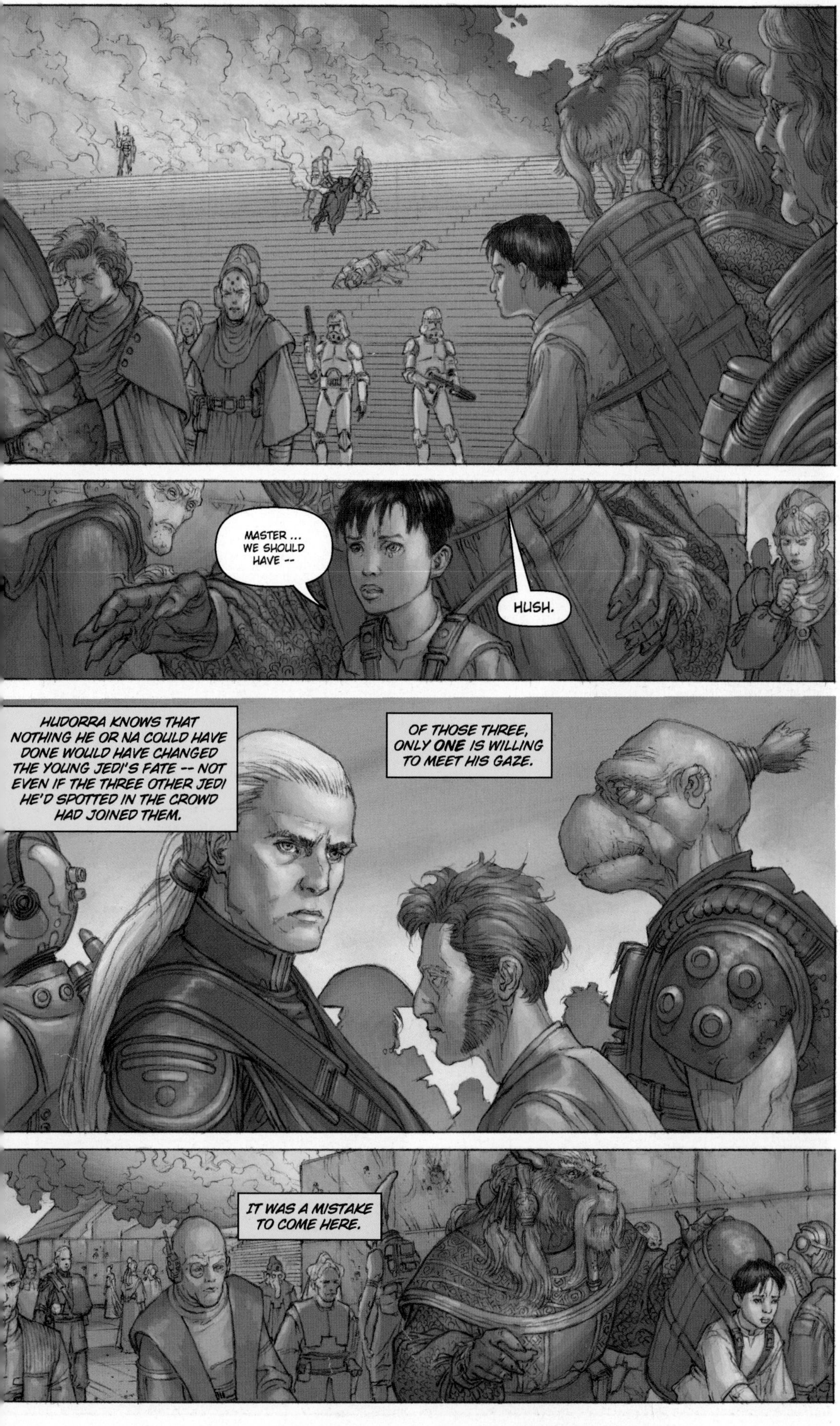
MASTER ... WE SHOULD HAVE --
HUSH.
HUDORRA KNOWS THAT NOTHING HE OR NA COULD HAVE DONE WOULD HAVE CHANGED THE YOUNG JEDI'S FATE -- NOT EVEN IF THE THREE OTHER JEDI HE'D SPOTTED IN THE CROWD HAD JOINED THEM.
OF THOSE THREE, ONLY ONE IS WILLING TO MEET HIS GAZE.
IT WAS A MISTAKE TO COME HERE.

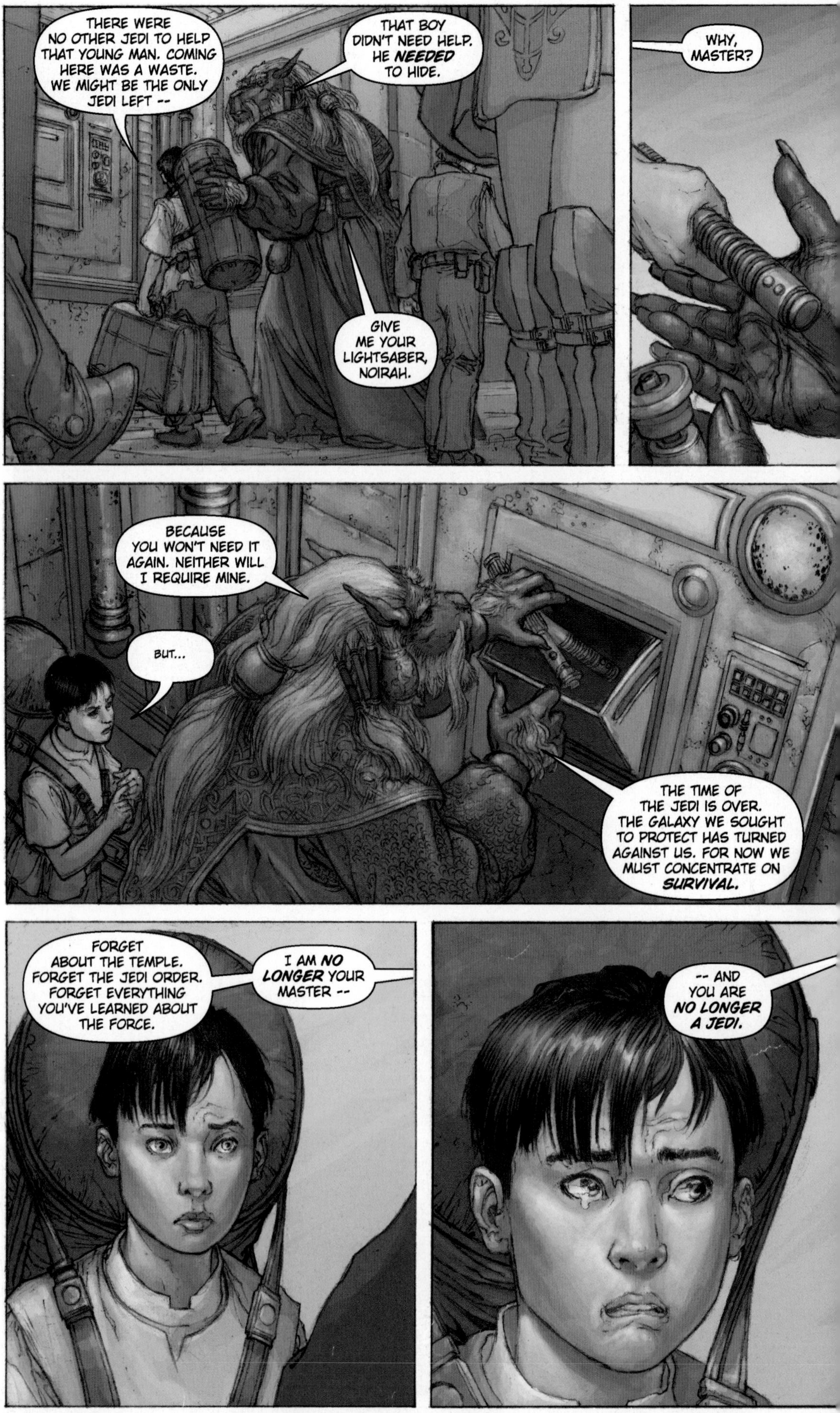
THERE WERE NO OTHER JEDI TO HELP THAT YOUNG MAN. COMING HERE WAS A WASTE. WE MIGHT BE THE ONLY JEDI LEFT --
THAT BOY DIDN'T NEED HELP. HE *NEEDED* TO HIDE.
GIVE ME YOUR LIGHTSABER, NOIRAH.
WHY, MASTER?
BECAUSE YOU WON'T NEED IT AGAIN. NEITHER WILL I REQUIRE MINE.
BUT...
THE TIME OF THE JEDI IS OVER. THE GALAXY WE SOUGHT TO PROTECT HAS TURNED AGAINST US. FOR NOW WE MUST CONCENTRATE ON *SURVIVAL.*
FORGET ABOUT THE TEMPLE. FORGET THE JEDI ORDER. FORGET EVERYTHING YOU'VE LEARNED ABOUT THE FORCE.
I AM *NO LONGER* YOUR MASTER --
-- AND YOU ARE *NO LONGER A JEDI.*

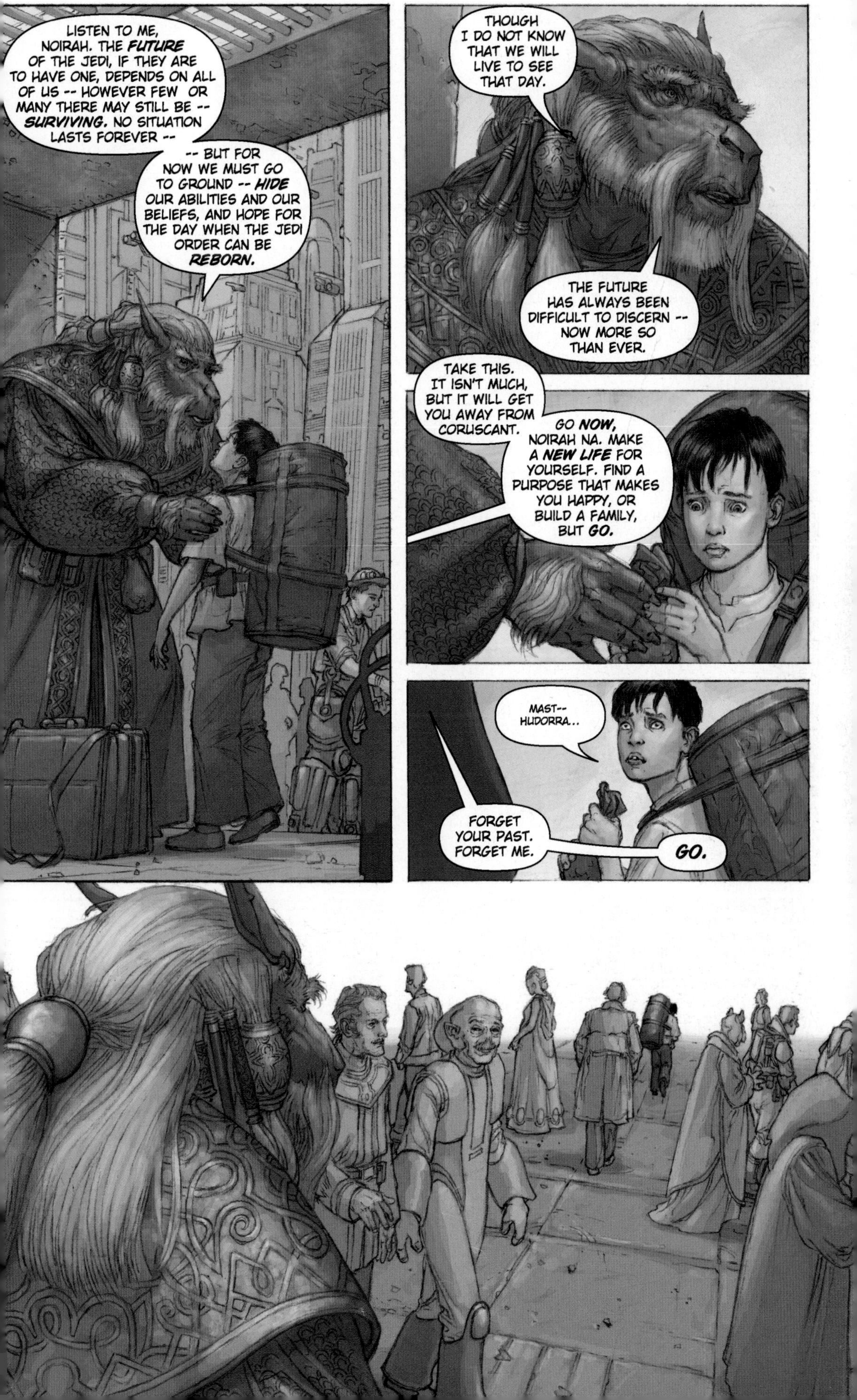
LISTEN TO ME, NOIRAH. THE *FUTURE* OF THE JEDI, IF THEY ARE TO HAVE ONE, DEPENDS ON ALL OF US -- HOWEVER FEW OR MANY THERE MAY STILL BE -- *SURVIVING.* NO SITUATION LASTS FOREVER --
-- BUT FOR NOW WE MUST GO TO GROUND -- *HIDE* OUR ABILITIES AND OUR BELIEFS, AND HOPE FOR THE DAY WHEN THE JEDI ORDER CAN BE *REBORN.*
THOUGH I DO NOT KNOW THAT WE WILL LIVE TO SEE THAT DAY.
THE FUTURE HAS ALWAYS BEEN DIFFICULT TO DISCERN -- NOW MORE SO THAN EVER.
TAKE THIS. IT ISN'T MUCH, BUT IT WILL GET YOU AWAY FROM CORUSCANT.
GO *NOW,* NOIRAH NA. MAKE A *NEW LIFE* FOR YOURSELF. FIND A PURPOSE THAT MAKES YOU HAPPY, OR BUILD A FAMILY, BUT *GO.*
MAST-- HUDORRA...
FORGET YOUR PAST. FORGET ME.
GO.

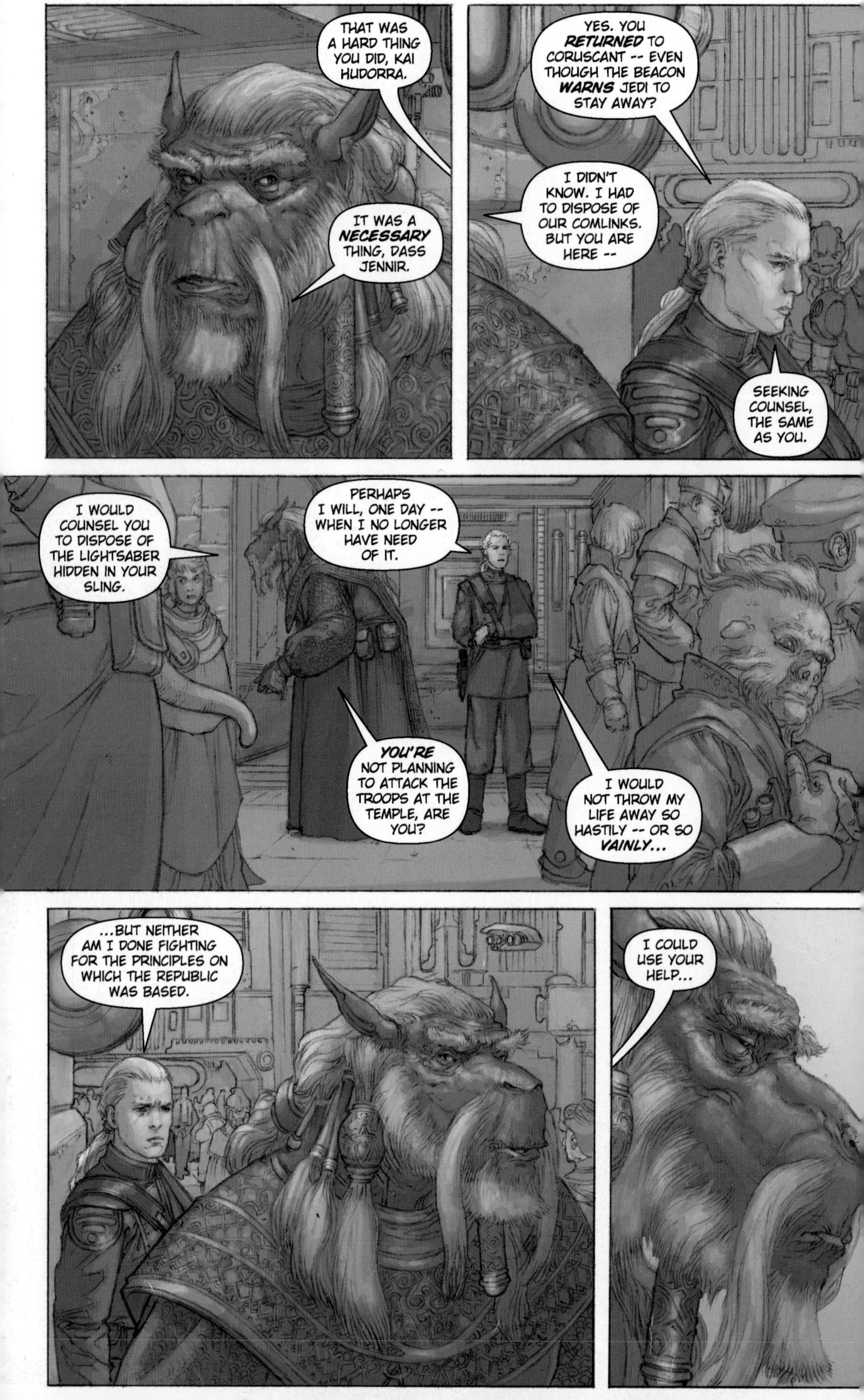

THAT WAS A HARD THING YOU DID, KAI HUDORRA.
IT WAS A NECESSARY THING, DASS JENNIR.
YES. YOU RETURNED TO CORUSCANT -- EVEN THOUGH THE BEACON WARNS JEDI TO STAY AWAY?
I DIDN'T KNOW. I HAD TO DISPOSE OF OUR COMLINKS. BUT YOU ARE HERE --
SEEKING COUNSEL, THE SAME AS YOU.
I WOULD COUNSEL YOU TO DISPOSE OF THE LIGHTSABER HIDDEN IN YOUR SLING.
PERHAPS I WILL, ONE DAY -- WHEN I NO LONGER HAVE NEED OF IT.
YOU'RE NOT PLANNING TO ATTACK THE TROOPS AT THE TEMPLE, ARE YOU?
I WOULD NOT THROW MY LIFE AWAY SO HASTILY -- OR SO VAINLY...
...BUT NEITHER AM I DONE FIGHTING FOR THE PRINCIPLES ON WHICH THE REPUBLIC WAS BASED.
I COULD USE YOUR HELP...

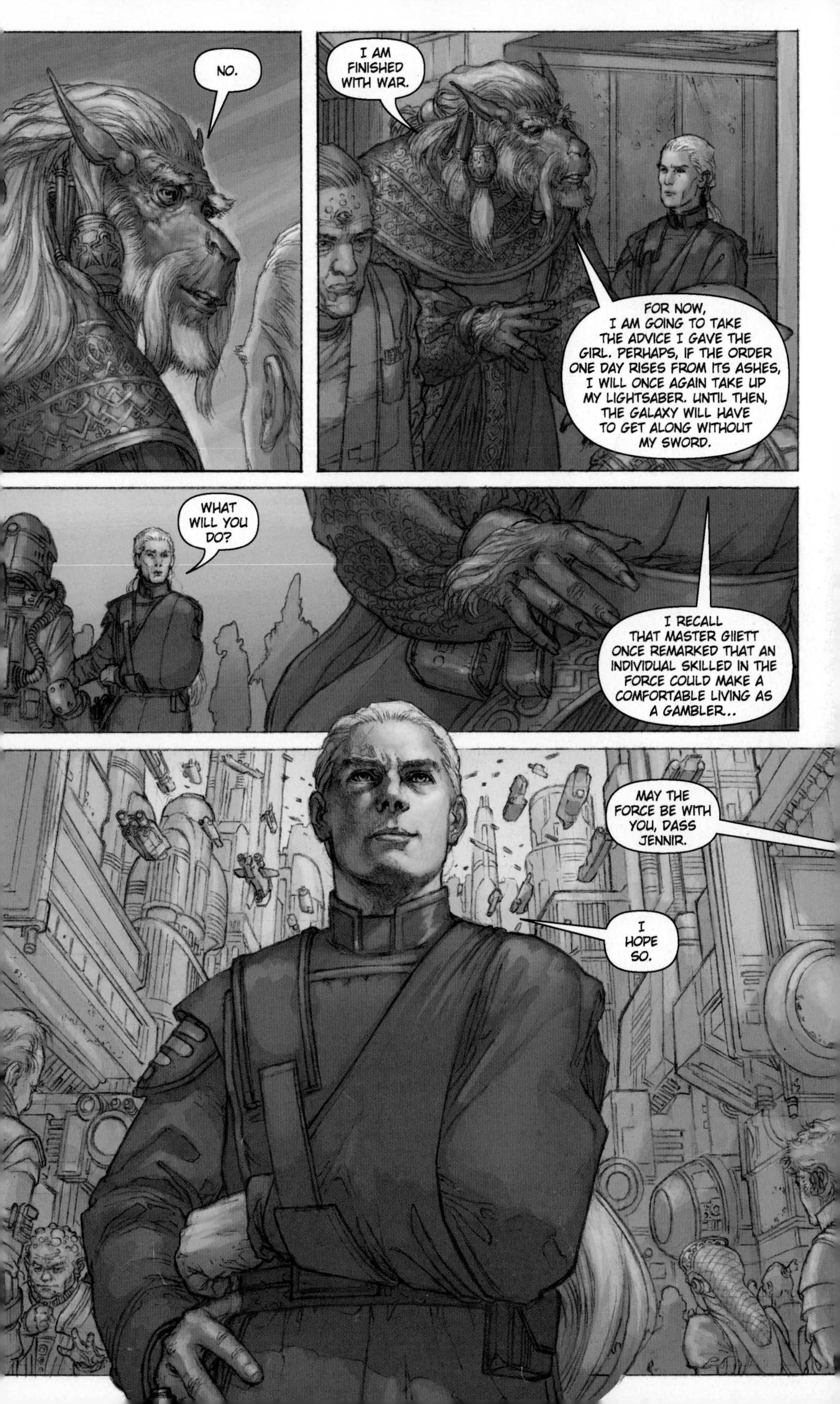
NO.
I AM FINISHED WITH WAR.
FOR NOW, I AM GOING TO TAKE THE ADVICE I GAVE THE GIRL. PERHAPS, IF THE ORDER ONE DAY RISES FROM ITS ASHES, I WILL ONCE AGAIN TAKE UP MY LIGHTSABER. UNTIL THEN, THE GALAXY WILL HAVE TO GET ALONG WITHOUT MY SWORD.
WHAT WILL YOU DO?
I RECALL THAT MASTER GIIETT ONCE REMARKED THAT AN INDIVIDUAL SKILLED IN THE FORCE COULD MAKE A COMFORTABLE LIVING AS A GAMBLER...
MAY THE FORCE BE WITH YOU, DASS JENNIR.
I HOPE SO.

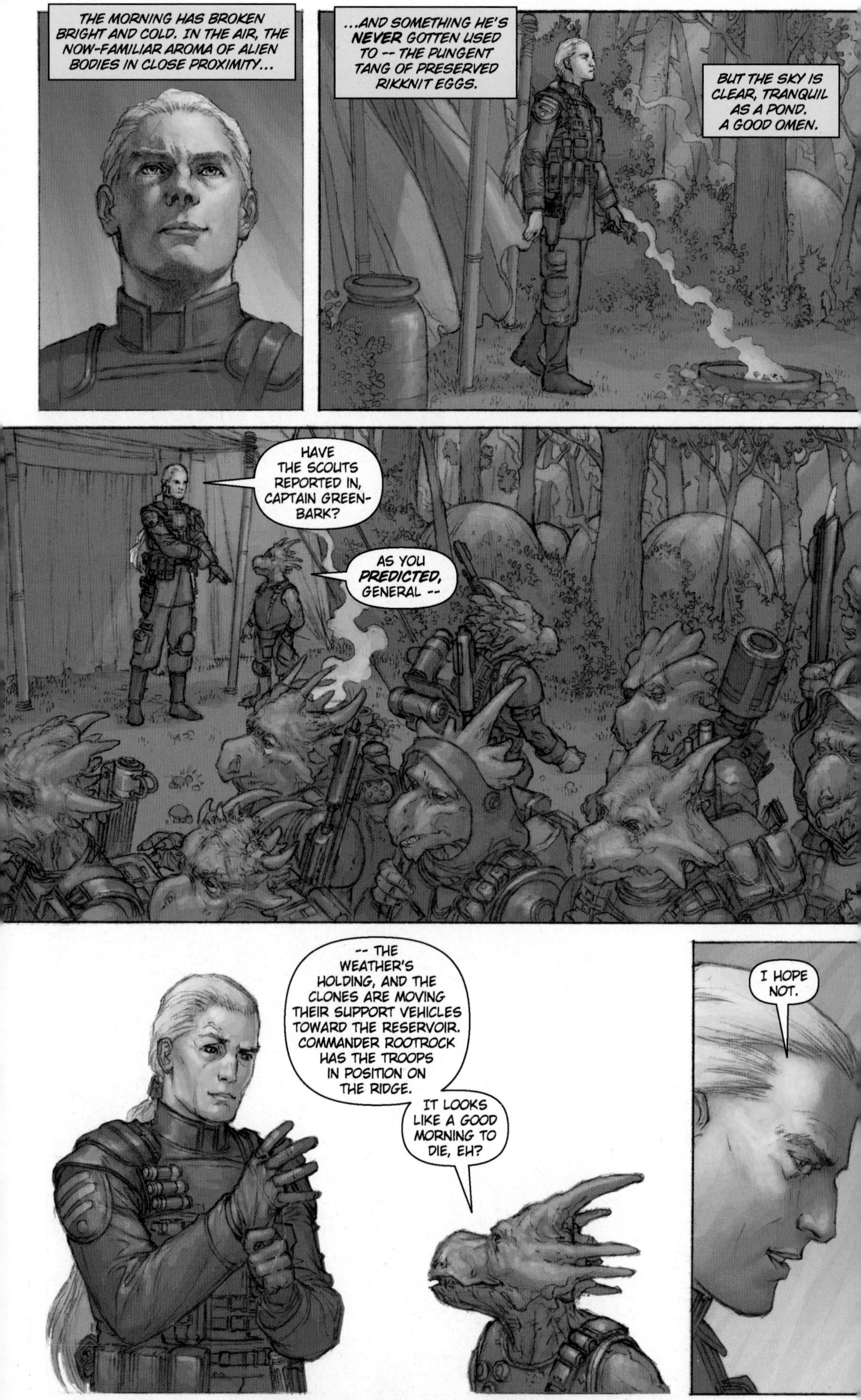
THE MORNING HAS BROKEN BRIGHT AND COLD. IN THE AIR, THE NOW-FAMILIAR AROMA OF ALIEN BODIES IN CLOSE PROXIMITY...
...AND SOMETHING HE'S NEVER GOTTEN USED TO -- THE PUNGENT TANG OF PRESERVED RIKKNIT EGGS.
BUT THE SKY IS CLEAR, TRANQUIL AS A POND. A GOOD OMEN.
HAVE THE SCOUTS REPORTED IN, CAPTAIN GREEN-BARK?
AS YOU PREDICTED, GENERAL --
-- THE WEATHER'S HOLDING, AND THE CLONES ARE MOVING THEIR SUPPORT VEHICLES TOWARD THE RESERVOIR. COMMANDER ROOTROCK HAS THE TROOPS IN POSITION ON THE RIDGE.
IT LOOKS LIKE A GOOD MORNING TO DIE, EH?
I HOPE NOT.

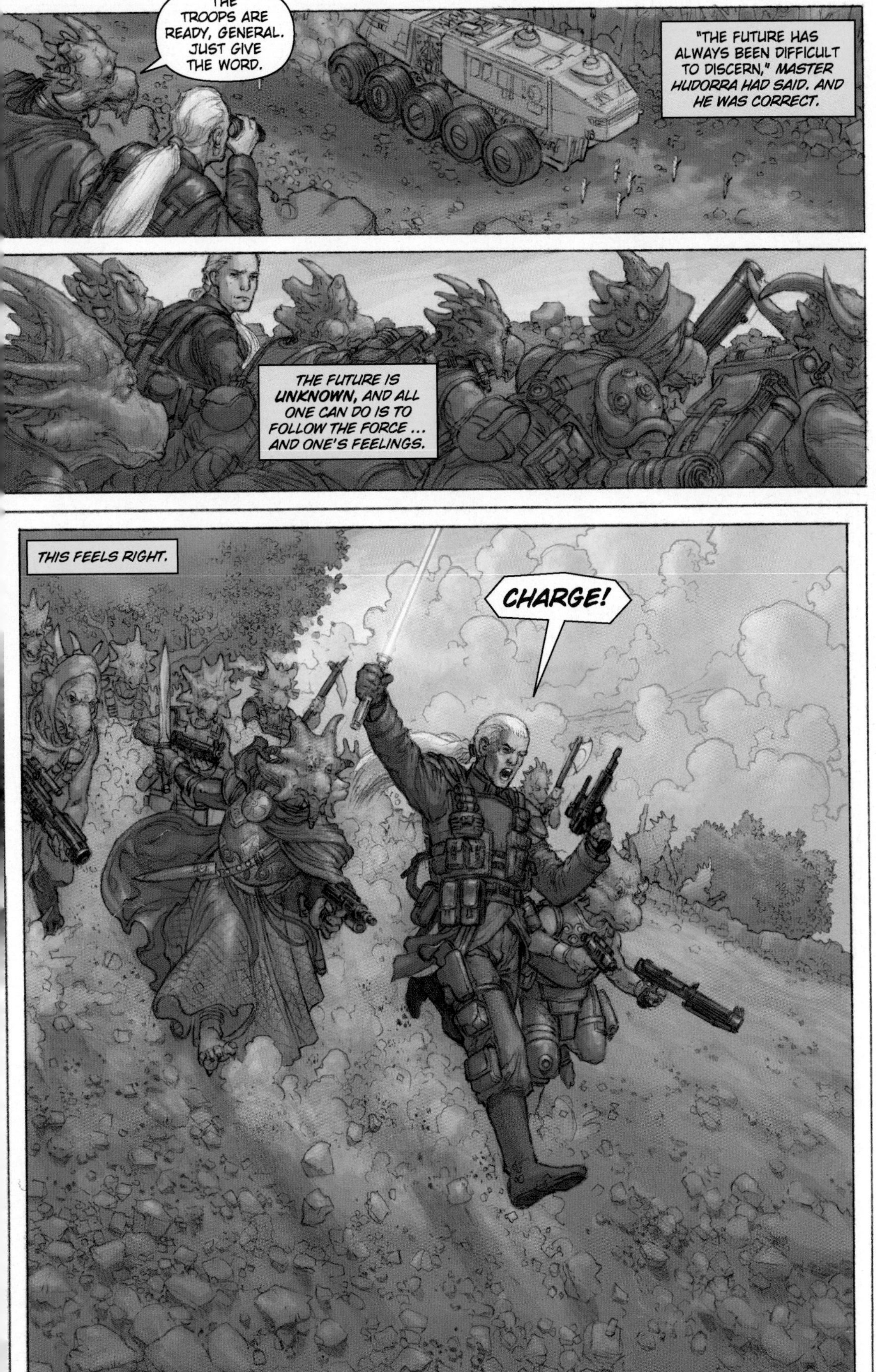

THE TROOPS ARE READY, GENERAL. JUST GIVE THE WORD.
"THE FUTURE HAS ALWAYS BEEN DIFFICULT TO DISCERN," MASTER HUDORRA HAD SAID. AND HE WAS CORRECT.
THE FUTURE IS UNKNOWN, AND ALL ONE CAN DO IS TO FOLLOW THE FORCE ... AND ONE'S FEELINGS.
THIS FEELS RIGHT.
CHARGE!
THE END.

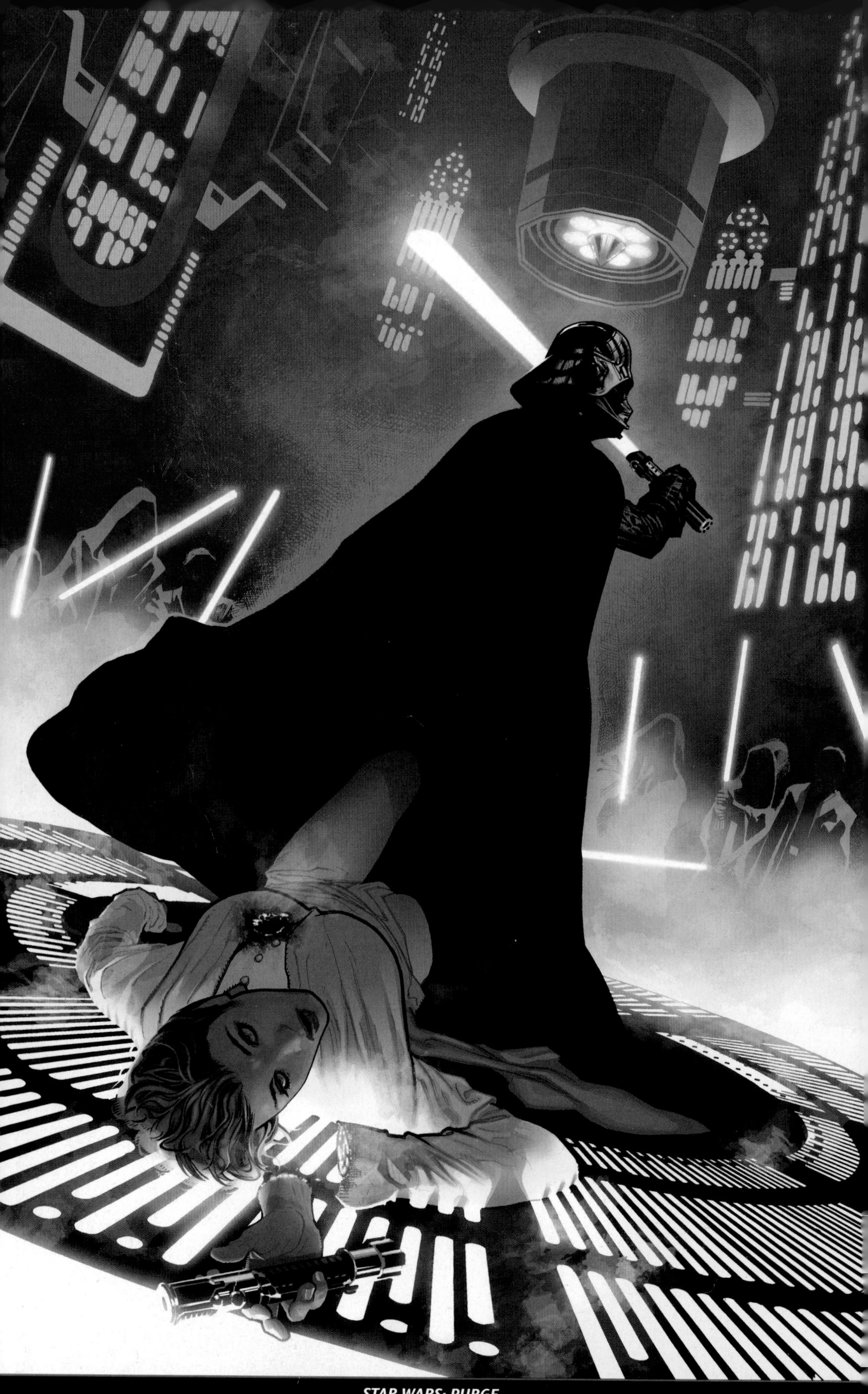

STAR WARS: PURGE

WRITER: JOHN OSTRANDER • ARTIST: DOUGLAS WHEATLEY • COLORIST: RONDA PATTISON • LETTERER: MICHAEL DAVID THOMAS • DESIGNER: TINA ALESS
ART DIRECTOR: LIA RIBACCHI • ASSISTANT EDITOR: DAVE MARSHALL • ASSOCIATE EDITOR: JEREMY BARLOW • EDITOR: RANDY STRADLEY

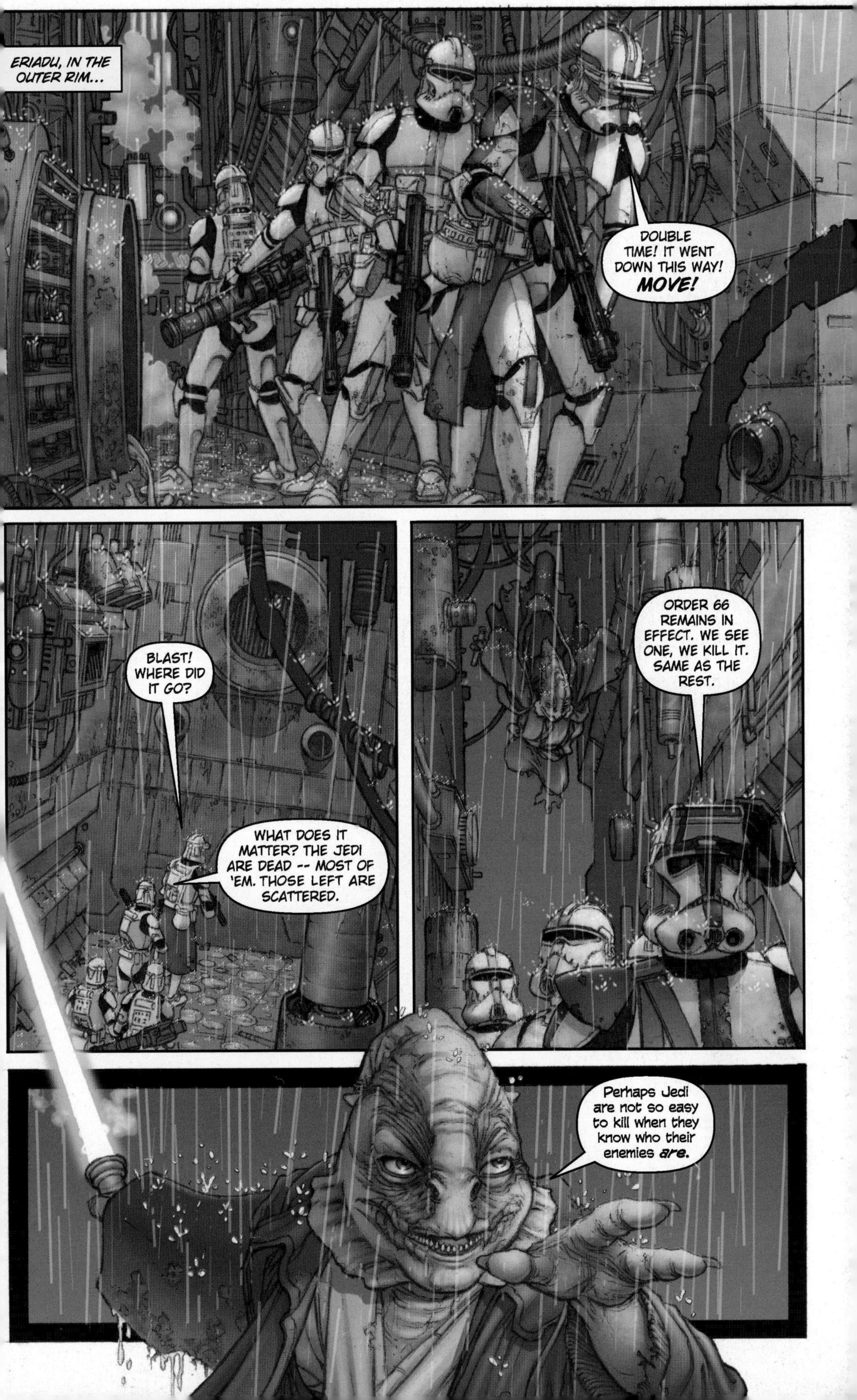
ERIADU, IN THE OUTER RIM...
DOUBLE TIME! IT WENT DOWN THIS WAY! MOVE!
BLAST! WHERE DID IT GO?
WHAT DOES IT MATTER? THE JEDI ARE DEAD -- MOST OF 'EM. THOSE LEFT ARE SCATTERED.
ORDER 66 REMAINS IN EFFECT. WE SEE ONE, WE KILL IT. SAME AS THE REST.
Perhaps Jedi are not so easy to kill when they know who their enemies are.

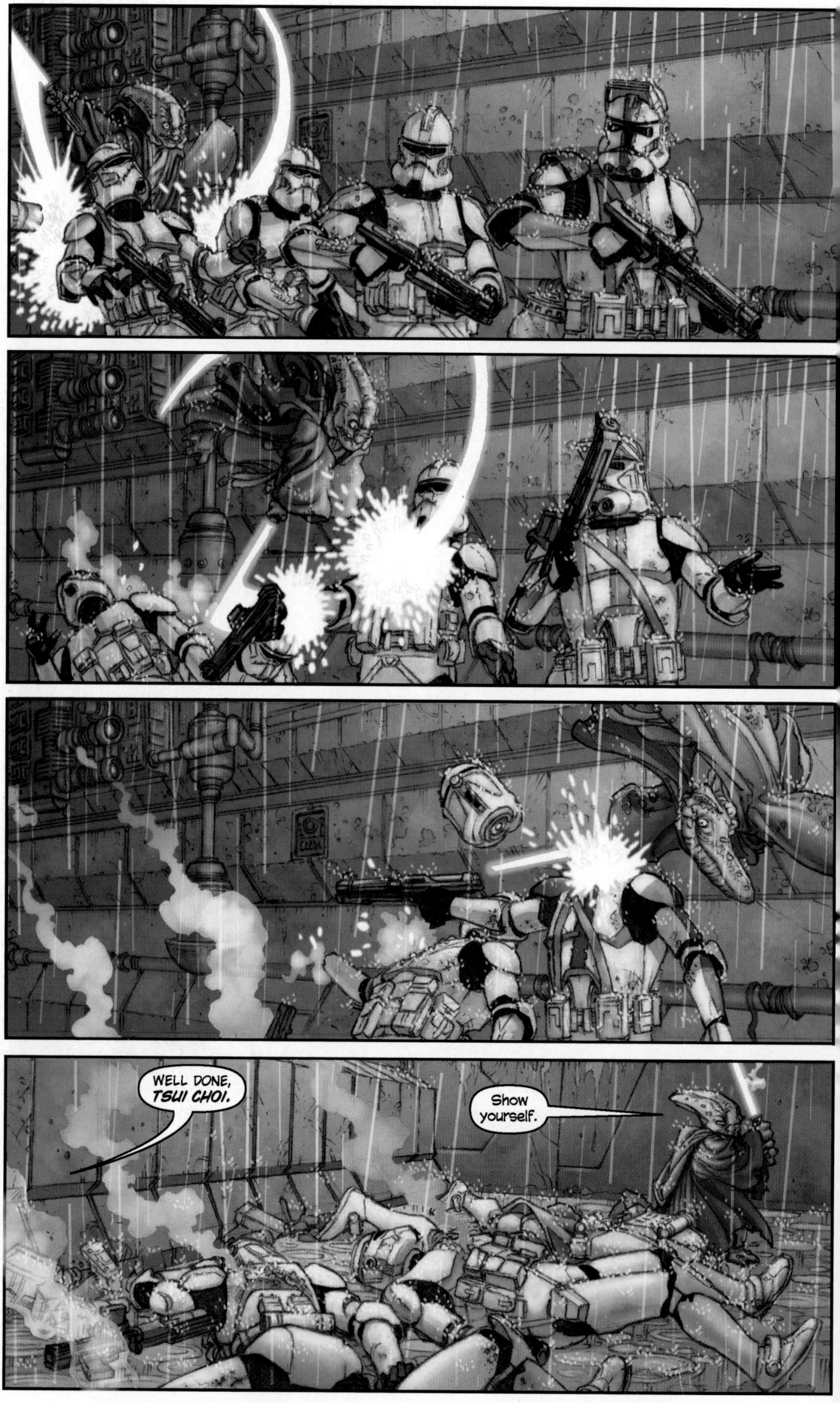
WELL DONE, TSUI CHOI.
Show yourself.

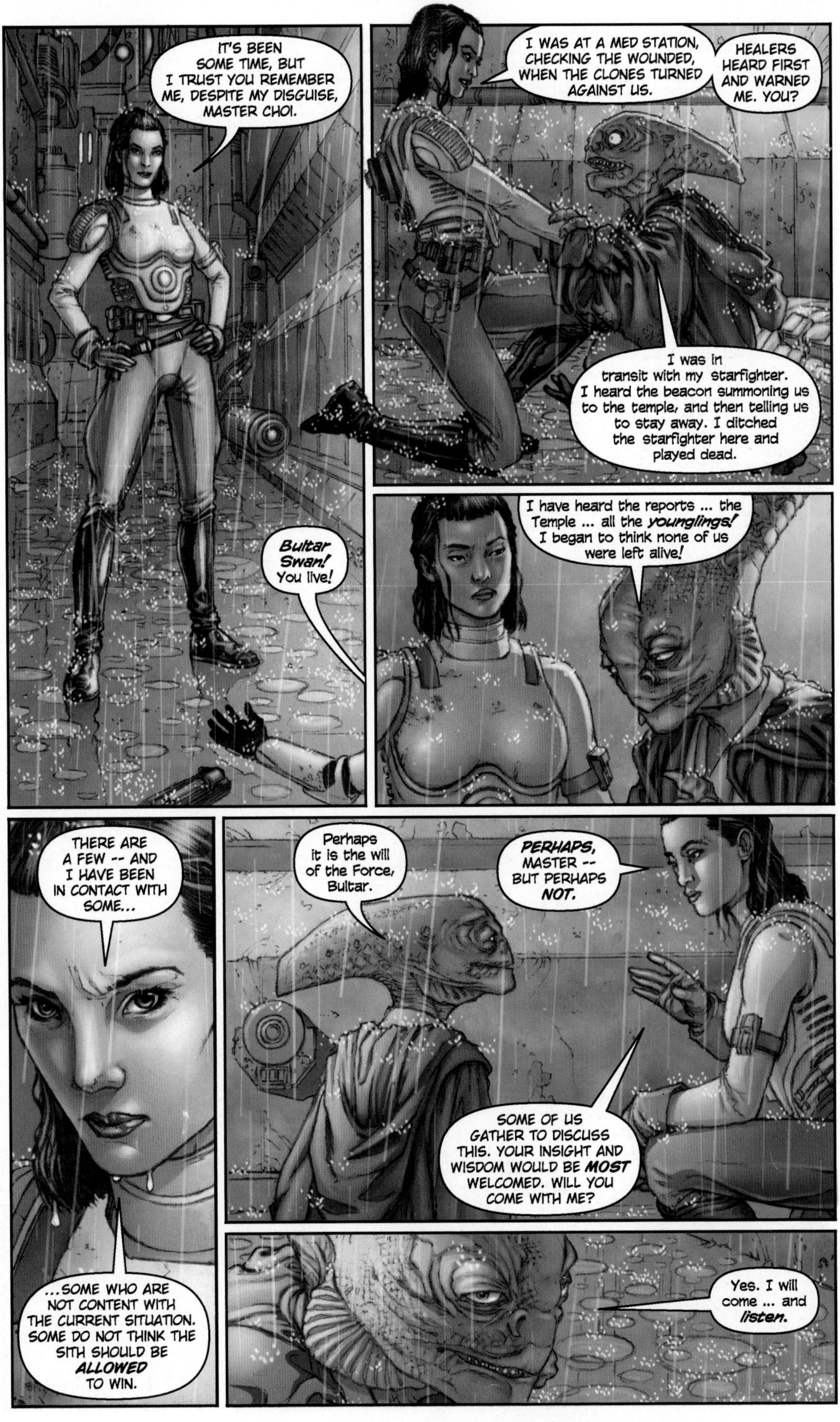
IT'S BEEN SOME TIME, BUT I TRUST YOU REMEMBER ME, DESPITE MY DISGUISE, MASTER CHOI.
Bultar Swan! You live!
I WAS AT A MED STATION, CHECKING THE WOUNDED, WHEN THE CLONES TURNED AGAINST US.
HEALERS HEARD FIRST AND WARNED ME. YOU?
I was in transit with my starfighter. I heard the beacon summoning us to the temple, and then telling us to stay away. I ditched the starfighter here and played dead.
I have heard the reports ... the Temple ... all the younglings! I began to think none of us were left alive!
THERE ARE A FEW -- AND I HAVE BEEN IN CONTACT WITH SOME...
...SOME WHO ARE NOT CONTENT WITH THE CURRENT SITUATION. SOME DO NOT THINK THE SITH SHOULD BE ALLOWED TO WIN.
Perhaps it is the will of the Force, Bultar.
PERHAPS, MASTER -- BUT PERHAPS NOT.
SOME OF US GATHER TO DISCUSS THIS. YOUR INSIGHT AND WISDOM WOULD BE MOST WELCOMED. WILL YOU COME WITH ME?
Yes. I will come ... and listen.

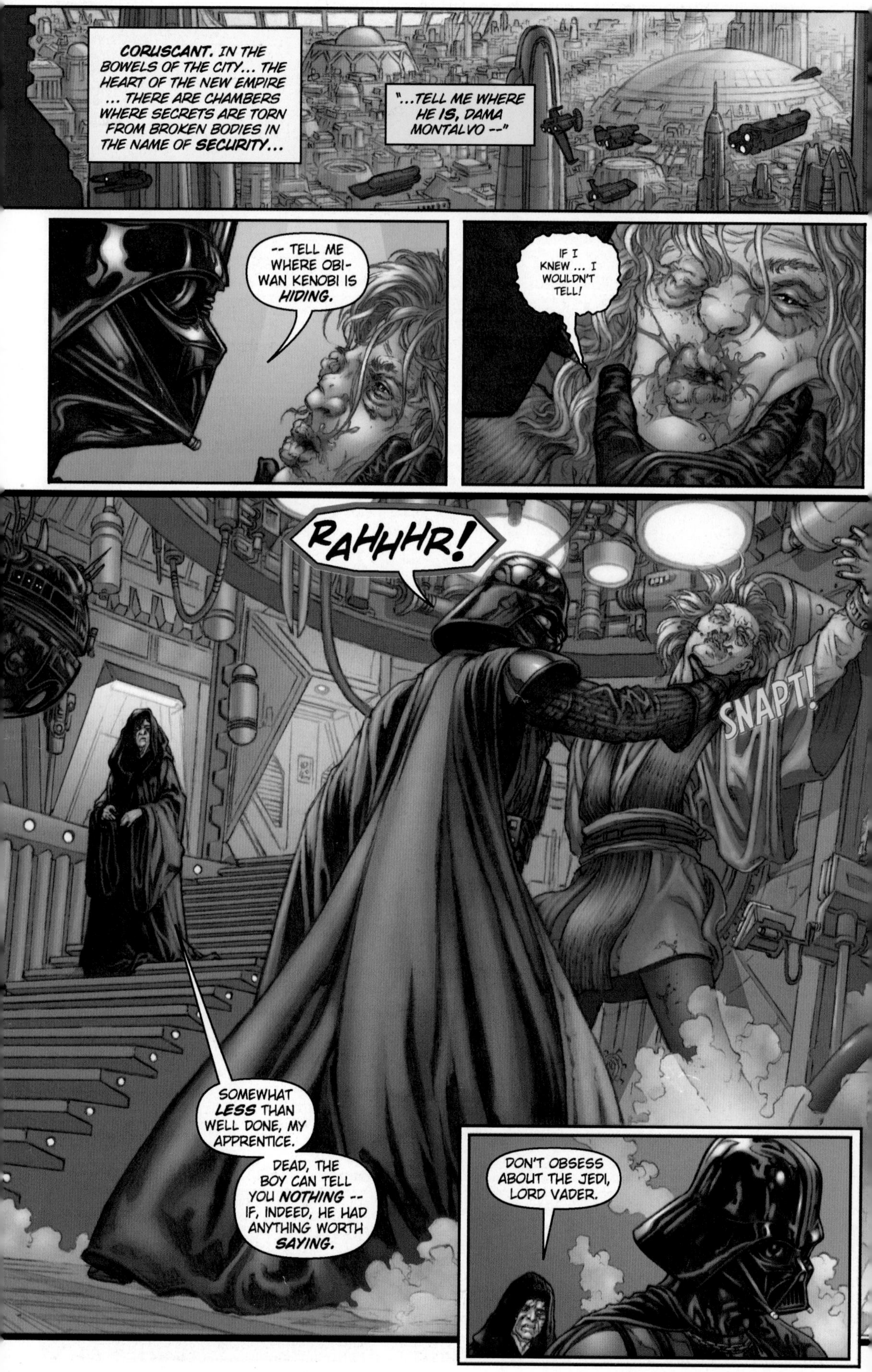
CORUSCANT. IN THE BOWELS OF THE CITY... THE HEART OF THE NEW EMPIRE ... THERE ARE CHAMBERS WHERE SECRETS ARE TORN FROM BROKEN BODIES IN THE NAME OF SECURITY...
"...TELL ME WHERE HE IS, DAMA MONTALVO --"
-- TELL ME WHERE OBI-WAN KENOBI IS HIDING.
IF I KNEW ... I WOULDN'T TELL!
RAHHHR!
SNAPT!
SOMEWHAT LESS THAN WELL DONE, MY APPRENTICE.
DEAD, THE BOY CAN TELL YOU NOTHING -- IF, INDEED, HE HAD ANYTHING WORTH SAYING.
DON'T OBSESS ABOUT THE JEDI, LORD VADER.

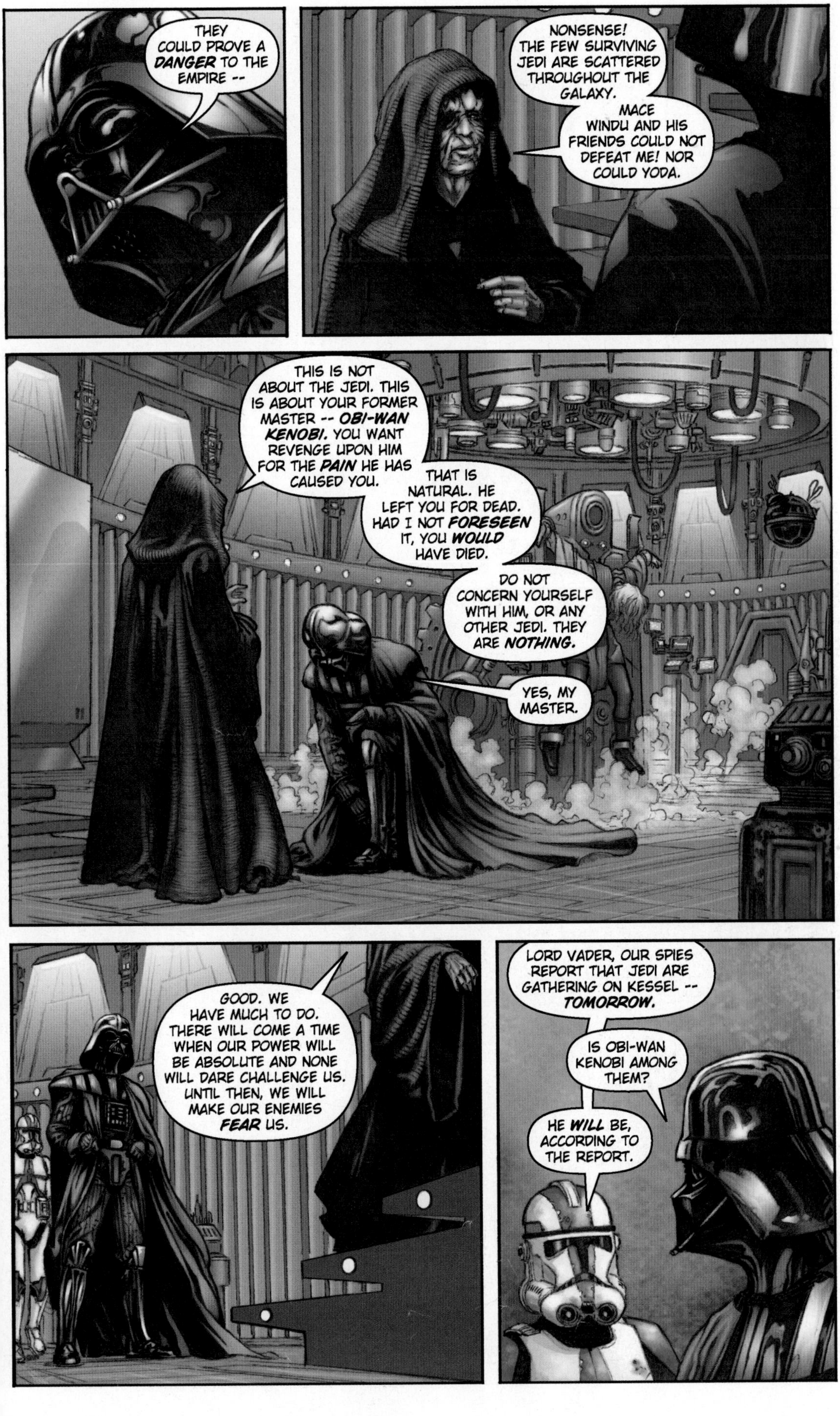

THEY COULD PROVE A DANGER TO THE EMPIRE --
NONSENSE! THE FEW SURVIVING JEDI ARE SCATTERED THROUGHOUT THE GALAXY.
MACE WINDU AND HIS FRIENDS COULD NOT DEFEAT ME! NOR COULD YODA.
THIS IS NOT ABOUT THE JEDI. THIS IS ABOUT YOUR FORMER MASTER -- OBI-WAN KENOBI. YOU WANT REVENGE UPON HIM FOR THE PAIN HE HAS CAUSED YOU.
THAT IS NATURAL. HE LEFT YOU FOR DEAD. HAD I NOT FORESEEN IT, YOU WOULD HAVE DIED.
DO NOT CONCERN YOURSELF WITH HIM, OR ANY OTHER JEDI. THEY ARE NOTHING.
YES, MY MASTER.
GOOD. WE HAVE MUCH TO DO. THERE WILL COME A TIME WHEN OUR POWER WILL BE ABSOLUTE AND NONE WILL DARE CHALLENGE US. UNTIL THEN, WE WILL MAKE OUR ENEMIES FEAR US.
LORD VADER, OUR SPIES REPORT THAT JEDI ARE GATHERING ON KESSEL -- TOMORROW.
IS OBI-WAN KENOBI AMONG THEM?
HE WILL BE, ACCORDING TO THE REPORT.

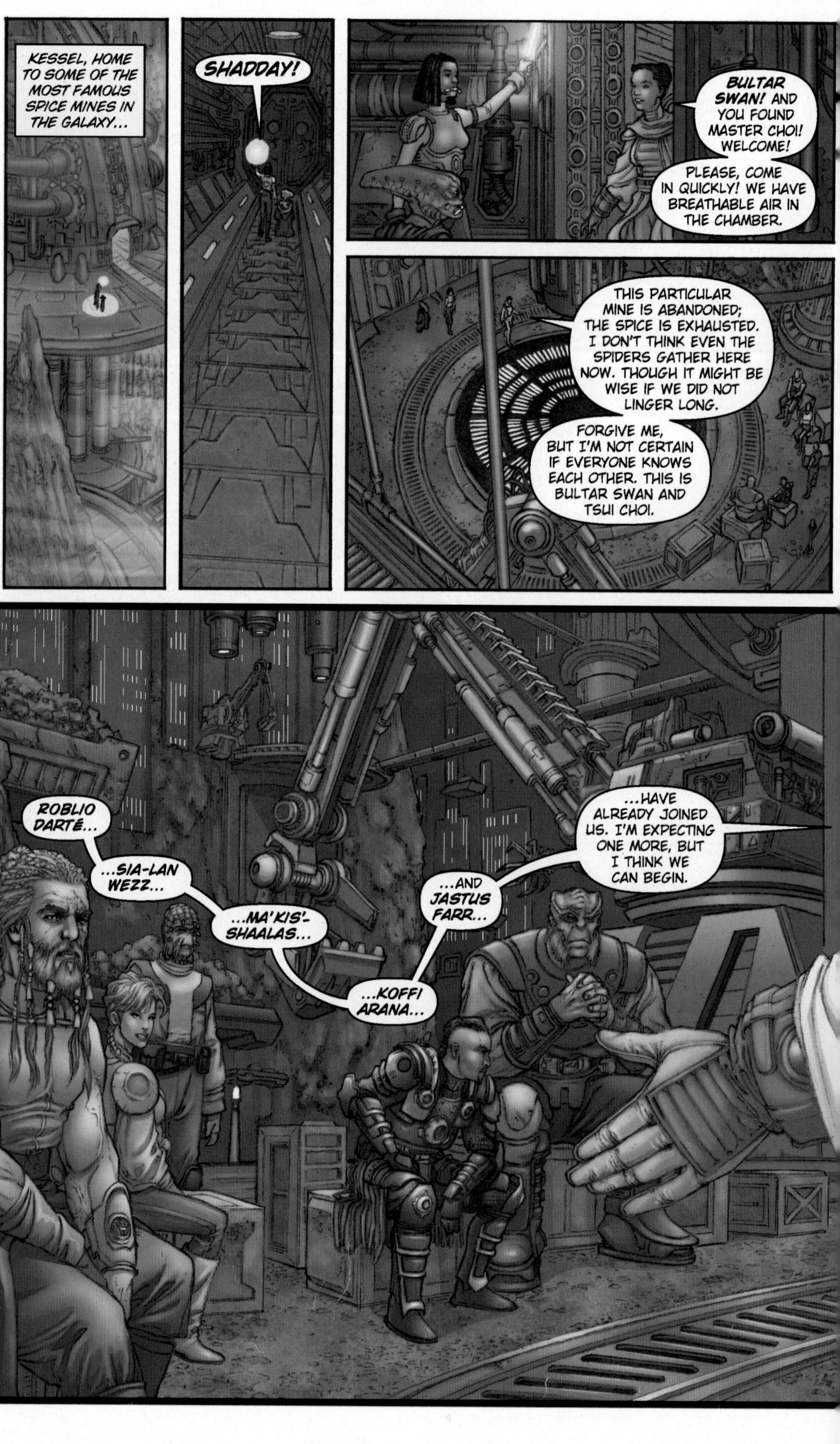

KESSEL, HOME TO SOME OF THE MOST FAMOUS SPICE MINES IN THE GALAXY...
SHADDAY!
BULTAR SWAN! AND YOU FOUND MASTER CHOI! WELCOME!
PLEASE, COME IN QUICKLY! WE HAVE BREATHABLE AIR IN THE CHAMBER.
THIS PARTICULAR MINE IS ABANDONED; THE SPICE IS EXHAUSTED. I DON'T THINK EVEN THE SPIDERS GATHER HERE NOW. THOUGH IT MIGHT BE WISE IF WE DID NOT LINGER LONG.
FORGIVE ME, BUT I'M NOT CERTAIN IF EVERYONE KNOWS EACH OTHER. THIS IS BULTAR SWAN AND TSUI CHOI.
ROBLIO DARTÉ...
...SIA-LAN WEZZ...
...MA'KIS'-SHAALAS...
...KOFFI ARANA...
...AND JASTUS FARR...
...HAVE ALREADY JOINED US. I'M EXPECTING ONE MORE, BUT I THINK WE CAN BEGIN.

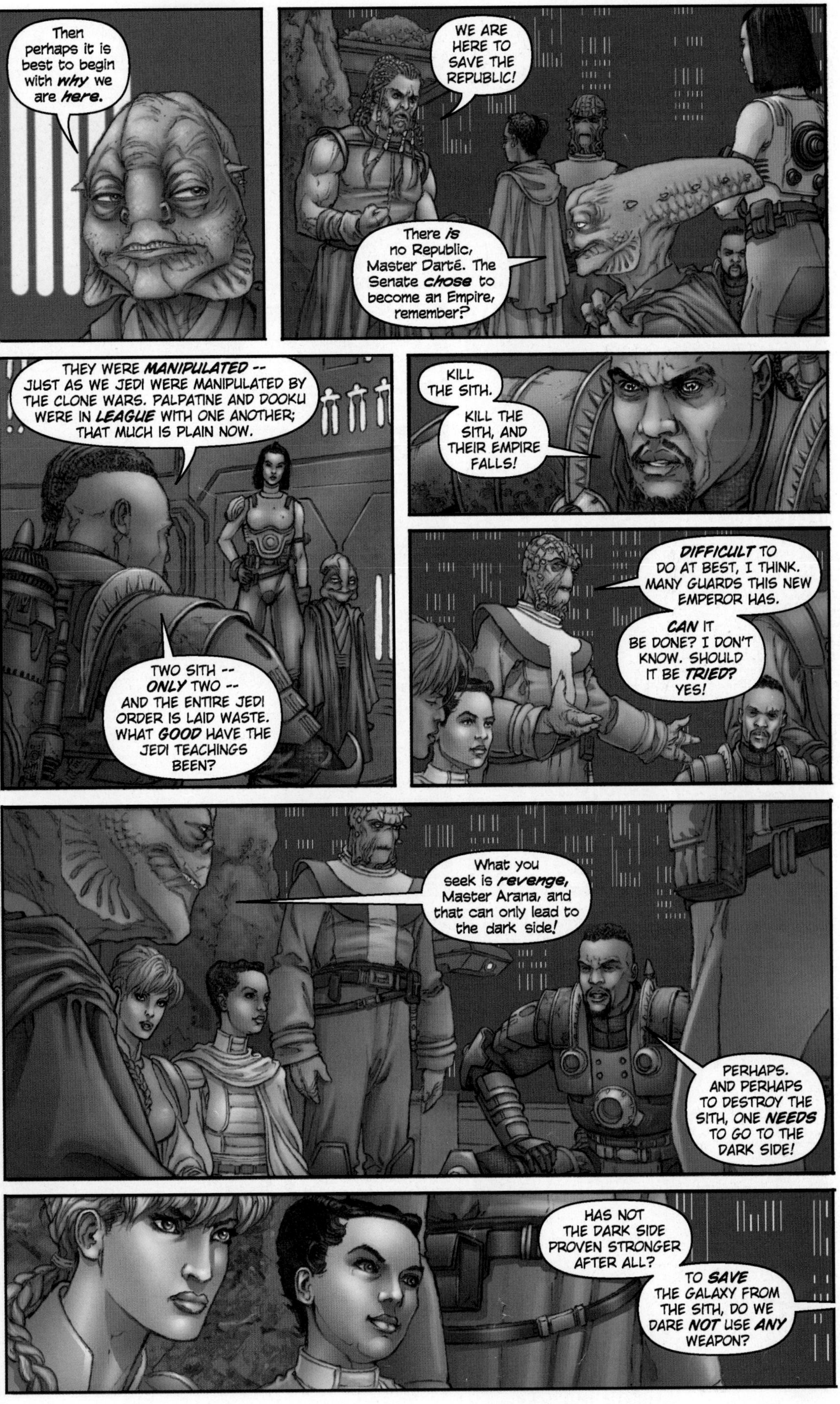

Then perhaps it is best to begin with *why* we are *here.*
WE ARE HERE TO SAVE THE REPUBLIC!
There *is* no Republic, Master Darté. The Senate *chose* to become an Empire, remember?
THEY WERE *MANIPULATED* -- JUST AS WE JEDI WERE MANIPULATED BY THE CLONE WARS. PALPATINE AND DOOKU WERE IN *LEAGUE* WITH ONE ANOTHER; THAT MUCH IS PLAIN NOW.
TWO SITH -- *ONLY* TWO -- AND THE ENTIRE JEDI ORDER IS LAID WASTE. WHAT *GOOD* HAVE THE JEDI TEACHINGS BEEN?
KILL THE SITH.
KILL THE SITH, AND THEIR EMPIRE FALLS!
DIFFICULT TO DO AT BEST, I THINK. MANY GUARDS THIS NEW EMPEROR HAS.
CAN IT BE DONE? I DON'T KNOW. SHOULD IT BE *TRIED?* YES!
What you seek is *revenge,* Master Arana, and that can only lead to the dark side!
PERHAPS. AND PERHAPS TO DESTROY THE SITH, ONE *NEEDS* TO GO TO THE DARK SIDE!
HAS NOT THE DARK SIDE PROVEN STRONGER AFTER ALL?
TO *SAVE* THE GALAXY FROM THE SITH, DO WE DARE *NOT* USE *ANY* WEAPON?

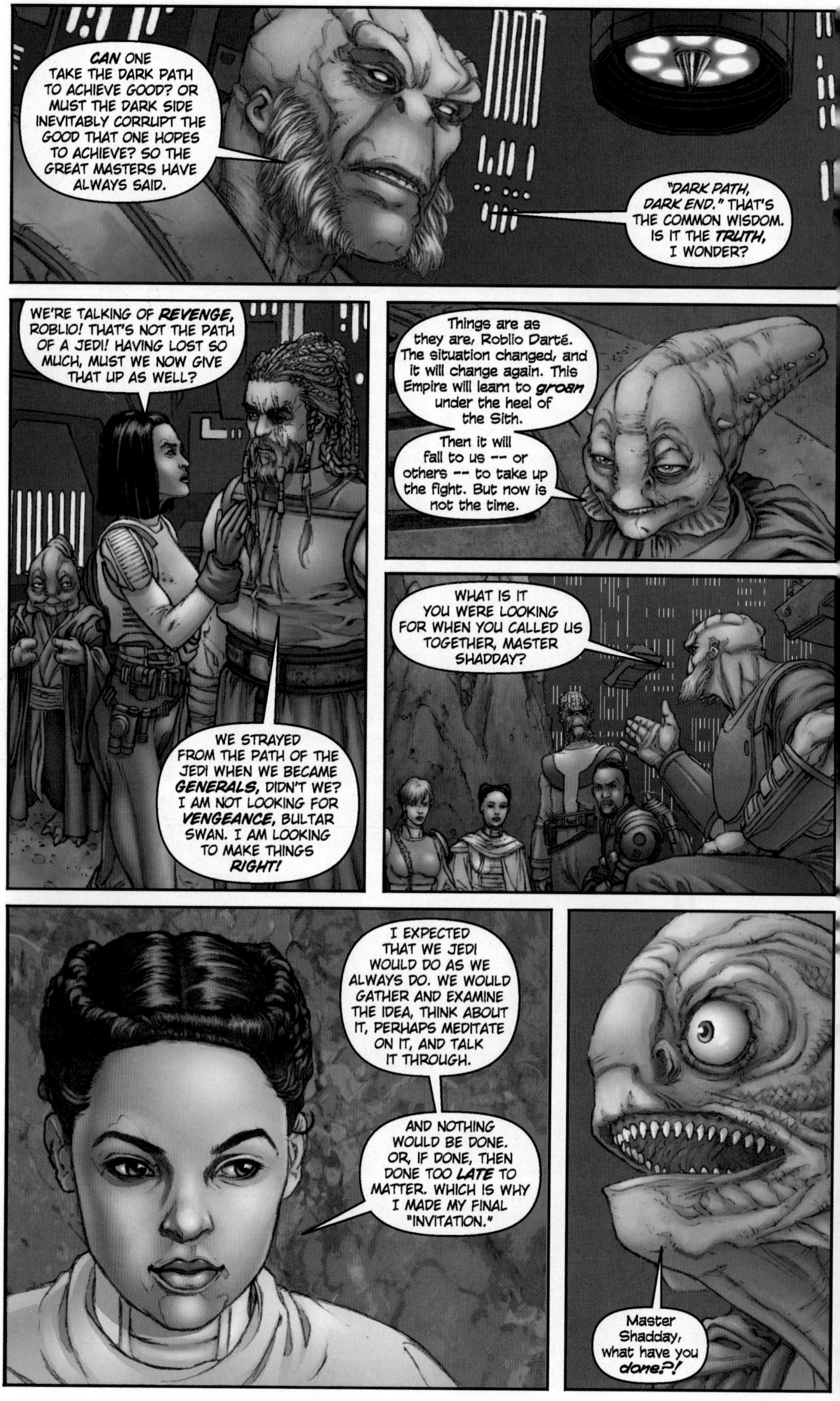
CAN ONE TAKE THE DARK PATH TO ACHIEVE GOOD? OR MUST THE DARK SIDE INEVITABLY CORRUPT THE GOOD THAT ONE HOPES TO ACHIEVE? SO THE GREAT MASTERS HAVE ALWAYS SAID.
"DARK PATH, DARK END." THAT'S THE COMMON WISDOM. IS IT THE TRUTH, I WONDER?
WE'RE TALKING OF REVENGE, ROBLIO! THAT'S NOT THE PATH OF A JEDI! HAVING LOST SO MUCH, MUST WE NOW GIVE THAT UP AS WELL?
WE STRAYED FROM THE PATH OF THE JEDI WHEN WE BECAME GENERALS, DIDN'T WE? I AM NOT LOOKING FOR VENGEANCE, BULTAR SWAN. I AM LOOKING TO MAKE THINGS RIGHT!
Things are as they are, Roblio Darté. The situation changed, and it will change again. This Empire will learn to groan under the heel of the Sith.
Then it will fall to us -- or others -- to take up the fight. But now is not the time.
WHAT IS IT YOU WERE LOOKING FOR WHEN YOU CALLED US TOGETHER, MASTER SHADDAY?
I EXPECTED THAT WE JEDI WOULD DO AS WE ALWAYS DO. WE WOULD GATHER AND EXAMINE THE IDEA, THINK ABOUT IT, PERHAPS MEDITATE ON IT, AND TALK IT THROUGH.
AND NOTHING WOULD BE DONE. OR, IF DONE, THEN DONE TOO LATE TO MATTER. WHICH IS WHY I MADE MY FINAL "INVITATION."
Master Shadday, what have you done?!

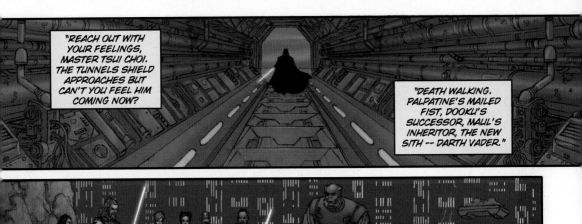

"REACH OUT WITH YOUR FEELINGS, MASTER TSUI CHOI. THE TUNNELS SHIELD APPROACHES BUT CAN'T YOU FEEL HIM COMING NOW?"

"DEATH WALKING. PALPATINE'S MAILED FIST, DOOKU'S SUCCESSOR, MAUL'S INHERITOR, THE NEW SITH -- DARTH VADER."

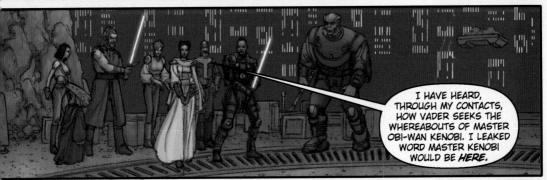

I HAVE HEARD, THROUGH MY CONTACTS, HOW VADER SEEKS THE WHEREABOUTS OF MASTER OBI-WAN KENOBI. I LEAKED WORD MASTER KENOBI WOULD BE *HERE*.

"I DO NOT KNOW THE *REASON* FOR VADER'S HATRED OF MASTER KENOBI. I ONLY KNOW IT DRAWS HIM HERE -- *ALONE*."

HOWEVER POWERFUL, VADER IS *ONE*, AND WE ARE *MANY*.

NO MORE DEBATE. NO MORE "REFLECTION." NO NEED OF PLANNING. OUR PREY COMES TO US. WHEN HE IS DEAD, THE EMPEROR WILL BE CRIPPLED AND KNOW *FEAR*.

AND THE GALAXY WILL KNOW THE JEDI *LIVE*.

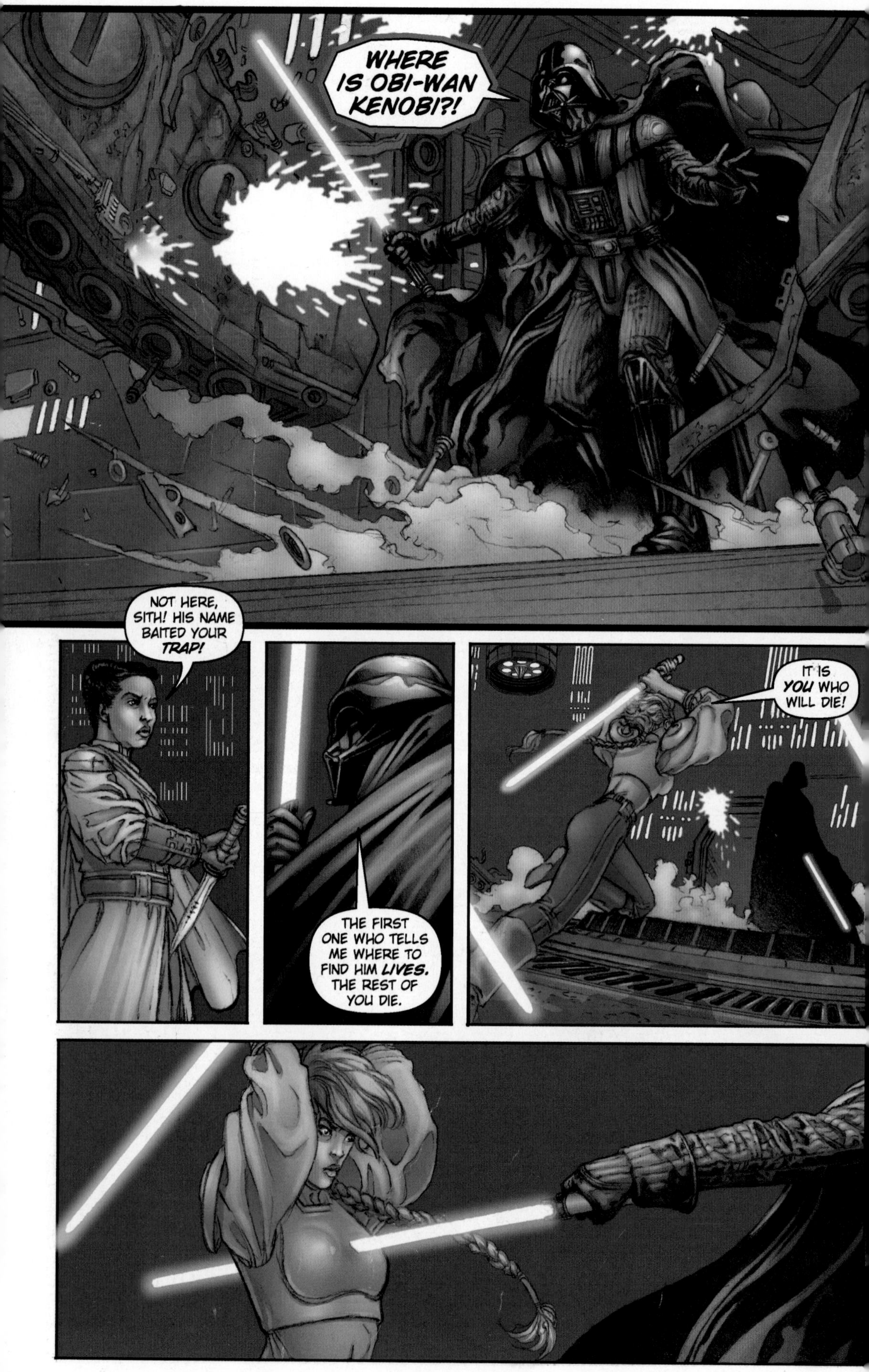
WHERE IS OBI-WAN KENOBI?!
NOT HERE, SITH! HIS NAME BAITED YOUR TRAP!
THE FIRST ONE WHO TELLS ME WHERE TO FIND HIM LIVES. THE REST OF YOU DIE.
IT IS YOU WHO WILL DIE!

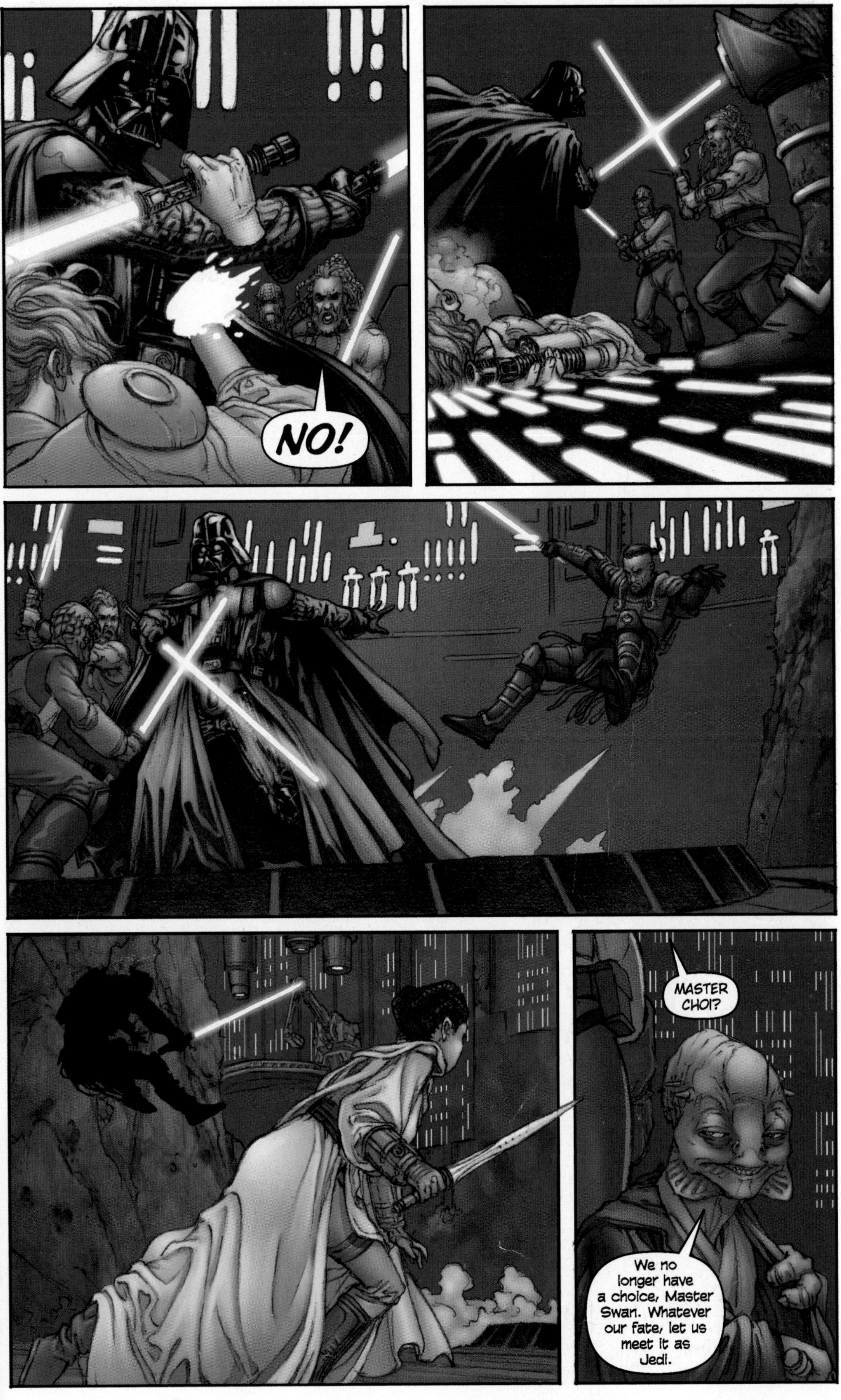
NO!
MASTER CHOI?
We no longer have a choice, Master Swan. Whatever our fate, let us meet it as Jedi.

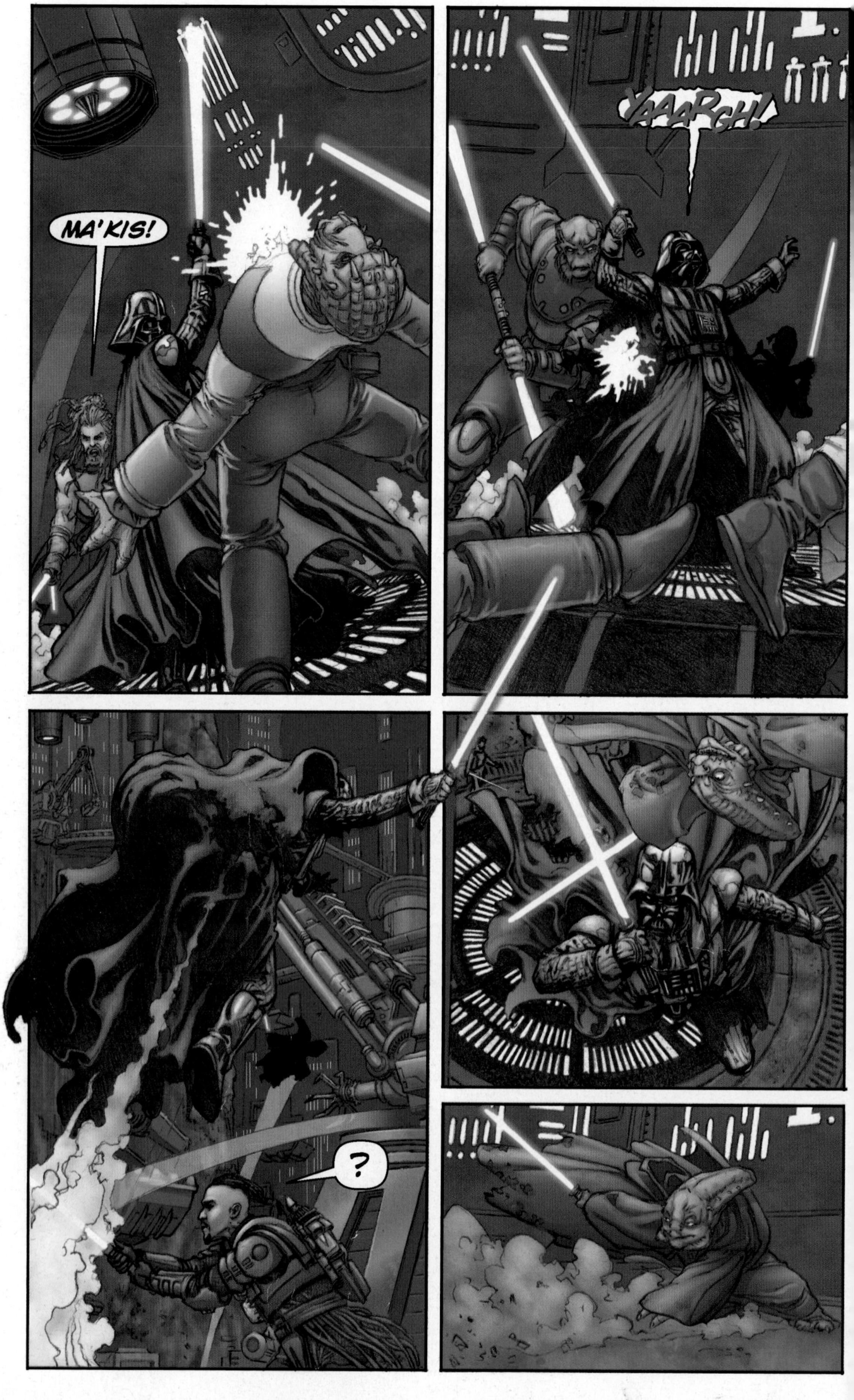
MA'KIS!
YAAARGH!
?

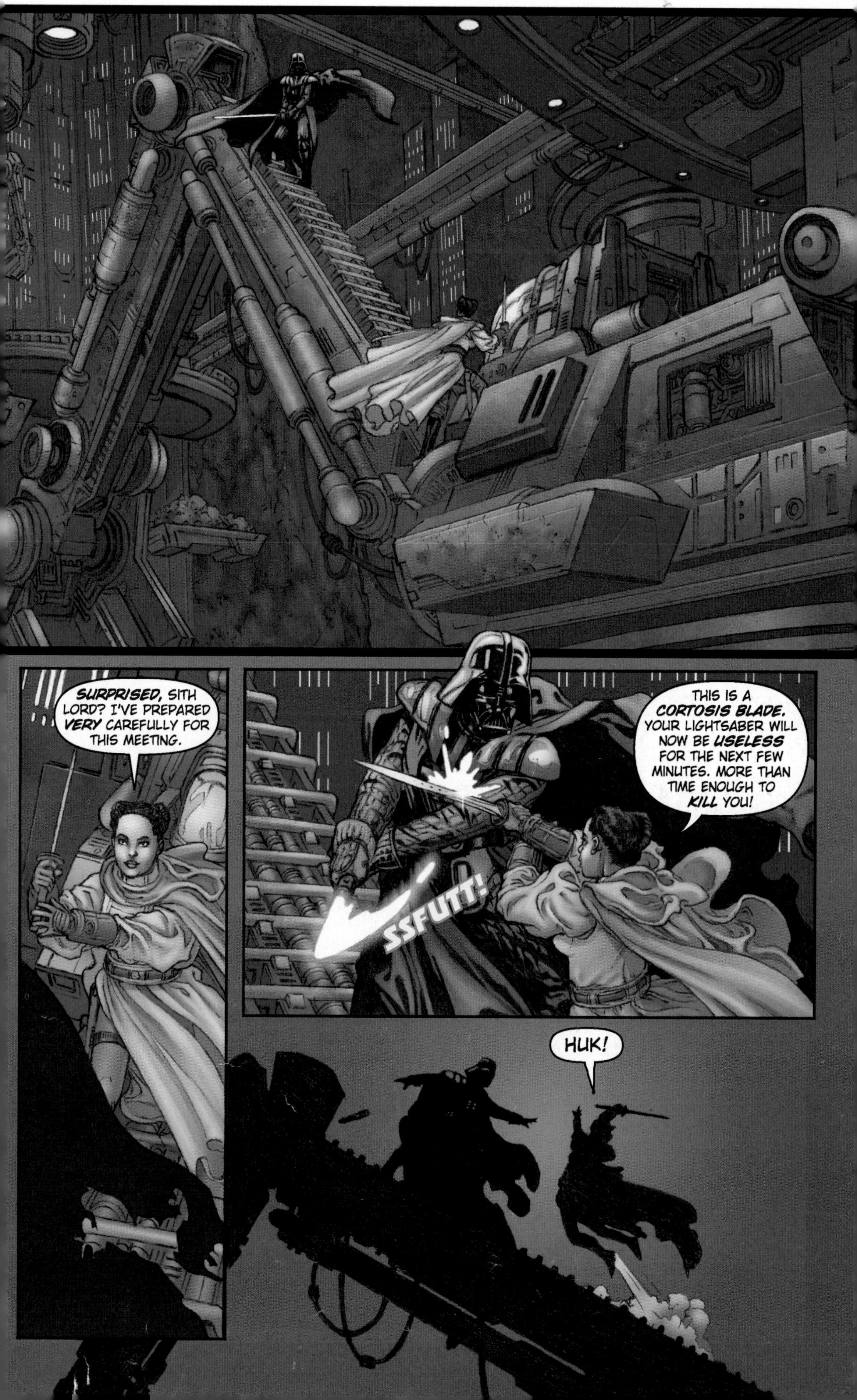
SURPRISED, SITH LORD? I'VE PREPARED VERY CAREFULLY FOR THIS MEETING.
THIS IS A CORTOSIS BLADE. YOUR LIGHTSABER WILL NOW BE USELESS FOR THE NEXT FEW MINUTES. MORE THAN TIME ENOUGH TO KILL YOU!
SSFUTT!
HUK!

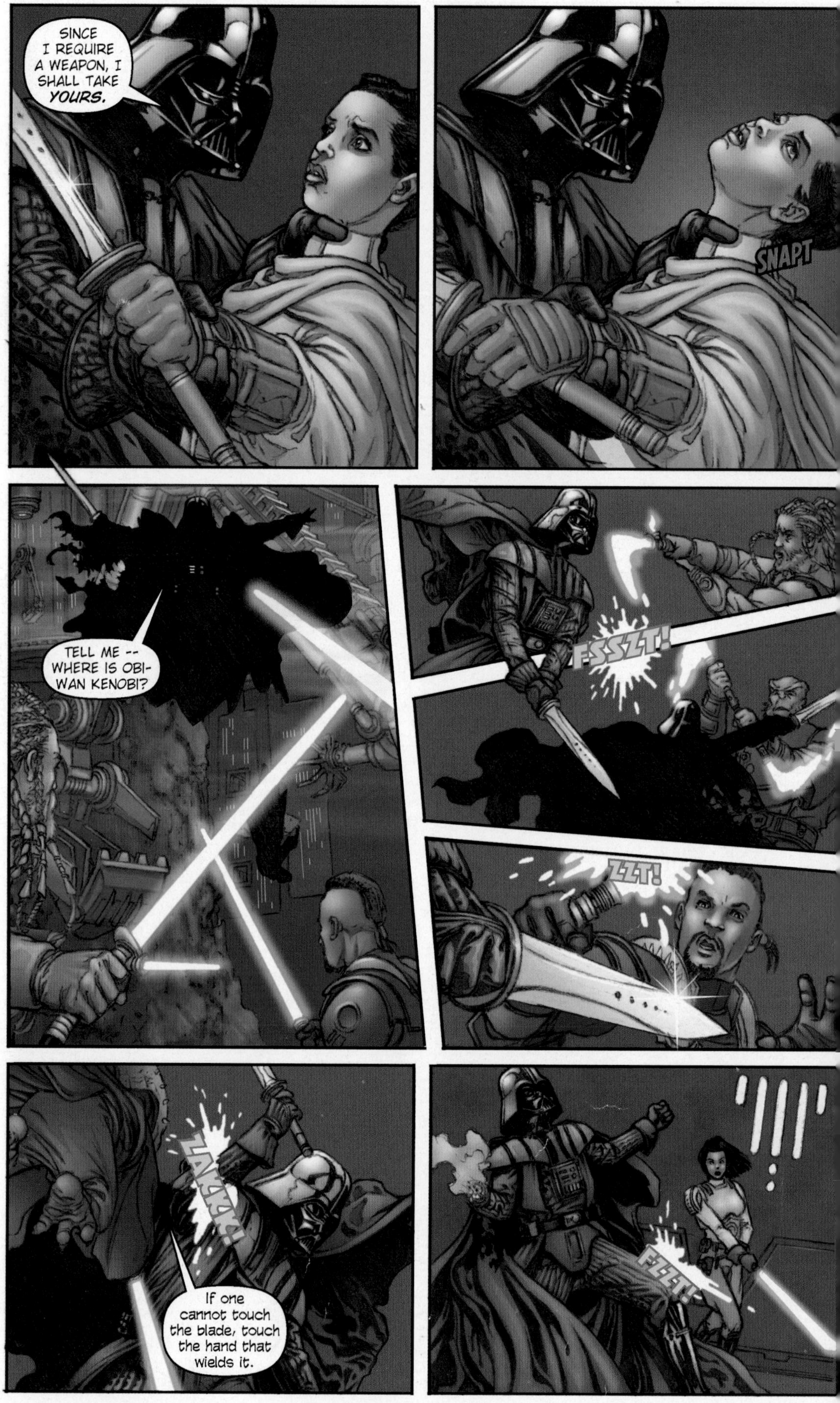

SINCE I REQUIRE A WEAPON, I SHALL TAKE *YOURS.*
SNAPT
TELL ME -- WHERE IS OBI-WAN KENOBI?
FSSZT!
ZZT!
ZAKKK!
If one cannot touch the blade, touch the hand that wields it.
FZZT!
!!!

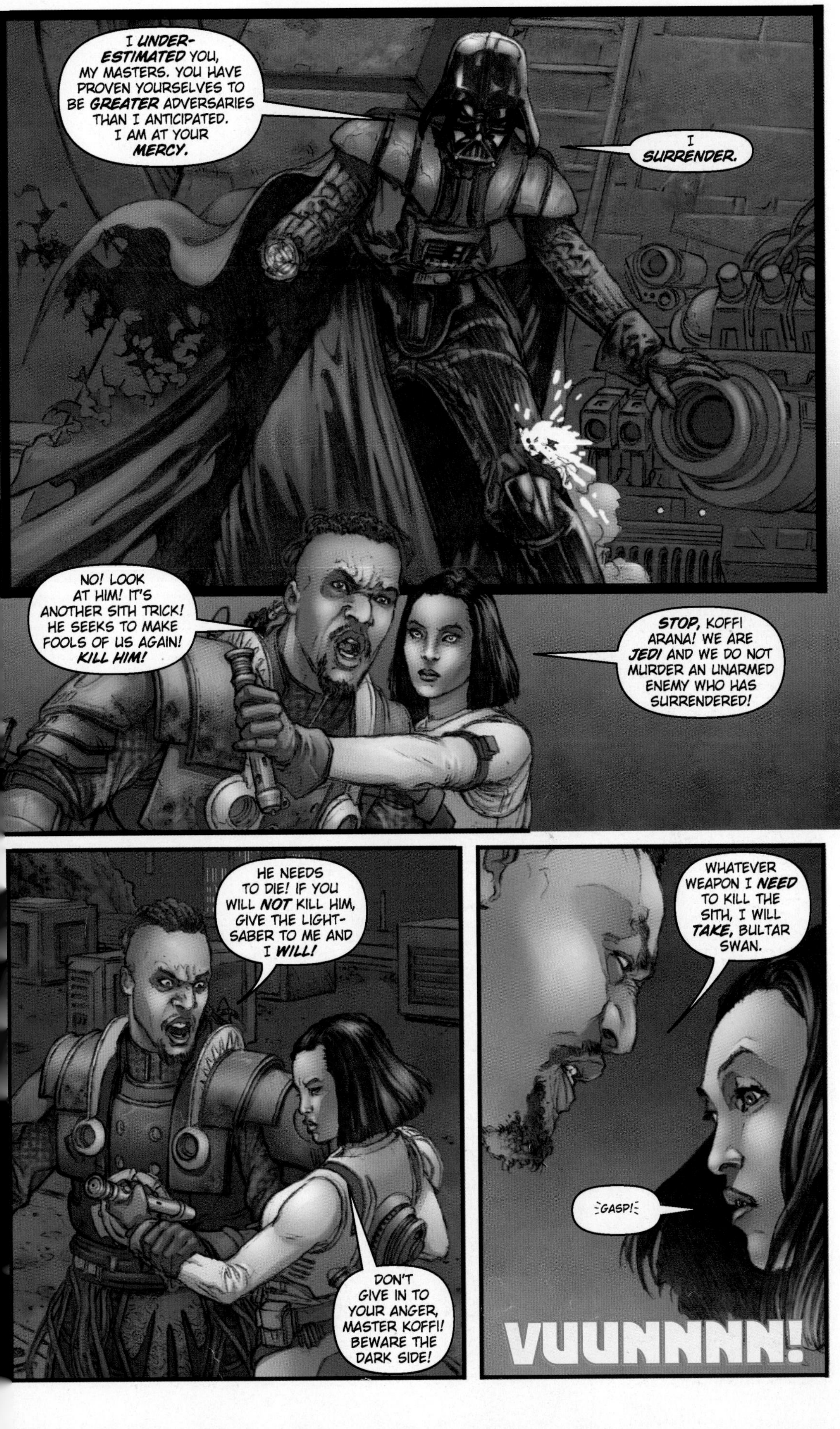
I UNDER-ESTIMATED YOU, MY MASTERS. YOU HAVE PROVEN YOURSELVES TO BE GREATER ADVERSARIES THAN I ANTICIPATED. I AM AT YOUR MERCY.
I SURRENDER.
NO! LOOK AT HIM! IT'S ANOTHER SITH TRICK! HE SEEKS TO MAKE FOOLS OF US AGAIN! KILL HIM!
STOP, KOFFI ARANA! WE ARE JEDI AND WE DO NOT MURDER AN UNARMED ENEMY WHO HAS SURRENDERED!
HE NEEDS TO DIE! IF YOU WILL NOT KILL HIM, GIVE THE LIGHT-SABER TO ME AND I WILL!
DON'T GIVE IN TO YOUR ANGER, MASTER KOFFI! BEWARE THE DARK SIDE!
WHATEVER WEAPON I NEED TO KILL THE SITH, I WILL TAKE, BULTAR SWAN.
GASP!
VUUNNNN!

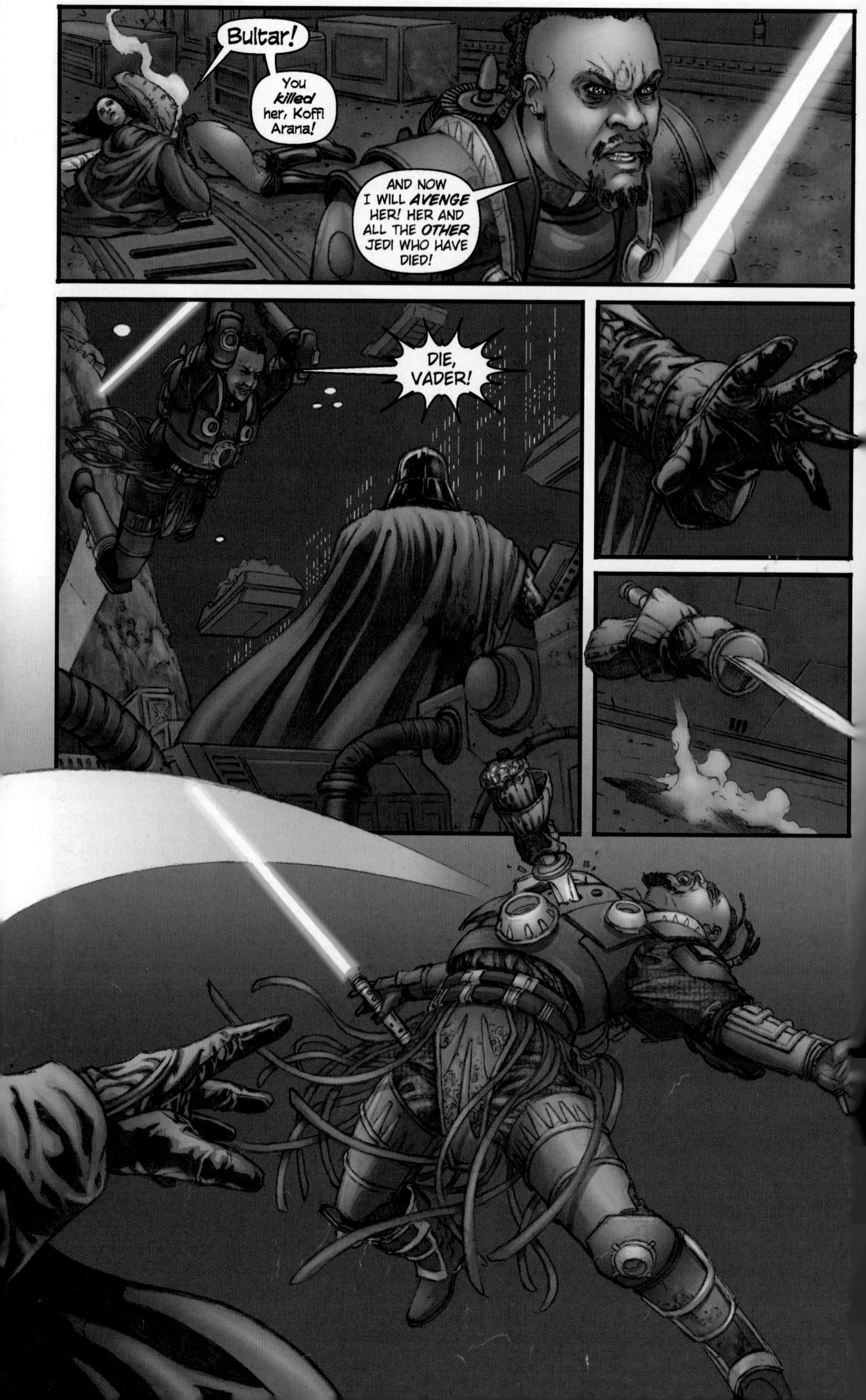
Bultar!
You killed her, Koffi Arana!
AND NOW I WILL AVENGE HER! HER AND ALL THE OTHER JEDI WHO HAVE DIED!
DIE, VADER!

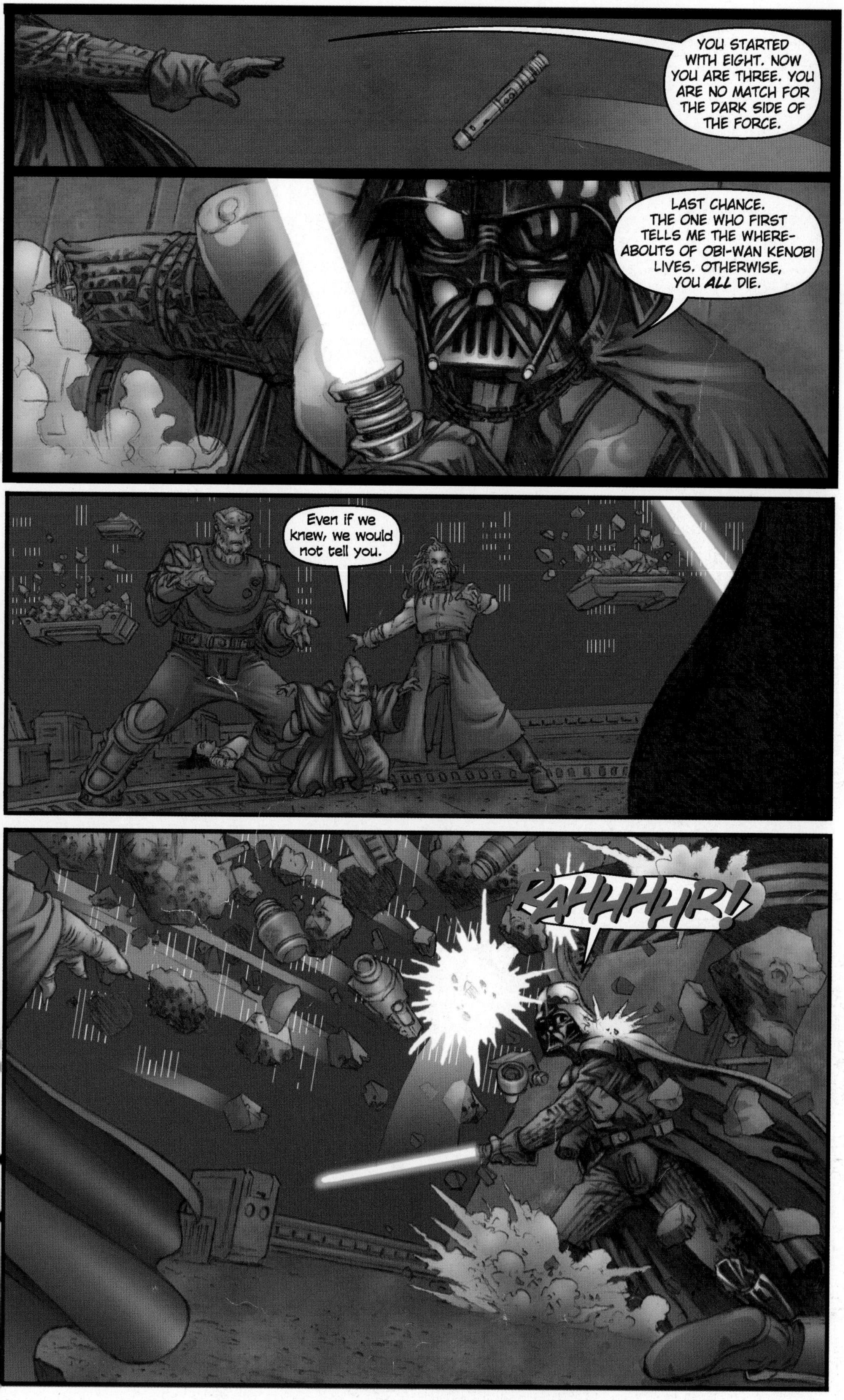
YOU STARTED WITH EIGHT. NOW YOU ARE THREE. YOU ARE NO MATCH FOR THE DARK SIDE OF THE FORCE.
LAST CHANCE. THE ONE WHO FIRST TELLS ME THE WHERE-ABOUTS OF OBI-WAN KENOBI LIVES. OTHERWISE, YOU ALL DIE.
Even if we knew, we would not tell you.
RAHHHHR!

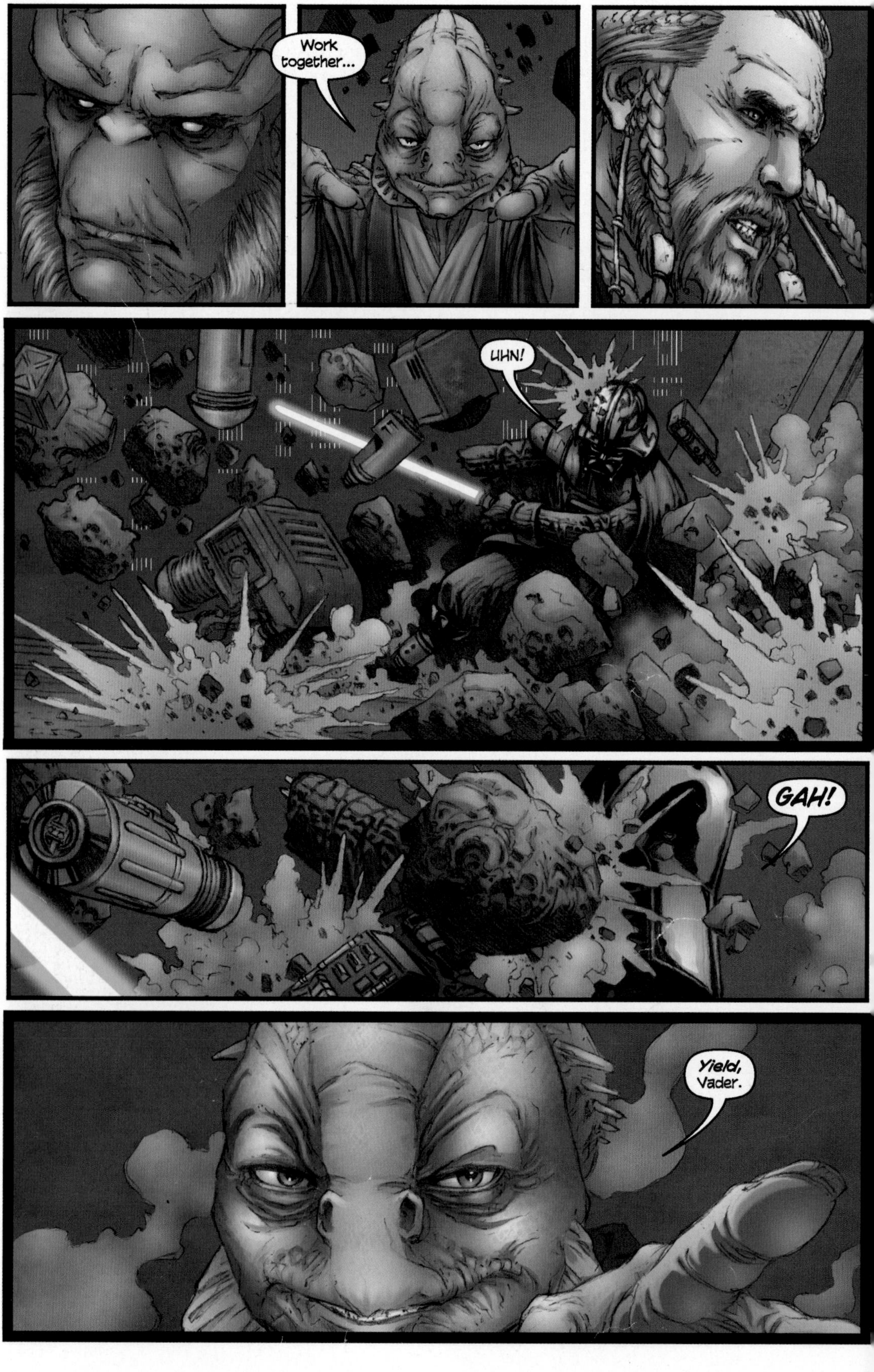
Work together...
UHN!
GAH!
Yield, Vader.

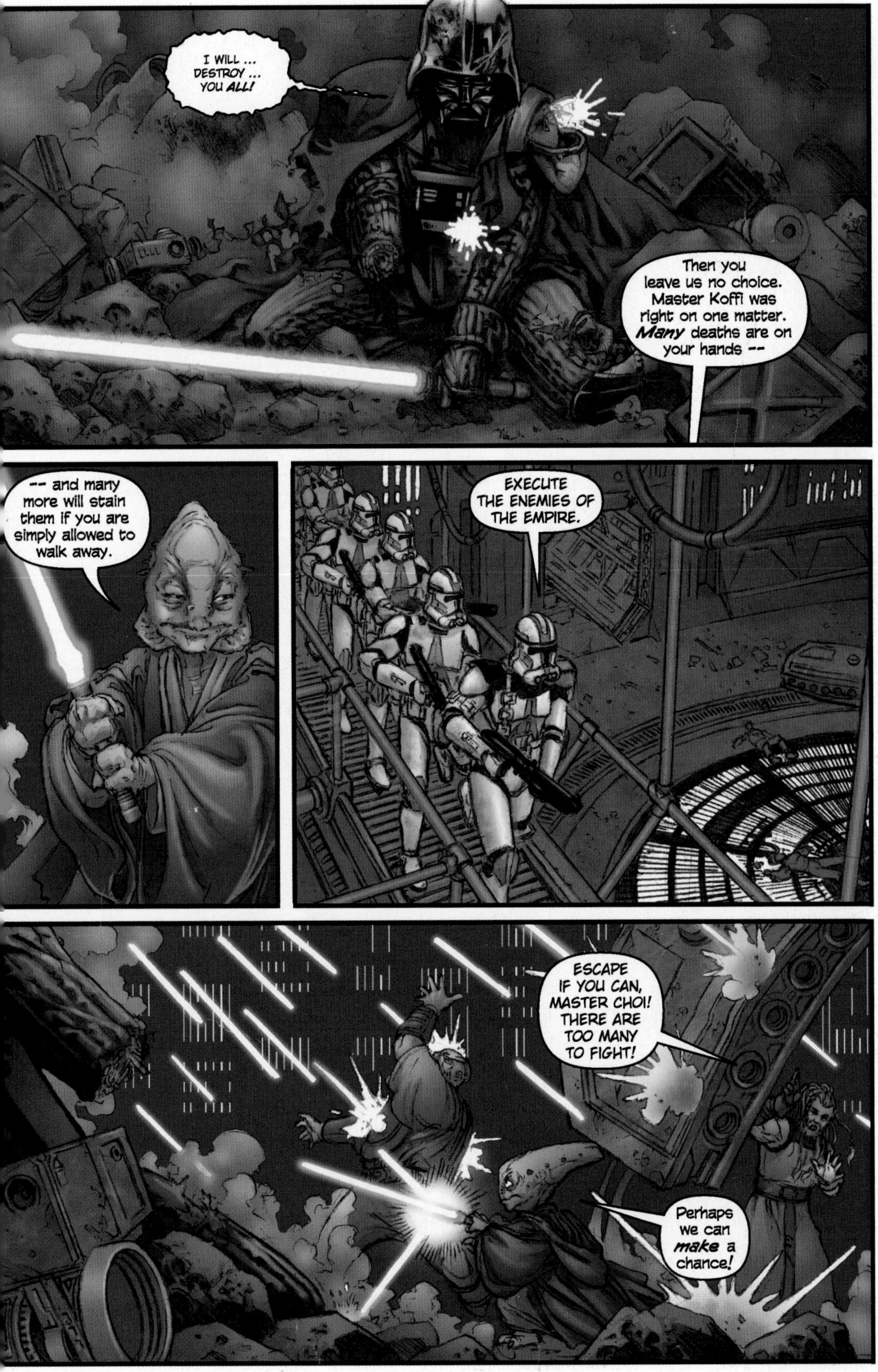
I WILL ... DESTROY ... YOU ALL!
Then you leave us no choice. Master Koffi was right on one matter. Many deaths are on your hands --
-- and many more will stain them if you are simply allowed to walk away.
EXECUTE THE ENEMIES OF THE EMPIRE.
ESCAPE IF YOU CAN, MASTER CHOI! THERE ARE TOO MANY TO FIGHT!
Perhaps we can make a chance!

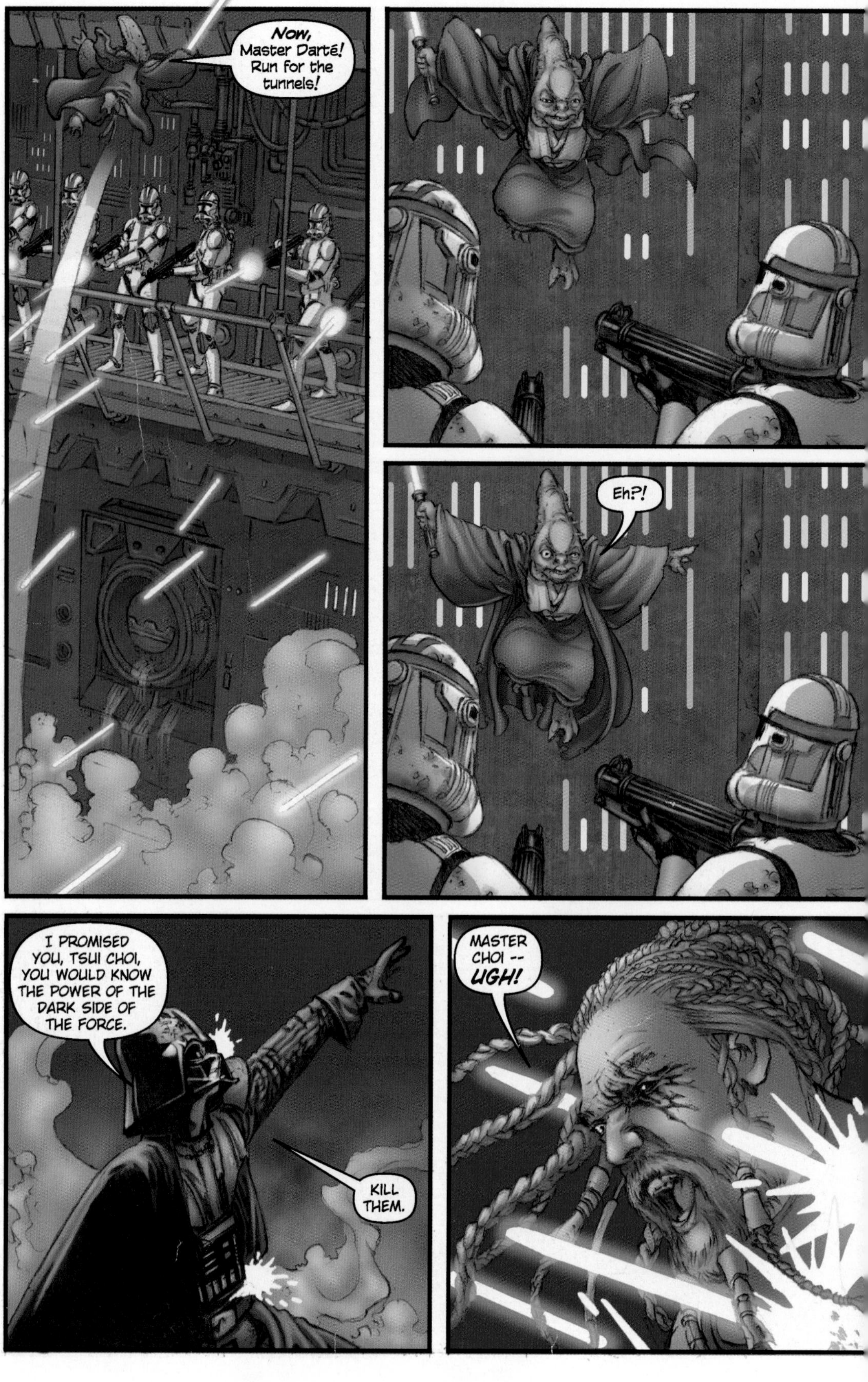

Now, Master Darté! Run for the tunnels!
Eh?!
I PROMISED YOU, TSUI CHOI, YOU WOULD KNOW THE POWER OF THE DARK SIDE OF THE FORCE.
KILL THEM.
MASTER CHOI -- UGH!

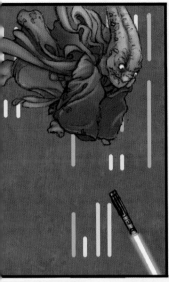

VSSSHT!

BDOW! DOW! DOW!

BDEW!

WHAT ... BRINGS YOU HERE, COMMANDER?

ORDERS, MY LORD. THE *EMPEROR* REQUESTS YOUR PRESENCE.

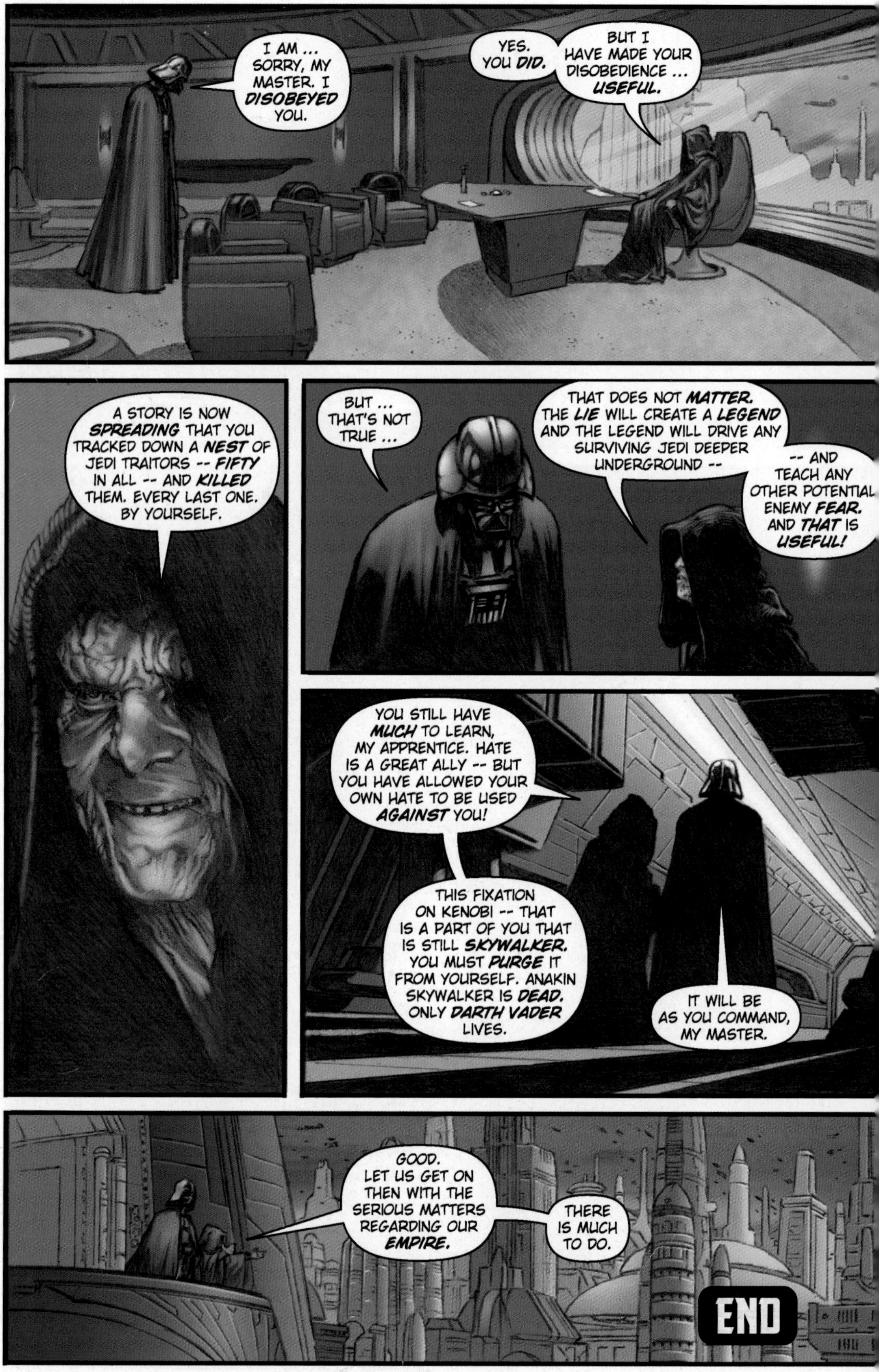
I AM ... SORRY, MY MASTER. I DISOBEYED YOU.
YES. YOU DID.
BUT I HAVE MADE YOUR DISOBEDIENCE ... USEFUL.
A STORY IS NOW SPREADING THAT YOU TRACKED DOWN A NEST OF JEDI TRAITORS -- FIFTY IN ALL -- AND KILLED THEM. EVERY LAST ONE. BY YOURSELF.
BUT ... THAT'S NOT TRUE ...
THAT DOES NOT MATTER. THE LIE WILL CREATE A LEGEND AND THE LEGEND WILL DRIVE ANY SURVIVING JEDI DEEPER UNDERGROUND --
-- AND TEACH ANY OTHER POTENTIAL ENEMY FEAR. AND THAT IS USEFUL!
YOU STILL HAVE MUCH TO LEARN, MY APPRENTICE. HATE IS A GREAT ALLY -- BUT YOU HAVE ALLOWED YOUR OWN HATE TO BE USED AGAINST YOU!
THIS FIXATION ON KENOBI -- THAT IS A PART OF YOU THAT IS STILL SKYWALKER. YOU MUST PURGE IT FROM YOURSELF. ANAKIN SKYWALKER IS DEAD. ONLY DARTH VADER LIVES.
IT WILL BE AS YOU COMMAND, MY MASTER.
GOOD. LET US GET ON THEN WITH THE SERIOUS MATTERS REGARDING OUR EMPIRE.
THERE IS MUCH TO DO.
END

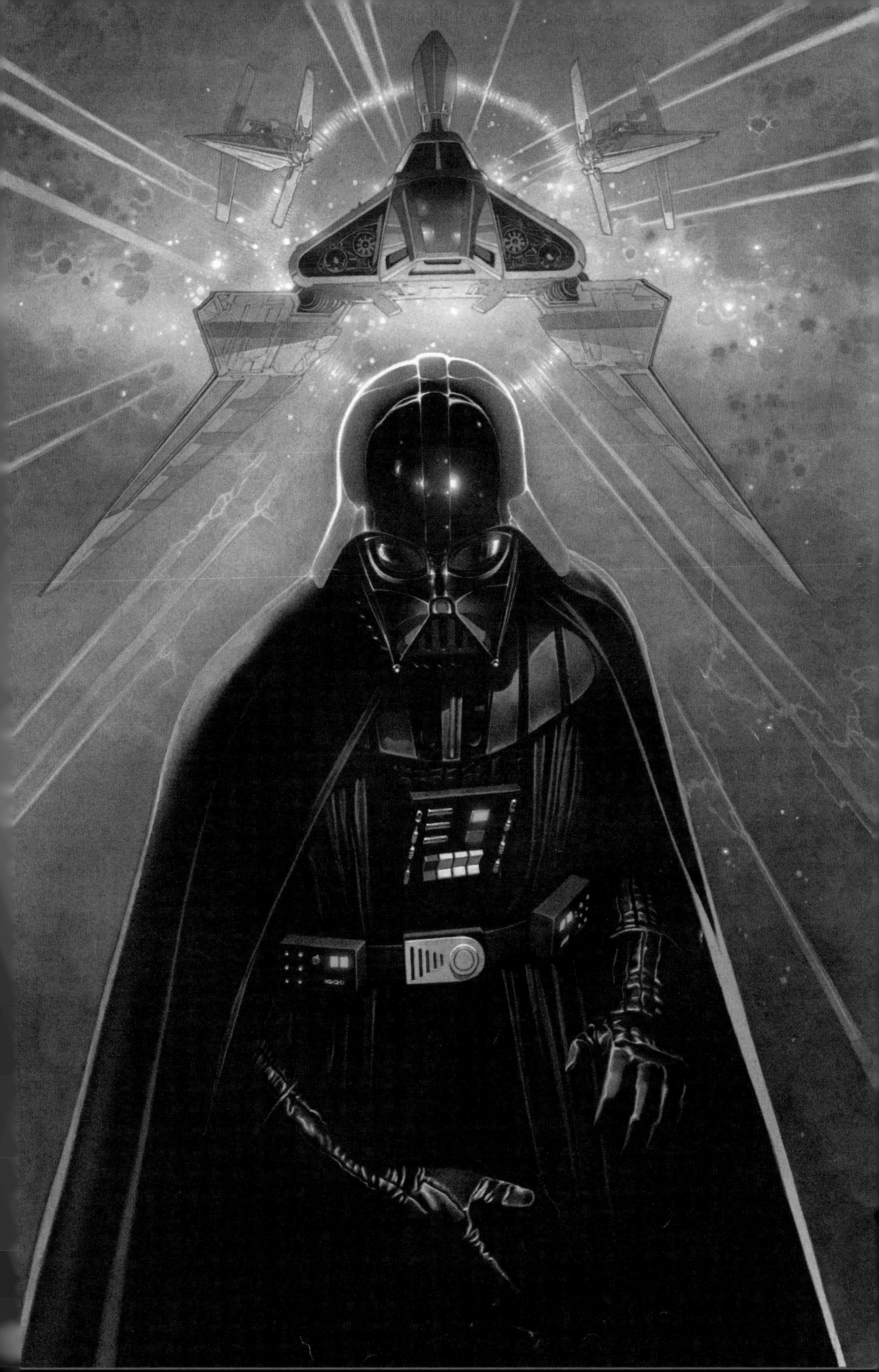

STAR WARS: PURGE — SECONDS TO DIE

WRITER: JOHN OSTRANDER • PENCILER: JIM HALL • INKERS: ALEX LEI & MARK MCKENNA • COLORIST: RONDA PATTISON • LETTERER: MICHAEL HEISLER
DESIGNER: DAVID NESTELLE • ASSISTANT EDITOR: FREDDYE LINS • EDITOR: RANDY STRADLEY • COVER ARTIST: TRAVIS CHAREST

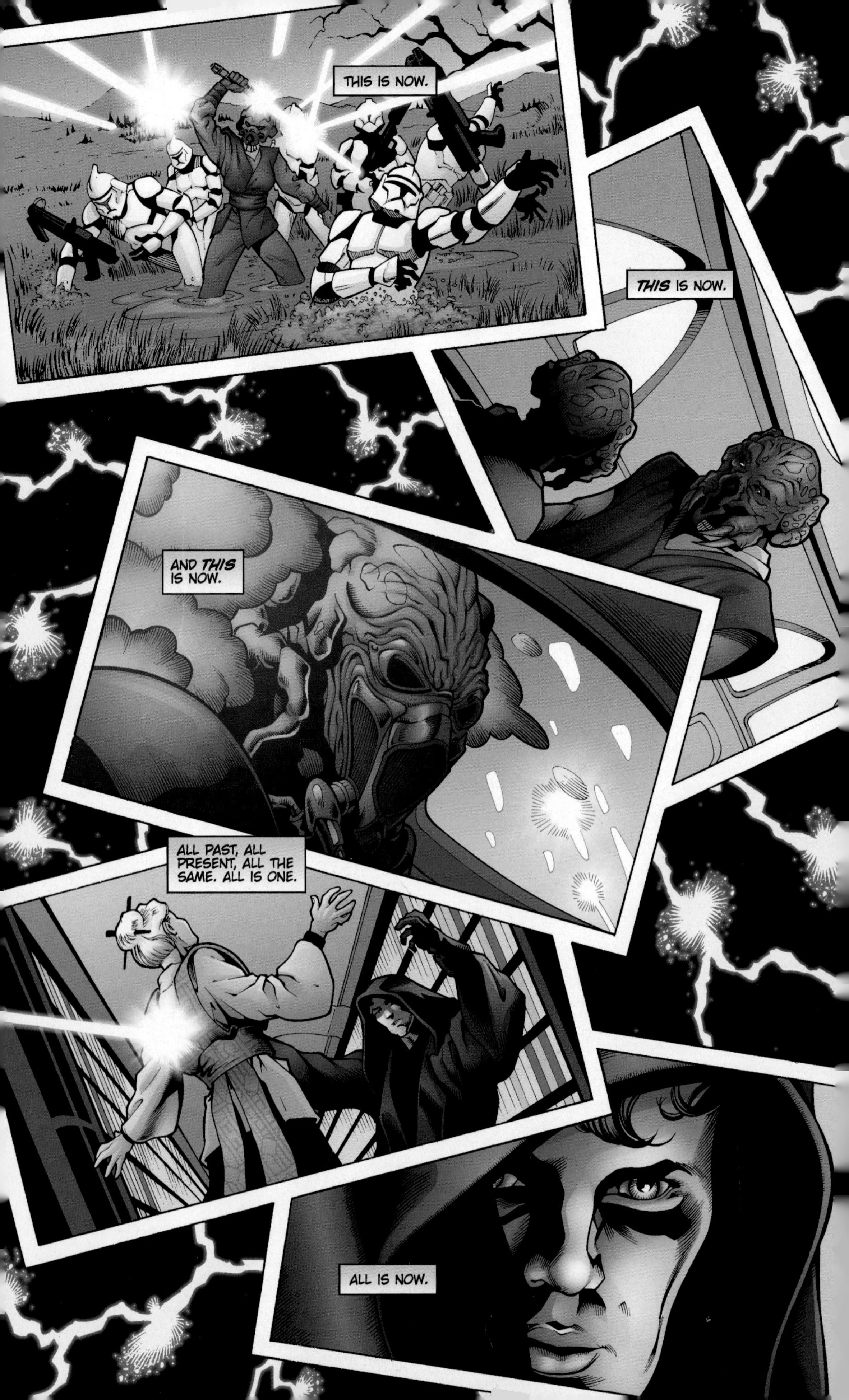
THIS IS NOW.
THIS IS NOW.
AND THIS IS NOW.
ALL PAST, ALL PRESENT, ALL THE SAME. ALL IS ONE.
ALL IS NOW.

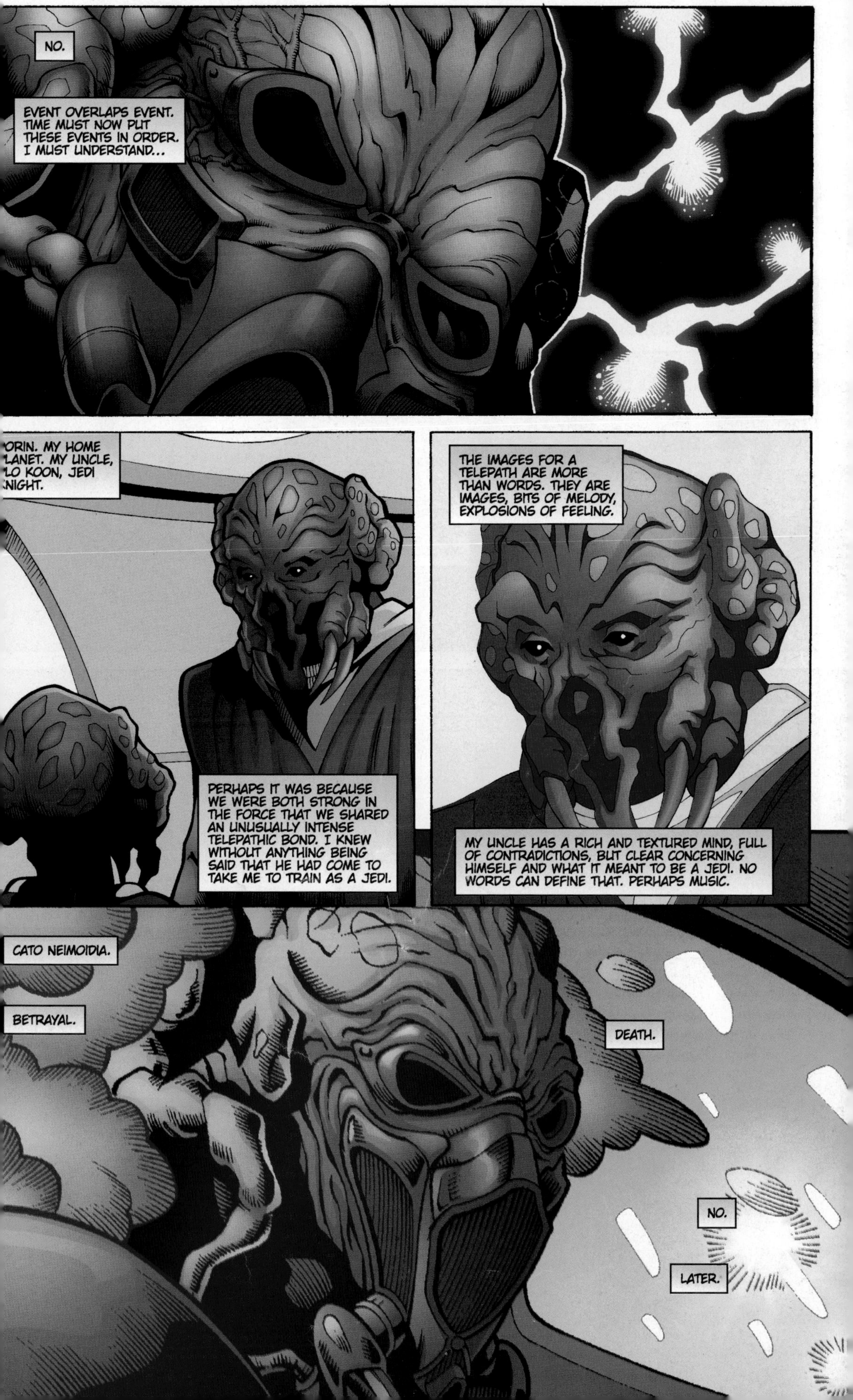

NO.
EVENT OVERLAPS EVENT. TIME MUST NOW PUT THESE EVENTS IN ORDER. I MUST UNDERSTAND...
ORIN. MY HOME LANET. MY UNCLE, LO KOON, JEDI NIGHT.
PERHAPS IT WAS BECAUSE WE WERE BOTH STRONG IN THE FORCE THAT WE SHARED AN UNUSUALLY INTENSE TELEPATHIC BOND. I KNEW WITHOUT ANYTHING BEING SAID THAT HE HAD COME TO TAKE ME TO TRAIN AS A JEDI.
THE IMAGES FOR A TELEPATH ARE MORE THAN WORDS. THEY ARE IMAGES, BITS OF MELODY, EXPLOSIONS OF FEELING.
MY UNCLE HAS A RICH AND TEXTURED MIND, FULL OF CONTRADICTIONS, BUT CLEAR CONCERNING HIMSELF AND WHAT IT MEANT TO BE A JEDI. NO WORDS CAN DEFINE THAT. PERHAPS MUSIC.
CATO NEIMOIDIA.
BETRAYAL.
DEATH.
NO.
LATER.

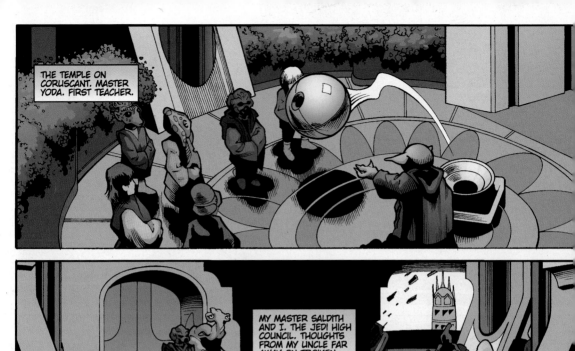

THE TEMPLE ON CORUSCANT. MASTER YODA. FIRST TEACHER.

MY MASTER SALDITH AND I. THE JEDI HIGH COUNCIL. THOUGHTS FROM MY UNCLE FAR AWAY ON TROIKEN DURING THE STARK HYPERSPACE WAR REACH ME. I TELL THE JEDI. I SAVE MY UNCLE.

LATER, WHEN I AM A JEDI KNIGHT, I AM GIVEN A PADAWAN -- BAYLIS ARCHAN. CORELLIAN BORN, HE TOO HAD A TOUCH OF TELEPATHY AND SO MY TRAINING HIM SEEMED NATURAL.

HE HAD SUCH A PLAYFUL MIND. LIKE A FAST MOVING RIVER, IN WHICH HIS THOUGHTS WERE LIKE FISH, DARTING AND SPARKLING.

HE DIED ON THE PLANET GIJU DURING THE WAR -- ALONG WITH THE REST OF MY COMMAND. A STUPID, USELESS BATTLE IN AN INCREASINGLY VIOLENT AND USELESS WAR.

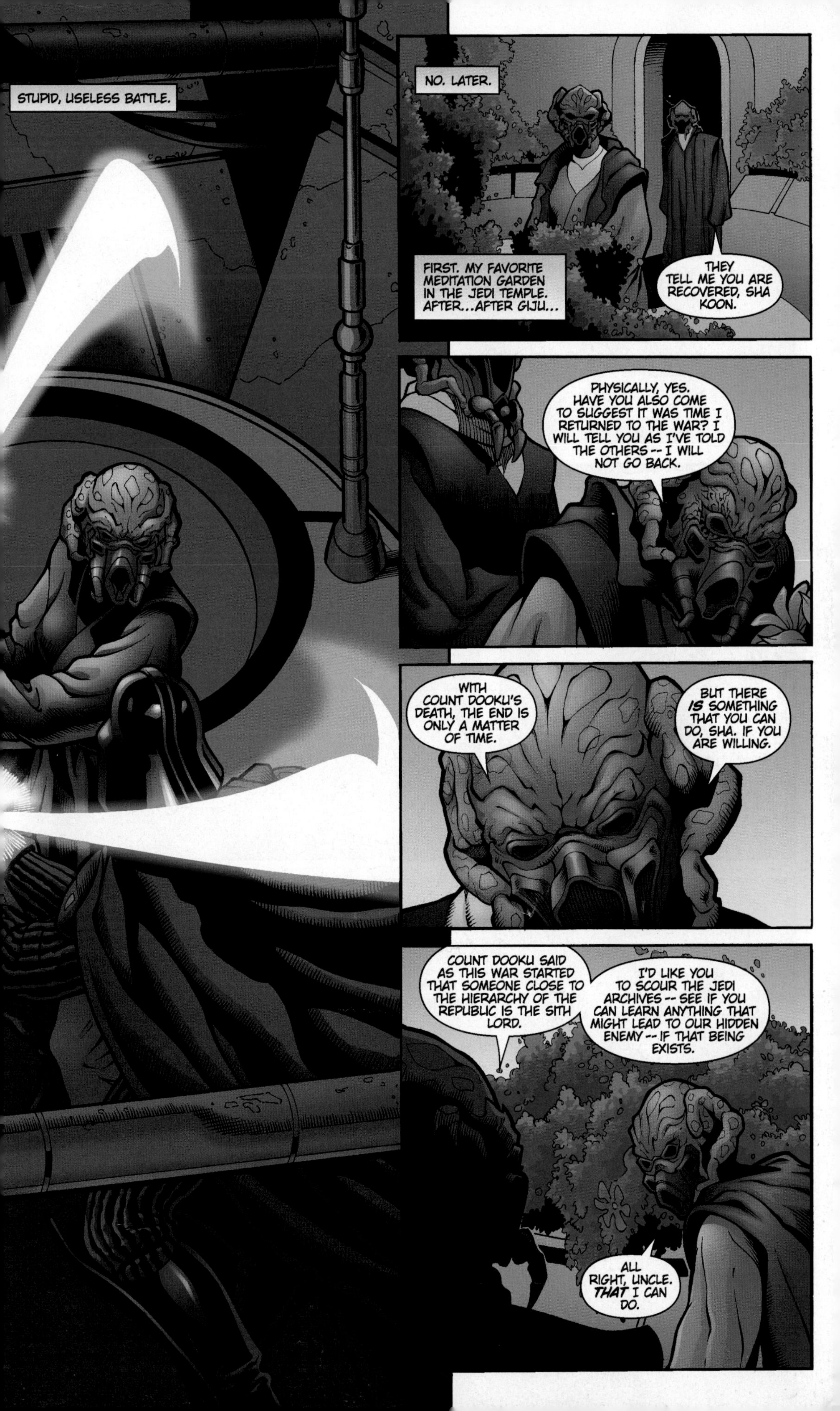
STUPID, USELESS BATTLE.
NO. LATER.
FIRST. MY FAVORITE MEDITATION GARDEN IN THE JEDI TEMPLE. AFTER...AFTER GIJU...
THEY TELL ME YOU ARE RECOVERED, SHA KOON.
PHYSICALLY, YES. HAVE YOU ALSO COME TO SUGGEST IT WAS TIME I RETURNED TO THE WAR? I WILL TELL YOU AS I'VE TOLD THE OTHERS -- I WILL NOT GO BACK.
WITH COUNT DOOKU'S DEATH, THE END IS ONLY A MATTER OF TIME.
BUT THERE *IS* SOMETHING THAT YOU CAN DO, SHA. IF YOU ARE WILLING.
COUNT DOOKU SAID AS THIS WAR STARTED THAT SOMEONE CLOSE TO THE HIERARCHY OF THE REPUBLIC IS THE SITH LORD.
I'D LIKE YOU TO SCOUR THE JEDI ARCHIVES -- SEE IF YOU CAN LEARN ANYTHING THAT MIGHT LEAD TO OUR HIDDEN ENEMY -- IF THAT BEING EXISTS.
ALL RIGHT, UNCLE. *THAT* I CAN DO.

THE ARCHIVES. THE LIBRARY. THE FIRST HALL -- HISTORY OF THE REPUBLIC, CHRONICLES OF THE JEDI GOING BACK OVER THOUSANDS OF YEARS. THEIR GUARDIAN, THEIR PROTECTOR -- MASTER *JOCASTA NU*.

IF YOU WOULD *TELL* ME WHAT YOU ARE *LOOKING* FOR, MASTER SHA, I MIGHT BE ABLE TO HELP YOU *FIND* IT.

WHAT I LOOK FOR, MASTER NU, MAY NOT BE *IN* THE LINES BUT *BETWEEN* THEM.

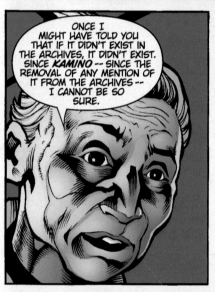

ONCE I MIGHT HAVE TOLD YOU THAT IF IT DIDN'T EXIST IN THE ARCHIVES, IT DIDN'T EXIST. SINCE *KAMINO* -- SINCE THE REMOVAL OF ANY MENTION OF IT FROM THE ARCHIVES -- I CANNOT BE SO SURE.

WHO CAN WE TRUST ANYMORE? I THOUGHT COUNT DOOKU ONE OF OUR VERY BEST -- AND LOOK AT WHAT HE BECAME. STILL, OTHERS HAVE RISEN LIKE MASTER SKYWALKER. SO YOUNG AND SUCH A HERO!

I MUST SEE WHAT MY OWN PADAWAN, JIN-LO RAYCE, IS DOING. LOST IN THE ARCHIVES OR EXPLORING THE SECRET PASSAGEWAYS BELOW, NO DOUBT. LET ME KNOW IF I CAN BE OF ASSISTANCE.

YES. I WILL. THANK YOU.

TIME PASSED. I WAS OBLIVIOUS TO IT. I WAS IMMERSED -- OBSESSED -- WITH MY HUNT.

NO!

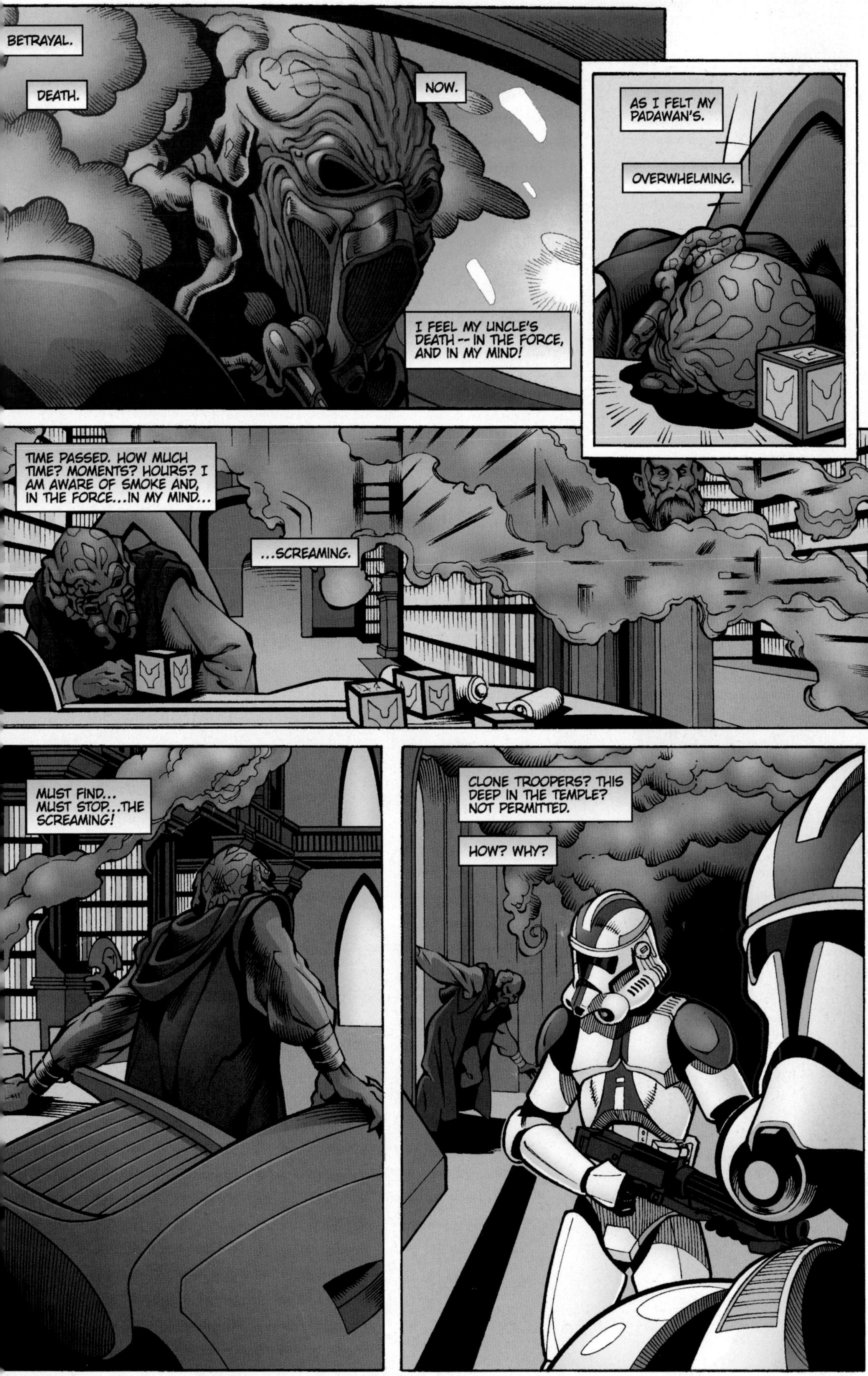
BETRAYAL.
DEATH.
NOW.
I FEEL MY UNCLE'S DEATH -- IN THE FORCE, AND IN MY MIND!
AS I FELT MY PADAWAN'S.
OVERWHELMING.
TIME PASSED. HOW MUCH TIME? MOMENTS? HOURS? I AM AWARE OF SMOKE AND, IN THE FORCE...IN MY MIND...
...SCREAMING.
MUST FIND... MUST STOP...THE SCREAMING!
CLONE TROOPERS? THIS DEEP IN THE TEMPLE? NOT PERMITTED.
HOW? WHY?

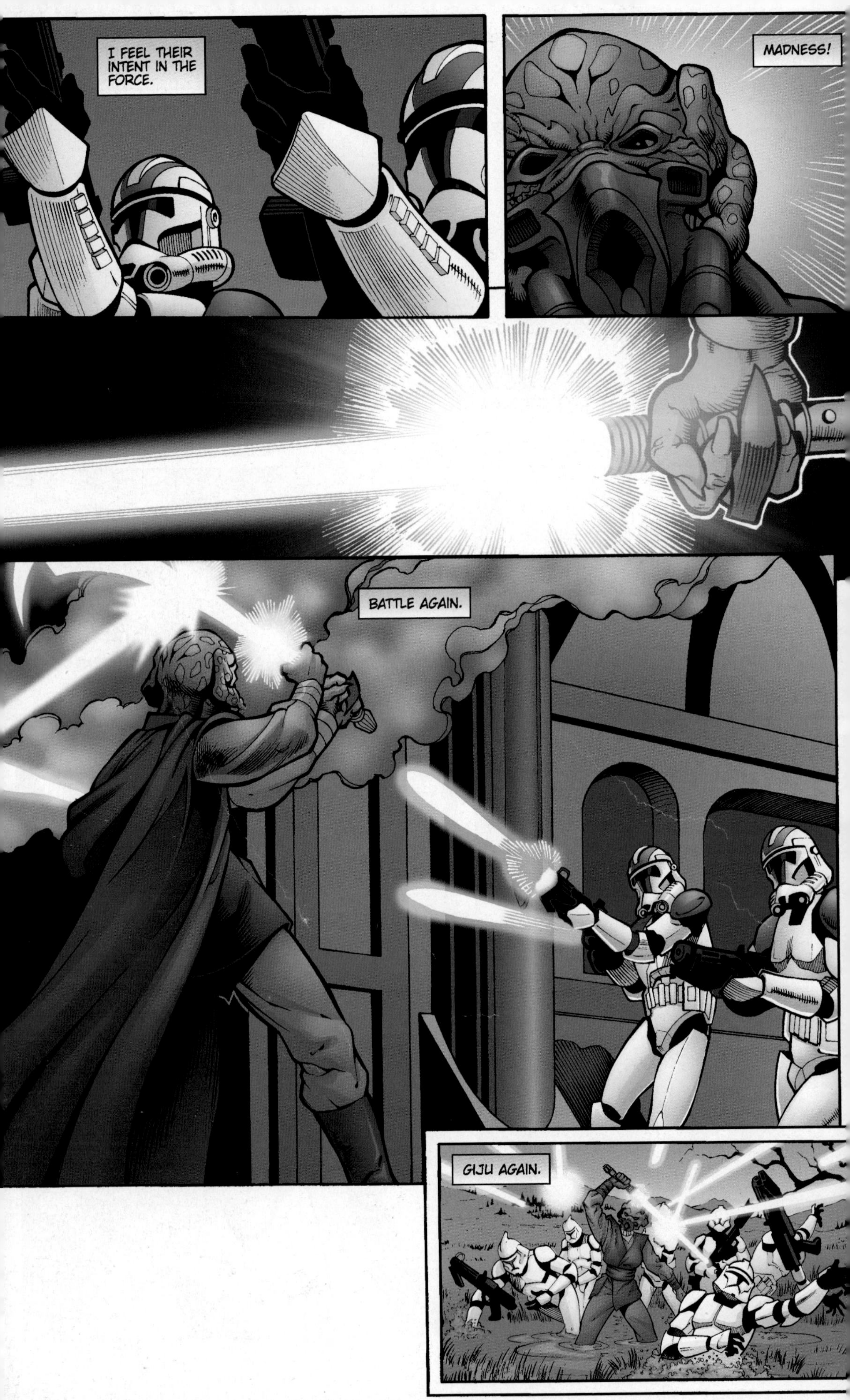
I FEEL THEIR INTENT IN THE FORCE.
MADNESS!
BATTLE AGAIN.
GIJU AGAIN.

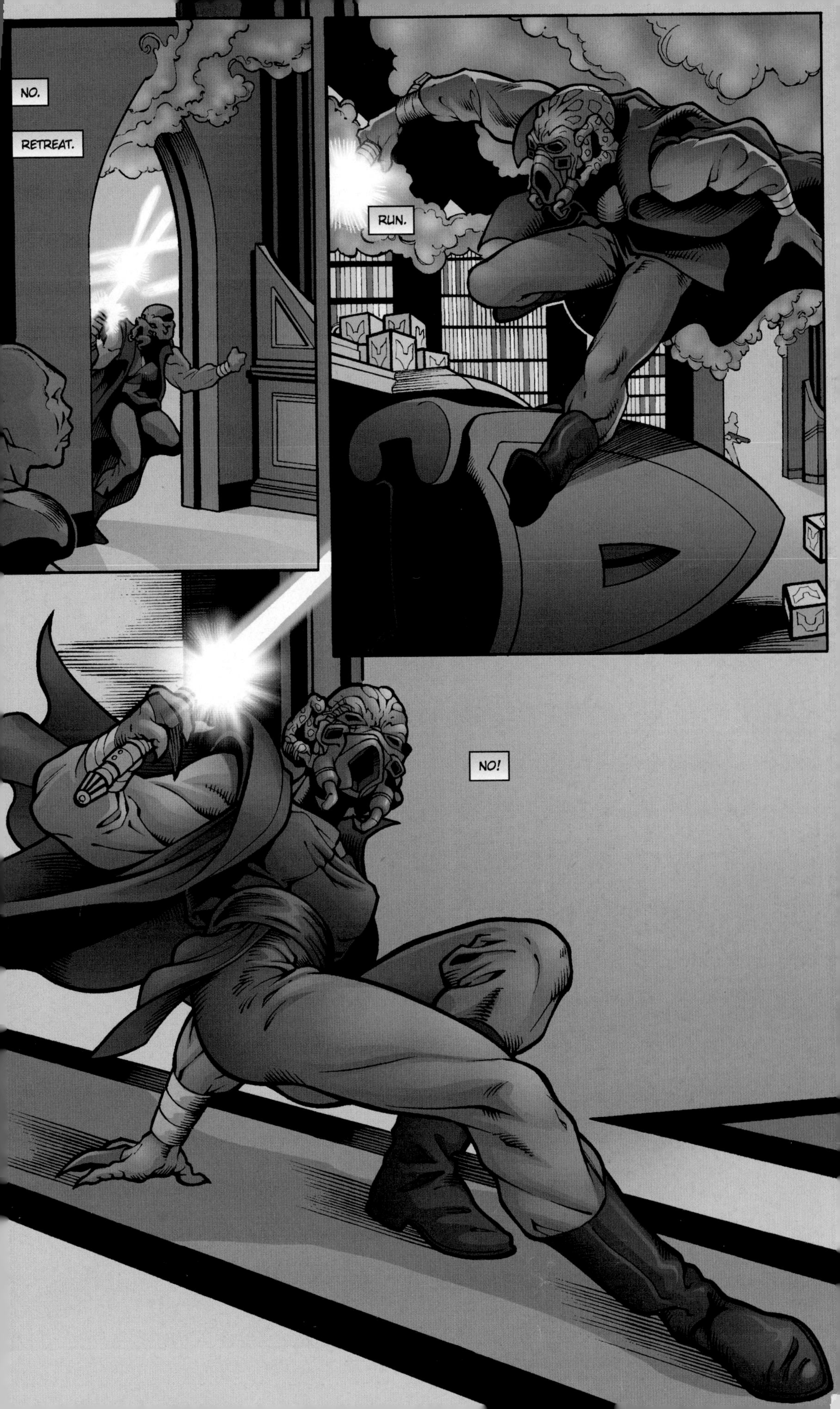
NO.
RETREAT.
RUN.
NO!

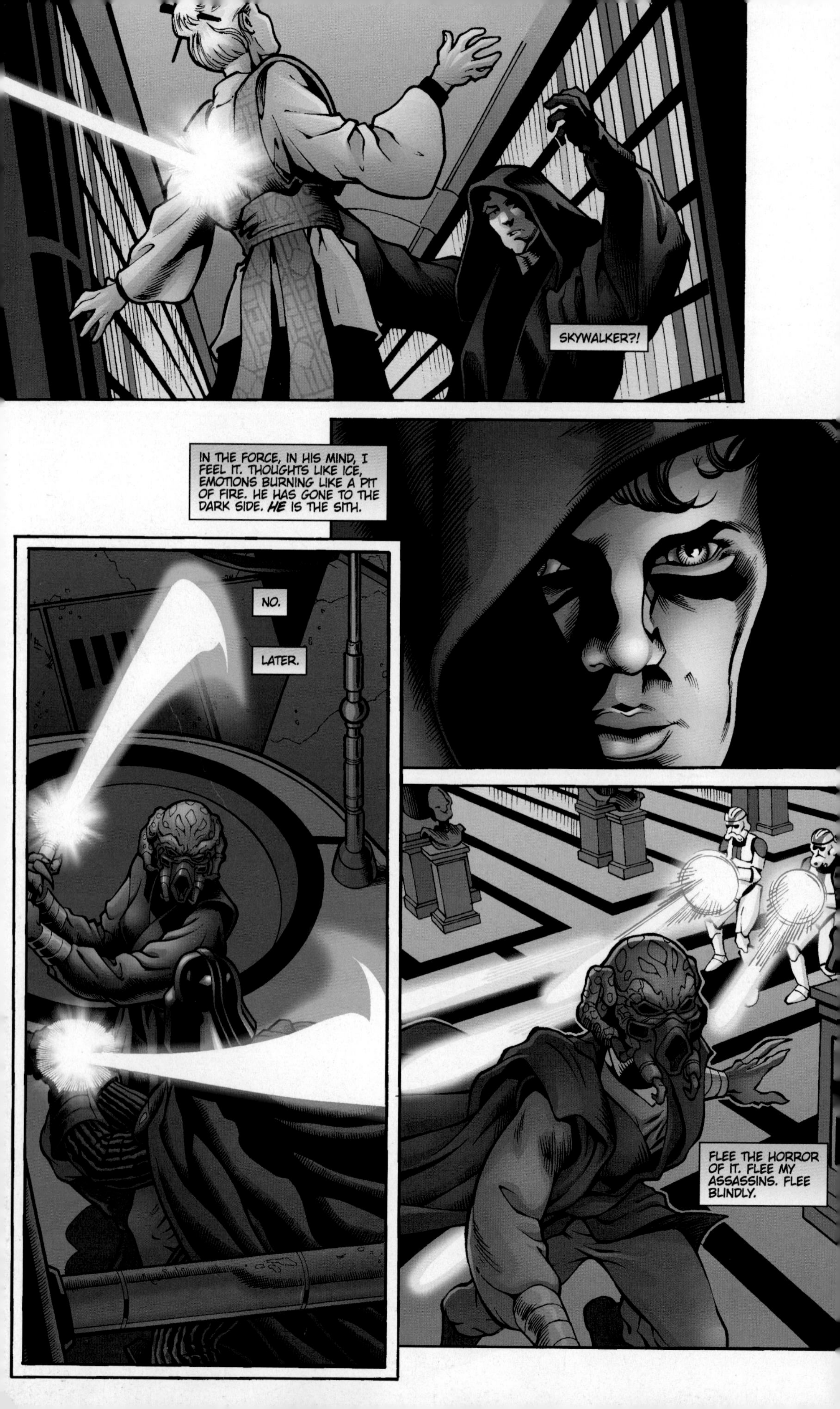
SKYWALKER?!
IN THE FORCE, IN HIS MIND, I FEEL IT. THOUGHTS LIKE ICE, EMOTIONS BURNING LIKE A PIT OF FIRE. HE HAS GONE TO THE DARK SIDE. HE IS THE SITH.
NO.
LATER.
FLEE THE HORROR OF IT. FLEE MY ASSASSINS. FLEE BLINDLY.

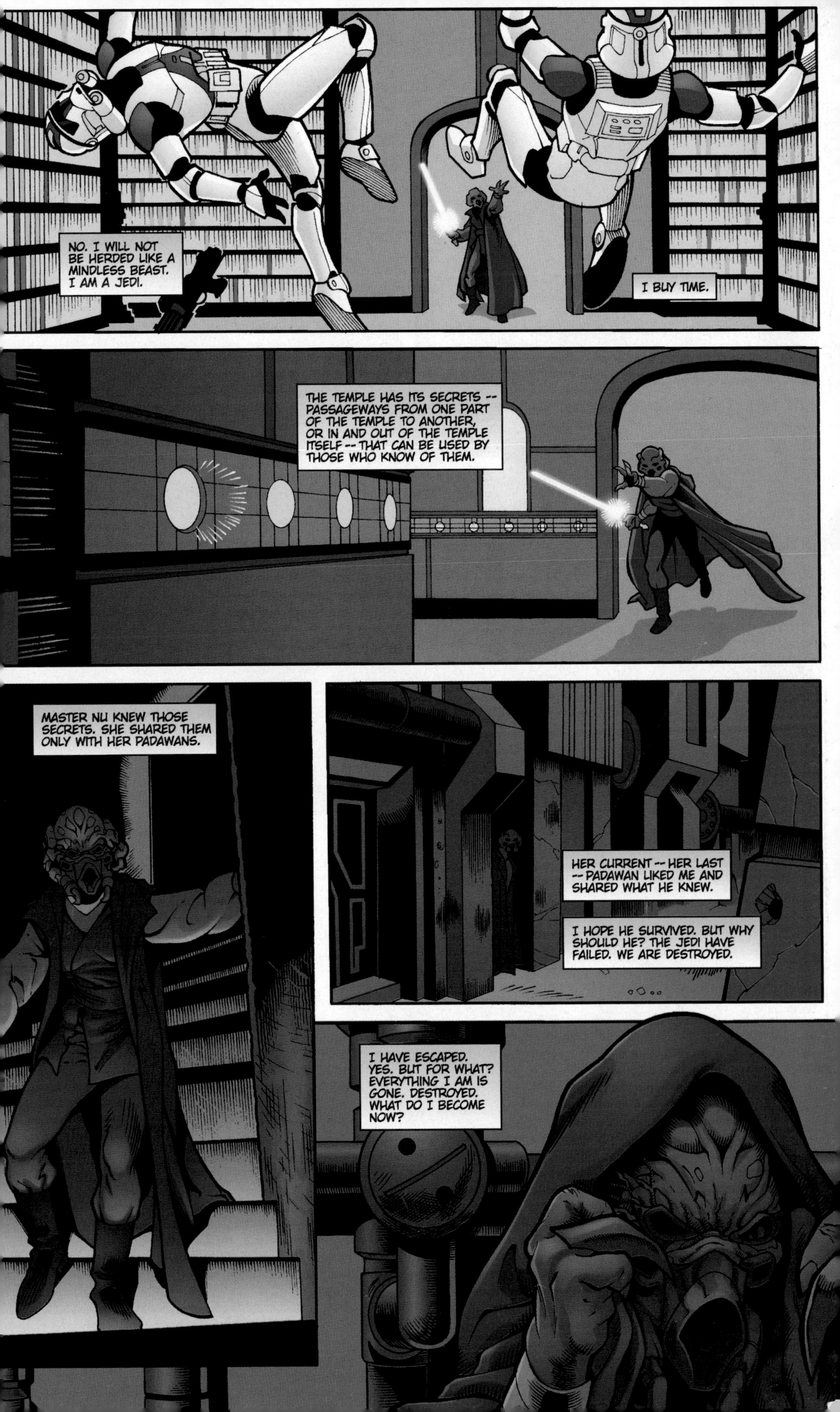
NO. I WILL NOT BE HERDED LIKE A MINDLESS BEAST. I AM A JEDI.
I BUY TIME.
THE TEMPLE HAS ITS SECRETS -- PASSAGEWAYS FROM ONE PART OF THE TEMPLE TO ANOTHER, OR IN AND OUT OF THE TEMPLE ITSELF -- THAT CAN BE USED BY THOSE WHO KNOW OF THEM.
MASTER NU KNEW THOSE SECRETS. SHE SHARED THEM ONLY WITH HER PADAWANS.
HER CURRENT -- HER LAST -- PADAWAN LIKED ME AND SHARED WHAT HE KNEW.
I HOPE HE SURVIVED. BUT WHY SHOULD HE? THE JEDI HAVE FAILED. WE ARE DESTROYED.
I HAVE ESCAPED. YES. BUT FOR WHAT? EVERYTHING I AM IS GONE. DESTROYED. WHAT DO I BECOME NOW?

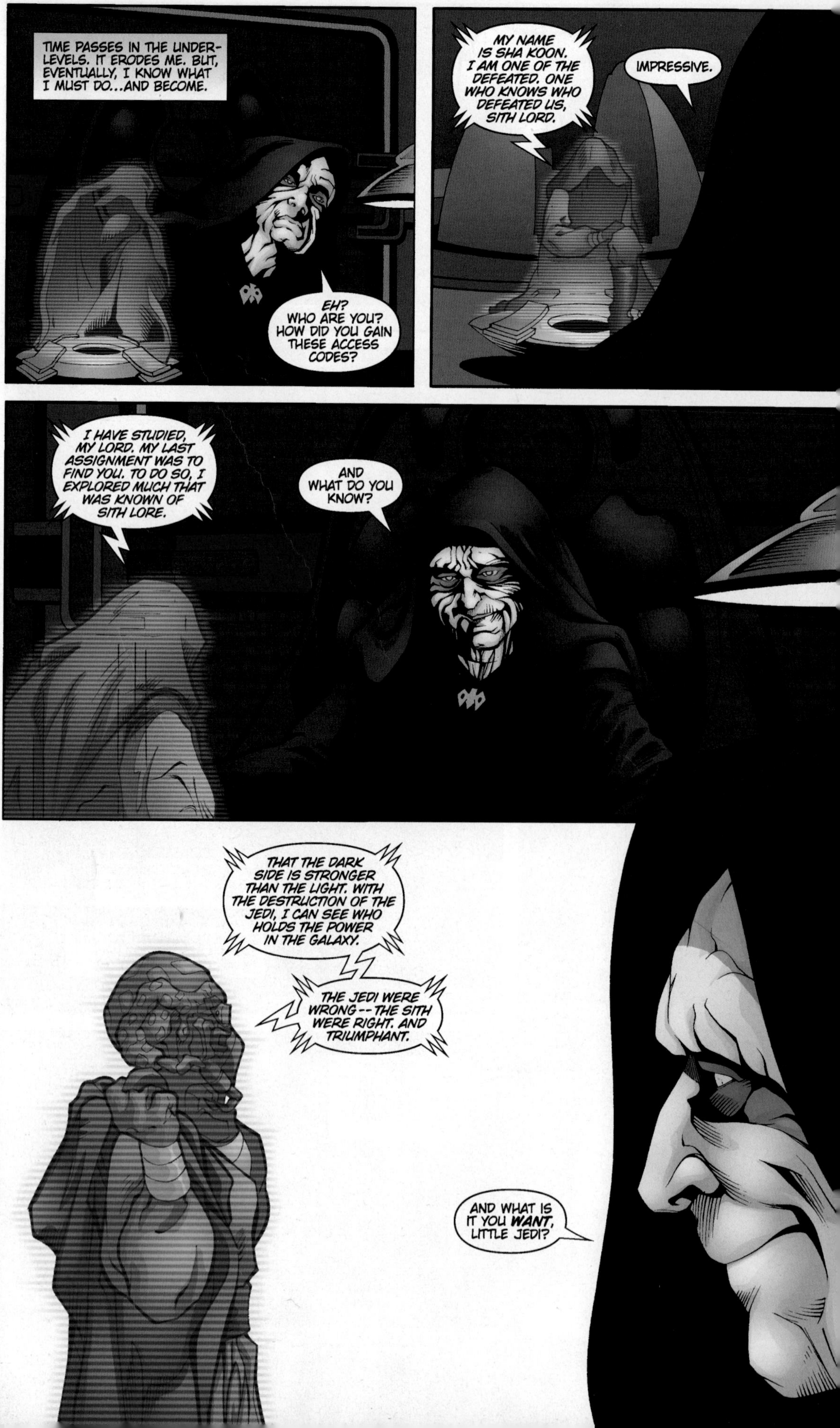
TIME PASSES IN THE UNDER-LEVELS. IT ERODES ME. BUT, EVENTUALLY, I KNOW WHAT I MUST DO...AND BECOME.
EH? WHO ARE YOU? HOW DID YOU GAIN THESE ACCESS CODES?
MY NAME IS SHA KOON. I AM ONE OF THE DEFEATED. ONE WHO KNOWS WHO DEFEATED US, SITH LORD.
IMPRESSIVE.
I HAVE STUDIED, MY LORD. MY LAST ASSIGNMENT WAS TO FIND YOU. TO DO SO, I EXPLORED MUCH THAT WAS KNOWN OF SITH LORE.
AND WHAT DO YOU KNOW?
THAT THE DARK SIDE IS STRONGER THAN THE LIGHT. WITH THE DESTRUCTION OF THE JEDI, I CAN SEE WHO HOLDS THE POWER IN THE GALAXY.
THE JEDI WERE WRONG--THE SITH WERE RIGHT. AND TRIUMPHANT.
AND WHAT IS IT YOU *WANT*, LITTLE JEDI?

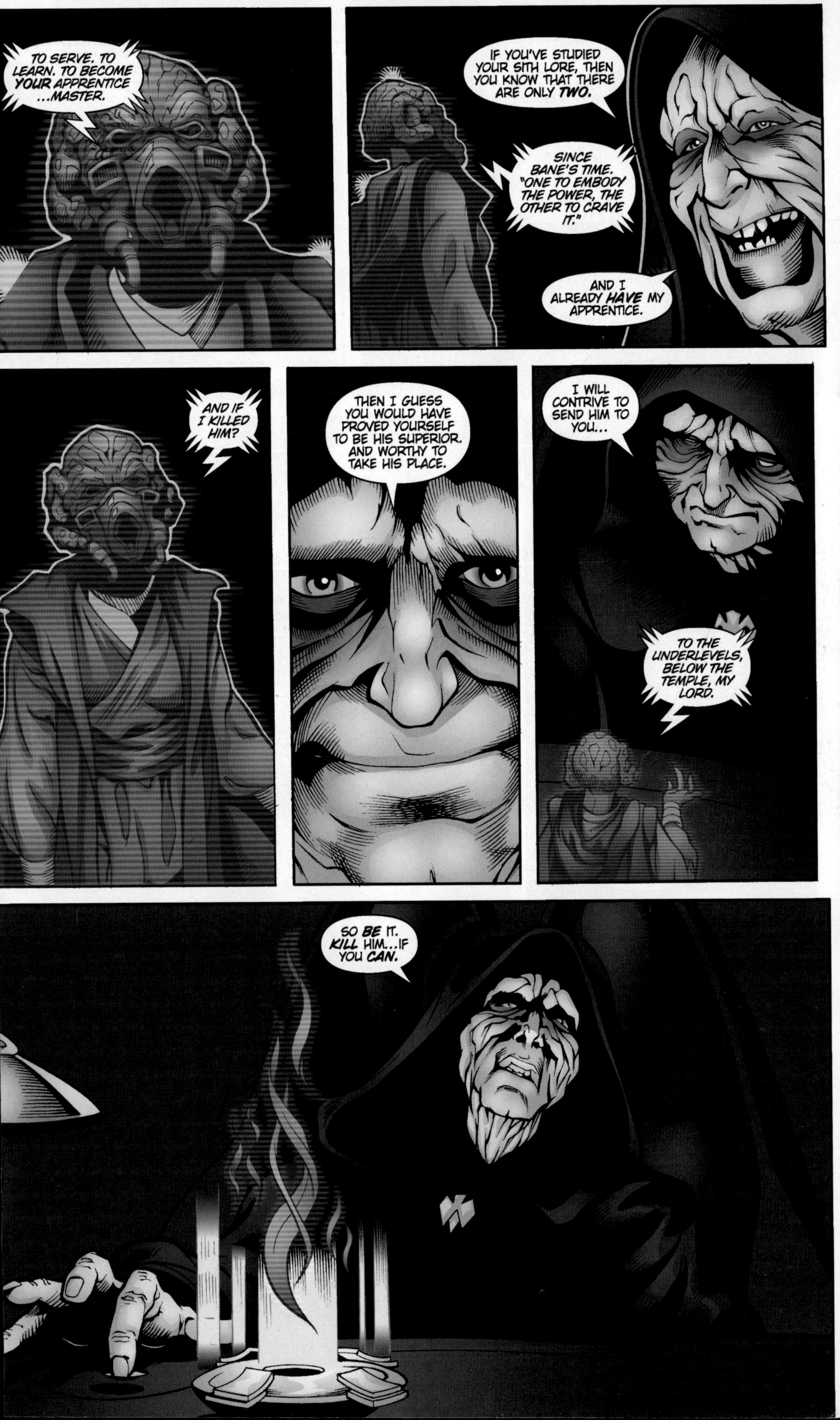
TO SERVE. TO LEARN. TO BECOME YOUR APPRENTICE ...MASTER.
IF YOU'VE STUDIED YOUR SITH LORE, THEN YOU KNOW THAT THERE ARE ONLY TWO.
SINCE BANE'S TIME. "ONE TO EMBODY THE POWER, THE OTHER TO CRAVE IT."
AND I ALREADY HAVE MY APPRENTICE.
AND IF I KILLED HIM?
THEN I GUESS YOU WOULD HAVE PROVED YOURSELF TO BE HIS SUPERIOR. AND WORTHY TO TAKE HIS PLACE.
I WILL CONTRIVE TO SEND HIM TO YOU...
TO THE UNDERLEVELS, BELOW THE TEMPLE, MY LORD.
SO BE IT. KILL HIM...IF YOU CAN.

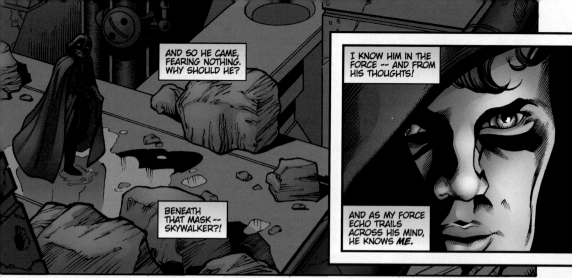

AND SO HE CAME, FEARING NOTHING. WHY SHOULD HE?

BENEATH THAT MASK -- SKYWALKER?!

I KNOW HIM IN THE FORCE -- AND FROM HIS THOUGHTS!

AND AS MY FORCE ECHO TRAILS ACROSS HIS MIND, HE KNOWS ME.

YOUR EMOTIONS REVEAL YOU, SHA KOON. YES, I REMEMBER YOU FROM THAT DAY IN THE ARCHIVES. I WOULD HAVE KILLED YOU THEN, BUT YOU CHOSE TO FLEE.

MY MASTER BID ME COME HERE. YOU WANT TO KILL ME AND TAKE MY PLACE.

OR SO YOU SAID. YOUR LIE AMUSED LORD SIDIOUS.

YOU SPOKE VIA HOLOCOMM TO HIDE YOUR TRUE INTENT -- TO KILL HIM. YOUR PLAN IS AS PATHETICALLY SIMPLE AS IT IS DOOMED.

I HAVE A FALLBACK PLAN. CRIPPLE HIM BY KILLING YOU.

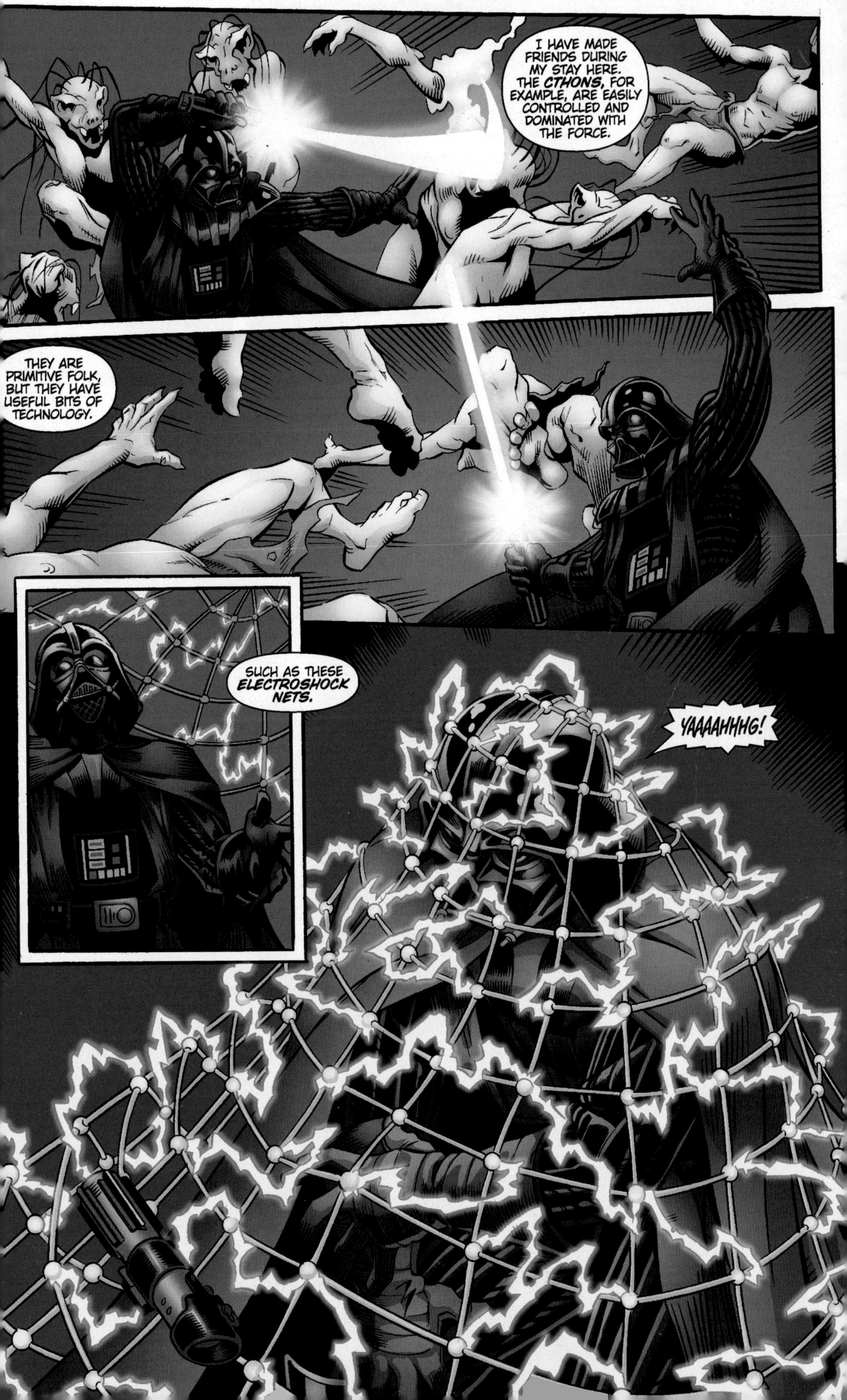
I HAVE MADE FRIENDS DURING MY STAY HERE. THE *CTHONS*, FOR EXAMPLE, ARE EASILY CONTROLLED AND DOMINATED WITH THE FORCE.
THEY ARE PRIMITIVE FOLK, BUT THEY HAVE USEFUL BITS OF TECHNOLOGY.
SUCH AS THESE *ELECTROSHOCK NETS.*
YAAAAHHHG!

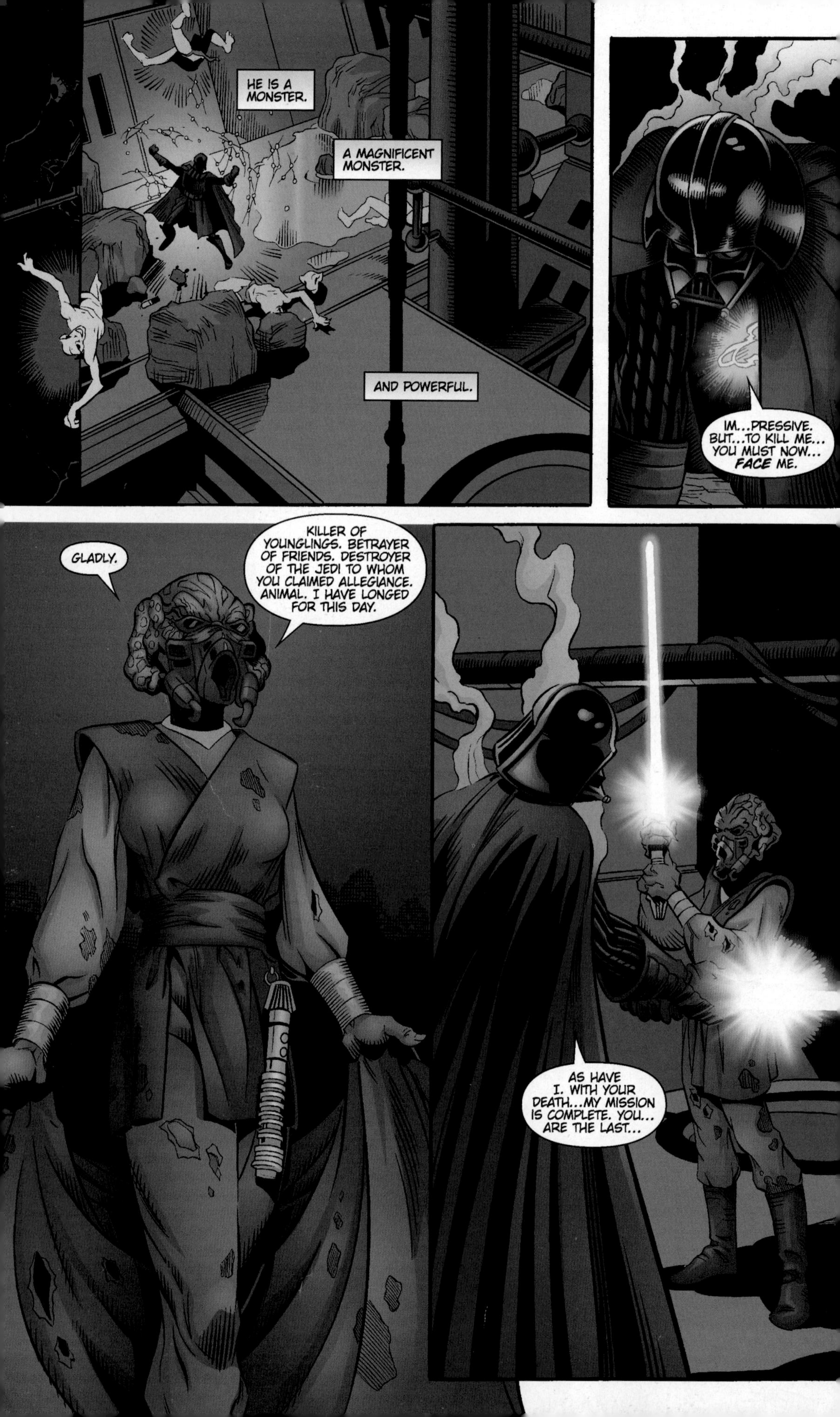
HE IS A MONSTER.
A MAGNIFICENT MONSTER.
AND POWERFUL.
IM...PRESSIVE. BUT...TO KILL ME... YOU MUST NOW... FACE ME.
GLADLY.
KILLER OF YOUNGLINGS. BETRAYER OF FRIENDS. DESTROYER OF THE JEDI TO WHOM YOU CLAIMED ALLEGIANCE. ANIMAL. I HAVE LONGED FOR THIS DAY.
AS HAVE I. WITH YOUR DEATH...MY MISSION IS COMPLETE. YOU... ARE THE LAST...

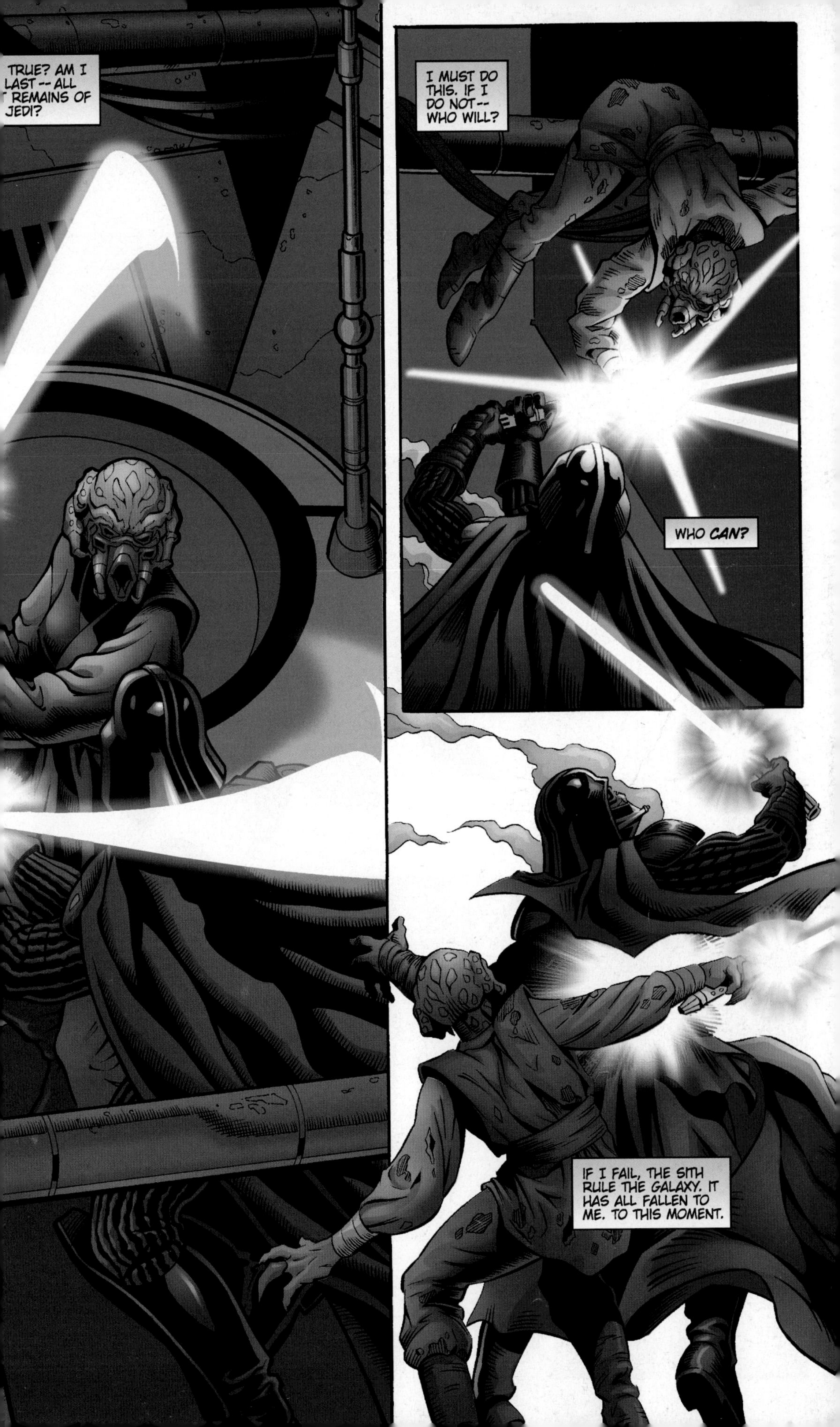
TRUE? AM I
LAST -- ALL
T REMAINS OF
JEDI?
I MUST DO THIS. IF I DO NOT-- WHO WILL?
WHO CAN?
IF I FAIL, THE SITH RULE THE GALAXY. IT HAS ALL FALLEN TO ME. TO THIS MOMENT.

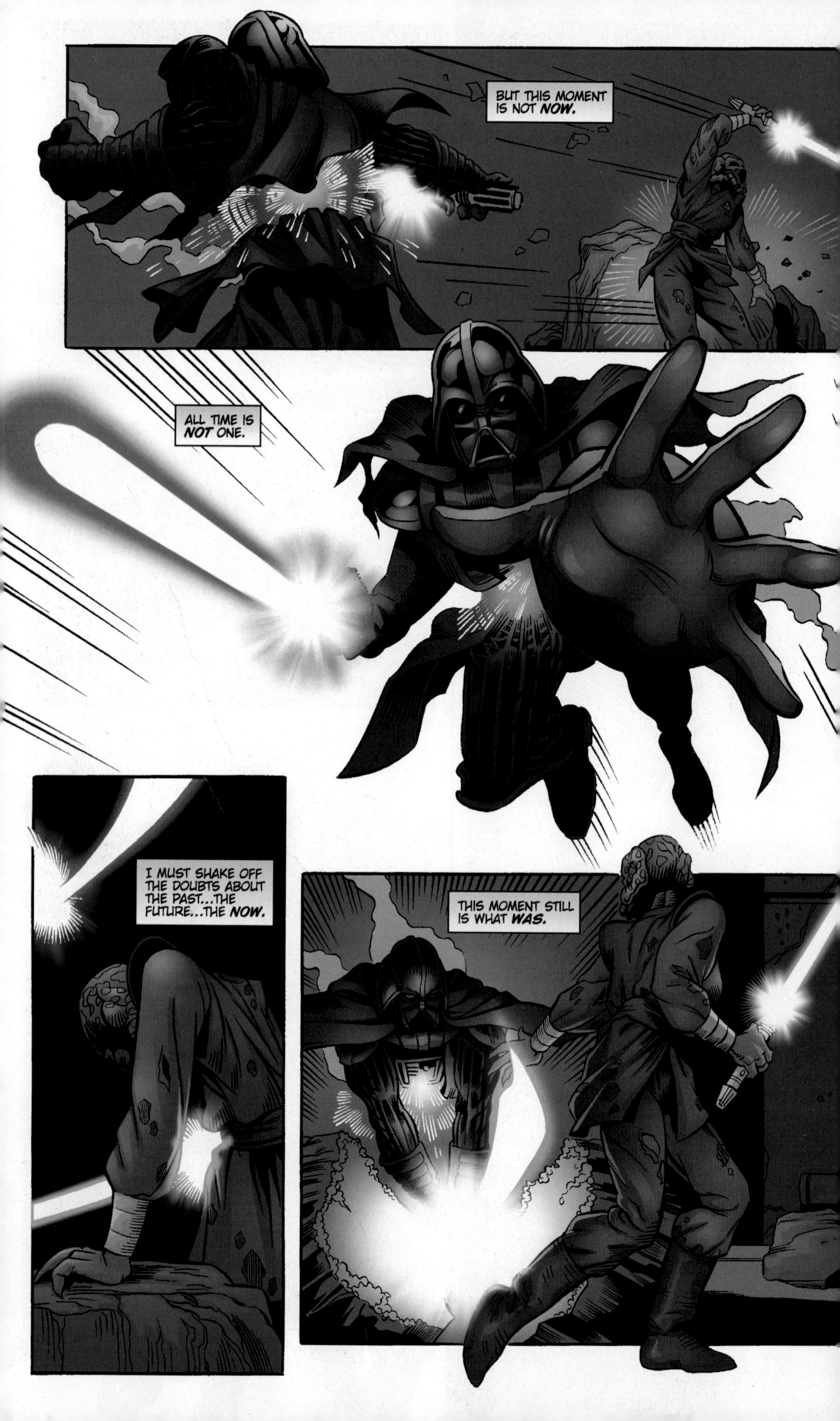
BUT THIS MOMENT IS NOT NOW.
ALL TIME IS NOT ONE.
I MUST SHAKE OFF THE DOUBTS ABOUT THE PAST...THE FUTURE...THE NOW.
THIS MOMENT STILL IS WHAT WAS.

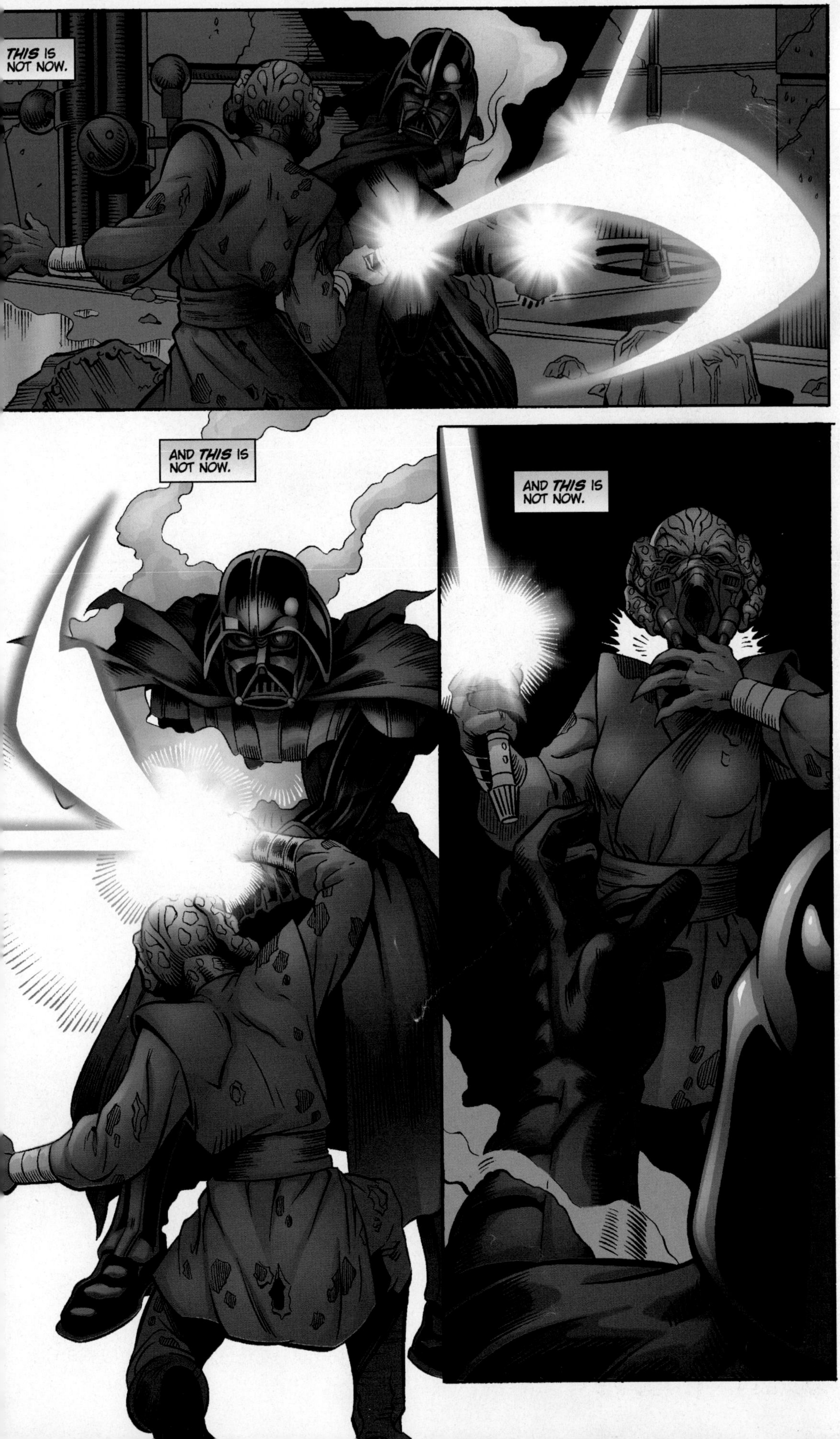
THIS IS NOT NOW.
AND THIS IS NOT NOW.
AND THIS IS NOT NOW.

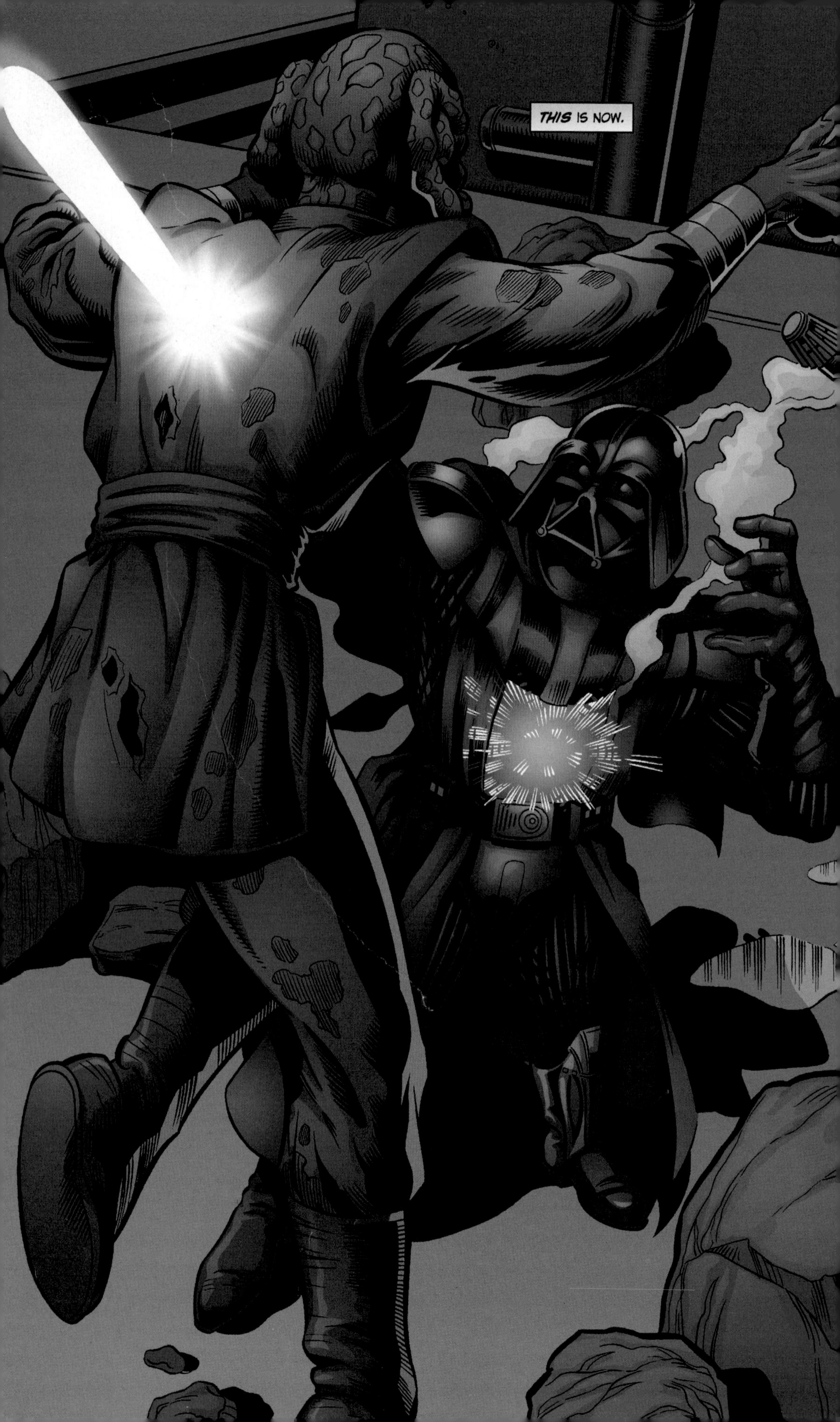
THIS IS NOW.

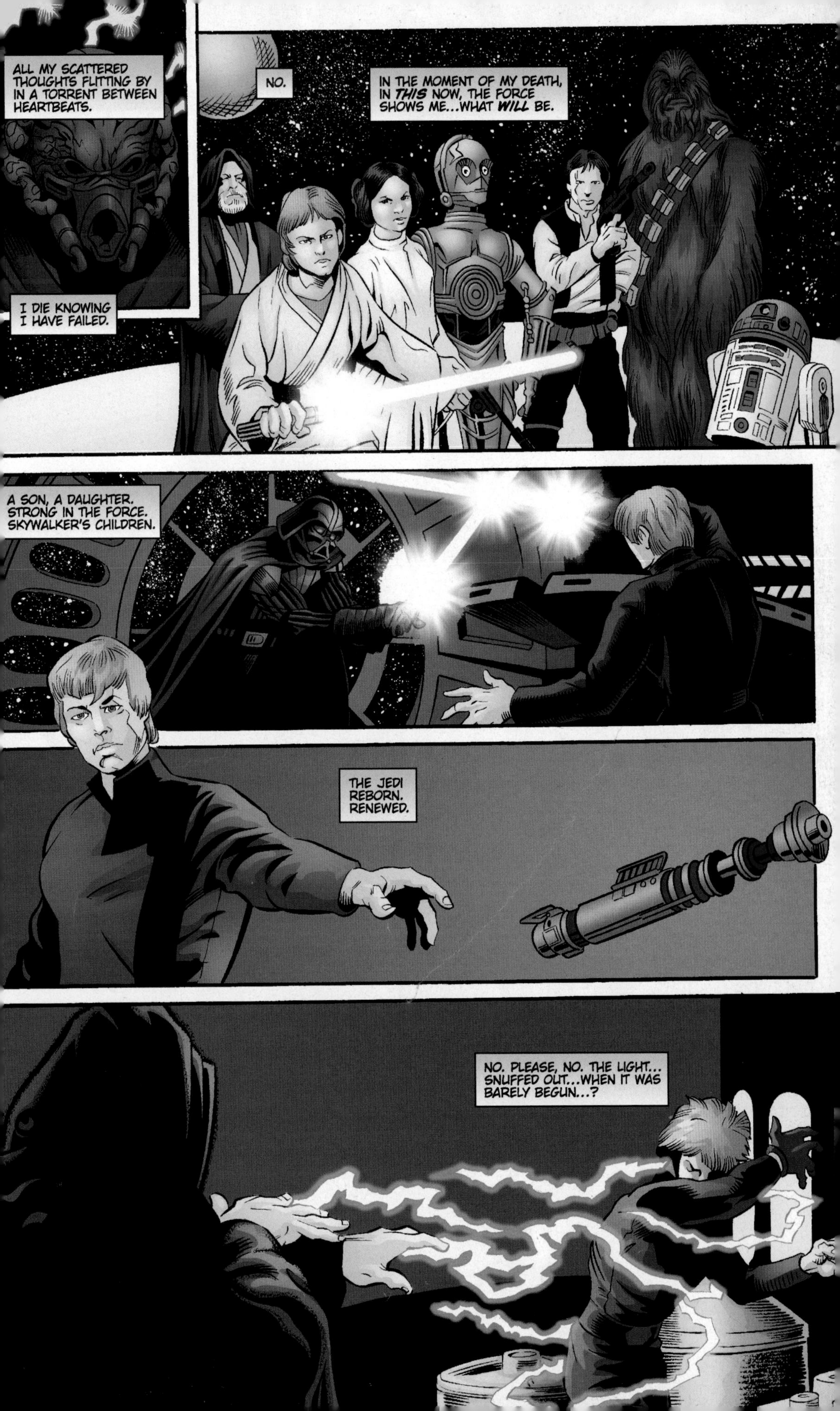

ALL MY SCATTERED THOUGHTS FLITTING BY IN A TORRENT BETWEEN HEARTBEATS.
I DIE KNOWING I HAVE FAILED.
NO.
IN THE MOMENT OF MY DEATH, IN THIS NOW, THE FORCE SHOWS ME...WHAT WILL BE.
A SON, A DAUGHTER. STRONG IN THE FORCE. SKYWALKER'S CHILDREN.
THE JEDI REBORN. RENEWED.
NO. PLEASE, NO. THE LIGHT... SNUFFED OUT...WHEN IT WAS BARELY BEGUN...?

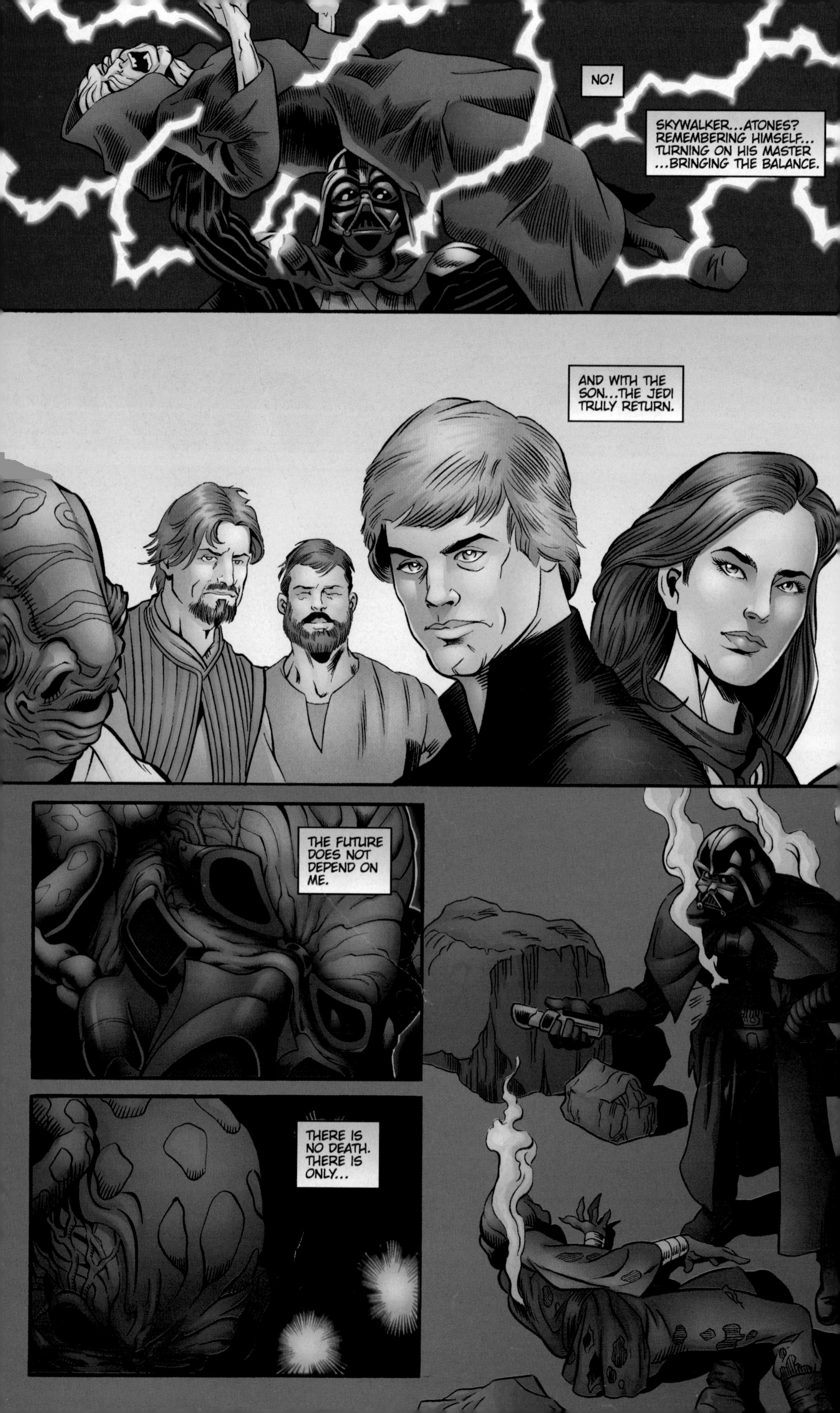
NO!
SKYWALKER...ATONES? REMEMBERING HIMSELF... TURNING ON HIS MASTER ...BRINGING THE BALANCE.
AND WITH THE SON...THE JEDI TRULY RETURN.
THE FUTURE DOES NOT DEPEND ON ME.
THERE IS NO DEATH. THERE IS ONLY...

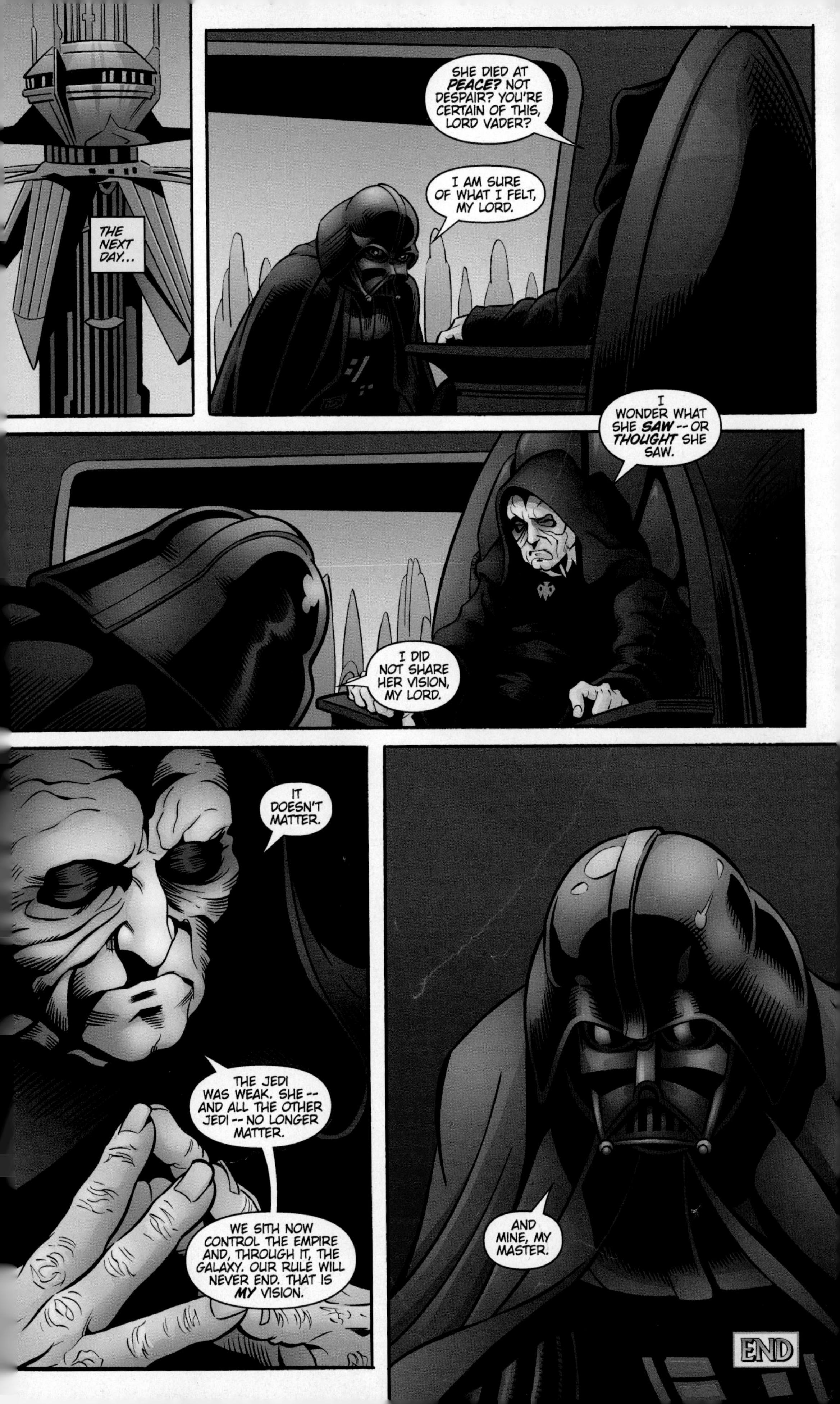
THE NEXT DAY...
SHE DIED AT PEACE? NOT DESPAIR? YOU'RE CERTAIN OF THIS, LORD VADER?
I AM SURE OF WHAT I FELT, MY LORD.
I WONDER WHAT SHE SAW -- OR THOUGHT SHE SAW.
I DID NOT SHARE HER VISION, MY LORD.
IT DOESN'T MATTER.
THE JEDI WAS WEAK. SHE -- AND ALL THE OTHER JEDI -- NO LONGER MATTER.
WE SITH NOW CONTROL THE EMPIRE AND, THROUGH IT, THE GALAXY. OUR RULE WILL NEVER END. THAT IS MY VISION.
AND MINE, MY MASTER.
END

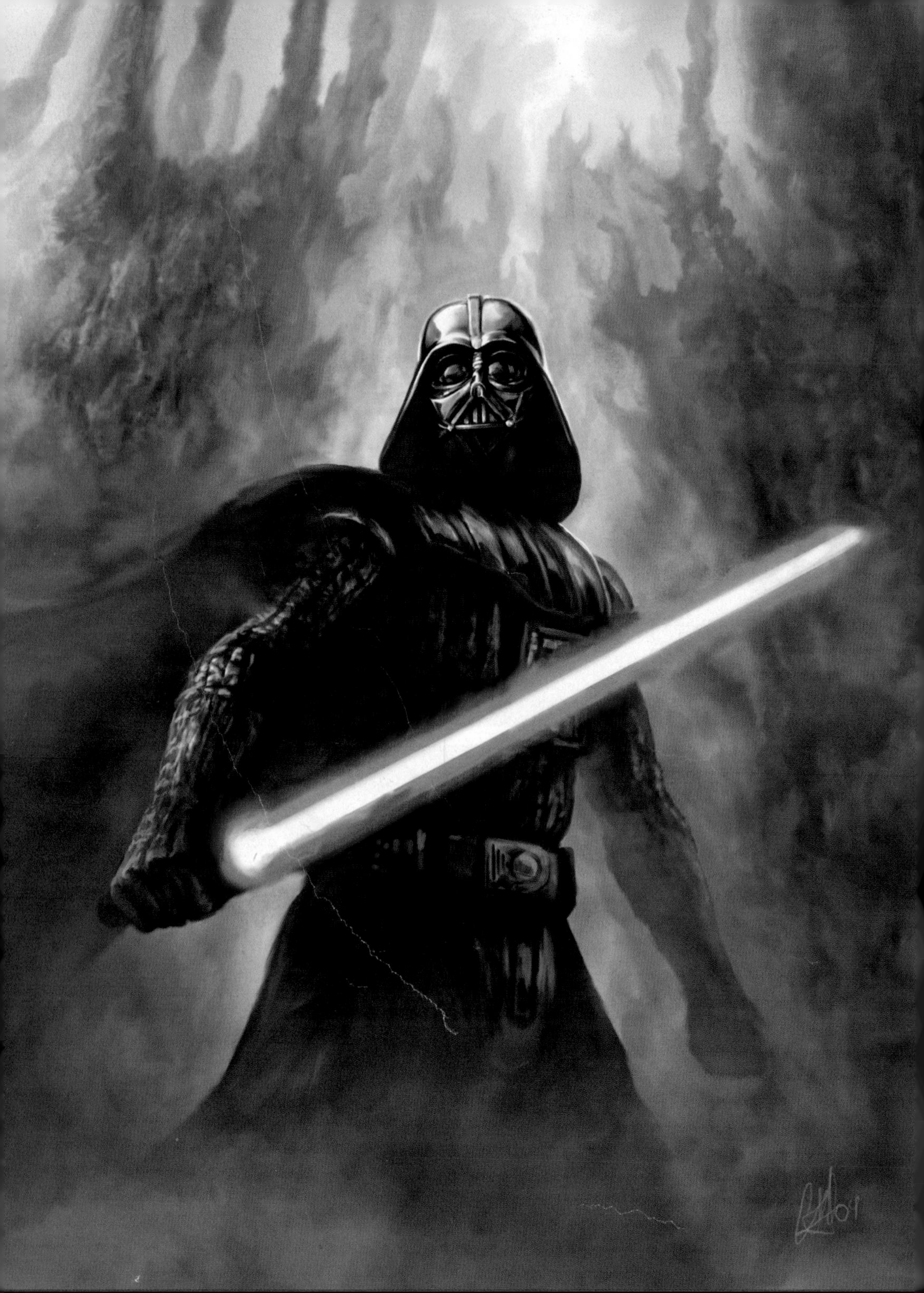

STAR WARS: PURGE — THE HIDDEN BLADE

WRITER: HADEN BLACKMAN • ARTIST & COLORIST: CHRIS SCALF • LETTERER: MICHAEL HEISLER • DESIGNER & PRODUCTION: JOSH ELLIOTT
ASSISTANT EDITOR: FREDDYE LINS • EDITOR: RANDY STRADLEY • COVER ARTIST: CHRIS SCALF

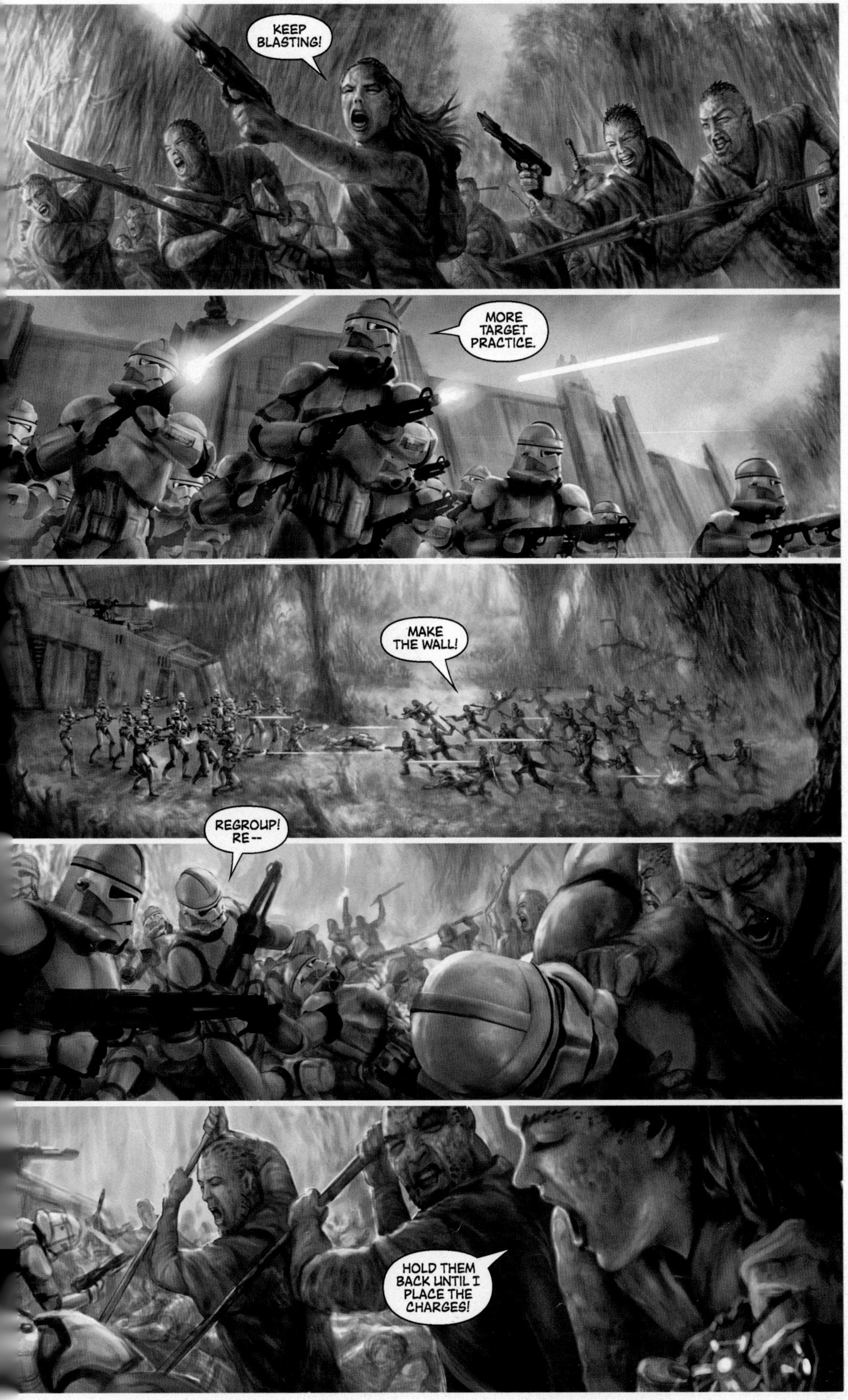
KEEP BLASTING!
MORE TARGET PRACTICE.
MAKE THE WALL!
REGROUP! RE--
HOLD THEM BACK UNTIL I PLACE THE CHARGES!

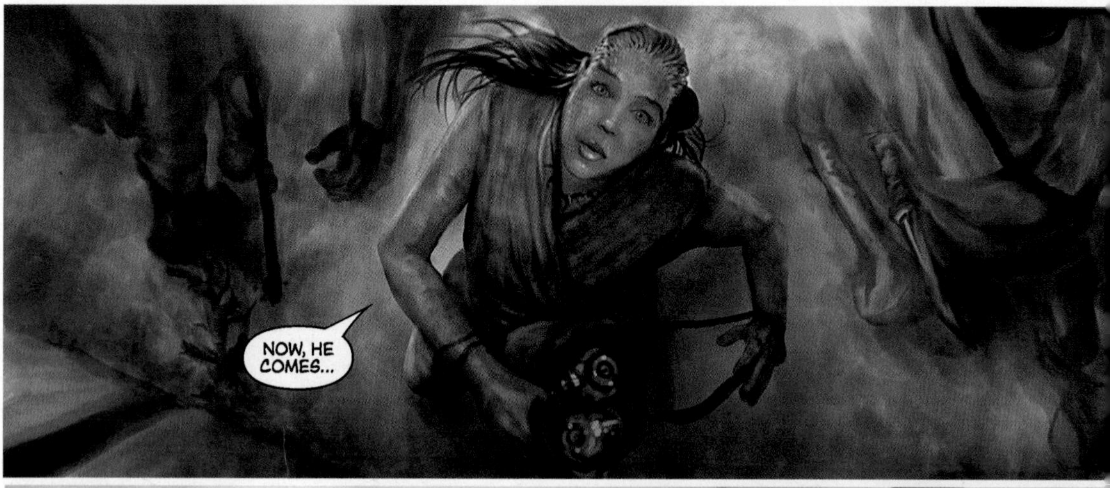
NOW, HE COMES...

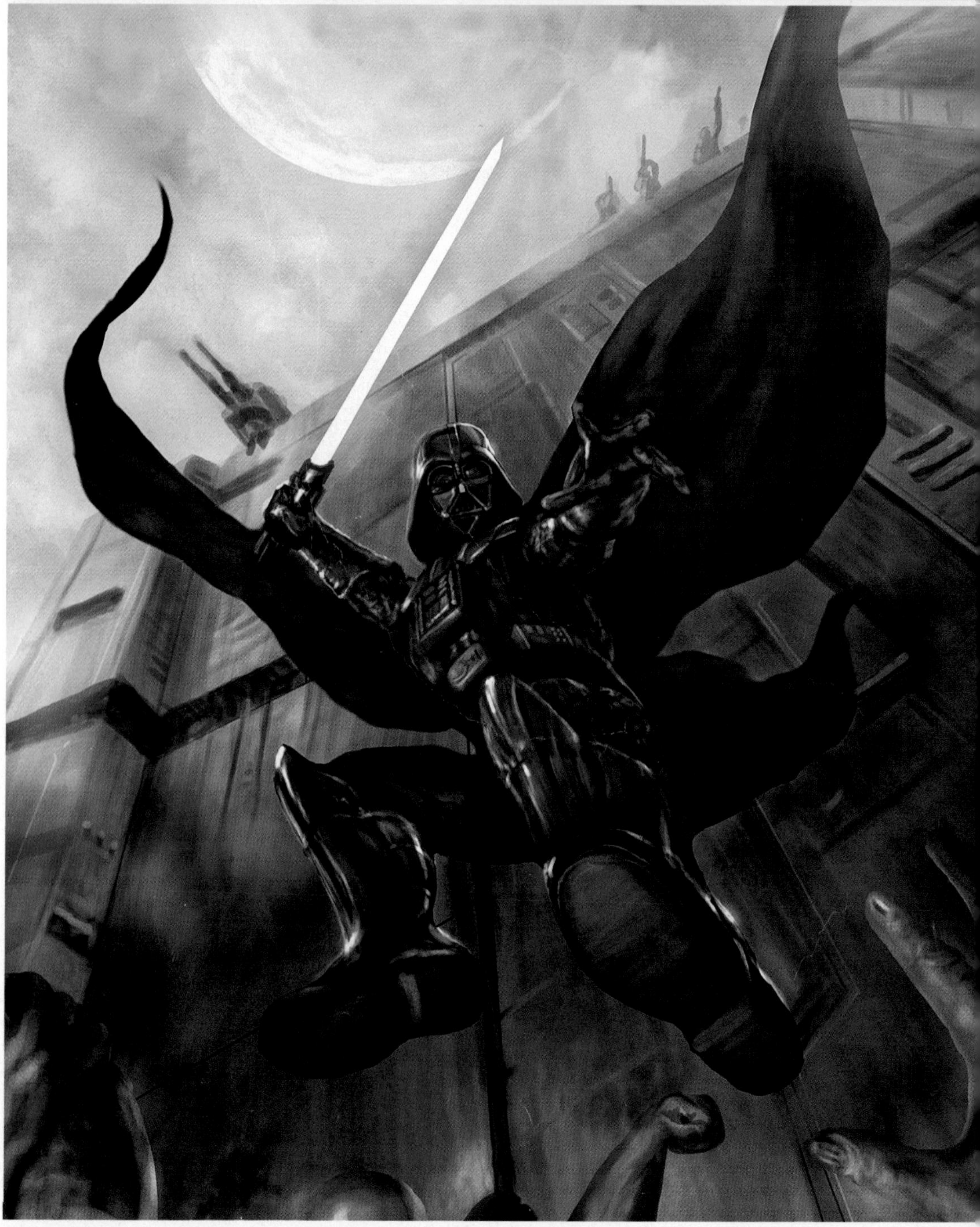

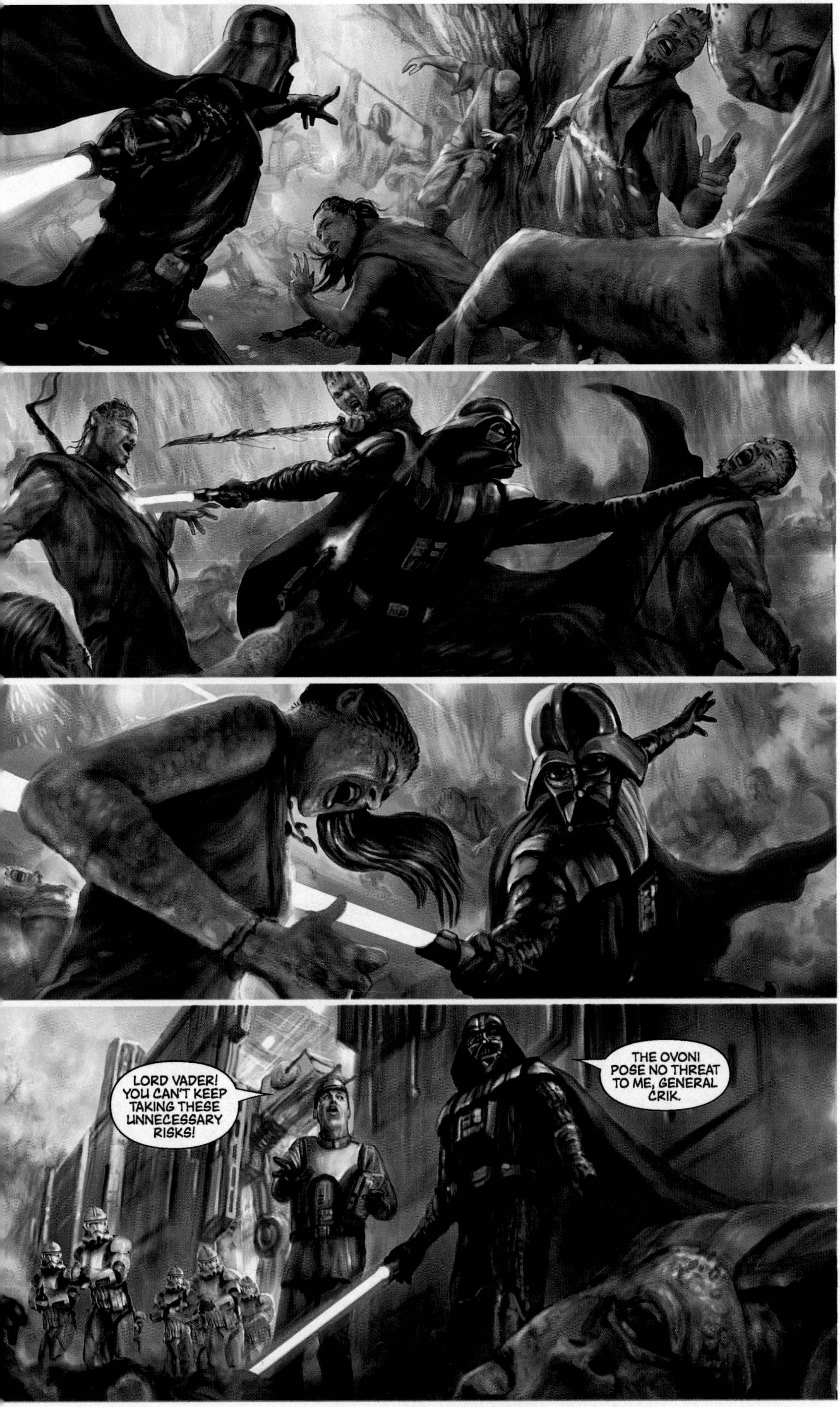
LORD VADER! YOU CAN'T KEEP TAKING THESE UNNECESSARY RISKS!
THE OVONI POSE NO THREAT TO ME, GENERAL CRIK.

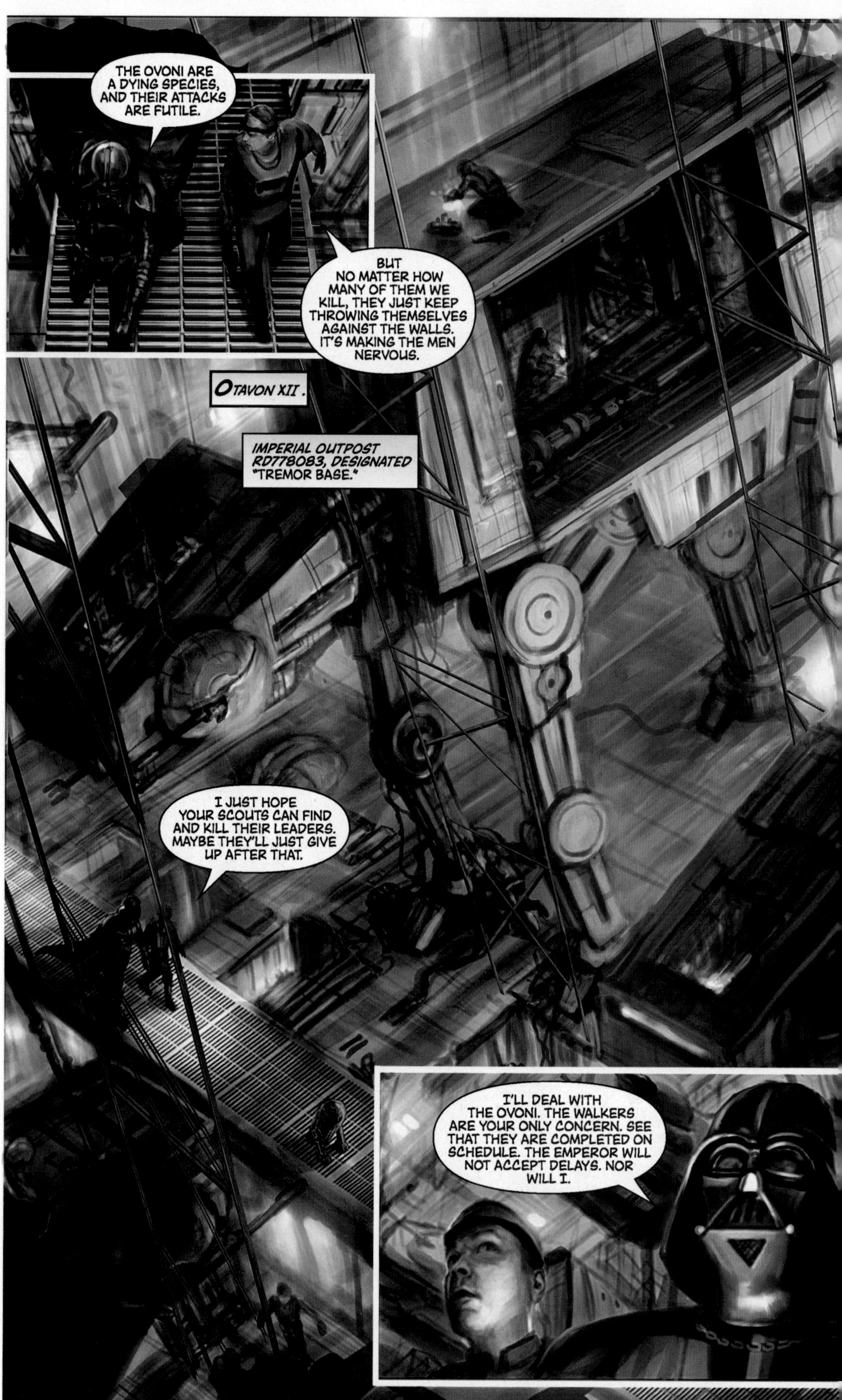
THE OVONI ARE A DYING SPECIES, AND THEIR ATTACKS ARE FUTILE.
BUT NO MATTER HOW MANY OF THEM WE KILL, THEY JUST KEEP THROWING THEMSELVES AGAINST THE WALLS. IT'S MAKING THE MEN NERVOUS.
OTAVON XII.
IMPERIAL OUTPOST RD778083, DESIGNATED "TREMOR BASE."
I JUST HOPE YOUR SCOUTS CAN FIND AND KILL THEIR LEADERS. MAYBE THEY'LL JUST GIVE UP AFTER THAT.
I'LL DEAL WITH THE OVONI. THE WALKERS ARE YOUR ONLY CONCERN. SEE THAT THEY ARE COMPLETED ON SCHEDULE. THE EMPEROR WILL NOT ACCEPT DELAYS. NOR WILL I.

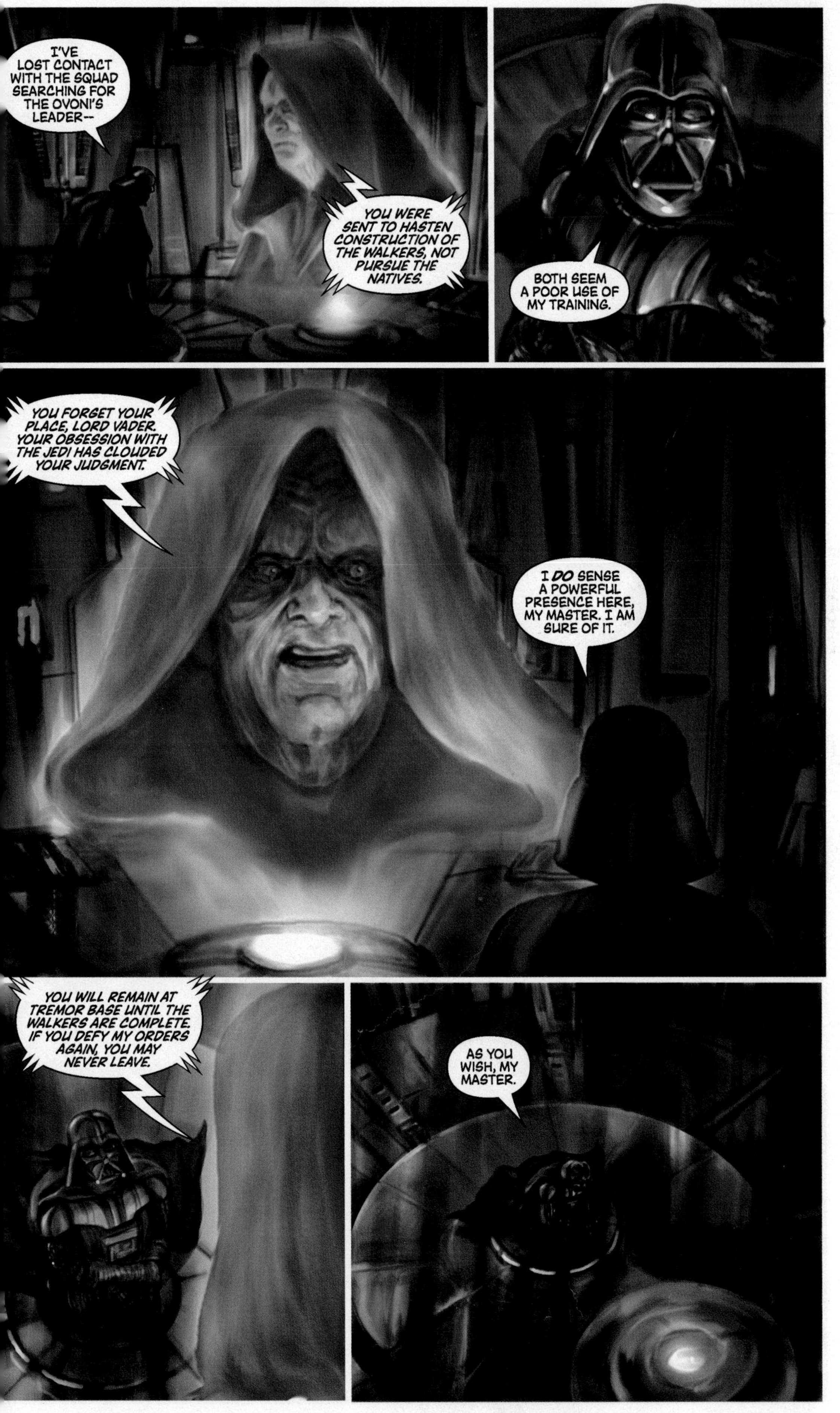
I'VE LOST CONTACT WITH THE SQUAD SEARCHING FOR THE OVONI'S LEADER--
YOU WERE SENT TO HASTEN CONSTRUCTION OF THE WALKERS, NOT PURSUE THE NATIVES.
BOTH SEEM A POOR USE OF MY TRAINING.
YOU FORGET YOUR PLACE, LORD VADER. YOUR OBSESSION WITH THE JEDI HAS CLOUDED YOUR JUDGMENT.
I *DO* SENSE A POWERFUL PRESENCE HERE, MY MASTER. I AM SURE OF IT.
YOU WILL REMAIN AT TREMOR BASE UNTIL THE WALKERS ARE COMPLETE. IF YOU DEFY MY ORDERS AGAIN, YOU MAY NEVER LEAVE.
AS YOU WISH, MY MASTER.

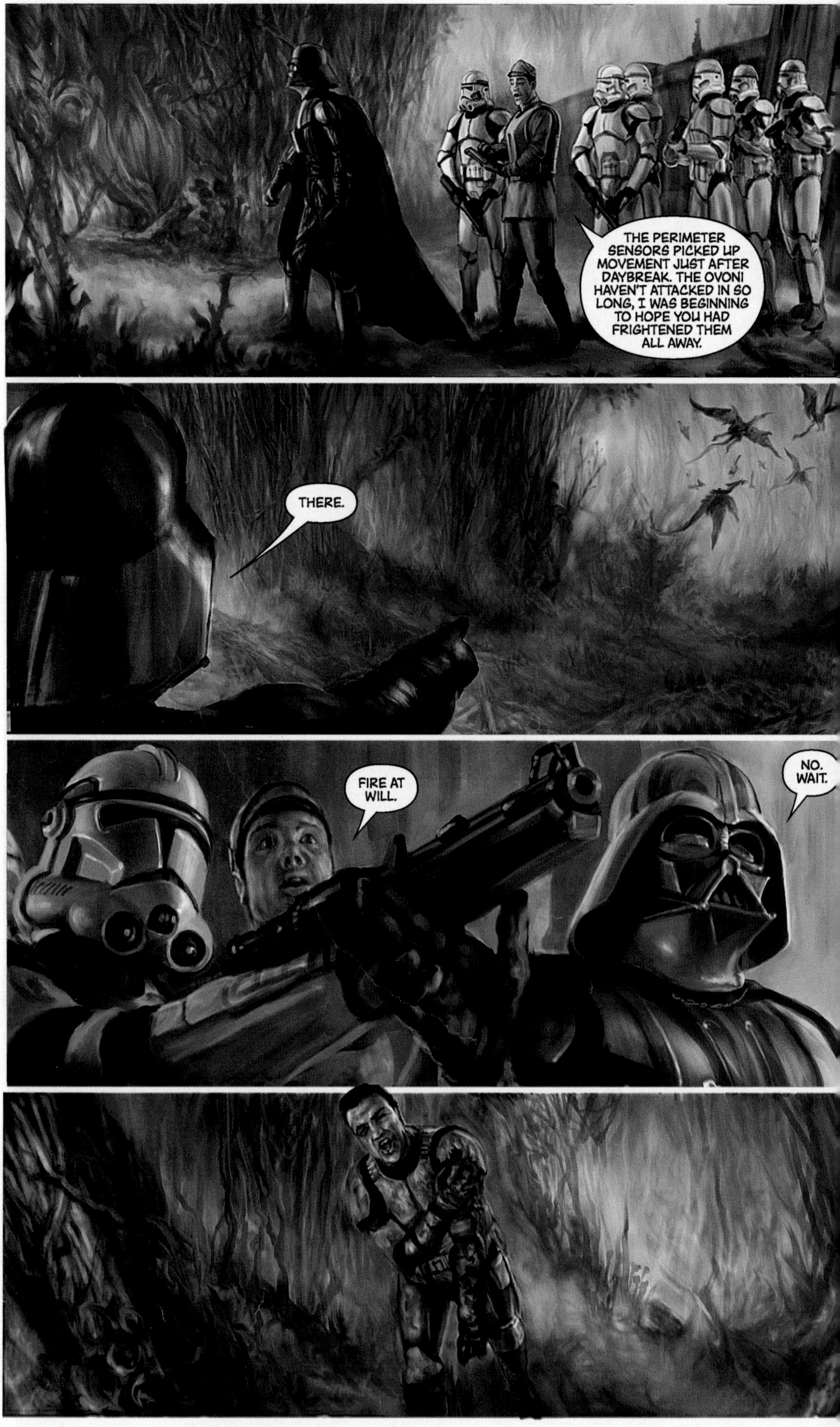
THE PERIMETER SENSORS PICKED UP MOVEMENT JUST AFTER DAYBREAK. THE OVONI HAVEN'T ATTACKED IN SO LONG, I WAS BEGINNING TO HOPE YOU HAD FRIGHTENED THEM ALL AWAY.
THERE.
FIRE AT WILL.
NO. WAIT.

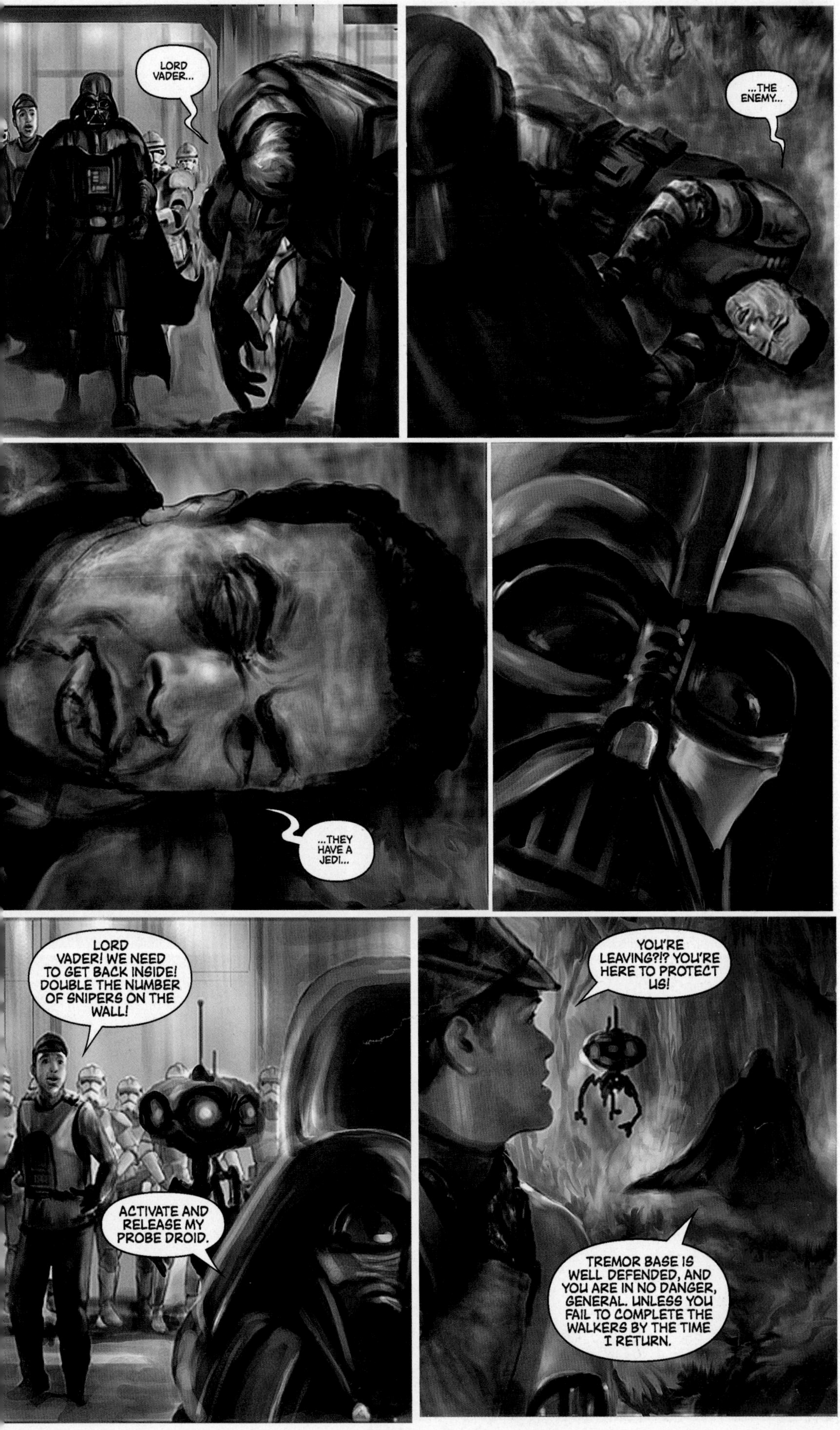

LORD VADER...
...THE ENEMY...
...THEY HAVE A JEDI...
LORD VADER! WE NEED TO GET BACK INSIDE! DOUBLE THE NUMBER OF SNIPERS ON THE WALL!
ACTIVATE AND RELEASE MY PROBE DROID.
YOU'RE LEAVING?!? YOU'RE HERE TO PROTECT US!
TREMOR BASE IS WELL DEFENDED, AND YOU ARE IN NO DANGER, GENERAL. UNLESS YOU FAIL TO COMPLETE THE WALKERS BY THE TIME I RETURN.

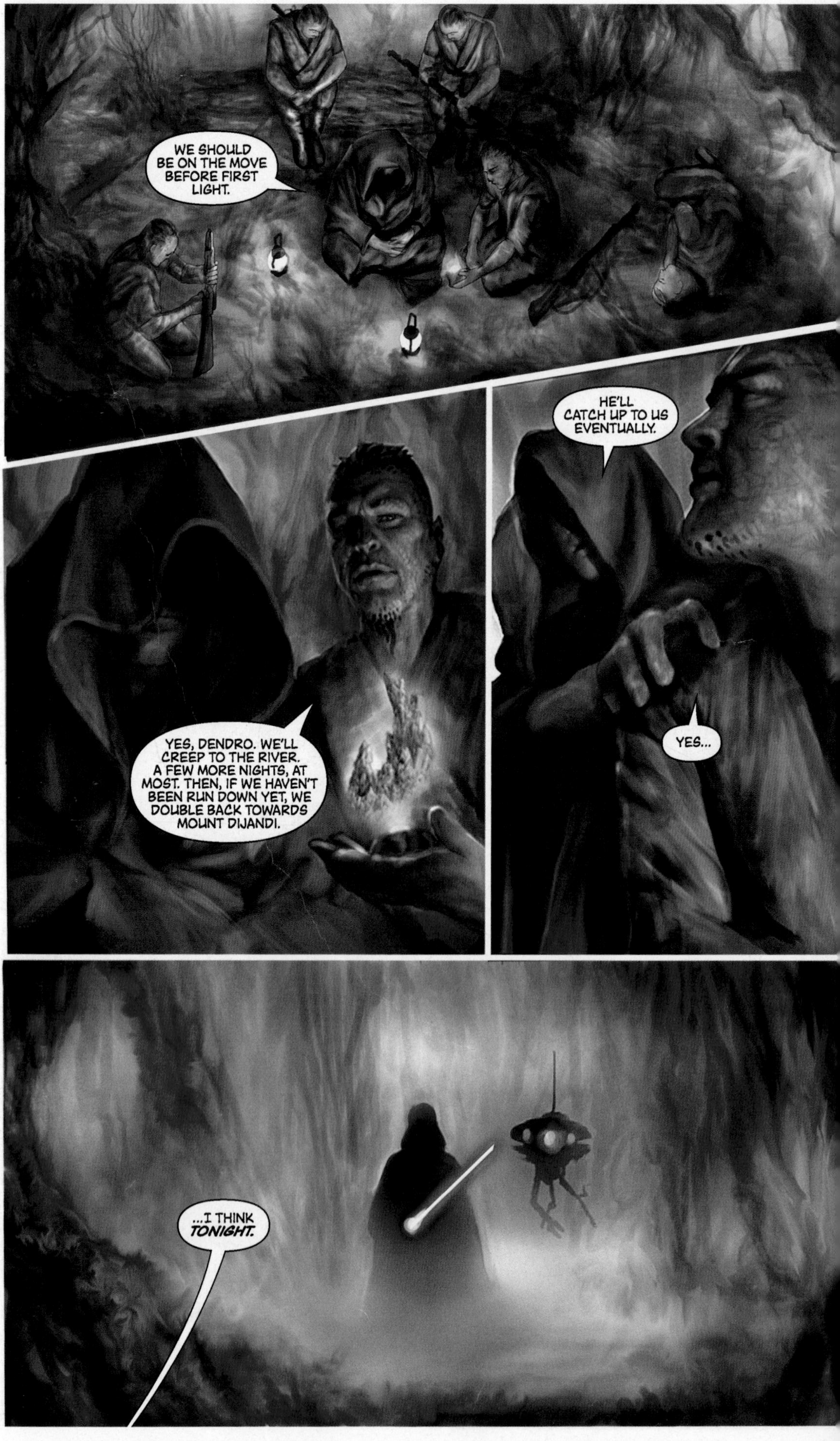
WE SHOULD BE ON THE MOVE BEFORE FIRST LIGHT.
HE'LL CATCH UP TO US EVENTUALLY.
YES, DENDRO. WE'LL CREEP TO THE RIVER. A FEW MORE NIGHTS, AT MOST. THEN, IF WE HAVEN'T BEEN RUN DOWN YET, WE DOUBLE BACK TOWARDS MOUNT DIJANDI.
YES...
...I THINK *TONIGHT.*

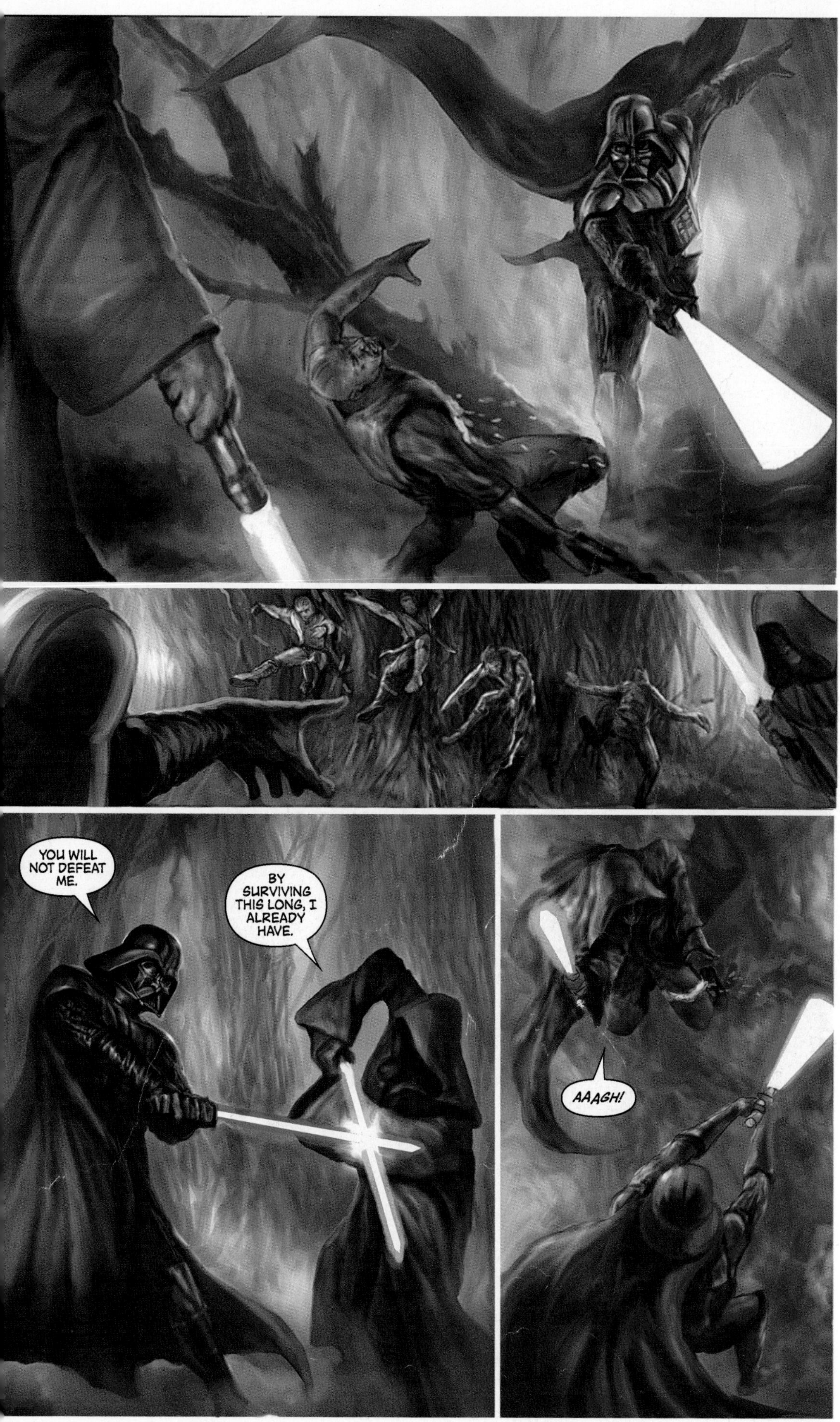
YOU WILL NOT DEFEAT ME.
BY SURVIVING THIS LONG, I ALREADY HAVE.
AAAGH!

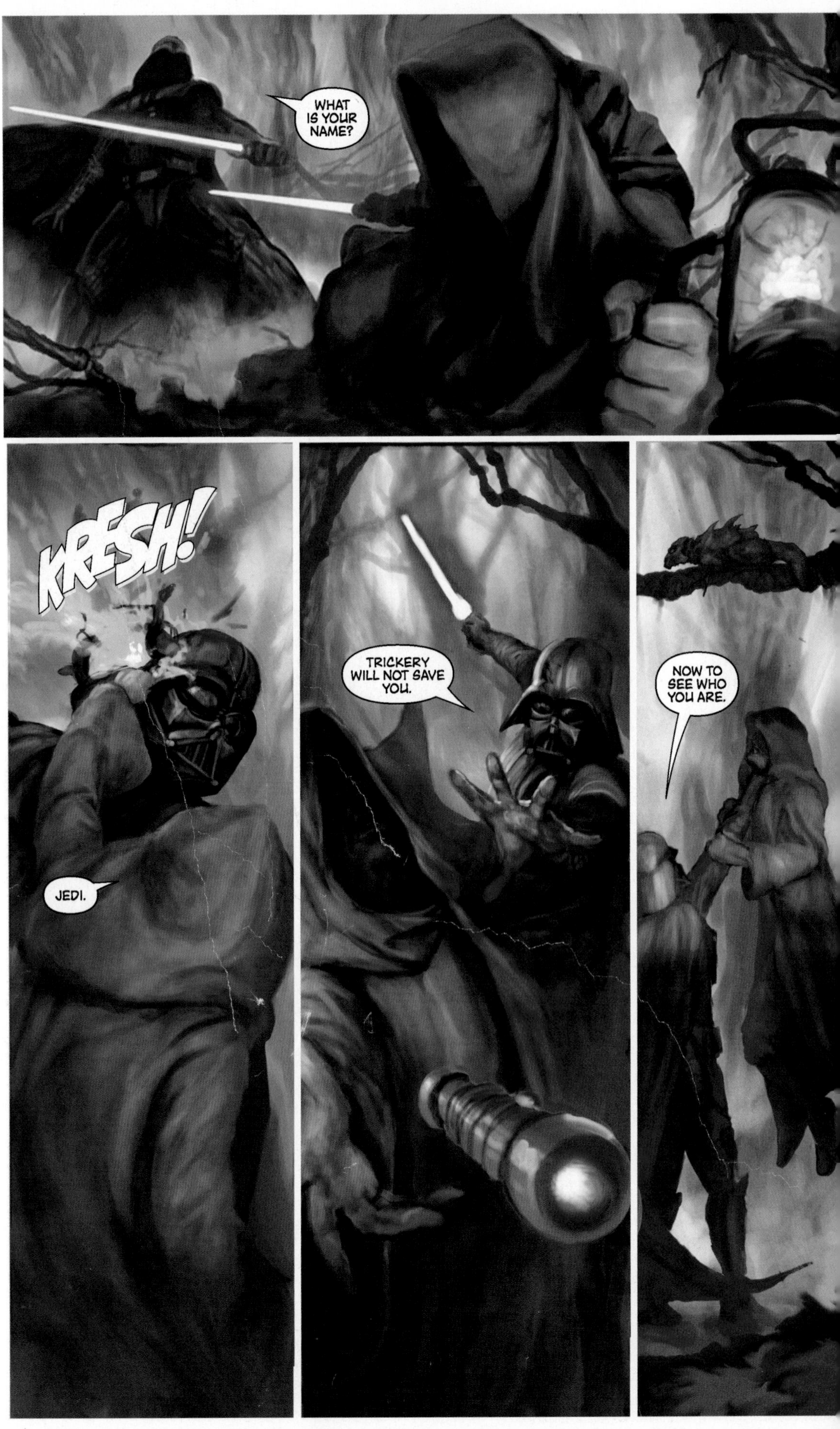
WHAT IS YOUR NAME?
KRESH!
JEDI.
TRICKERY WILL NOT SAVE YOU.
NOW TO SEE WHO YOU ARE.

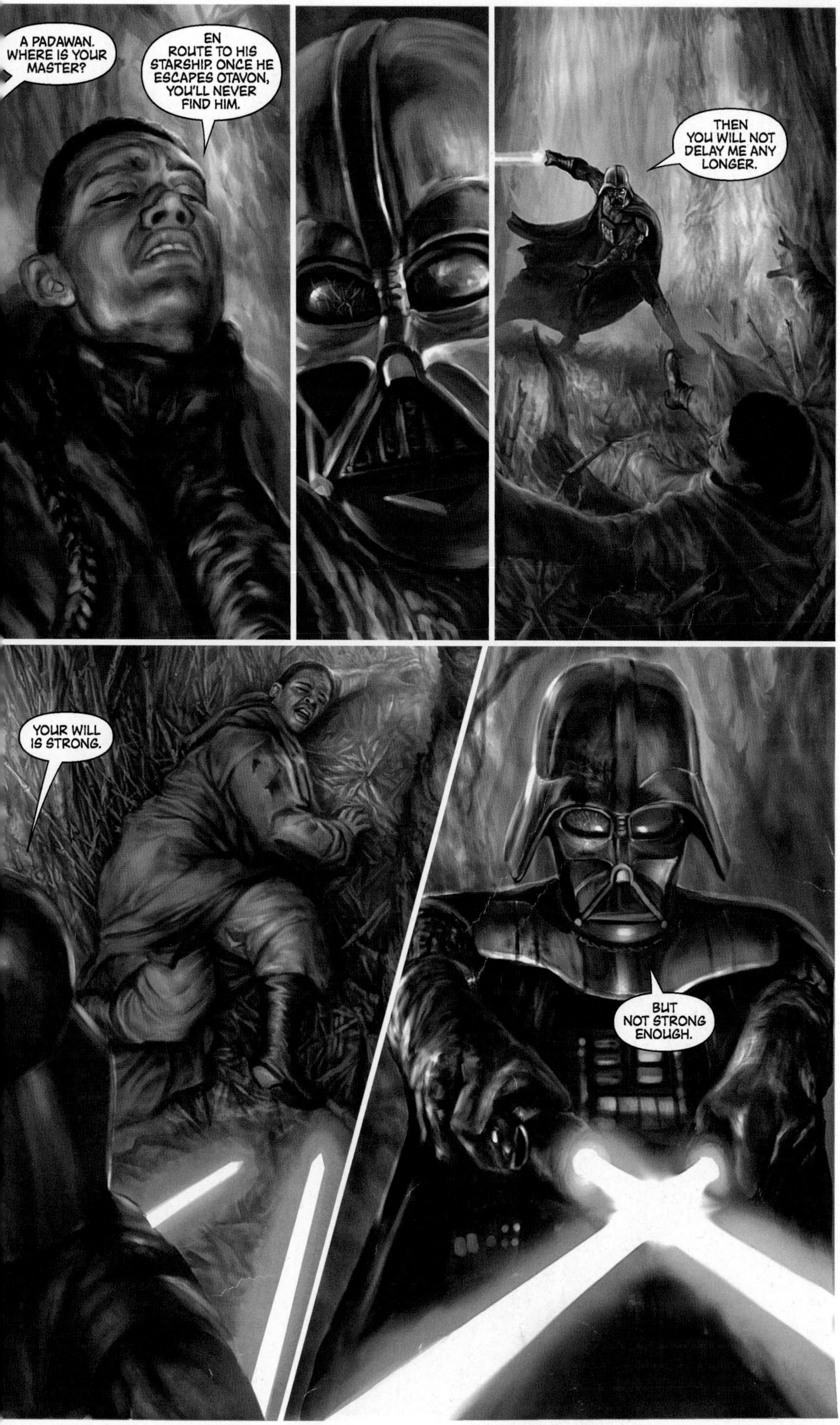
A PADAWAN. WHERE IS YOUR MASTER?
EN ROUTE TO HIS STARSHIP. ONCE HE ESCAPES OTAVON, YOU'LL NEVER FIND HIM.
THEN YOU WILL NOT DELAY ME ANY LONGER.
YOUR WILL IS STRONG.
BUT NOT STRONG ENOUGH.

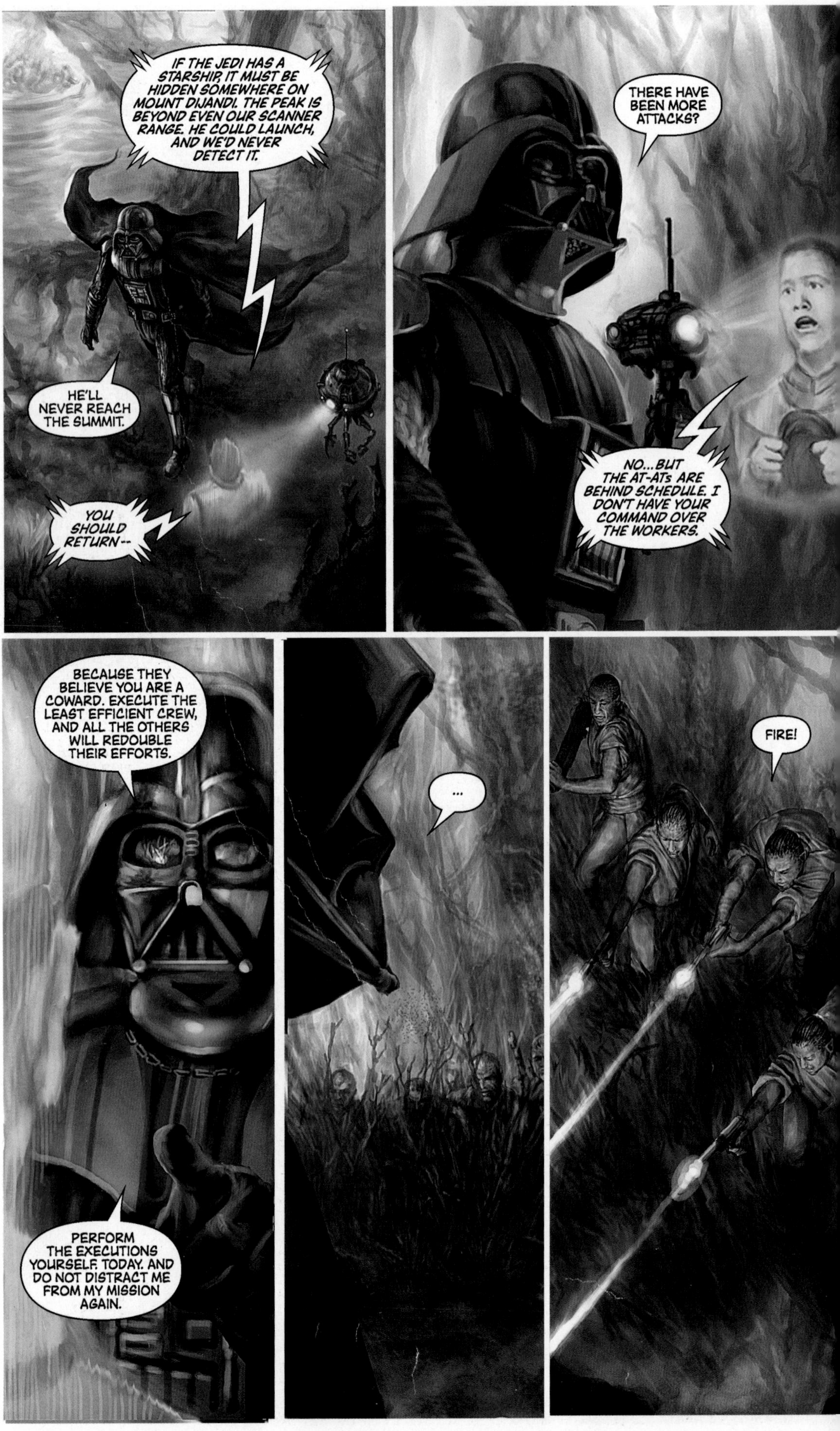
IF THE JEDI HAS A STARSHIP, IT MUST BE HIDDEN SOMEWHERE ON MOUNT DIJANDI. THE PEAK IS BEYOND EVEN OUR SCANNER RANGE. HE COULD LAUNCH, AND WE'D NEVER DETECT IT.
HE'LL NEVER REACH THE SUMMIT.
YOU SHOULD RETURN--
THERE HAVE BEEN MORE ATTACKS?
NO...BUT THE AT-ATs ARE BEHIND SCHEDULE. I DON'T HAVE YOUR COMMAND OVER THE WORKERS.
BECAUSE THEY BELIEVE YOU ARE A COWARD. EXECUTE THE LEAST EFFICIENT CREW, AND ALL THE OTHERS WILL REDOUBLE THEIR EFFORTS.
PERFORM THE EXECUTIONS YOURSELF. TODAY. AND DO NOT DISTRACT ME FROM MY MISSION AGAIN.
...
FIRE!

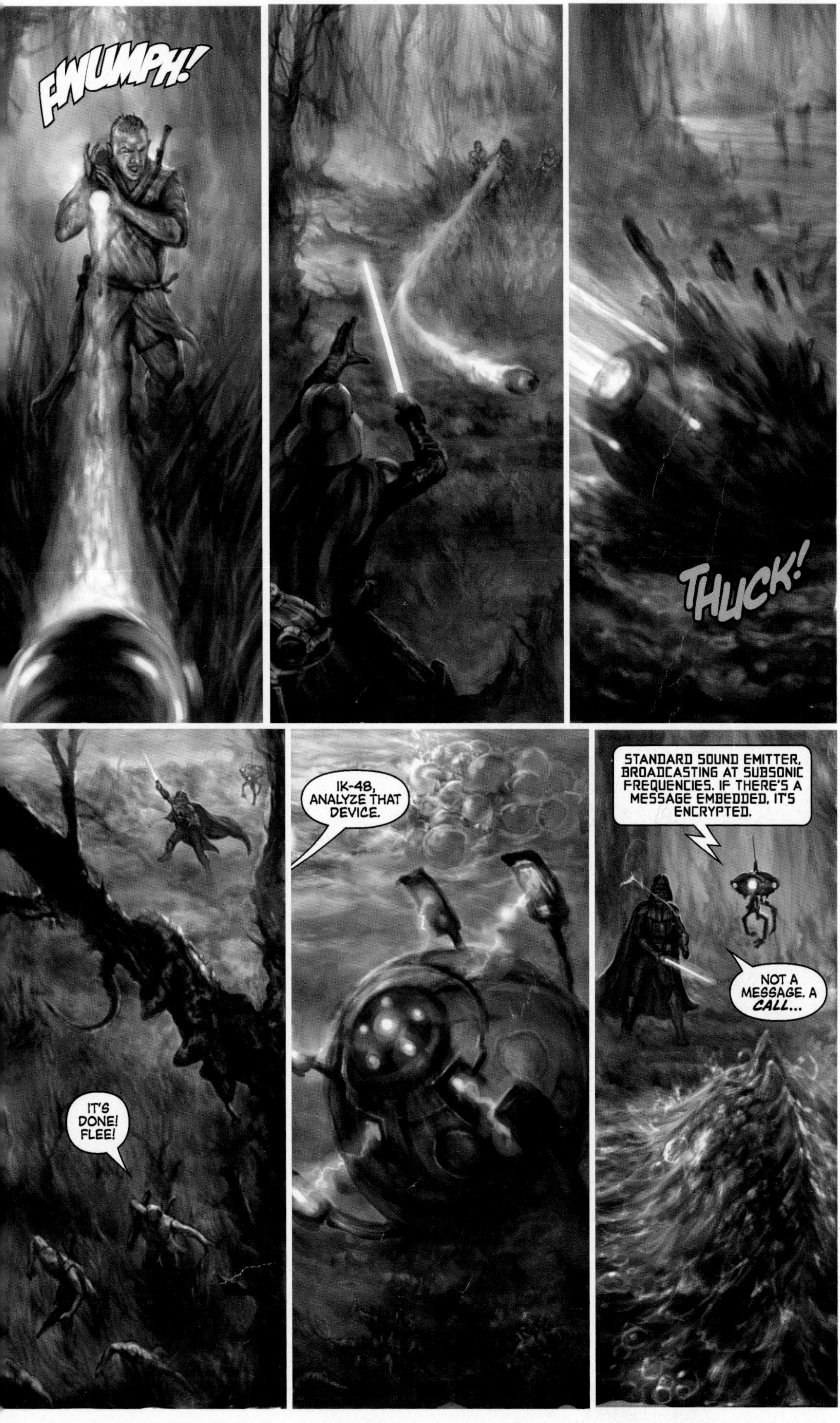
FWUMPH!
THUCK!
IT'S DONE! FLEE!
IK-48, ANALYZE THAT DEVICE.
STANDARD SOUND EMITTER, BROADCASTING AT SUBSONIC FREQUENCIES. IF THERE'S A MESSAGE EMBEDDED, IT'S ENCRYPTED.
NOT A MESSAGE. A *CALL*...

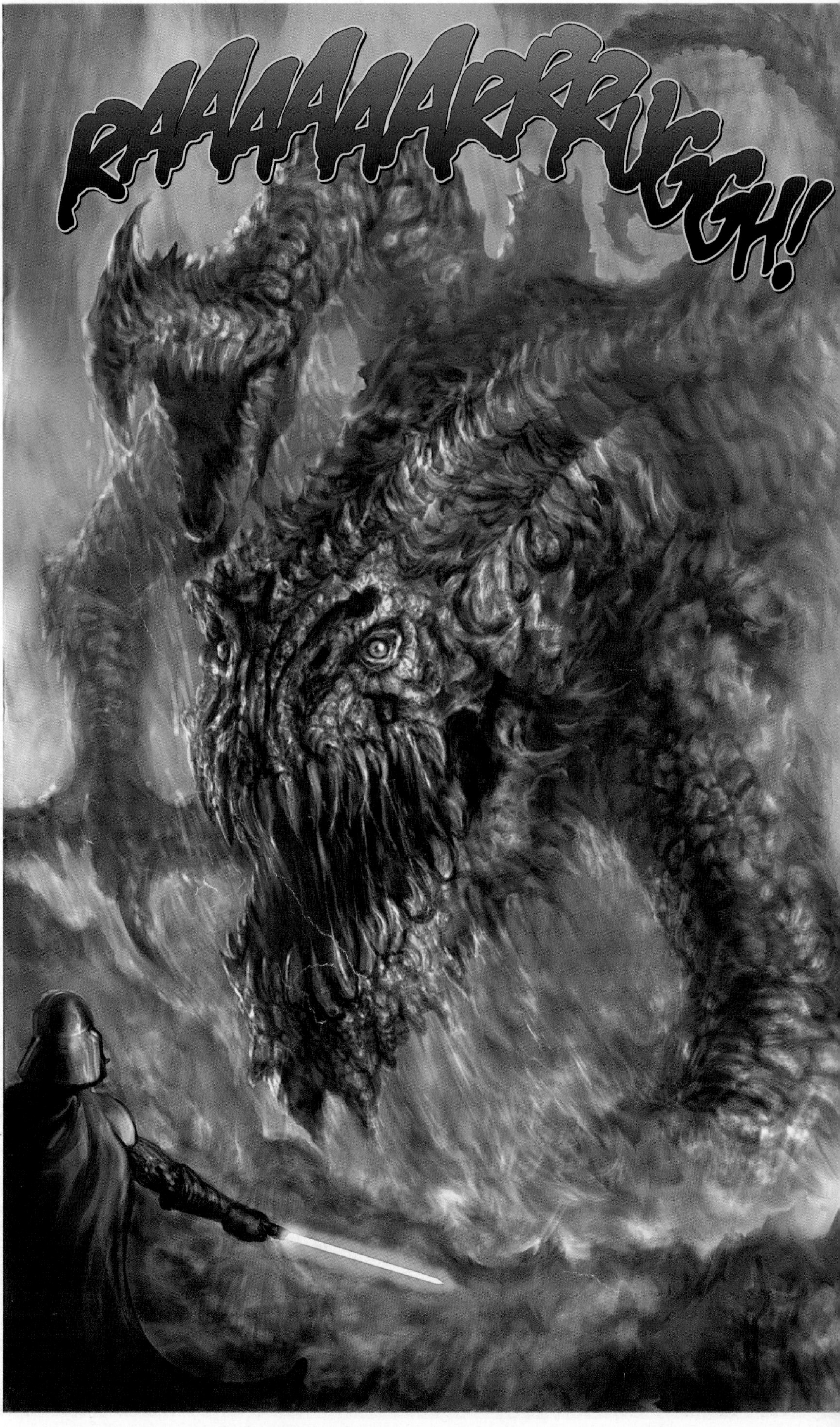
RAAAAAARRRUGGH!

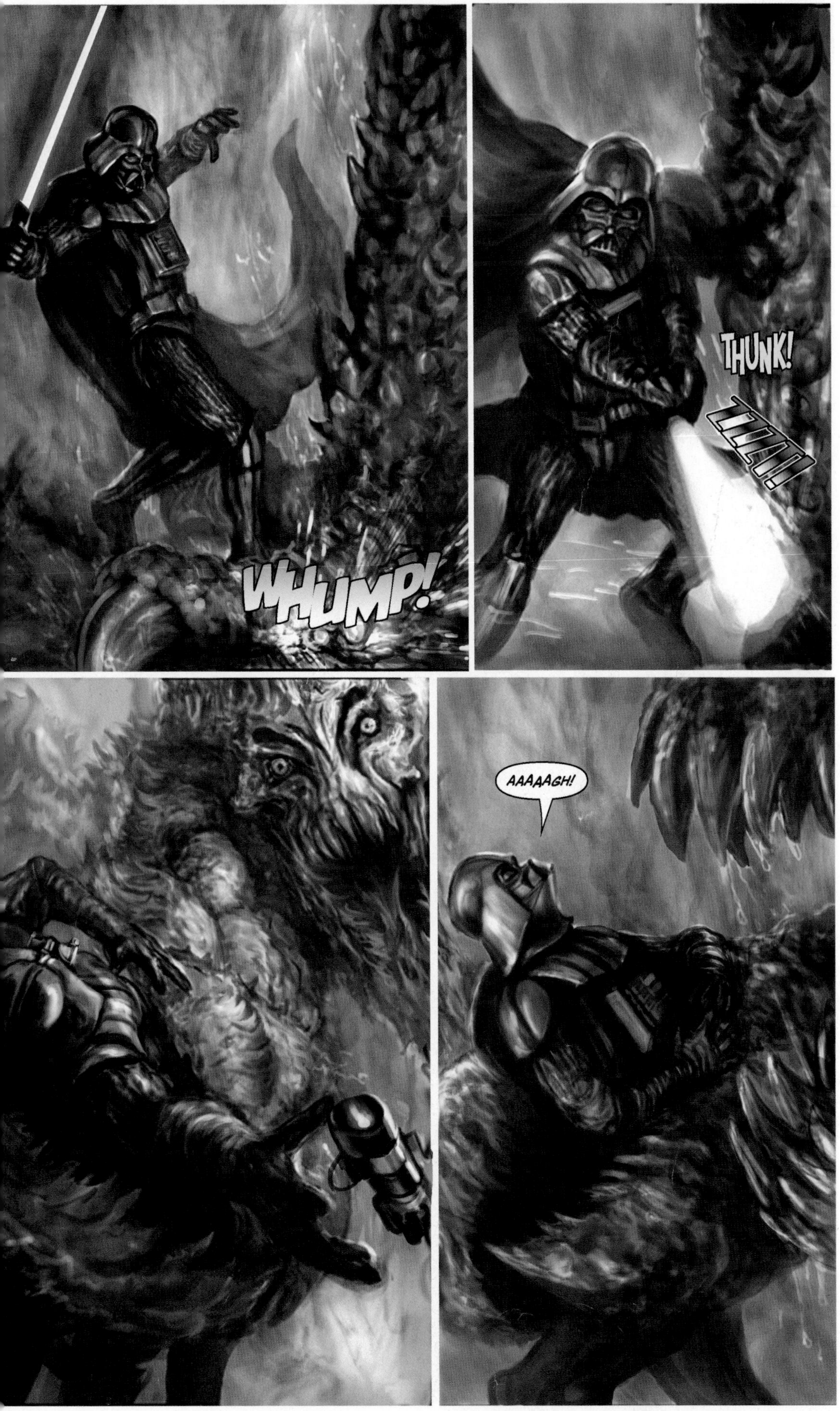
WHUMP!
THUNK!
AAAAAGH!

UNGH... STOP!

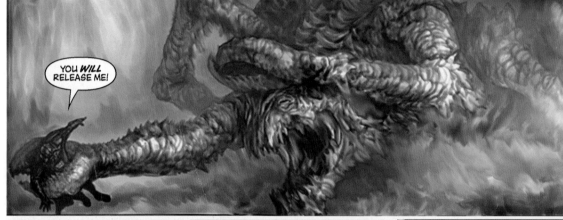

YOU *WILL* RELEASE ME!

YOU DO *NOT* WANT TO KILL ME...

...ANY MORE THAN I WANT TO KILL YOU.

KRUNCH!

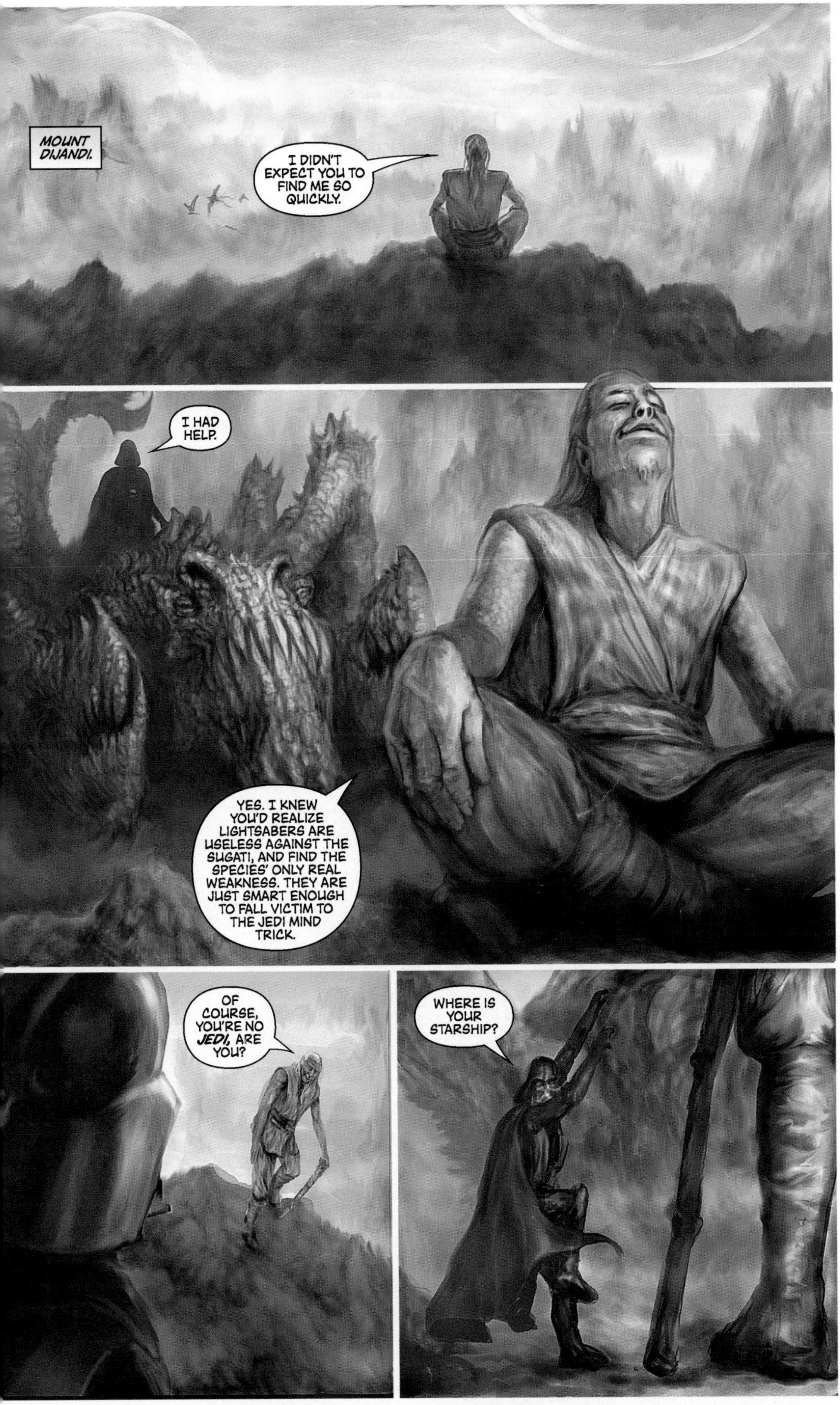
MOUNT DIJANDI.
I DIDN'T EXPECT YOU TO FIND ME SO QUICKLY.
I HAD HELP.
YES. I KNEW YOU'D REALIZE LIGHTSABERS ARE USELESS AGAINST THE SUGATI, AND FIND THE SPECIES' ONLY REAL WEAKNESS. THEY ARE JUST SMART ENOUGH TO FALL VICTIM TO THE JEDI MIND TRICK.
OF COURSE, YOU'RE NO *JEDI*, ARE YOU?
WHERE IS YOUR STARSHIP?

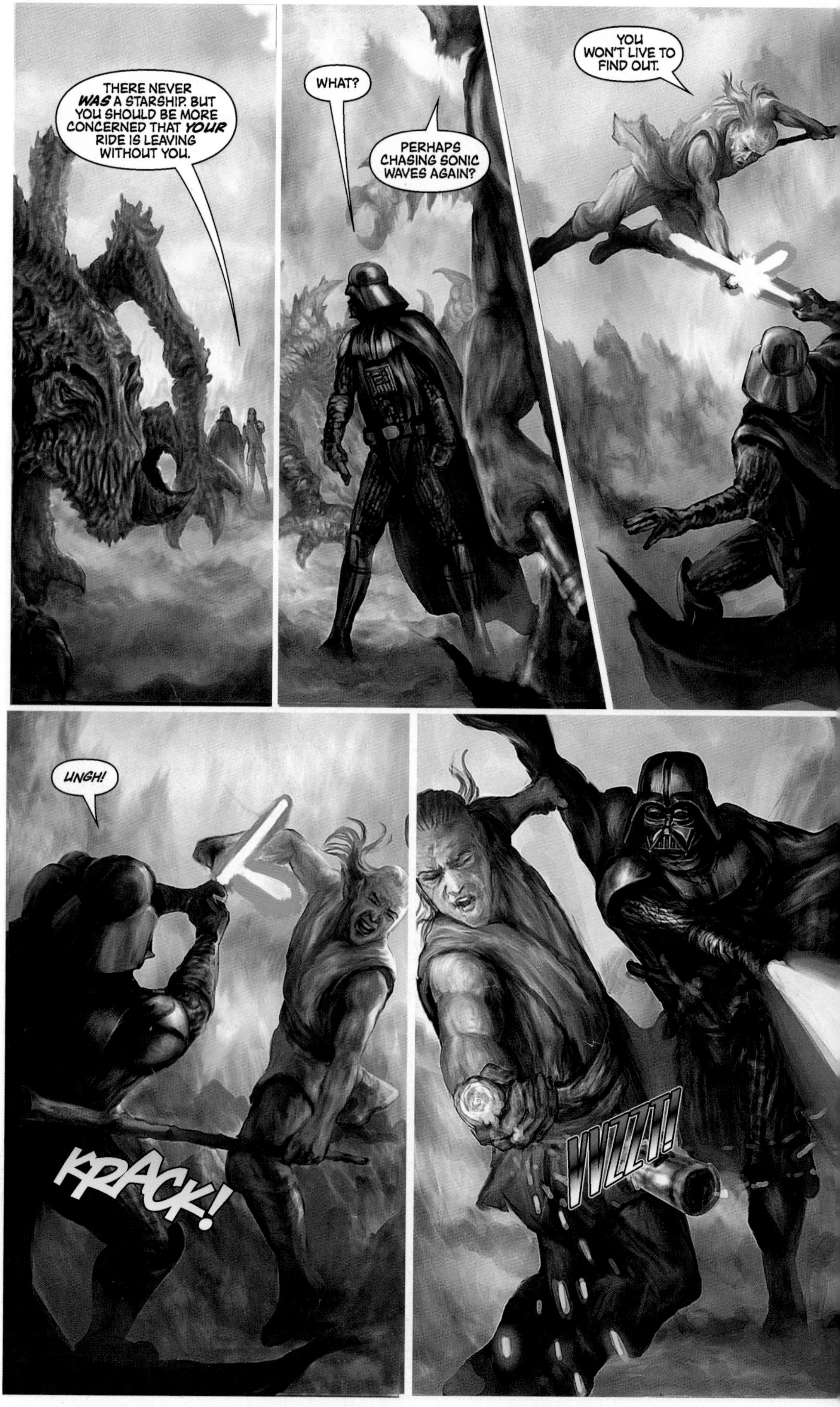
THERE NEVER WAS A STARSHIP. BUT YOU SHOULD BE MORE CONCERNED THAT YOUR RIDE IS LEAVING WITHOUT YOU.
WHAT?
PERHAPS CHASING SONIC WAVES AGAIN?
YOU WON'T LIVE TO FIND OUT.
UNGH!
KRACK!
VVZZZT!

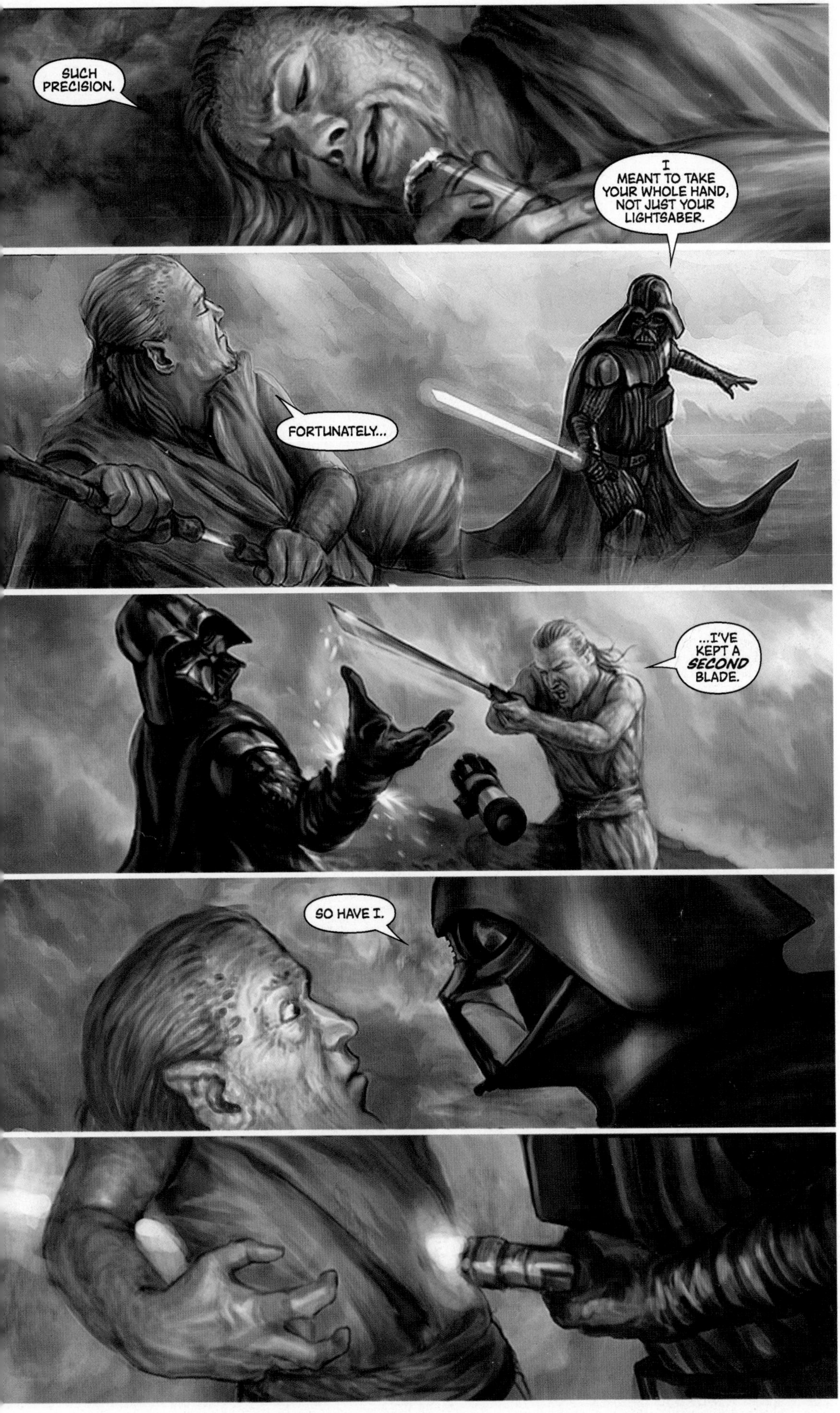
SUCH PRECISION.
I MEANT TO TAKE YOUR WHOLE HAND, NOT JUST YOUR LIGHTSABER.
FORTUNATELY...
...I'VE KEPT A SECOND BLADE.
SO HAVE I.

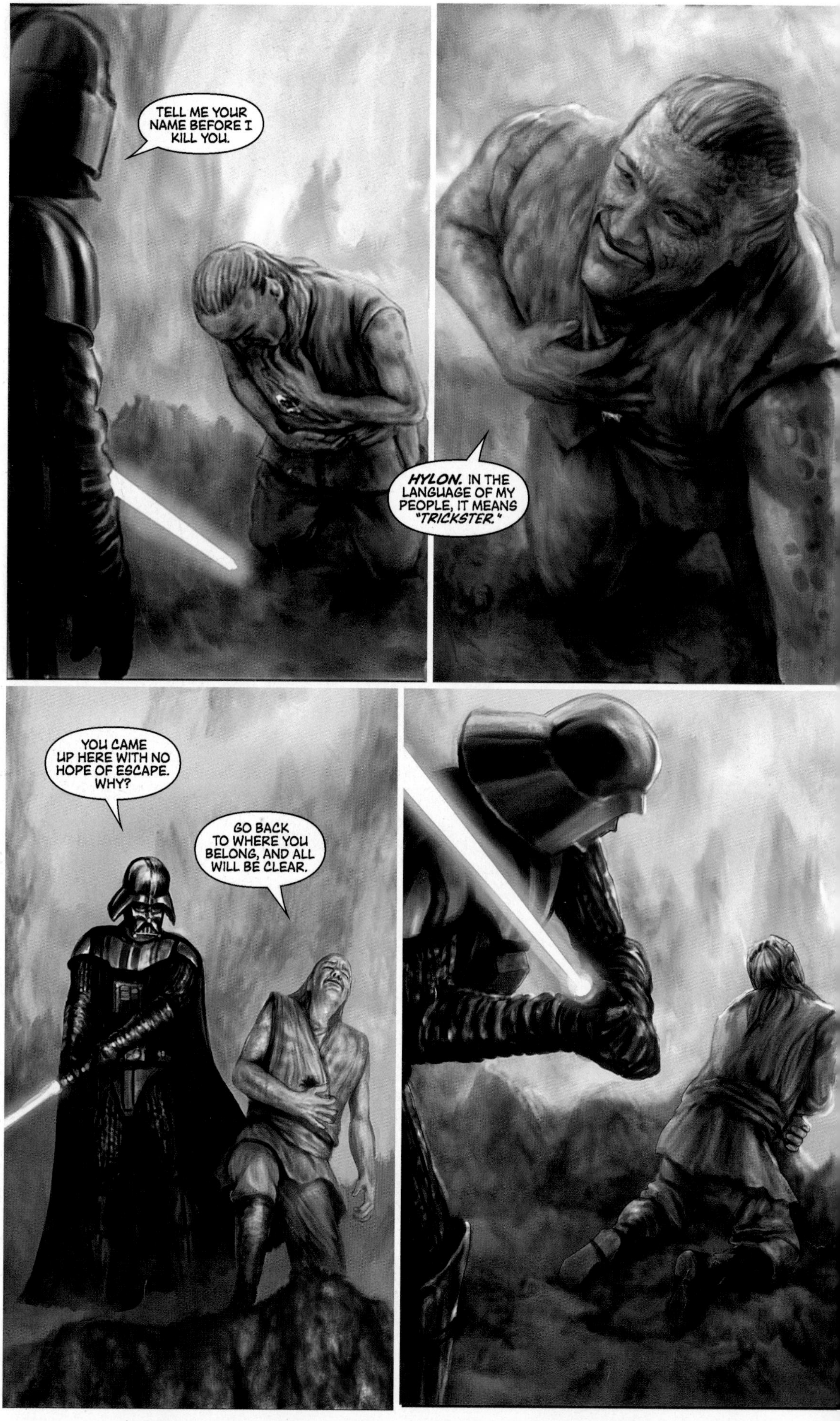
TELL ME YOUR NAME BEFORE I KILL YOU.
HYLON. IN THE LANGUAGE OF MY PEOPLE, IT MEANS "TRICKSTER."
YOU CAME UP HERE WITH NO HOPE OF ESCAPE. WHY?
GO BACK TO WHERE YOU BELONG, AND ALL WILL BE CLEAR.

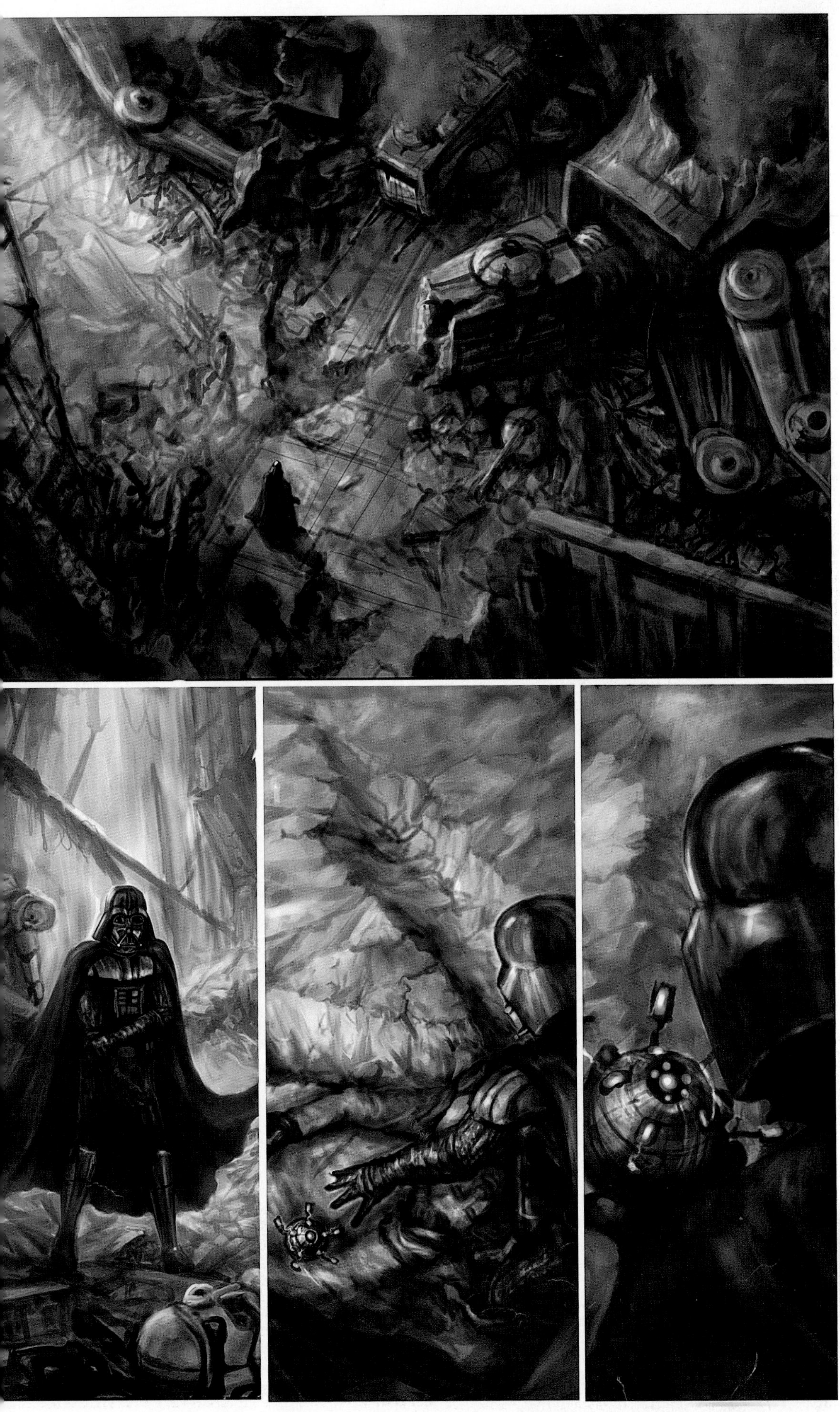

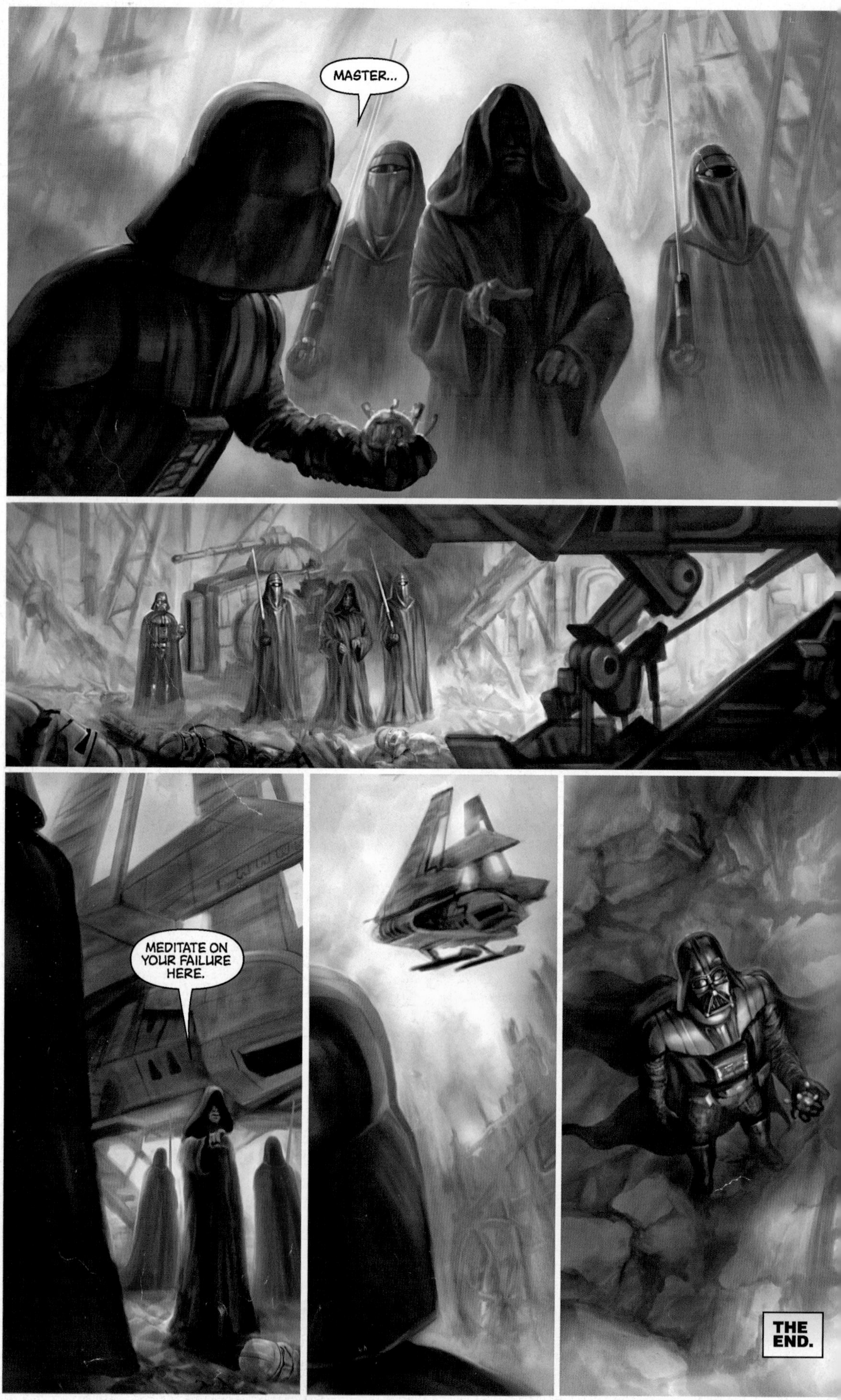
MASTER...
MEDITATE ON YOUR FAILURE HERE.
THE END.

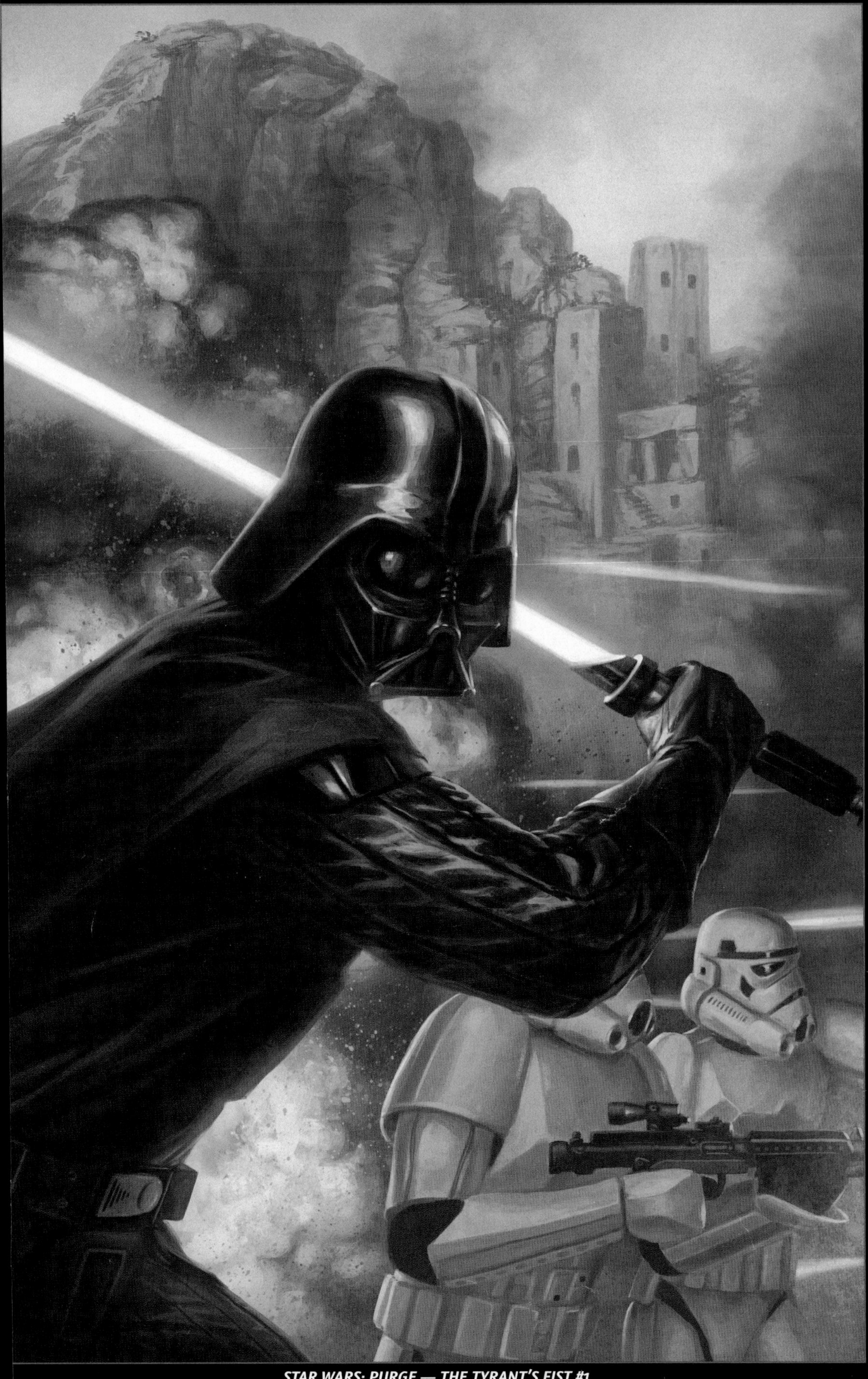

STAR WARS: PURGE — THE TYRANT'S FIST #1

WRITER: ALEXANDER FREED • ARTISTS: MARCO CASTIELLO & ANDREA CHELLA • COLORIST: MICHAEL ATIYEH • LETTERER: MICHAEL HEISLER
DESIGNER: ALLYSON HALLER • ASSISTANT EDITOR: FREDDYE LINS • EDITOR: DAVE MARSHALL • COVER ARTIST: DAN SCOTT

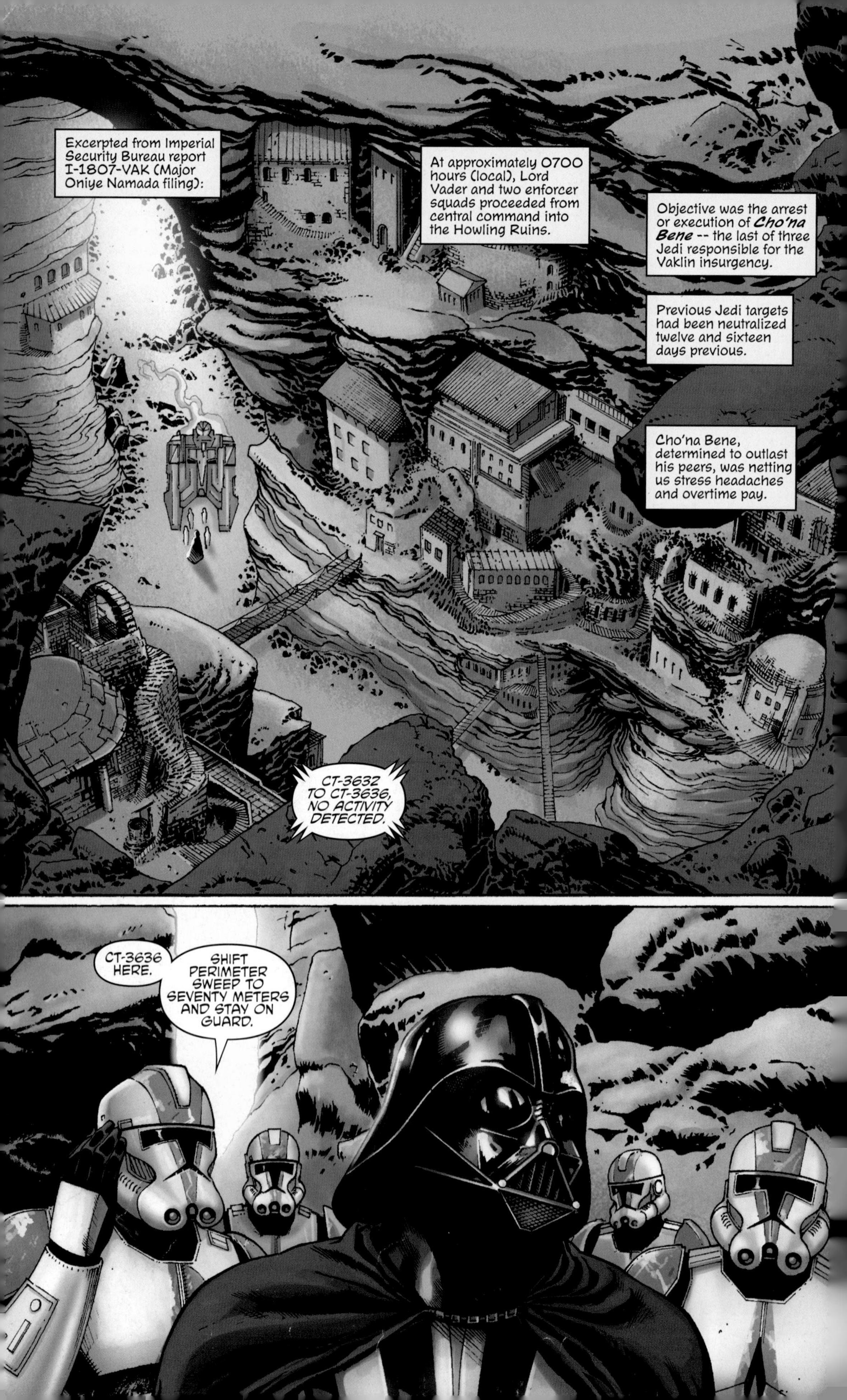
Excerpted from Imperial Security Bureau report I-1807-VAK (Major Oniye Namada filing):
At approximately 0700 hours (local), Lord Vader and two enforcer squads proceeded from central command into the Howling Ruins.
Objective was the arrest or execution of *Cho'na Bene* -- the last of three Jedi responsible for the Vaklin insurgency.
Previous Jedi targets had been neutralized twelve and sixteen days previous.
Cho'na Bene, determined to outlast his peers, was netting us stress headaches and overtime pay.
CT-3632 TO CT-3636, NO ACTIVITY DETECTED.
CT-3636 HERE.
SHIFT PERIMETER SWEEP TO SEVENTY METERS AND STAY ON GUARD.

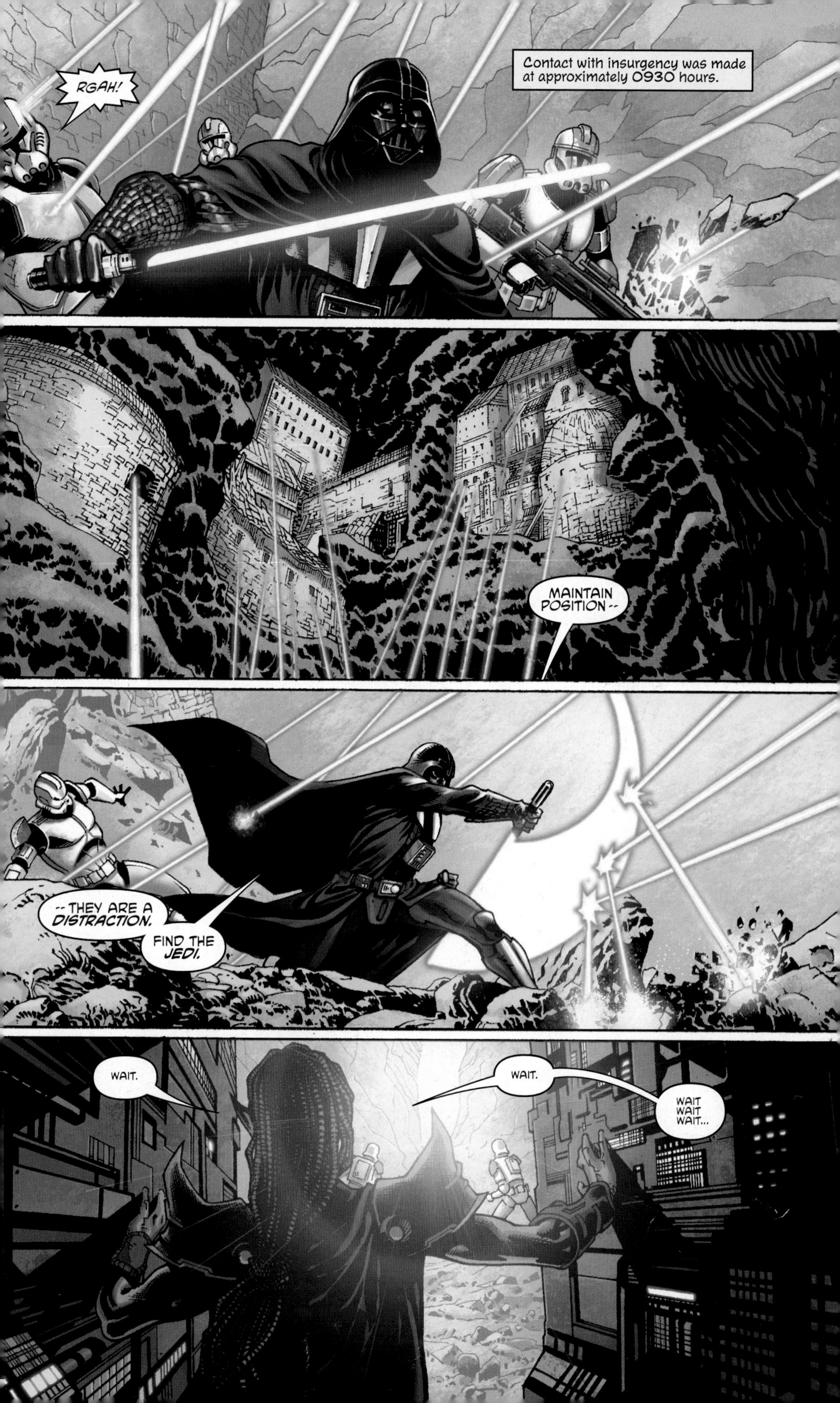
RGAH!
Contact with insurgency was made at approximately 0930 hours.
MAINTAIN POSITION --
-- THEY ARE A DISTRACTION.
FIND THE JEDI.
WAIT.
WAIT.
WAIT WAIT WAIT...

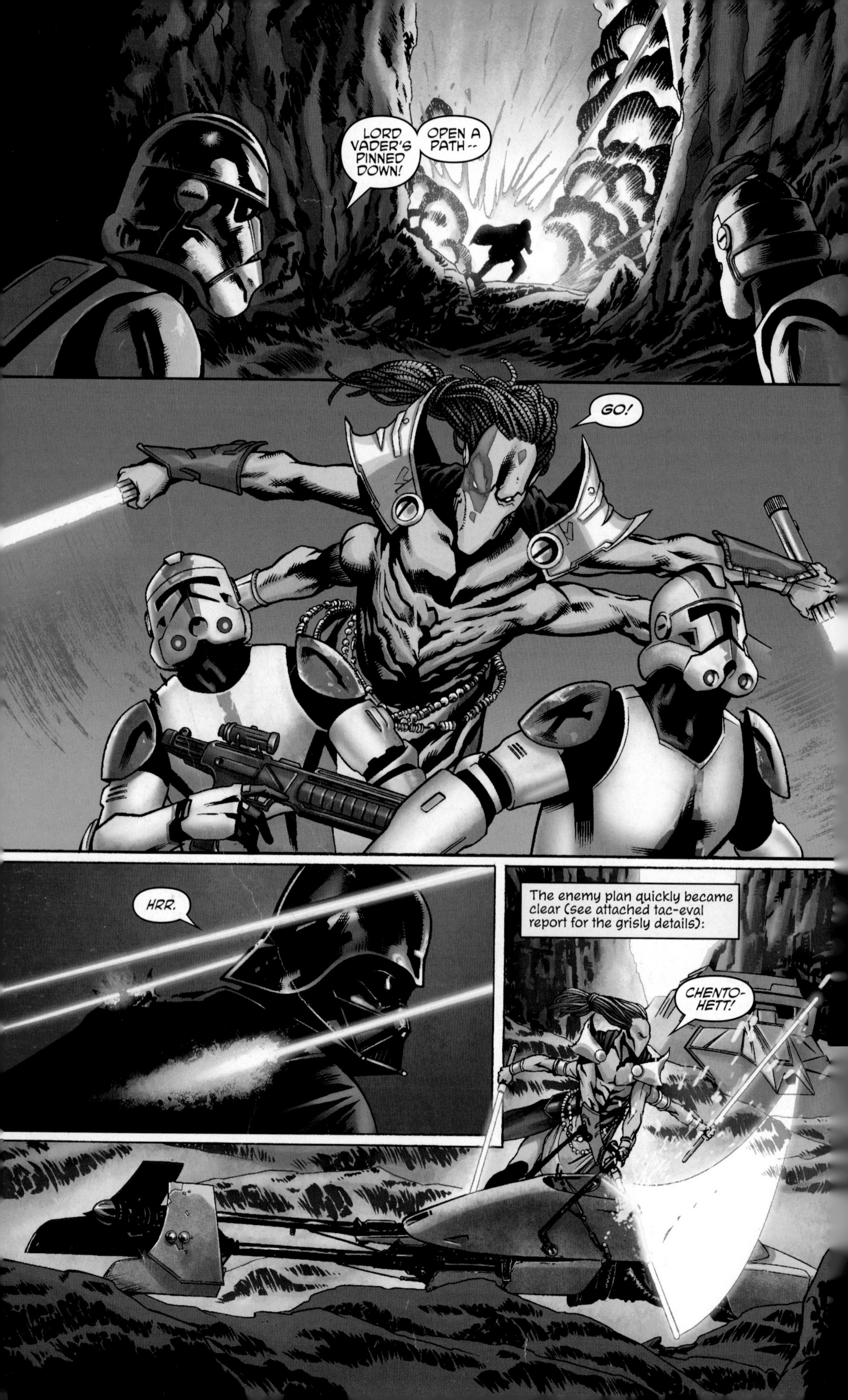
LORD VADER'S PINNED DOWN!
OPEN A PATH --
GO!
HRR.
The enemy plan quickly became clear (see attached tac-eval report for the grisly details):
CHENTO-HETT!

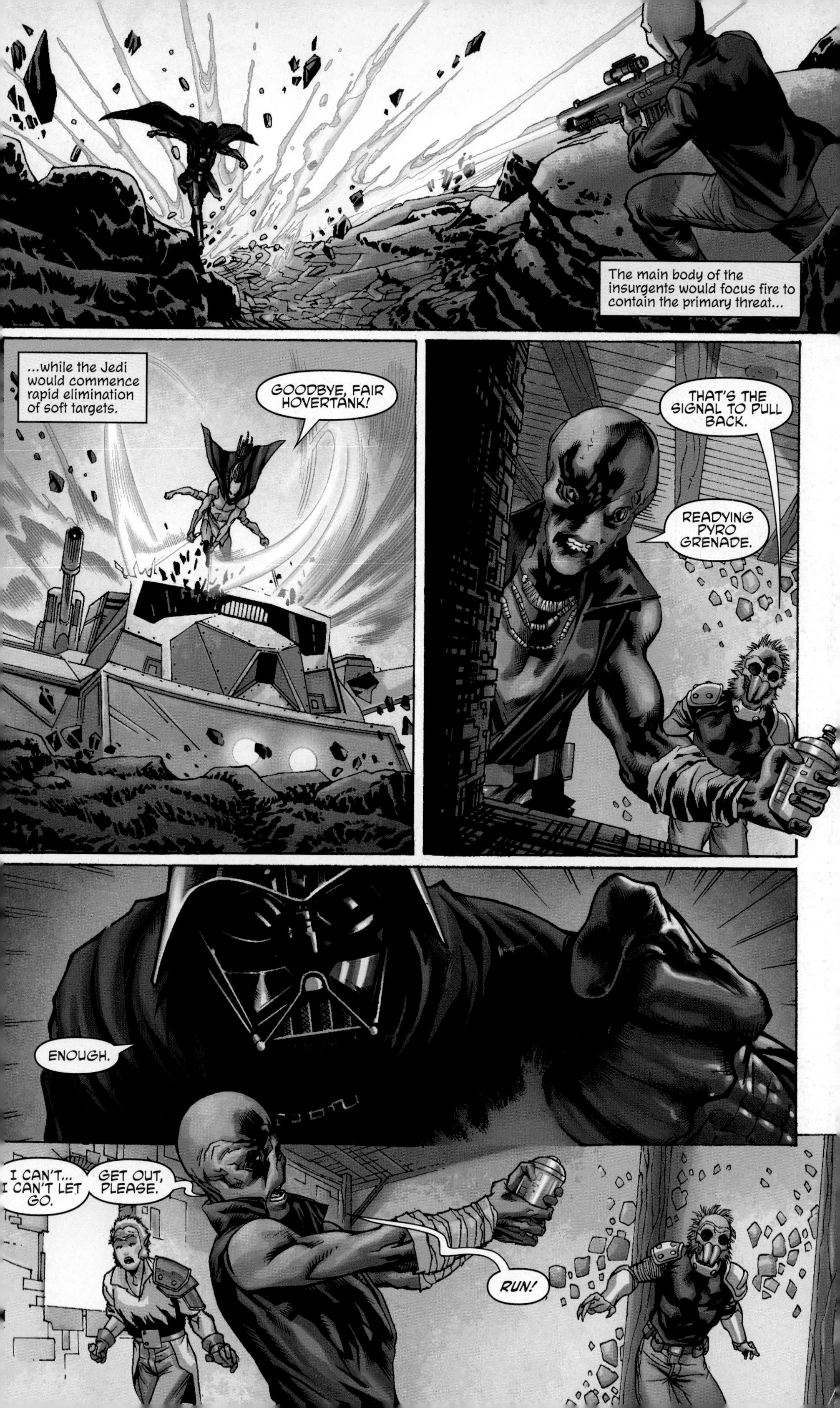
The main body of the insurgents would focus fire to contain the primary threat...
...while the Jedi would commence rapid elimination of soft targets.
GOODBYE, FAIR HOVERTANK!
THAT'S THE SIGNAL TO PULL BACK.
READYING PYRO GRENADE.
ENOUGH.
I CAN'T... I CAN'T LET GO.
GET OUT, PLEASE.
RUN!

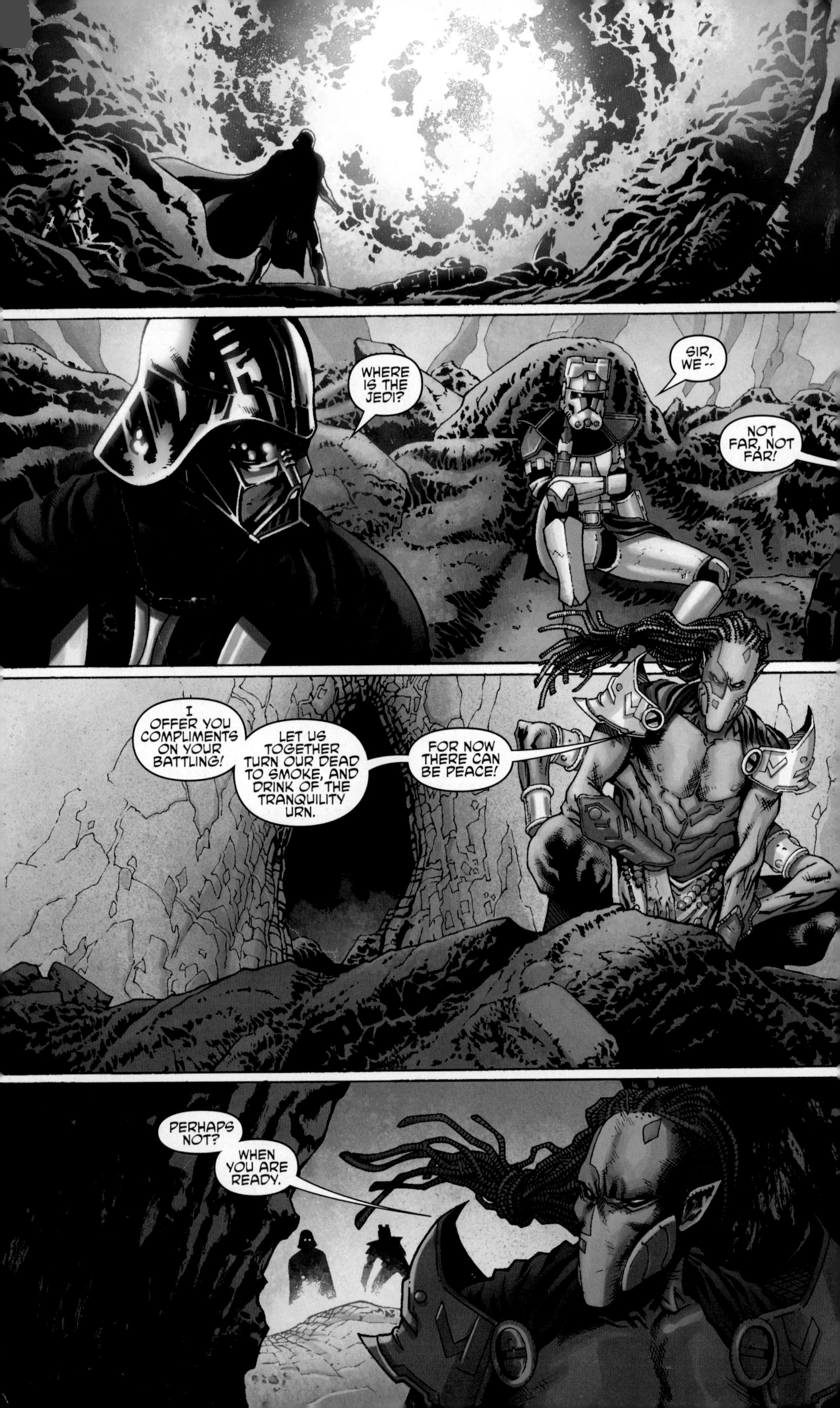

WHERE IS THE JEDI?
SIR, WE --
NOT FAR, NOT FAR!
I OFFER YOU COMPLIMENTS ON YOUR BATTLING!
LET US TOGETHER TURN OUR DEAD TO SMOKE, AND DRINK OF THE TRANQUILITY URN.
FOR NOW THERE CAN BE PEACE!
PERHAPS NOT?
WHEN YOU ARE READY.

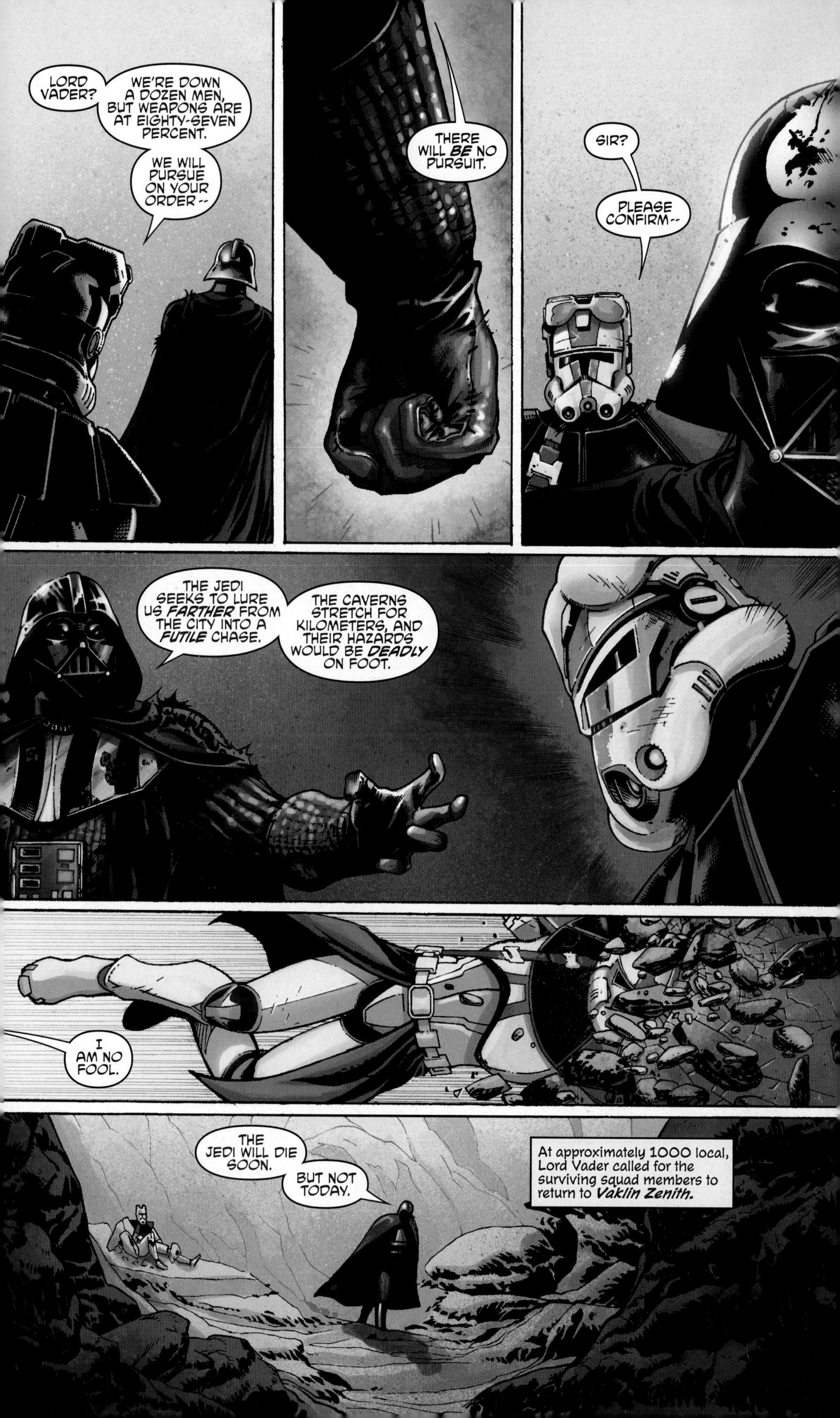
LORD VADER?
WE'RE DOWN A DOZEN MEN, BUT WEAPONS ARE AT EIGHTY-SEVEN PERCENT.
WE WILL PURSUE ON YOUR ORDER--
THERE WILL *BE* NO PURSUIT.
SIR?
PLEASE CONFIRM--
THE JEDI SEEKS TO LURE US *FARTHER* FROM THE CITY INTO A *FUTILE* CHASE.
THE CAVERNS STRETCH FOR KILOMETERS, AND THEIR HAZARDS WOULD BE *DEADLY* ON FOOT.
I AM NO FOOL.
THE JEDI WILL DIE SOON.
BUT NOT TODAY.
At approximately 1000 local, Lord Vader called for the surviving squad members to return to *Vaklin Zenith.*

Morning patrol through the plaza was uneventful. Daytime incidents within the city are rare since Lord Vader arrived.

People are nervous, but in this economy, the locals are *always* nervous.

They're one bad season away from selling their pets' organs to buy food.

Vaklin reminds me of *home.*

SAVE ME A SWEET ROLL, DJON?

BERRY AND TOK NUT -- LAST OF THE MORNING BATCH!

...I HATE TOK NUTS.

SO SCRAPE THE DAMN THINGS OFF.

CAN'T SAVE MY BEST FOR THE GIRL WHO SCARES MY CUSTOMERS.

NOW WHY WOULD YOUR CUSTOMERS BE SCARED OF THE IMPERIAL SECURITY BUREAU?

DON'T START NOW--

YOU BROUGHT IT UP.

YOU MAKE GOOD PASTRIES, AND I'VE GIVEN YOU A LOT OF LEEWAY, BUT YOU CAN'T KEEP COVERING FOR THESE PEOPLE.

LAST NIGHT, YOU WERE *IN THE CANTINA* WHEN KREN SALLO WAS COLLECTING DONATIONS FOR THE INSURGENCY.

MUST HAVE BEEN AFTER I LEFT.

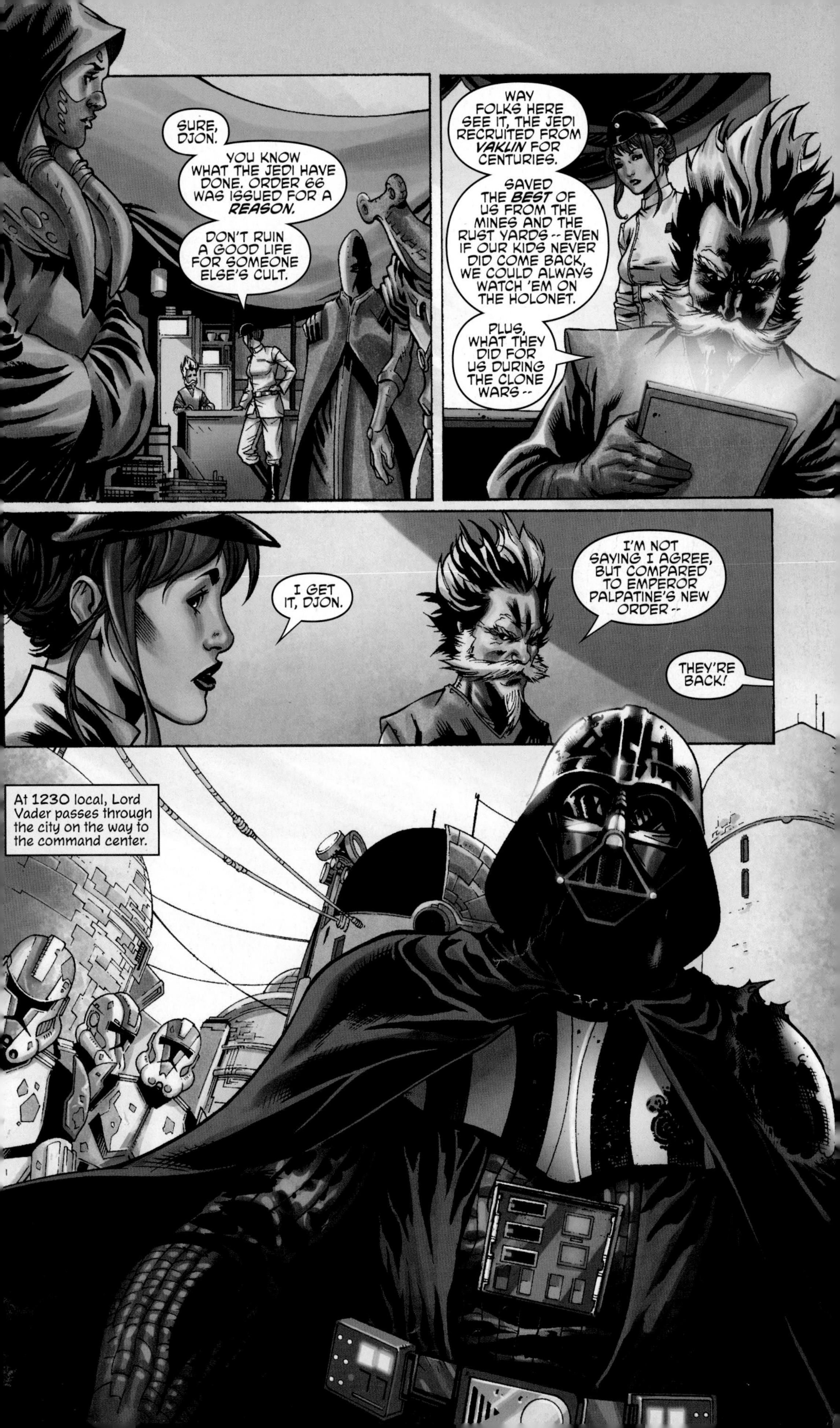
SURE, DJON.
YOU KNOW WHAT THE JEDI HAVE DONE. ORDER 66 WAS ISSUED FOR A REASON.
DON'T RUIN A GOOD LIFE FOR SOMEONE ELSE'S CULT.
WAY FOLKS HERE SEE IT, THE JEDI RECRUITED FROM VAKLIN FOR CENTURIES.
SAVED THE BEST OF US FROM THE MINES AND THE RUST YARDS -- EVEN IF OUR KIDS NEVER DID COME BACK, WE COULD ALWAYS WATCH 'EM ON THE HOLONET.
PLUS, WHAT THEY DID FOR US DURING THE CLONE WARS --
I GET IT, DJON.
I'M NOT SAYING I AGREE, BUT COMPARED TO EMPEROR PALPATINE'S NEW ORDER --
THEY'RE BACK!
At 1230 local, Lord Vader passes through the city on the way to the command center.

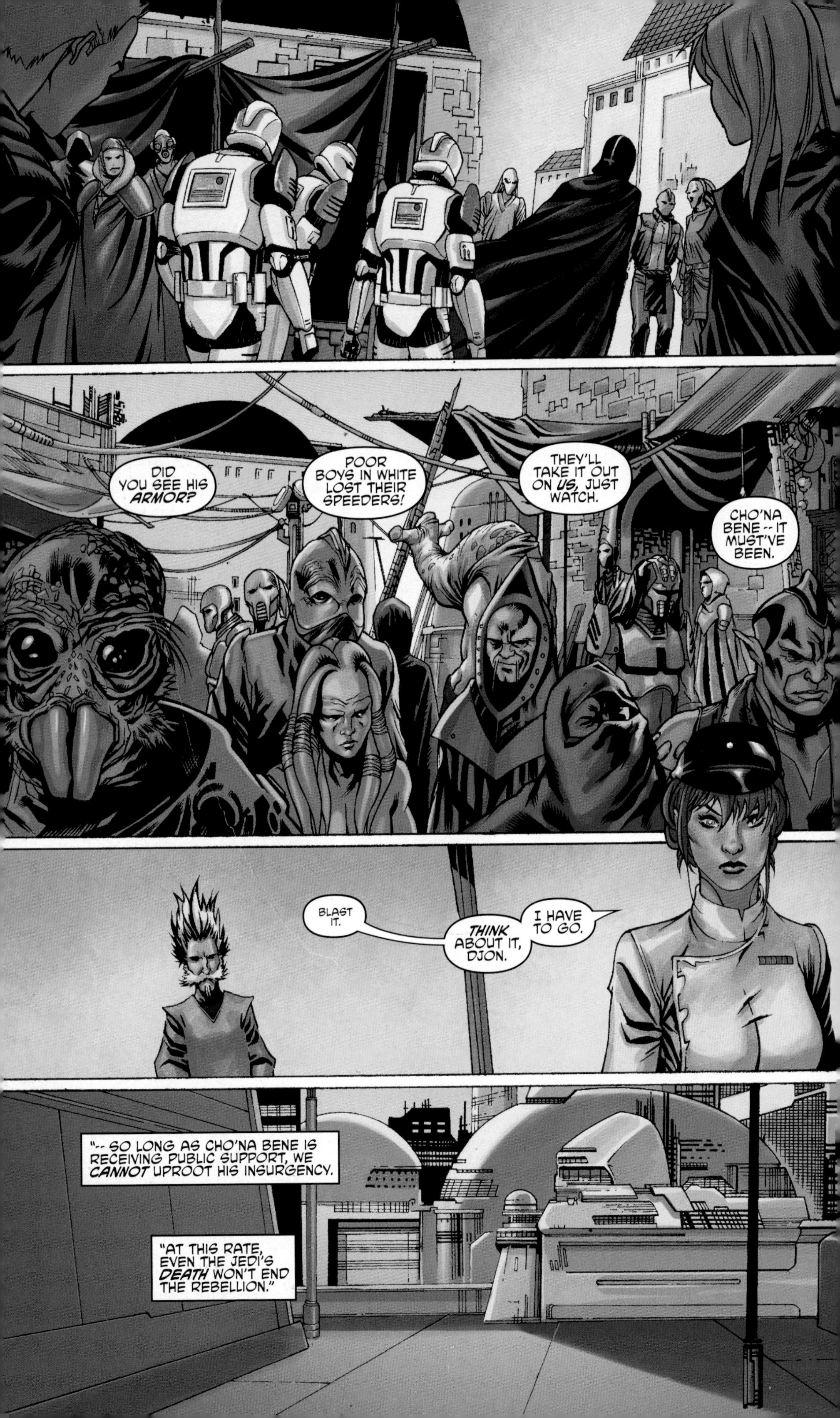
DID YOU SEE HIS *ARMOR?*
POOR BOYS IN WHITE LOST THEIR SPEEDERS!
THEY'LL TAKE IT OUT ON *US,* JUST WATCH.
CHO'NA BENE -- IT MUST'VE BEEN.
BLAST IT.
THINK ABOUT IT, DJON.
I HAVE TO GO.
"-- SO LONG AS CHO'NA BENE IS RECEIVING PUBLIC SUPPORT, WE *CANNOT* UPROOT HIS INSURGENCY.
"AT THIS RATE, EVEN THE JEDI'S *DEATH* WON'T END THE REBELLION."

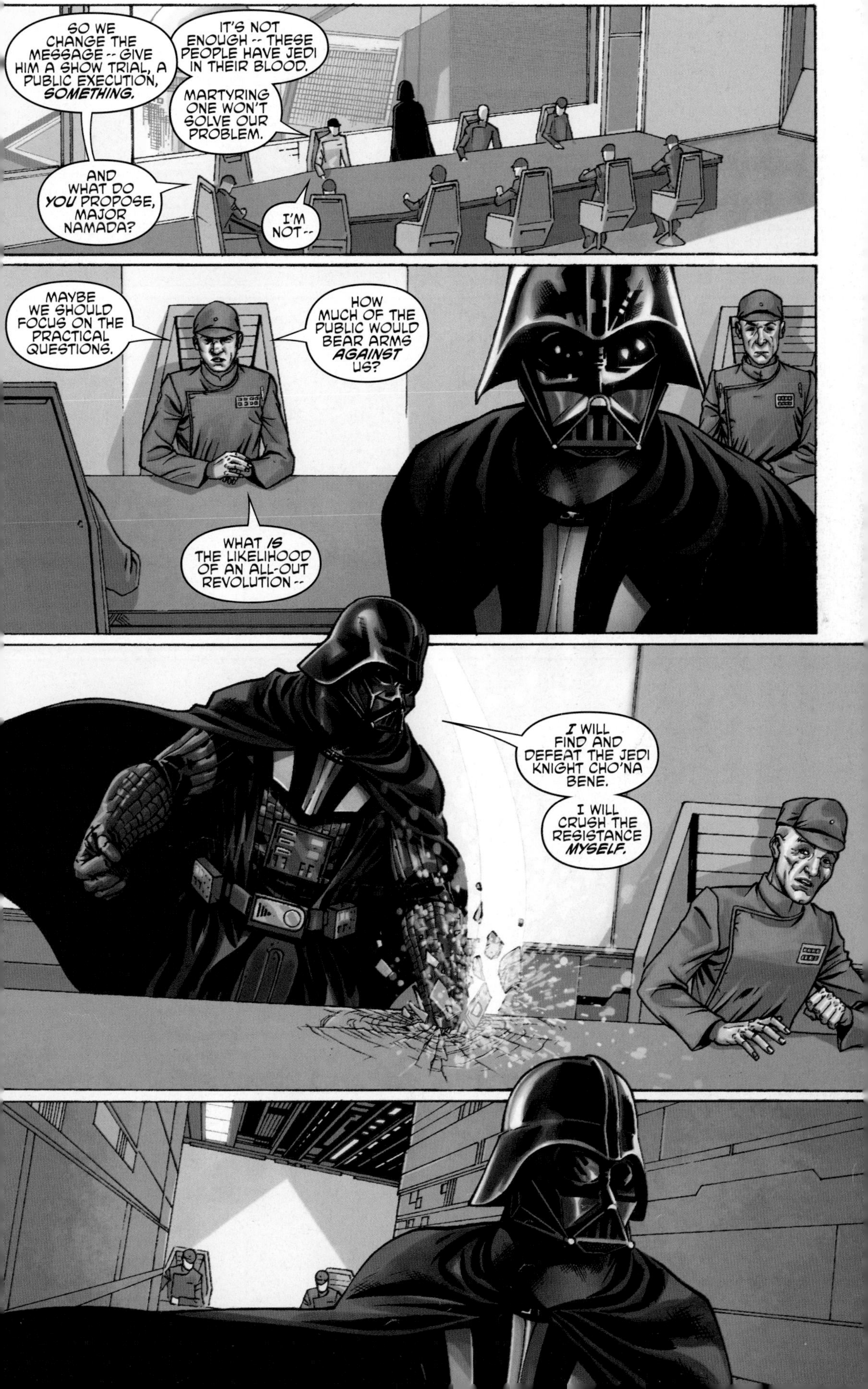
SO WE CHANGE THE MESSAGE -- GIVE HIM A SHOW TRIAL, A PUBLIC EXECUTION, SOMETHING.
IT'S NOT ENOUGH -- THESE PEOPLE HAVE JEDI IN THEIR BLOOD.
MARTYRING ONE WON'T SOLVE OUR PROBLEM.
AND WHAT DO YOU PROPOSE, MAJOR NAMADA?
I'M NOT--
MAYBE WE SHOULD FOCUS ON THE PRACTICAL QUESTIONS.
HOW MUCH OF THE PUBLIC WOULD BEAR ARMS AGAINST US?
WHAT IS THE LIKELIHOOD OF AN ALL-OUT REVOLUTION --
I WILL FIND AND DEFEAT THE JEDI KNIGHT CHO'NA BENE.
I WILL CRUSH THE RESISTANCE MYSELF.

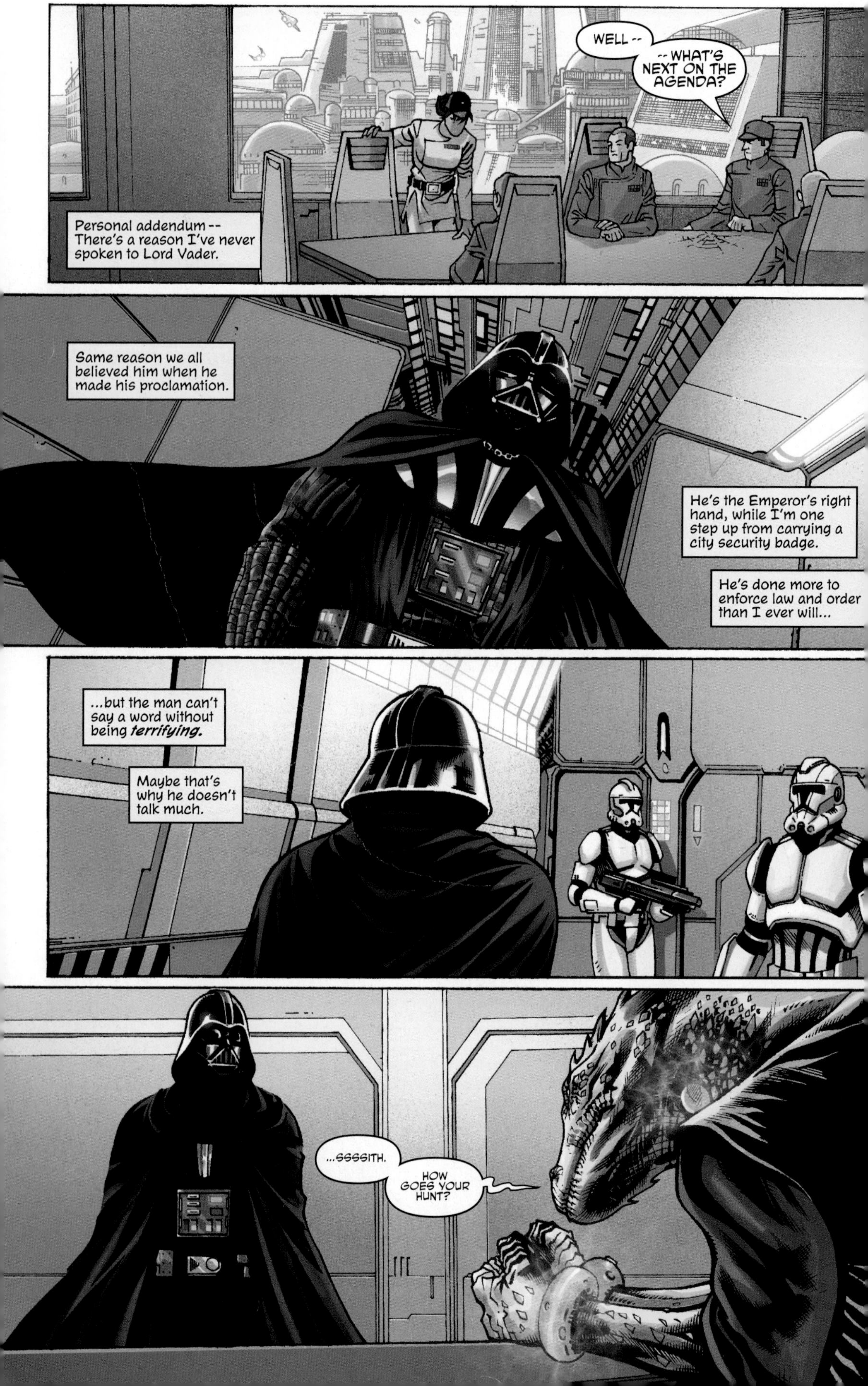
WELL --
-- WHAT'S NEXT ON THE AGENDA?
Personal addendum -- There's a reason I've never spoken to Lord Vader.
Same reason we all believed him when he made his proclamation.
He's the Emperor's right hand, while I'm one step up from carrying a city security badge.
He's done more to enforce law and order than I ever will...
...but the man can't say a word without being *terrifying.*
Maybe that's why he doesn't talk much.
...SSSSITH.
HOW GOES YOUR HUNT?

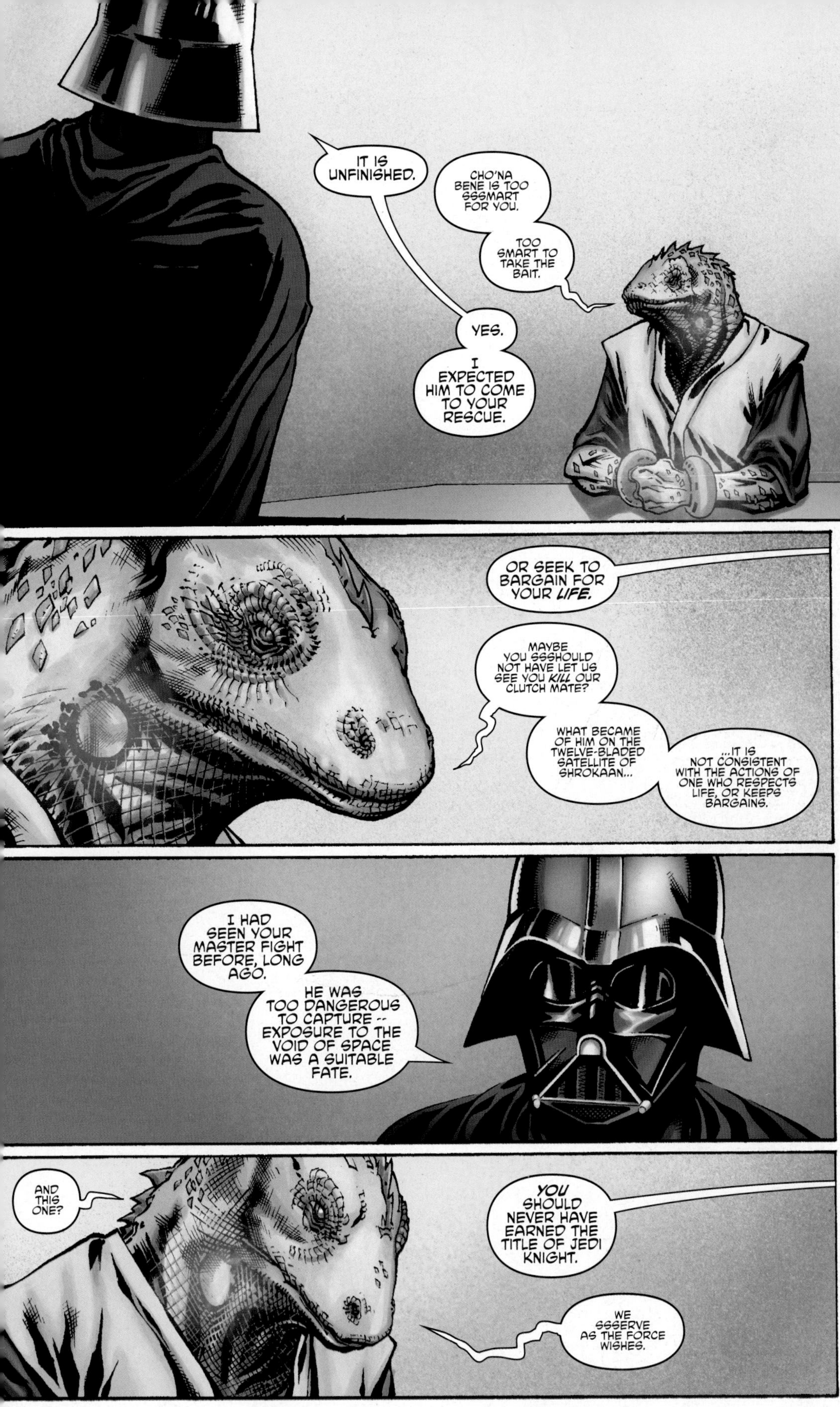
IT IS UNFINISHED.
CHO'NA BENE IS TOO SSSMART FOR YOU.
TOO SMART TO TAKE THE BAIT.
YES.
I EXPECTED HIM TO COME TO YOUR RESCUE.
OR SEEK TO BARGAIN FOR YOUR LIFE.
MAYBE YOU SSSHOULD NOT HAVE LET US SEE YOU KILL OUR CLUTCH MATE?
WHAT BECAME OF HIM ON THE TWELVE-BLADED SATELLITE OF SHROKAAN...
...IT IS NOT CONSISTENT WITH THE ACTIONS OF ONE WHO RESPECTS LIFE, OR KEEPS BARGAINS.
I HAD SEEN YOUR MASTER FIGHT BEFORE, LONG AGO.
HE WAS TOO DANGEROUS TO CAPTURE -- EXPOSURE TO THE VOID OF SPACE WAS A SUITABLE FATE.
AND THIS ONE?
YOU SHOULD NEVER HAVE EARNED THE TITLE OF JEDI KNIGHT.
WE SSSERVE AS THE FORCE WISHES.

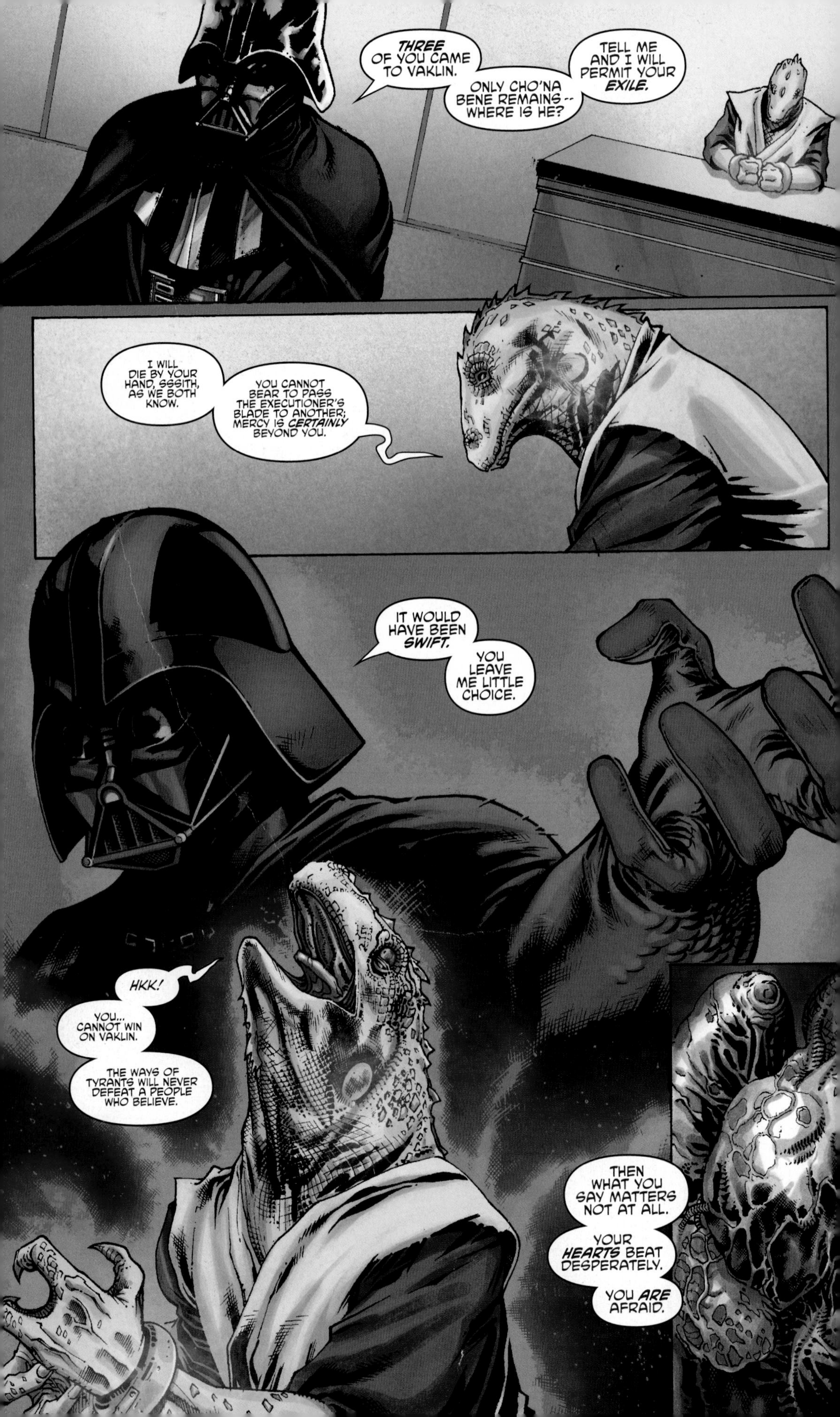
THREE OF YOU CAME TO VAKLIN.
ONLY CHO'NA BENE REMAINS-- WHERE IS HE?
TELL ME AND I WILL PERMIT YOUR EXILE.
I WILL DIE BY YOUR HAND, SSSITH, AS WE BOTH KNOW.
YOU CANNOT BEAR TO PASS THE EXECUTIONER'S BLADE TO ANOTHER; MERCY IS CERTAINLY BEYOND YOU.
IT WOULD HAVE BEEN SWIFT.
YOU LEAVE ME LITTLE CHOICE.
HKK!
YOU... CANNOT WIN ON VAKLIN.
THE WAYS OF TYRANTS WILL NEVER DEFEAT A PEOPLE WHO BELIEVE.
THEN WHAT YOU SAY MATTERS NOT AT ALL.
YOUR HEARTS BEAT DESPERATELY.
YOU ARE AFRAID.

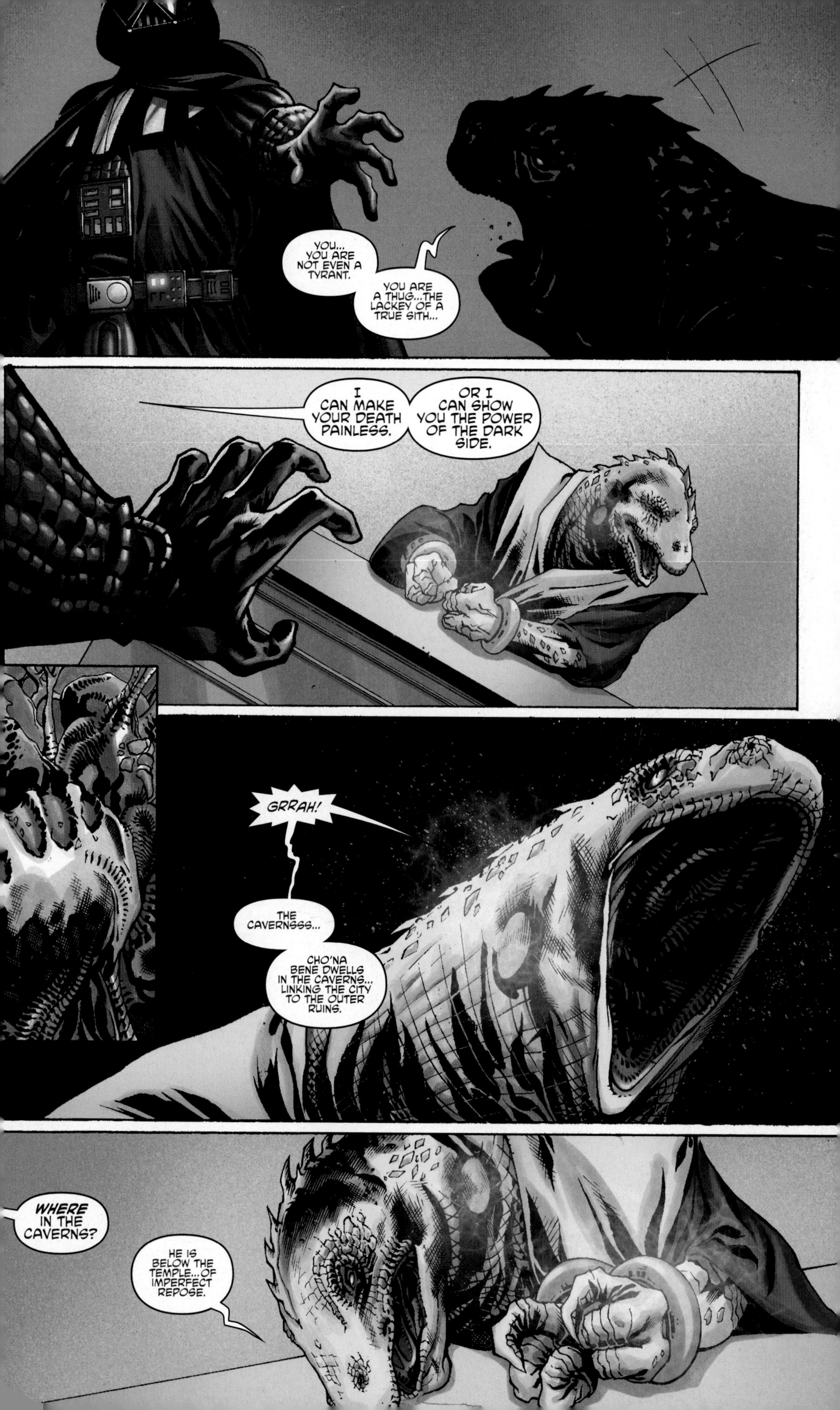
YOU... YOU ARE NOT EVEN A TYRANT.
YOU ARE A THUG...THE LACKEY OF A TRUE SITH...
I CAN MAKE YOUR DEATH PAINLESS.
OR I CAN SHOW YOU THE POWER OF THE DARK SIDE.
GRRAH!
THE CAVERNSSS...
CHO'NA BENE DWELLS IN THE CAVERNS... LINKING THE CITY TO THE OUTER RUINS.
WHERE IN THE CAVERNS?
HE IS BELOW THE TEMPLE...OF IMPERFECT REPOSE.

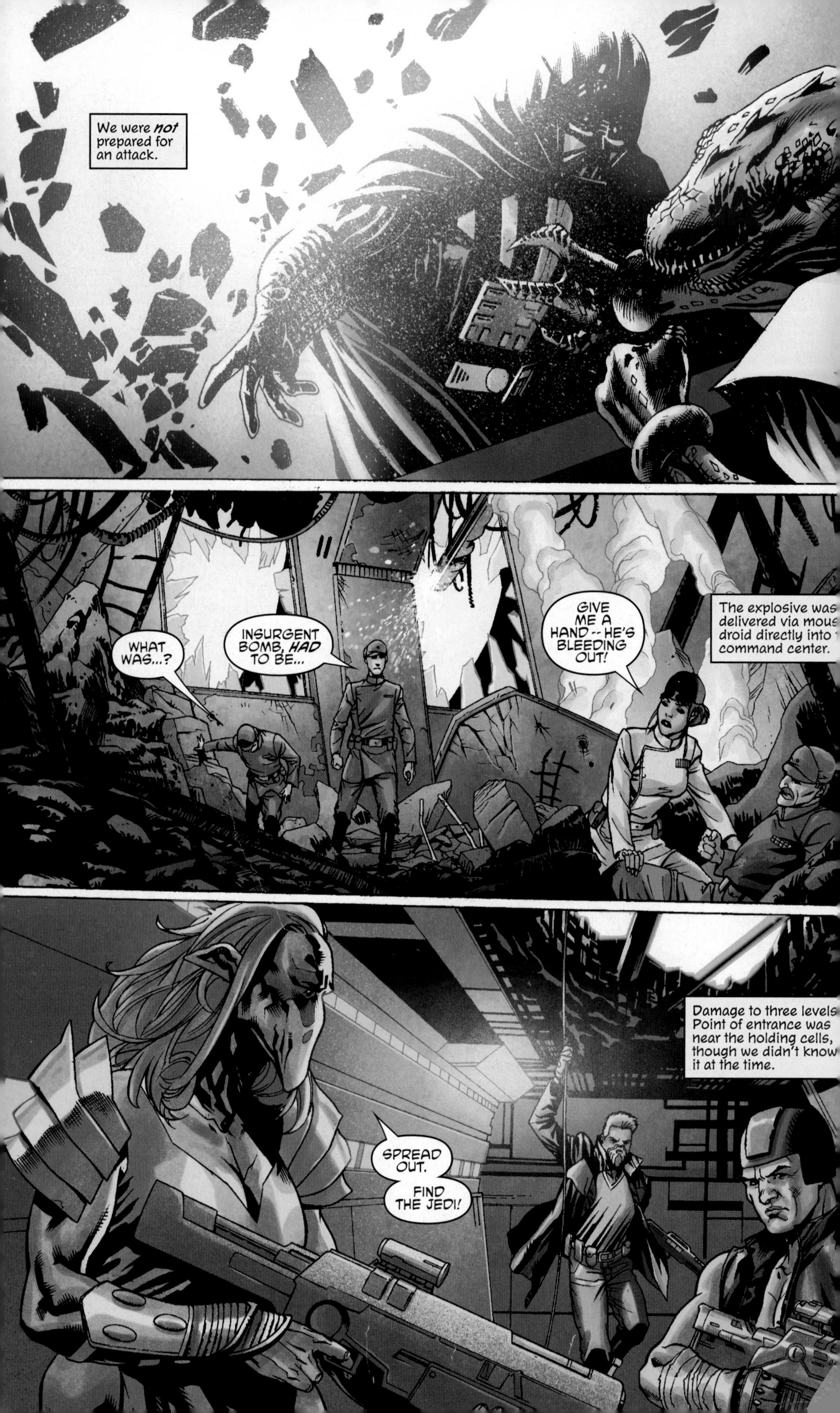

We were *not* prepared for an attack.
WHAT WAS...?
INSURGENT BOMB, *HAD* TO BE...
GIVE ME A HAND -- HE'S BLEEDING OUT!
The explosive was delivered via mous droid directly into command center.
Damage to three levels Point of entrance was near the holding cells, though we didn't know it at the time.
SPREAD OUT.
FIND THE JEDI!

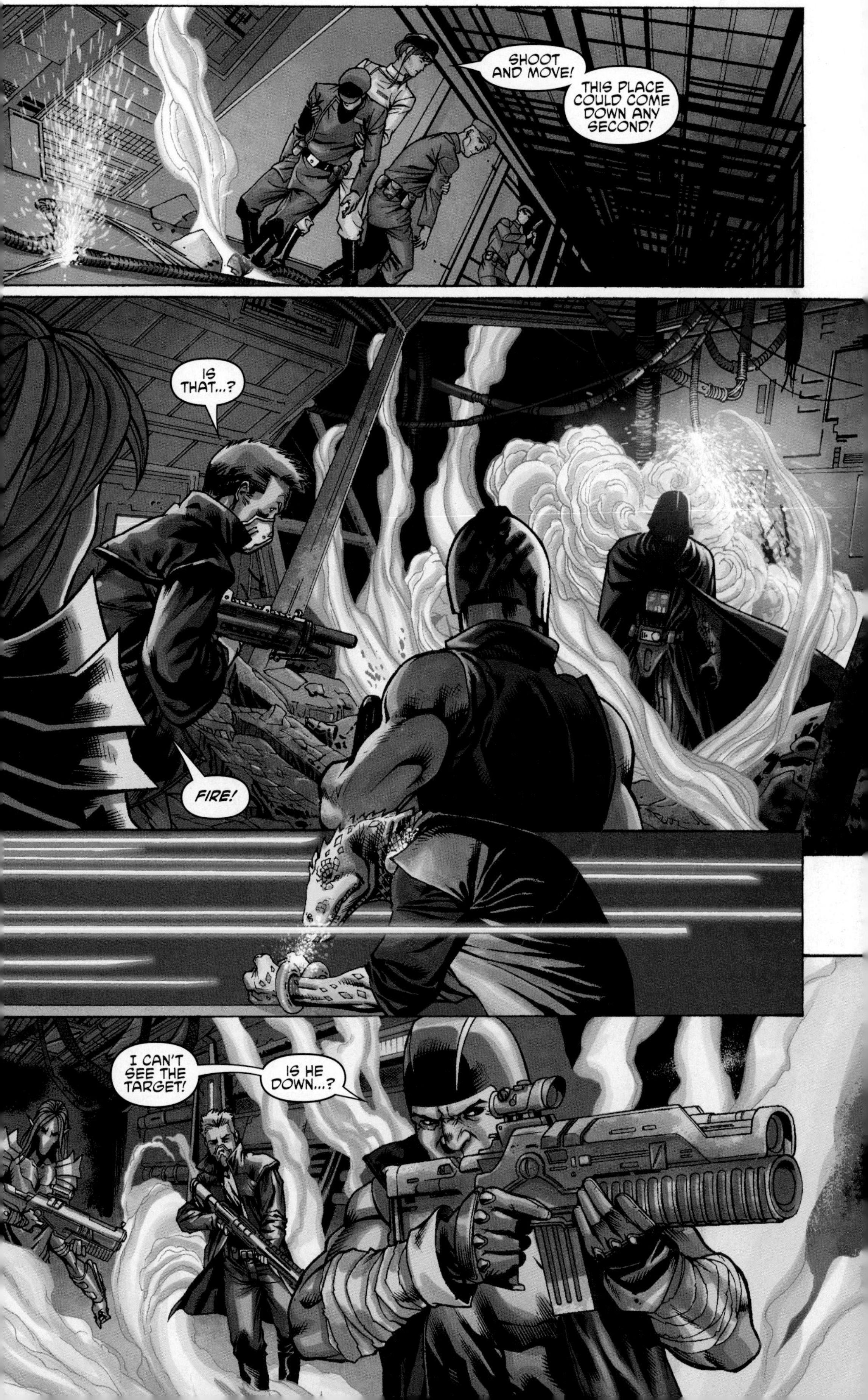
SHOOT AND MOVE!
THIS PLACE COULD COME DOWN ANY SECOND!
IS THAT...?
FIRE!
I CAN'T SEE THE TARGET!
IS HE DOWN...?

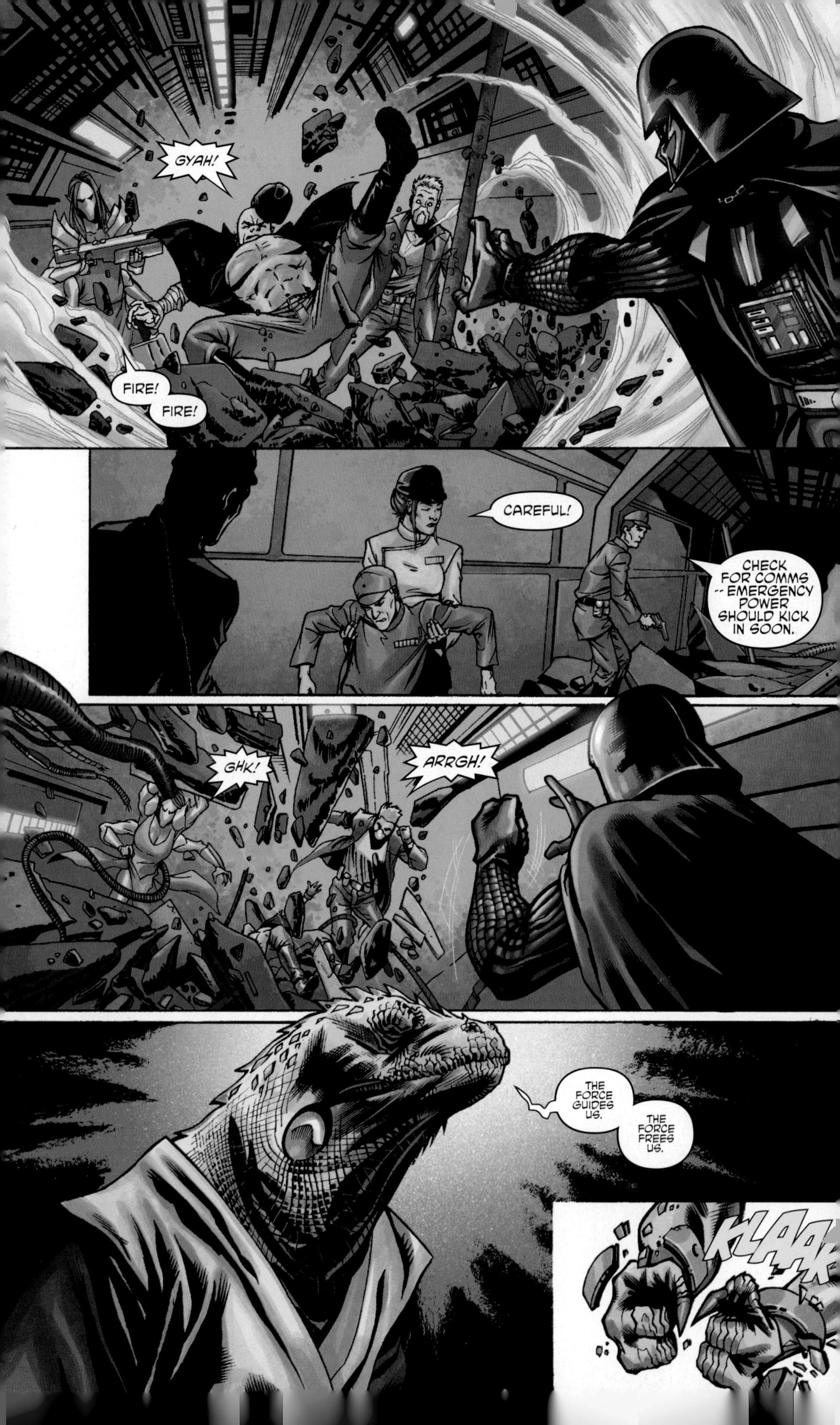
GYAH!
FIRE!
FIRE!
CAREFUL!
CHECK FOR COMMS -- EMERGENCY POWER SHOULD KICK IN SOON.
GHK!
ARRGH!
THE FORCE GUIDES US.
THE FORCE FREES US.

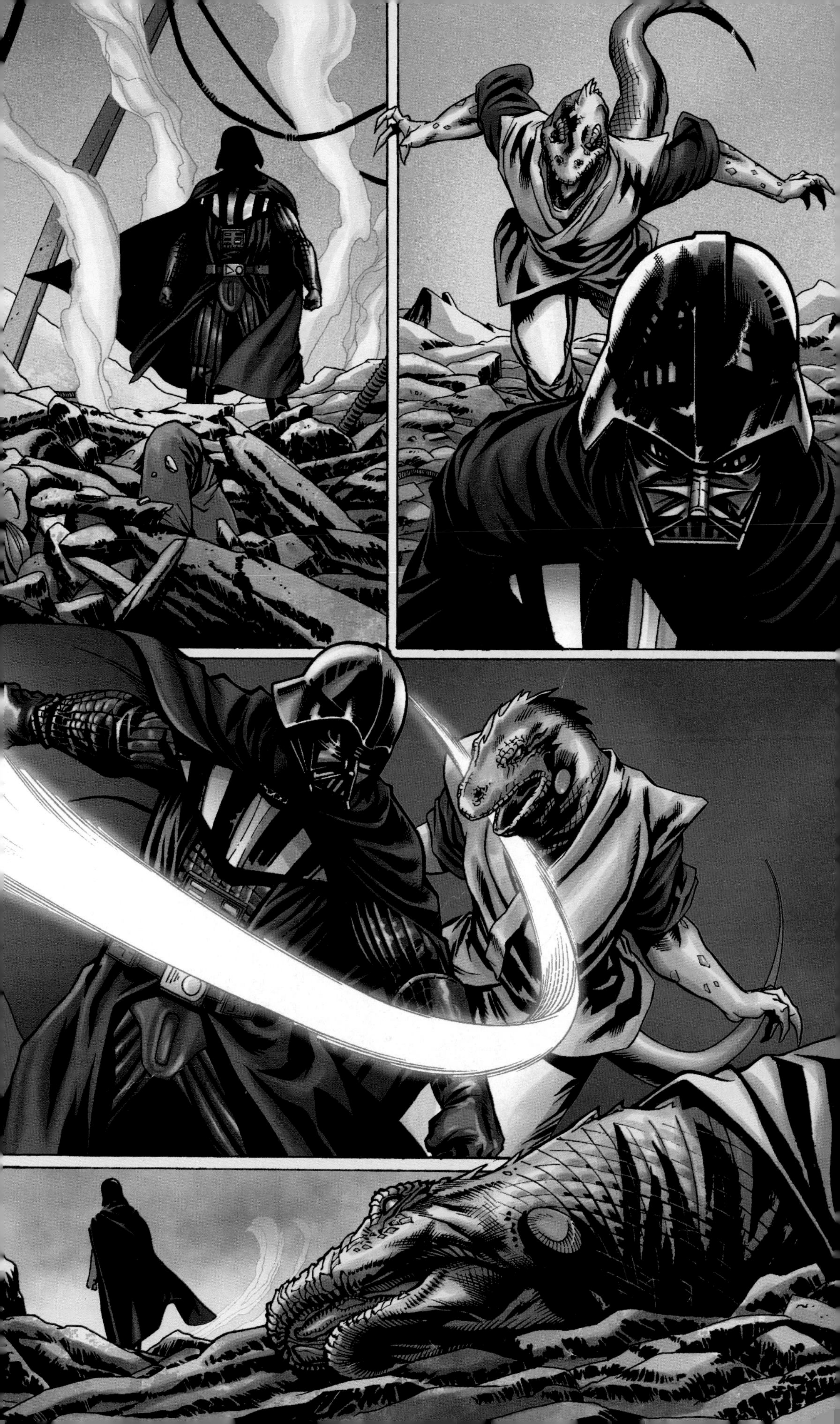

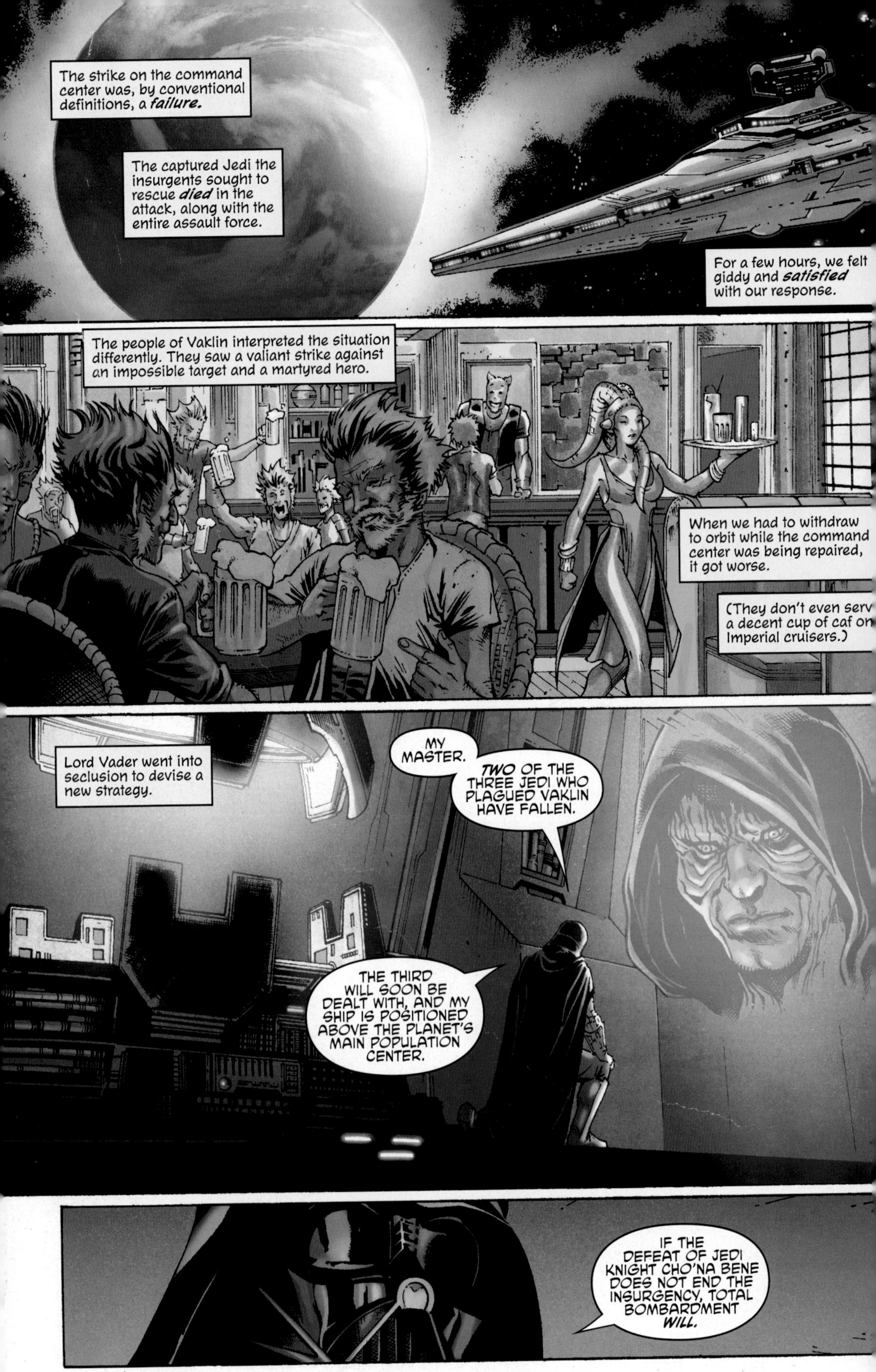
The strike on the command center was, by conventional definitions, a *failure.*
The captured Jedi the insurgents sought to rescue *died* in the attack, along with the entire assault force.
For a few hours, we felt giddy and *satisfied* with our response.
The people of Vaklin interpreted the situation differently. They saw a valiant strike against an impossible target and a martyred hero.
When we had to withdraw to orbit while the command center was being repaired, it got worse.
(They don't even serv a decent cup of caf on Imperial cruisers.)
Lord Vader went into seclusion to devise a new strategy.
MY MASTER.
TWO OF THE THREE JEDI WHO PLAGUED VAKLIN HAVE FALLEN.
THE THIRD WILL SOON BE DEALT WITH, AND MY SHIP IS POSITIONED ABOVE THE PLANET'S MAIN POPULATION CENTER.
IF THE DEFEAT OF JEDI KNIGHT CHO'NA BENE DOES NOT END THE INSURGENCY, TOTAL BOMBARDMENT *WILL.*

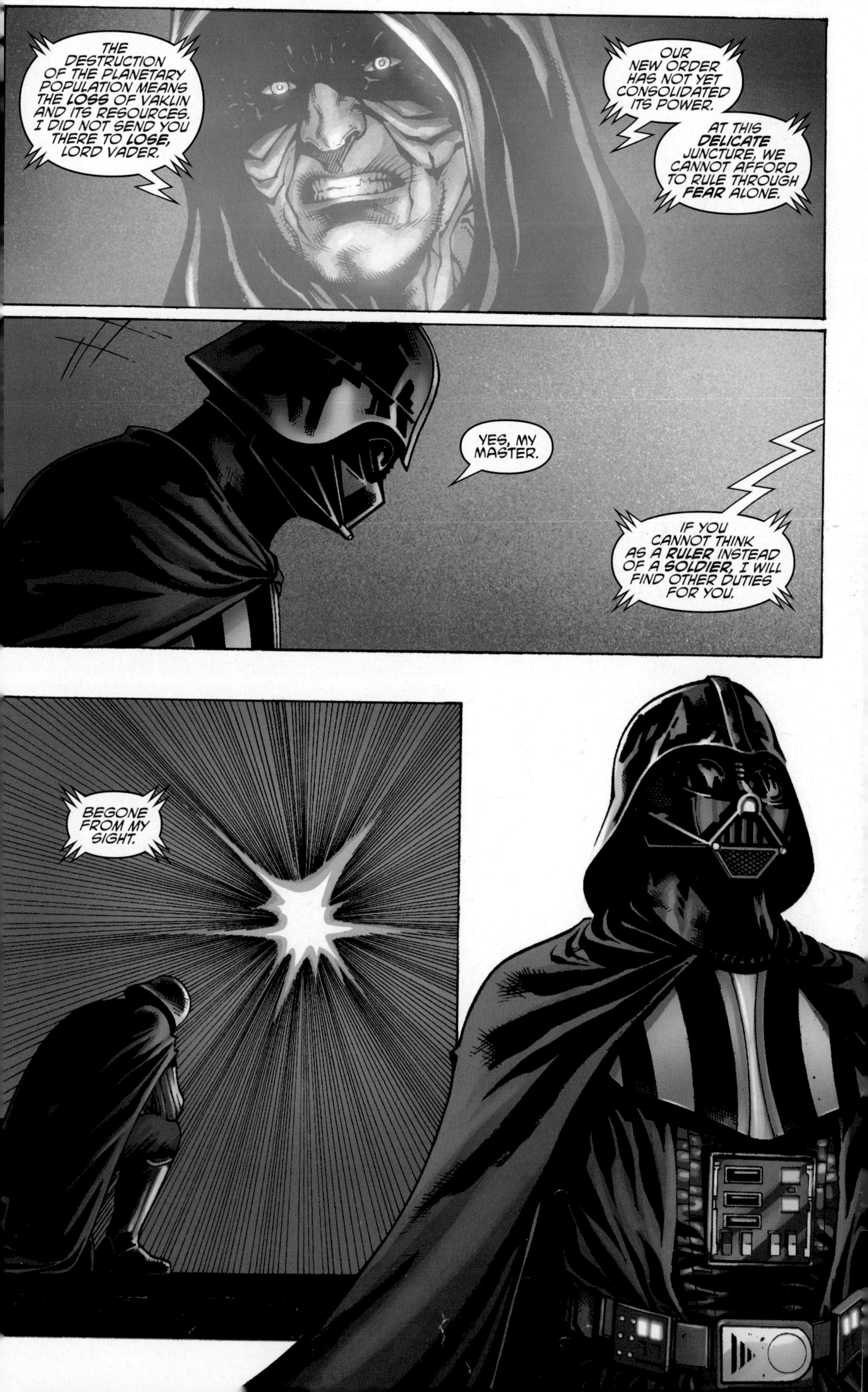
THE DESTRUCTION OF THE PLANETARY POPULATION MEANS THE LOSS OF VAKLIN AND ITS RESOURCES. I DID NOT SEND YOU THERE TO LOSE, LORD VADER.
OUR NEW ORDER HAS NOT YET CONSOLIDATED ITS POWER.
AT THIS DELICATE JUNCTURE, WE CANNOT AFFORD TO RULE THROUGH FEAR ALONE.
YES, MY MASTER.
IF YOU CANNOT THINK AS A RULER INSTEAD OF A SOLDIER, I WILL FIND OTHER DUTIES FOR YOU.
BEGONE FROM MY SIGHT.

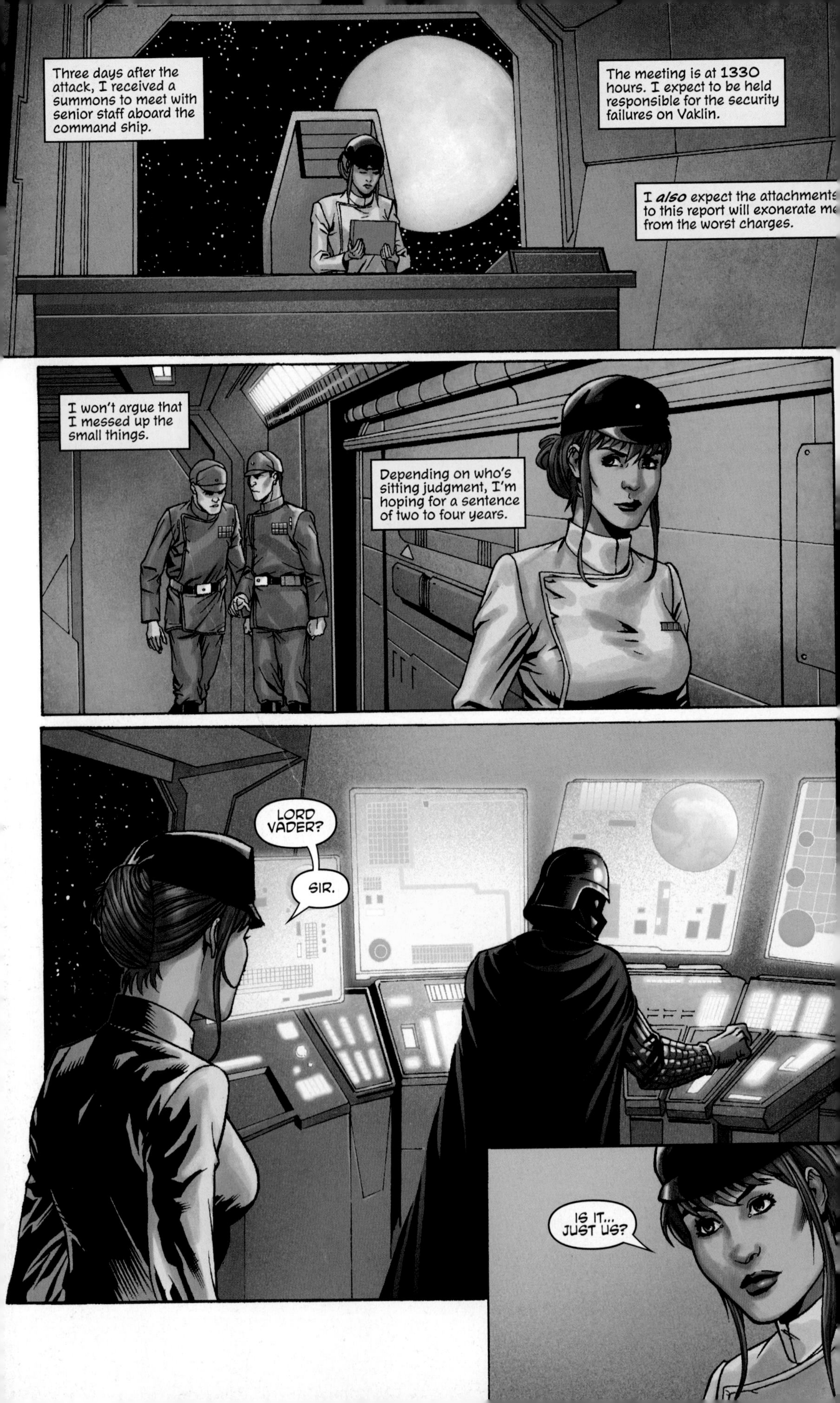
Three days after the attack, I received a summons to meet with senior staff aboard the command ship.
The meeting is at 1330 hours. I expect to be held responsible for the security failures on Vaklin.
I *also* expect the attachments to this report will exonerate me from the worst charges.
I won't argue that I messed up the small things.
Depending on who's sitting judgment, I'm hoping for a sentence of two to four years.
LORD VADER?
SIR.
IS IT... JUST US?

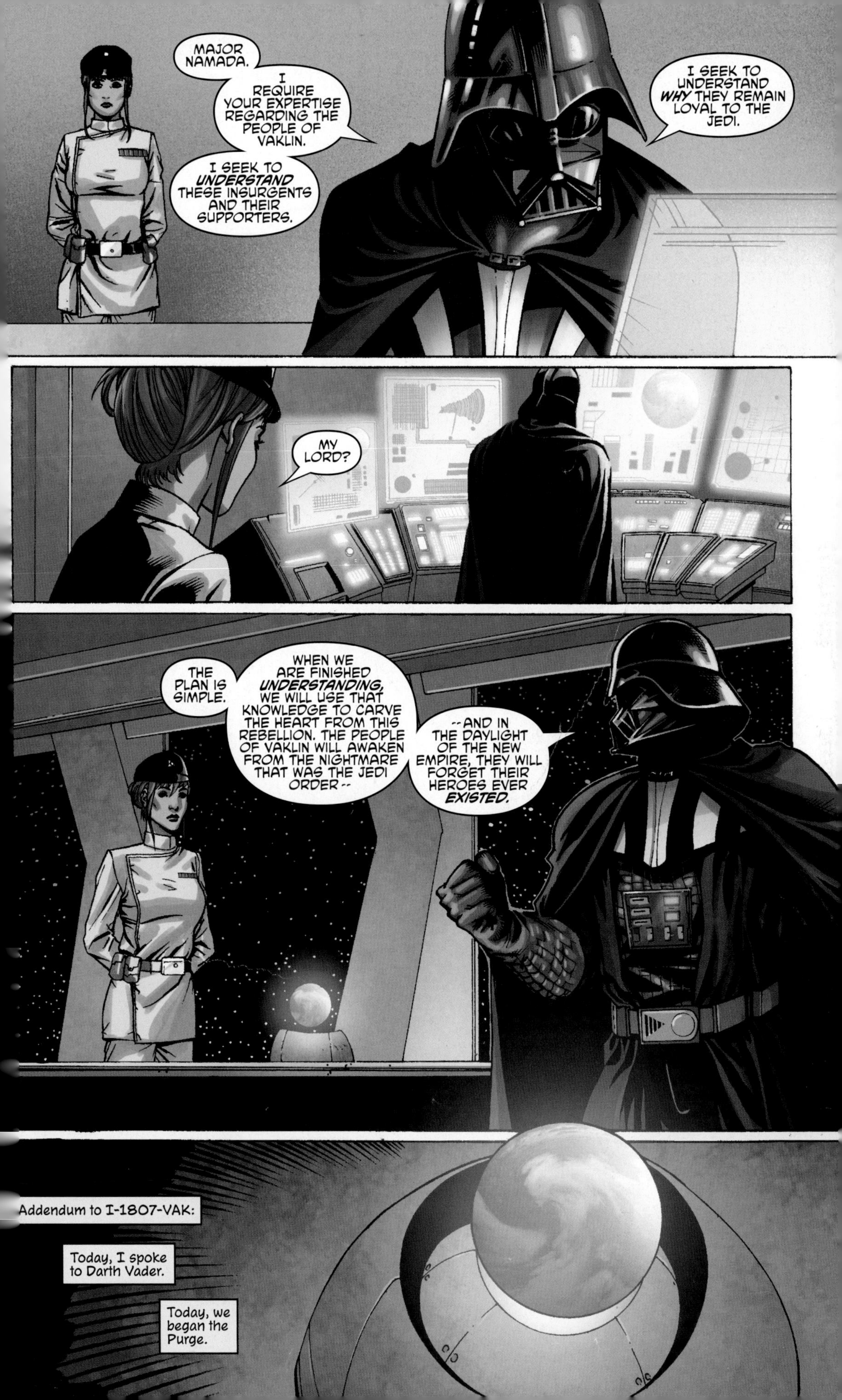

MAJOR NAMADA.
I REQUIRE YOUR EXPERTISE REGARDING THE PEOPLE OF VAKLIN.
I SEEK TO UNDERSTAND THESE INSURGENTS AND THEIR SUPPORTERS.
I SEEK TO UNDERSTAND WHY THEY REMAIN LOYAL TO THE JEDI.
MY LORD?
THE PLAN IS SIMPLE.
WHEN WE ARE FINISHED UNDERSTANDING, WE WILL USE THAT KNOWLEDGE TO CARVE THE HEART FROM THIS REBELLION. THE PEOPLE OF VAKLIN WILL AWAKEN FROM THE NIGHTMARE THAT WAS THE JEDI ORDER--
--AND IN THE DAYLIGHT OF THE NEW EMPIRE, THEY WILL FORGET THEIR HEROES EVER EXISTED.
Addendum to I-1807-VAK:
Today, I spoke to Darth Vader.
Today, we began the Purge.

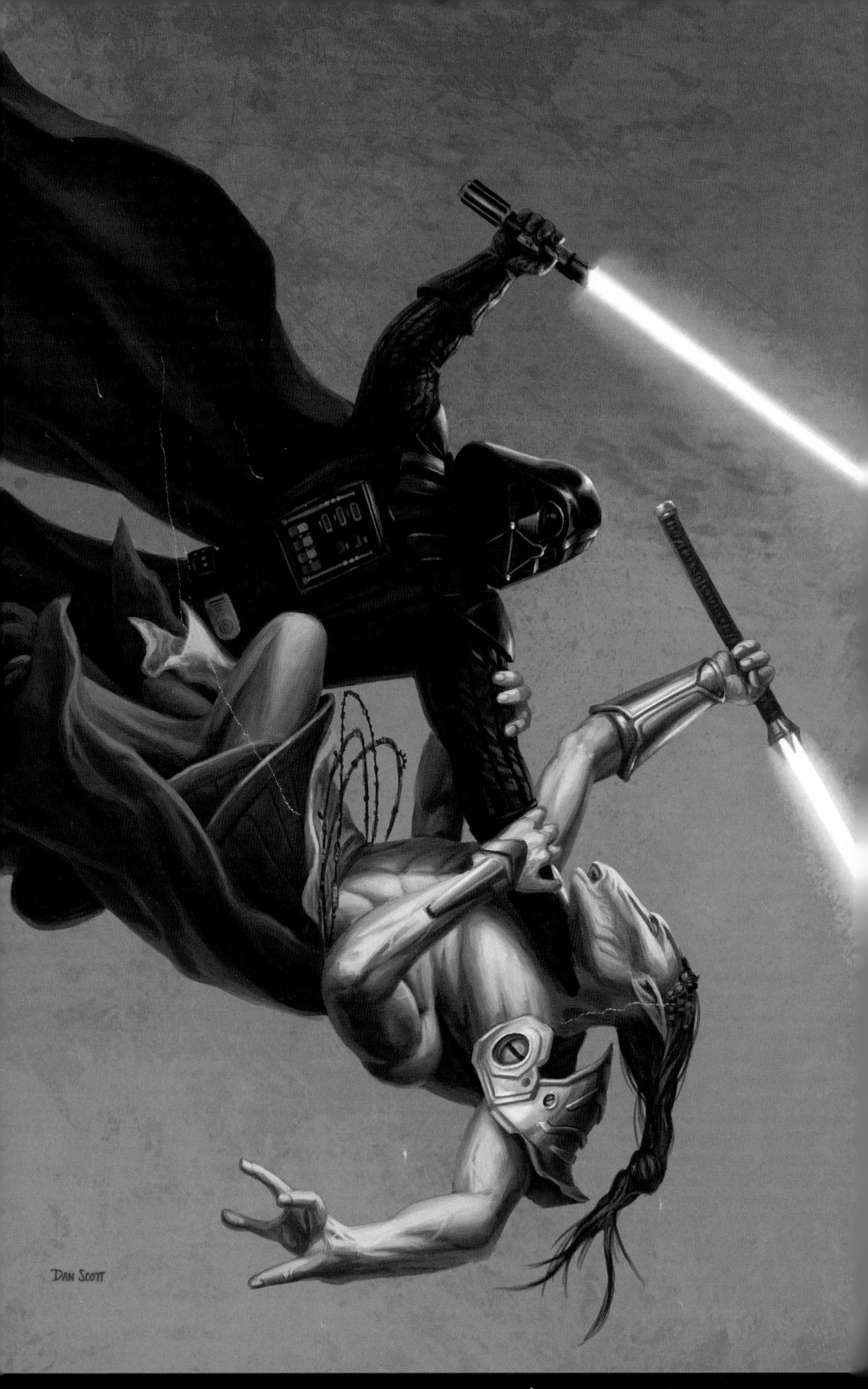
DAN SCOTT

STAR WARS: PURGE — THE TYRANT'S FIST #2

WRITER: ALEXANDER FREED • ARTISTS: MARCO CASTIELLO & ANDREA CHELLA • COLORIST: MICHAEL ATIYEH • LETTERER: MICHAEL HEISLER
DESIGNER: ALLYSON HALLER • ASSISTANT EDITOR: FREDDYE LINS • EDITOR: DAVE MARSHALL • COVER ARTIST: DAN SCOTT

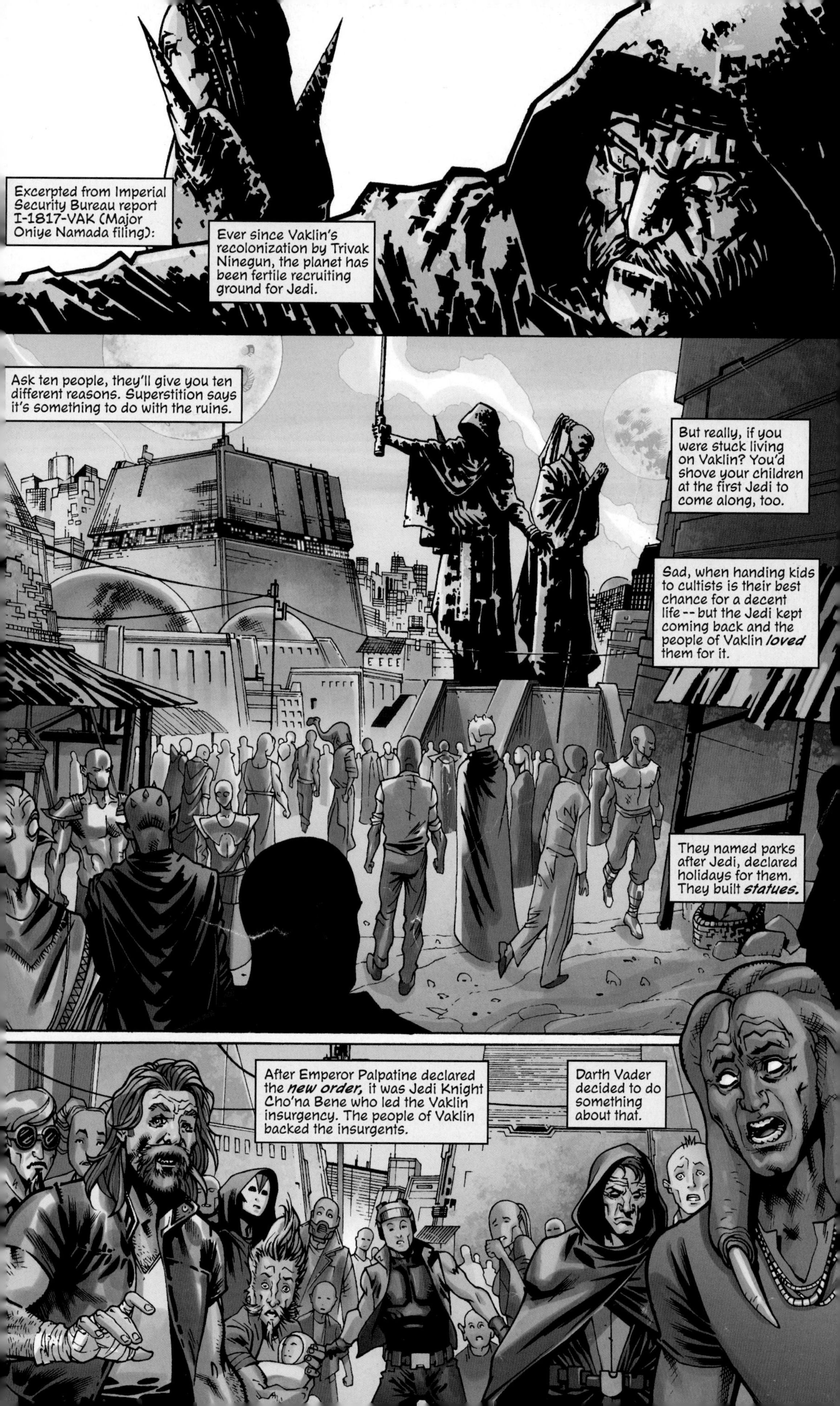
Excerpted from Imperial Security Bureau report I-1817-VAK (Major Oniye Namada filing):
Ever since Vaklin's recolonization by Trivak Ninegun, the planet has been fertile recruiting ground for Jedi.
Ask ten people, they'll give you ten different reasons. Superstition says it's something to do with the ruins.
But really, if you were stuck living on Vaklin? You'd shove your children at the first Jedi to come along, too.
Sad, when handing kids to cultists is their best chance for a decent life -- but the Jedi kept coming back and the people of Vaklin *loved* them for it.
They named parks after Jedi, declared holidays for them. They built ***statues.***
After Emperor Palpatine declared the ***new order,*** it was Jedi Knight Cho'na Bene who led the Vaklin insurgency. The people of Vaklin backed the insurgents.
Darth Vader decided to do something about that.

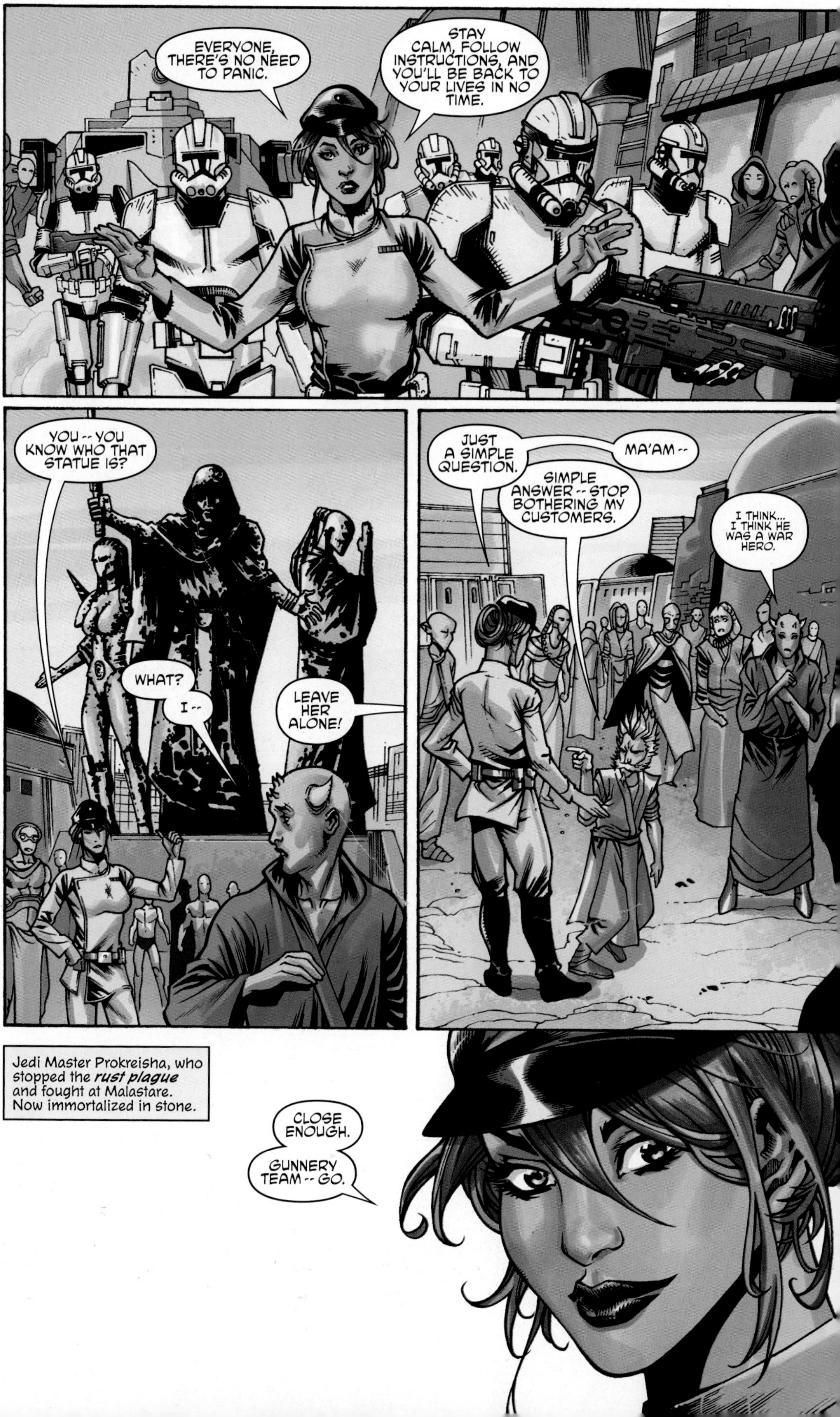
EVERYONE, THERE'S NO NEED TO PANIC.
STAY CALM, FOLLOW INSTRUCTIONS, AND YOU'LL BE BACK TO YOUR LIVES IN NO TIME.
YOU -- YOU KNOW WHO THAT STATUE IS?
WHAT?
I --
LEAVE HER ALONE!
JUST A SIMPLE QUESTION.
MA'AM --
SIMPLE ANSWER -- STOP BOTHERING MY CUSTOMERS.
I THINK... I THINK HE WAS A WAR HERO.
Jedi Master Prokreisha, who stopped the ***rust plague*** and fought at Malastare. Now immortalized in stone.
CLOSE ENOUGH.
GUNNERY TEAM -- GO.

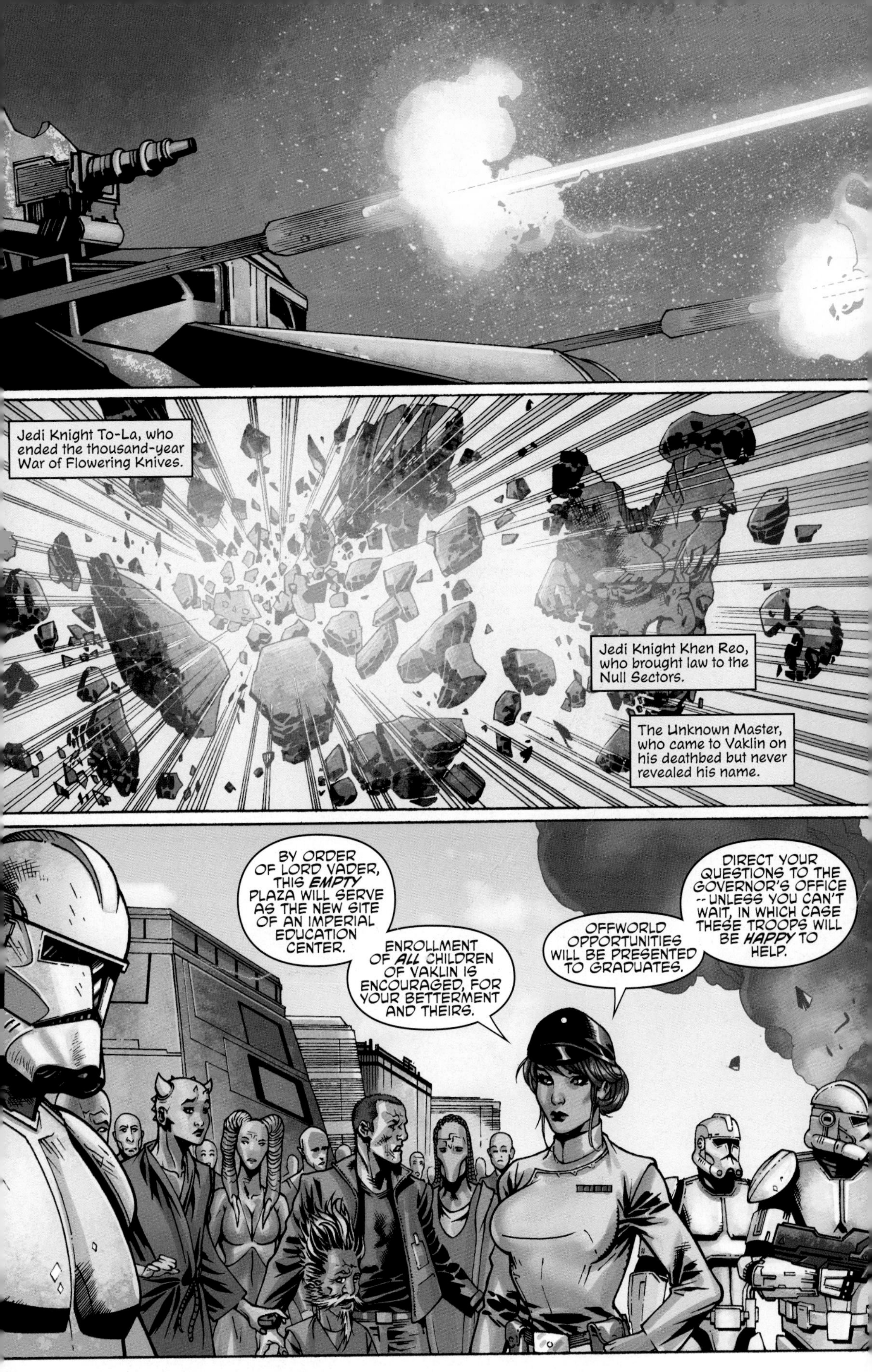
Jedi Knight To-La, who ended the thousand-year War of Flowering Knives.
Jedi Knight Khen Reo, who brought law to the Null Sectors.
The Unknown Master, who came to Vaklin on his deathbed but never revealed his name.
BY ORDER OF LORD VADER, THIS EMPTY PLAZA WILL SERVE AS THE NEW SITE OF AN IMPERIAL EDUCATION CENTER.
ENROLLMENT OF ALL CHILDREN OF VAKLIN IS ENCOURAGED, FOR YOUR BETTERMENT AND THEIRS.
OFFWORLD OPPORTUNITIES WILL BE PRESENTED TO GRADUATES.
DIRECT YOUR QUESTIONS TO THE GOVERNOR'S OFFICE -- UNLESS YOU CAN'T WAIT, IN WHICH CASE THESE TROOPS WILL BE HAPPY TO HELP.

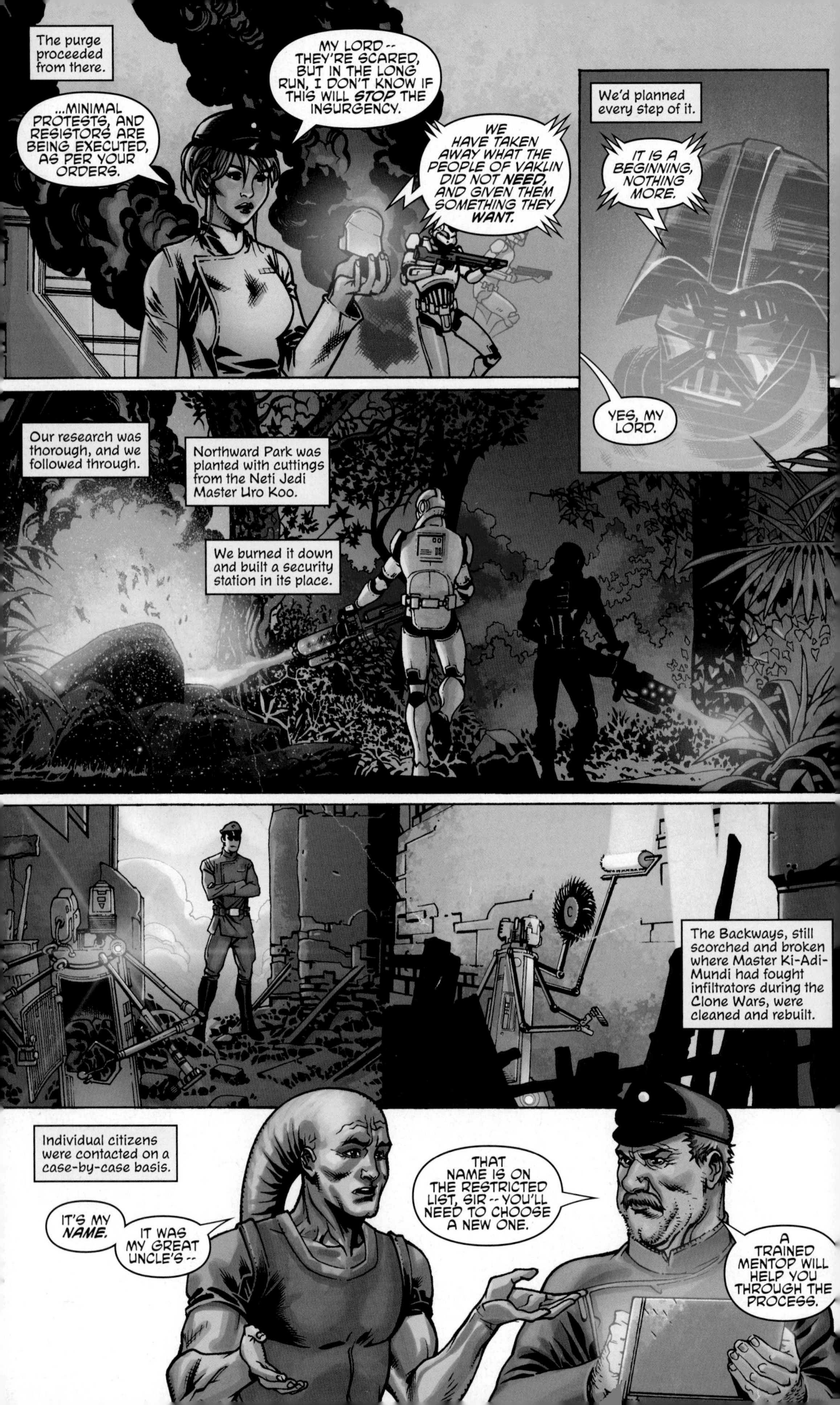

The purge proceeded from there.
...MINIMAL PROTESTS, AND RESISTORS ARE BEING EXECUTED, AS PER YOUR ORDERS.
MY LORD -- THEY'RE SCARED, BUT IN THE LONG RUN, I DON'T KNOW IF THIS WILL STOP THE INSURGENCY.
WE HAVE TAKEN AWAY WHAT THE PEOPLE OF VAKLIN DID NOT NEED, AND GIVEN THEM SOMETHING THEY WANT.
We'd planned every step of it.
IT IS A BEGINNING, NOTHING MORE.
YES, MY LORD.
Our research was thorough, and we followed through.
Northward Park was planted with cuttings from the Neti Jedi Master Uro Koo.
We burned it down and built a security station in its place.
The Backways, still scorched and broken where Master Ki-Adi-Mundi had fought infiltrators during the Clone Wars, were cleaned and rebuilt.
Individual citizens were contacted on a case-by-case basis.
IT'S MY NAME.
IT WAS MY GREAT UNCLE'S --
THAT NAME IS ON THE RESTRICTED LIST, SIR -- YOU'LL NEED TO CHOOSE A NEW ONE.
A TRAINED MENTOP WILL HELP YOU THROUGH THE PROCESS.

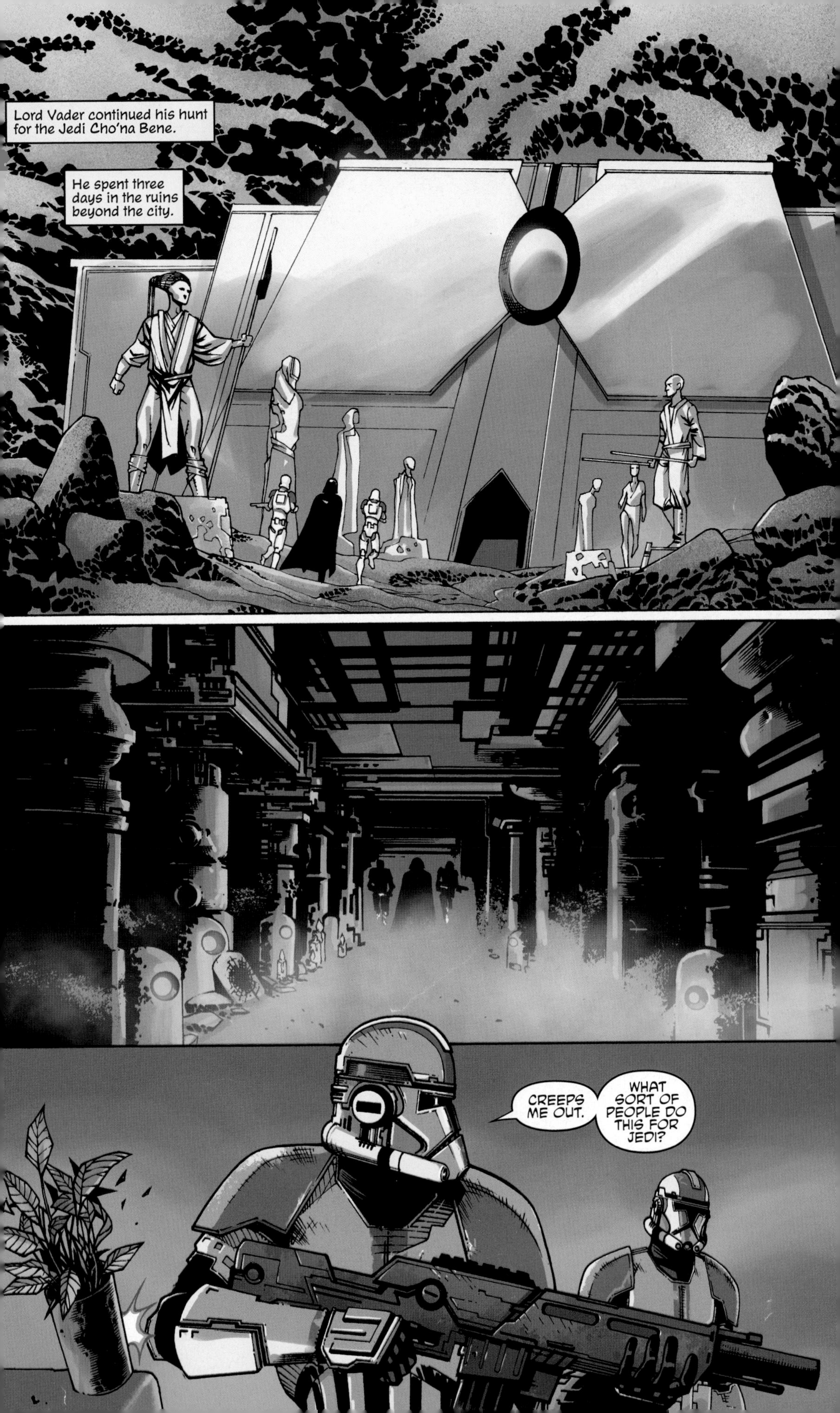
Lord Vader continued his hunt for the Jedi Cho'na Bene.
He spent three days in the ruins beyond the city.
CREEPS ME OUT.
WHAT SORT OF PEOPLE DO THIS FOR JEDI?

"THEY ARE CALLED *TUK'ATA NOBILIS*.

"THE GALAXY'S ONLY PAIR, *GIFTED* TO US THREE CENTURIES AGO.

"KANZHEI OPLI WAS TRULY THE *GREATEST* OF THE JEDI BEAST MASTERS."

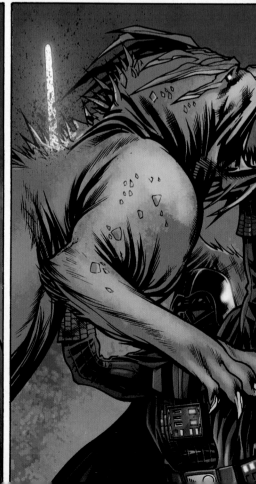

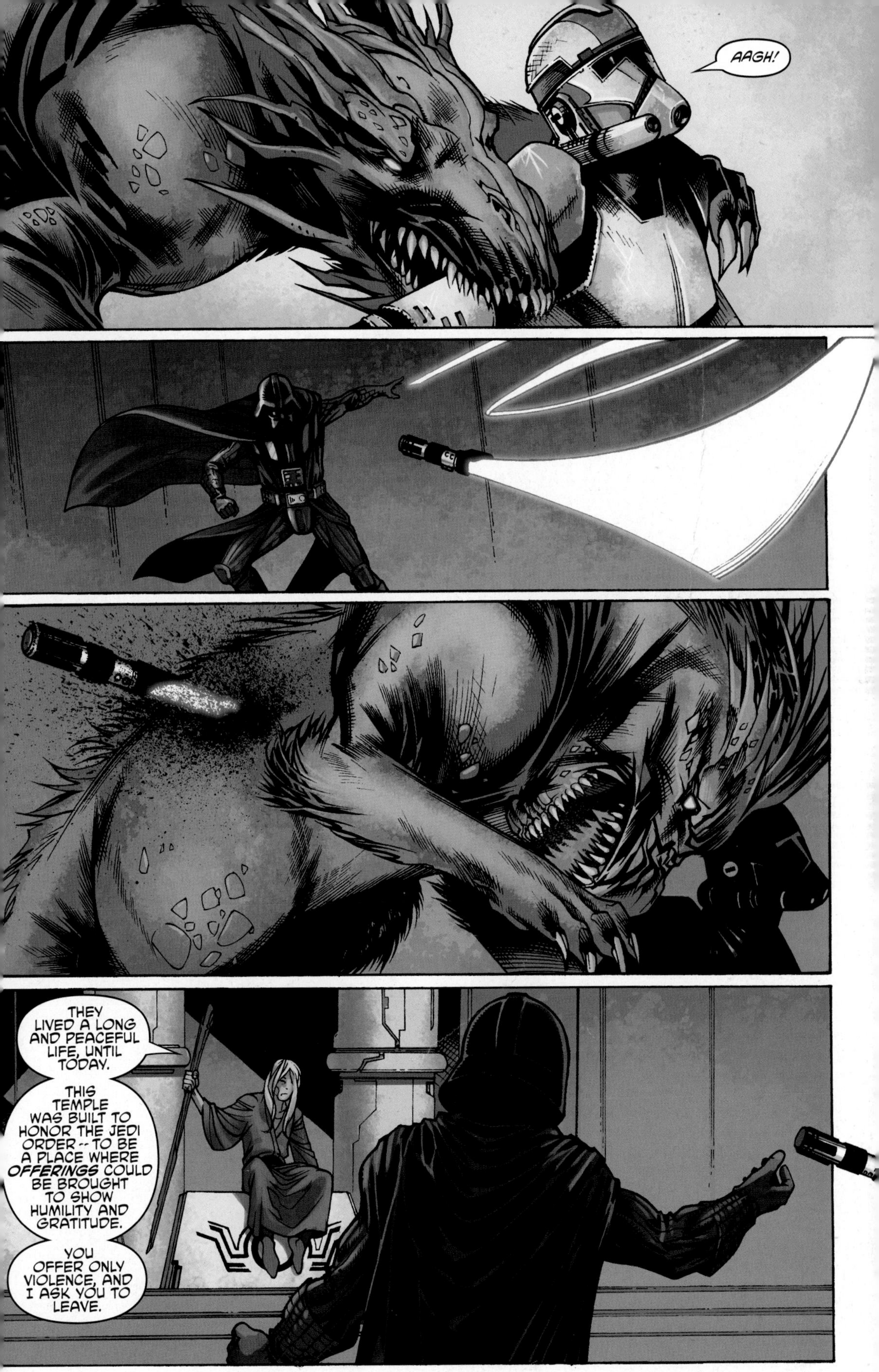
AAGH!
THEY LIVED A LONG AND PEACEFUL LIFE, UNTIL TODAY.
THIS TEMPLE WAS BUILT TO HONOR THE JEDI ORDER -- TO BE A PLACE WHERE OFFERINGS COULD BE BROUGHT TO SHOW HUMILITY AND GRATITUDE.
YOU OFFER ONLY VIOLENCE, AND I ASK YOU TO LEAVE.

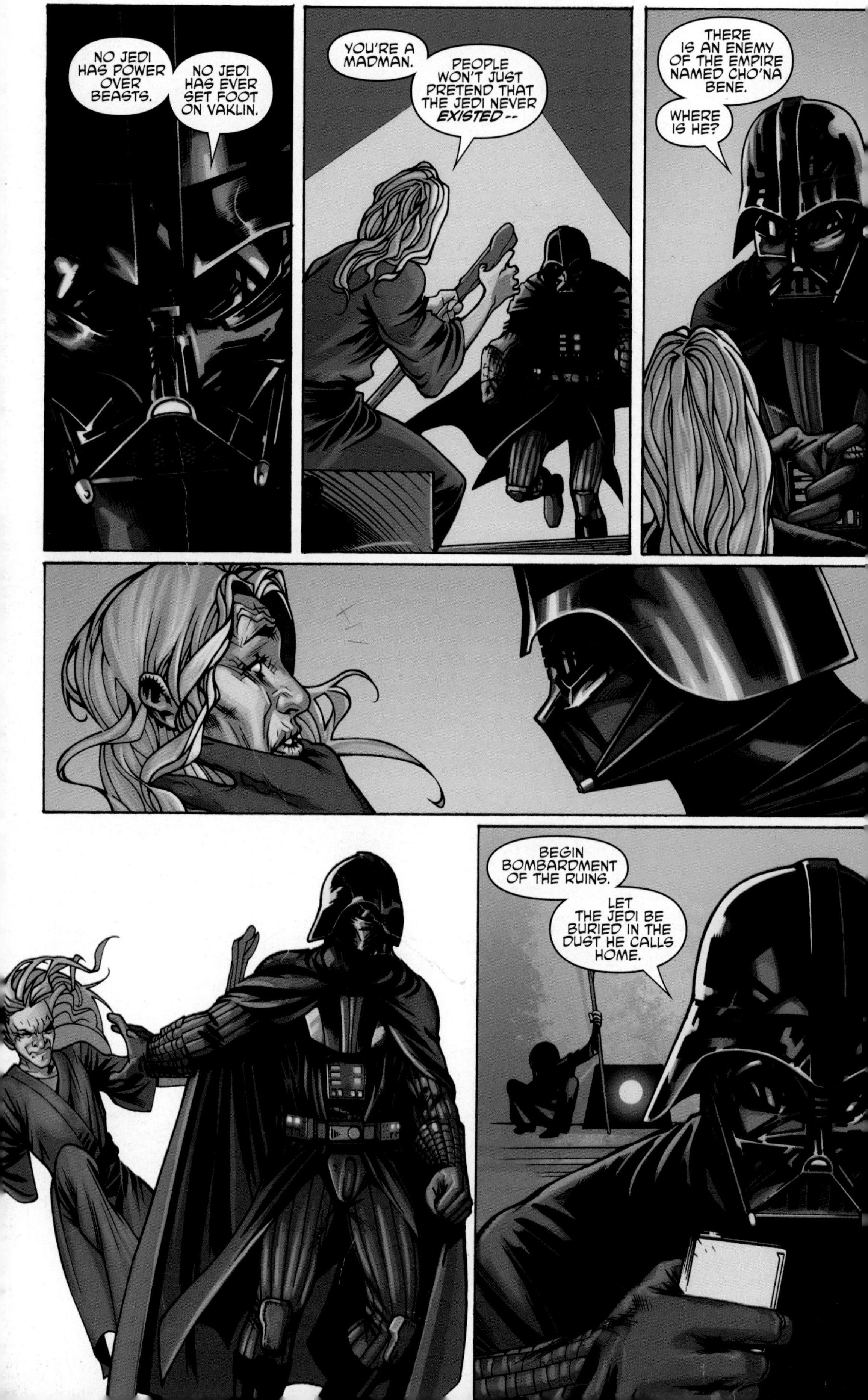
NO JEDI HAS POWER OVER BEASTS.
NO JEDI HAS EVER SET FOOT ON VAKLIN.
YOU'RE A MADMAN.
PEOPLE WON'T JUST PRETEND THAT THE JEDI NEVER *EXISTED* --
THERE IS AN ENEMY OF THE EMPIRE NAMED CHO'NA BENE.
WHERE IS HE?
BEGIN BOMBARDMENT OF THE RUINS.
LET THE JEDI BE BURIED IN THE DUST HE CALLS HOME.

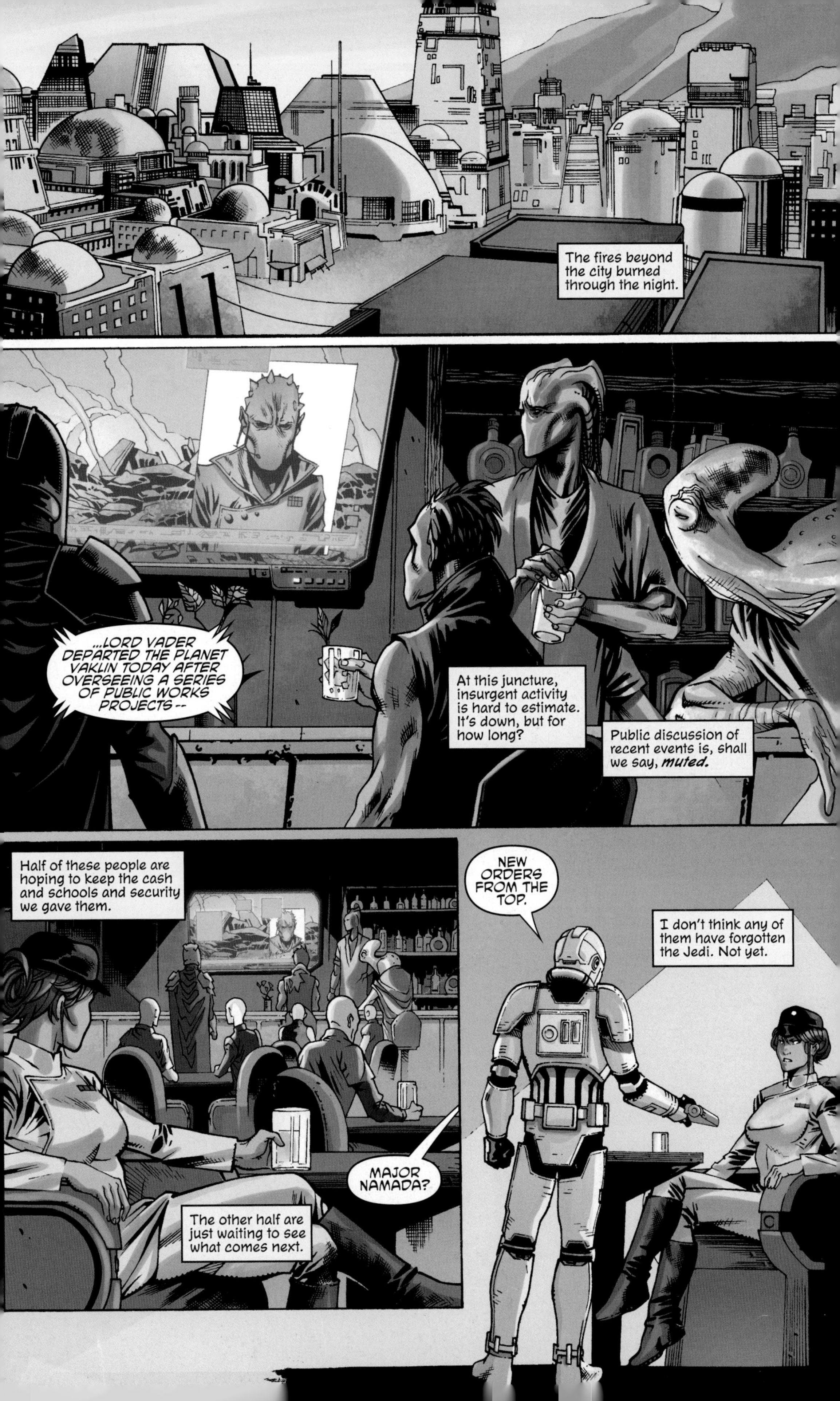
The fires beyond the city burned through the night.
...LORD VADER DEPARTED THE PLANET VAKLIN TODAY AFTER OVERSEEING A SERIES OF PUBLIC WORKS PROJECTS --
At this juncture, insurgent activity is hard to estimate. It's down, but for how long?
Public discussion of recent events is, shall we say, *muted.*
Half of these people are hoping to keep the cash and schools and security we gave them.
MAJOR NAMADA?
The other half are just waiting to see what comes next.
NEW ORDERS FROM THE TOP.
I don't think any of them have forgotten the Jedi. Not yet.

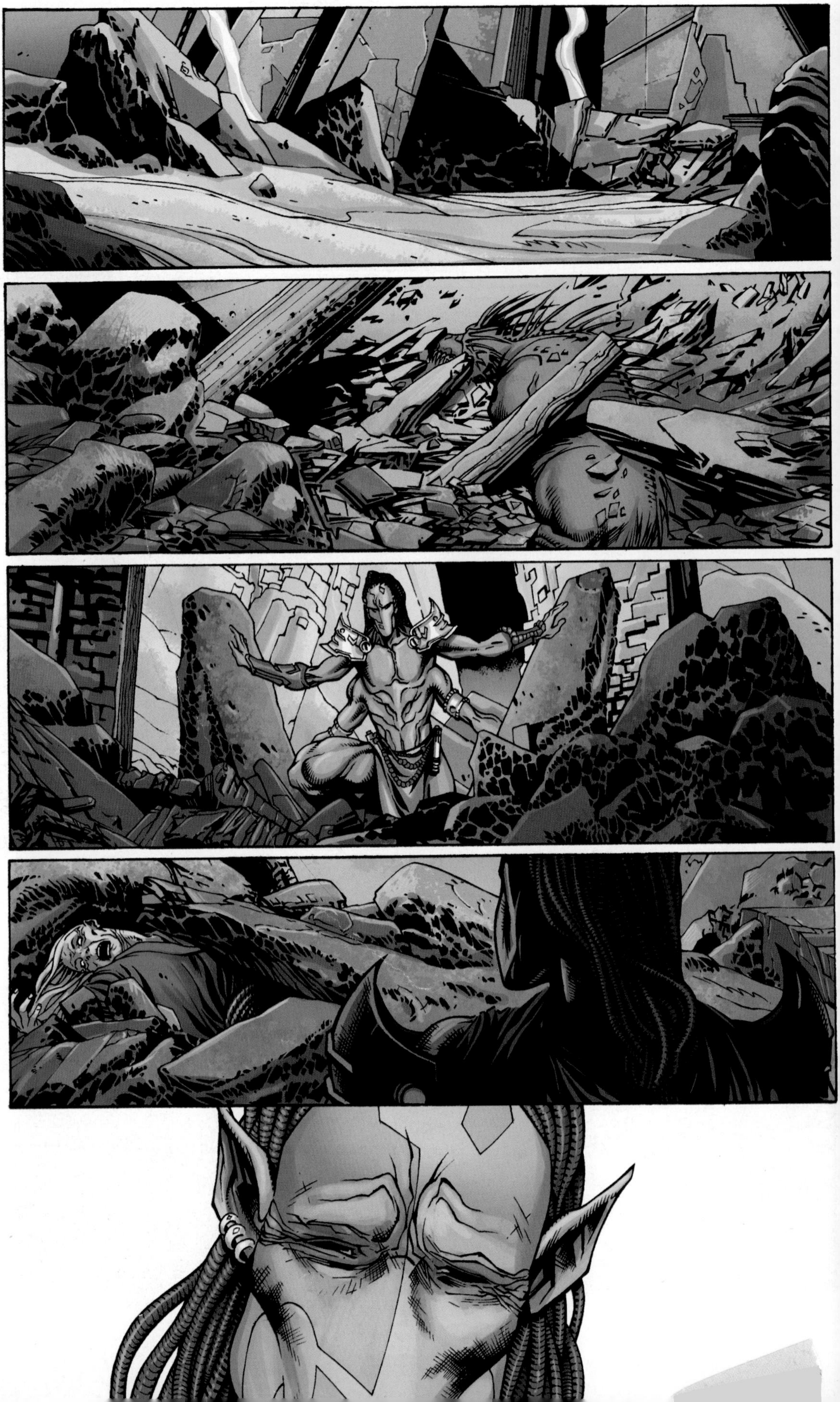

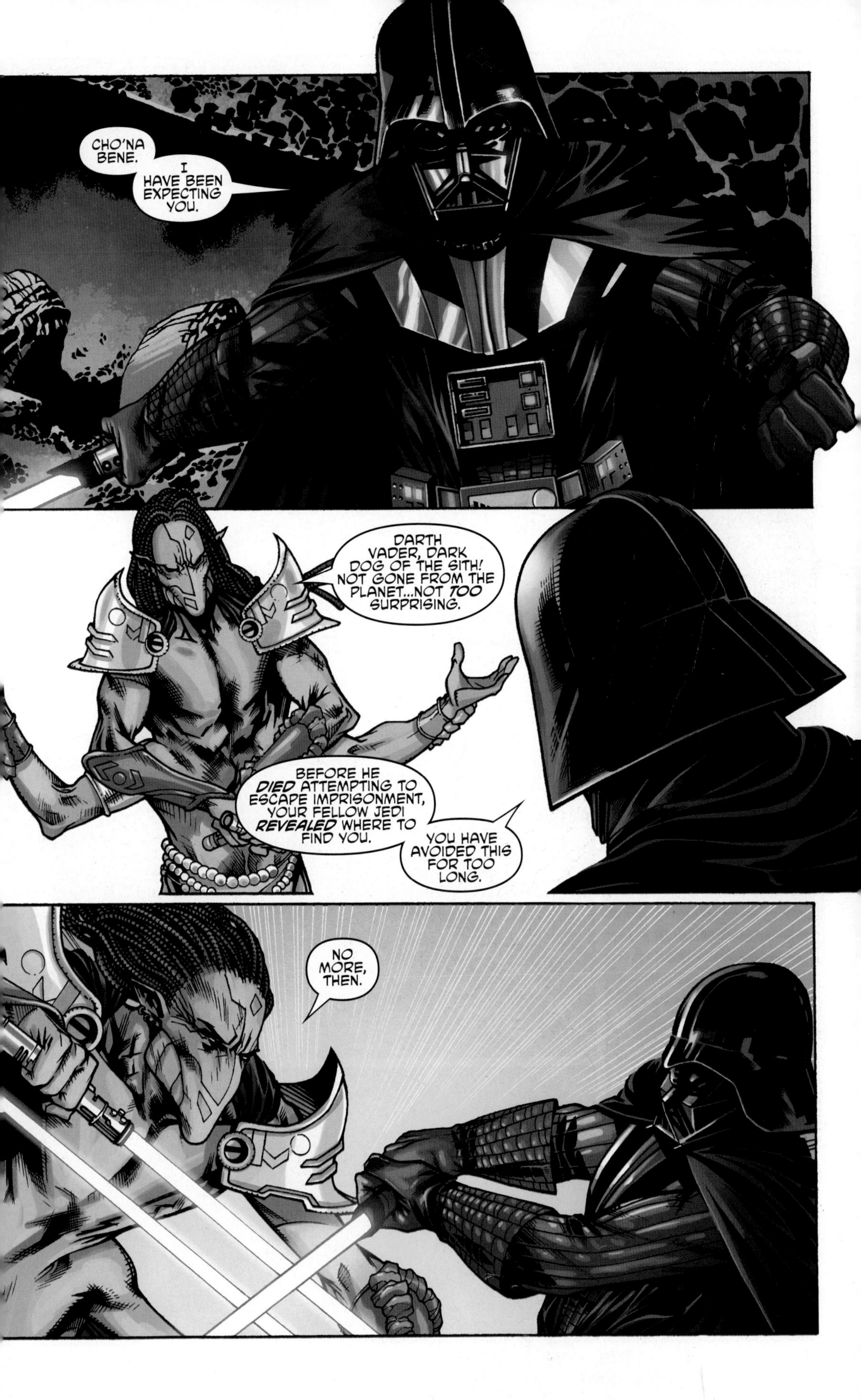
CHO'NA BENE.
I HAVE BEEN EXPECTING YOU.
DARTH VADER, DARK DOG OF THE SITH! NOT GONE FROM THE PLANET...NOT *TOO* SURPRISING.
BEFORE HE *DIED* ATTEMPTING TO ESCAPE IMPRISONMENT, YOUR FELLOW JEDI *REVEALED* WHERE TO FIND YOU.
YOU HAVE AVOIDED THIS FOR TOO LONG.
NO MORE, THEN.

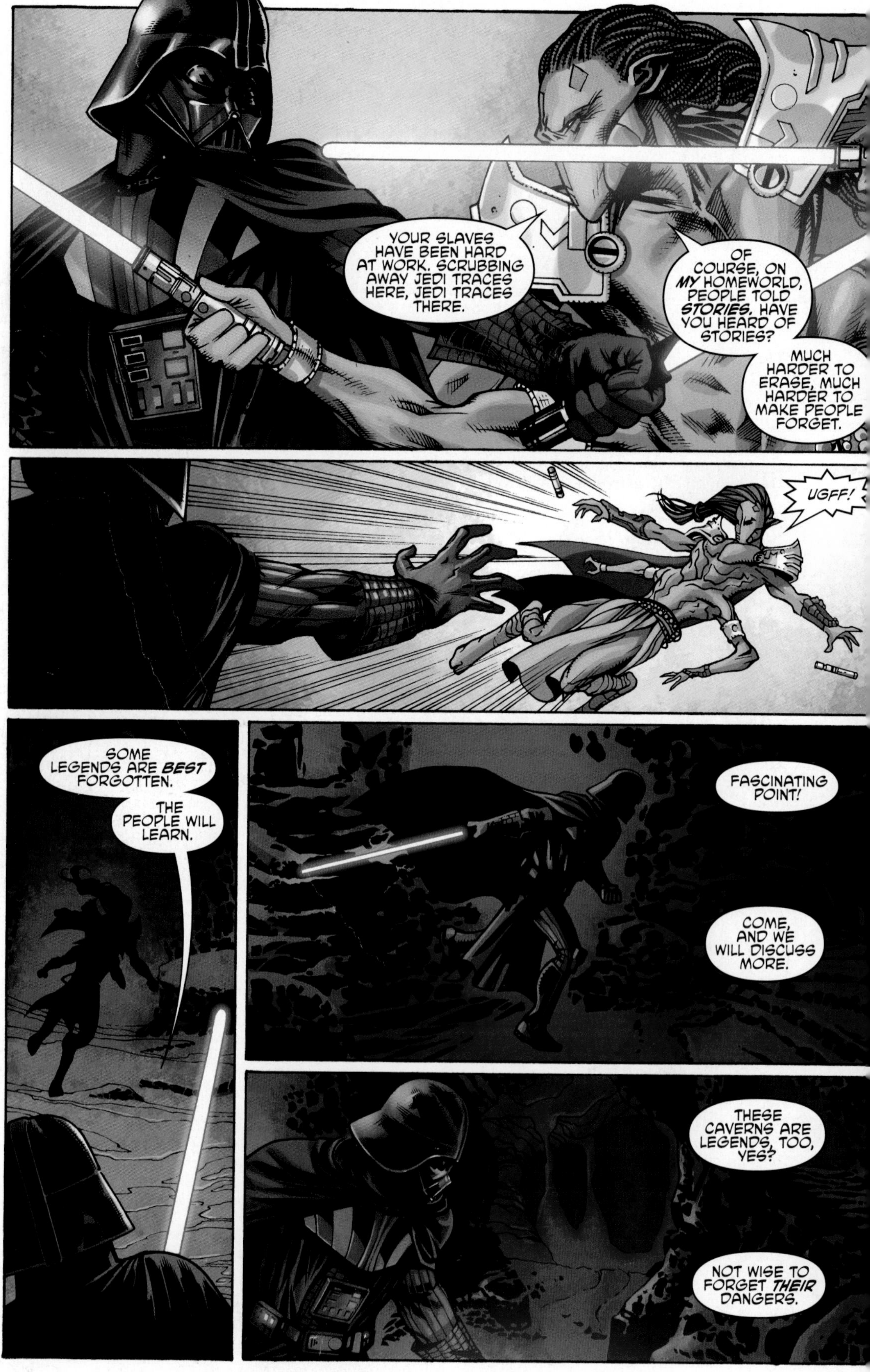
YOUR SLAVES HAVE BEEN HARD AT WORK. SCRUBBING AWAY JEDI TRACES HERE, JEDI TRACES THERE.
OF COURSE, ON *MY* HOMEWORLD, PEOPLE TOLD *STORIES*. HAVE YOU HEARD OF STORIES?
MUCH HARDER TO ERASE, MUCH HARDER TO MAKE PEOPLE FORGET.
UGFF!
SOME LEGENDS ARE *BEST* FORGOTTEN.
THE PEOPLE WILL LEARN.
FASCINATING POINT!
COME, AND WE WILL DISCUSS MORE.
THESE CAVERNS ARE LEGENDS, TOO, YES?
NOT WISE TO FORGET *THEIR* DANGERS.

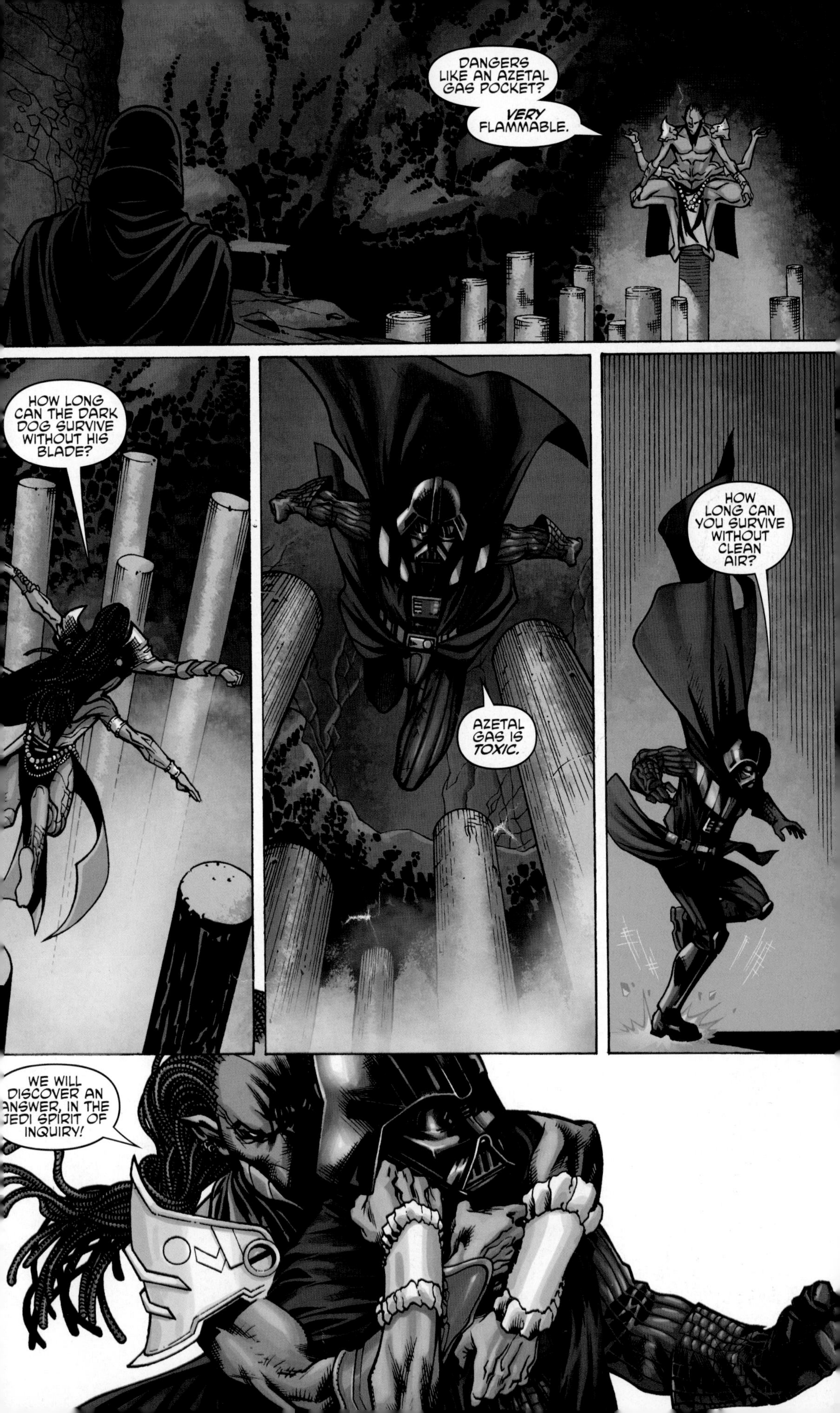
DANGERS LIKE AN AZETAL GAS POCKET?
VERY FLAMMABLE.
HOW LONG CAN THE DARK DOG SURVIVE WITHOUT HIS BLADE?
AZETAL GAS IS *TOXIC.*
HOW LONG CAN YOU SURVIVE WITHOUT CLEAN AIR?
WE WILL DISCOVER AN ANSWER, IN THE JEDI SPIRIT OF INQUIRY!

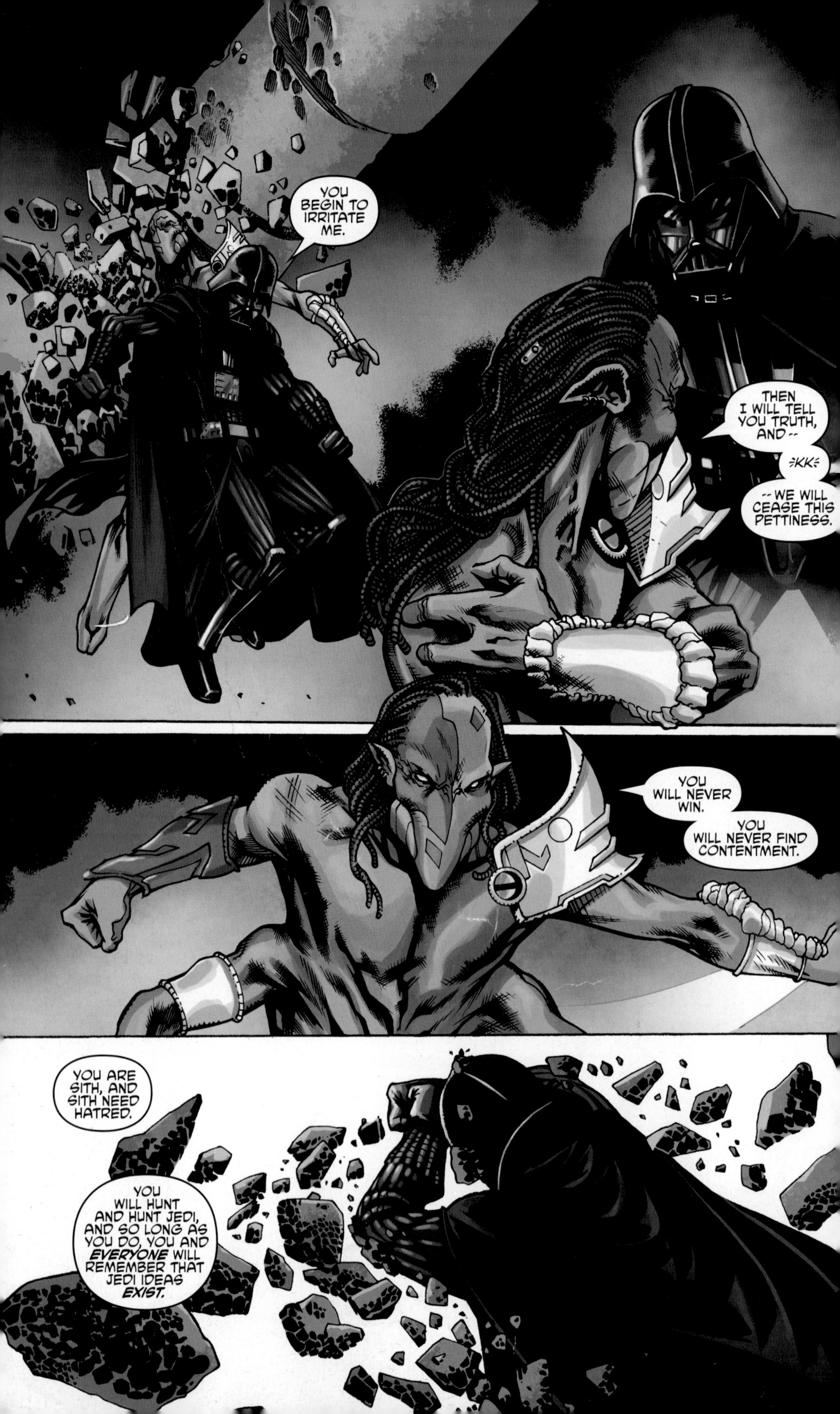
YOU BEGIN TO IRRITATE ME.
THEN I WILL TELL YOU TRUTH, AND--
KK
--WE WILL CEASE THIS PETTINESS.
YOU WILL NEVER WIN.
YOU WILL NEVER FIND CONTENTMENT.
YOU ARE SITH, AND SITH NEED HATRED.
YOU WILL HUNT AND HUNT JEDI, AND SO LONG AS YOU DO, YOU AND *EVERYONE* WILL REMEMBER THAT JEDI IDEAS *EXIST.*

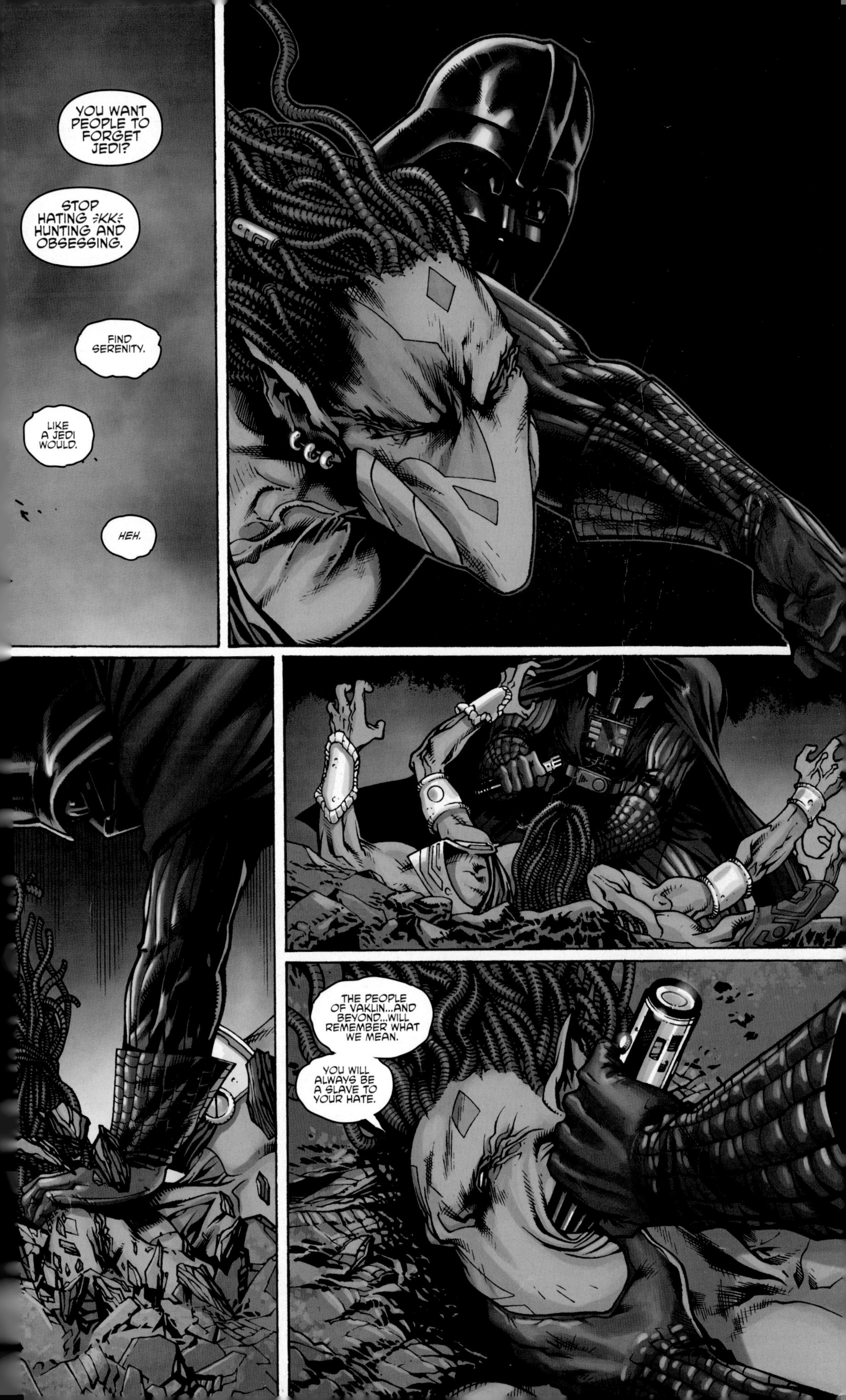
YOU WANT PEOPLE TO FORGET JEDI?
STOP HATING ≠KK≠ HUNTING AND OBSESSING.
FIND SERENITY.
LIKE A JEDI WOULD.
HEH.
THE PEOPLE OF VAKLIN...AND BEYOND...WILL REMEMBER WHAT WE MEAN.
YOU WILL ALWAYS BE A SLAVE TO YOUR HATE.

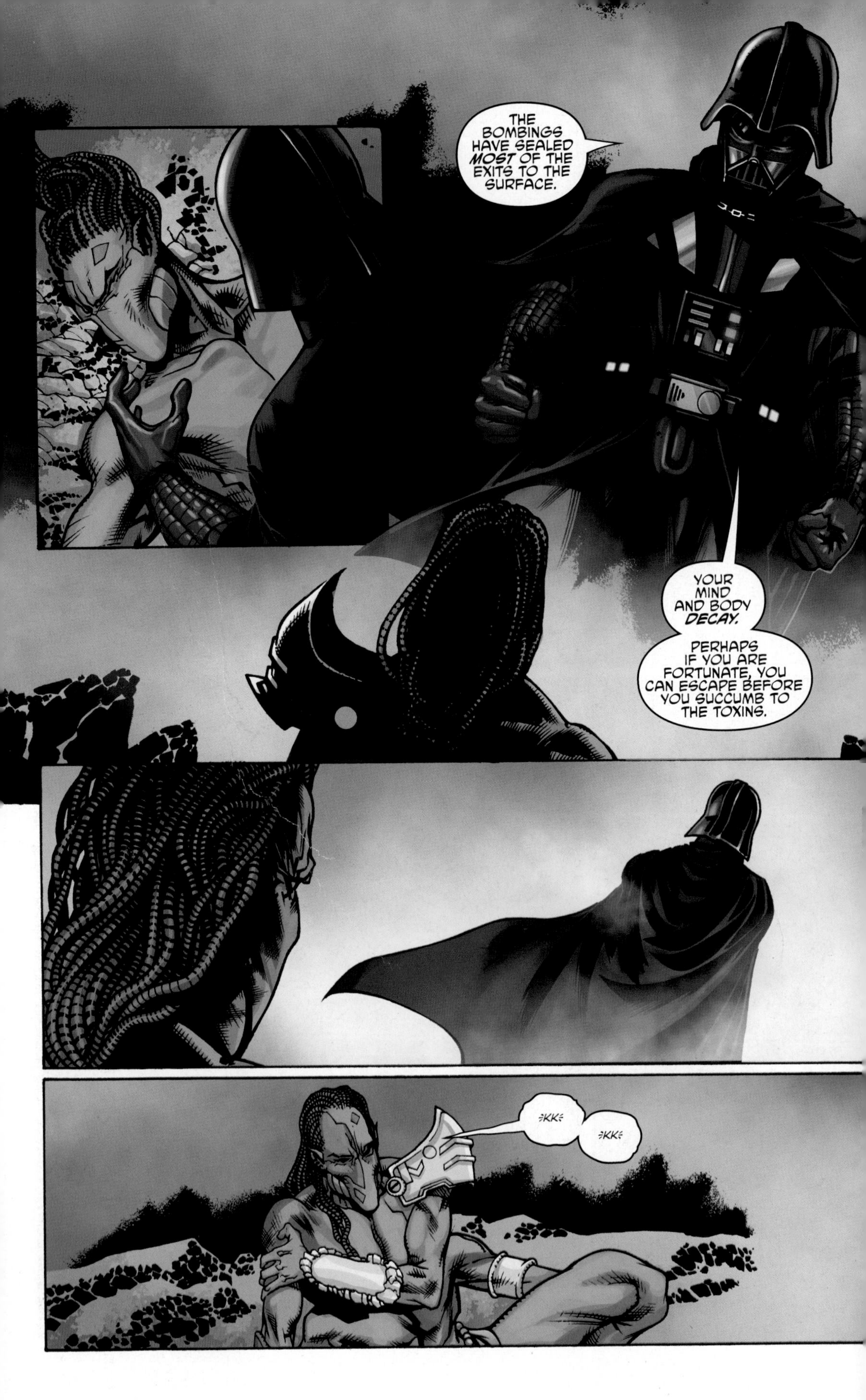
THE BOMBINGS HAVE SEALED *MOST* OF THE EXITS TO THE SURFACE.
YOUR MIND AND BODY *DECAY.*
PERHAPS IF YOU ARE FORTUNATE, YOU CAN ESCAPE BEFORE YOU SUCCUMB TO THE TOXINS.
KK
KK

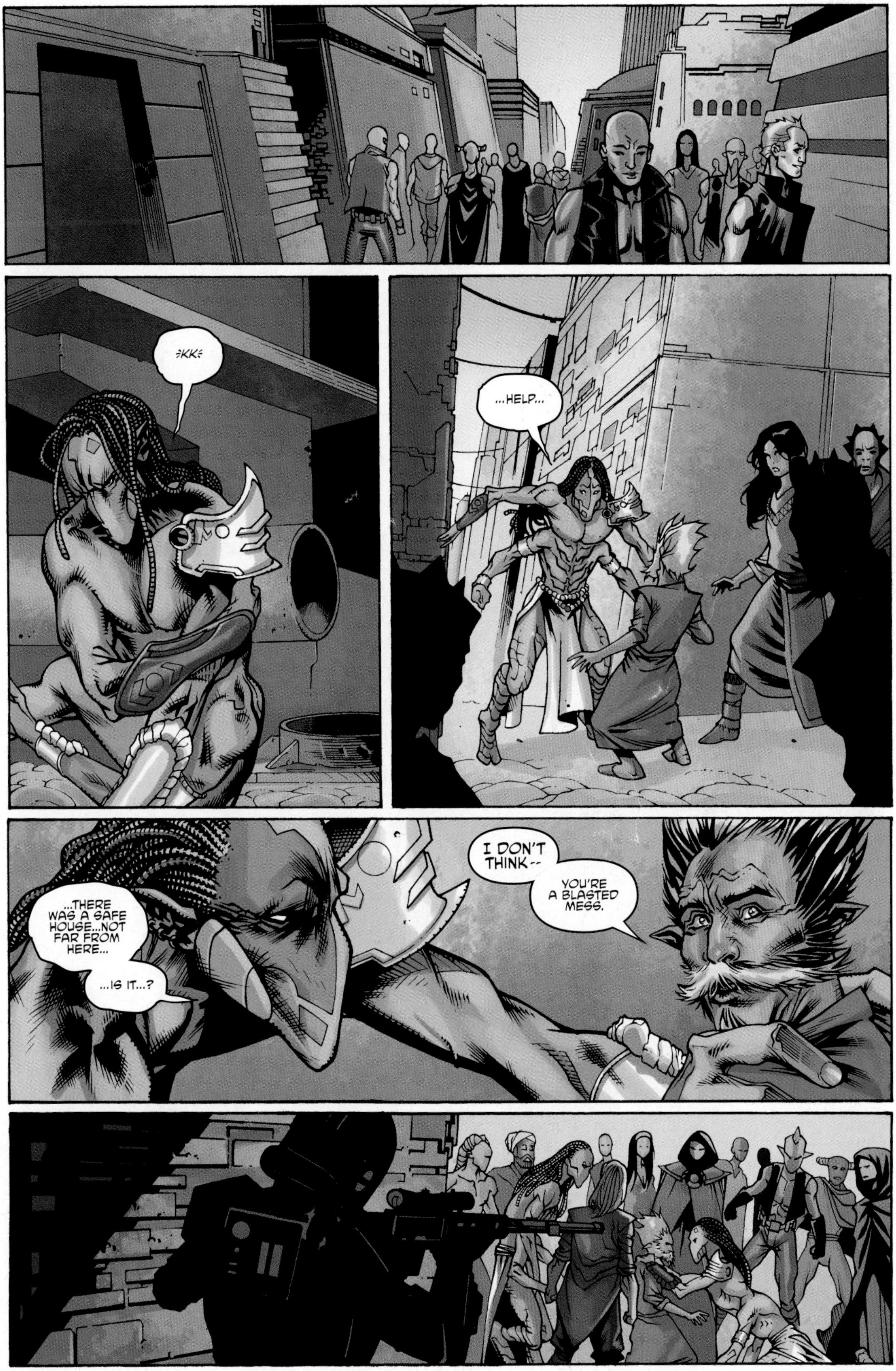

≥KK≤
...HELP...
I DON'T THINK--
YOU'RE A BLASTED MESS.
...THERE WAS A SAFE HOUSE...NOT FAR FROM HERE...
...IS IT...?

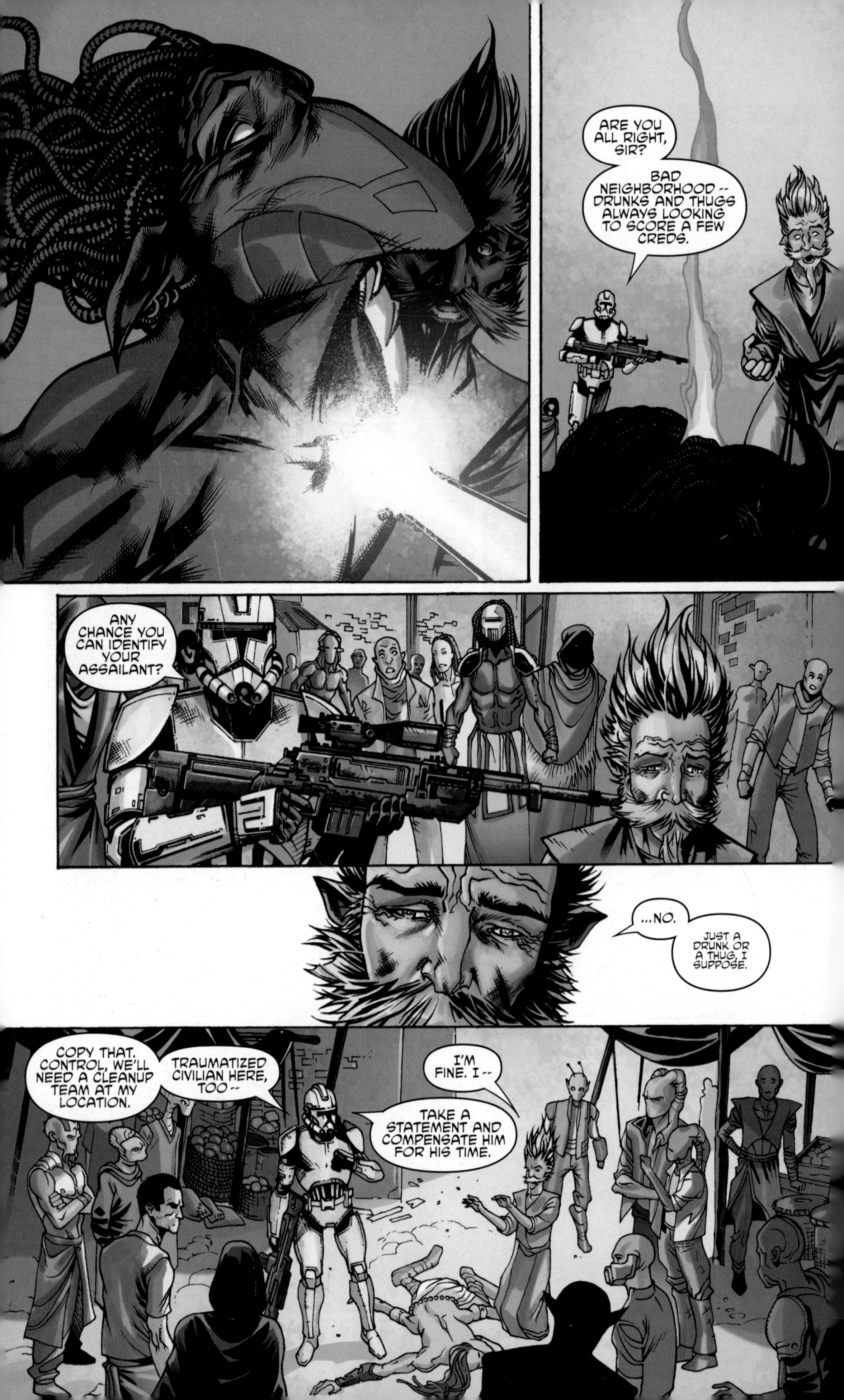
ARE YOU ALL RIGHT, SIR?
BAD NEIGHBORHOOD -- DRUNKS AND THUGS ALWAYS LOOKING TO SCORE A FEW CREDS.
ANY CHANCE YOU CAN IDENTIFY YOUR ASSAILANT?
...NO.
JUST A DRUNK OR A THUG, I SUPPOSE.
COPY THAT. CONTROL, WE'LL NEED A CLEANUP TEAM AT MY LOCATION.
TRAUMATIZED CIVILIAN HERE, TOO --
I'M FINE. I --
TAKE A STATEMENT AND COMPENSATE HIM FOR HIS TIME.

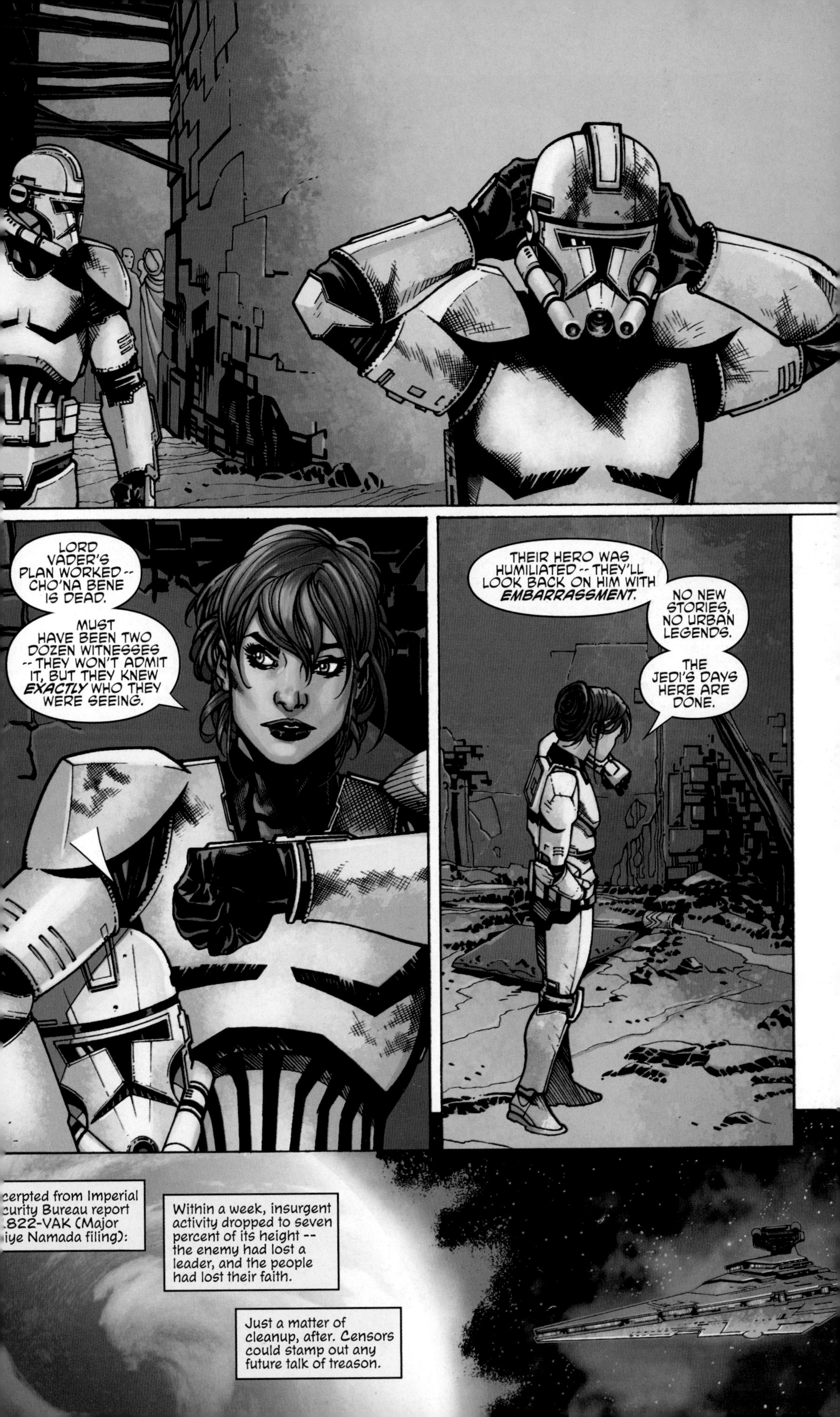
LORD VADER'S PLAN WORKED -- CHO'NA BENE IS DEAD.
MUST HAVE BEEN TWO DOZEN WITNESSES -- THEY WON'T ADMIT IT, BUT THEY KNEW *EXACTLY* WHO THEY WERE SEEING.
THEIR HERO WAS HUMILIATED -- THEY'LL LOOK BACK ON HIM WITH *EMBARRASSMENT*.
NO NEW STORIES, NO URBAN LEGENDS.
THE JEDI'S DAYS HERE ARE DONE.
cerpted from Imperial curity Bureau report 822-VAK (Major iye Namada filing):
Within a week, insurgent activity dropped to seven percent of its height -- the enemy had lost a leader, and the people had lost their faith.
Just a matter of cleanup, after. Censors could stamp out any future talk of treason.

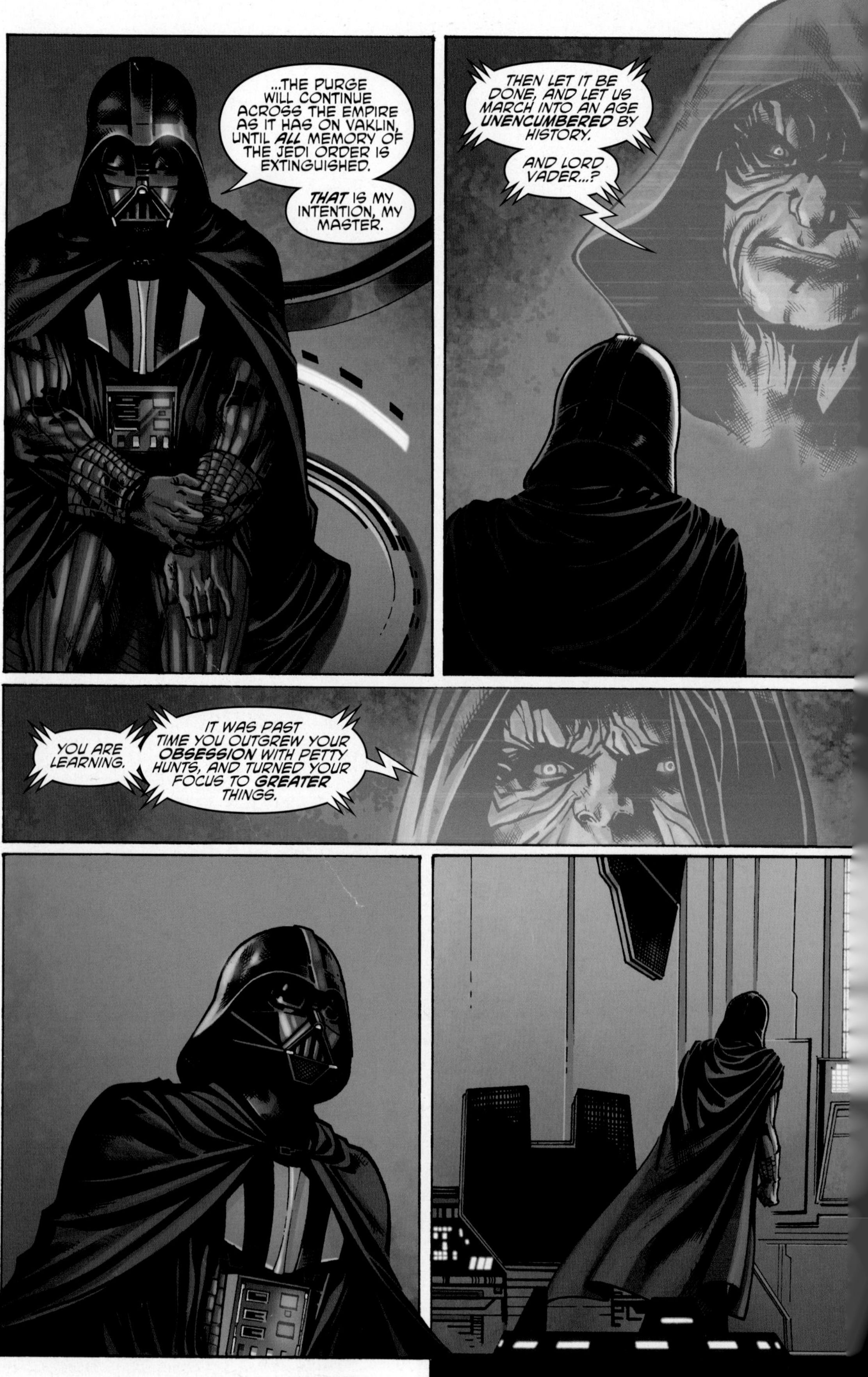
...THE PURGE WILL CONTINUE ACROSS THE EMPIRE AS IT HAS ON VAKLIN, UNTIL ALL MEMORY OF THE JEDI ORDER IS EXTINGUISHED.
THAT IS MY INTENTION, MY MASTER.
THEN LET IT BE DONE, AND LET US MARCH INTO AN AGE UNENCUMBERED BY HISTORY.
AND LORD VADER...?
YOU ARE LEARNING.
IT WAS PAST TIME YOU OUTGREW YOUR OBSESSION WITH PETTY HUNTS, AND TURNED YOUR FOCUS TO GREATER THINGS.

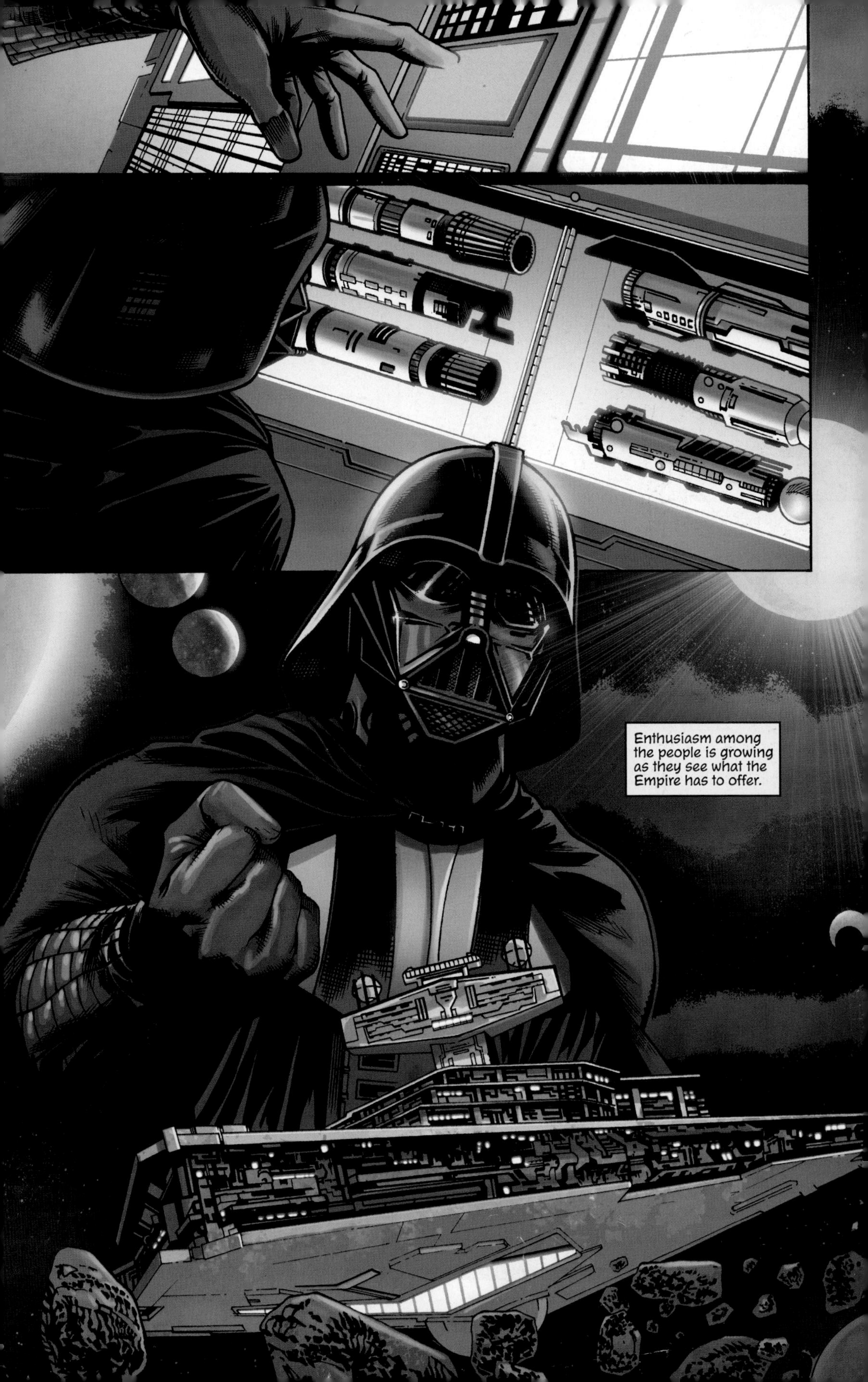
Enthusiasm among the people is growing as they see what the Empire has to offer.

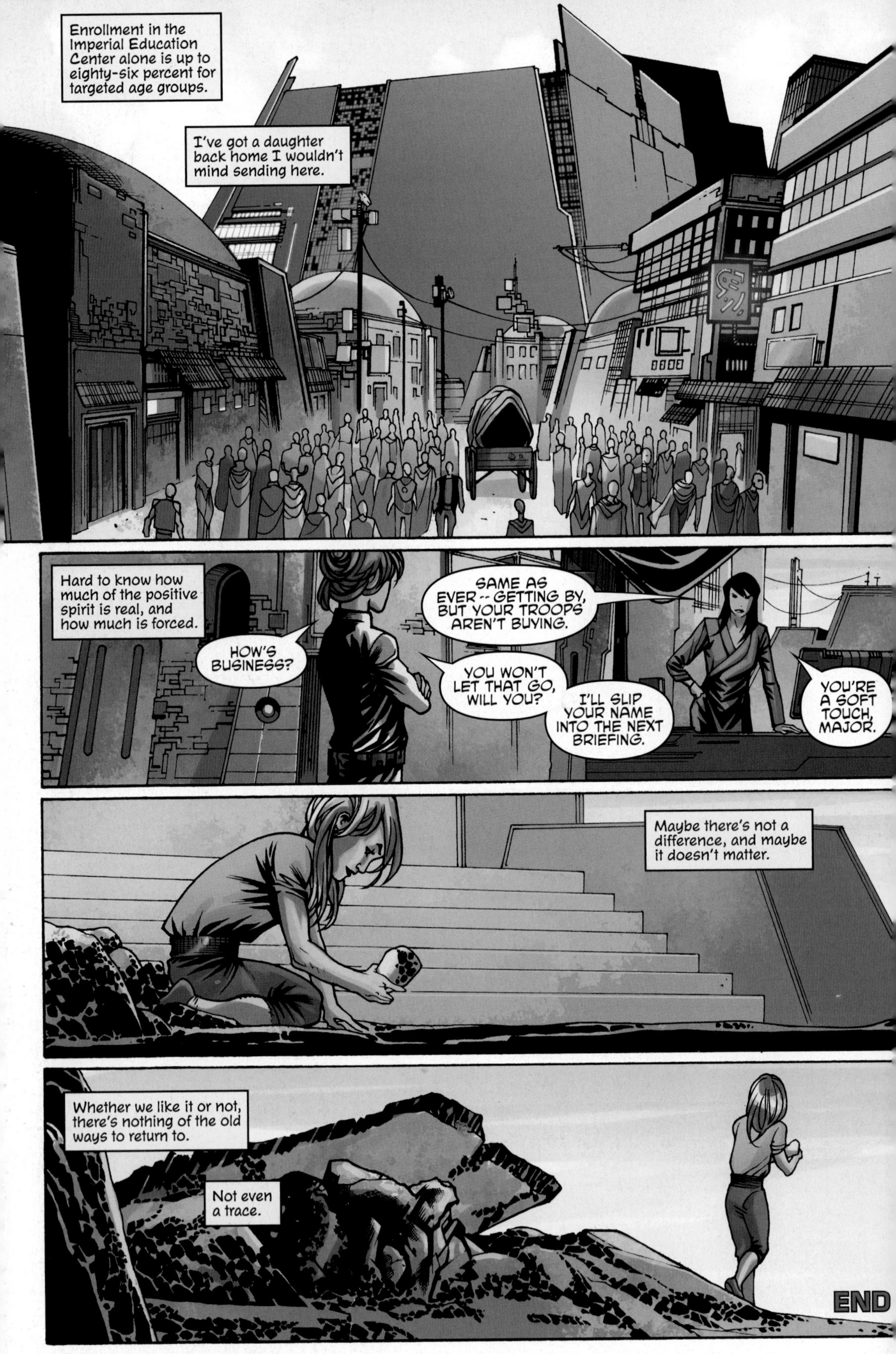

Enrollment in the Imperial Education Center alone is up to eighty-six percent for targeted age groups.
I've got a daughter back home I wouldn't mind sending here.
Hard to know how much of the positive spirit is real, and how much is forced.
HOW'S BUSINESS?
SAME AS EVER -- GETTING BY, BUT YOUR TROOPS AREN'T BUYING.
YOU WON'T LET THAT GO, WILL YOU?
I'LL SLIP YOUR NAME INTO THE NEXT BRIEFING.
YOU'RE A SOFT TOUCH, MAJOR.
Maybe there's not a difference, and maybe it doesn't matter.
Whether we like it or not, there's nothing of the old ways to return to.
Not even a trace.
END

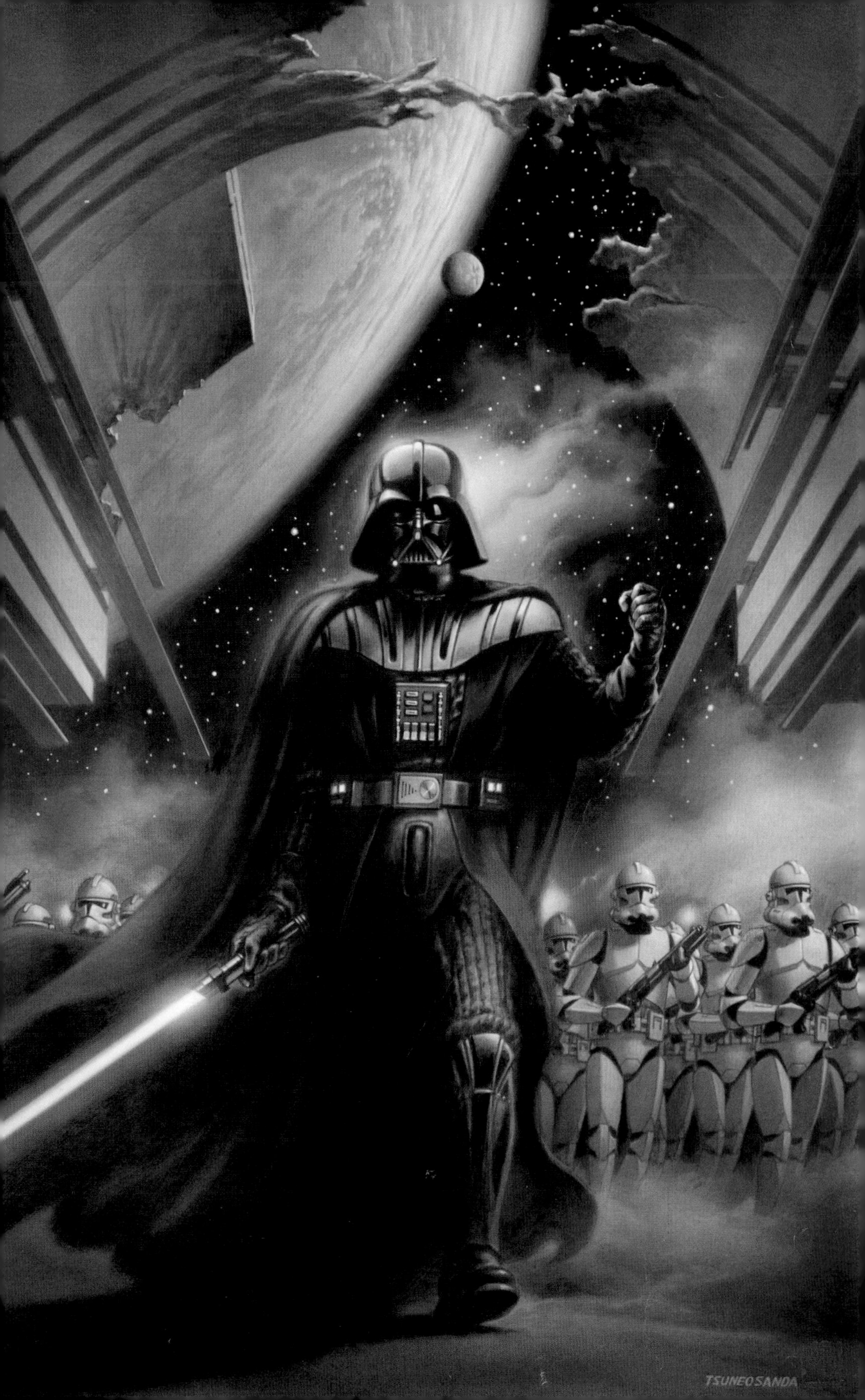
TSUNEO SANDA

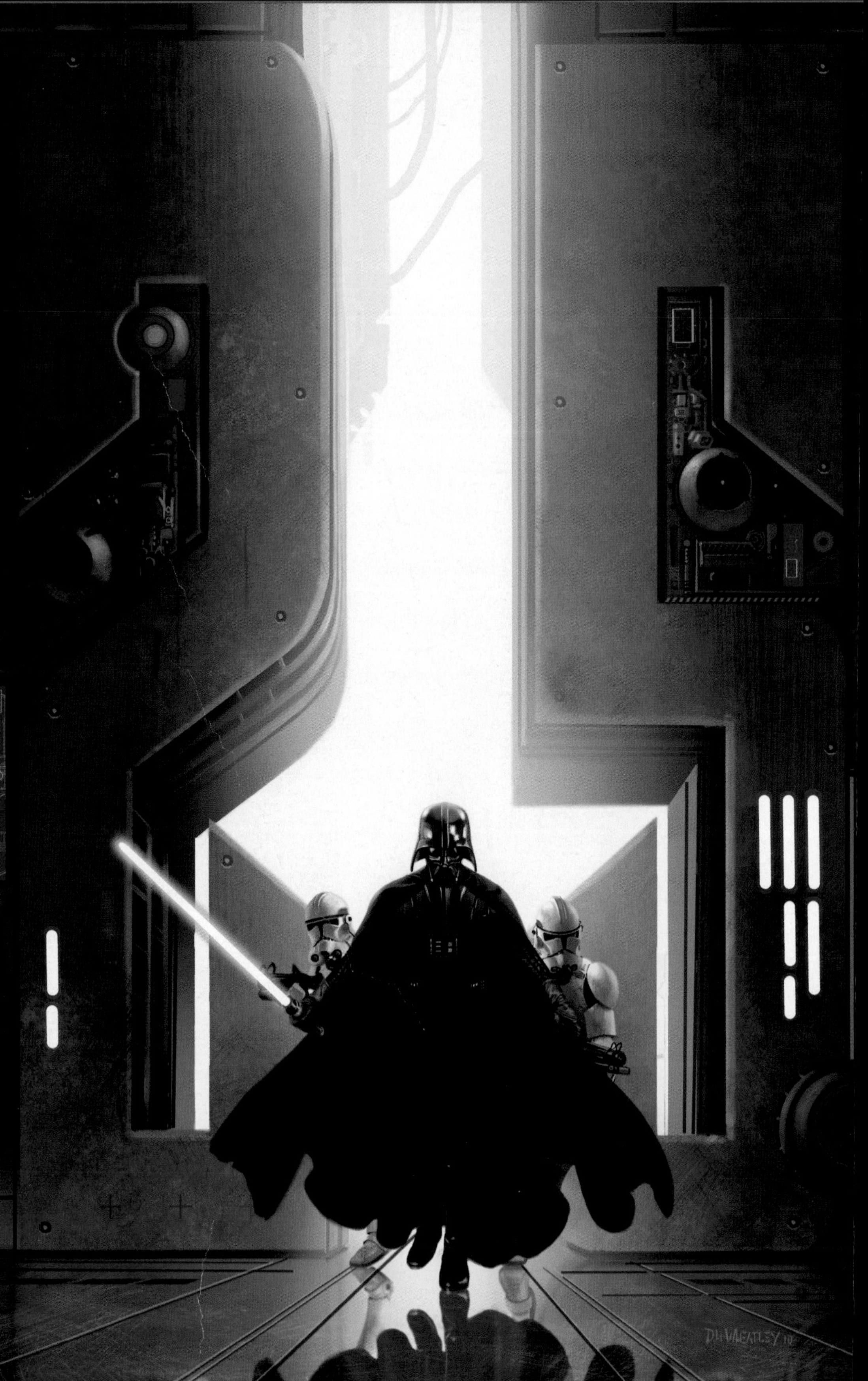

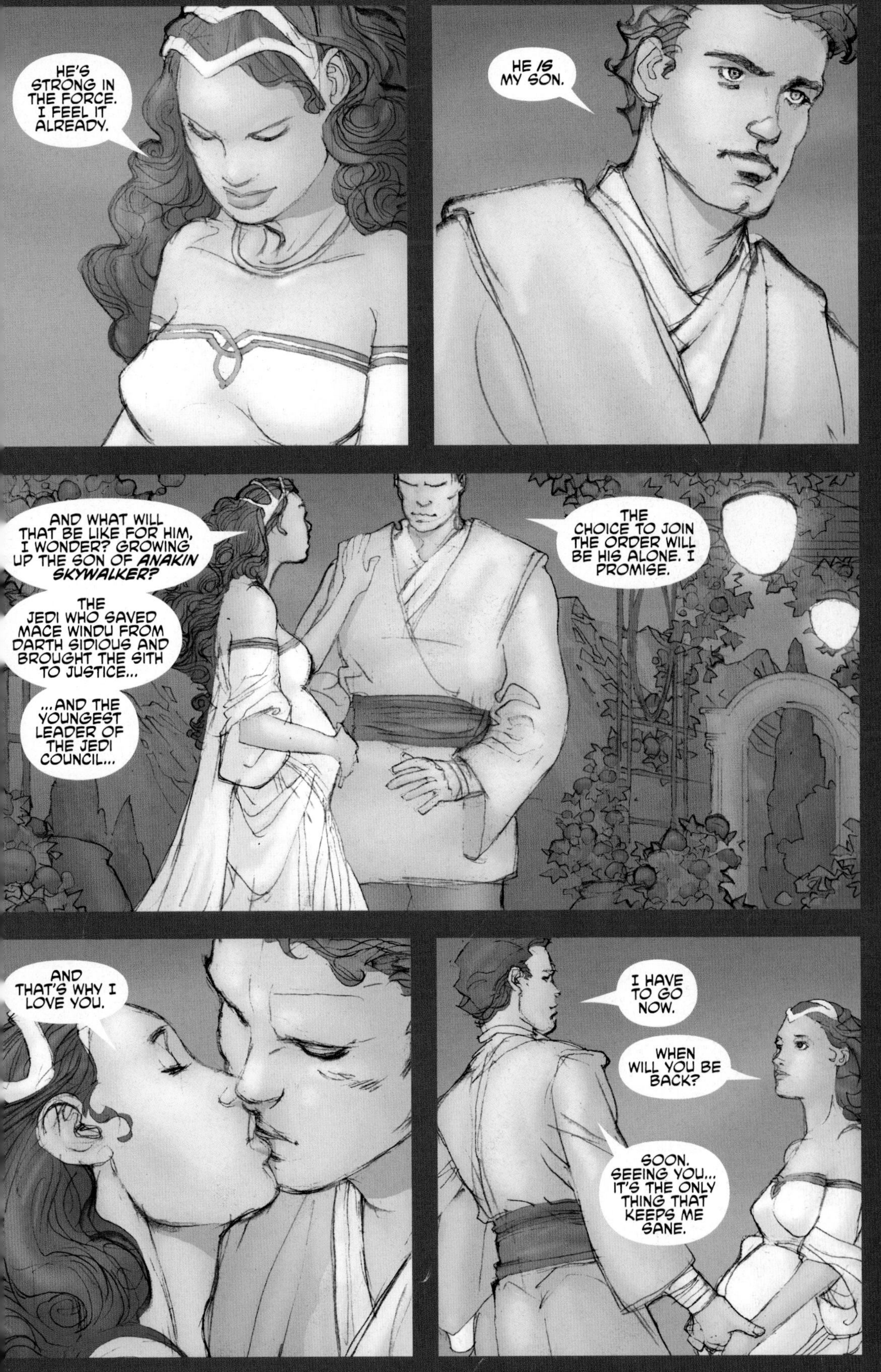
HE'S STRONG IN THE FORCE. I FEEL IT ALREADY.
HE IS MY SON.
AND WHAT WILL THAT BE LIKE FOR HIM, I WONDER? GROWING UP THE SON OF ANAKIN SKYWALKER?
THE JEDI WHO SAVED MACE WINDU FROM DARTH SIDIOUS AND BROUGHT THE SITH TO JUSTICE...
...AND THE YOUNGEST LEADER OF THE JEDI COUNCIL...
THE CHOICE TO JOIN THE ORDER WILL BE HIS ALONE. I PROMISE.
AND THAT'S WHY I LOVE YOU.
I HAVE TO GO NOW.
WHEN WILL YOU BE BACK?
SOON. SEEING YOU... IT'S THE ONLY THING THAT KEEPS ME SANE.

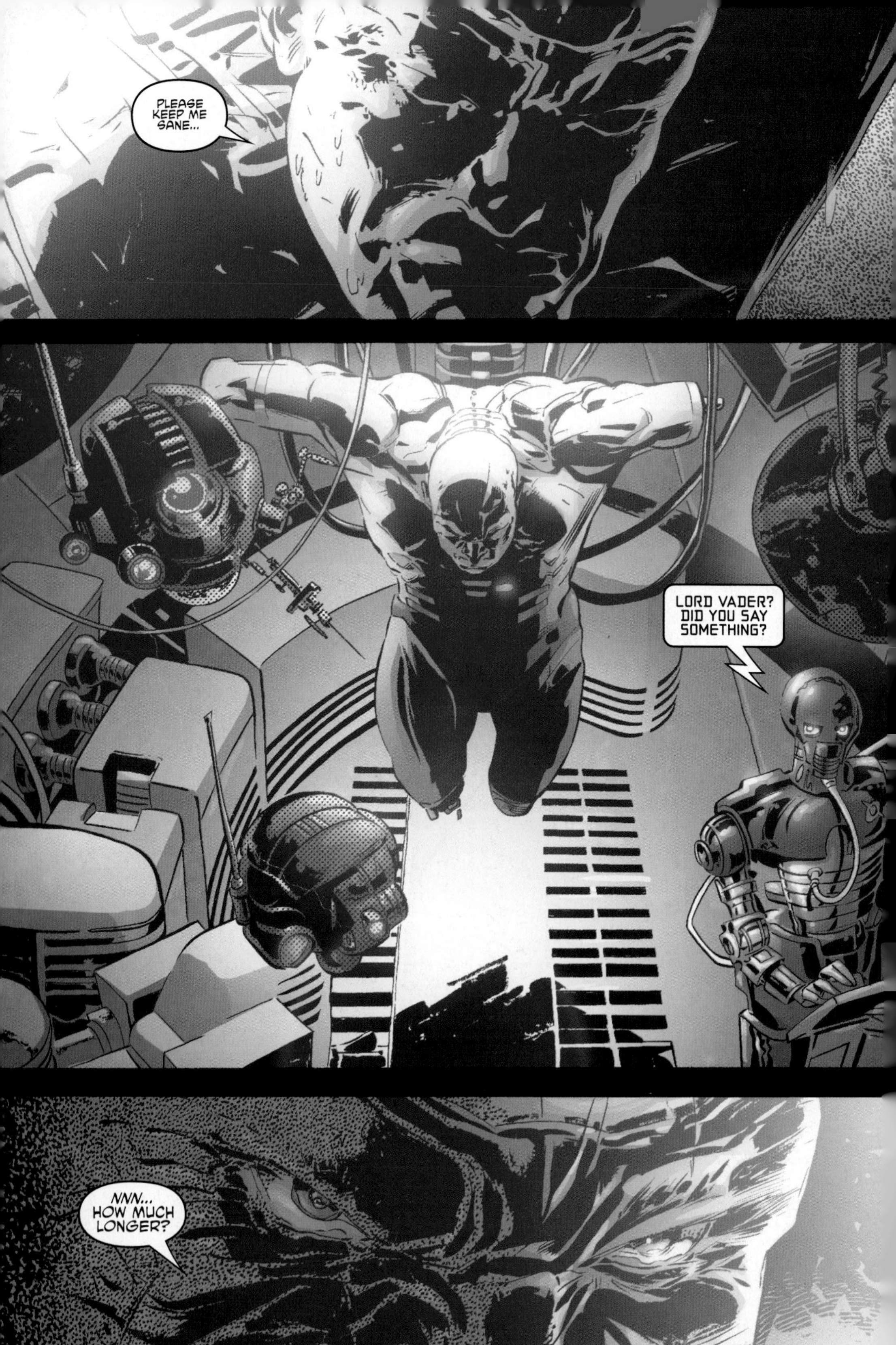
PLEASE KEEP ME SANE...
LORD VADER? DID YOU SAY SOMETHING?
NNN... HOW MUCH LONGER?

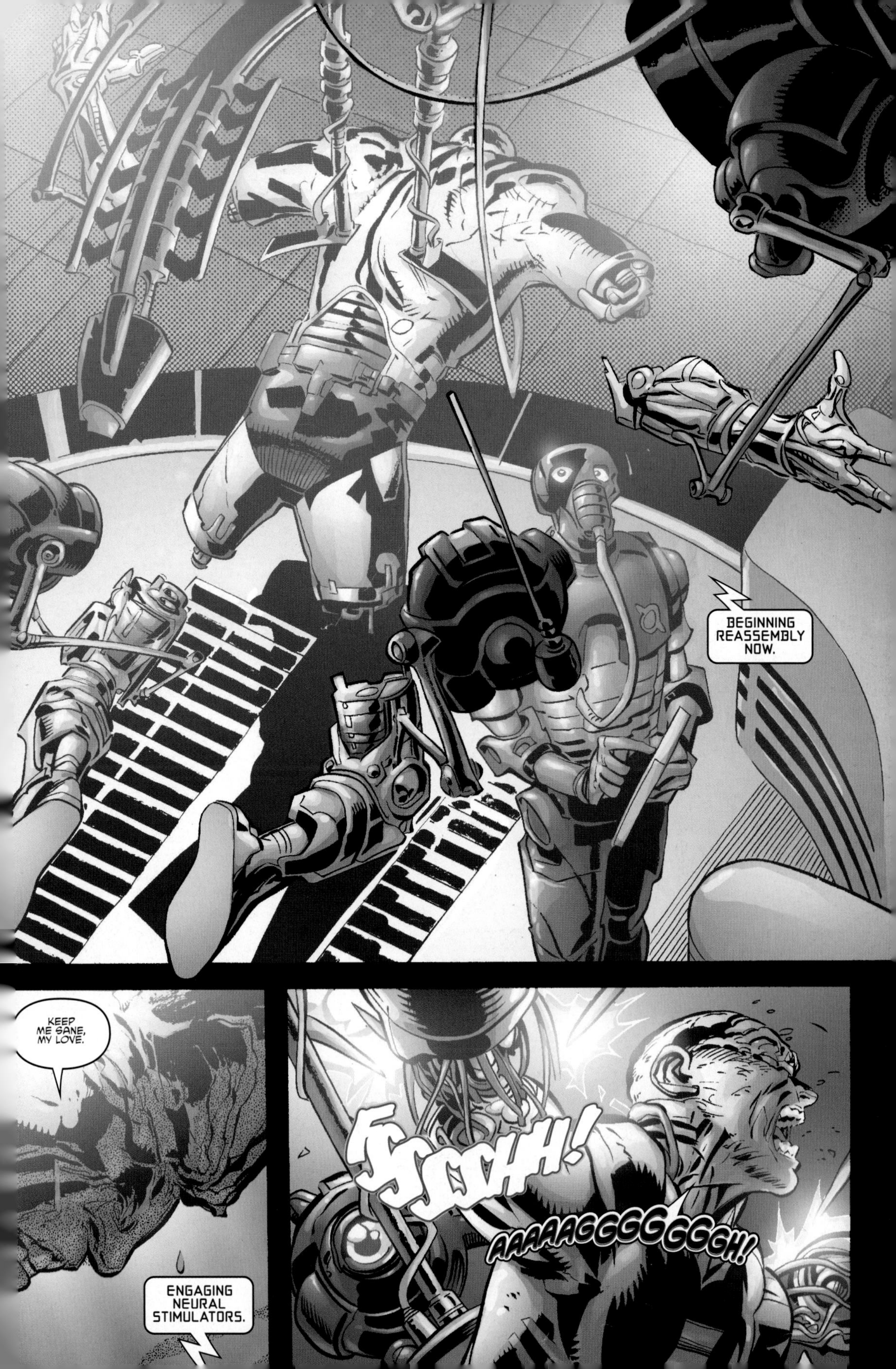
BEGINNING REASSEMBLY NOW.
KEEP ME SANE, MY LOVE.
ENGAGING NEURAL STIMULATORS.
SSSCHH!
AAAAAGGGGGGGGH!

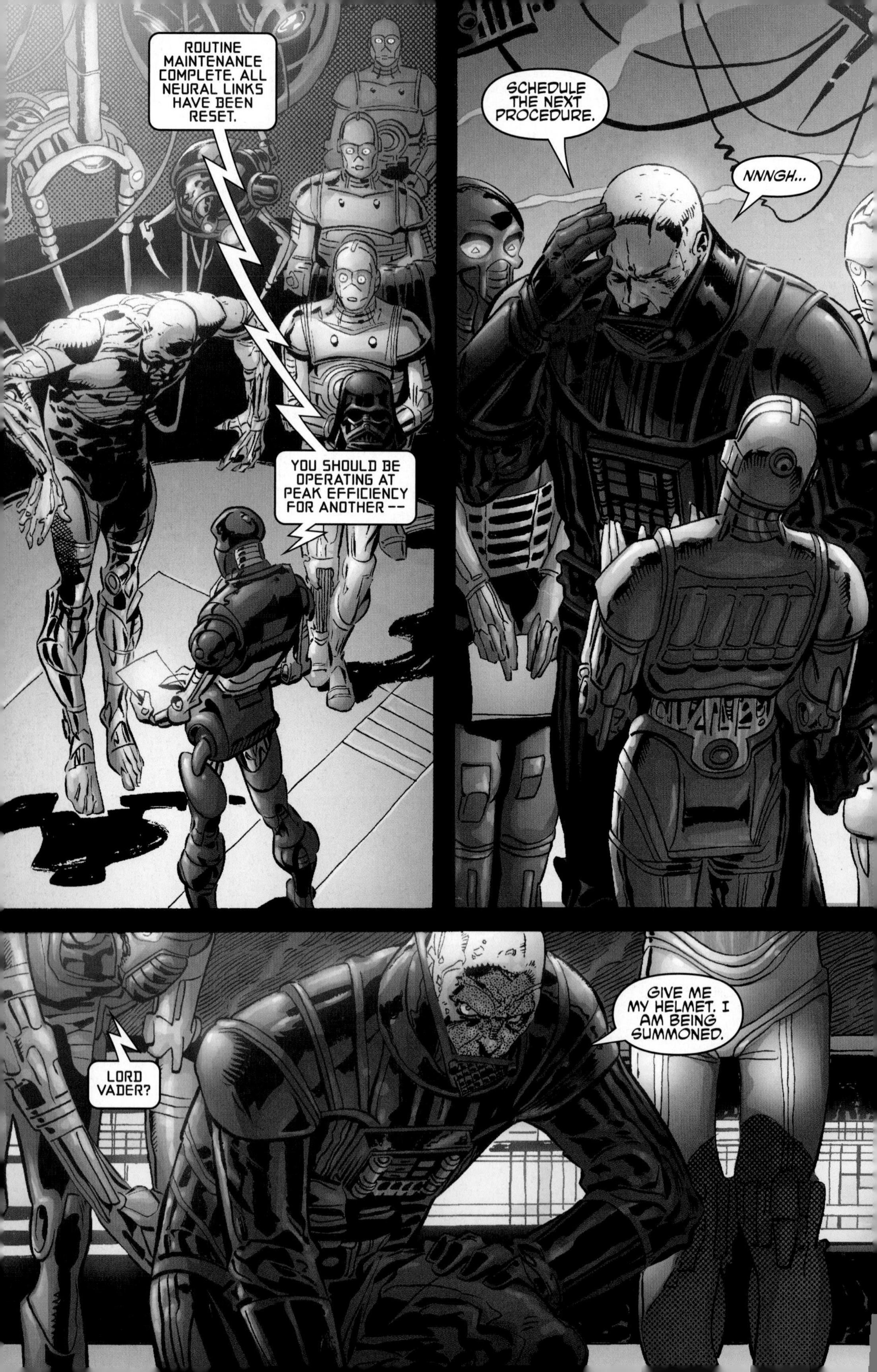
ROUTINE MAINTENANCE COMPLETE. ALL NEURAL LINKS HAVE BEEN RESET.
YOU SHOULD BE OPERATING AT PEAK EFFICIENCY FOR ANOTHER --
SCHEDULE THE NEXT PROCEDURE.
NNNGH...
LORD VADER?
GIVE ME MY HELMET. I AM BEING SUMMONED.

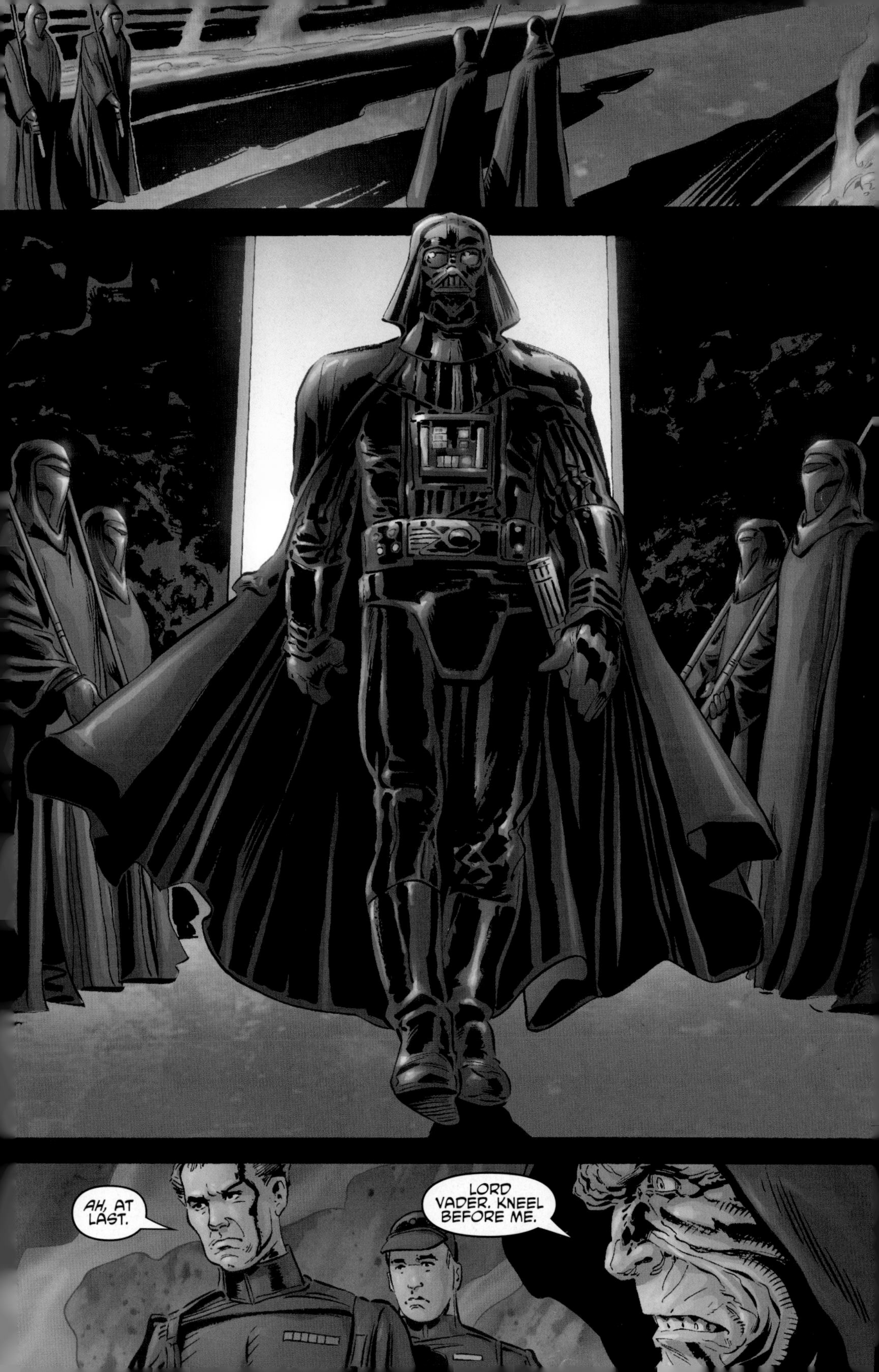
AH, AT LAST.
LORD VADER. KNEEL BEFORE ME.

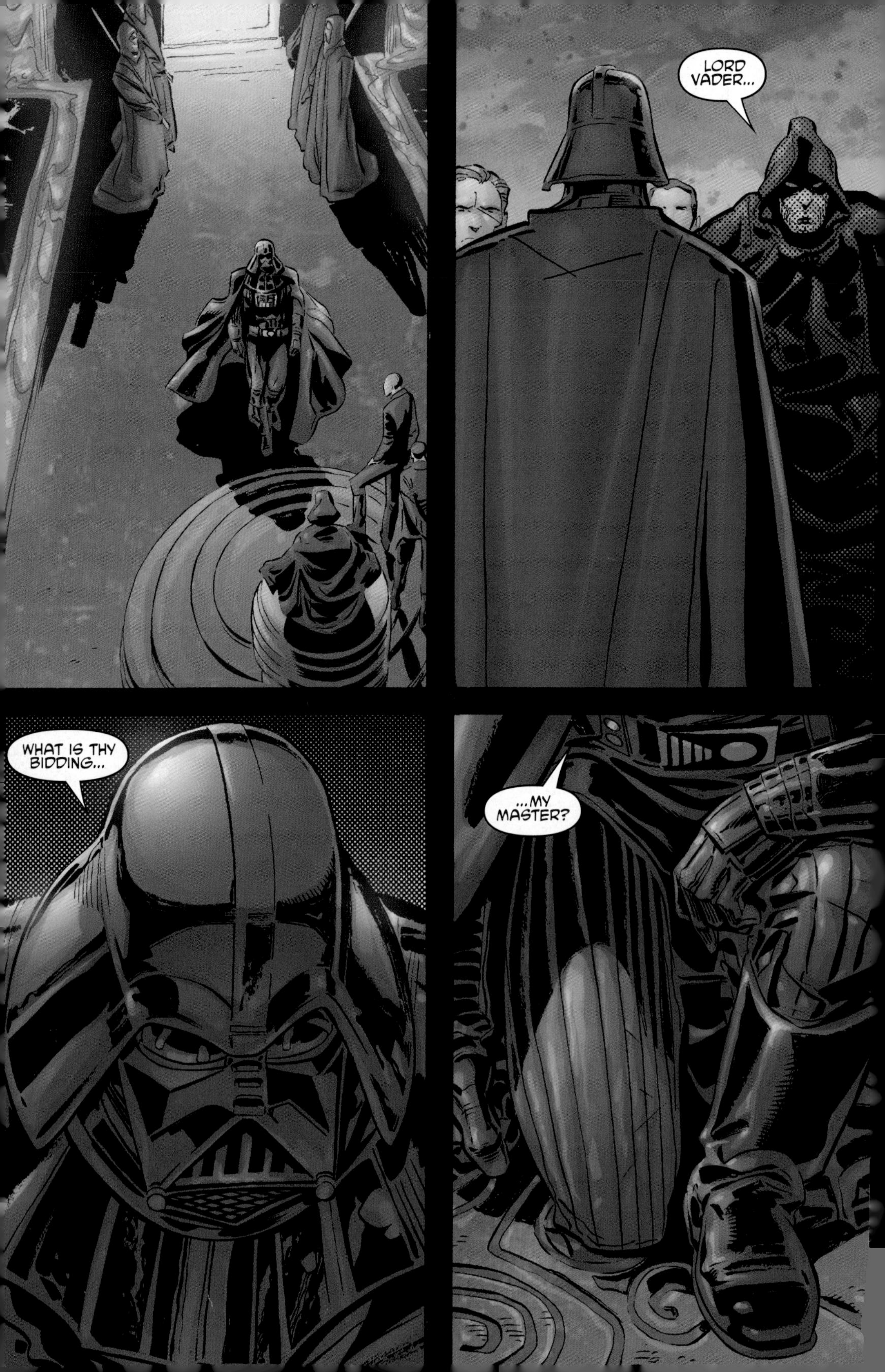
LORD VADER...
WHAT IS THY BIDDING...
...MY MASTER?

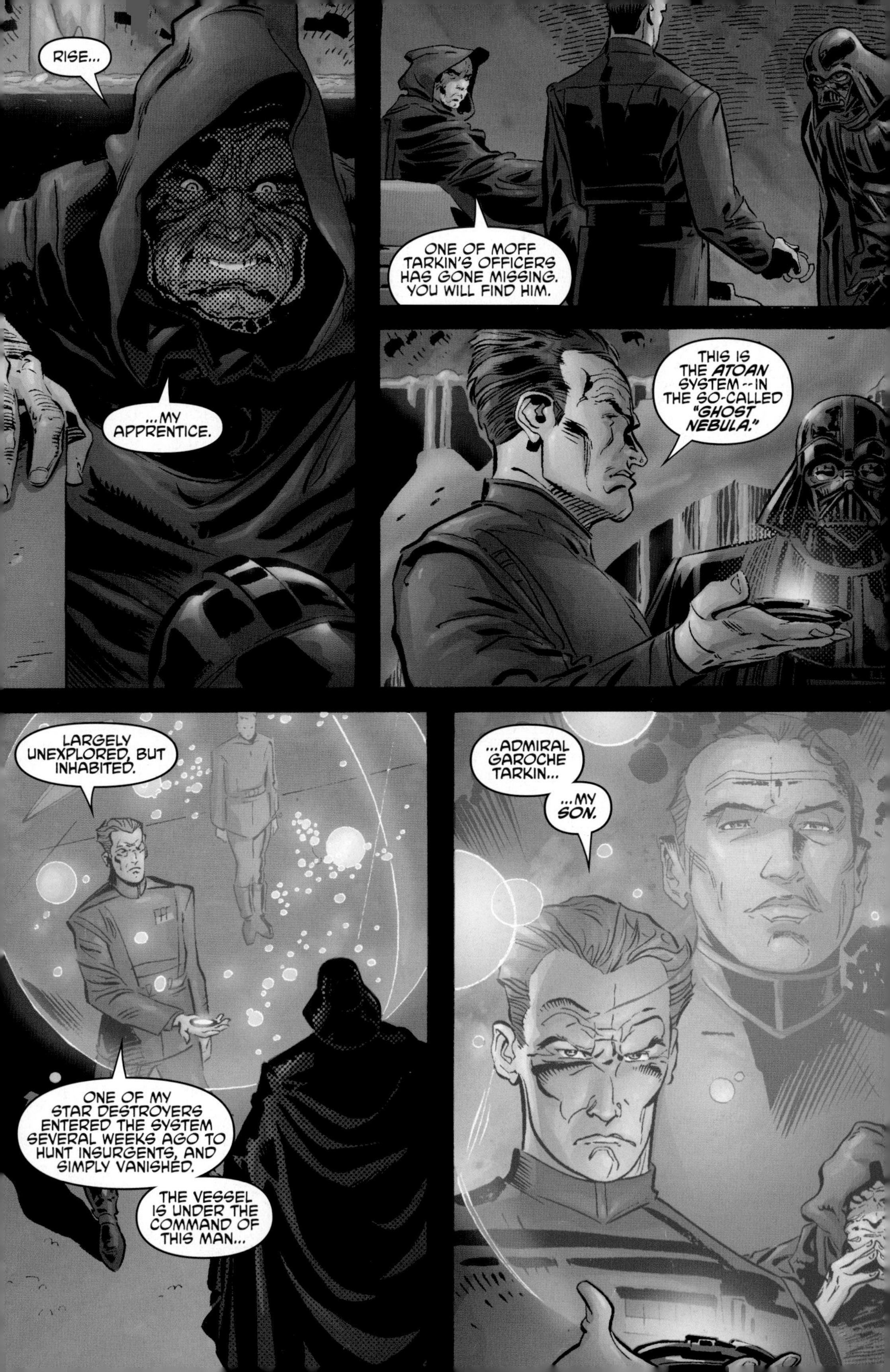
RISE...
...MY APPRENTICE.
ONE OF MOFF TARKIN'S OFFICERS HAS GONE MISSING. YOU WILL FIND HIM.
THIS IS THE *ATOAN* SYSTEM -- IN THE SO-CALLED *"GHOST NEBULA."*
LARGELY UNEXPLORED, BUT INHABITED.
ONE OF MY STAR DESTROYERS ENTERED THE SYSTEM SEVERAL WEEKS AGO TO HUNT INSURGENTS, AND SIMPLY VANISHED.
THE VESSEL IS UNDER THE COMMAND OF THIS MAN...
...ADMIRAL GAROCHE TARKIN...
...MY *SON.*

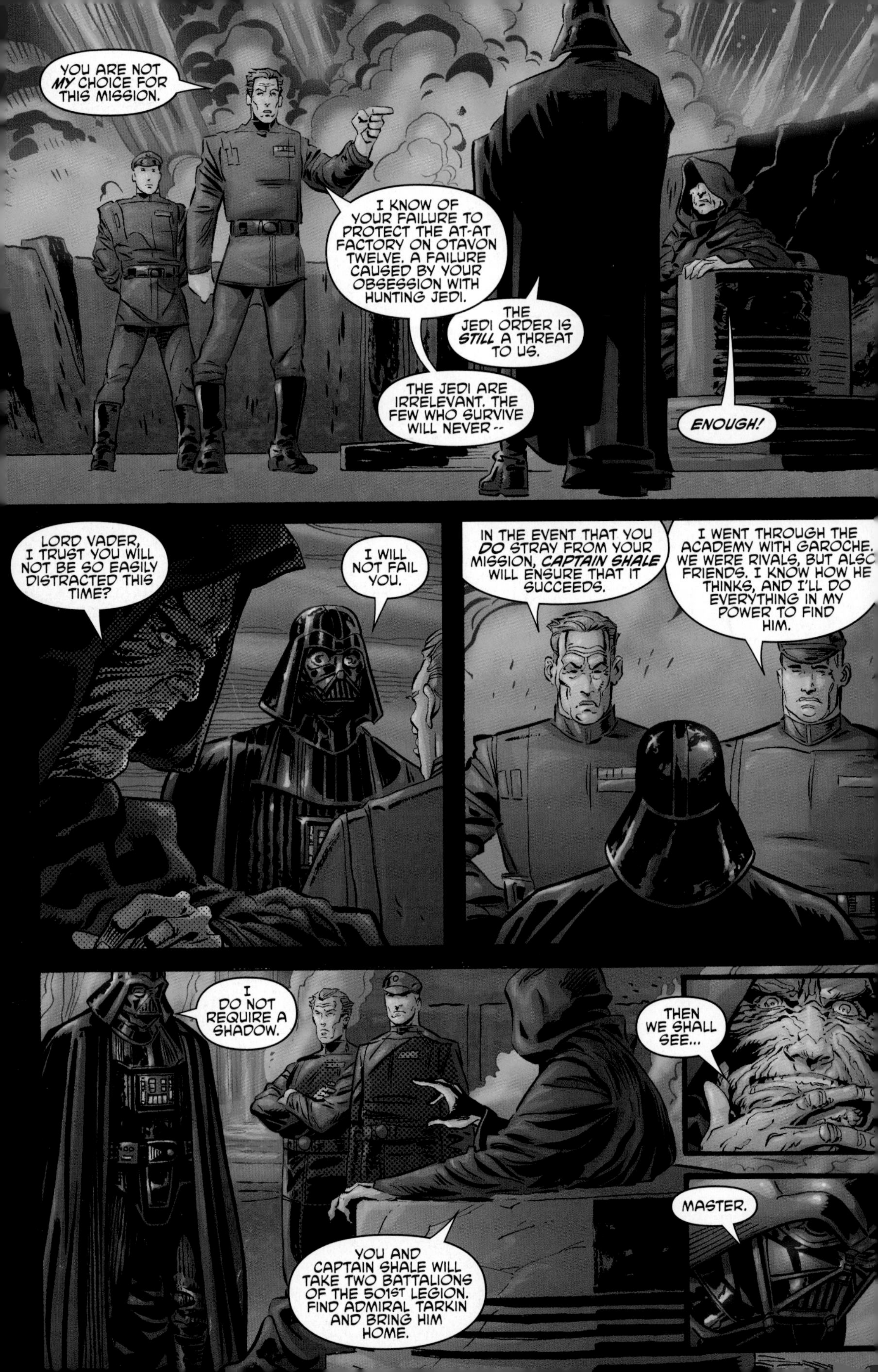
YOU ARE NOT MY CHOICE FOR THIS MISSION.
I KNOW OF YOUR FAILURE TO PROTECT THE AT-AT FACTORY ON OTAVON TWELVE. A FAILURE CAUSED BY YOUR OBSESSION WITH HUNTING JEDI.
THE JEDI ORDER IS STILL A THREAT TO US.
THE JEDI ARE IRRELEVANT. THE FEW WHO SURVIVE WILL NEVER --
ENOUGH!
LORD VADER, I TRUST YOU WILL NOT BE SO EASILY DISTRACTED THIS TIME?
I WILL NOT FAIL YOU.
IN THE EVENT THAT YOU DO STRAY FROM YOUR MISSION, CAPTAIN SHALE WILL ENSURE THAT IT SUCCEEDS.
I WENT THROUGH THE ACADEMY WITH GAROCHE. WE WERE RIVALS, BUT ALSO FRIENDS. I KNOW HOW HE THINKS, AND I'LL DO EVERYTHING IN MY POWER TO FIND HIM.
I DO NOT REQUIRE A SHADOW.
THEN WE SHALL SEE...
YOU AND CAPTAIN SHALE WILL TAKE TWO BATTALIONS OF THE 501ST LEGION. FIND ADMIRAL TARKIN AND BRING HIM HOME.
MASTER.

THE ATOAN SYSTEM. FOUR DAYS LATER.

OUR INTELLIGENCE ON ATOAN IS LIMITED.

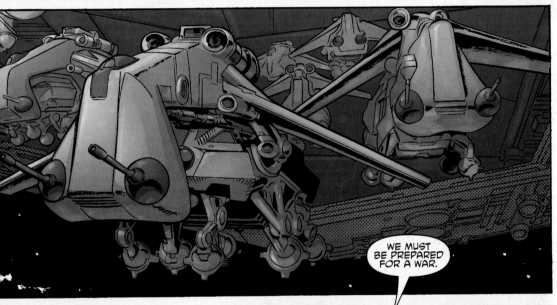

WE MUST BE PREPARED FOR A WAR.

CRUSH ANY RESISTANCE, BUT LEAVE THE OFFICERS ALIVE. FOR INTERROGATION.

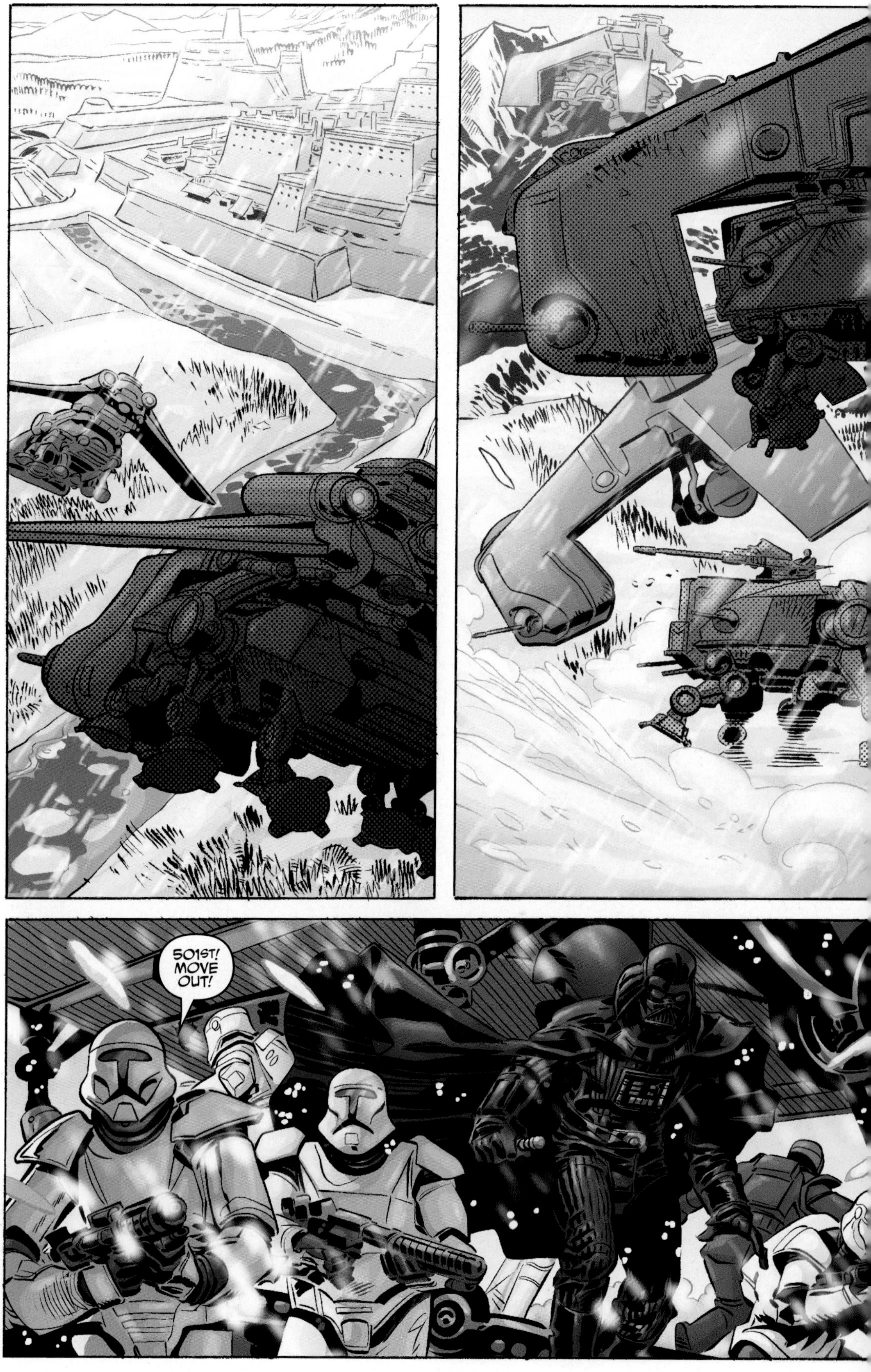
501ST! MOVE OUT!

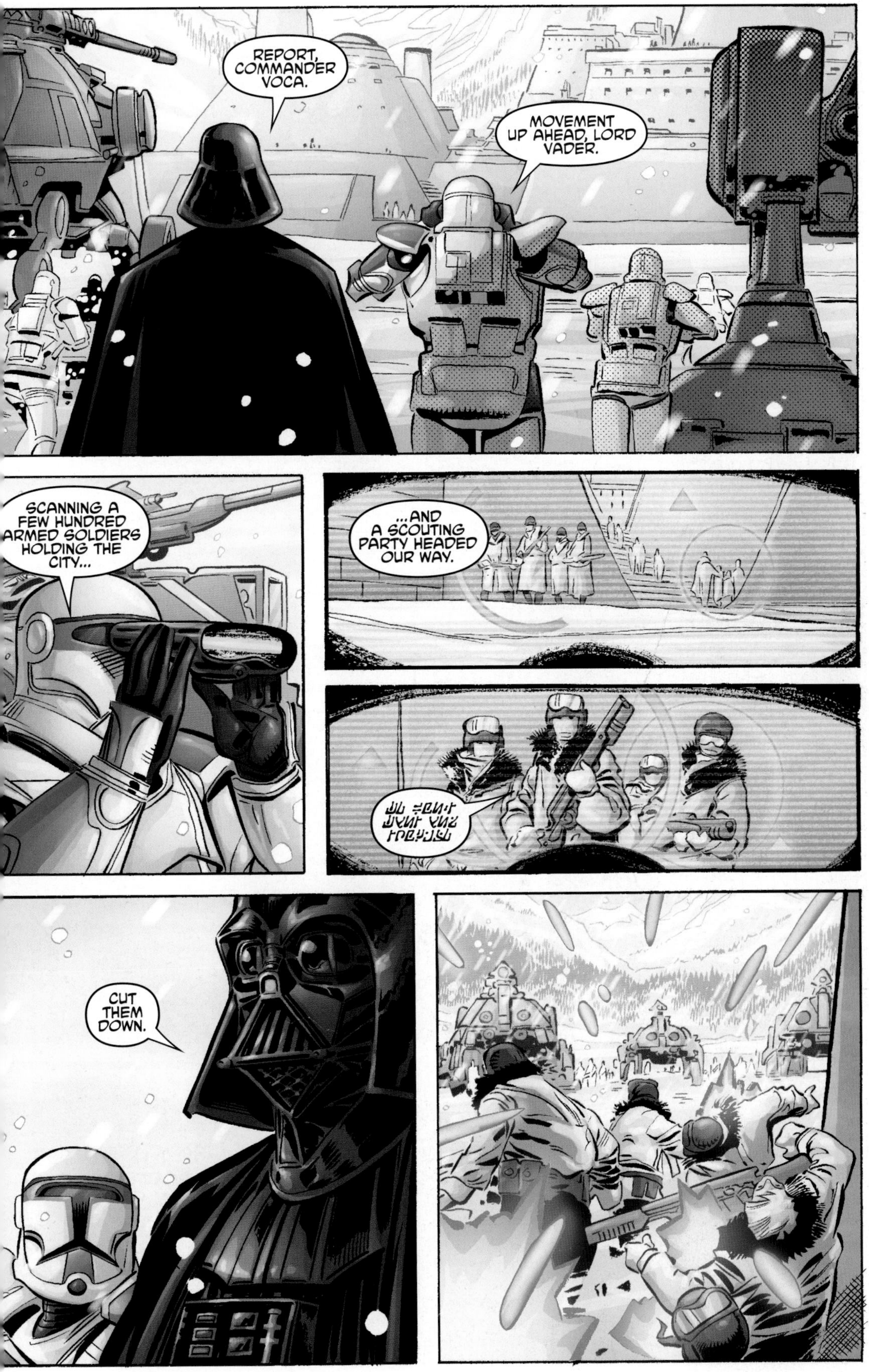
REPORT, COMMANDER VOCA.
MOVEMENT UP AHEAD, LORD VADER.
SCANNING A FEW HUNDRED ARMED SOLDIERS HOLDING THE CITY...
...AND A SCOUTING PARTY HEADED OUR WAY.
CUT THEM DOWN.

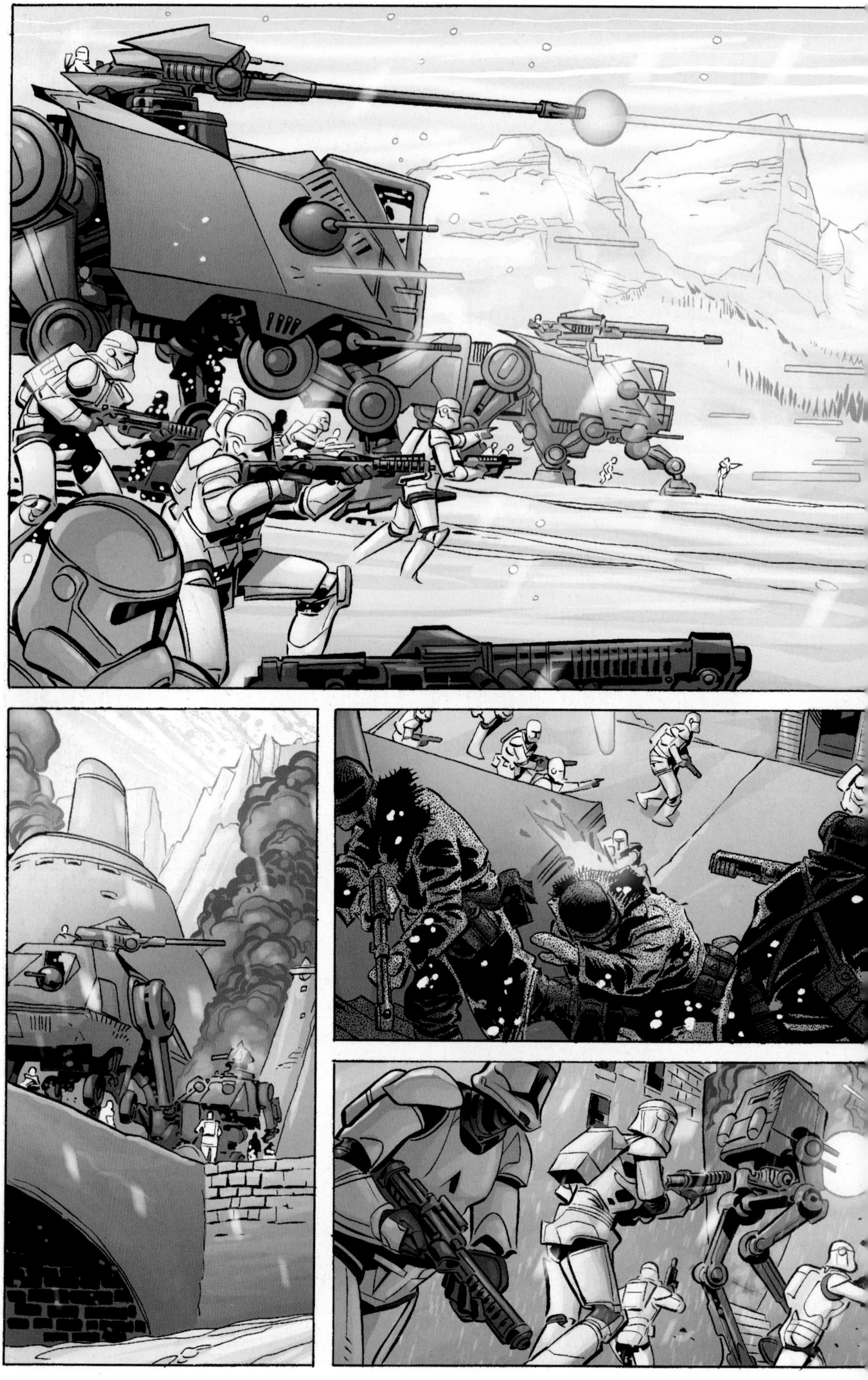

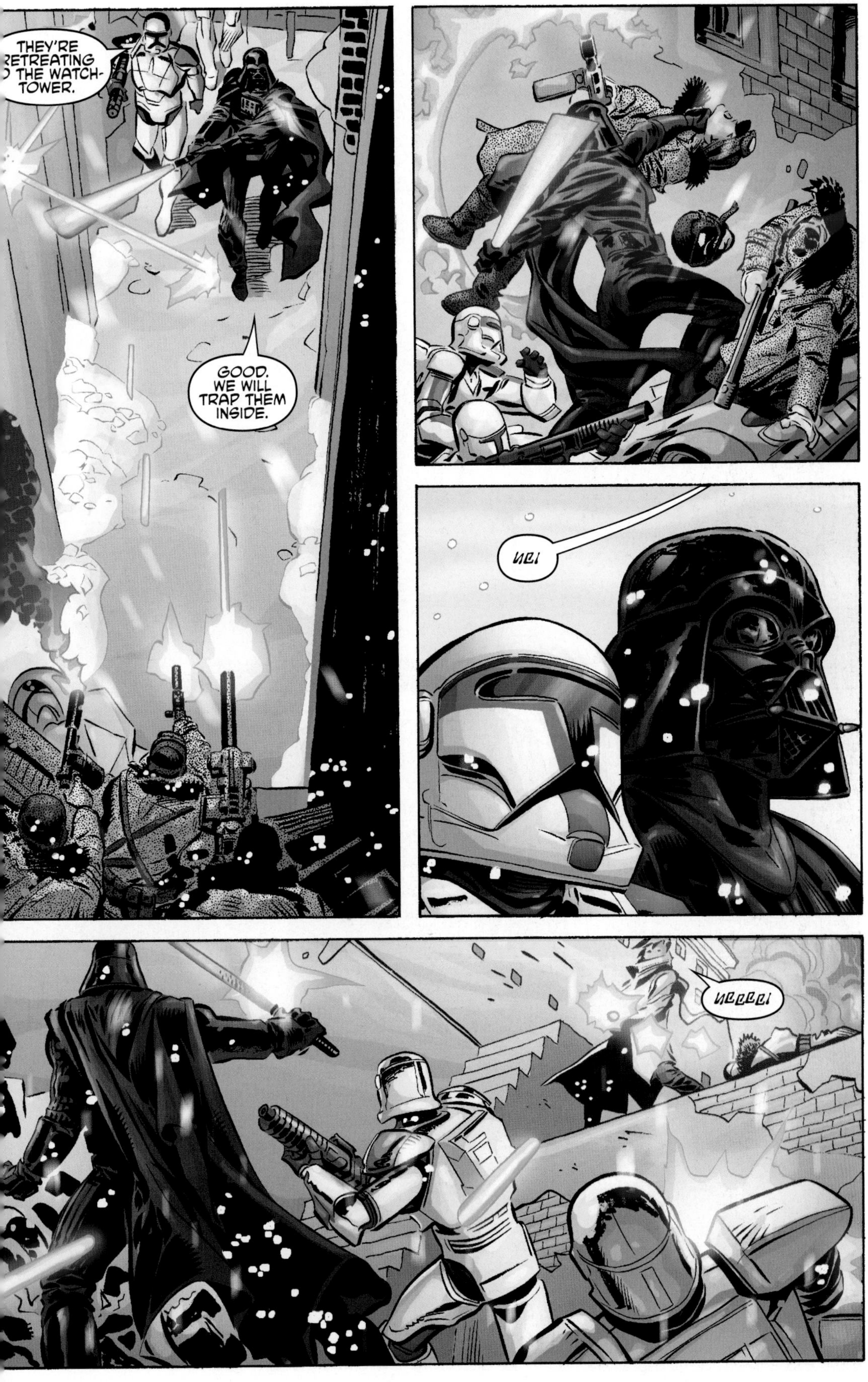

THEY'RE RETREATING TO THE WATCH-TOWER.
GOOD. WE WILL TRAP THEM INSIDE.

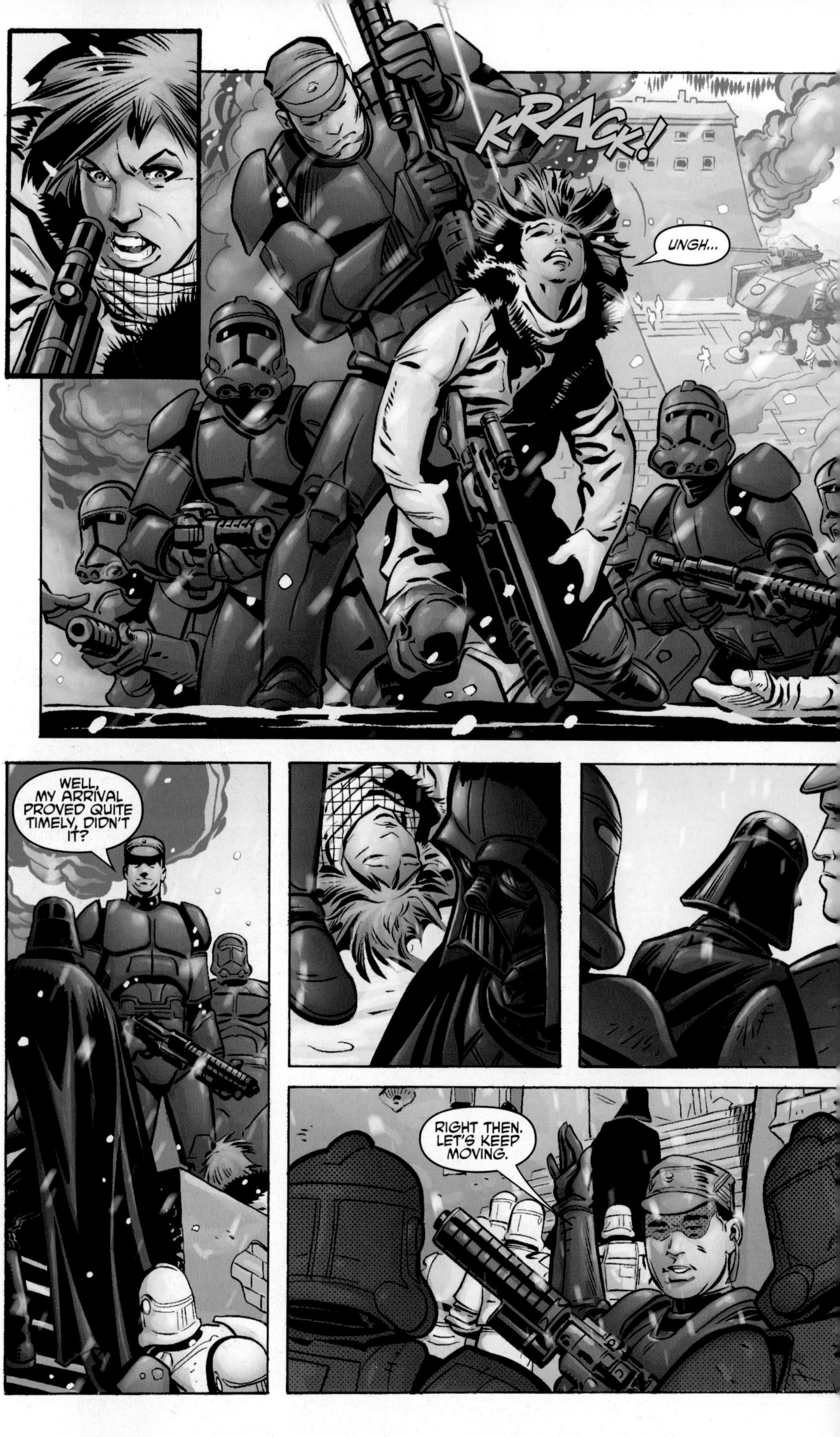
KRACK!
UNGH...
WELL, MY ARRIVAL PROVED QUITE TIMELY, DIDN'T IT?
RIGHT THEN. LET'S KEEP MOVING.

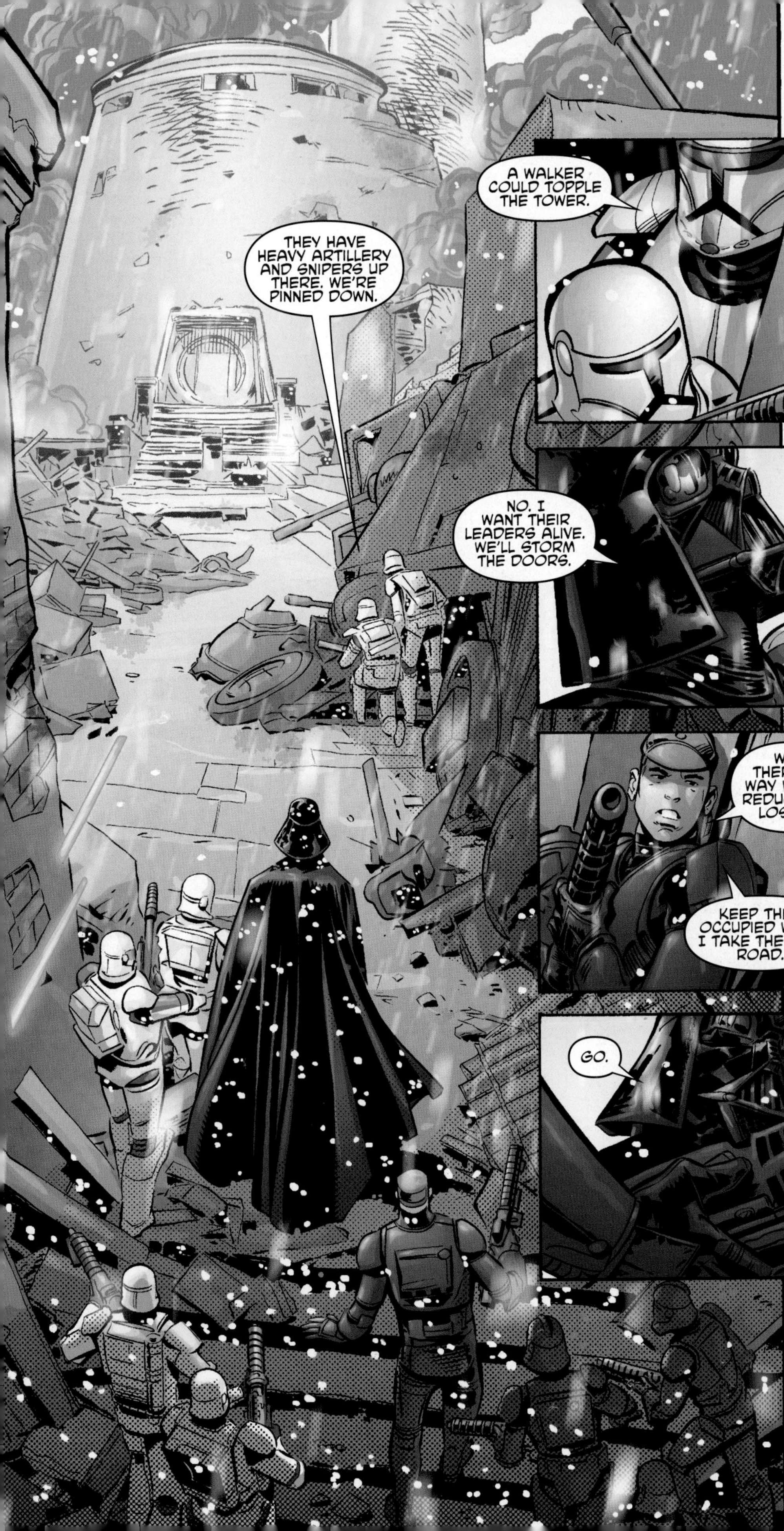
THEY HAVE HEAVY ARTILLERY AND SNIPERS UP THERE. WE'RE PINNED DOWN.
A WALKER COULD TOPPLE THE TOWER.
NO. I WANT THEIR LEADERS ALIVE. WE'LL STORM THE DOORS.
WAIT. THERE'S A WAY WE CAN REDUCE OUR LOSSES.
KEEP THEM OCCUPIED WHILE I TAKE THE HIGH ROAD.
GO.

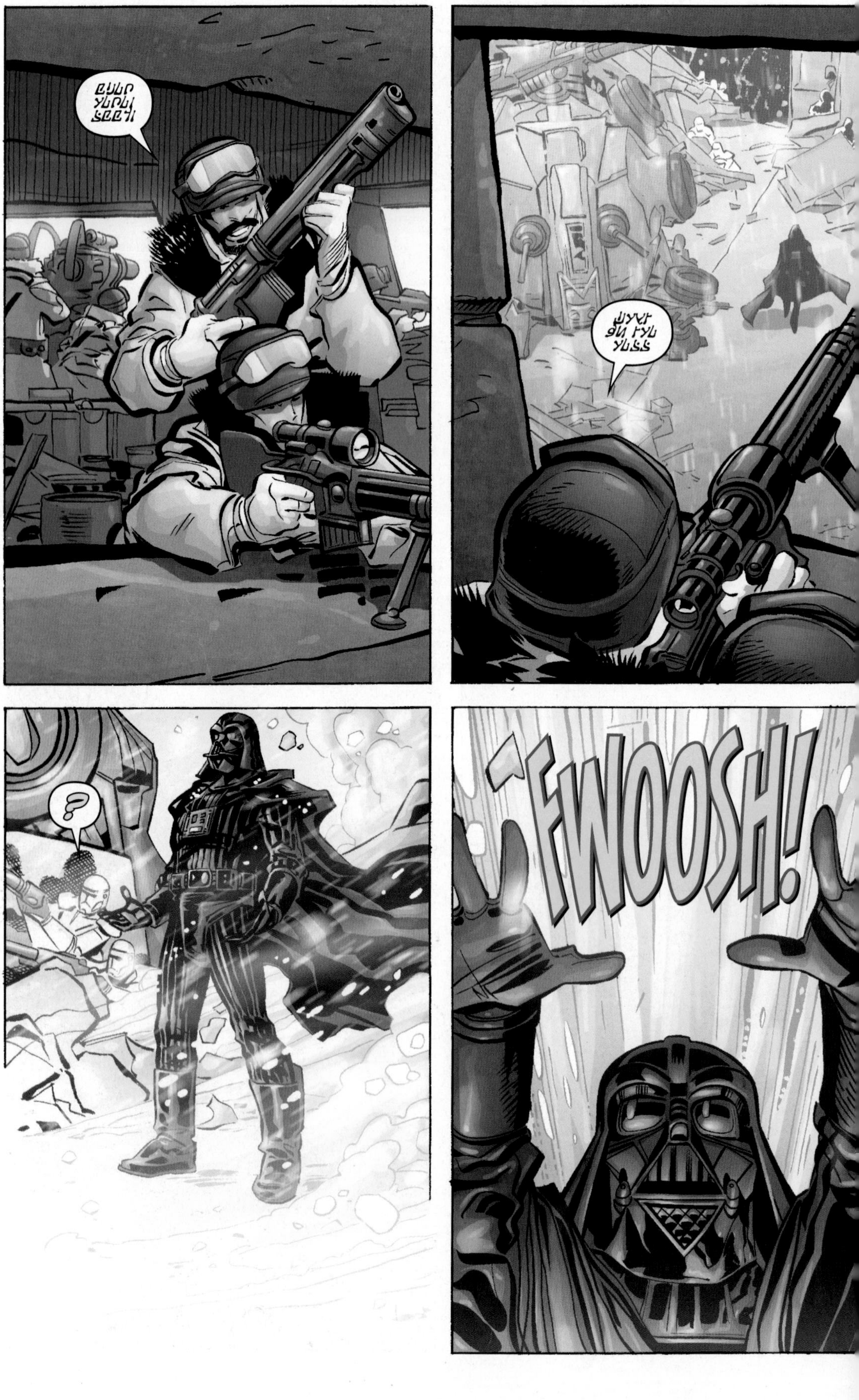
?
FWOOSH!

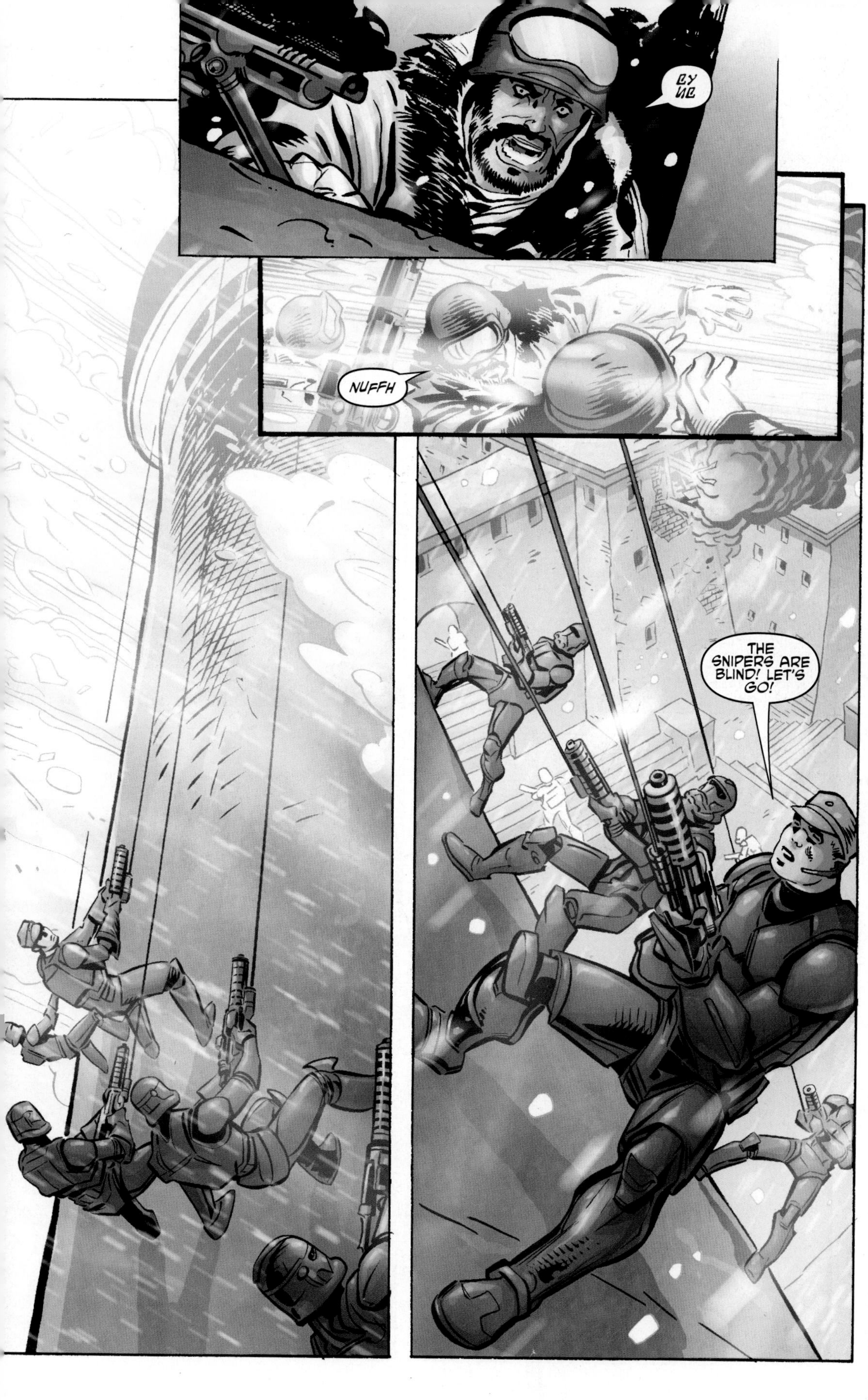
NUFFH
THE SNIPERS ARE BLIND! LET'S GO!

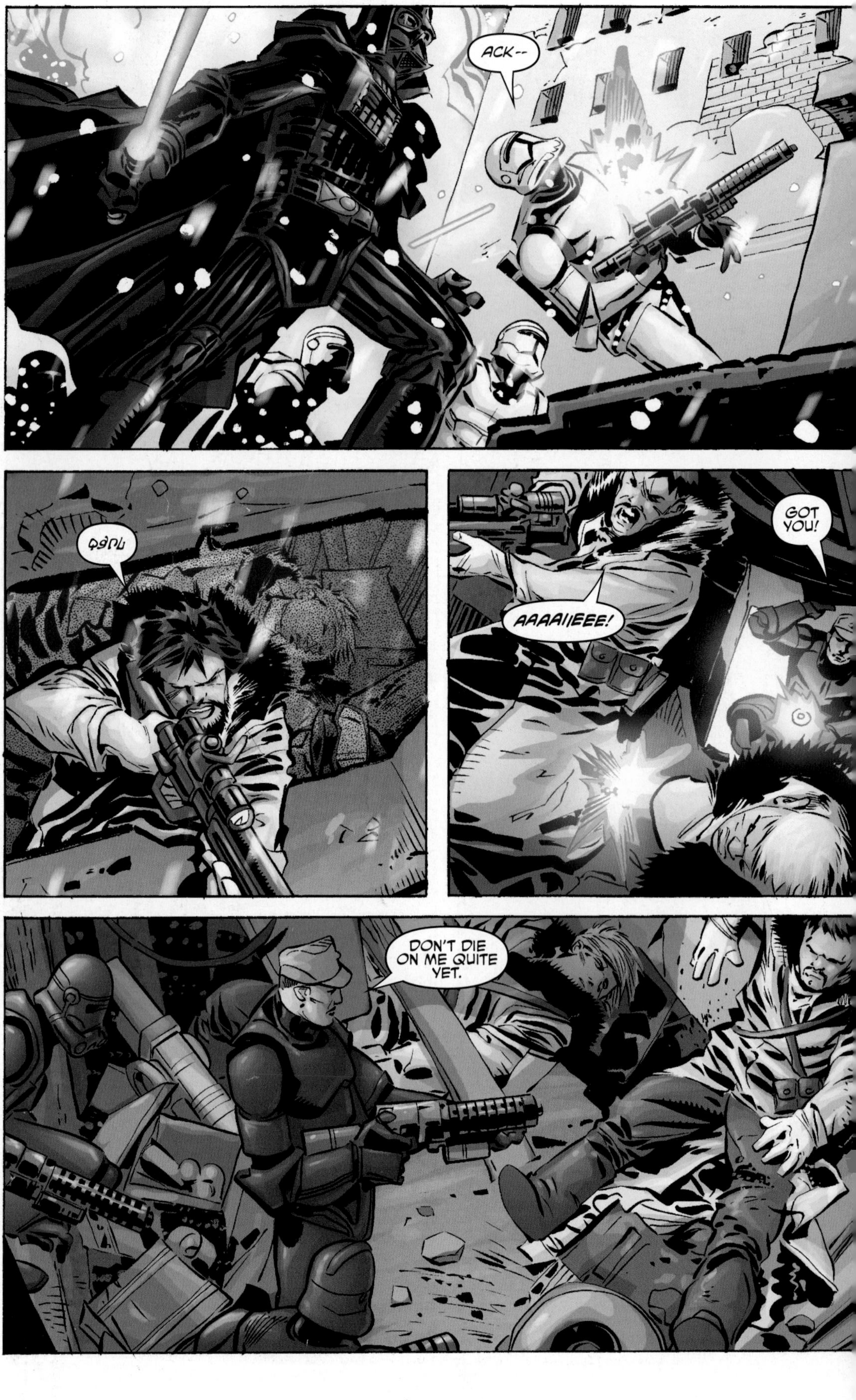
ACK--
GOT YOU!
AAAAIIEEE!
DON'T DIE ON ME QUITE YET.

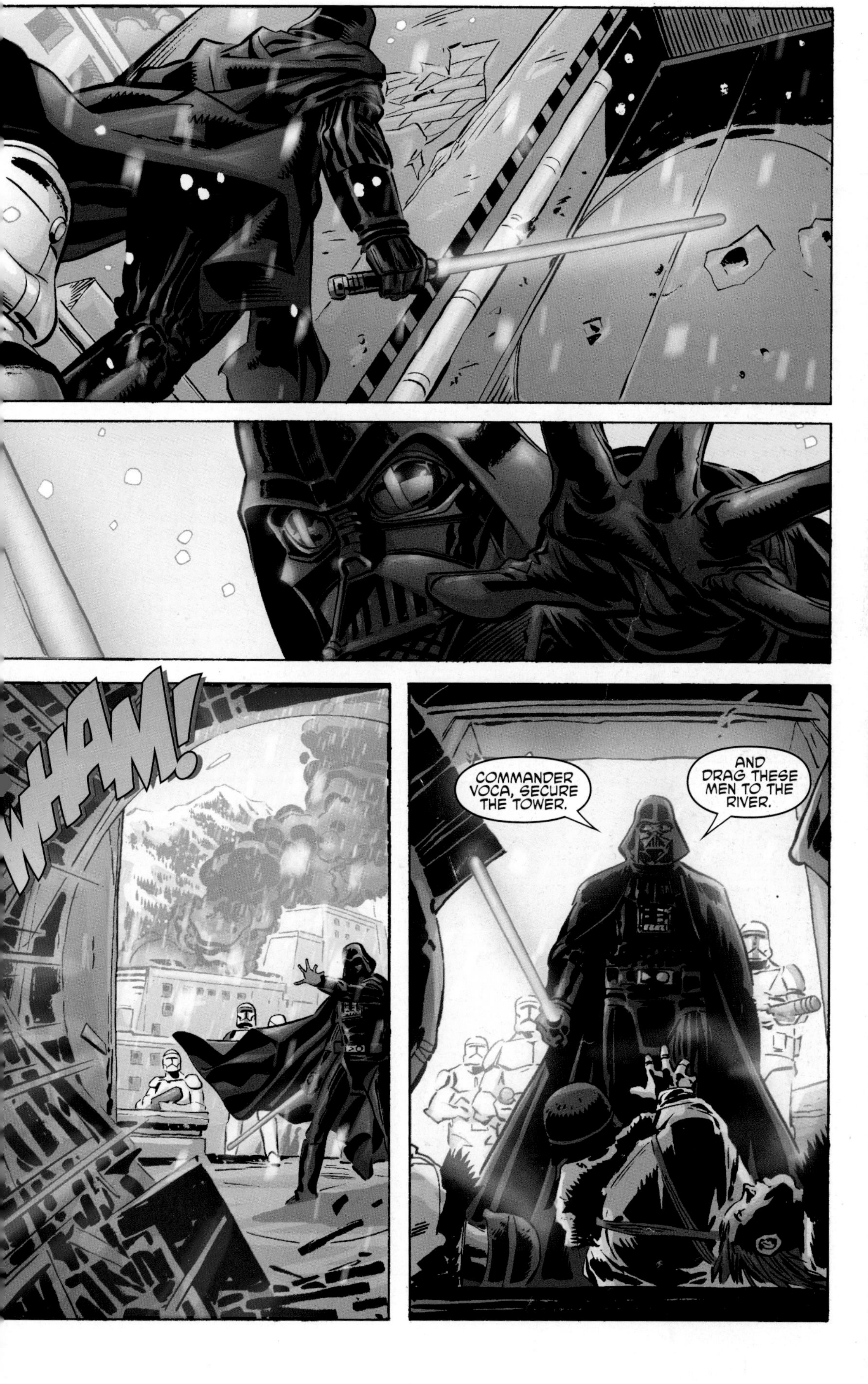
WHAM!
COMMANDER VOCA, SECURE THE TOWER.
AND DRAG THESE MEN TO THE RIVER.

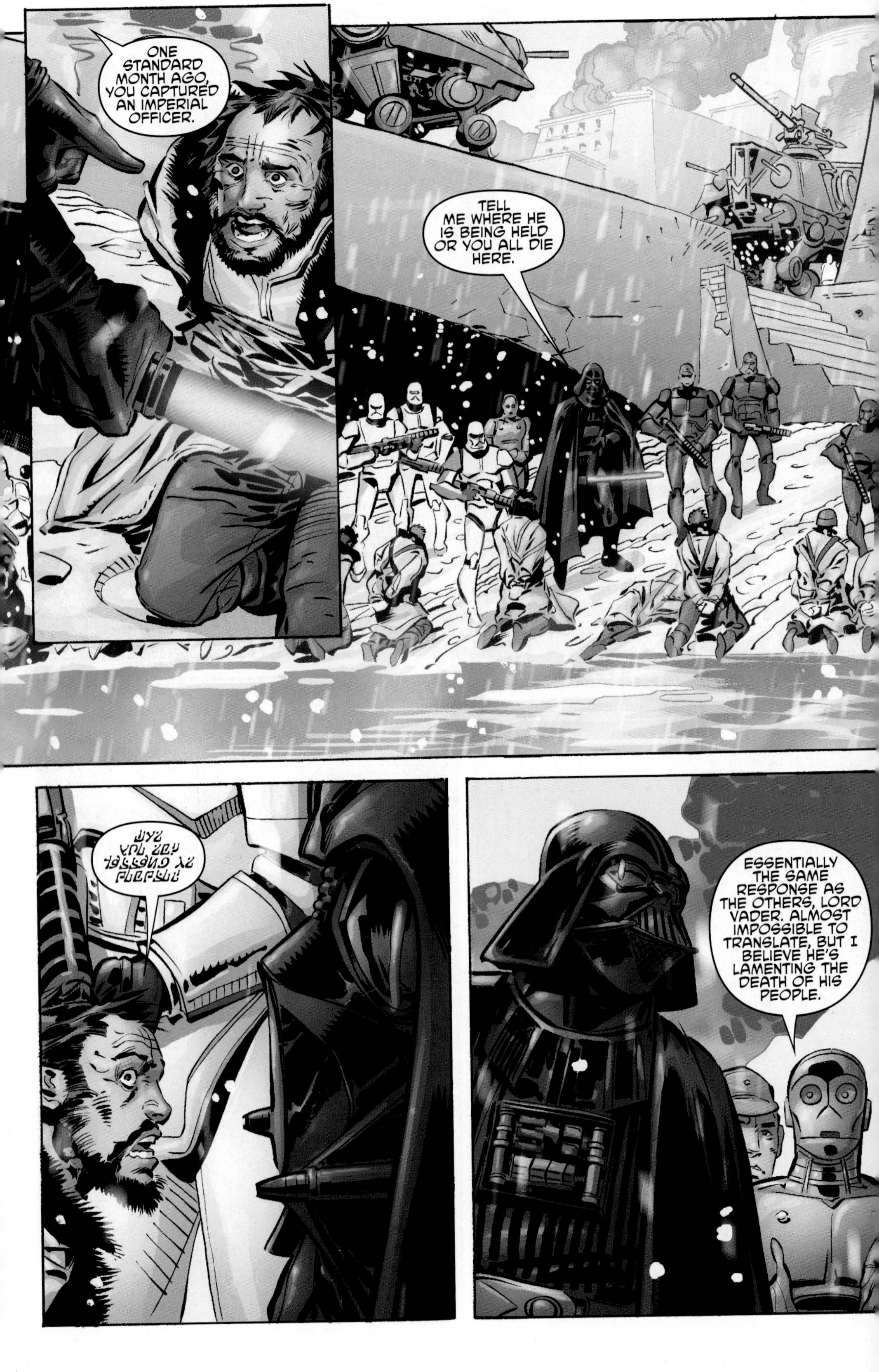
ONE STANDARD MONTH AGO, YOU CAPTURED AN IMPERIAL OFFICER.
TELL ME WHERE HE IS BEING HELD OR YOU ALL DIE HERE.
ESSENTIALLY THE SAME RESPONSE AS THE OTHERS, LORD VADER. ALMOST IMPOSSIBLE TO TRANSLATE, BUT I BELIEVE HE'S LAMENTING THE DEATH OF HIS PEOPLE.

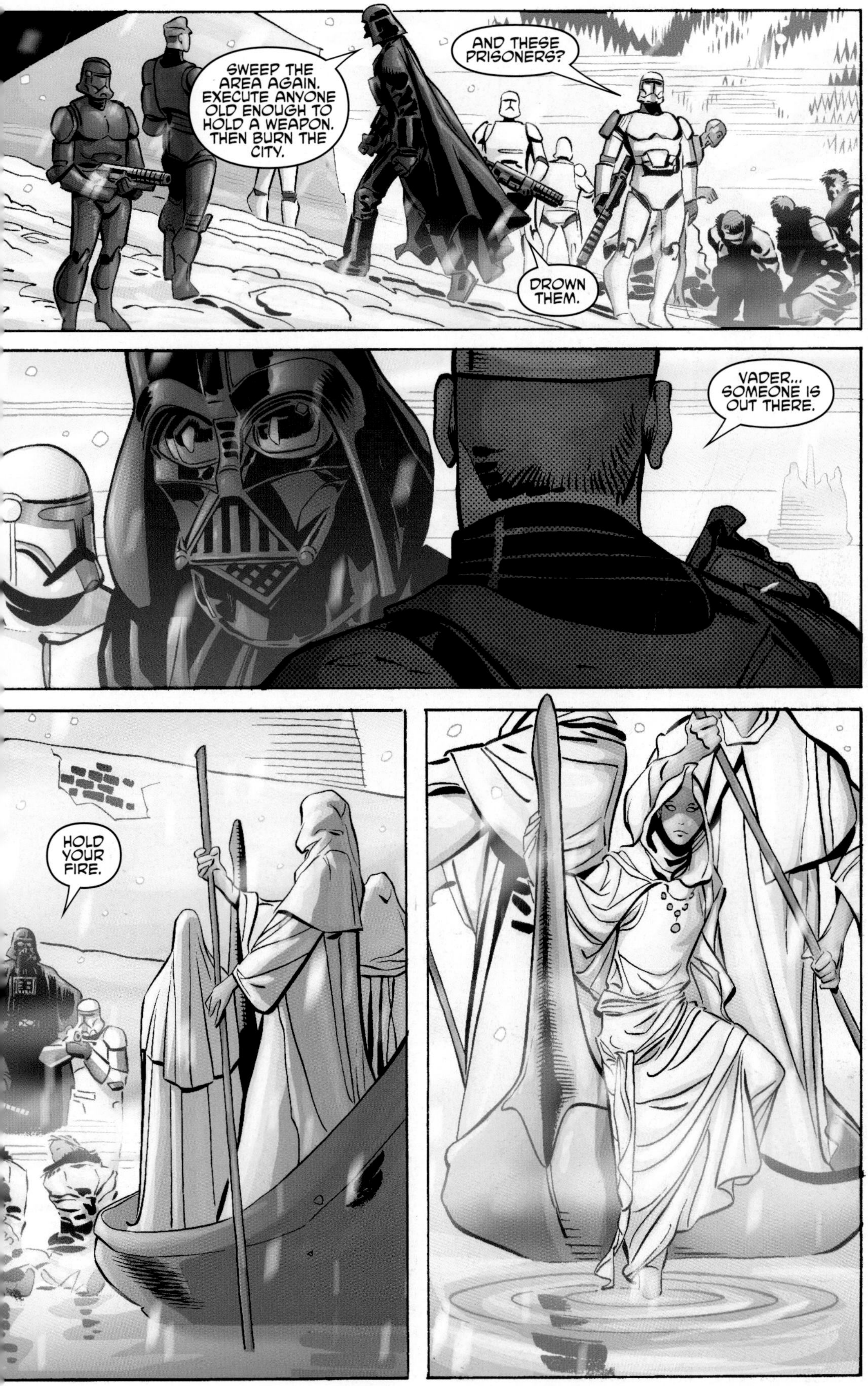
SWEEP THE AREA AGAIN. EXECUTE ANYONE OLD ENOUGH TO HOLD A WEAPON. THEN BURN THE CITY.
AND THESE PRISONERS?
DROWN THEM.
VADER... SOMEONE IS OUT THERE.
HOLD YOUR FIRE.

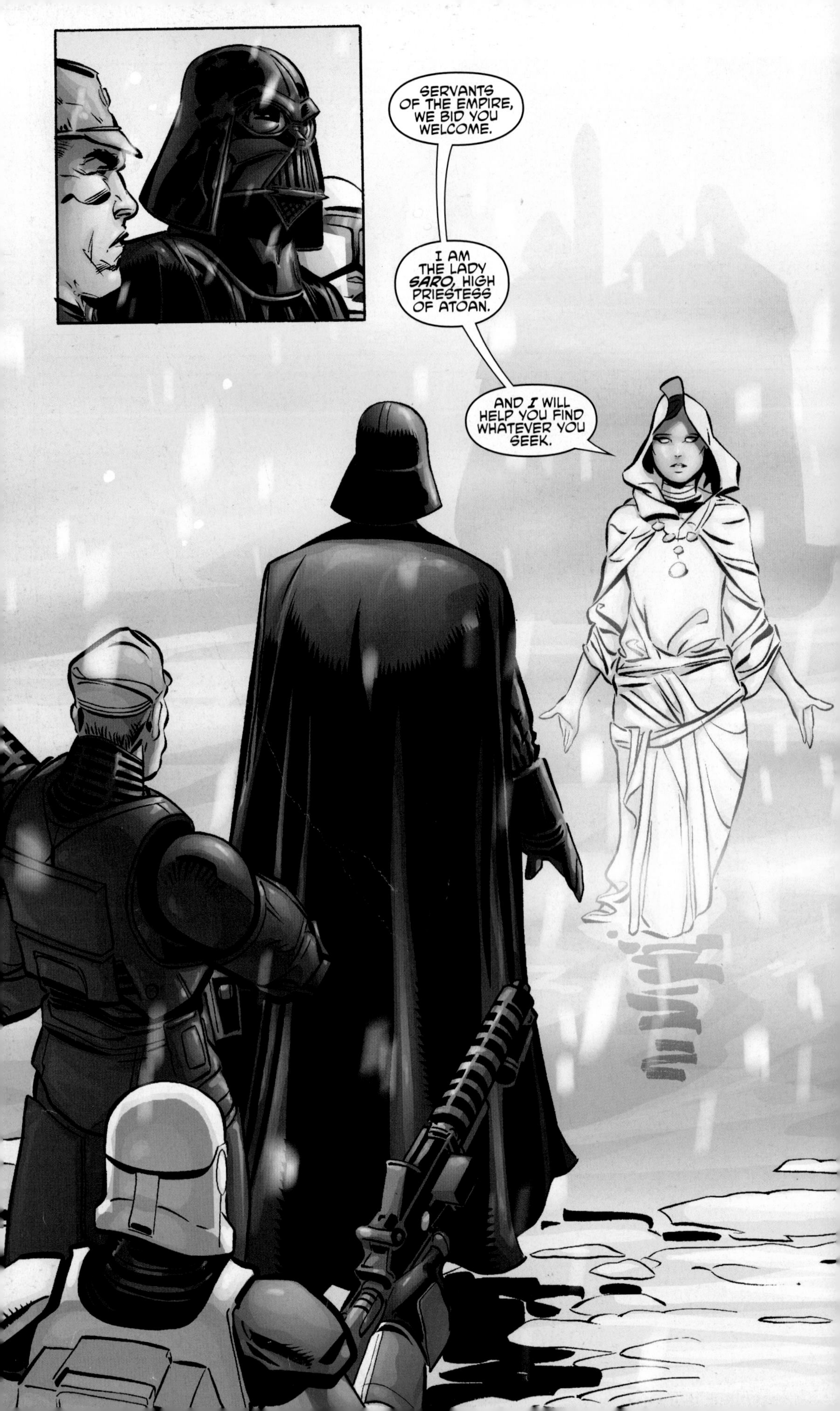
SERVANTS OF THE EMPIRE, WE BID YOU WELCOME.
I AM THE LADY SARO, HIGH PRIESTESS OF ATOAN.
AND I WILL HELP YOU FIND WHATEVER YOU SEEK.

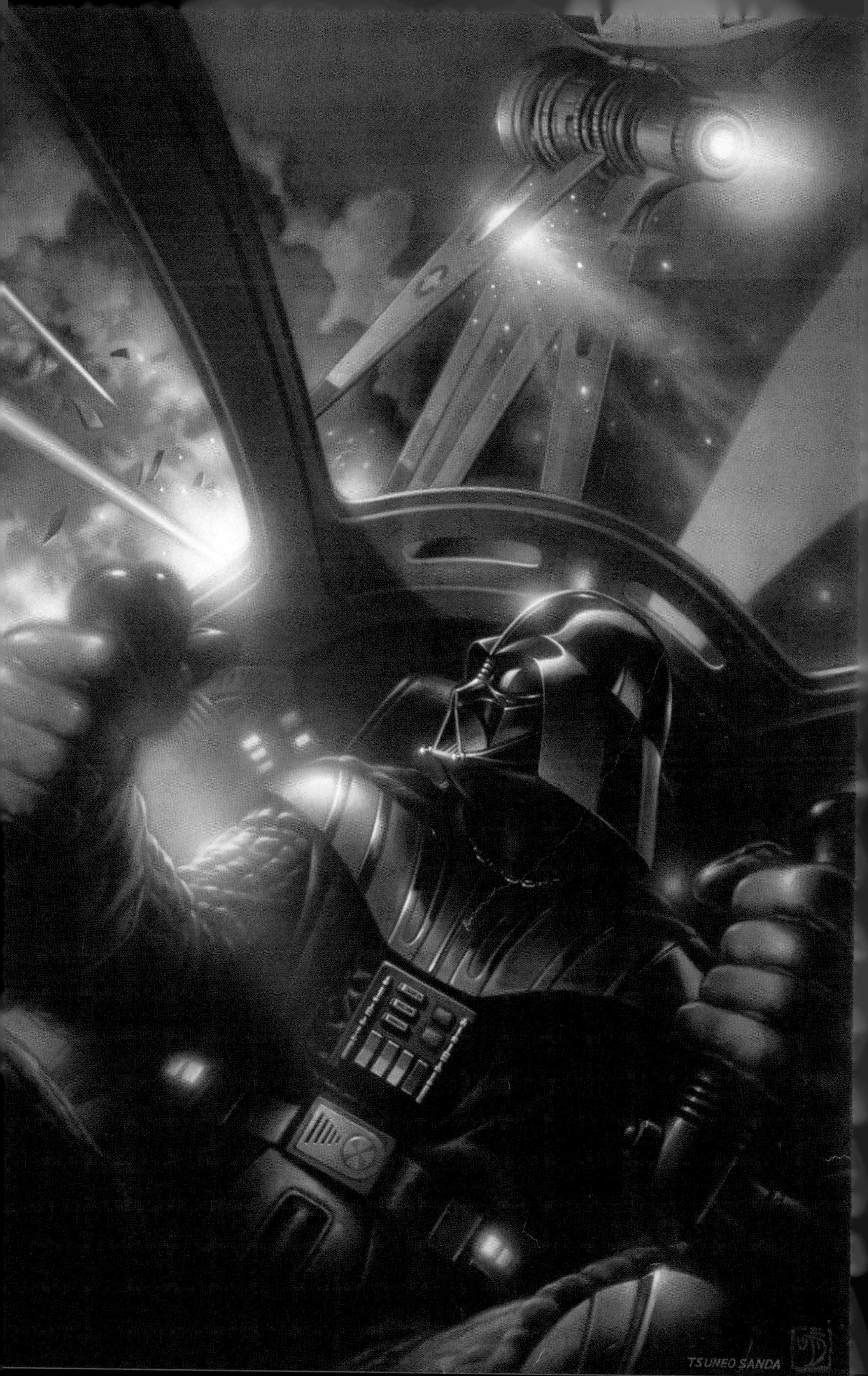
TSUNEO SANDA

STAR WARS: DARTH VADER AND THE LOST COMMAND #2

WRITER: HADEN BLACKMAN • PENCILER: RICK LEONARDI • INKER: DAN GREEN • COLORIST: WES DZIOBA • LETTERER: MICHAEL HEISLER
DESIGNER: STEPHEN REICHERT • ASSISTANT EDITOR: FREDDYE LINS • EDITOR: RANDY STRADLEY • COVER ARTIST: TSUNEO SANDA

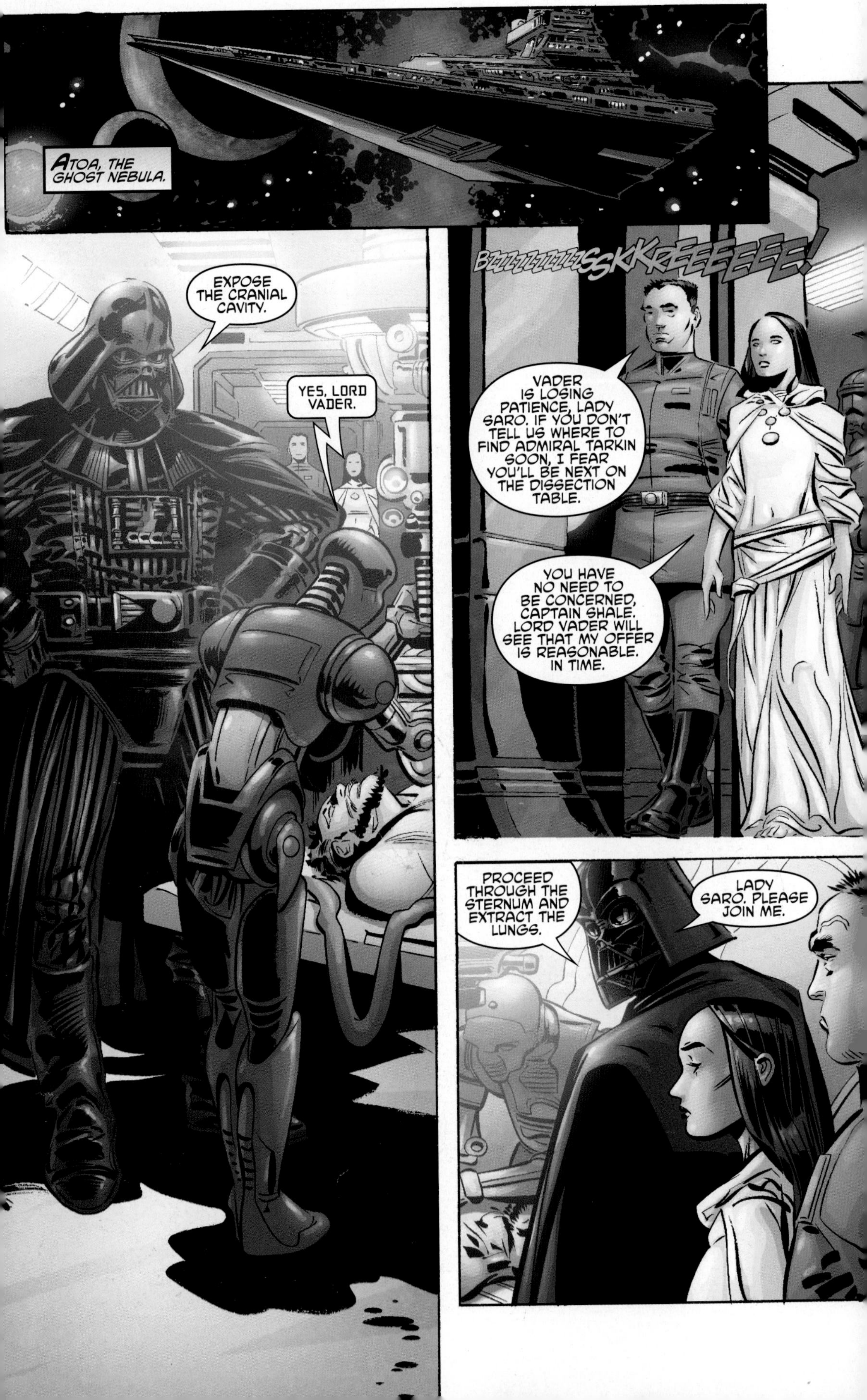

ATOA, THE GHOST NEBULA.
EXPOSE THE CRANIAL CAVITY.
YES, LORD VADER.
BZZZZZZZZZSSKKREEEEEEE!
VADER IS LOSING PATIENCE, LADY SARO. IF YOU DON'T TELL US WHERE TO FIND ADMIRAL TARKIN SOON, I FEAR YOU'LL BE NEXT ON THE DISSECTION TABLE.
YOU HAVE NO NEED TO BE CONCERNED, CAPTAIN SHALE. LORD VADER WILL SEE THAT MY OFFER IS REASONABLE. IN TIME.
PROCEED THROUGH THE STERNUM AND EXTRACT THE LUNGS.
LADY SARO. PLEASE JOIN ME.

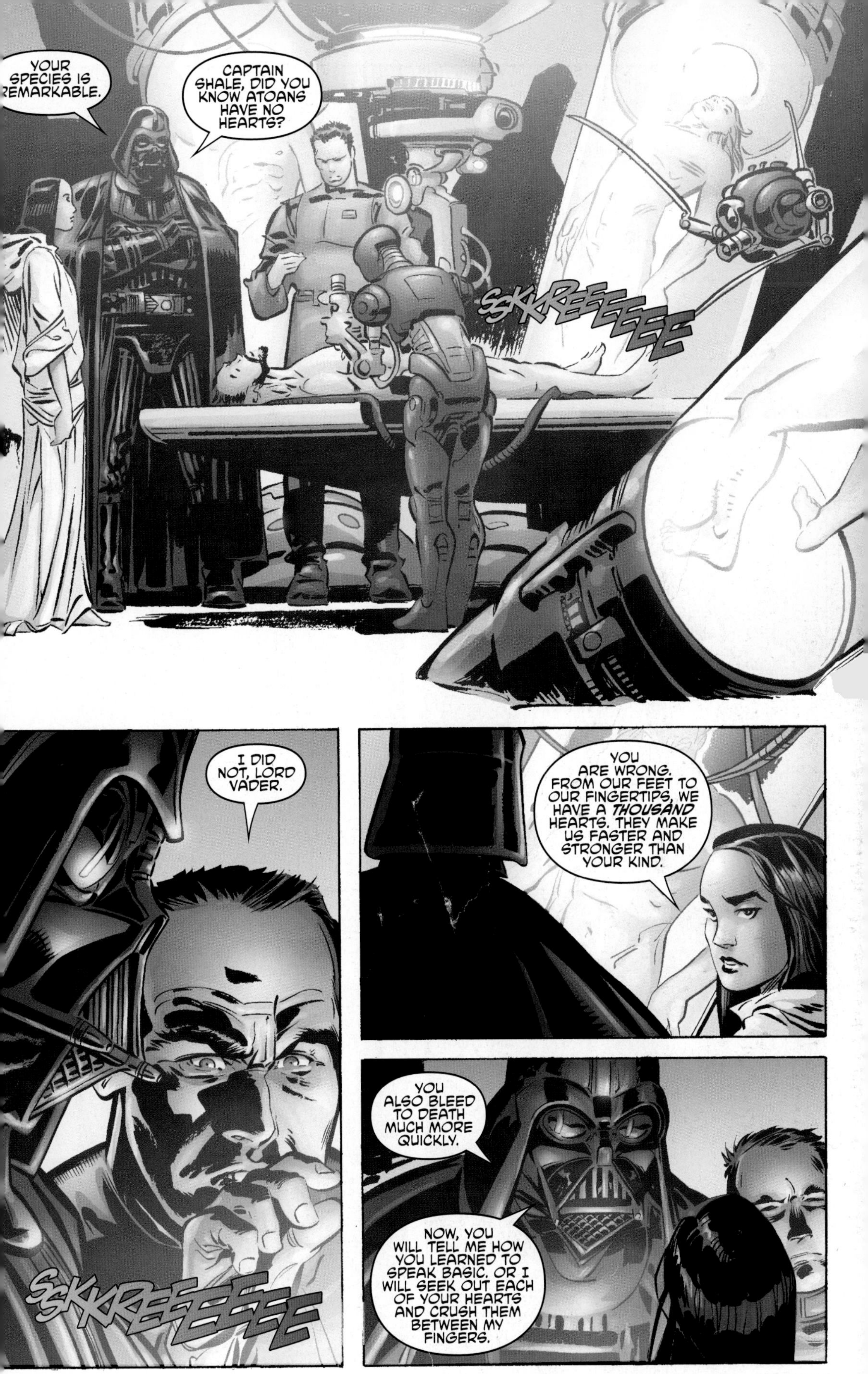
YOUR SPECIES IS REMARKABLE.
CAPTAIN SHALE, DID YOU KNOW ATOANS HAVE NO HEARTS?
SSKKREEEEEEEE
I DID NOT, LORD VADER.
SSKKREEEEEEEE
YOU ARE WRONG. FROM OUR FEET TO OUR FINGERTIPS, WE HAVE A *THOUSAND* HEARTS. THEY MAKE US FASTER AND STRONGER THAN YOUR KIND.
YOU ALSO BLEED TO DEATH MUCH MORE QUICKLY.
NOW, YOU WILL TELL ME HOW YOU LEARNED TO SPEAK BASIC. OR I WILL SEEK OUT EACH OF YOUR HEARTS AND CRUSH THEM BETWEEN MY FINGERS.

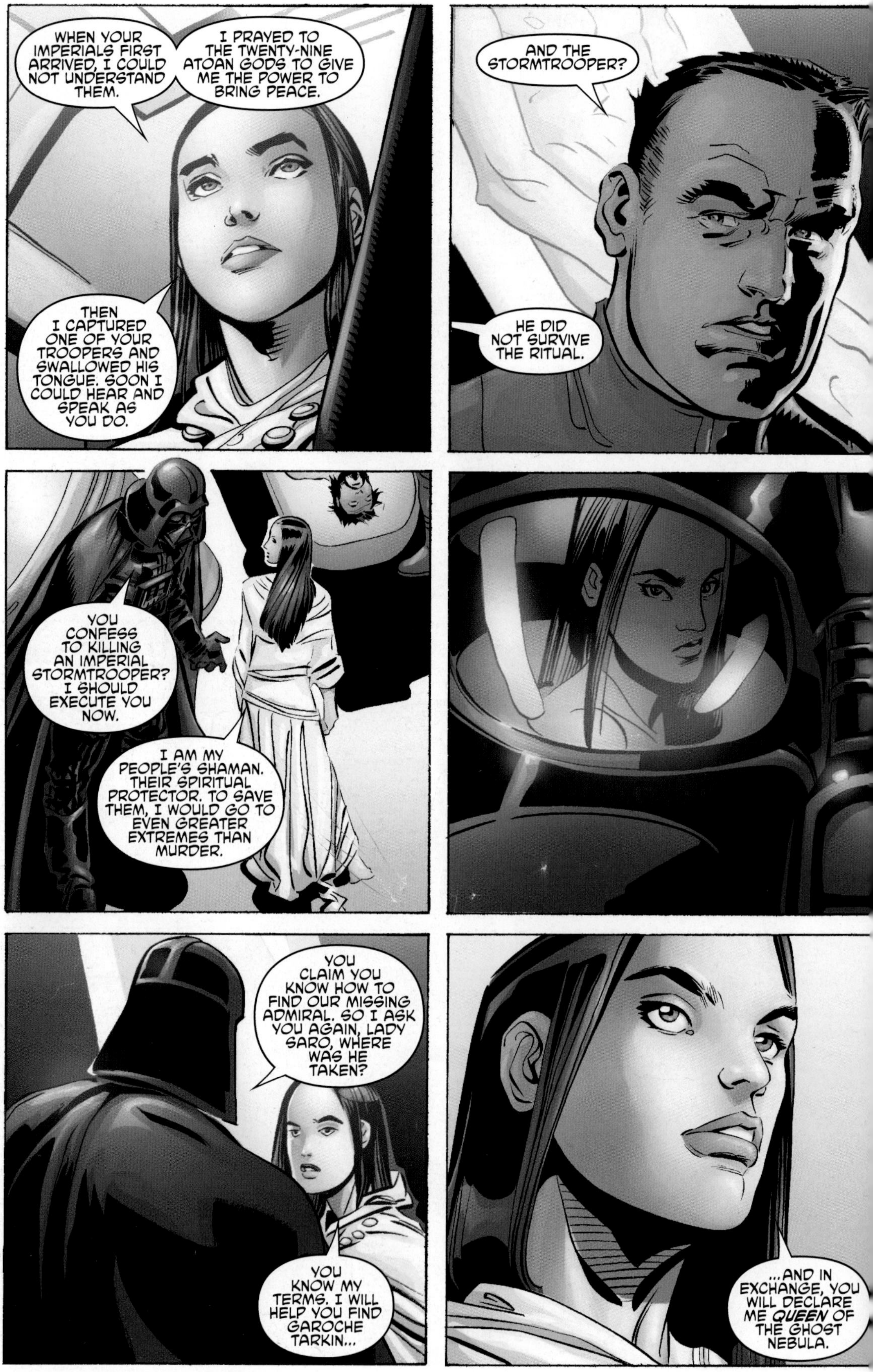
WHEN YOUR IMPERIALS FIRST ARRIVED, I COULD NOT UNDERSTAND THEM.
I PRAYED TO THE TWENTY-NINE ATOAN GODS TO GIVE ME THE POWER TO BRING PEACE.
THEN I CAPTURED ONE OF YOUR TROOPERS AND SWALLOWED HIS TONGUE. SOON I COULD HEAR AND SPEAK AS YOU DO.
AND THE STORMTROOPER?
HE DID NOT SURVIVE THE RITUAL.
YOU CONFESS TO KILLING AN IMPERIAL STORMTROOPER? I SHOULD EXECUTE YOU NOW.
I AM MY PEOPLE'S SHAMAN. THEIR SPIRITUAL PROTECTOR. TO SAVE THEM, I WOULD GO TO EVEN GREATER EXTREMES THAN MURDER.
YOU CLAIM YOU KNOW HOW TO FIND OUR MISSING ADMIRAL. SO I ASK YOU AGAIN, LADY SARO, WHERE WAS HE TAKEN?
YOU KNOW MY TERMS. I WILL HELP YOU FIND GAROCHE TARKIN...
...AND IN EXCHANGE, YOU WILL DECLARE ME *QUEEN* OF THE GHOST NEBULA.

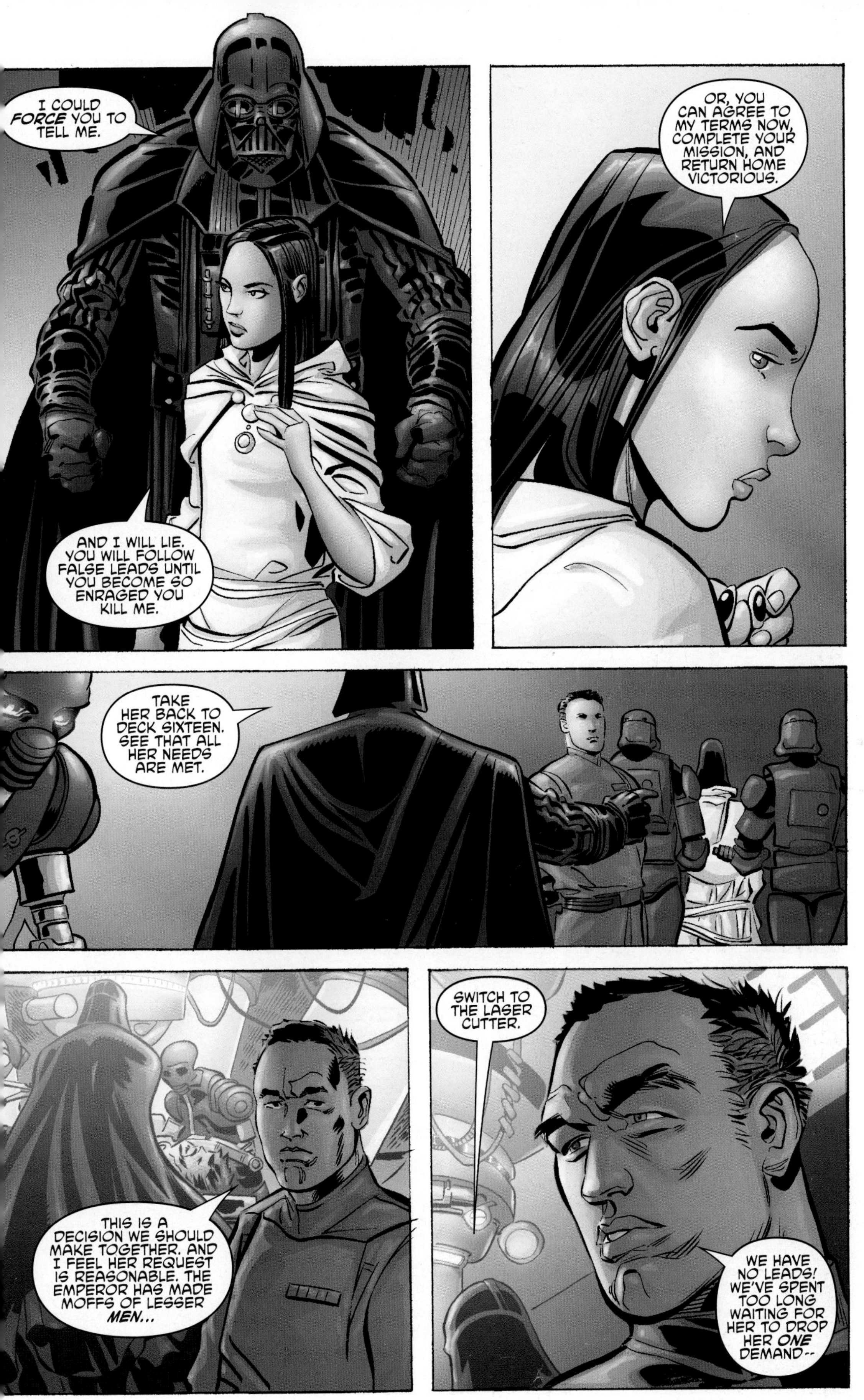
I COULD *FORCE* YOU TO TELL ME.
AND I WILL LIE. YOU WILL FOLLOW FALSE LEADS UNTIL YOU BECOME SO ENRAGED YOU KILL ME.
OR, YOU CAN AGREE TO MY TERMS NOW, COMPLETE YOUR MISSION, AND RETURN HOME VICTORIOUS.
TAKE HER BACK TO DECK SIXTEEN. SEE THAT ALL HER NEEDS ARE MET.
THIS IS A DECISION WE SHOULD MAKE TOGETHER. AND I FEEL HER REQUEST IS REASONABLE. THE EMPEROR HAS MADE MOFFS OF LESSER *MEN*...
SWITCH TO THE LASER CUTTER.
WE HAVE NO LEADS! WE'VE SPENT TOO LONG WAITING FOR HER TO DROP HER *ONE* DEMAND--

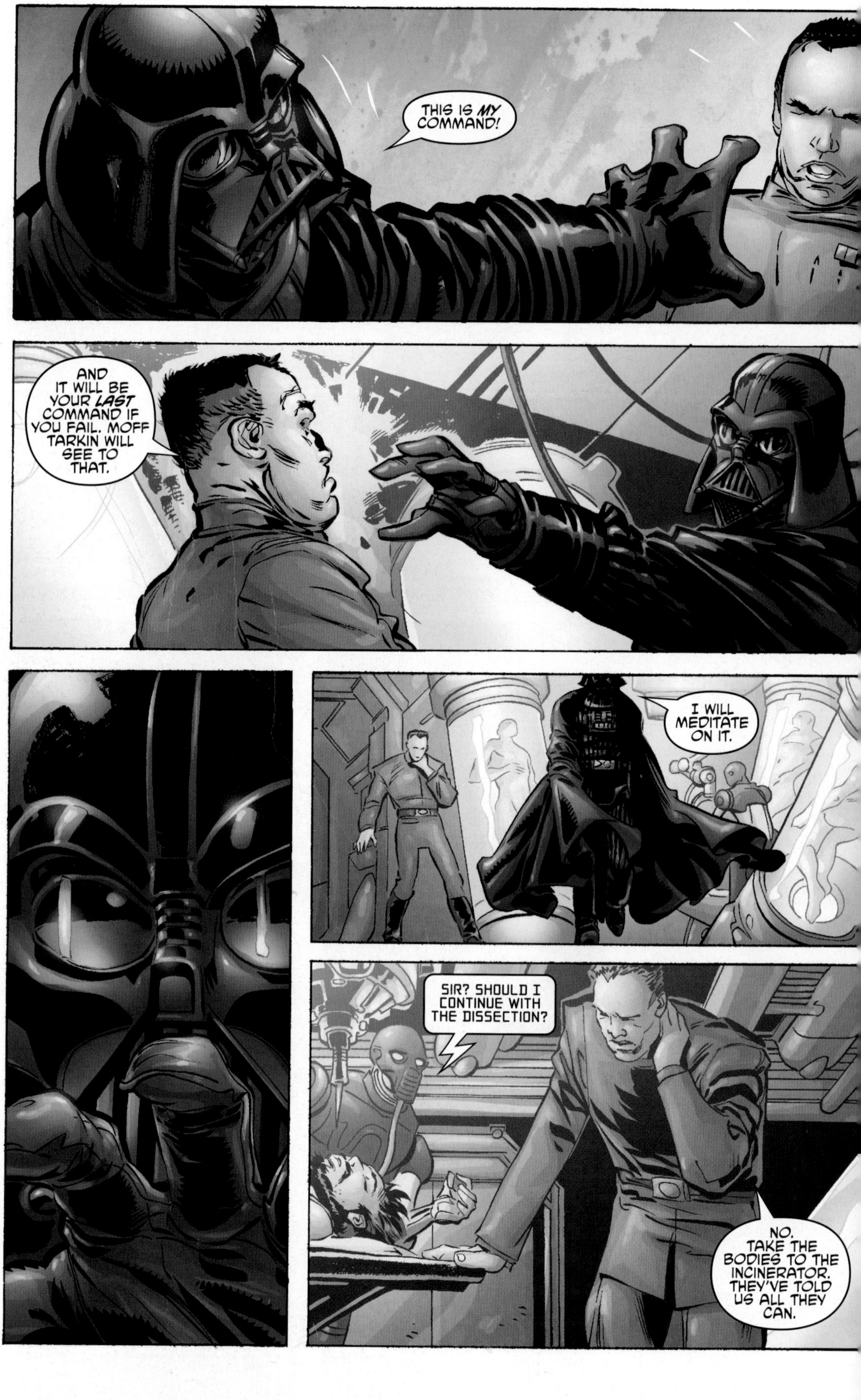
THIS IS *MY* COMMAND!
AND IT WILL BE YOUR *LAST* COMMAND IF YOU FAIL. MOFF TARKIN WILL SEE TO THAT.
I WILL MEDITATE ON IT.
SIR? SHOULD I CONTINUE WITH THE DISSECTION?
NO. TAKE THE BODIES TO THE INCINERATOR. THEY'VE TOLD US ALL THEY CAN.

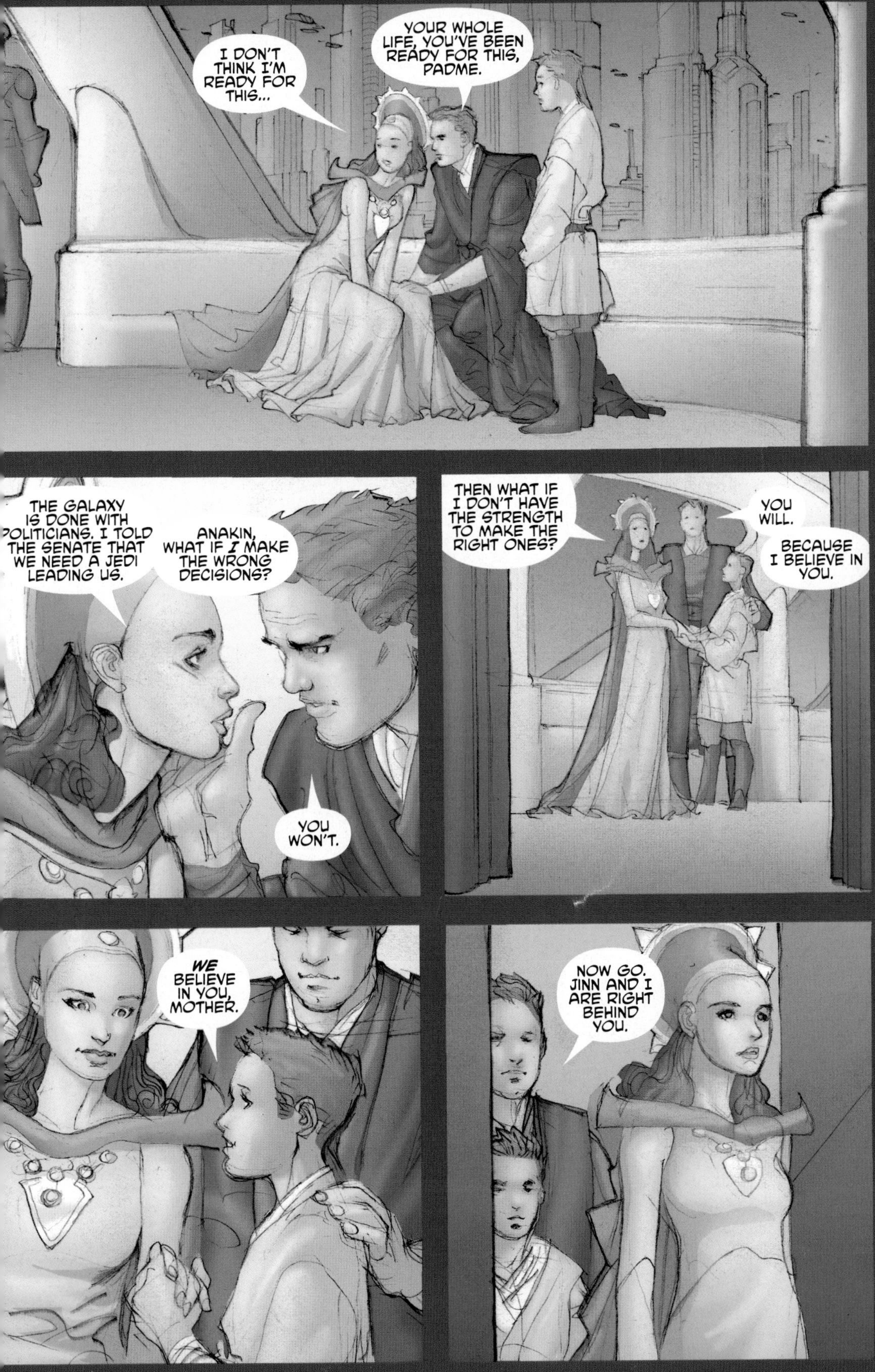
I DON'T THINK I'M READY FOR THIS...
YOUR WHOLE LIFE, YOU'VE BEEN READY FOR THIS, PADME.
THE GALAXY IS DONE WITH POLITICIANS. I TOLD THE SENATE THAT WE NEED A JEDI LEADING US.
ANAKIN, WHAT IF *I* MAKE THE WRONG DECISIONS?
YOU WON'T.
THEN WHAT IF I DON'T HAVE THE STRENGTH TO MAKE THE RIGHT ONES?
YOU WILL.
BECAUSE I BELIEVE IN YOU.
WE BELIEVE IN YOU, MOTHER.
NOW GO. JINN AND I ARE RIGHT BEHIND YOU.

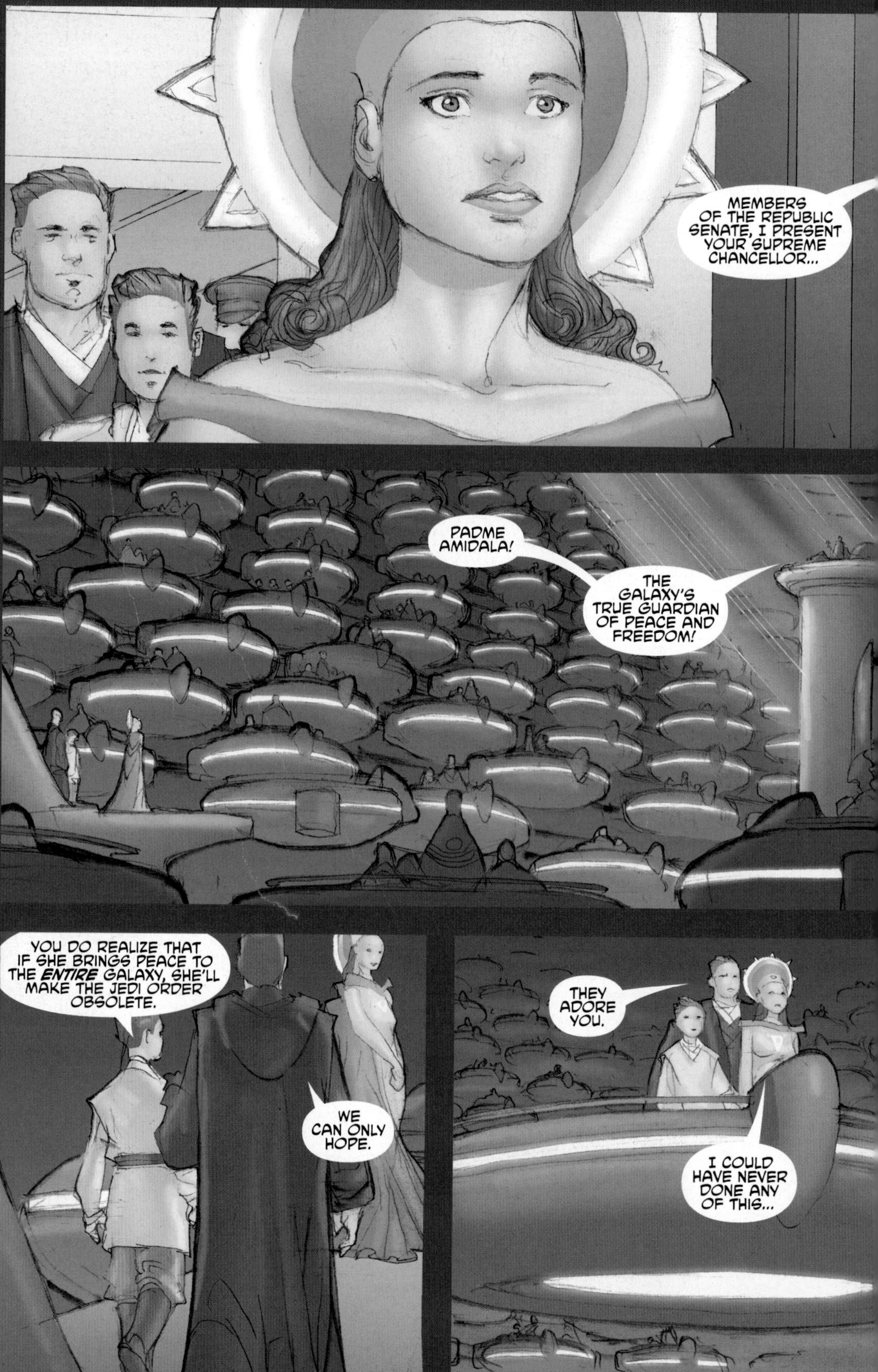
MEMBERS OF THE REPUBLIC SENATE, I PRESENT YOUR SUPREME CHANCELLOR...
PADME AMIDALA!
THE GALAXY'S TRUE GUARDIAN OF PEACE AND FREEDOM!
YOU DO REALIZE THAT IF SHE BRINGS PEACE TO THE *ENTIRE* GALAXY, SHE'LL MAKE THE JEDI ORDER OBSOLETE.
WE CAN ONLY HOPE.
THEY ADORE YOU.
I COULD HAVE NEVER DONE ANY OF THIS...

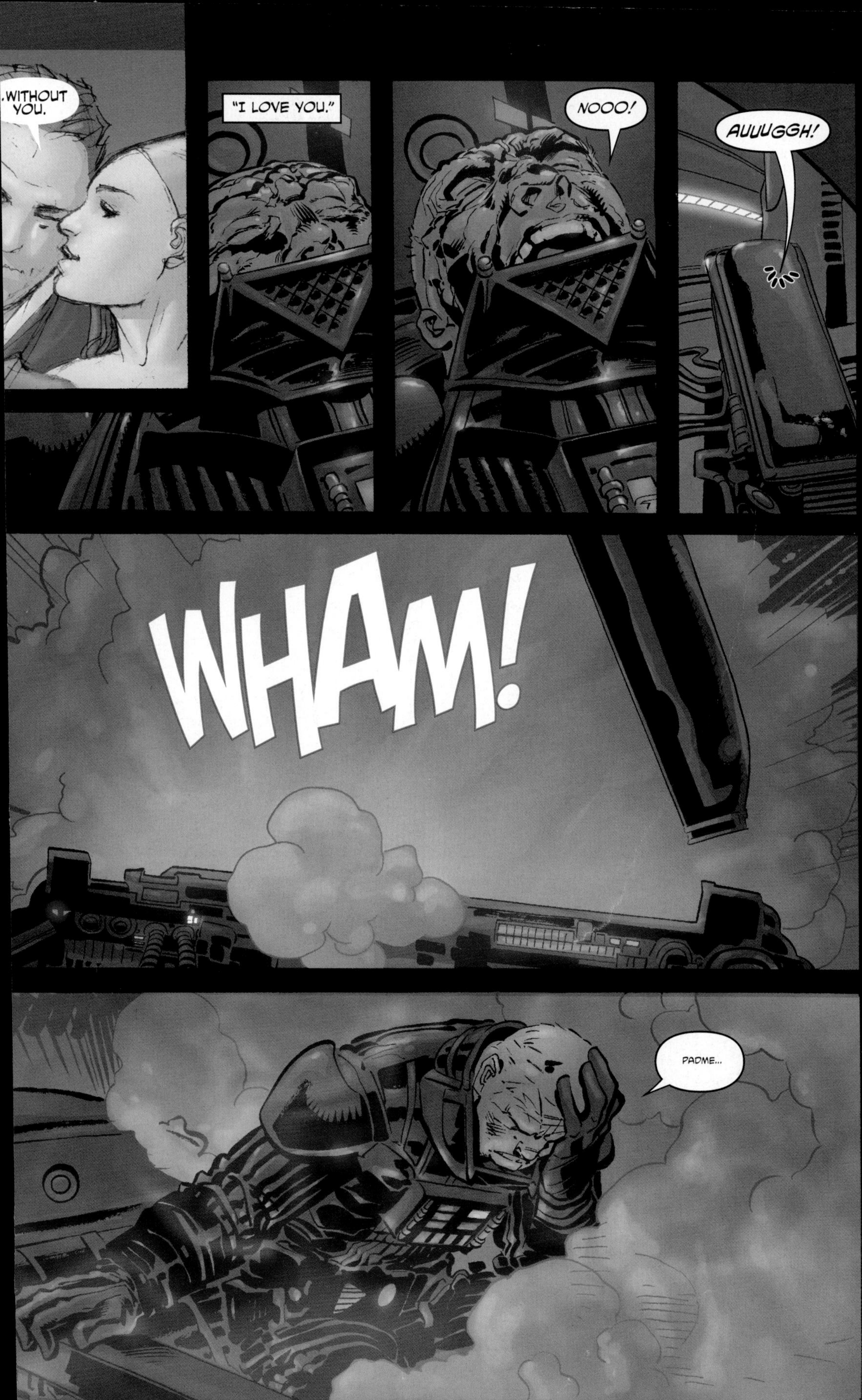
...WITHOUT YOU.
"I LOVE YOU."
NOOO!
AUUUGGH!
WHAM!
PADME...

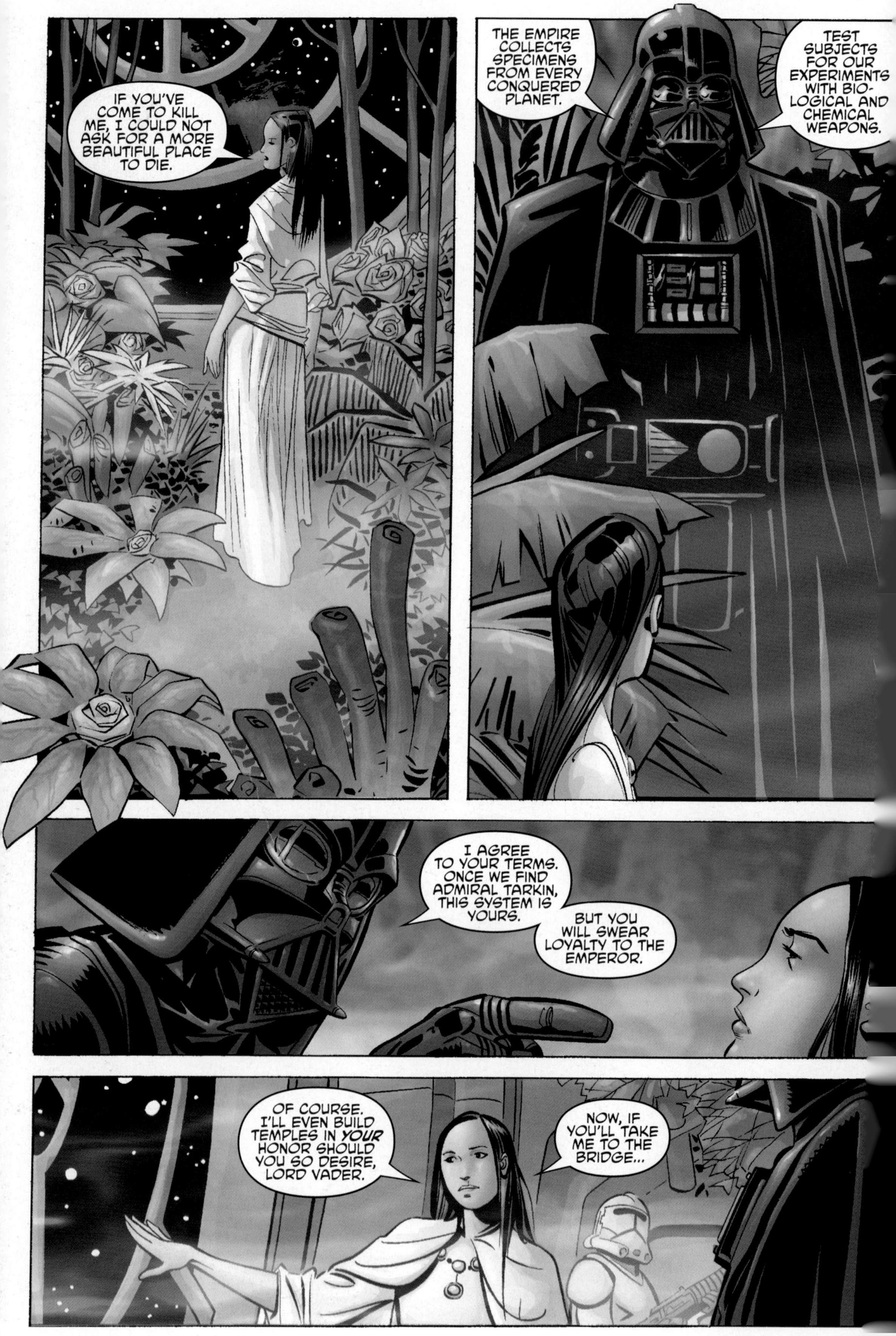
IF YOU'VE COME TO KILL ME, I COULD NOT ASK FOR A MORE BEAUTIFUL PLACE TO DIE.
THE EMPIRE COLLECTS SPECIMENS FROM EVERY CONQUERED PLANET.
TEST SUBJECTS FOR OUR EXPERIMENTS WITH BIO-LOGICAL AND CHEMICAL WEAPONS.
I AGREE TO YOUR TERMS. ONCE WE FIND ADMIRAL TARKIN, THIS SYSTEM IS YOURS.
BUT YOU WILL SWEAR LOYALTY TO THE EMPEROR.
OF COURSE. I'LL EVEN BUILD TEMPLES IN *YOUR* HONOR SHOULD YOU SO DESIRE, LORD VADER.
NOW, IF YOU'LL TAKE ME TO THE BRIDGE...

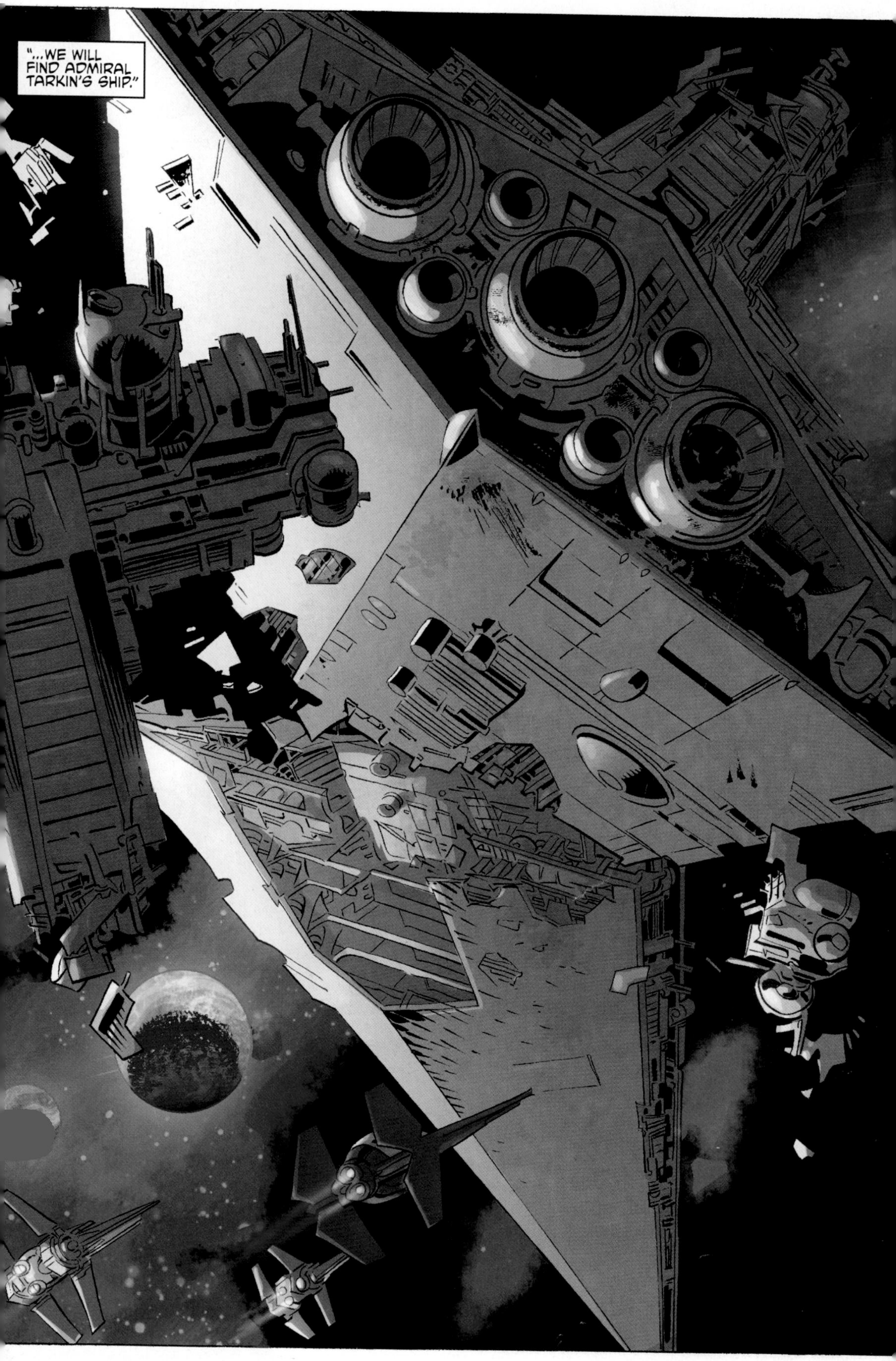
"...WE WILL FIND ADMIRAL TARKIN'S SHIP."

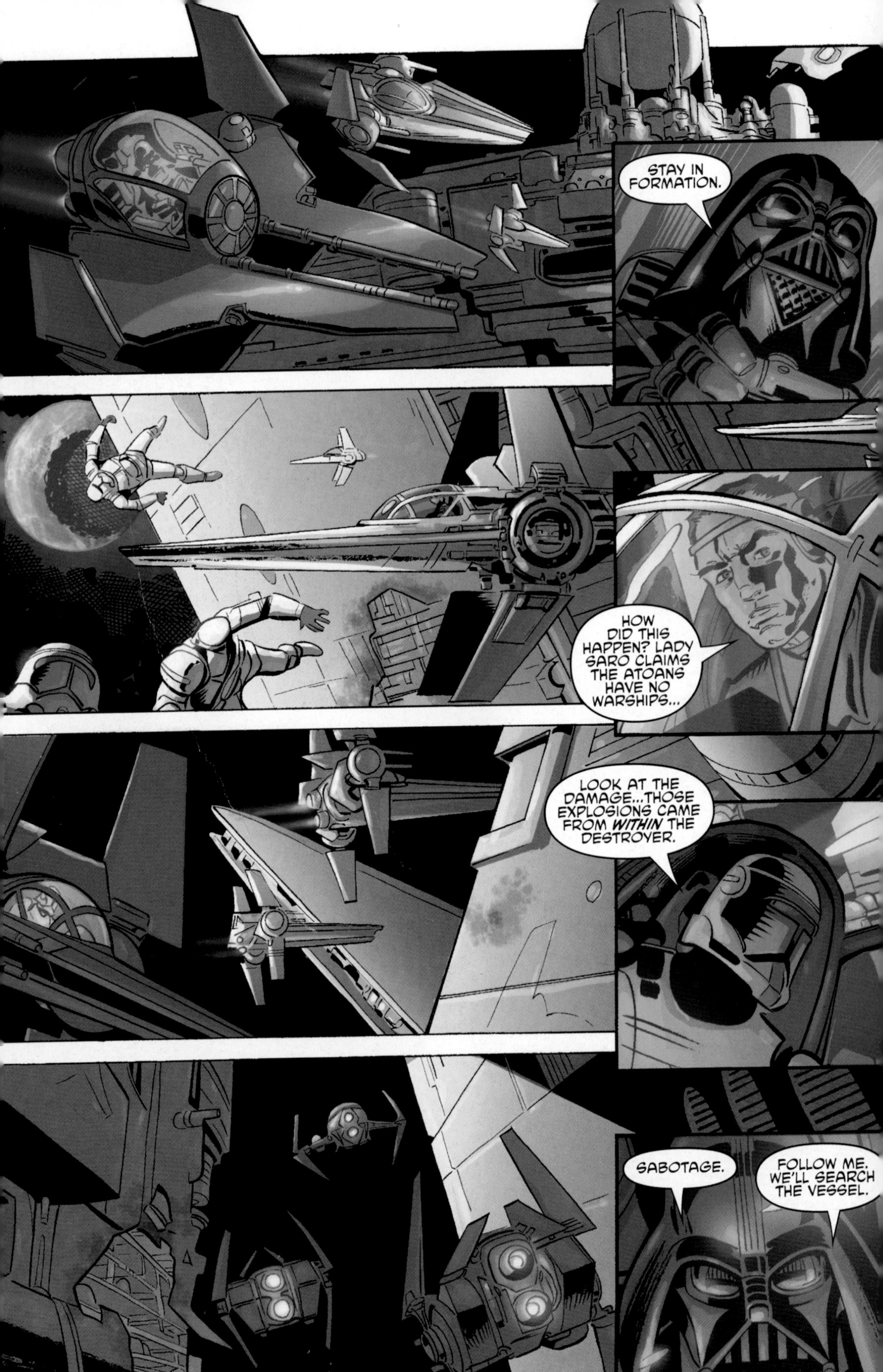
STAY IN FORMATION.
HOW DID THIS HAPPEN? LADY SARO CLAIMS THE ATOANS HAVE NO WARSHIPS...
LOOK AT THE DAMAGE...THOSE EXPLOSIONS CAME FROM *WITHIN* THE DESTROYER.
SABOTAGE.
FOLLOW ME. WE'LL SEARCH THE VESSEL.

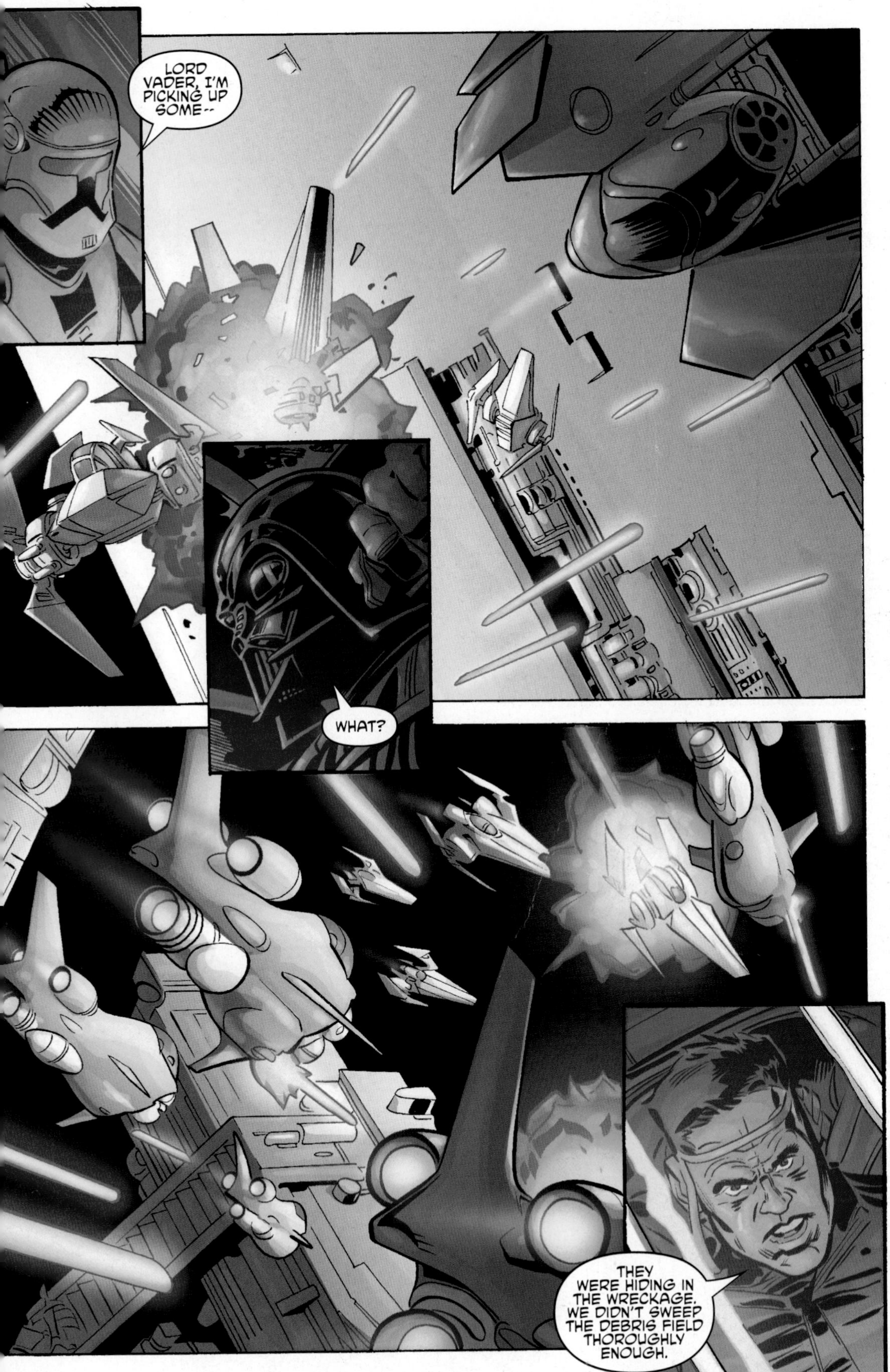
LORD VADER, I'M PICKING UP SOME--
WHAT?
THEY WERE HIDING IN THE WRECKAGE. WE DIDN'T SWEEP THE DEBRIS FIELD THOROUGHLY ENOUGH.

MOVE INTO
ATTACK
POSITIONS.

IGNEXAGNE
IGNEXAGNE

YYYYAAAAGHH!

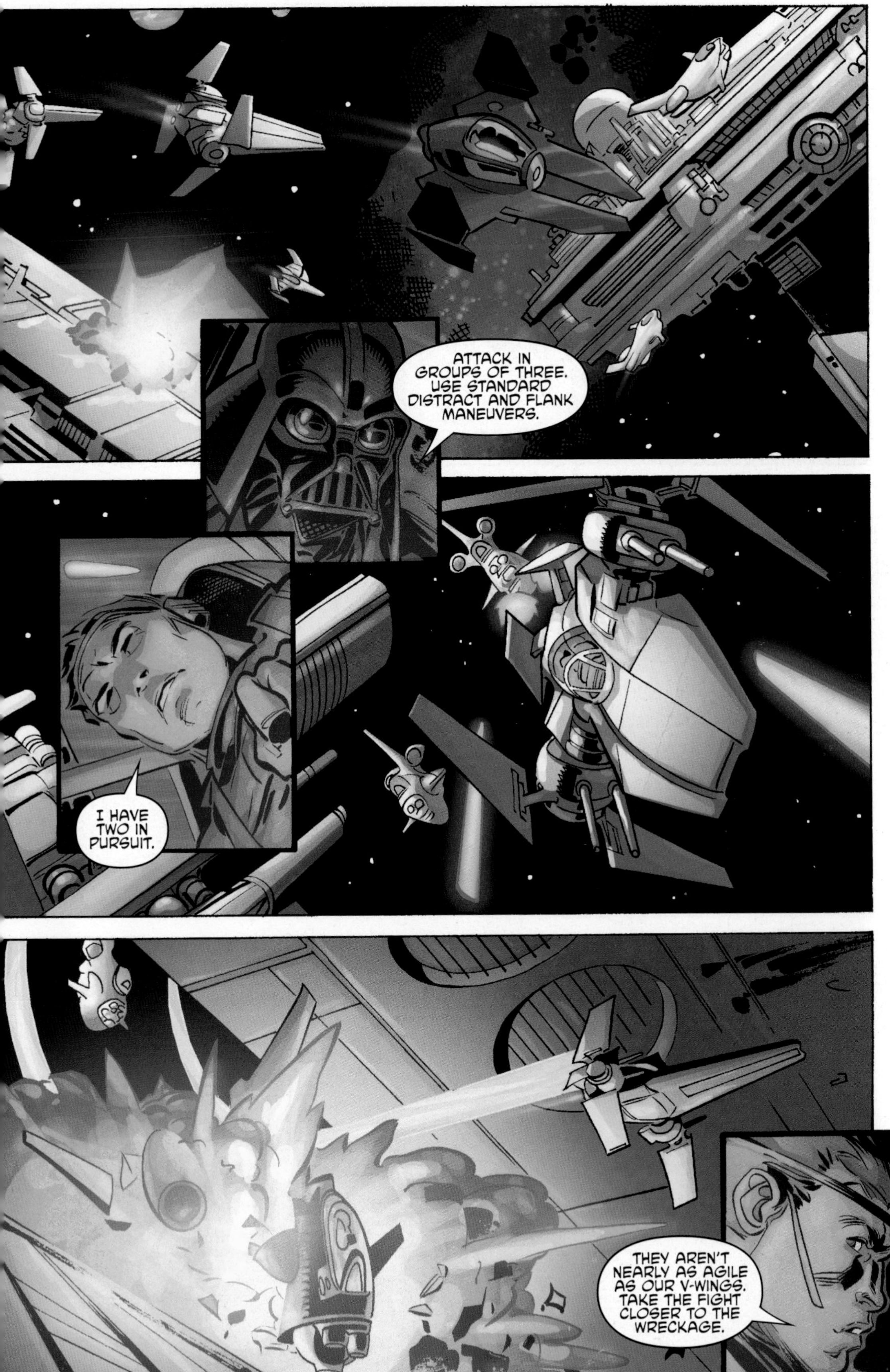
ATTACK IN GROUPS OF THREE. USE STANDARD DISTRACT AND FLANK MANEUVERS.
I HAVE TWO IN PURSUIT.
THEY AREN'T NEARLY AS AGILE AS OUR V-WINGS. TAKE THE FIGHT CLOSER TO THE WRECKAGE.

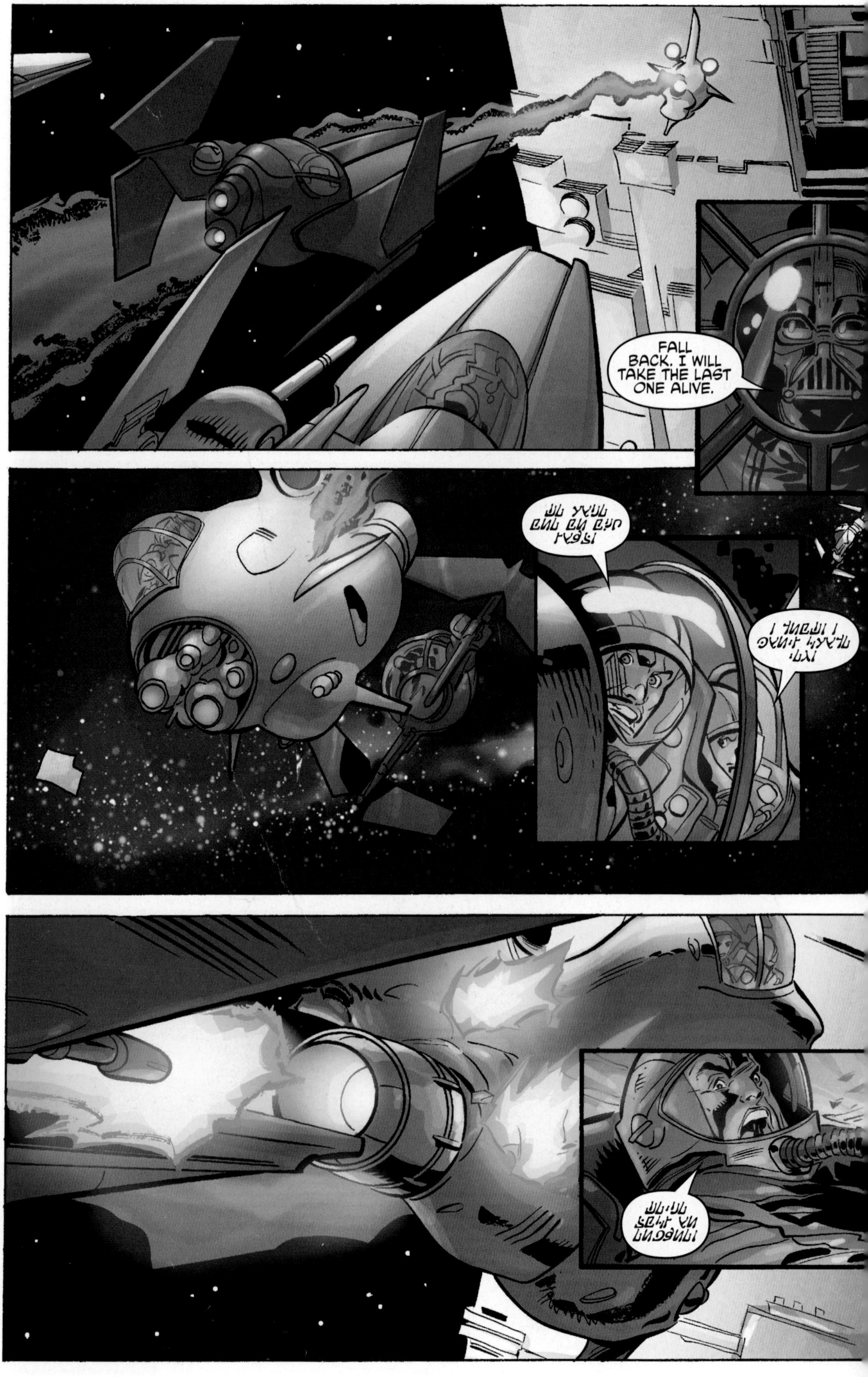
FALL BACK. I WILL TAKE THE LAST ONE ALIVE.

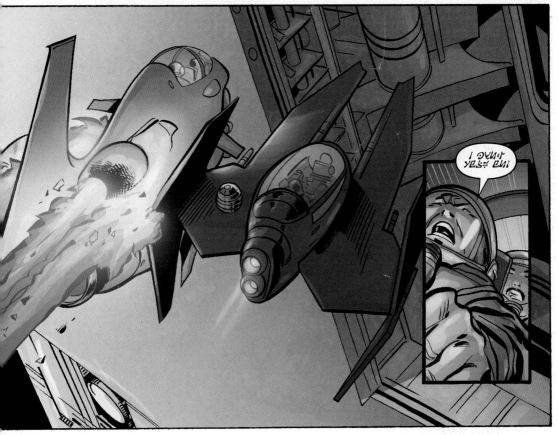

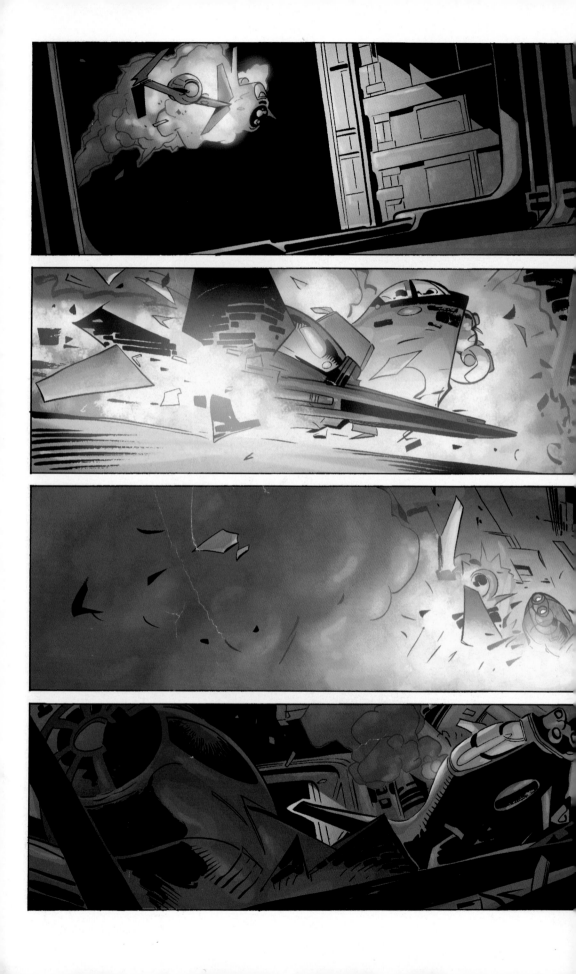

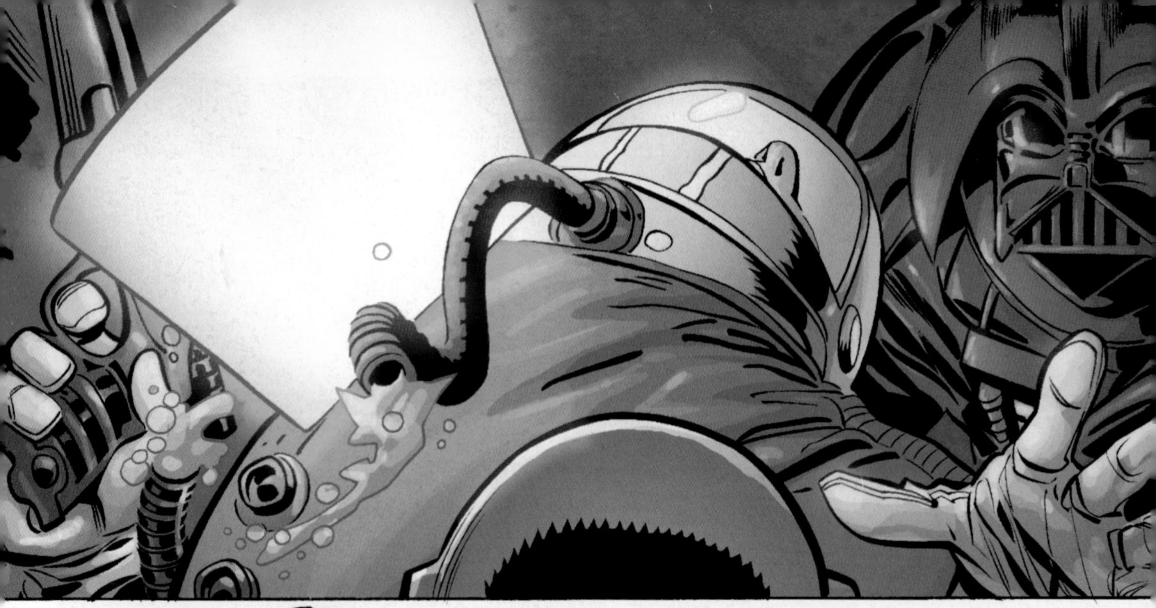

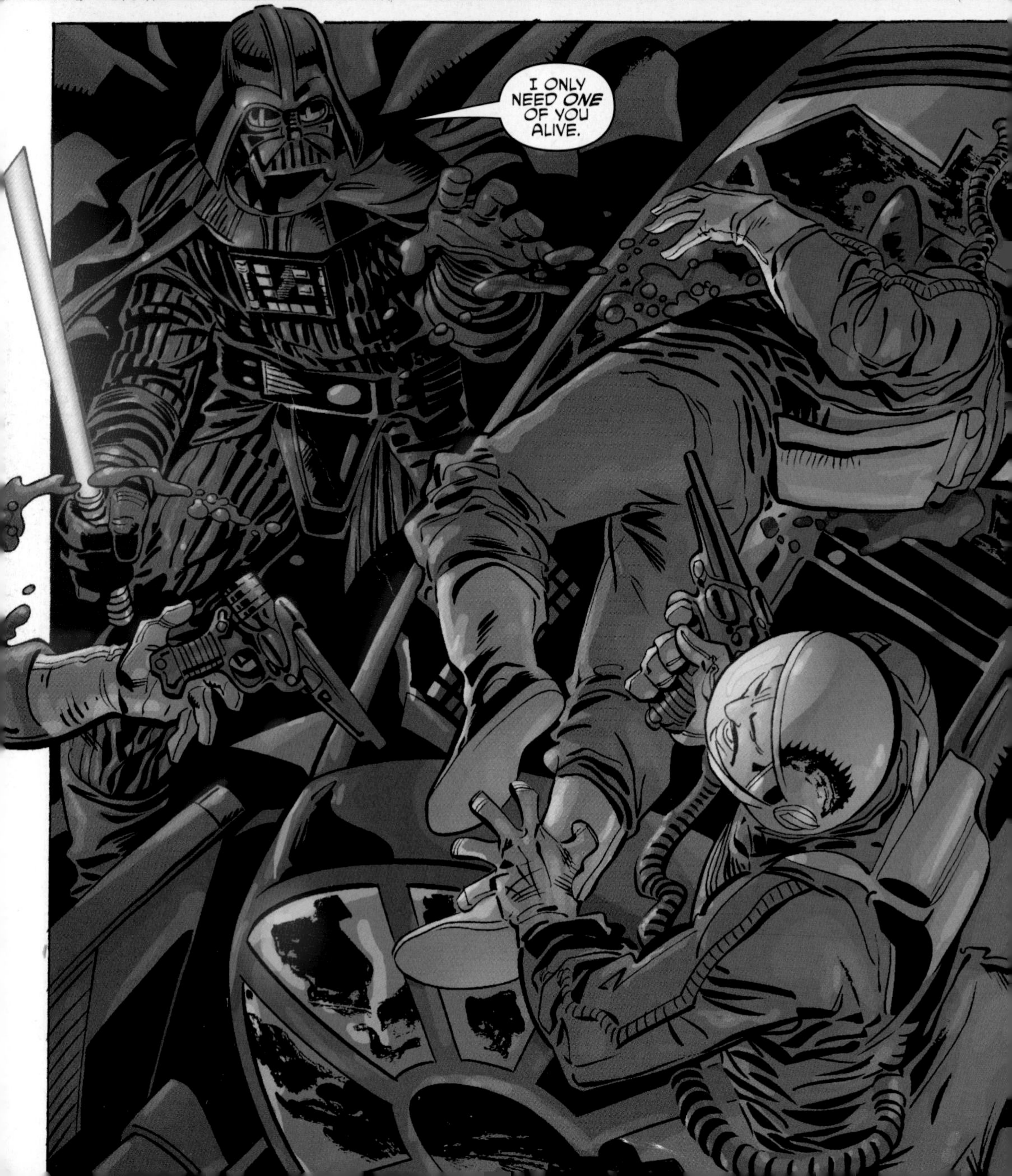

I ONLY NEED *ONE* OF YOU ALIVE.

THE PILOT REVEALED EVERYTHING BEFORE HE DIED. WE ARE ALREADY EN ROUTE TO OUR NEXT TARGET.

THIS MISSION IS VITAL, LORD VADER--

LIKE ALL OUR WORLDS, THIS ONE HAS NO NAME THAT YOU WOULD UNDERSTAND.

IT HAS ONLY RECENTLY BEEN SETTLED. MOST OF THE PLANET IS COVERED IN BLACK OCEANS.

-- GAROCHE TARKIN IS EASILY REPLACEABLE, BUT HIS FATHER IS A POWERFUL AND LOYAL ALLY.

HE EXCELS AT SPREADING FEAR. I WILL NOT HAVE HIM DISTRACTED.

OCEANS OF *WHAT?*

I DO NOT KNOW WHAT TO CALL IT IN YOUR LANGUAGE. BUT THE SEAS CONSUME ALL WHO ENTER.

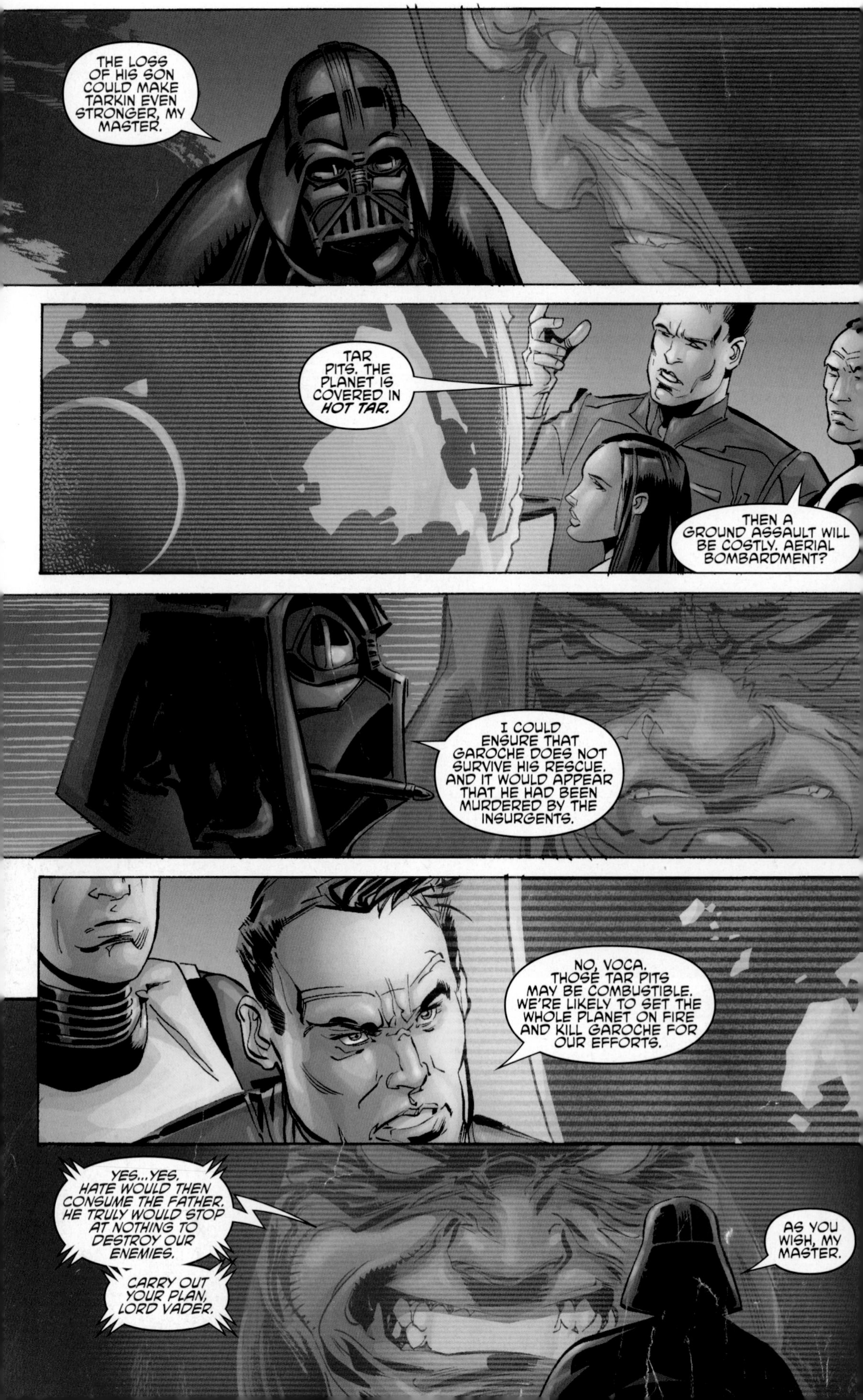
THE LOSS OF HIS SON COULD MAKE TARKIN EVEN STRONGER, MY MASTER.
TAR PITS. THE PLANET IS COVERED IN *HOT TAR.*
THEN A GROUND ASSAULT WILL BE COSTLY. AERIAL BOMBARDMENT?
I COULD ENSURE THAT GAROCHE DOES NOT SURVIVE HIS RESCUE. AND IT WOULD APPEAR THAT HE HAD BEEN MURDERED BY THE INSURGENTS.
NO, VOCA. THOSE TAR PITS MAY BE COMBUSTIBLE. WE'RE LIKELY TO SET THE WHOLE PLANET ON FIRE AND KILL GAROCHE FOR OUR EFFORTS.
YES...YES. HATE WOULD THEN CONSUME THE FATHER. HE TRULY WOULD STOP AT NOTHING TO DESTROY OUR ENEMIES.
CARRY OUT YOUR PLAN, LORD VADER.
AS YOU WISH, MY MASTER.

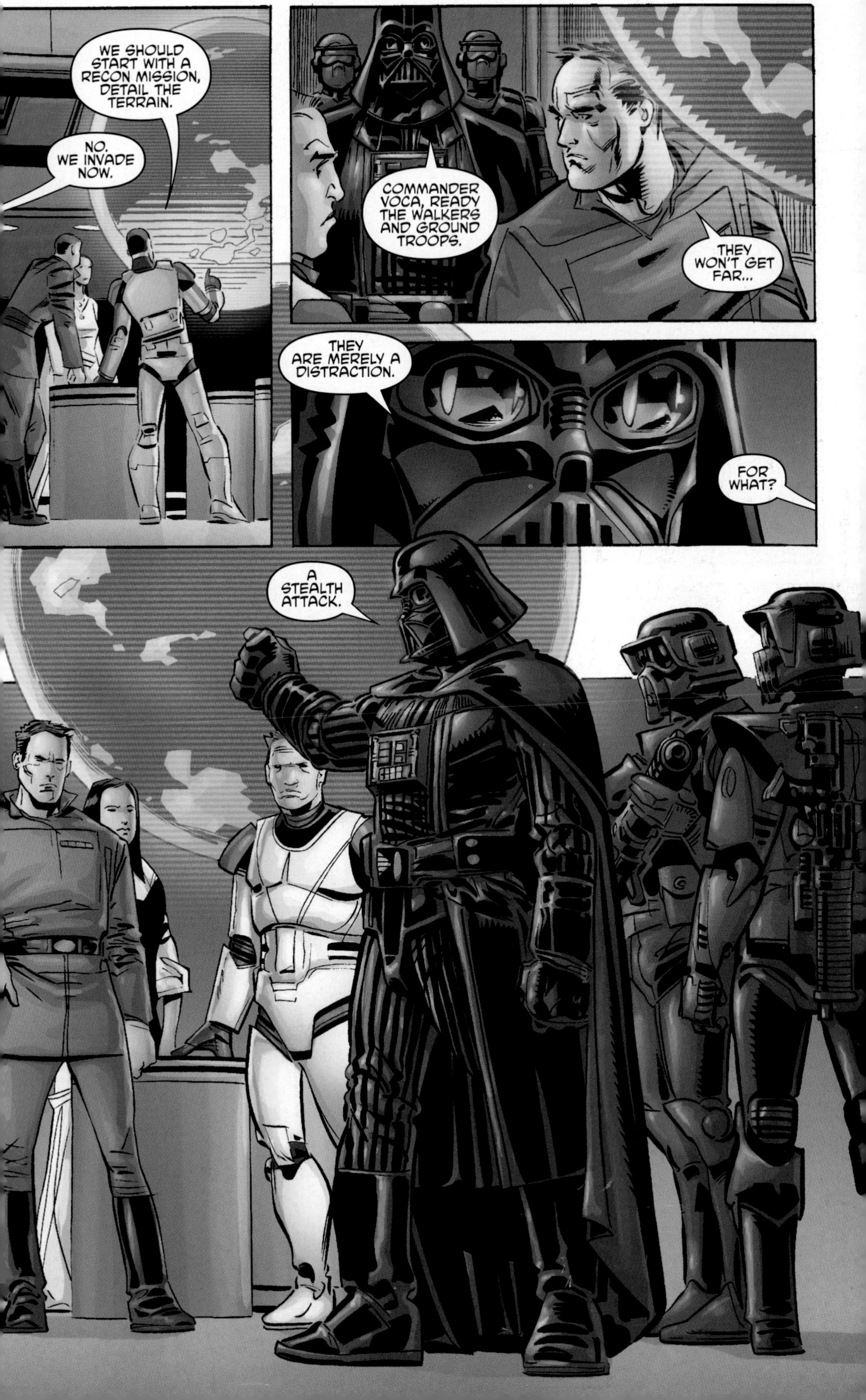
WE SHOULD START WITH A RECON MISSION, DETAIL THE TERRAIN.
NO. WE INVADE NOW.
COMMANDER VOCA, READY THE WALKERS AND GROUND TROOPS.
THEY WON'T GET FAR...
THEY ARE MERELY A DISTRACTION.
FOR WHAT?
A STEALTH ATTACK.

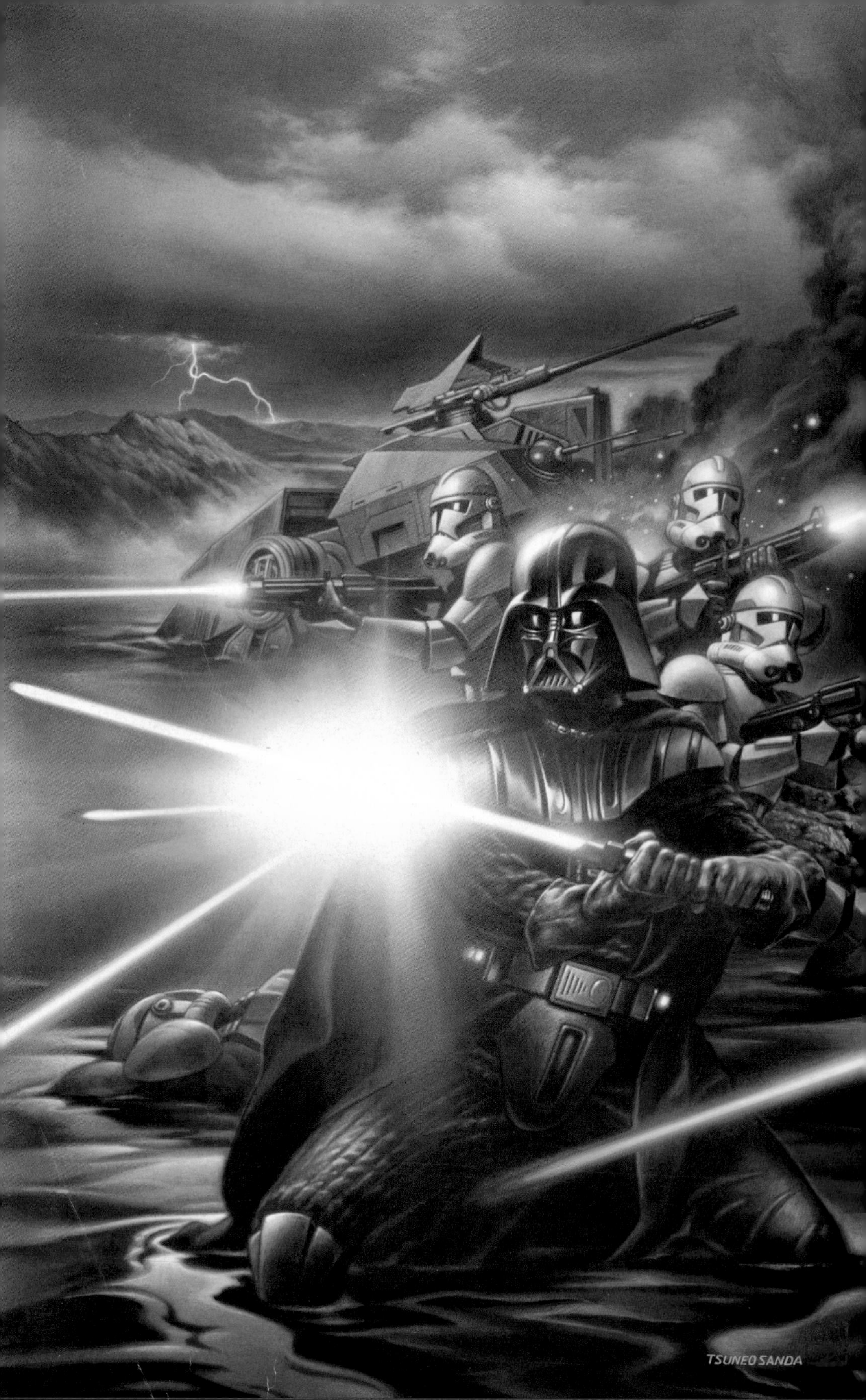
TSUNEO SANDA

STAR WARS: DARTH VADER AND THE LOST COMMAND #3

WRITER: HADEN BLACKMAN • PENCILER: RICK LEONARDI • INKER: DAN GREEN • COLORIST: WES DZIOBA • LETTERER: MICHAEL HEISLER
DESIGNER: STEPHEN REICHERT • ASSISTANT EDITOR: FREDDYE LINS • EDITOR: RANDY STRADLEY • COVER ARTIST: TSUNEO SANDA

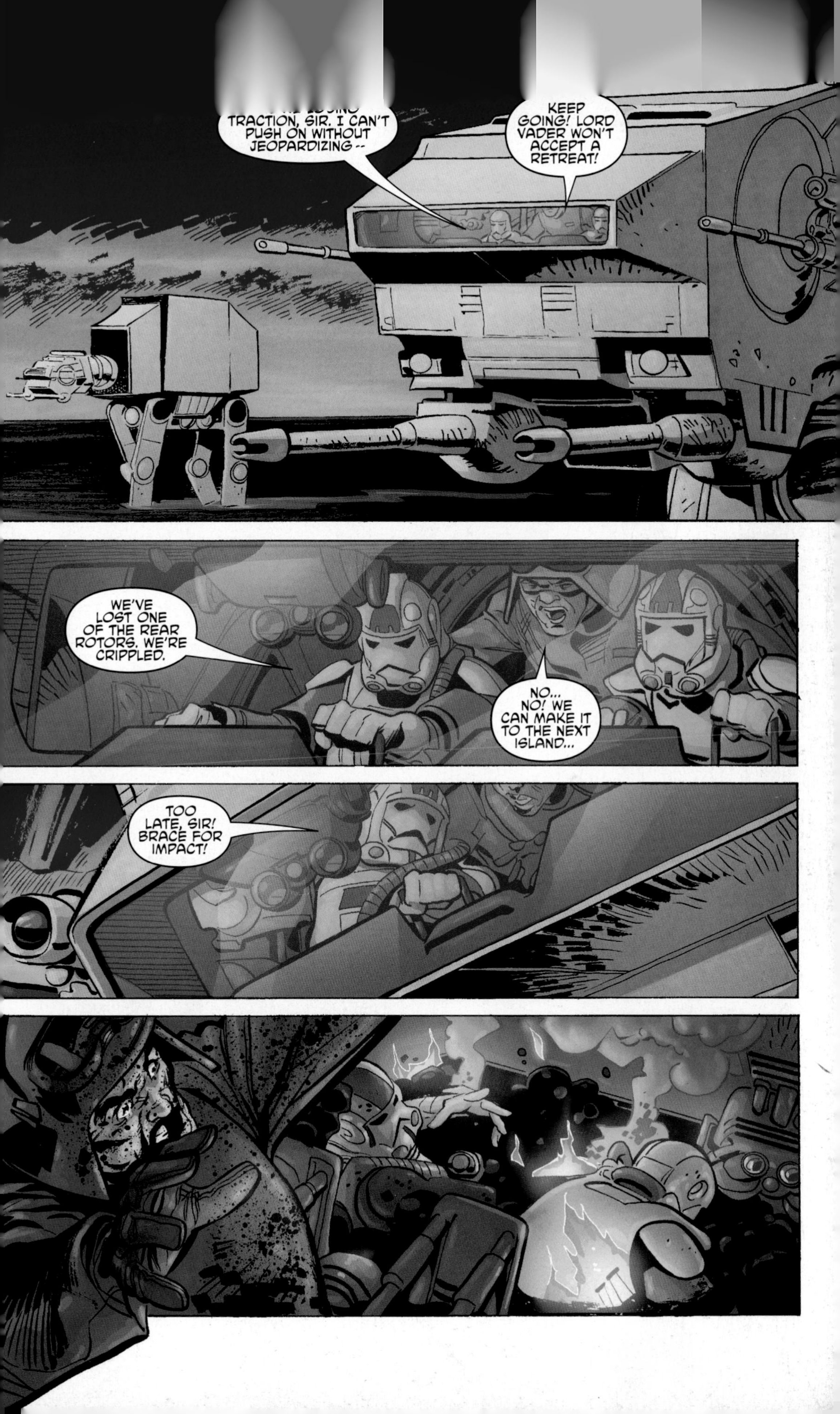
TRACTION, SIR. I CAN'T PUSH ON WITHOUT JEOPARDIZING --
KEEP GOING! LORD VADER WON'T ACCEPT A RETREAT!
WE'VE LOST ONE OF THE REAR ROTORS. WE'RE CRIPPLED.
NO... NO! WE CAN MAKE IT TO THE NEXT ISLAND...
TOO LATE, SIR! BRACE FOR IMPACT!

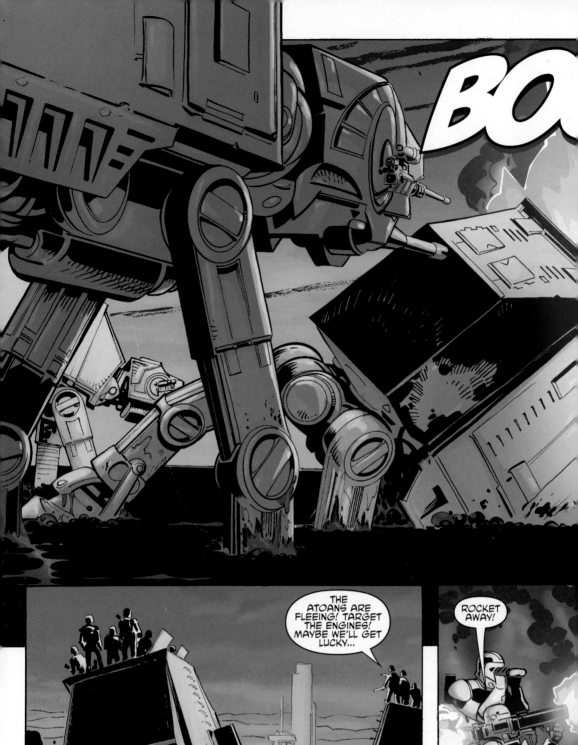

BO

THE ATOANS ARE FLEEING! TARGET THE ENGINES! MAYBE WE'LL GET LUCKY...

ROCKET AWAY!

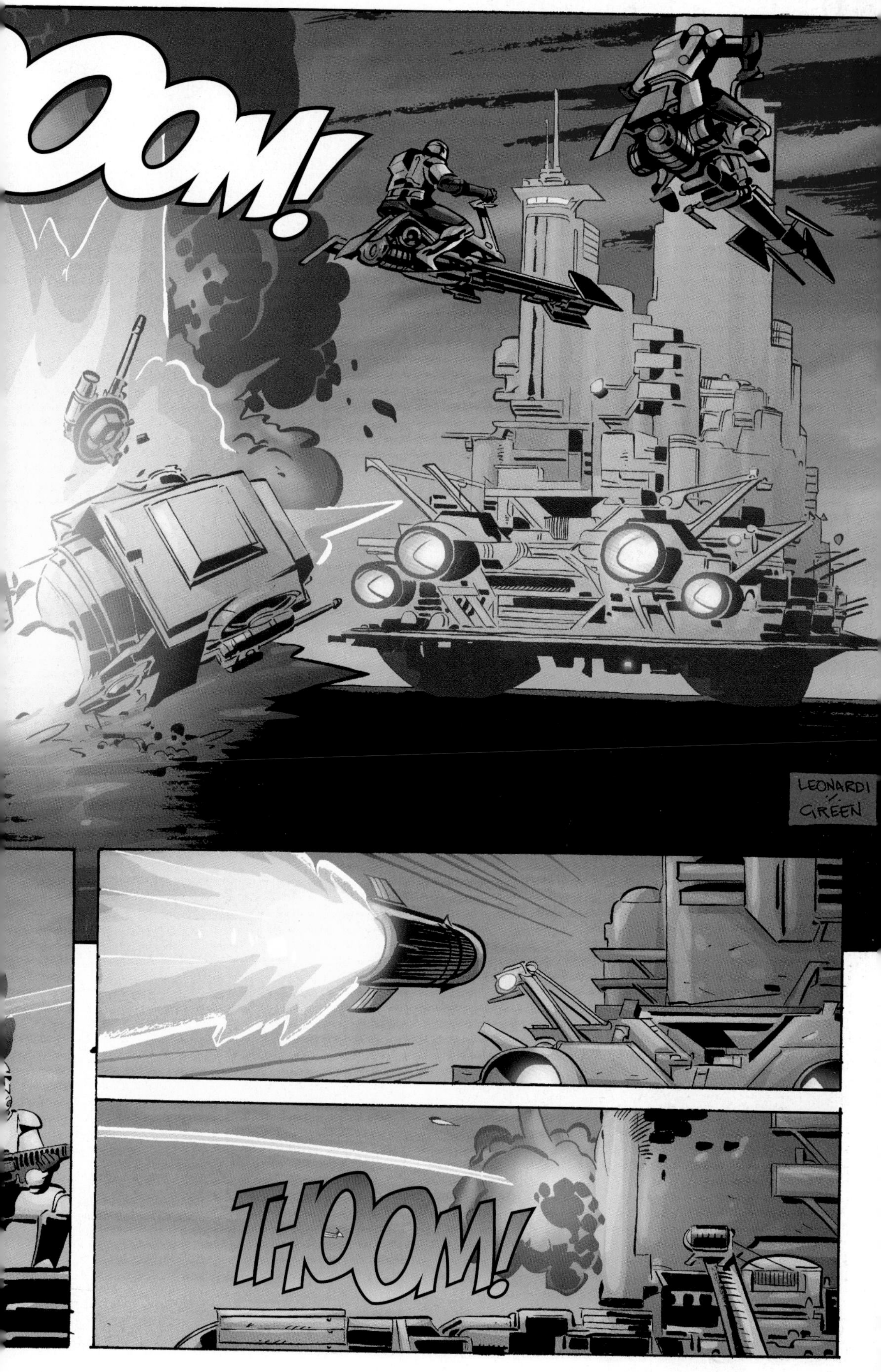

OOM!
LEONARDI
GREEN
THOOM!

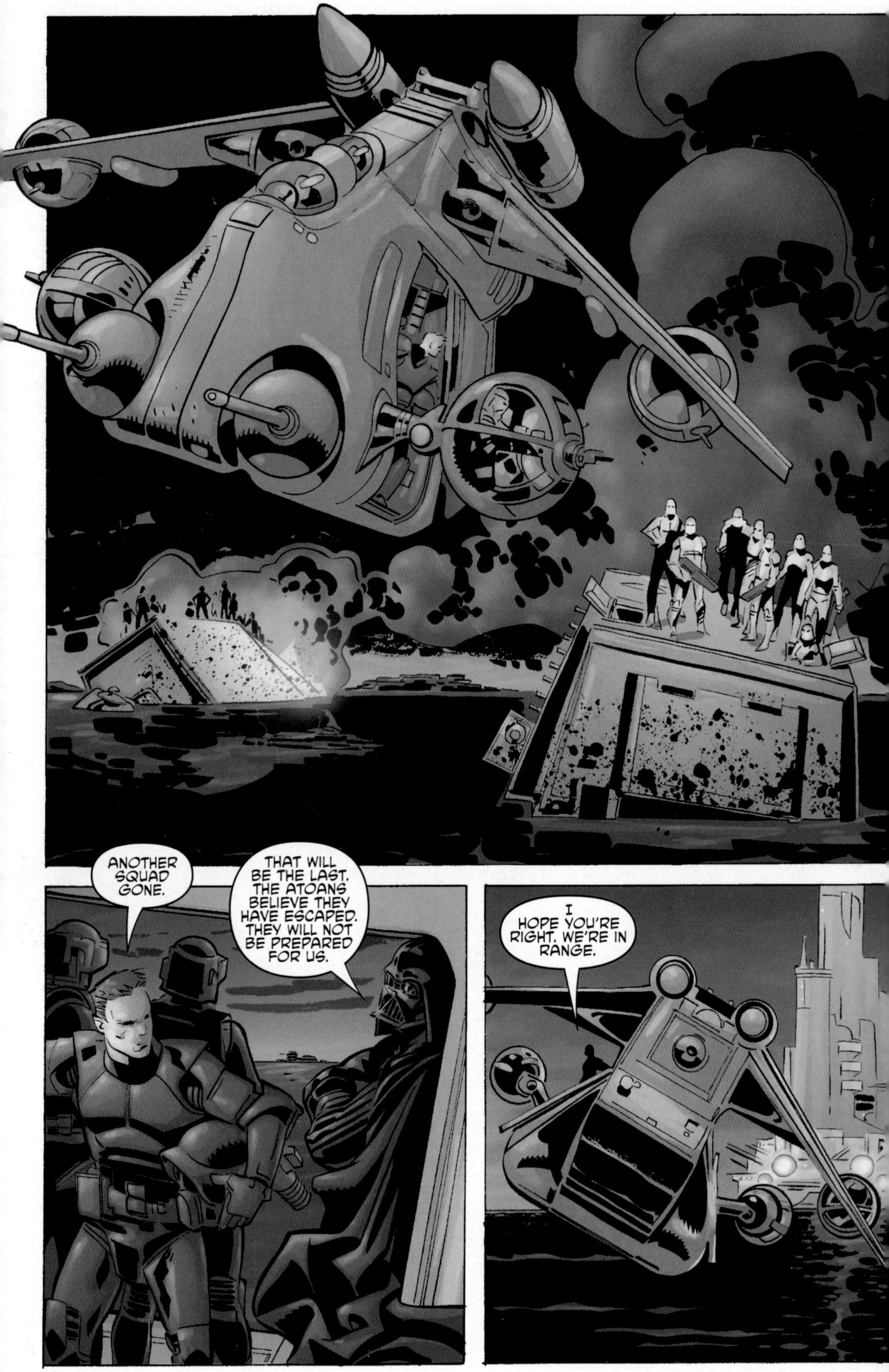
ANOTHER SQUAD GONE.
THAT WILL BE THE LAST. THE ATOANS BELIEVE THEY HAVE ESCAPED. THEY WILL NOT BE PREPARED FOR US.
I HOPE YOU'RE RIGHT. WE'RE IN RANGE.

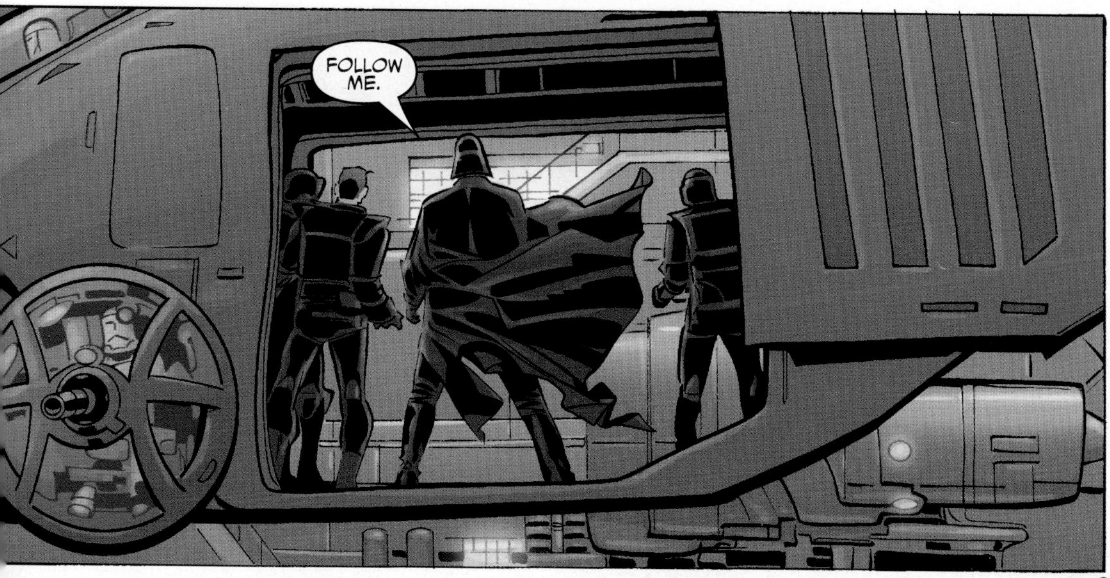
FOLLOW ME.

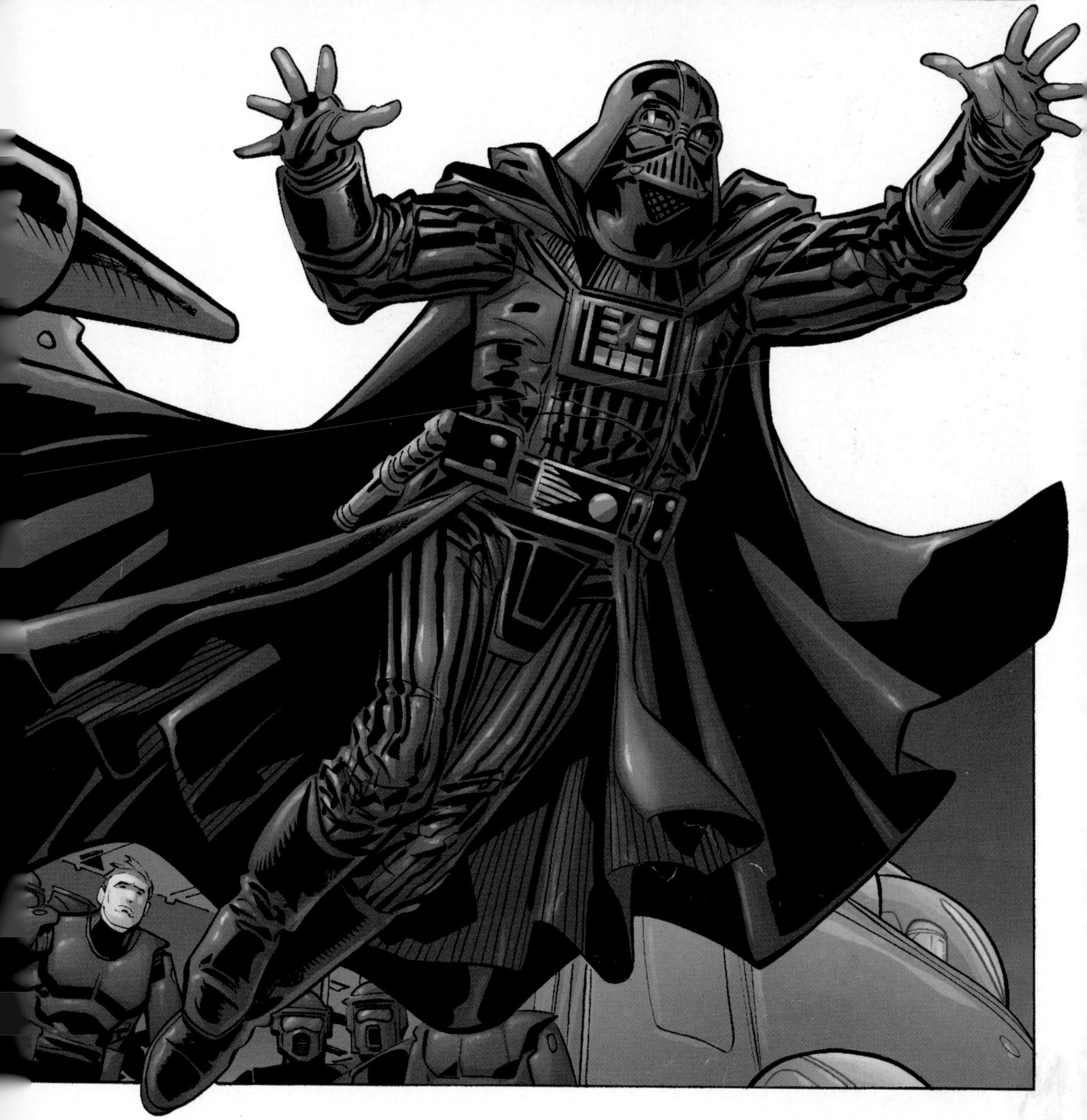

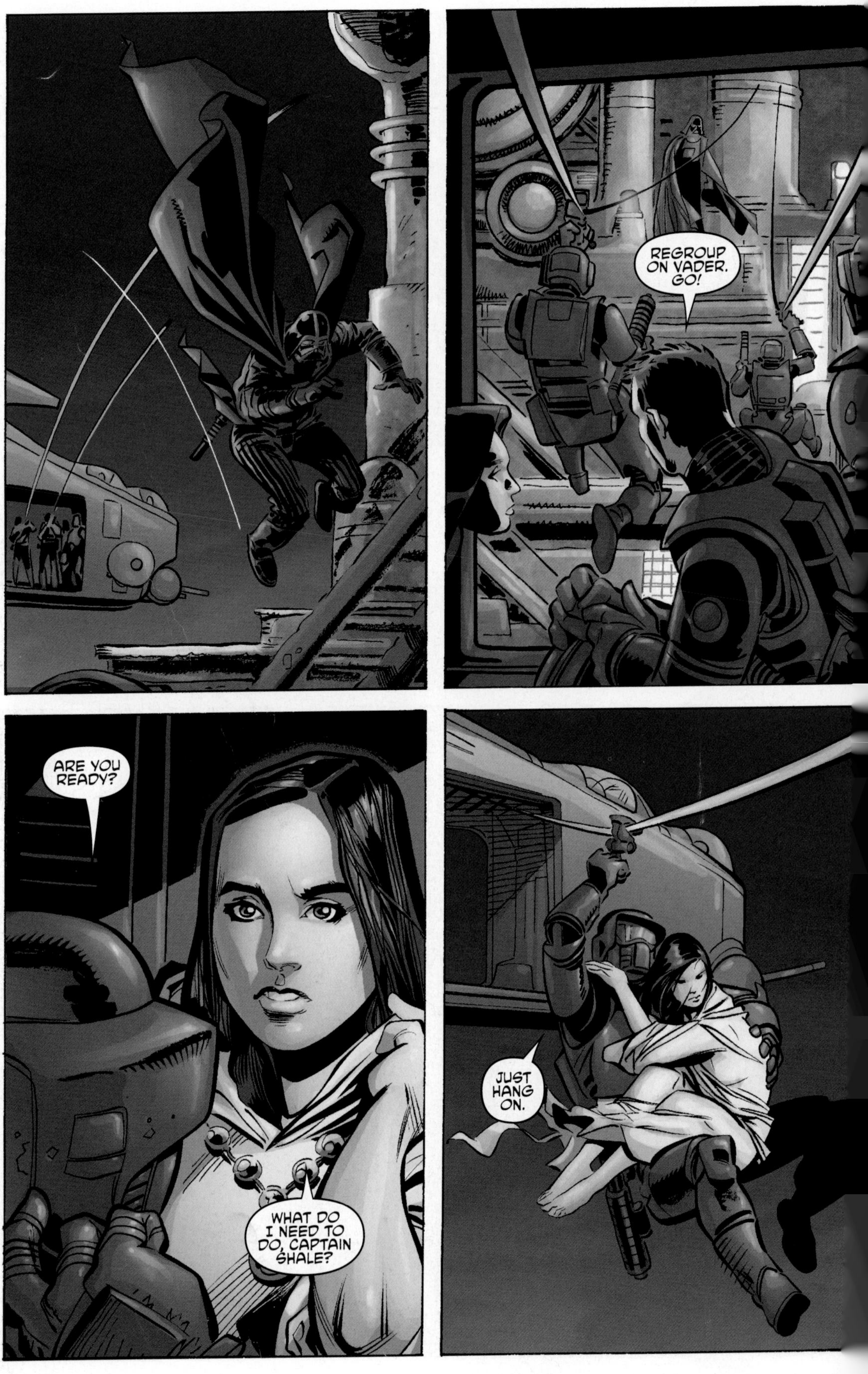
REGROUP ON VADER. GO!
ARE YOU READY?
WHAT DO I NEED TO DO, CAPTAIN SHALE?
JUST HANG ON.

ᓬᓂᒧ ᐁᑊᓬᑊ
ᒍᐁᑎ ᐁᓬ!

!

HURK!

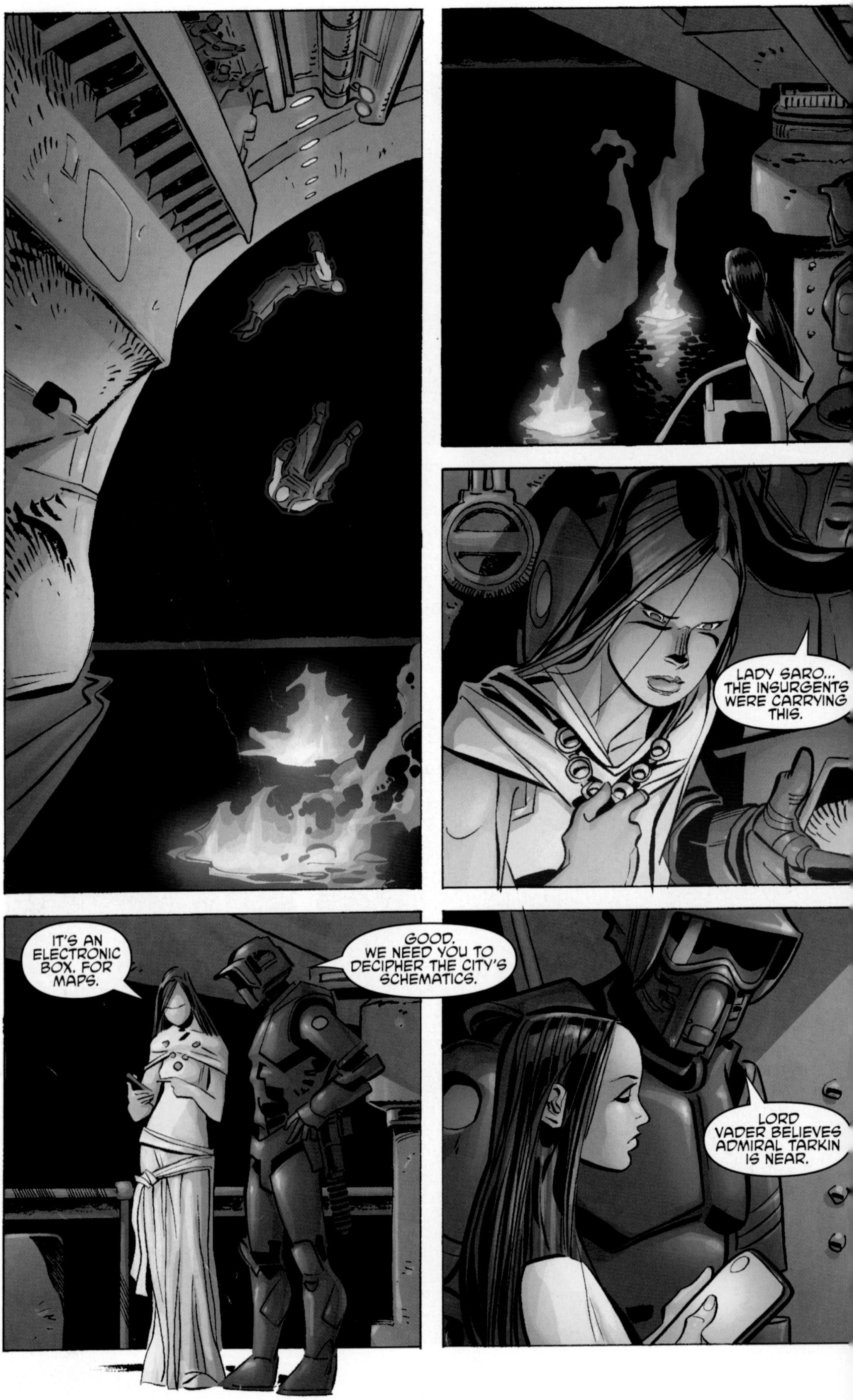
LADY SARO... THE INSURGENTS WERE CARRYING THIS.
IT'S AN ELECTRONIC BOX. FOR MAPS.
GOOD. WE NEED YOU TO DECIPHER THE CITY'S SCHEMATICS.
LORD VADER BELIEVES ADMIRAL TARKIN IS NEAR.

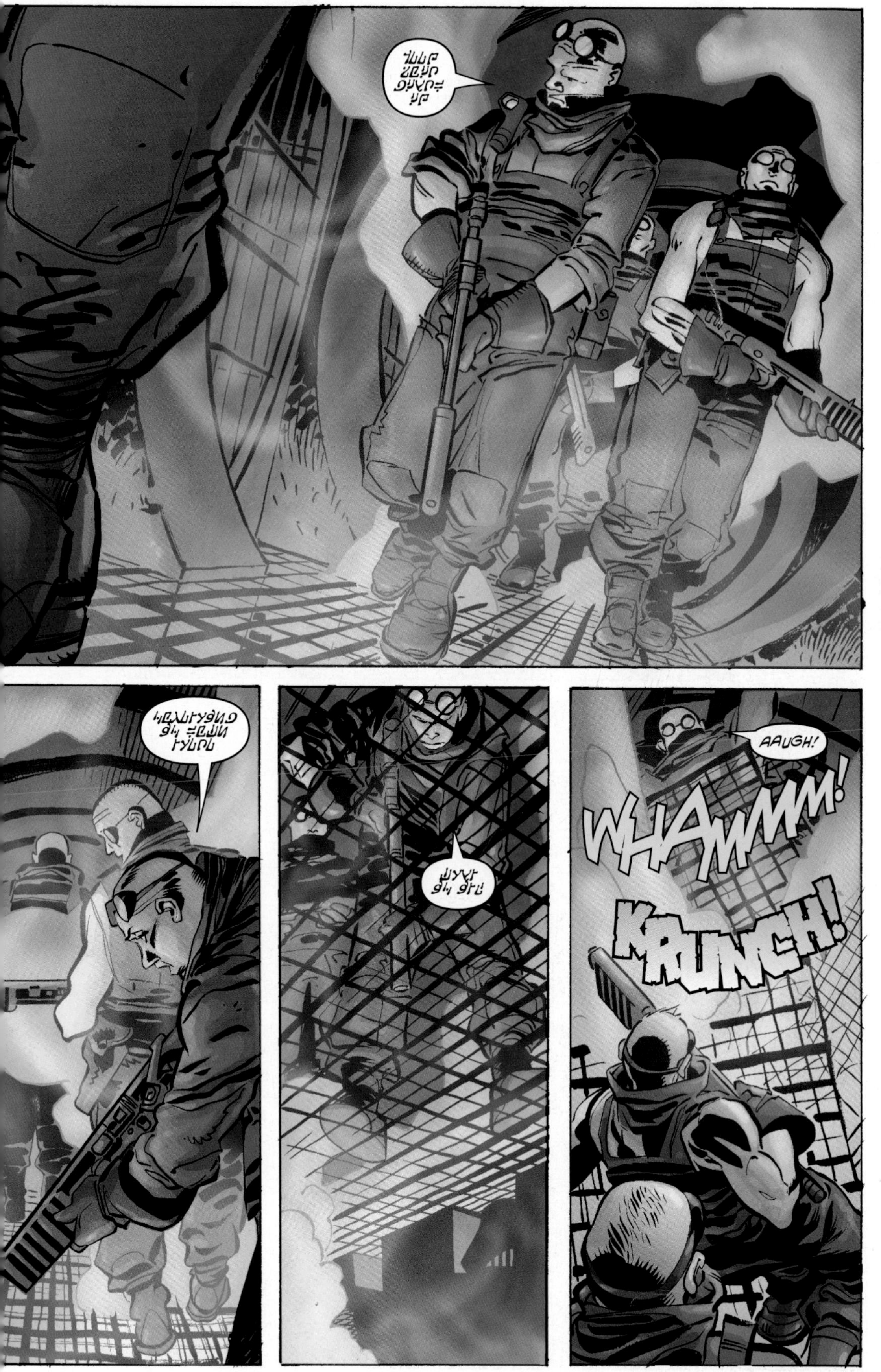
AAUGH!
WHAMMM!
KRUNCH!

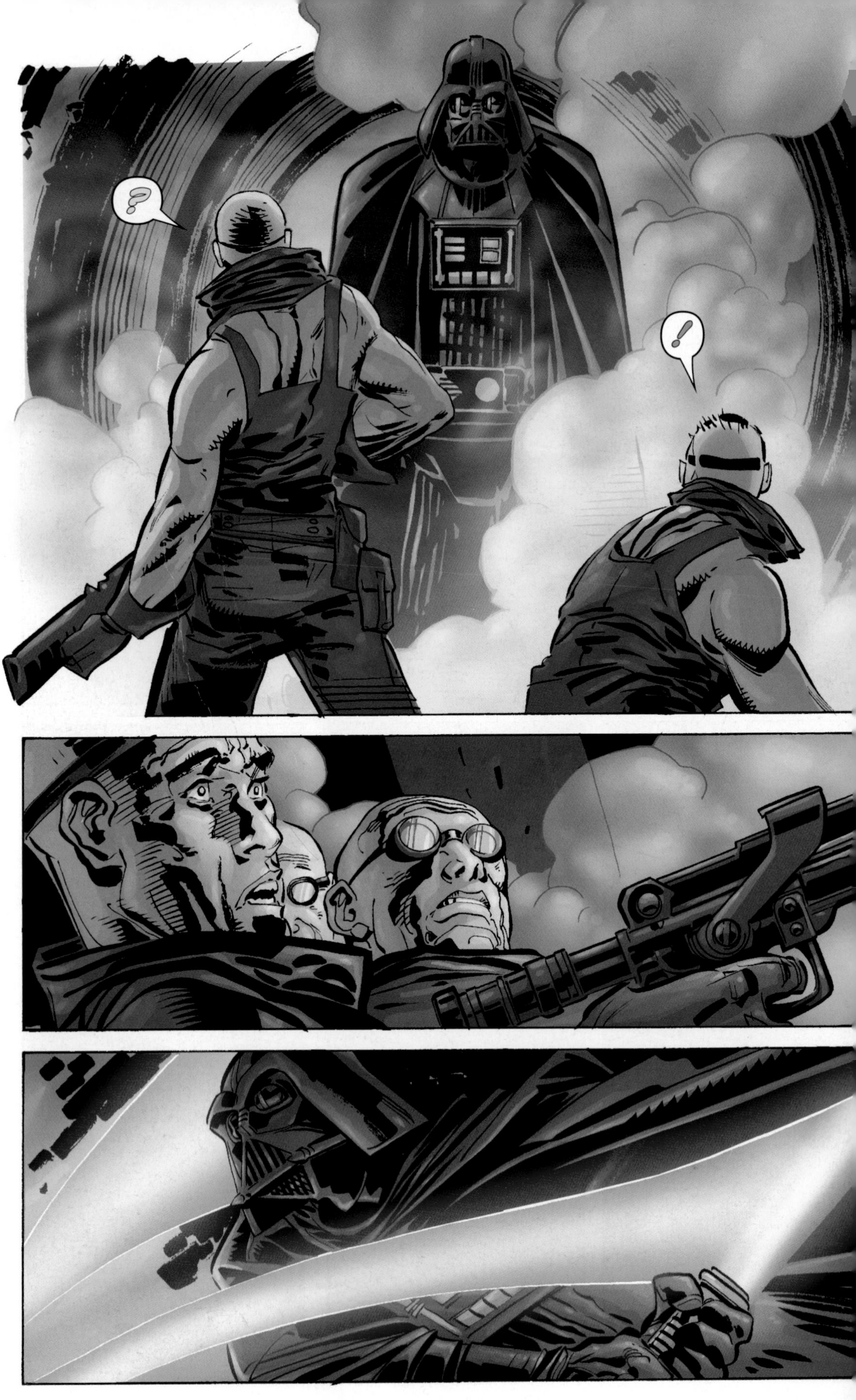
?
!

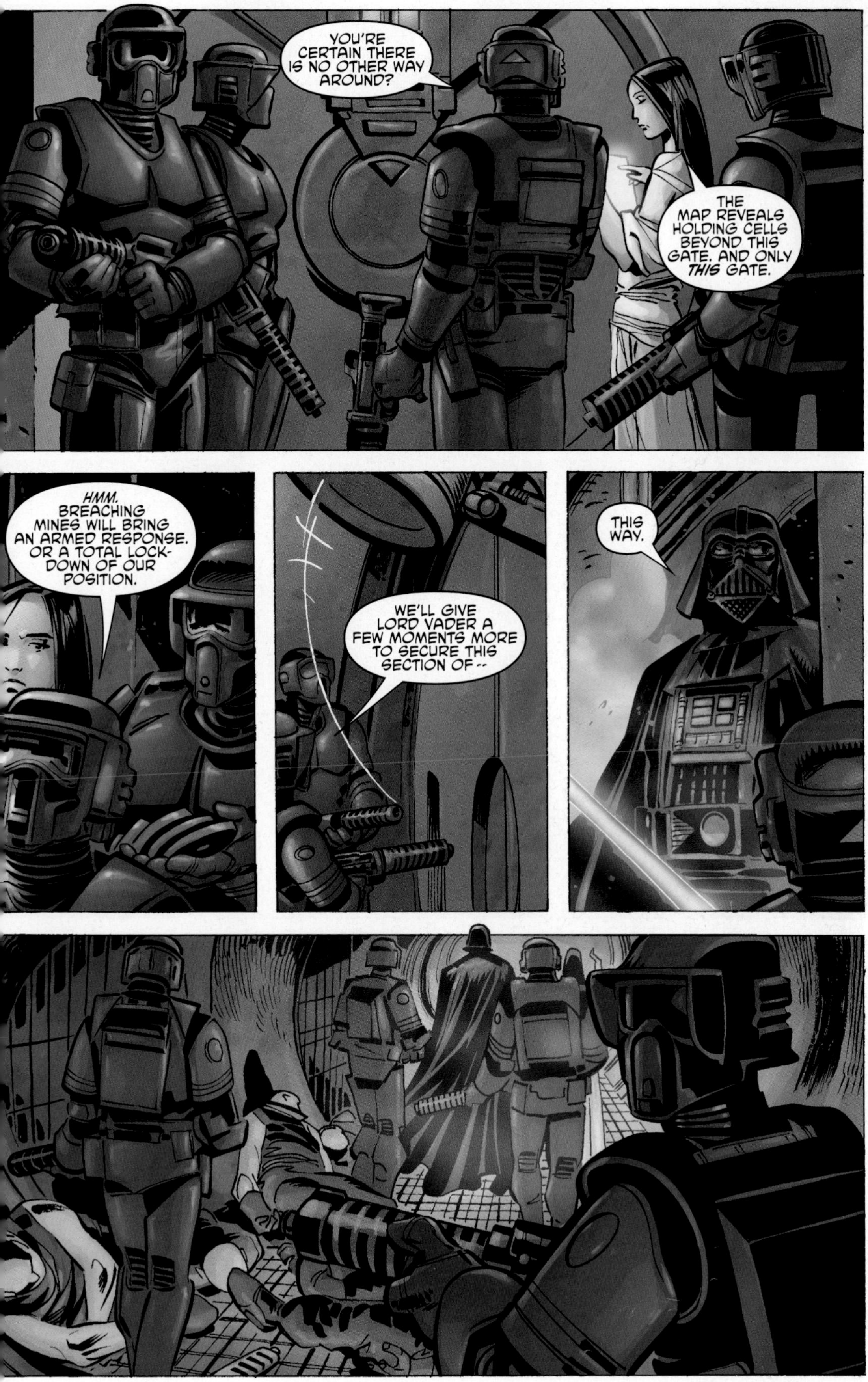
YOU'RE CERTAIN THERE IS NO OTHER WAY AROUND?
THE MAP REVEALS HOLDING CELLS BEYOND THIS GATE. AND ONLY *THIS* GATE.
HMM. BREACHING MINES WILL BRING AN ARMED RESPONSE. OR A TOTAL LOCK-DOWN OF OUR POSITION.
WE'LL GIVE LORD VADER A FEW MOMENTS MORE TO SECURE THIS SECTION OF --
THIS WAY.

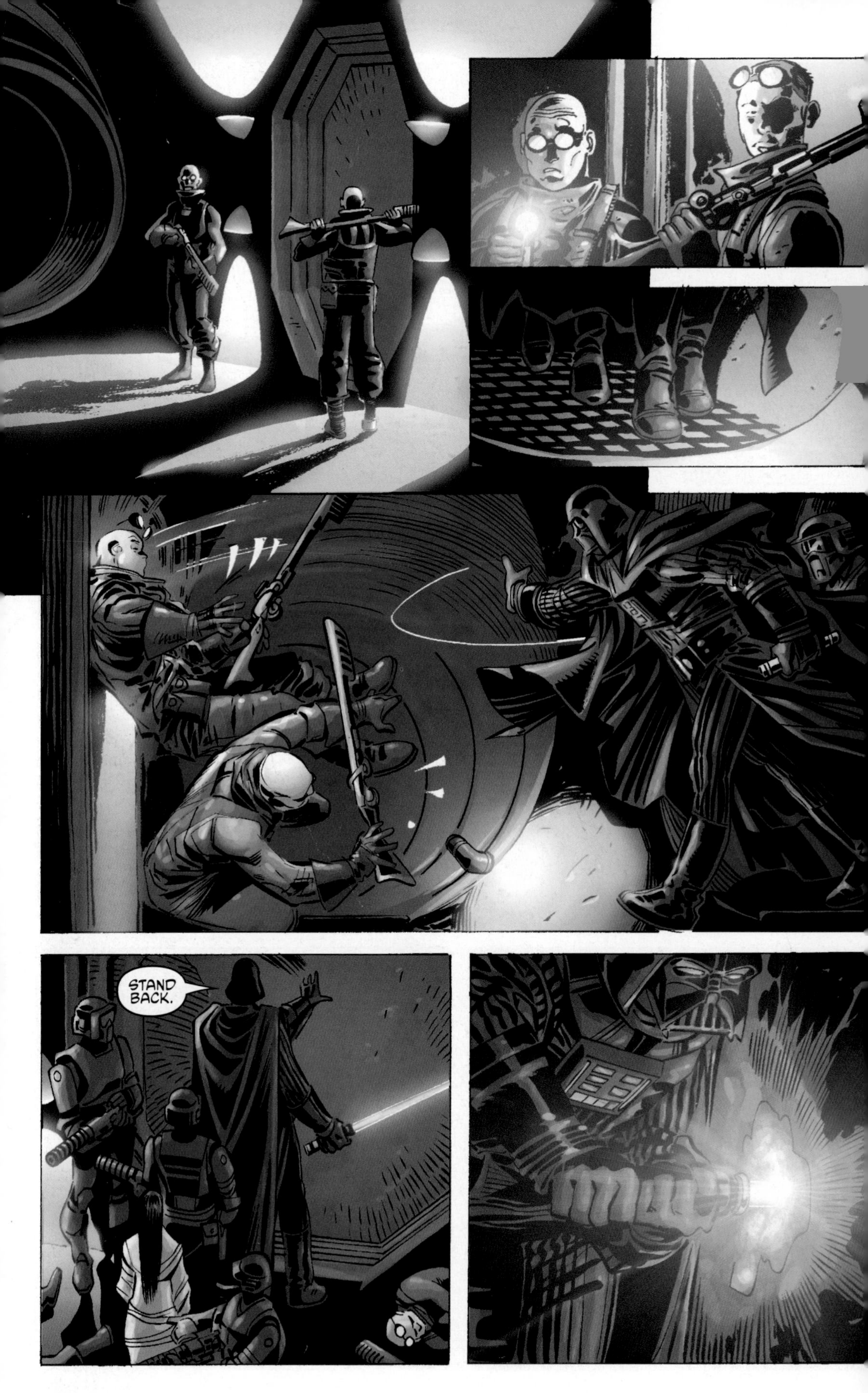
STAND BACK.

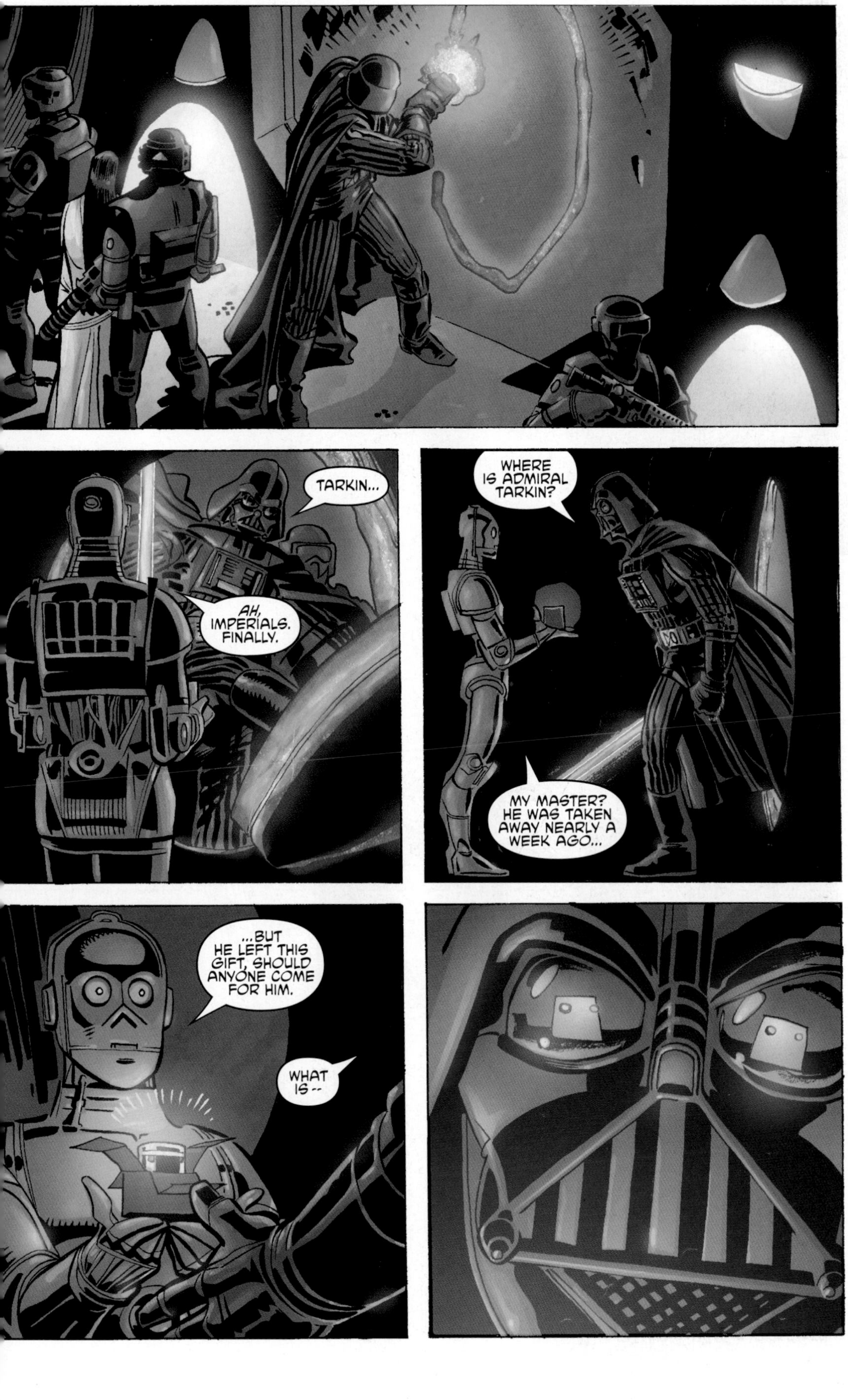
TARKIN...
AH, IMPERIALS. FINALLY.
WHERE IS ADMIRAL TARKIN?
MY MASTER? HE WAS TAKEN AWAY NEARLY A WEEK AGO...
...BUT HE LEFT THIS GIFT, SHOULD ANYONE COME FOR HIM.
WHAT IS --

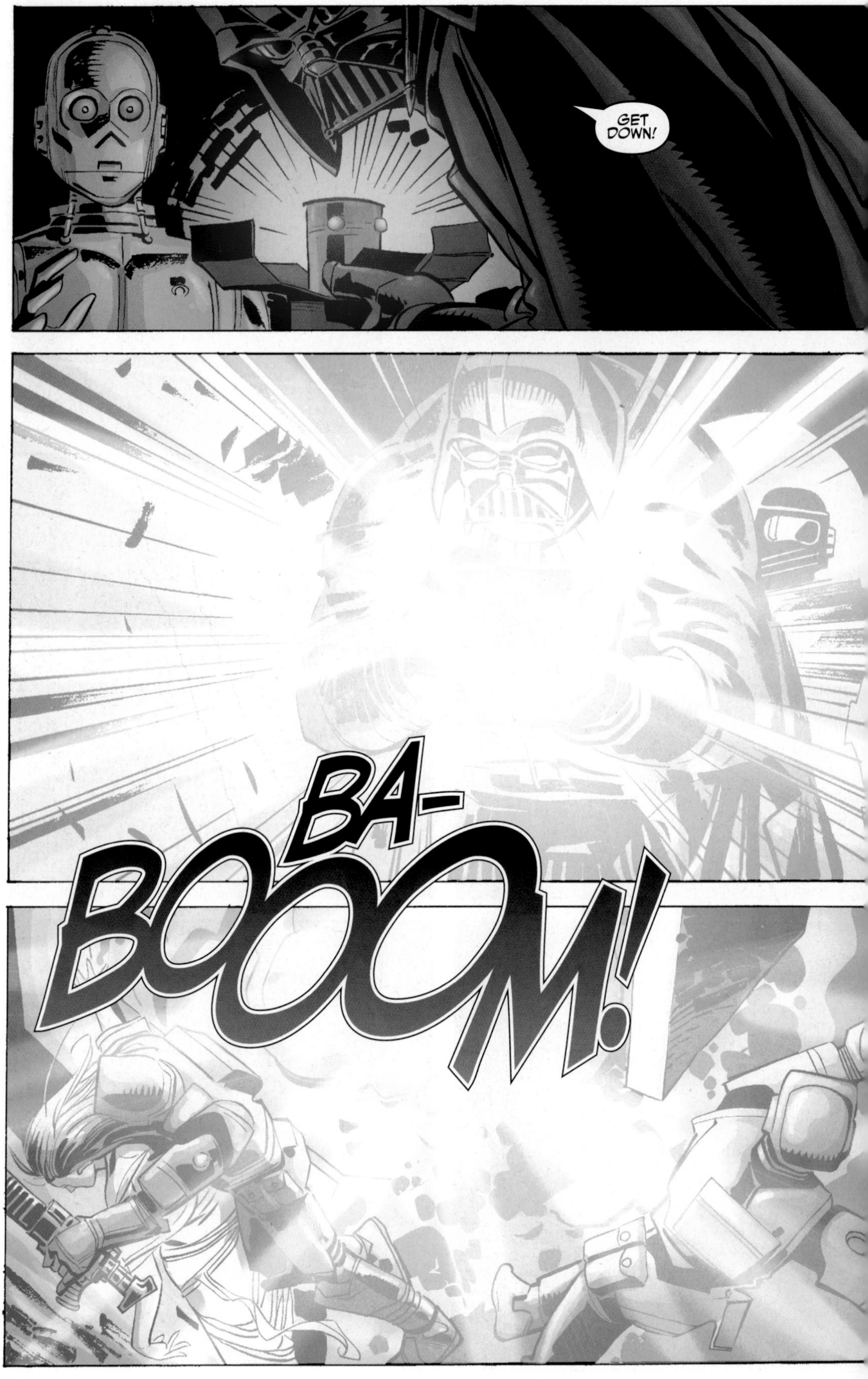
GET DOWN!
BA-BOOOM!

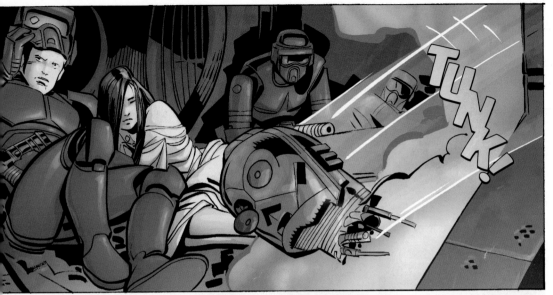

TUNK!

NO MORE ATTACKING FROM THE SHADOWS...

NOW WE TAKE THE BRIDGE.

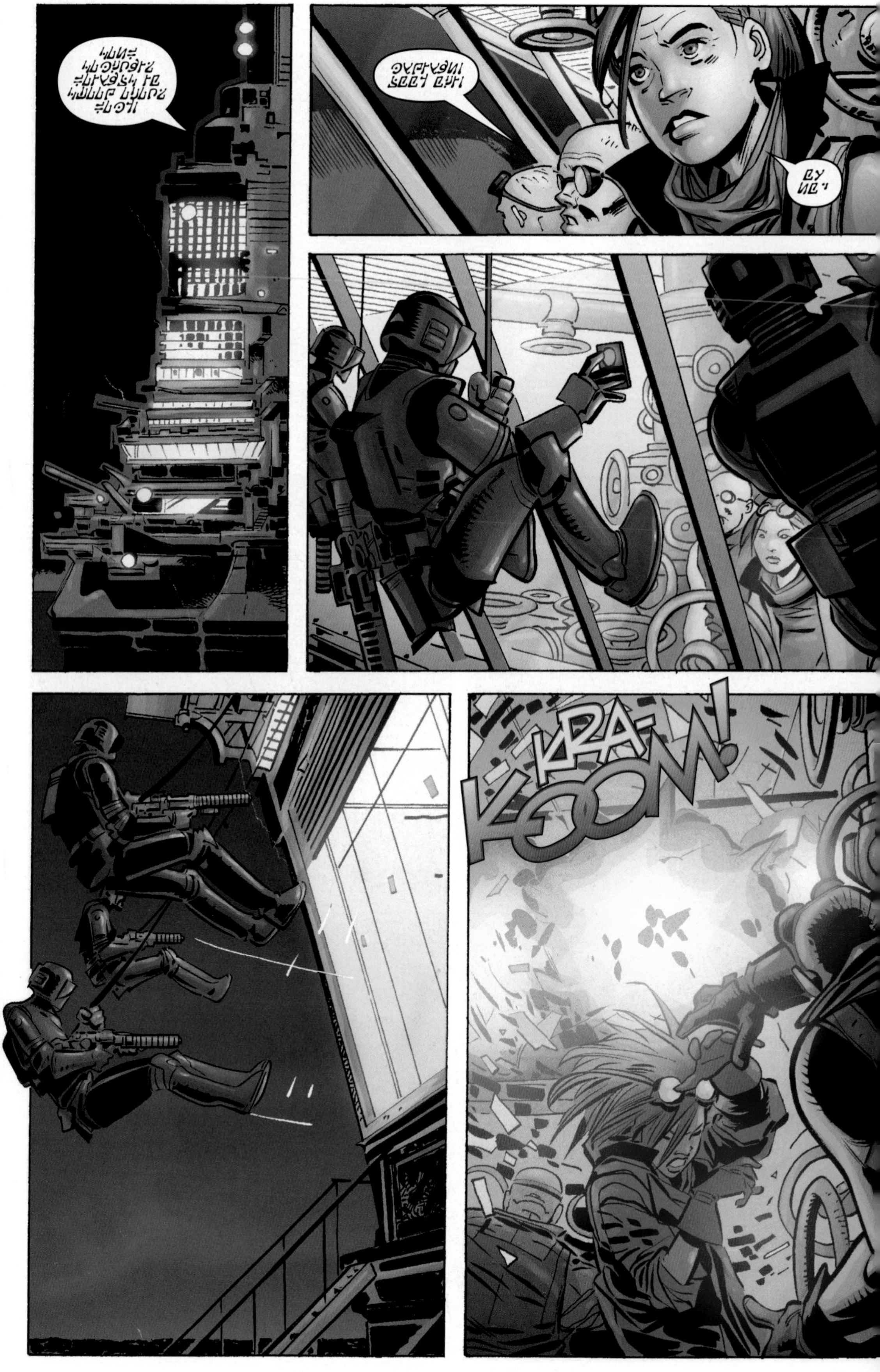
KRA-KOOM!

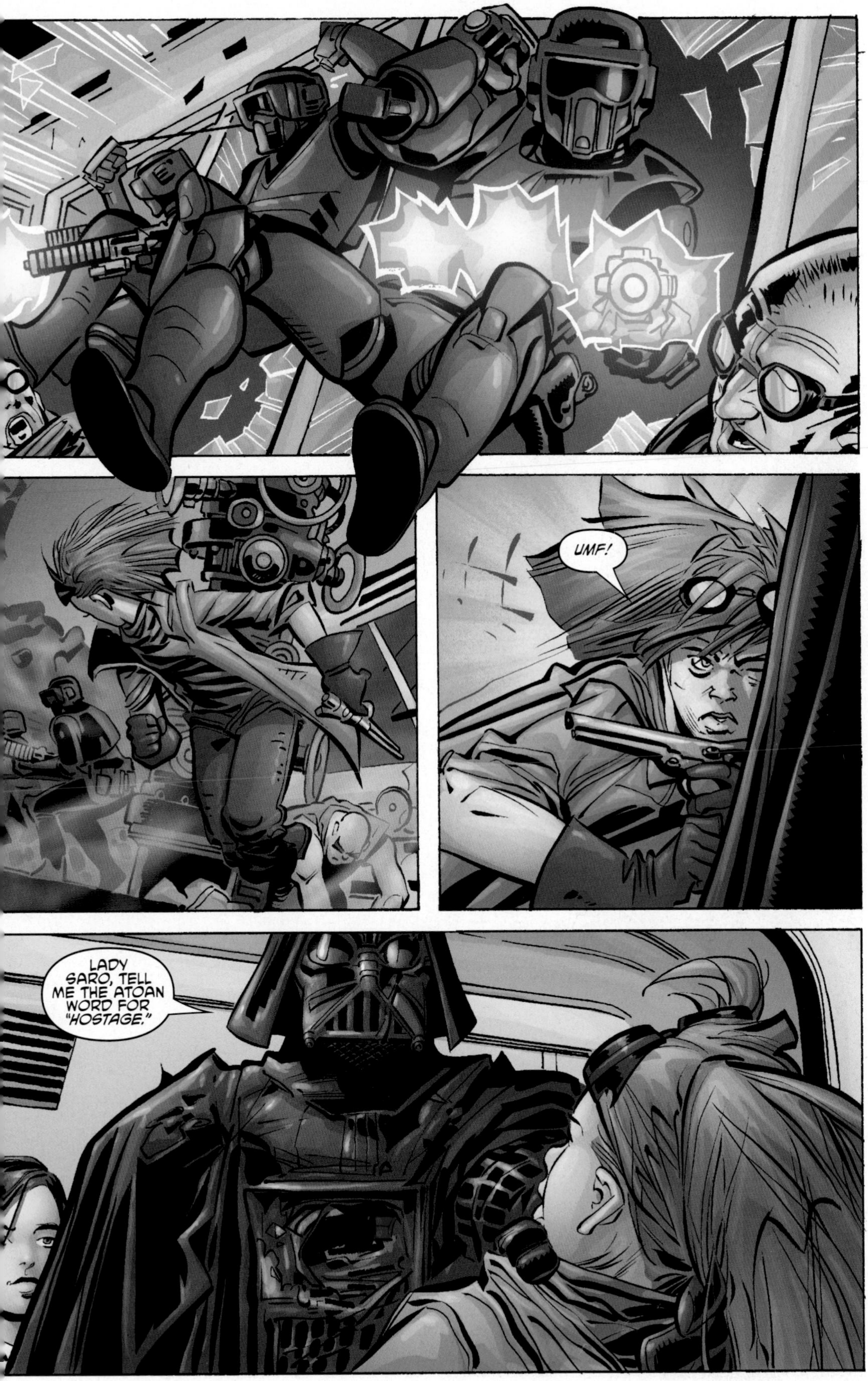
UMF!
LADY SARO, TELL ME THE ATOAN WORD FOR "HOSTAGE."

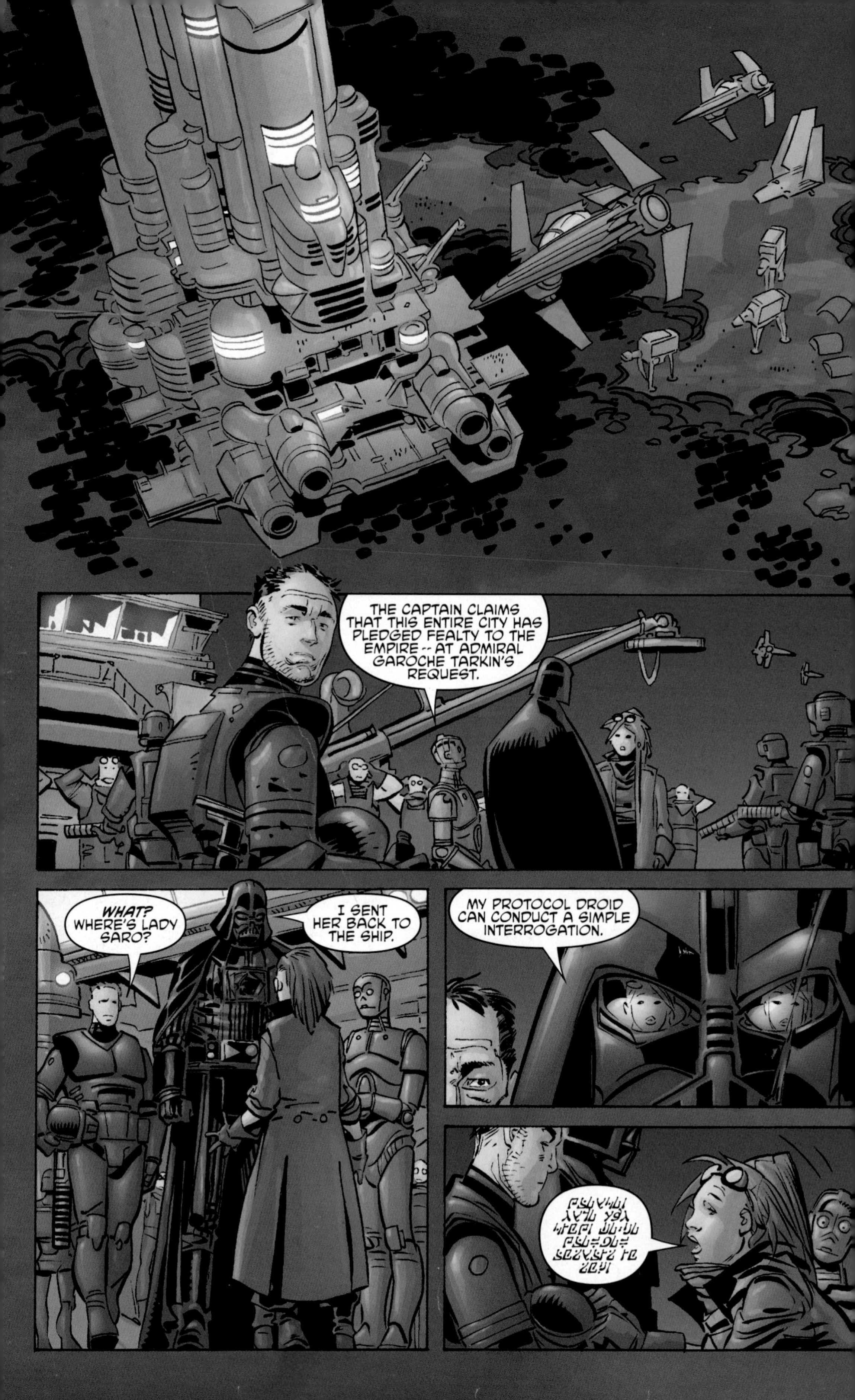
THE CAPTAIN CLAIMS THAT THIS ENTIRE CITY HAS PLEDGED FEALTY TO THE EMPIRE-- AT ADMIRAL GAROCHE TARKIN'S REQUEST.
WHAT? WHERE'S LADY SARO?
I SENT HER BACK TO THE SHIP.
MY PROTOCOL DROID CAN CONDUCT A SIMPLE INTERROGATION.

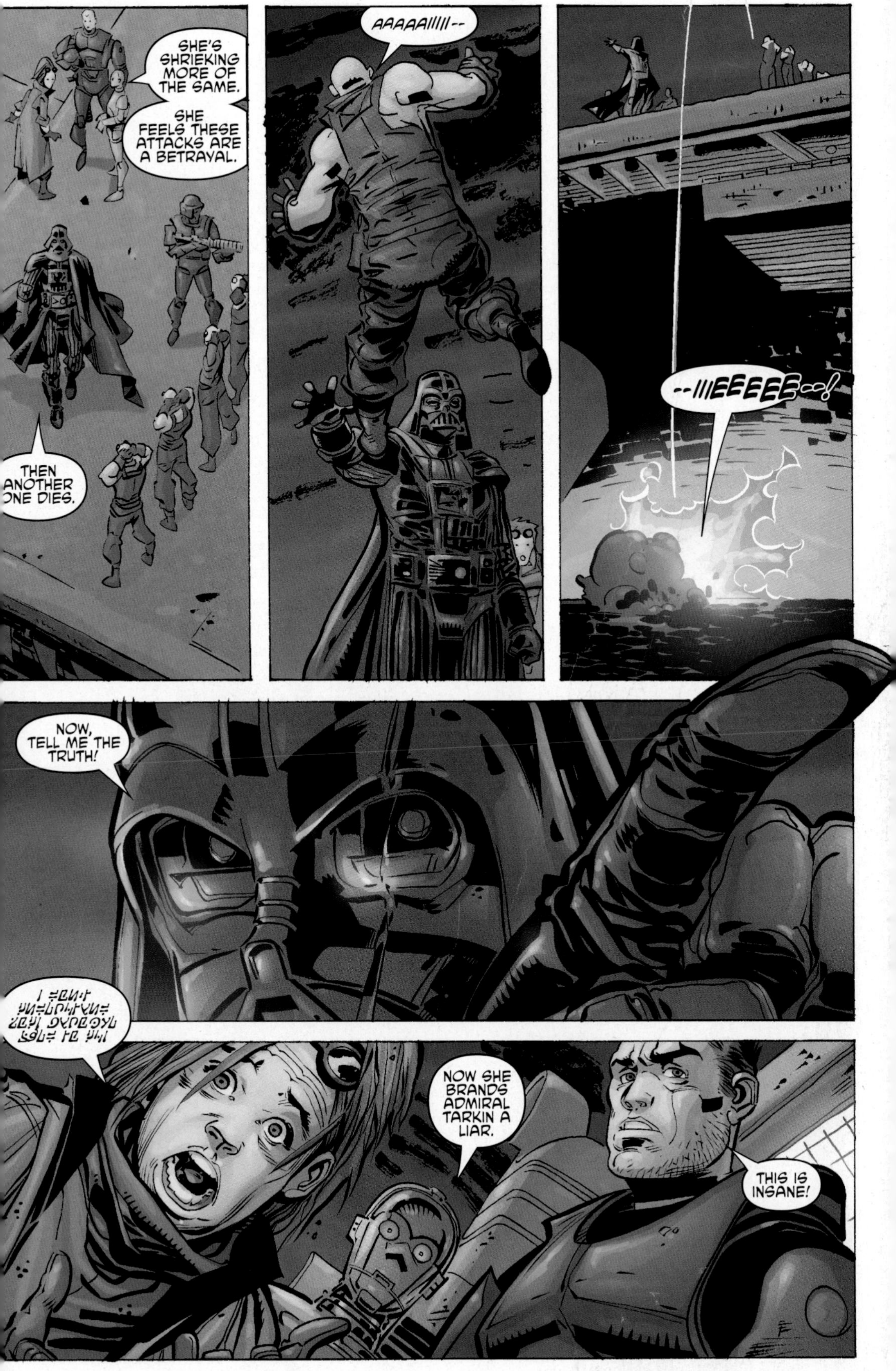
SHE'S SHRIEKING MORE OF THE SAME.
SHE FEELS THESE ATTACKS ARE A BETRAYAL.
THEN ANOTHER ONE DIES.
AAAAAIIIII--
--IIIEEEEEE--!
NOW, TELL ME THE TRUTH!
NOW SHE BRANDS ADMIRAL TARKIN A LIAR.
THIS IS INSANE!

AAAAAGH!

... ᒿᐁᐯᑕᐱᔭ ᑫᒣ ᑫᒣ ᒣᔭᒀ
ᔭᒀᐱᑕᒀ ᓇᑕ ᒣᑫᓇᒀᓇ

PSSHAK!

I....I THOUGHT SHE WAS ATTACKING YOU.

SINK THE CITY. BRING OUR FORCES BACK TO THE STAR DESTROYER.

AND THEN WE WILL DISCUSS THESE CHARGES AGAINST ADMIRAL TARKIN.

YOUR FRIEND.

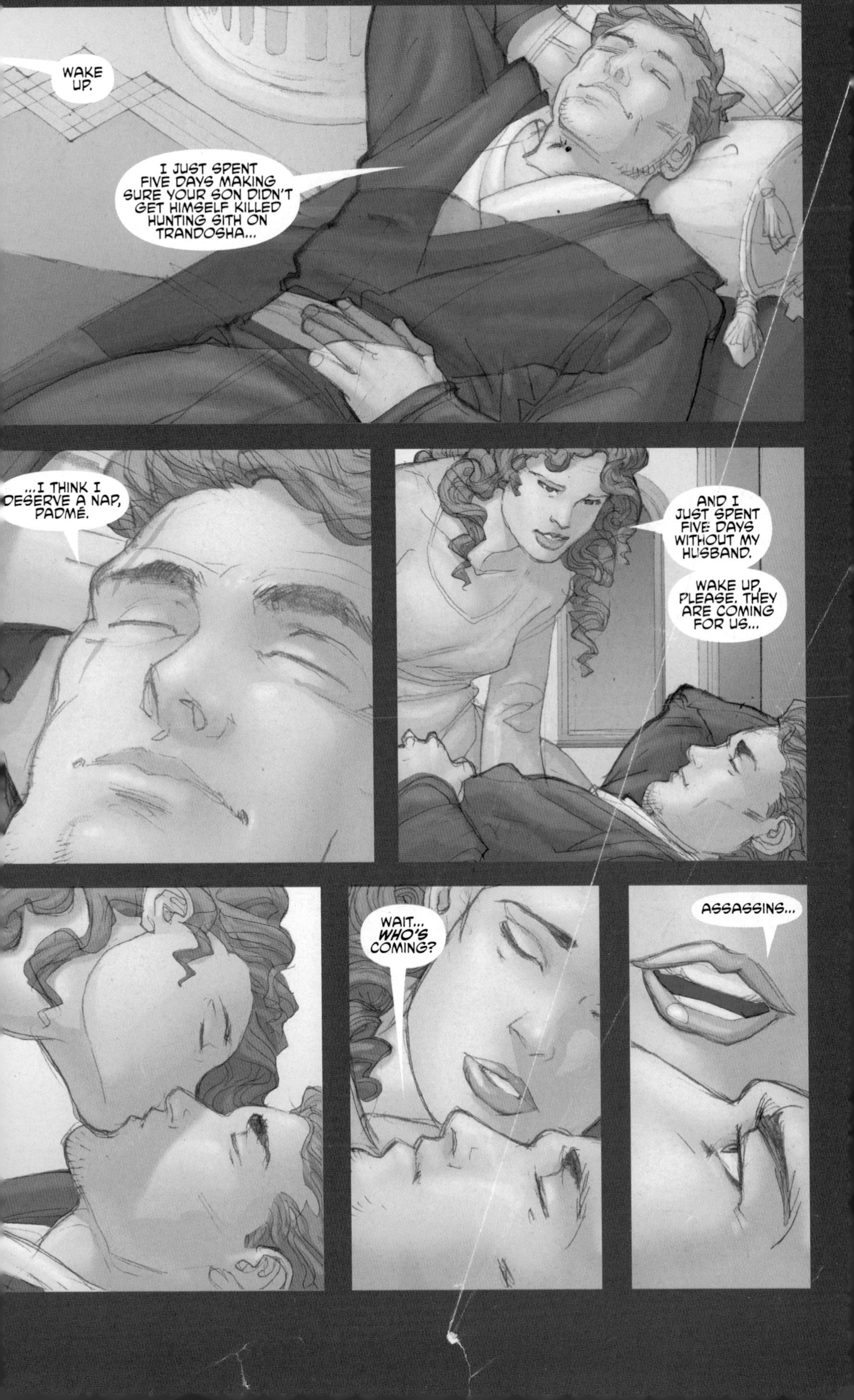
WAKE UP.
I JUST SPENT FIVE DAYS MAKING SURE YOUR SON DIDN'T GET HIMSELF KILLED HUNTING SITH ON TRANDOSHA...
...I THINK I DESERVE A NAP, PADMÉ.
AND I JUST SPENT FIVE DAYS WITHOUT MY HUSBAND.
WAKE UP, PLEASE. THEY ARE COMING FOR US...
WAIT... *WHO'S* COMING?
ASSASSINS...

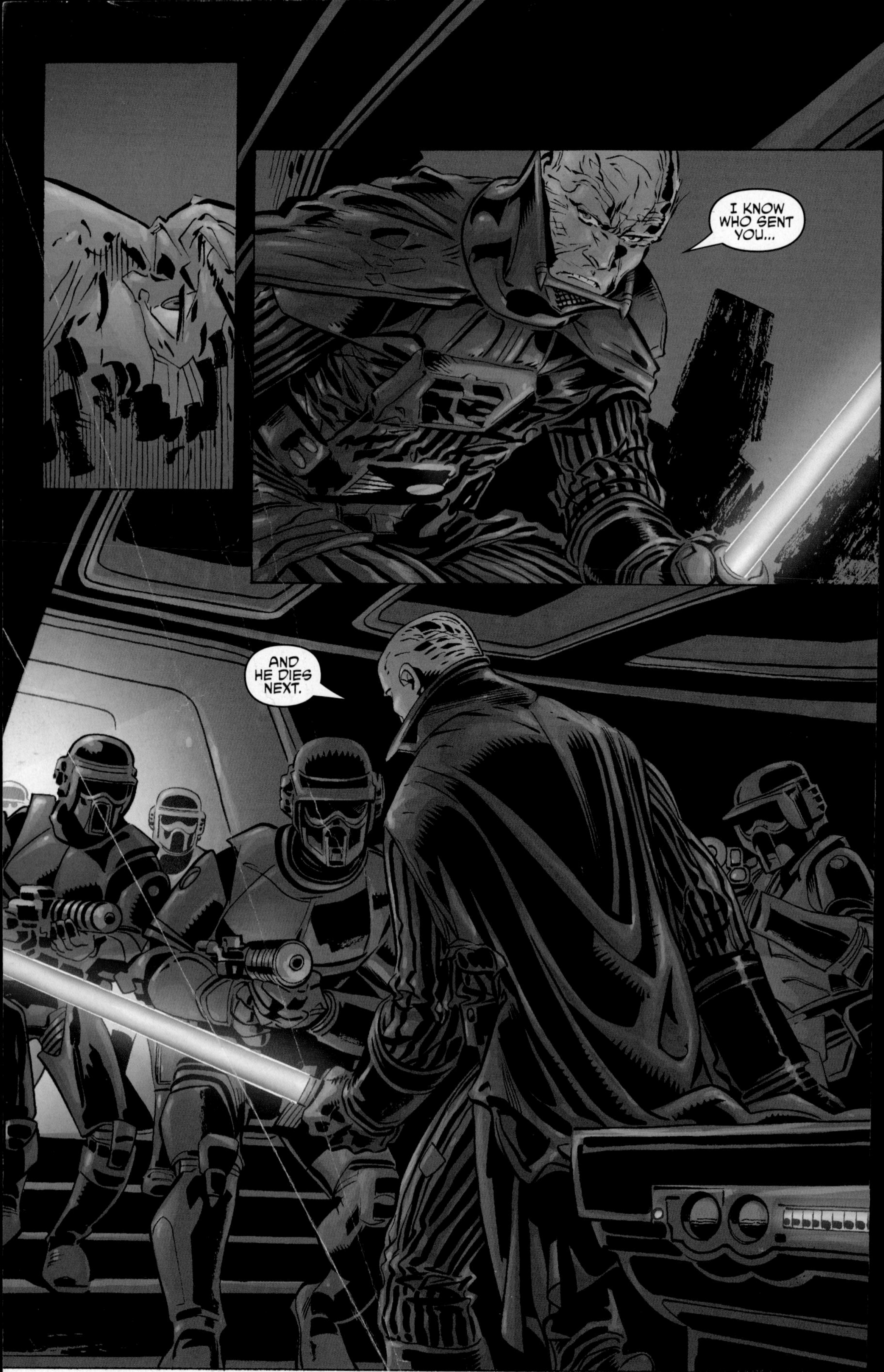
I KNOW WHO SENT YOU...
AND HE DIES NEXT.

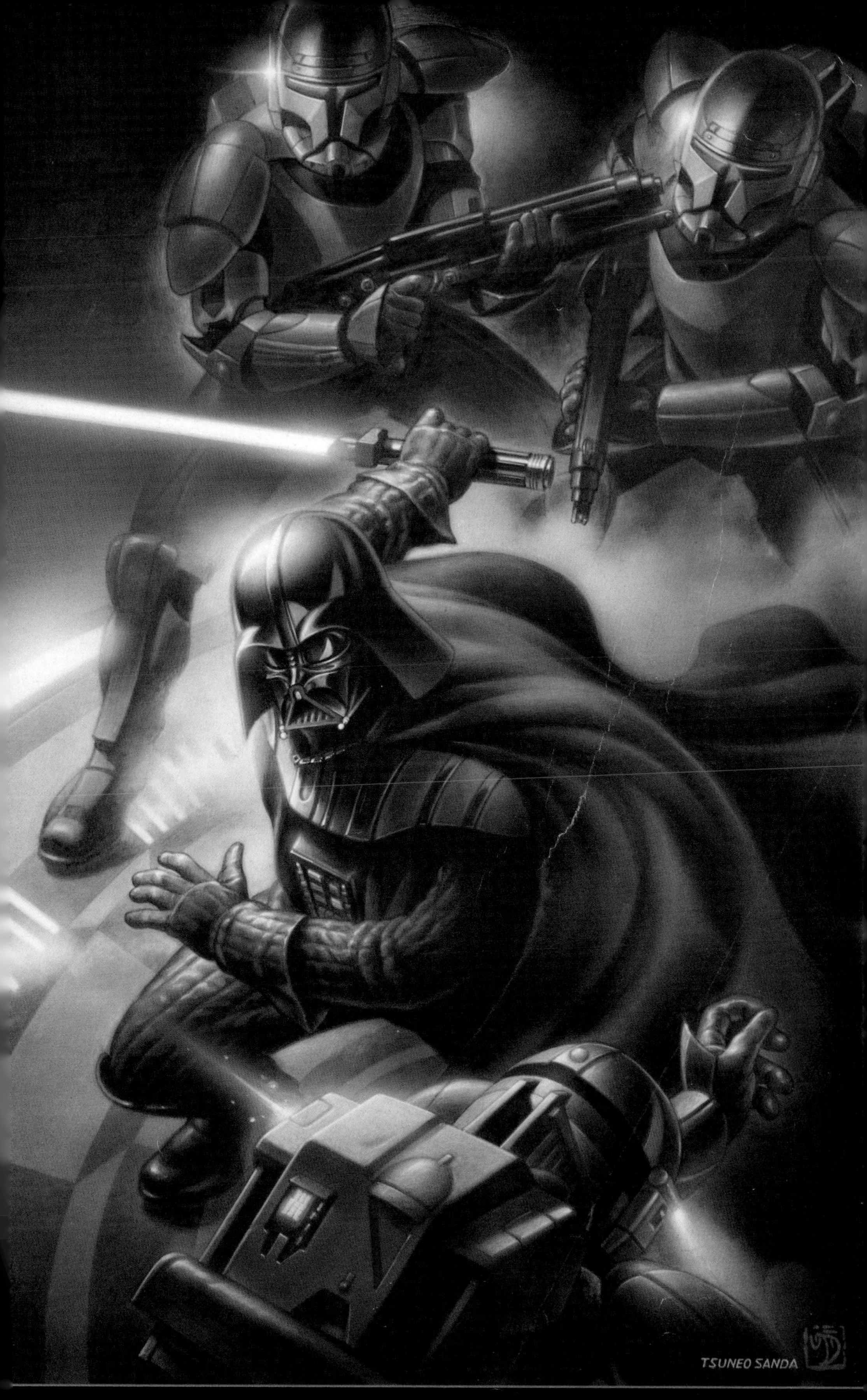
TSUNEO SANDA

STAR WARS: DARTH VADER AND THE LOST COMMAND #4

WRITER: HADEN BLACKMAN • PENCILER: RICK LEONARDI • INKER: DAN GREEN • COLORIST: WES DZIOBA • LETTERER: MICHAEL HEISLER
DESIGNER: KAT LARSON • ASSISTANT EDITOR: FREDDYE LINS • EDITOR: RANDY STRADLEY • COVER ARTIST: TSUNEO SANDA

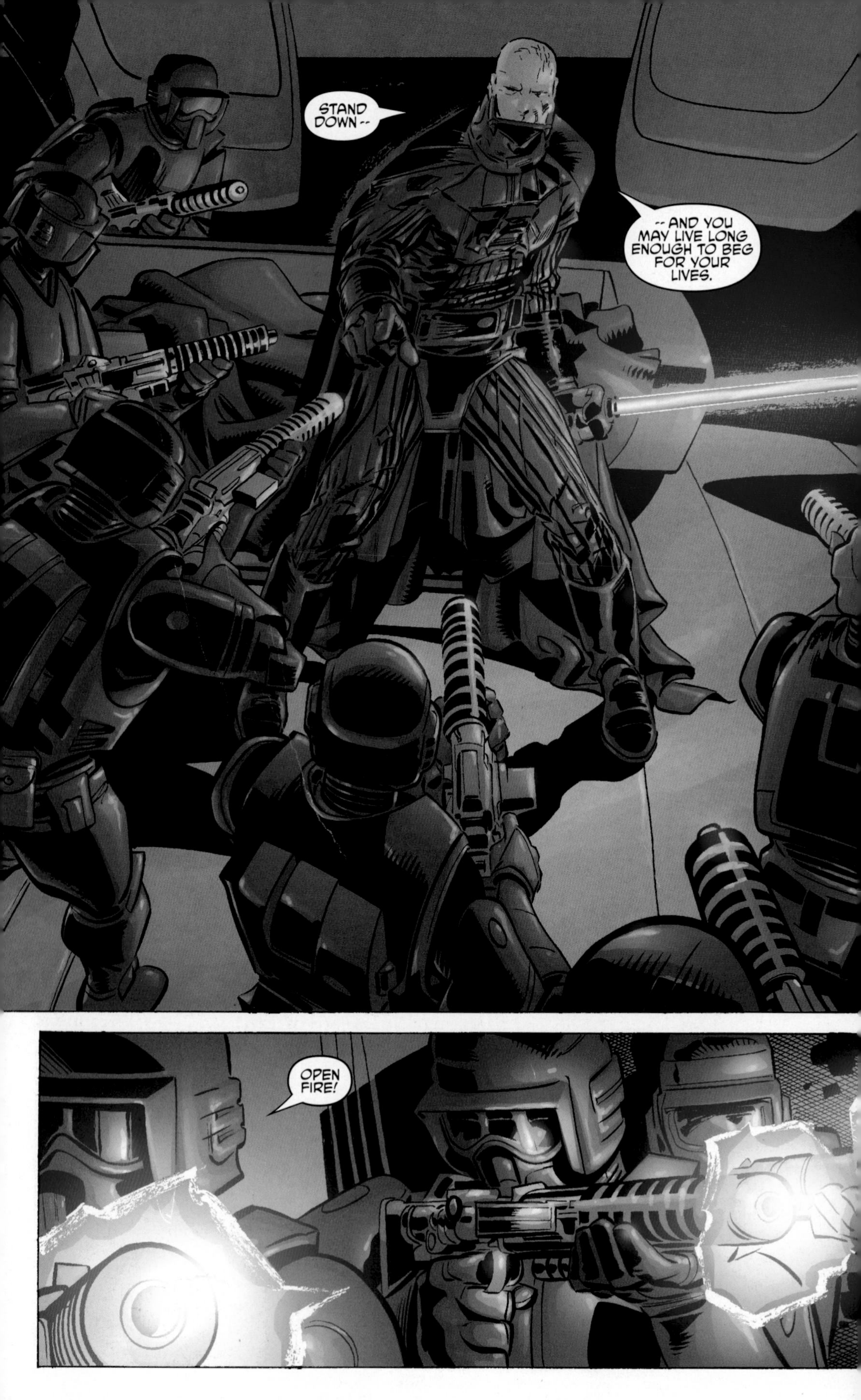
STAND DOWN --
-- AND YOU MAY LIVE LONG ENOUGH TO BEG FOR YOUR LIVES.
OPEN FIRE!

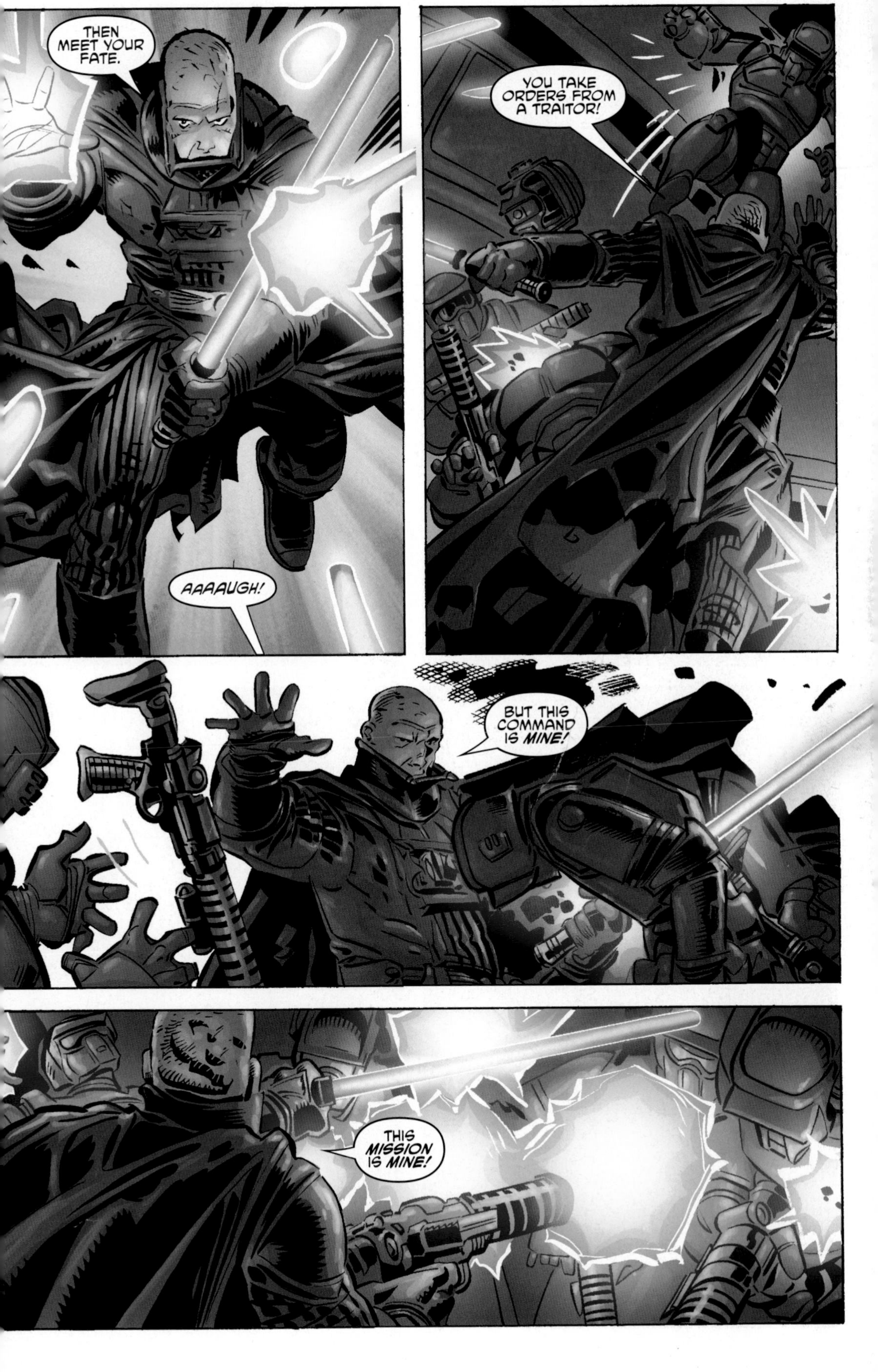
THEN MEET YOUR FATE.
AAAAUGH!
YOU TAKE ORDERS FROM A TRAITOR!
BUT THIS COMMAND IS *MINE!*
THIS *MISSION* IS *MINE!*

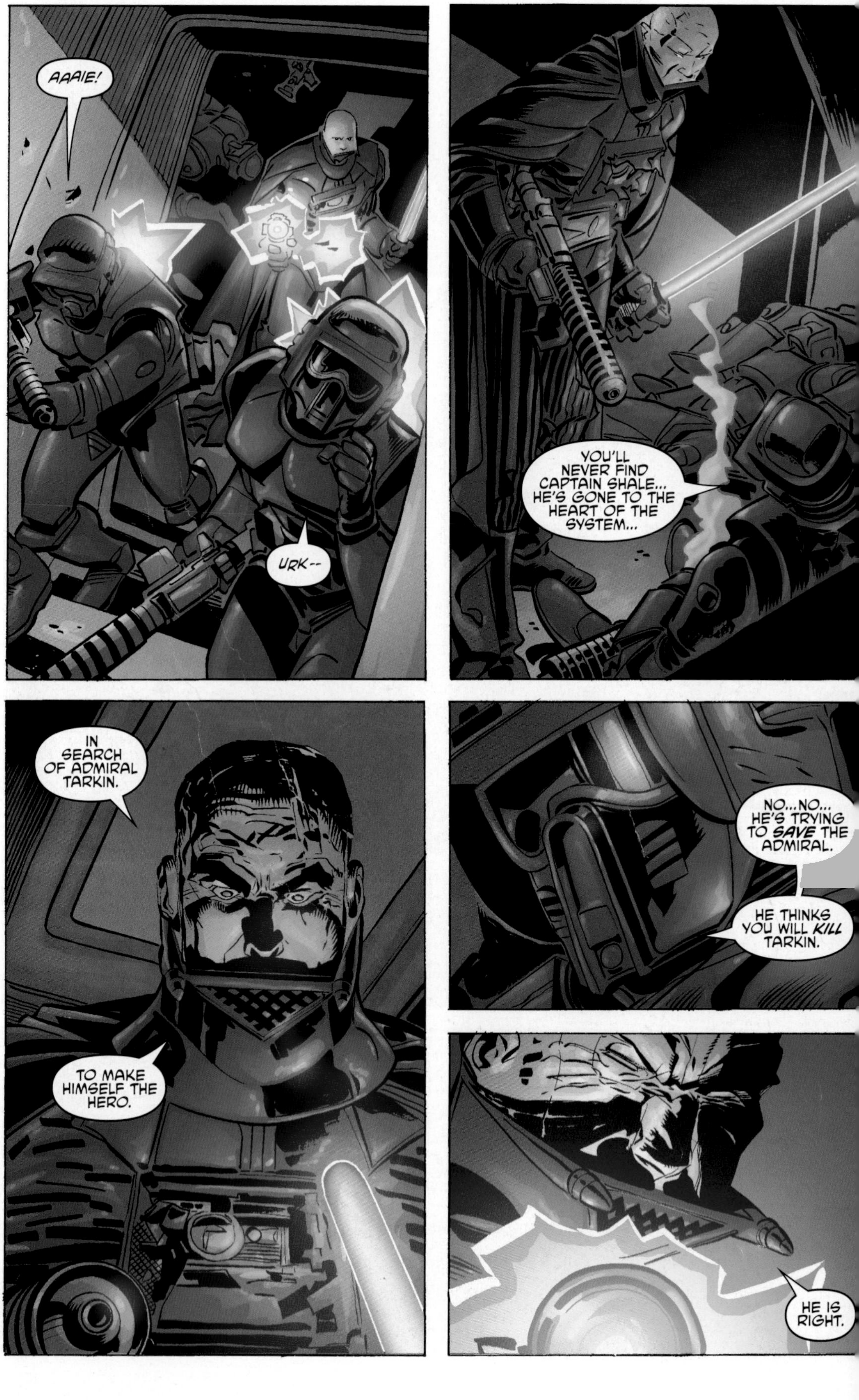
AAAIE!
URK--
YOU'LL NEVER FIND CAPTAIN SHALE... HE'S GONE TO THE HEART OF THE SYSTEM...
IN SEARCH OF ADMIRAL TARKIN.
TO MAKE HIMSELF THE HERO.
NO...NO... HE'S TRYING TO *SAVE* THE ADMIRAL.
HE THINKS YOU WILL *KILL* TARKIN.
HE IS RIGHT.

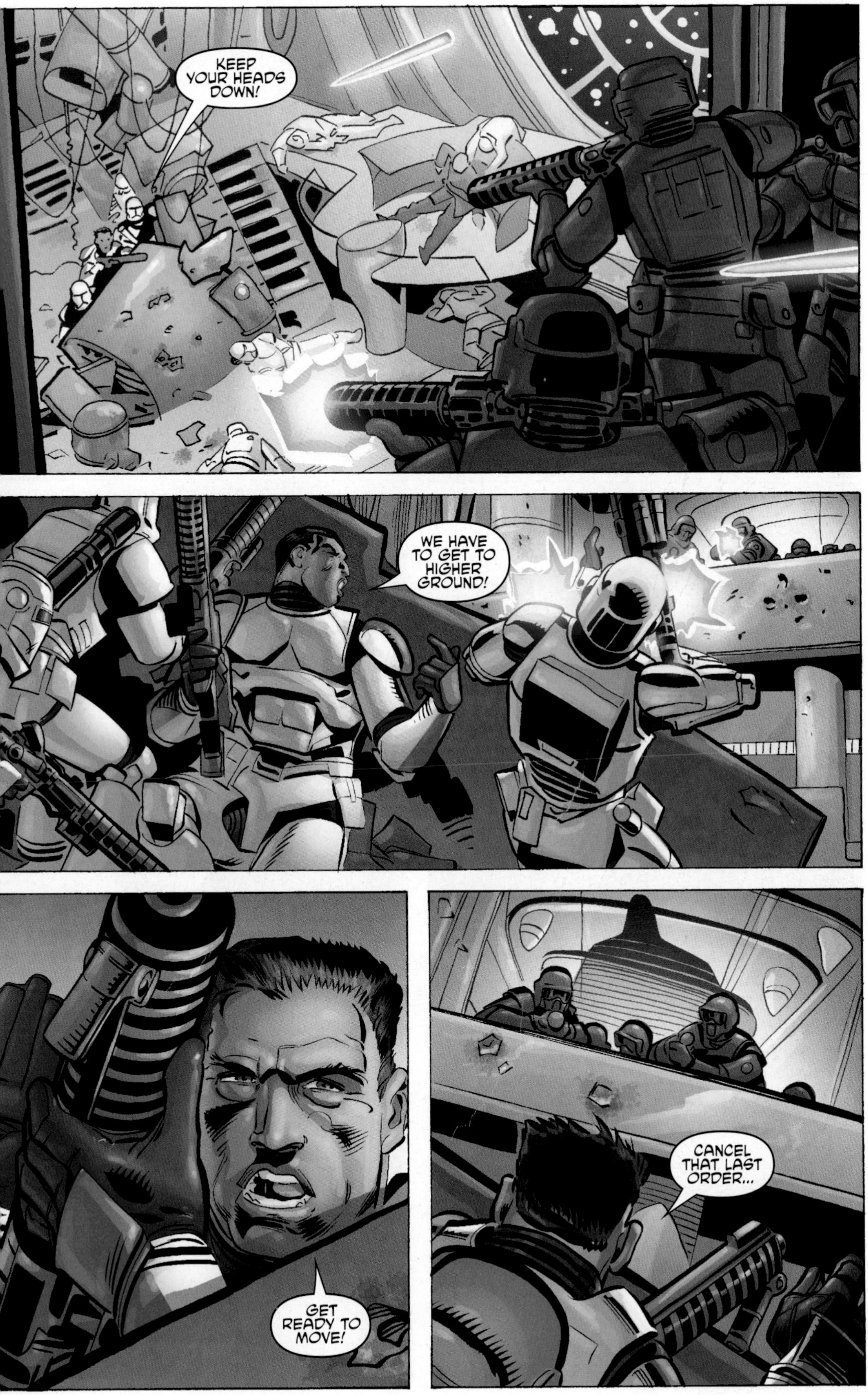
KEEP YOUR HEADS DOWN!
WE HAVE TO GET TO HIGHER GROUND!
GET READY TO MOVE!
CANCEL THAT LAST ORDER...

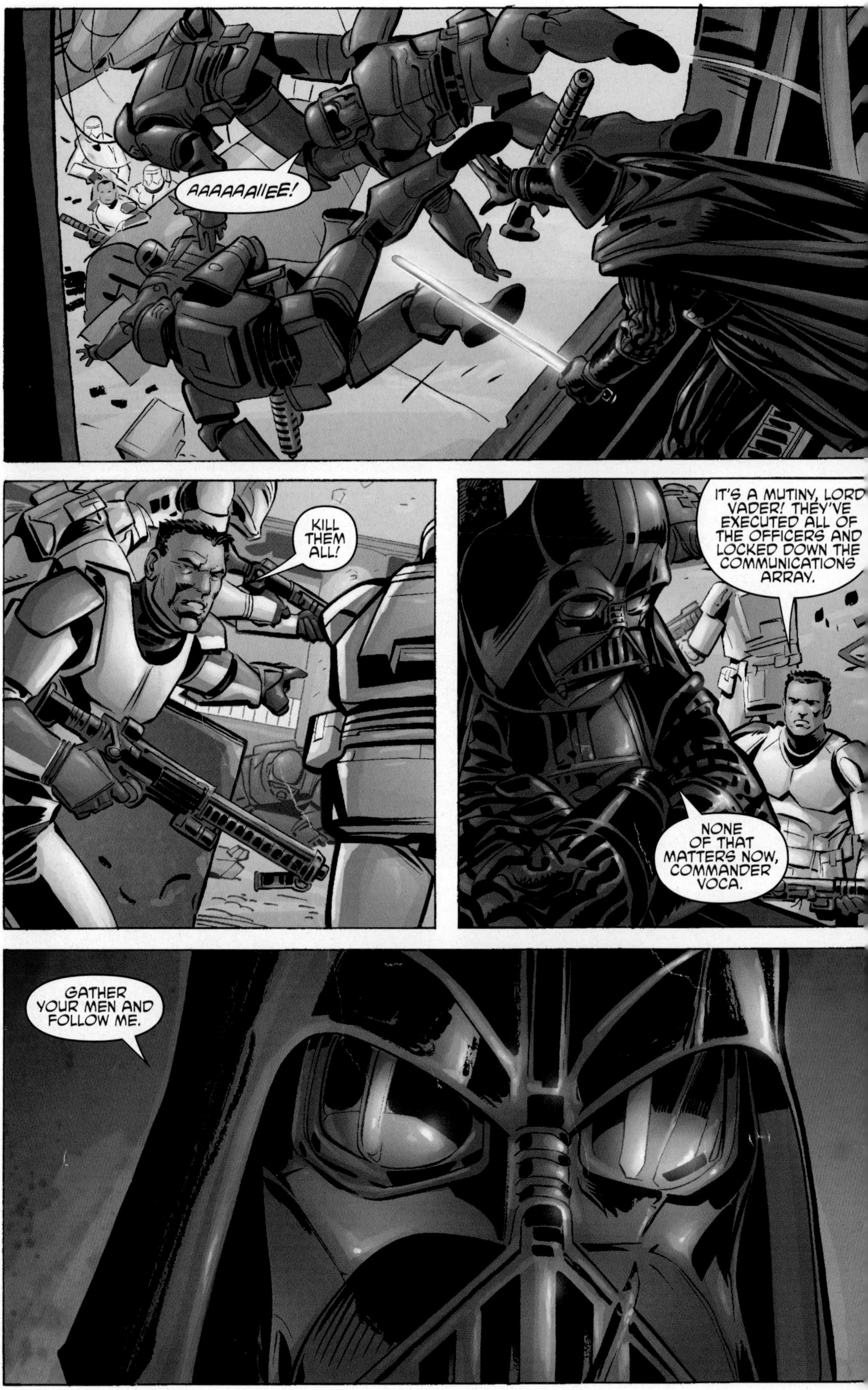
AAAAAAIIEE!
KILL THEM ALL!
IT'S A MUTINY, LORD VADER! THEY'VE EXECUTED ALL OF THE OFFICERS AND LOCKED DOWN THE COMMUNICATIONS ARRAY.
NONE OF THAT MATTERS NOW, COMMANDER VOCA.
GATHER YOUR MEN AND FOLLOW ME.

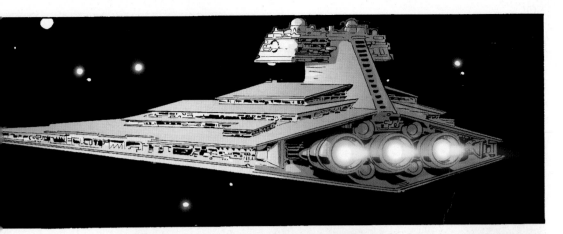

SEND YOUR ENGINEERS TO SHALE'S HANGAR AND ACTIVATE THE TRACKING DE--

BOOOOOOM!

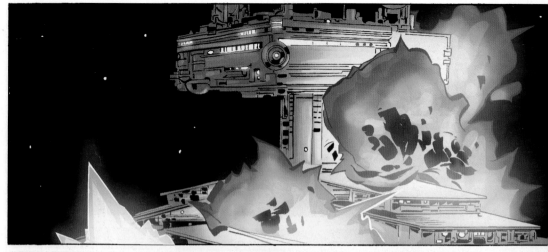

THE SHIP HAS BEEN SABOTAGED.

JUST LIKE TARKIN'S DESTROYER...

WE HAVE TO REACH THE HANGARS!

NOT YET. THE LADY SARO COMES WITH US.

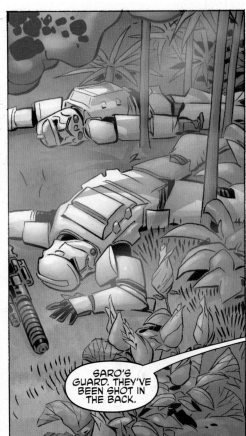

SARO'S GUARD. THEY'VE BEEN SHOT IN THE BACK.

SHALE MUST HAVE TAKEN THE LADY SARO BEFORE HE FLED.

THERE'S NOTHING MORE FOR US HERE.

NOW WE HUNT THESE COWARDS.

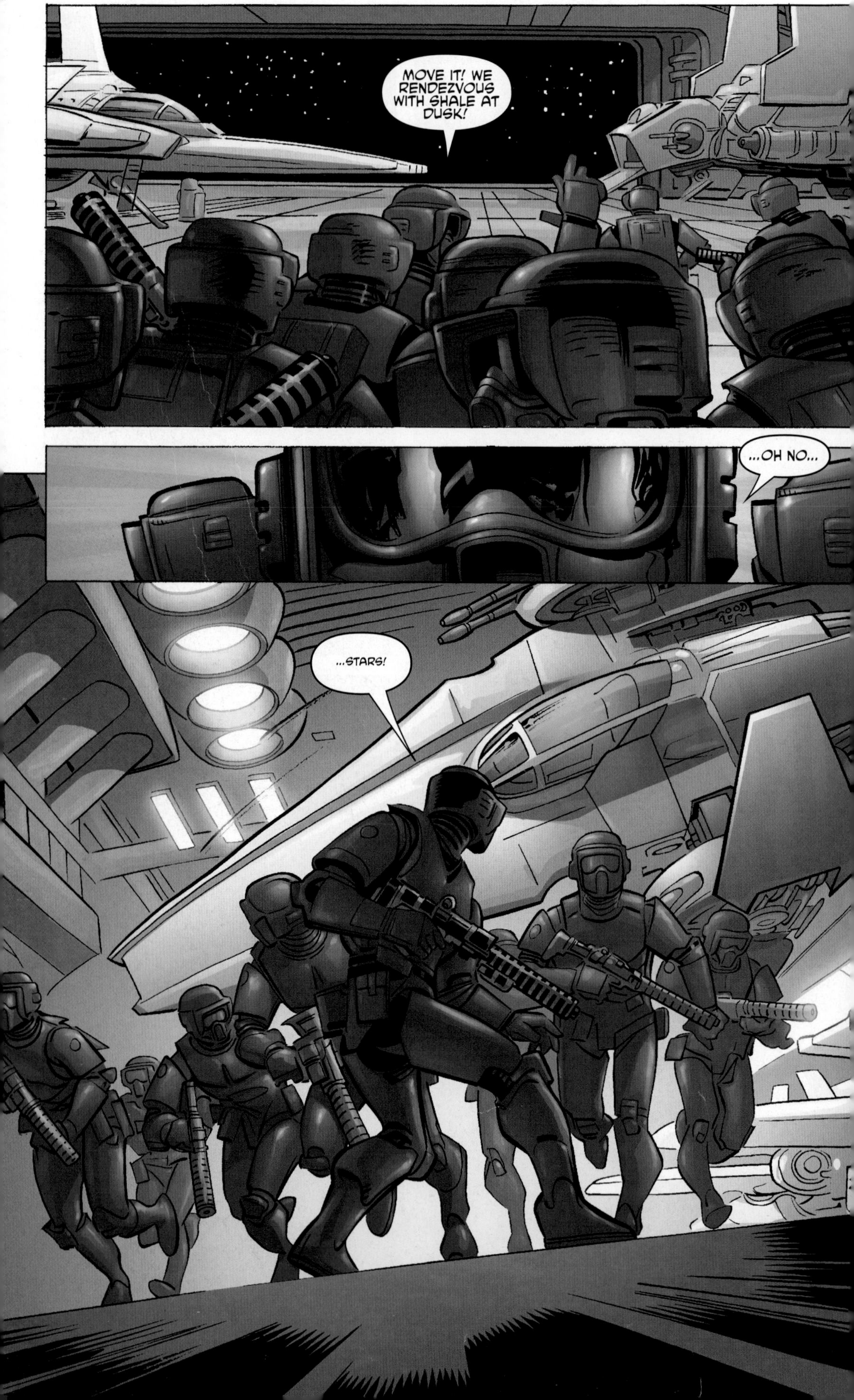
MOVE IT! WE RENDEZVOUS WITH SHALE AT DUSK!
...OH NO...
...STARS!

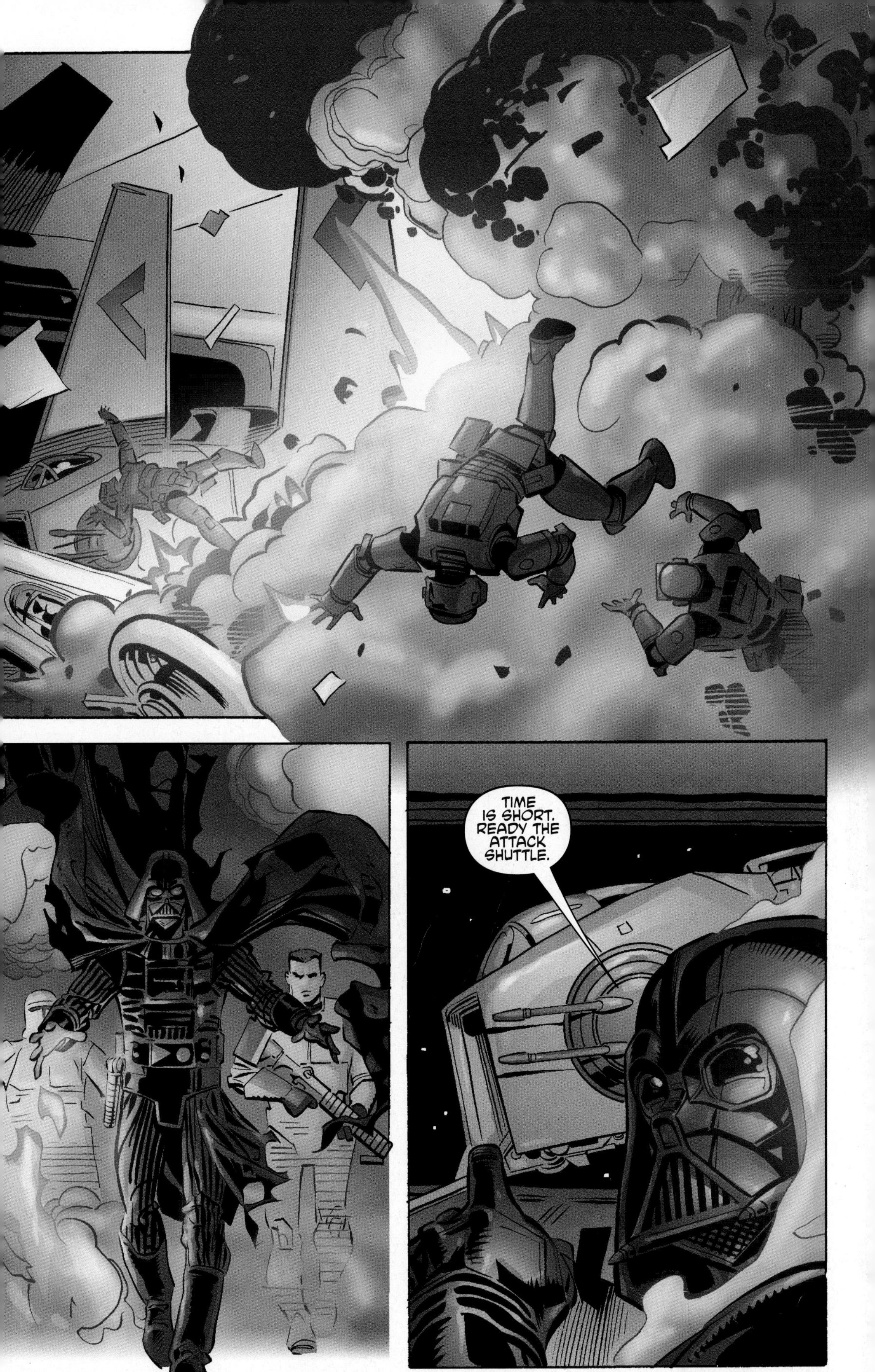
TIME IS SHORT. READY THE ATTACK SHUTTLE.

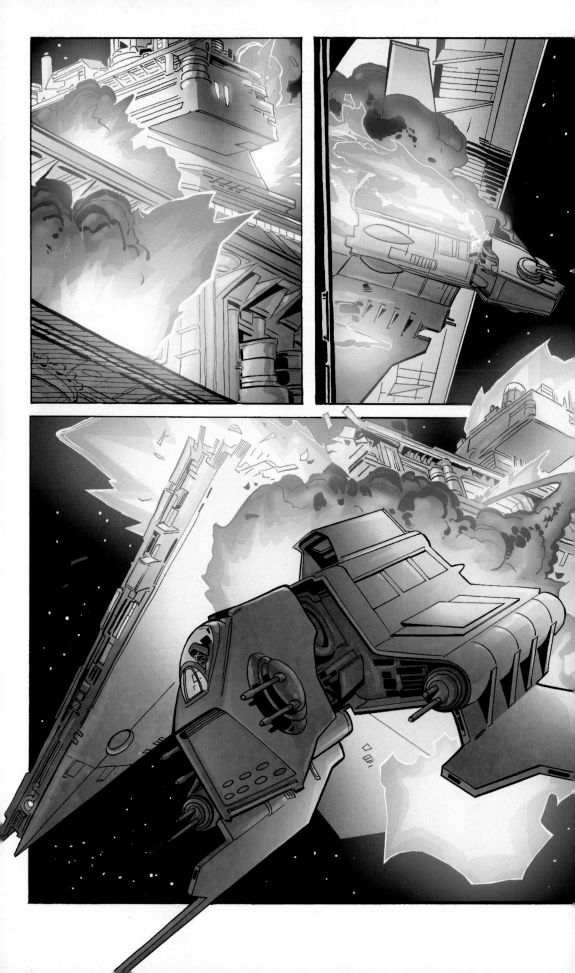

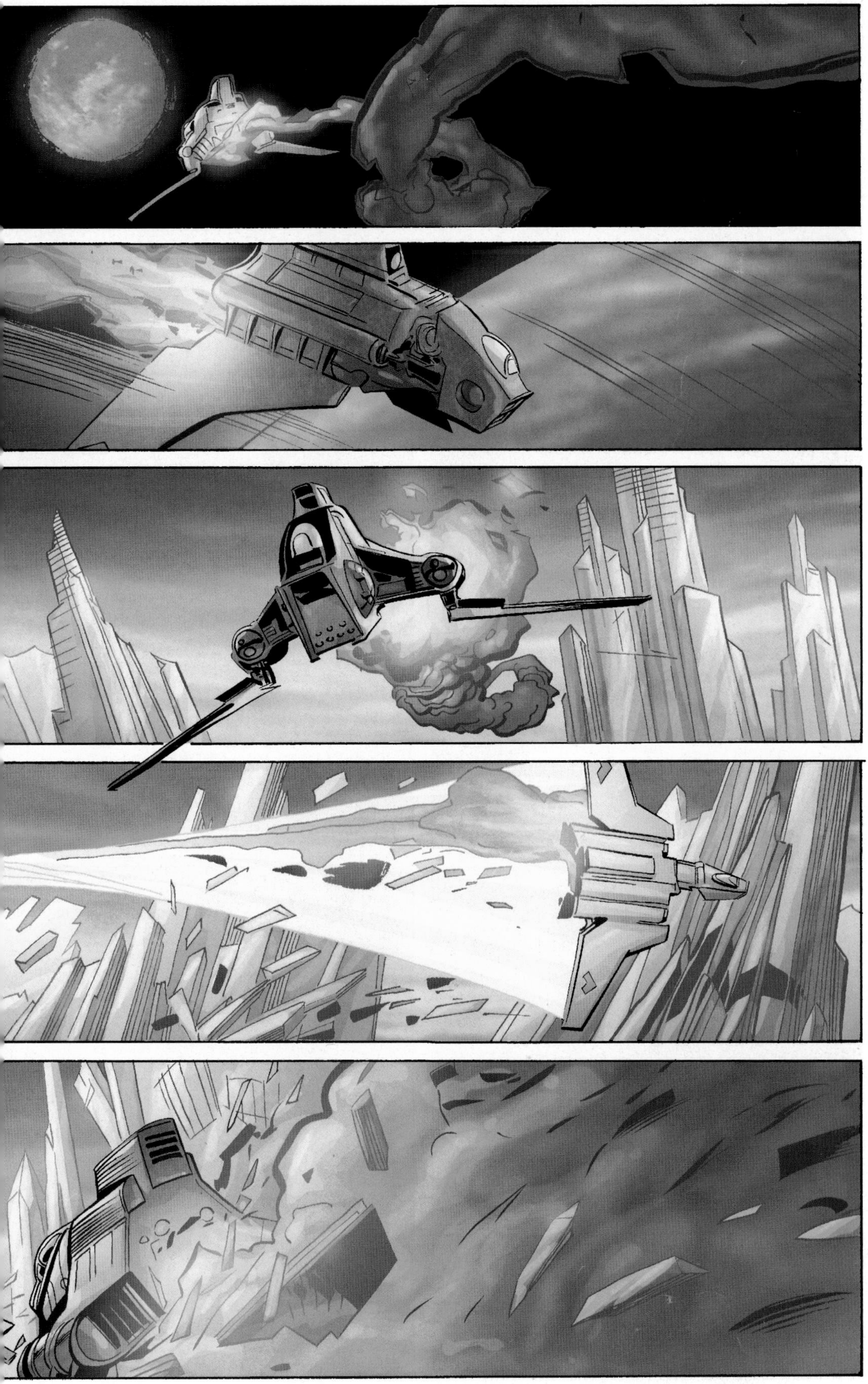

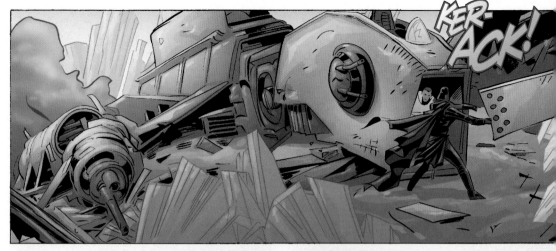

KER-ACK!

SECURE A PERIMETER! GO!

BLAST.

VOCA. HOW MANY OF YOUR SQUAD HAVE SURVIVED?

INCLUDING ME? JUST NINE. AND THE TRANSPORT IS A TOTAL LOSS.

GATHER WHATEVER SUPPLIES YOU NEED. WE'LL PURSUE SHALE ON FOOT.

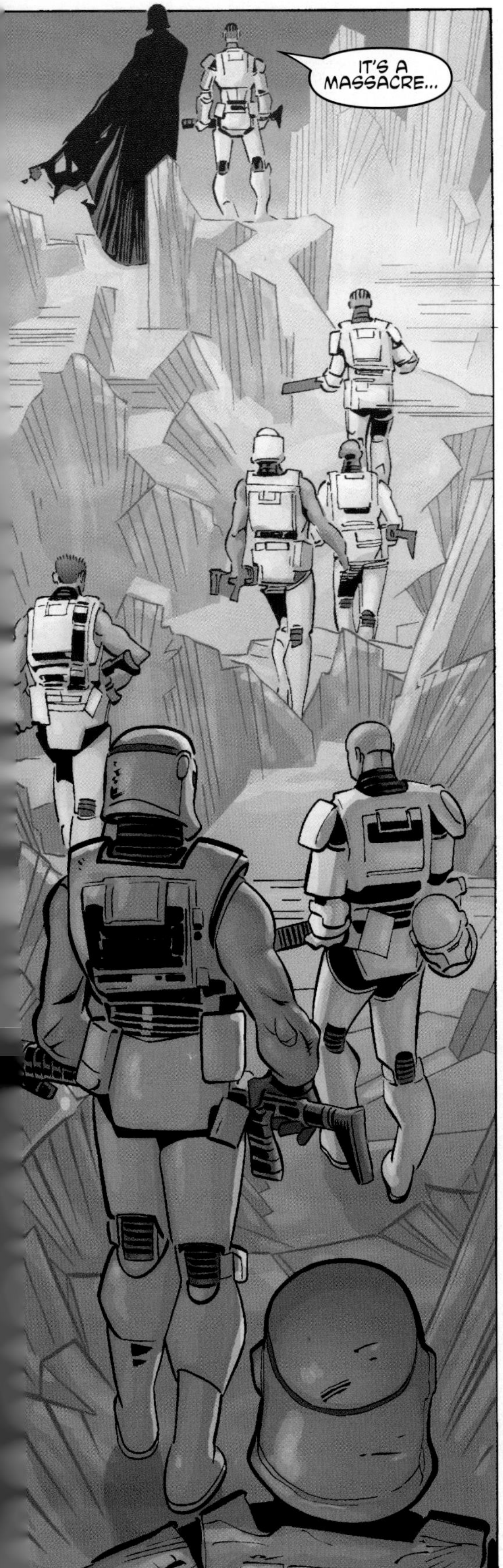
IT'S A MASSACRE...

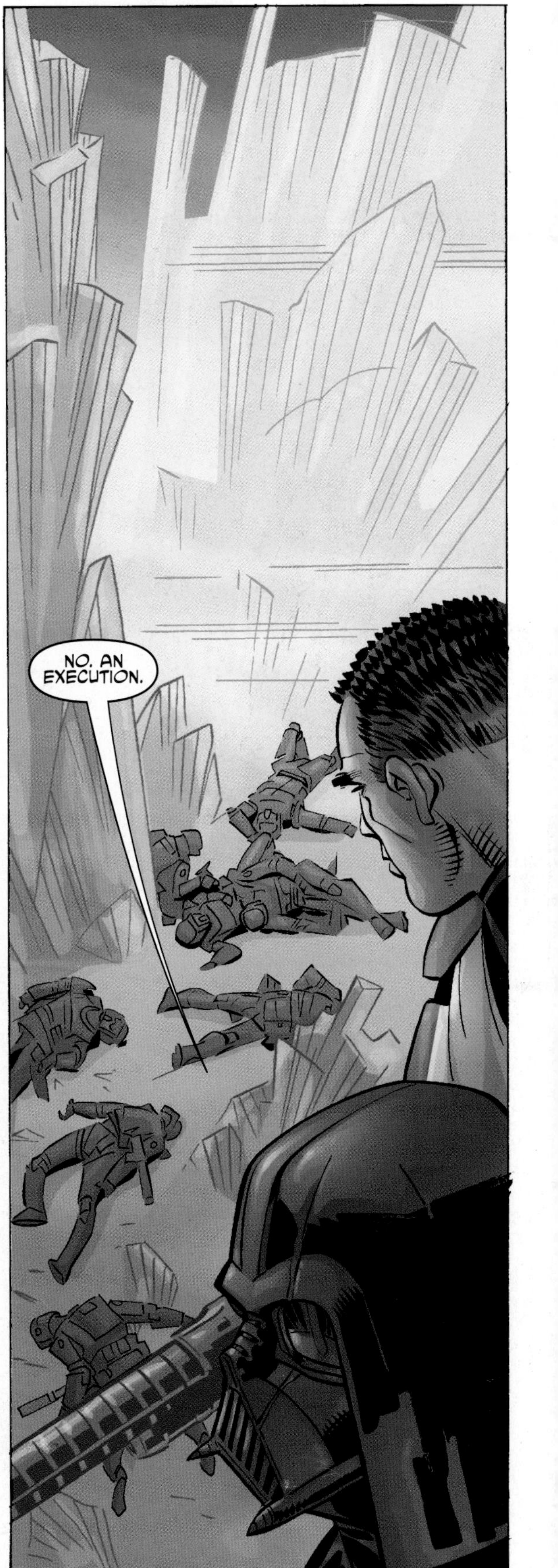
NO. AN EXECUTION.

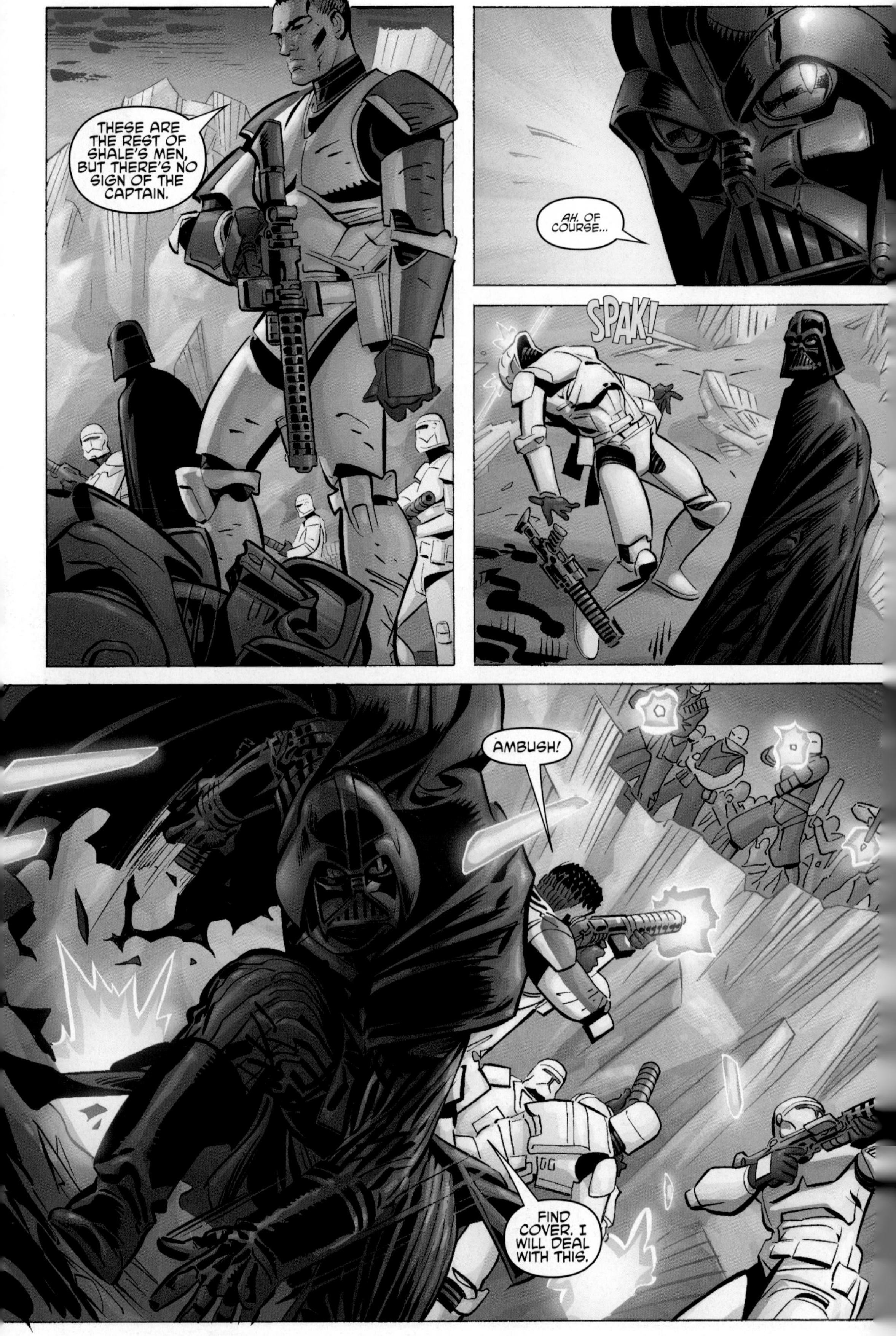
THESE ARE THE REST OF SHALE'S MEN, BUT THERE'S NO SIGN OF THE CAPTAIN.
AH. OF COURSE...
SPAK!
AMBUSH!
FIND COVER. I WILL DEAL WITH THIS.

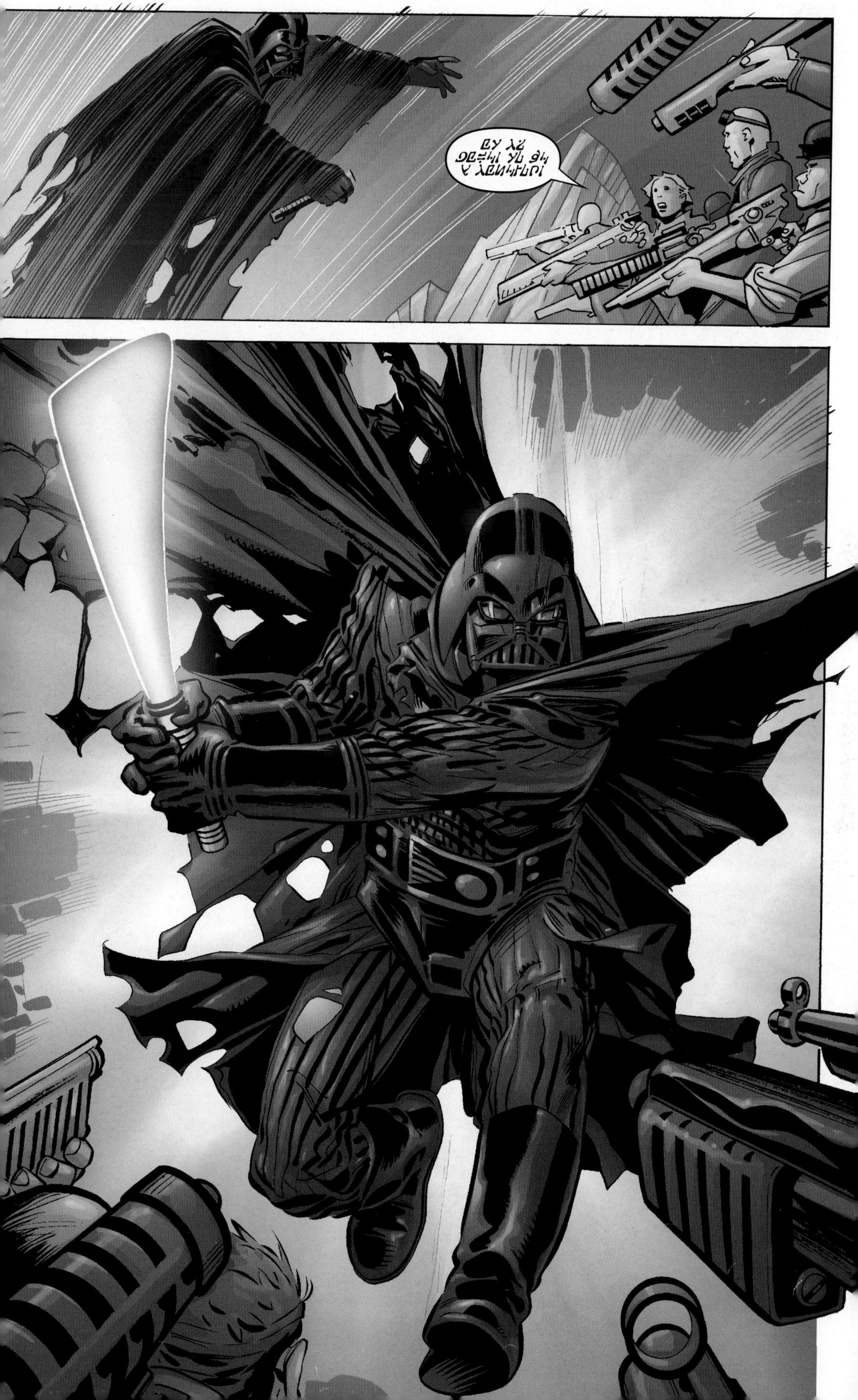

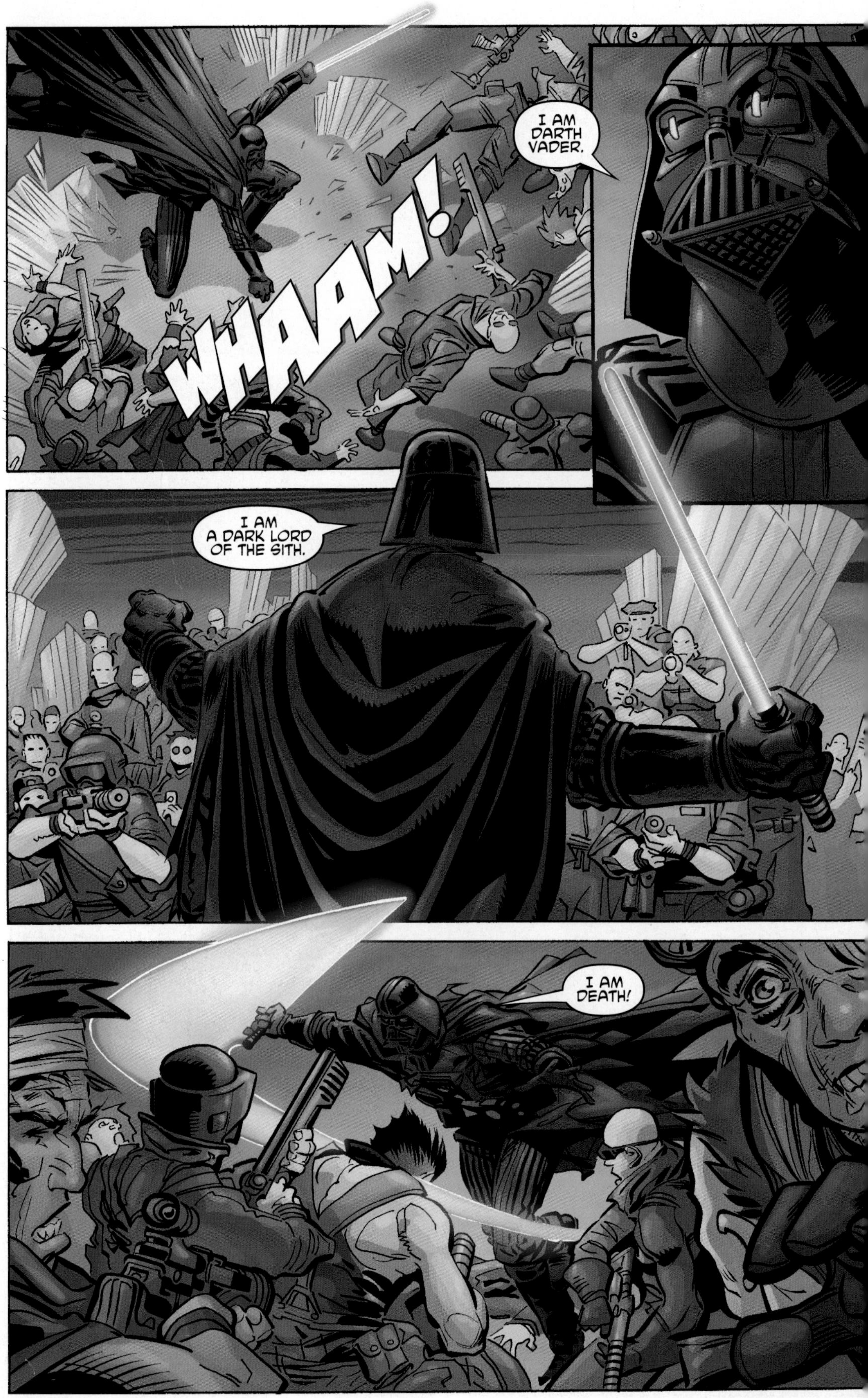
WHAAM!
I AM DARTH VADER.
I AM A DARK LORD OF THE SITH.
I AM DEATH!

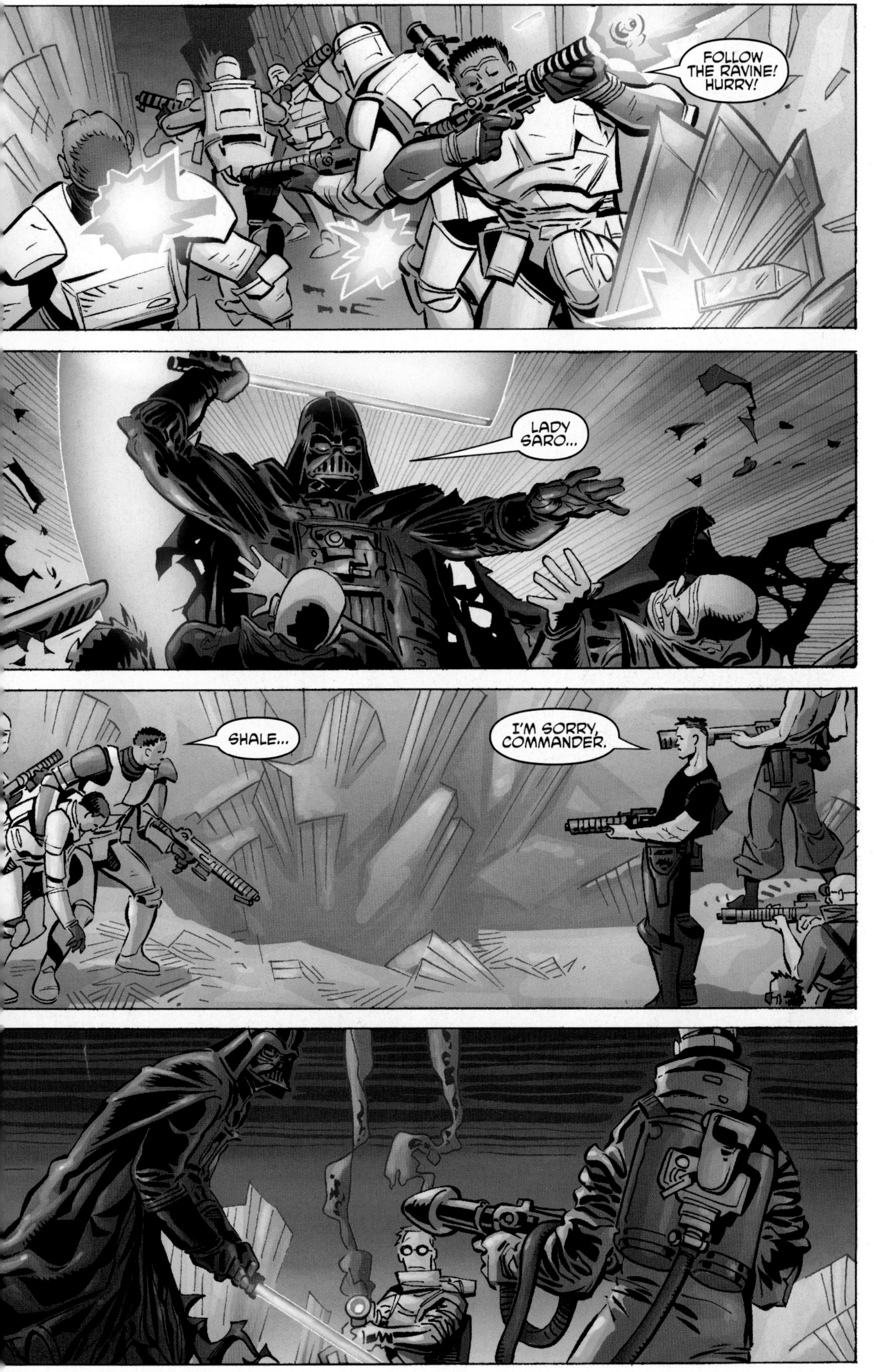
FOLLOW THE RAVINE! HURRY!
LADY SARO...
SHALE...
I'M SORRY, COMMANDER.

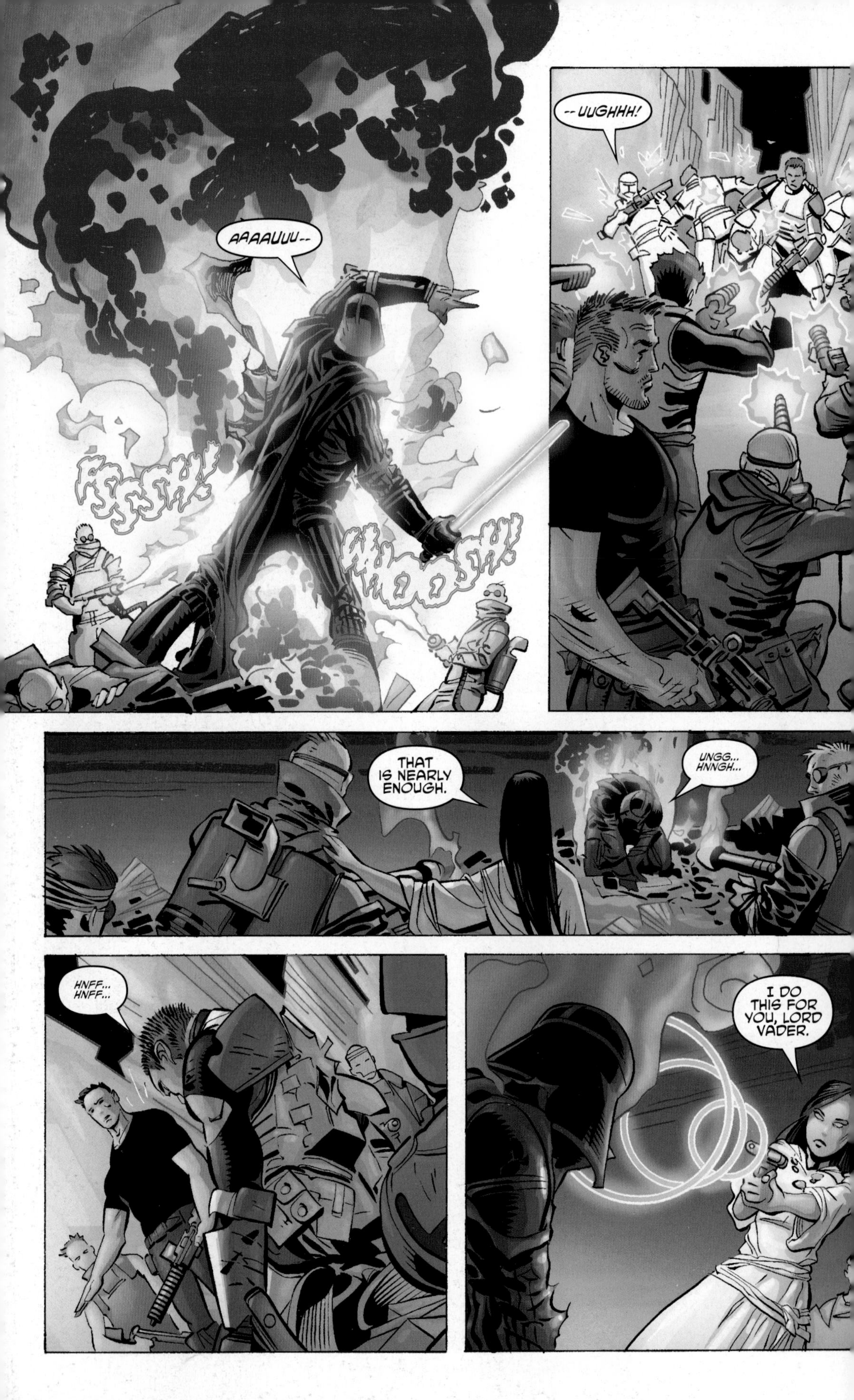
AAAAUUU--
FSSSH!
WHOOSH!
--UUGHHH!
THAT IS NEARLY ENOUGH.
UNGG... HNNGH...
HNFF... HNFF...
I DO THIS FOR YOU, LORD VADER.

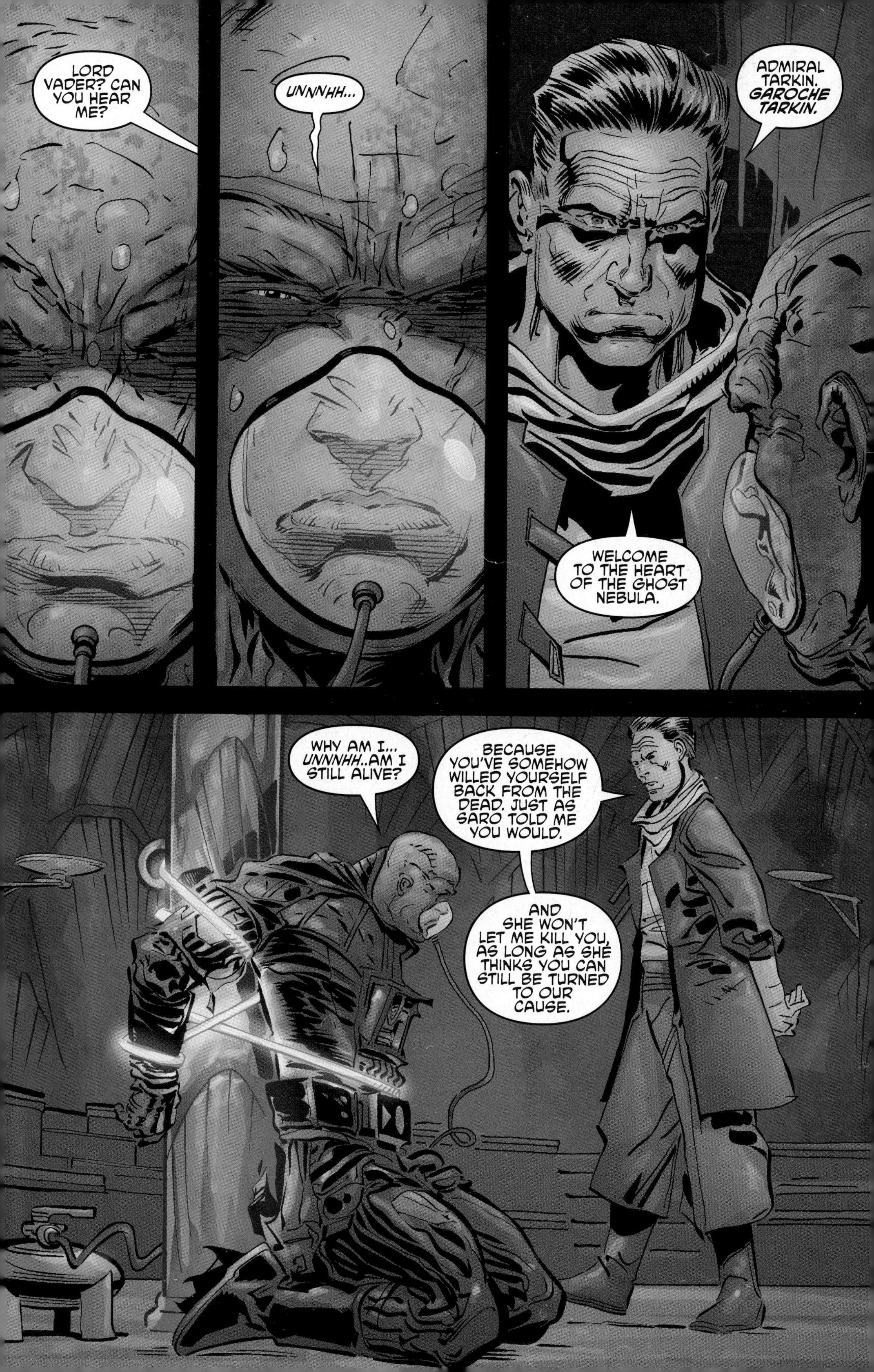
LORD VADER? CAN YOU HEAR ME?
UNNNHH...
ADMIRAL TARKIN. GAROCHE TARKIN.
WELCOME TO THE HEART OF THE GHOST NEBULA.
WHY AM I... UNNNHH..AM I STILL ALIVE?
BECAUSE YOU'VE SOMEHOW WILLED YOURSELF BACK FROM THE DEAD. JUST AS SARO TOLD ME YOU WOULD.
AND SHE WON'T LET ME KILL YOU, AS LONG AS SHE THINKS YOU CAN STILL BE TURNED TO OUR CAUSE.

WHAT... *CAUSE?*

THE ONLY ONE THAT MATTERS.

UNH... YOU THINK SHE... *UNH...*SHE LOVES YOU...

I *KNOW* SHE DOES. I CAME HERE TO CONQUER THIS SYSTEM FOR MY FATHER. I KILLED *CHILDREN* IN HIS NAME.

AND THEN THE LADY SARO CAME TO ME, AND OFFERED TO REVEAL ALL OF THE SYSTEM'S SECRETS IF I WOULD SPARE HER PEOPLE.

AT FIRST, I THOUGHT SHE MEANT HIDDEN RICHES, OR PERHAPS EVEN A NEW POWER SOURCE.

BUT SHE GAVE ME SO MUCH MORE THAN THAT...

SHE *FORGAVE* ME.

...YOU FOOL...SHE WANTS...

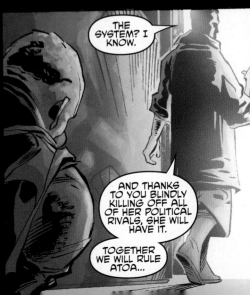

THE SYSTEM? I KNOW.

AND THANKS TO YOU BLINDLY KILLING OFF ALL OF HER POLITICAL RIVALS, SHE WILL HAVE IT.

TOGETHER WE WILL RULE ATOA...

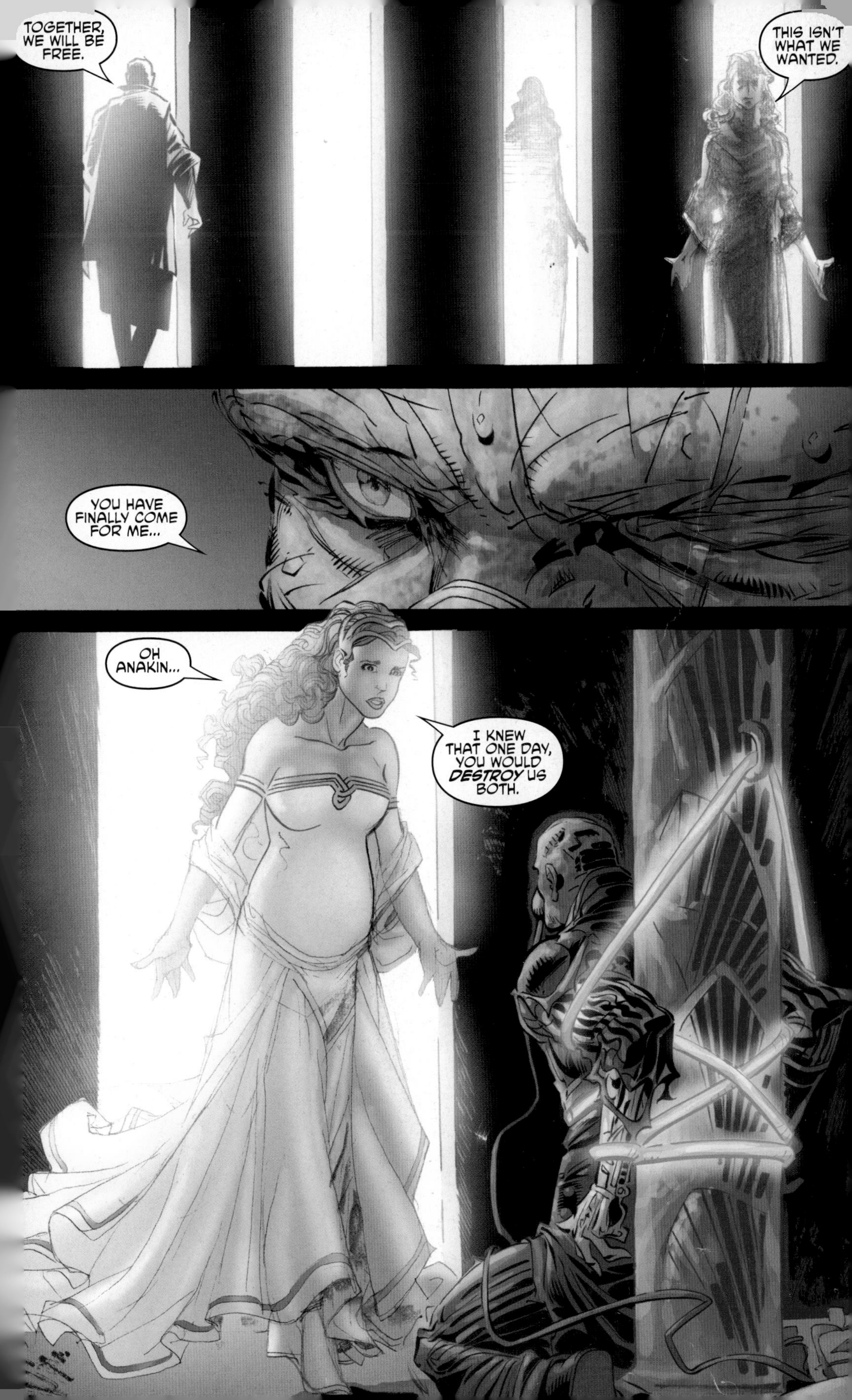
TOGETHER, WE WILL BE FREE.
THIS ISN'T WHAT WE WANTED.
YOU HAVE FINALLY COME FOR ME...
OH ANAKIN...
I KNEW THAT ONE DAY, YOU WOULD *DESTROY* US BOTH.

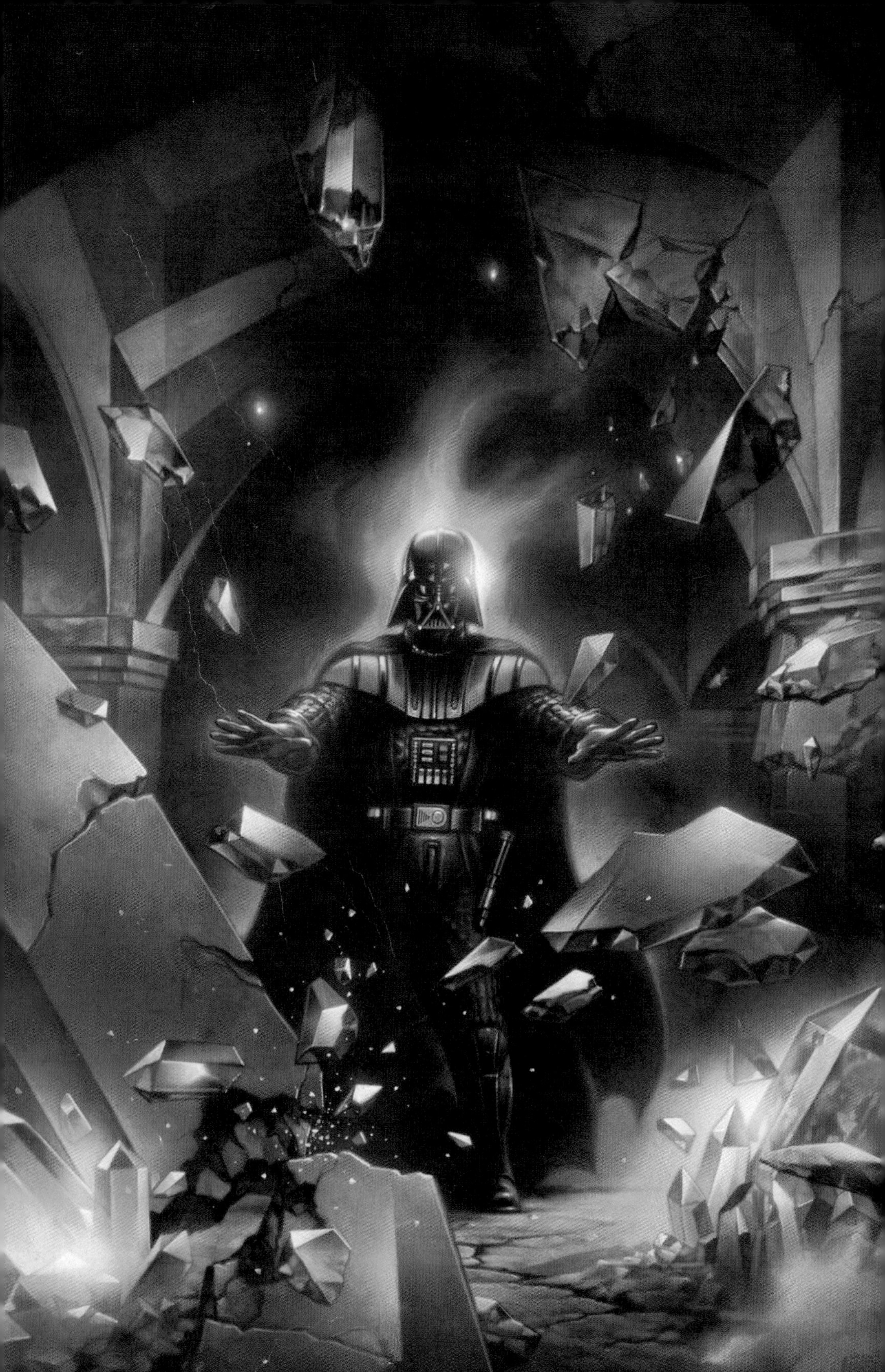
TSUNEO SANDA

STAR WARS: DARTH VADER AND THE LOST COMMAND #5

WRITER: HADEN BLACKMAN • PENCILER: RICK LEONARDI • INKER: DAN GREEN • COLORIST: WES DZIOBA • LETTERER: MICHAEL HEISLER
DESIGNER: KAT LARSON • ASSISTANT EDITOR: FREDDYE LINS • EDITOR: RANDY STRADLEY • COVER ARTIST: TSUNEO SANDA

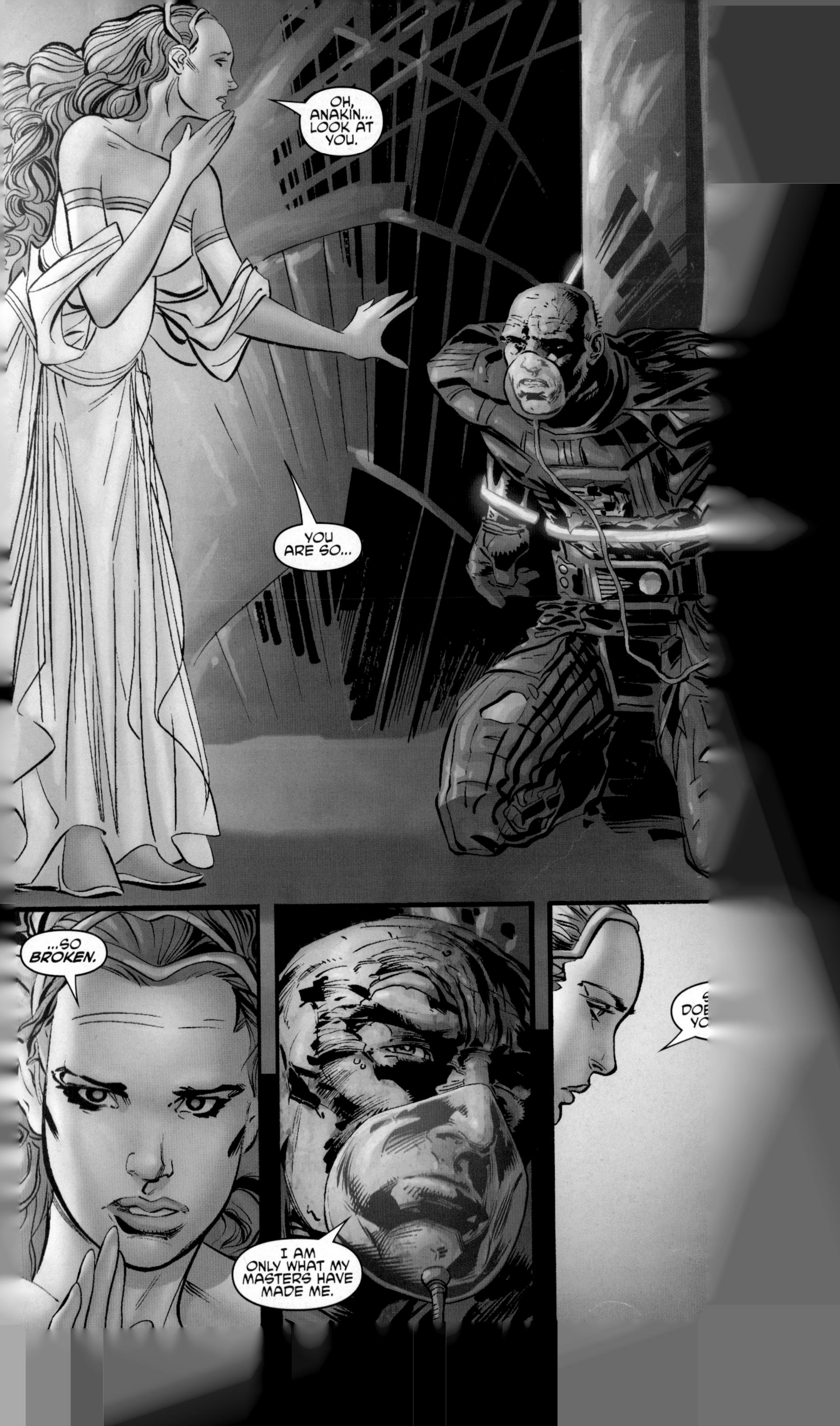
OH, ANAKIN... LOOK AT YOU.
YOU ARE SO...
...SO BROKEN.
I AM ONLY WHAT MY MASTERS HAVE MADE ME.

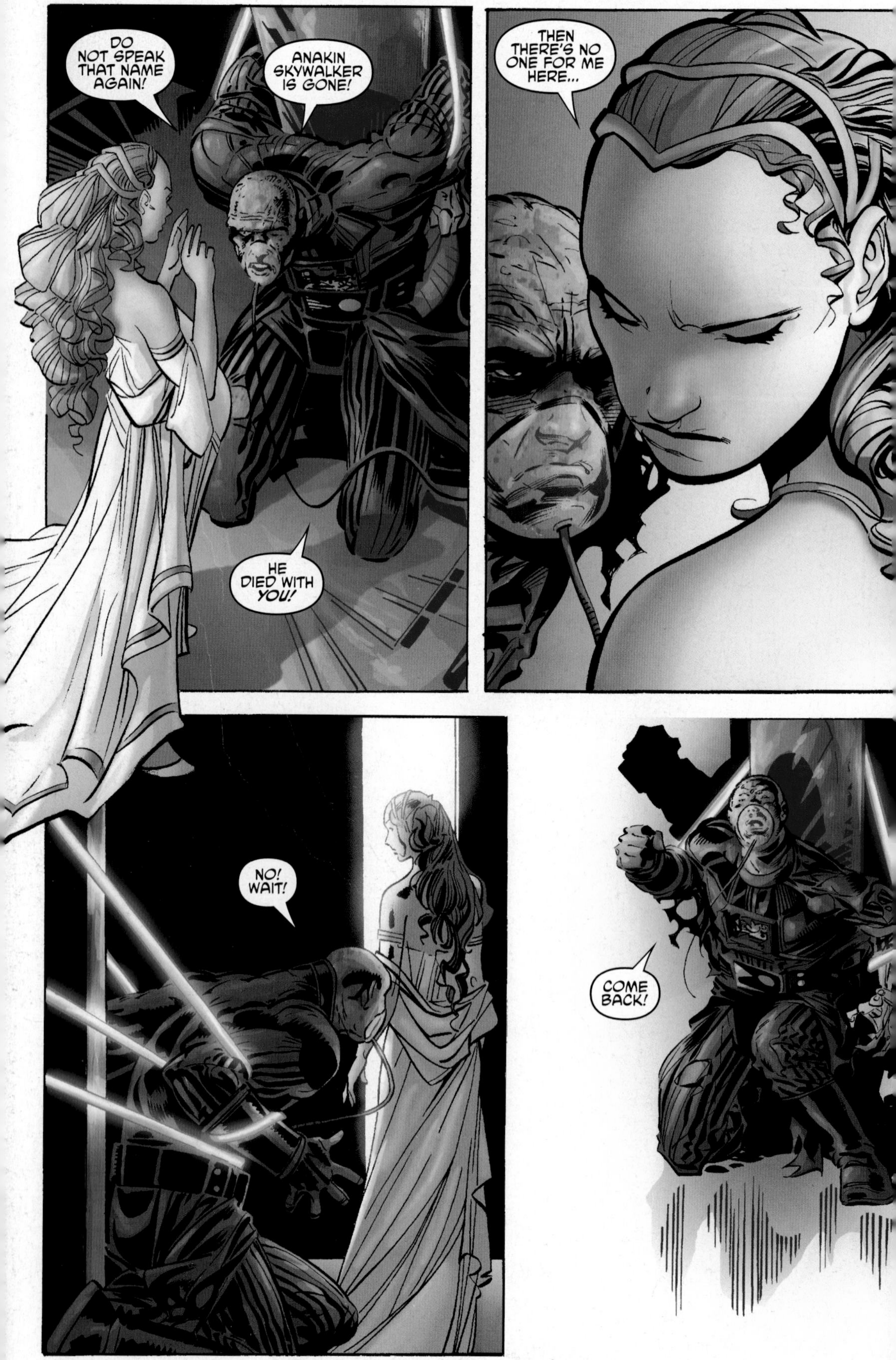
DO NOT SPEAK THAT NAME AGAIN!
ANAKIN SKYWALKER IS GONE!
HE DIED WITH YOU!
THEN THERE'S NO ONE FOR ME HERE...
NO! WAIT!
COME BACK!

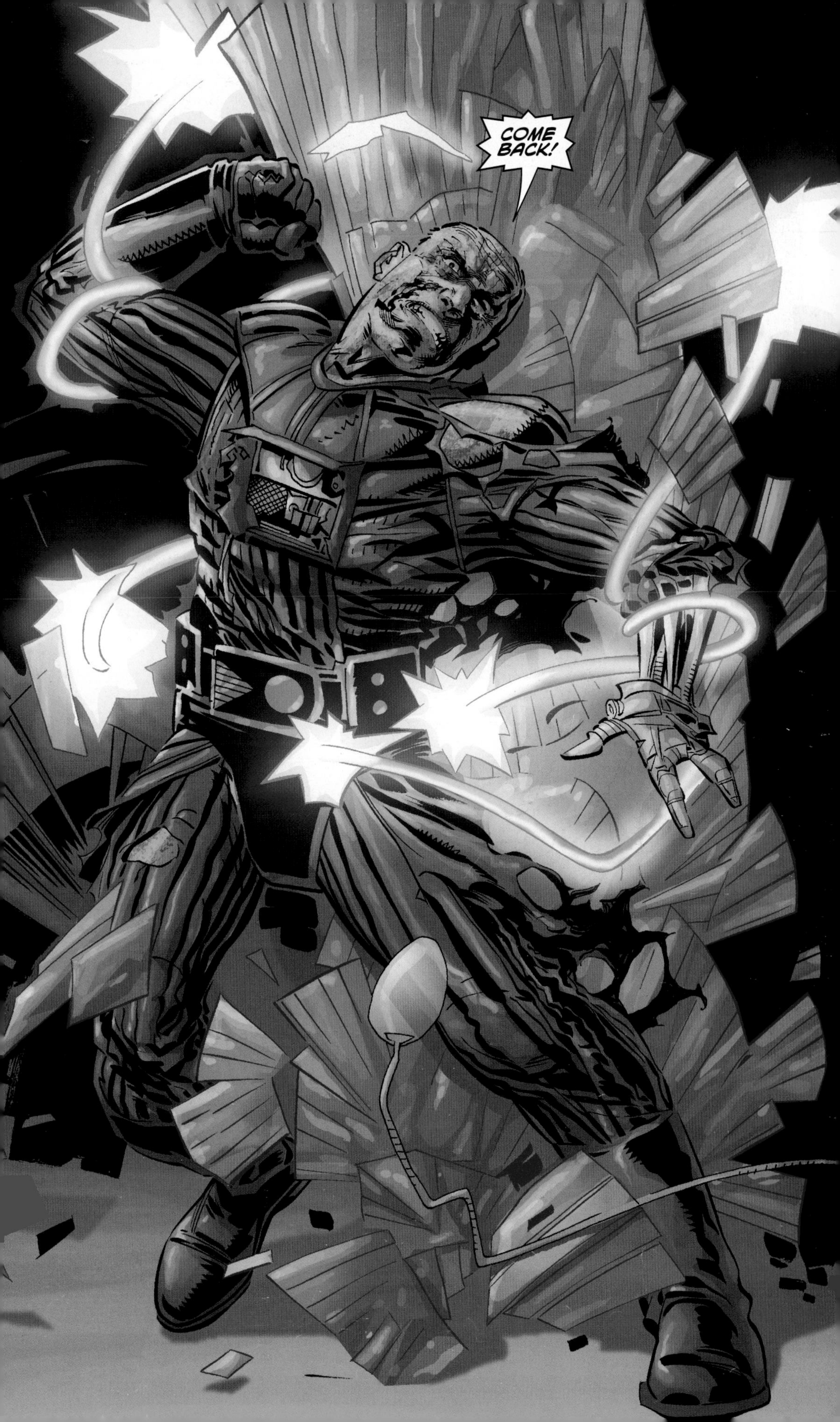
COME BACK!

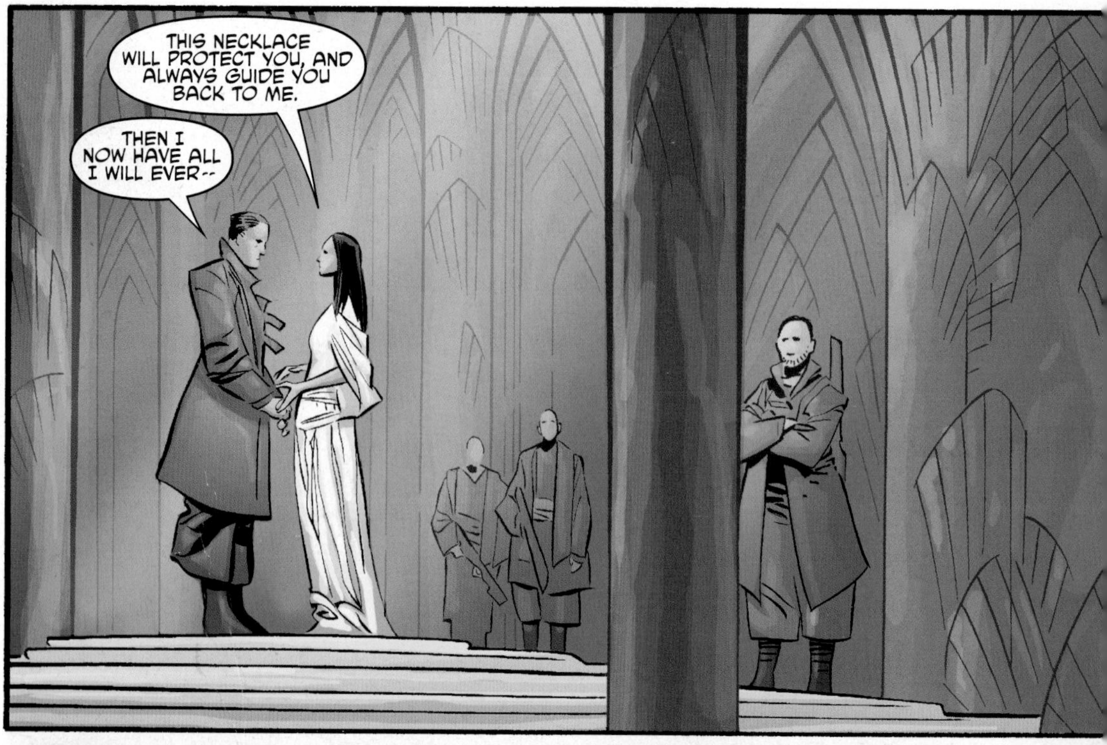
THIS NECKLACE WILL PROTECT YOU, AND ALWAYS GUIDE YOU BACK TO ME.
THEN I NOW HAVE ALL I WILL EVER--

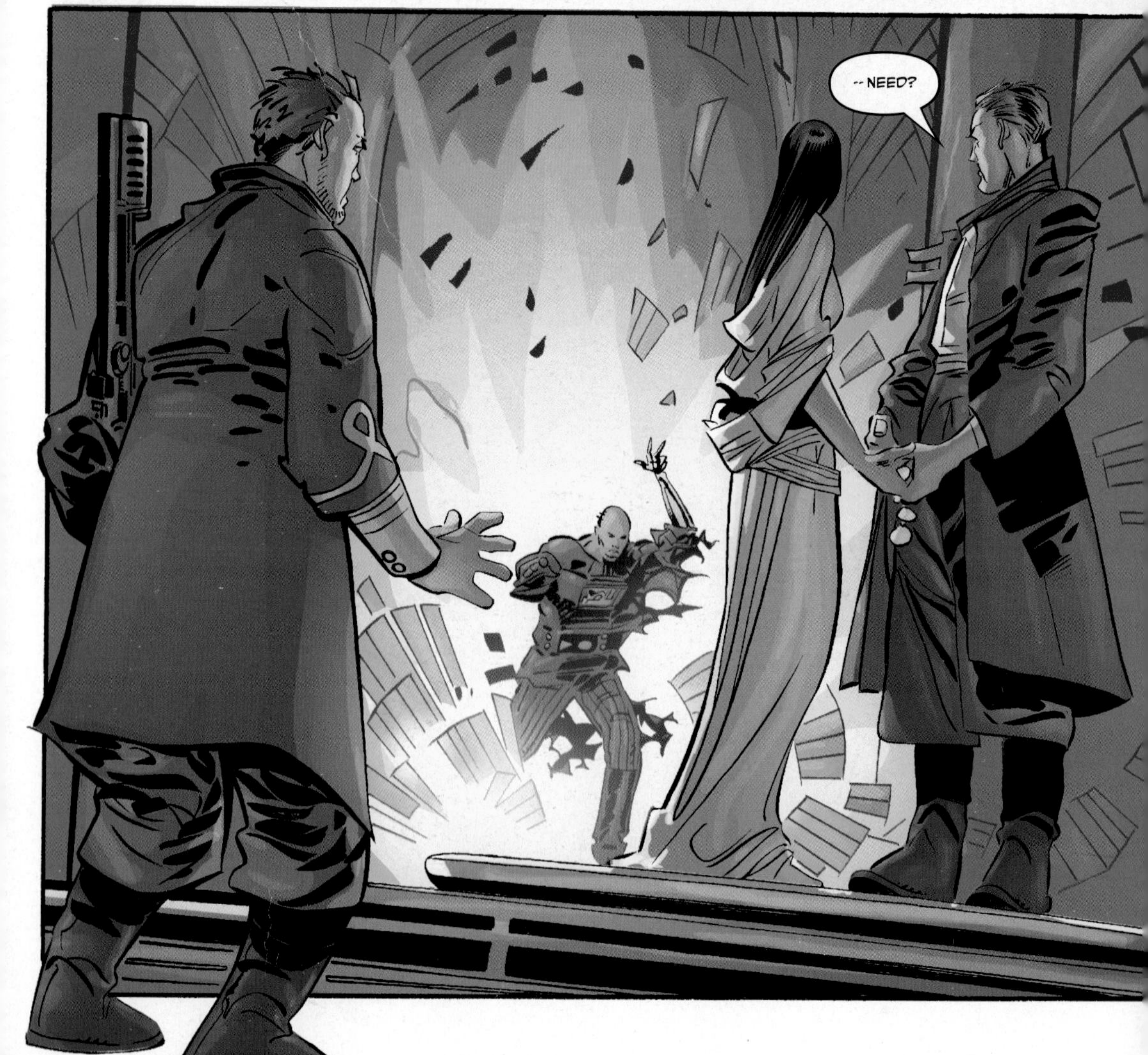
--NEED?

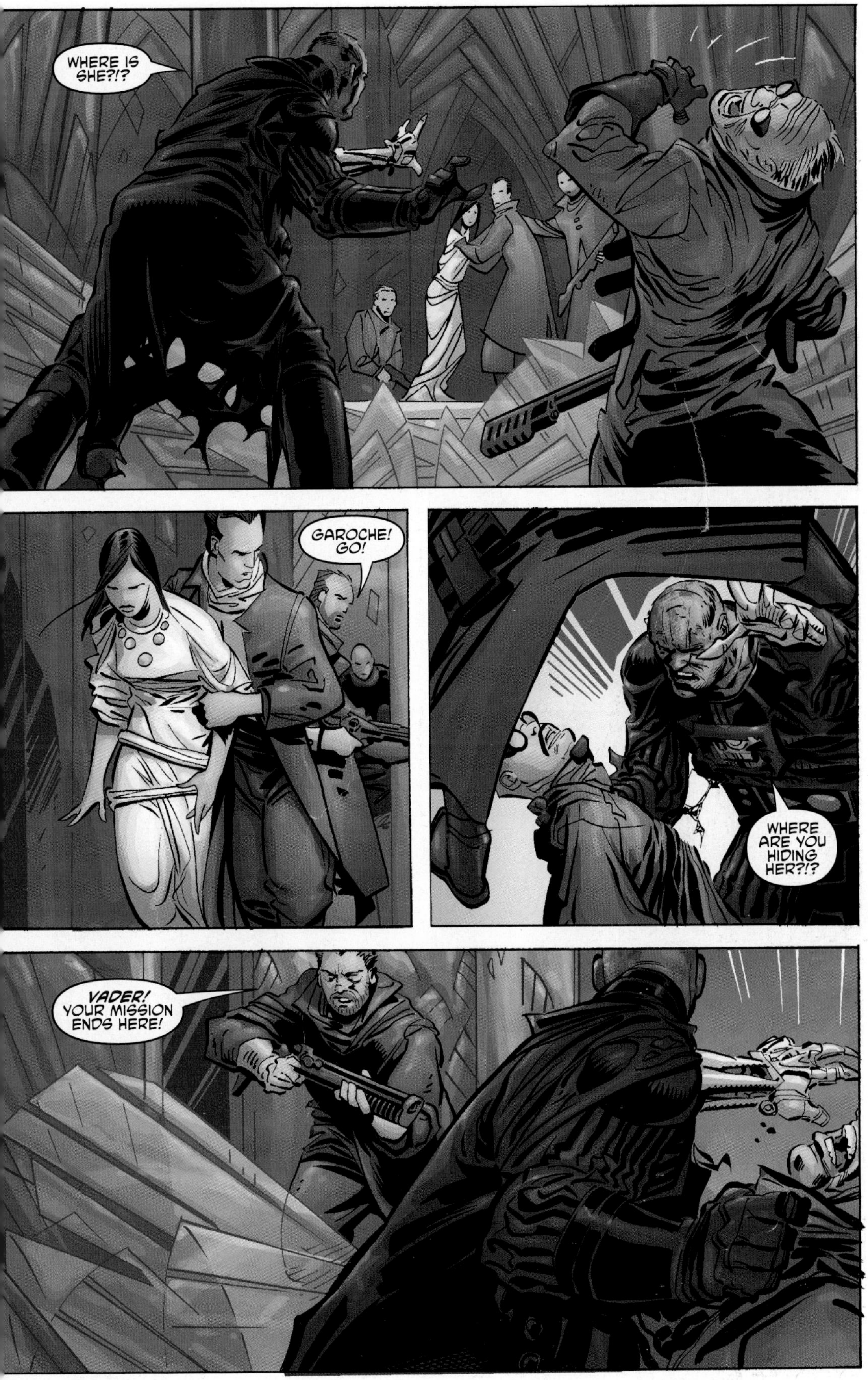
WHERE IS SHE?!?
GAROCHE! GO!
WHERE ARE YOU HIDING HER?!?
VADER! YOUR MISSION ENDS HERE!

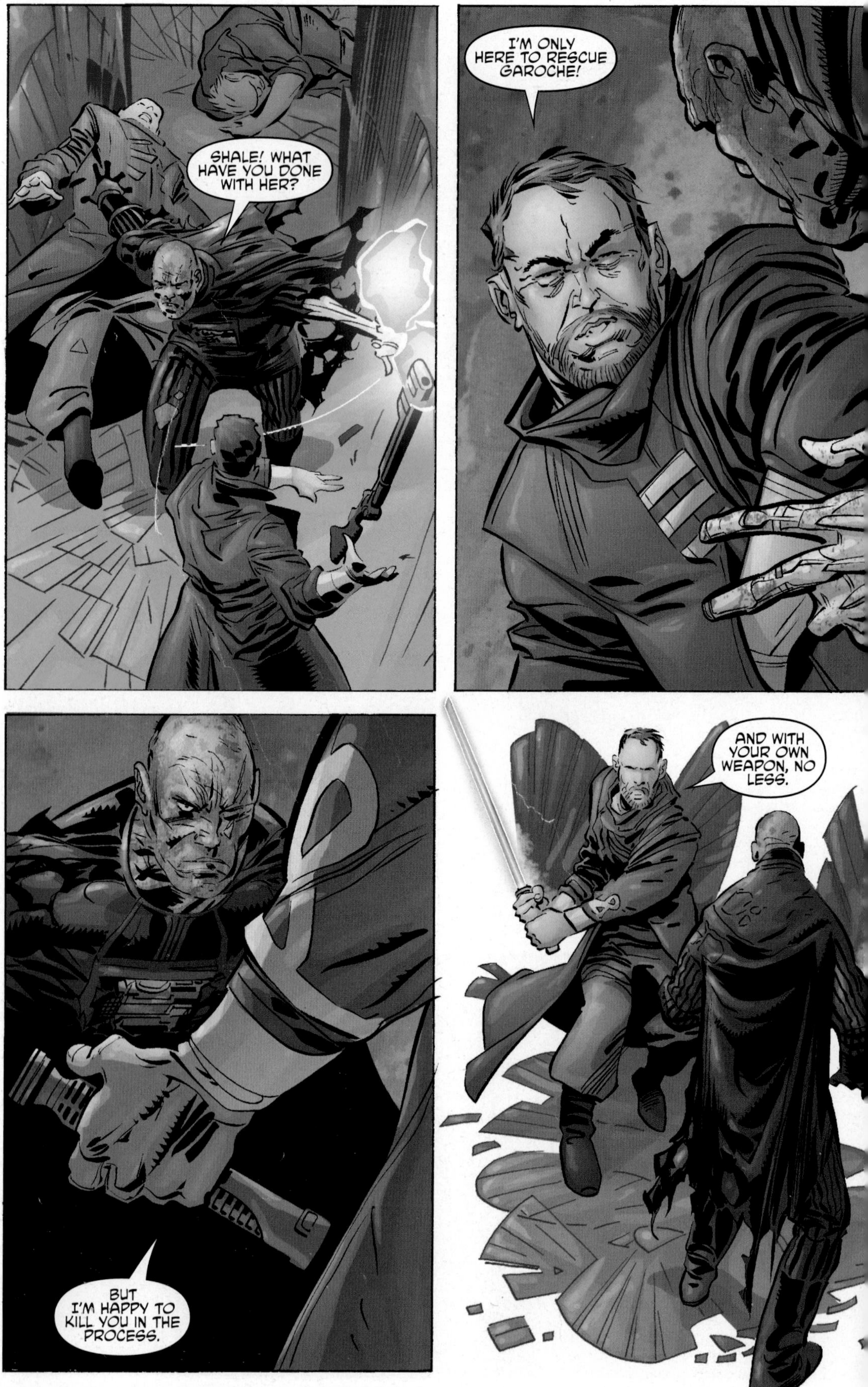
SHALE! WHAT HAVE YOU DONE WITH HER?
I'M ONLY HERE TO RESCUE GAROCHE!
BUT I'M HAPPY TO KILL YOU IN THE PROCESS.
AND WITH YOUR OWN WEAPON, NO LESS.

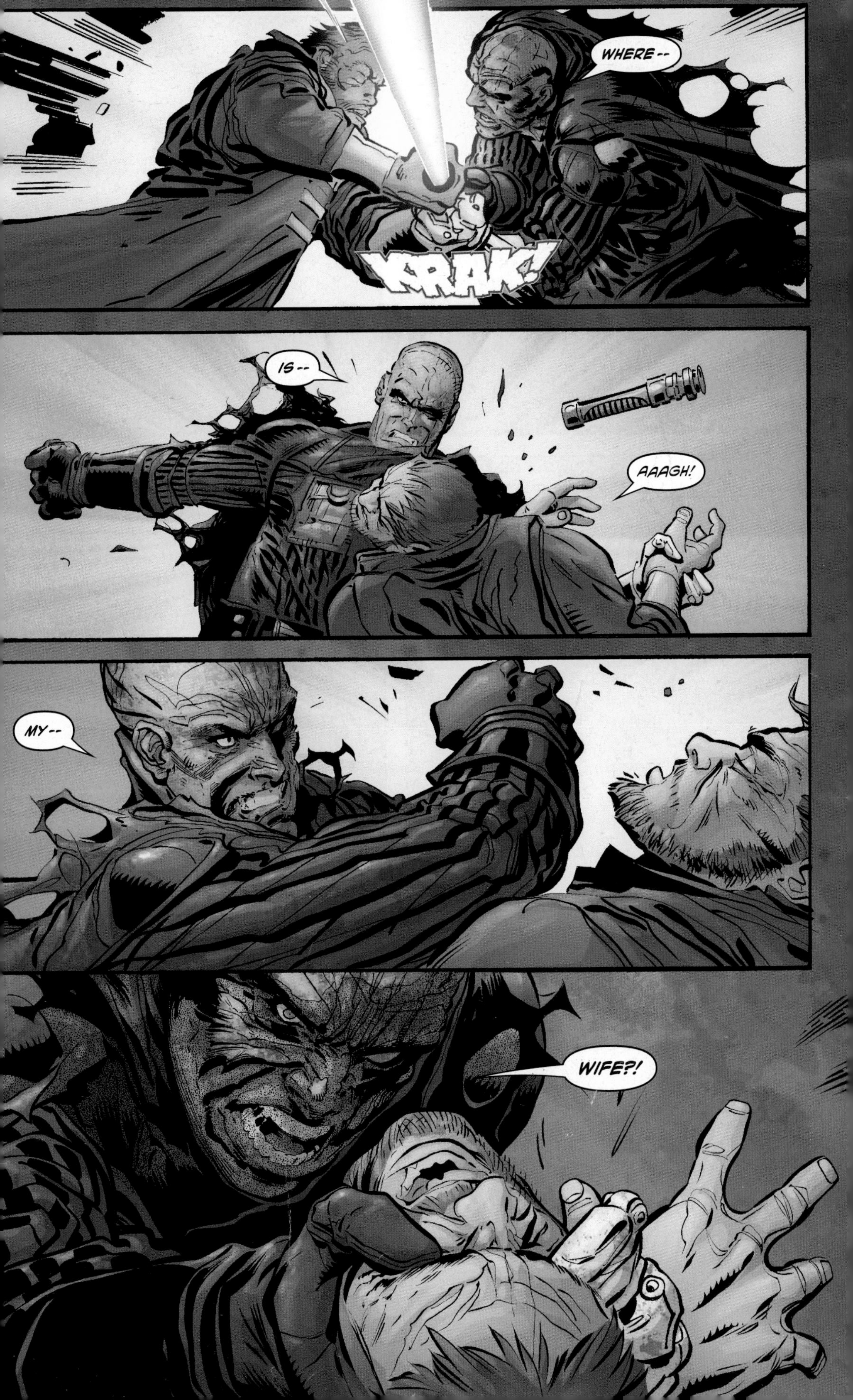
WHERE --
KRAK!
IS --
AAAGH!
MY --
WIFE?!

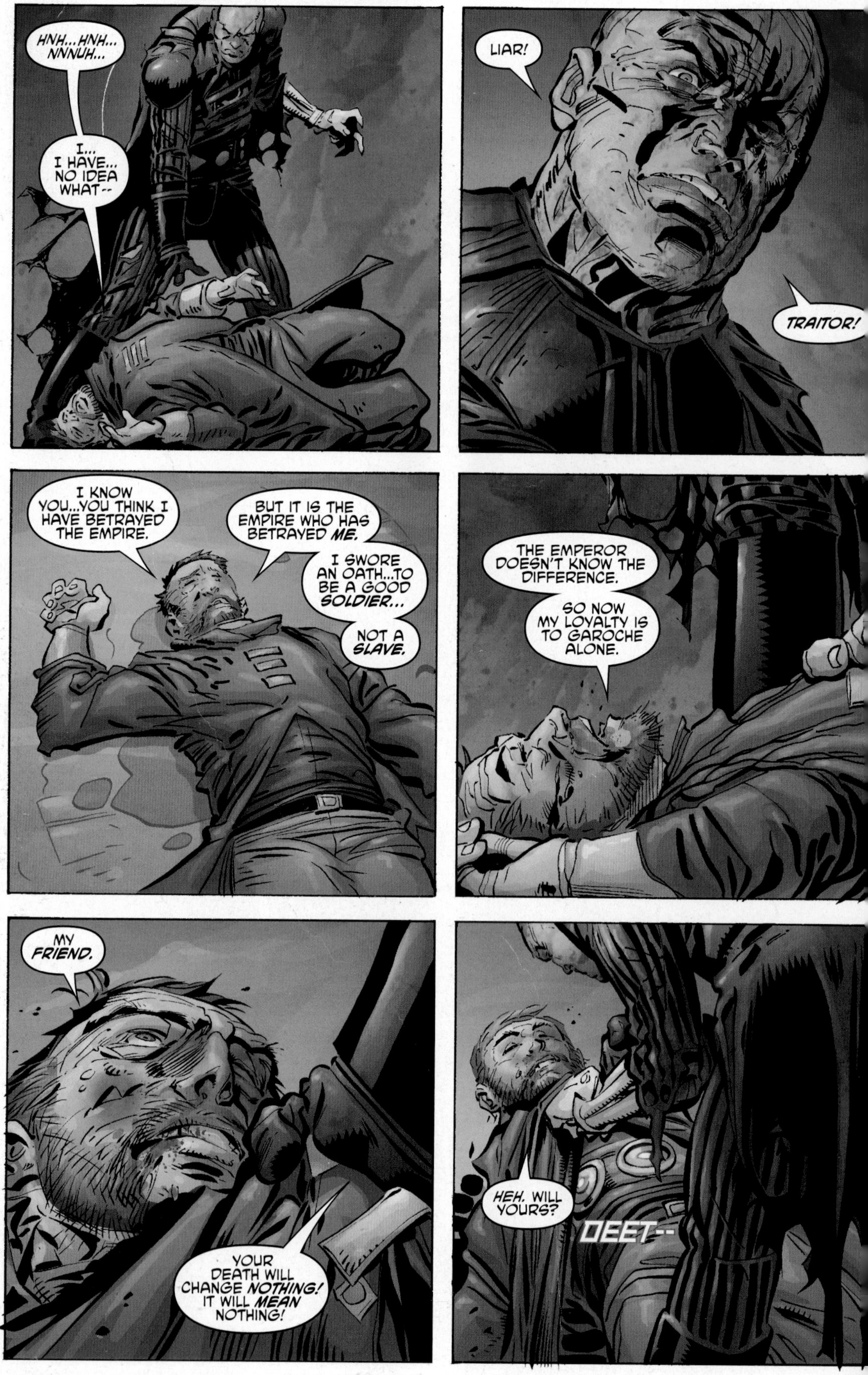
HNH...HNH... NNNUH...
I... I HAVE... NO IDEA WHAT--
LIAR!
TRAITOR!
I KNOW YOU...YOU THINK I HAVE BETRAYED THE EMPIRE.
BUT IT IS THE EMPIRE WHO HAS BETRAYED ME.
I SWORE AN OATH...TO BE A GOOD SOLDIER...
NOT A SLAVE.
THE EMPEROR DOESN'T KNOW THE DIFFERENCE.
SO NOW MY LOYALTY IS TO GAROCHE ALONE.
MY FRIEND.
YOUR DEATH WILL CHANGE NOTHING! IT WILL MEAN NOTHING!
HEH. WILL YOURS?
DEET--

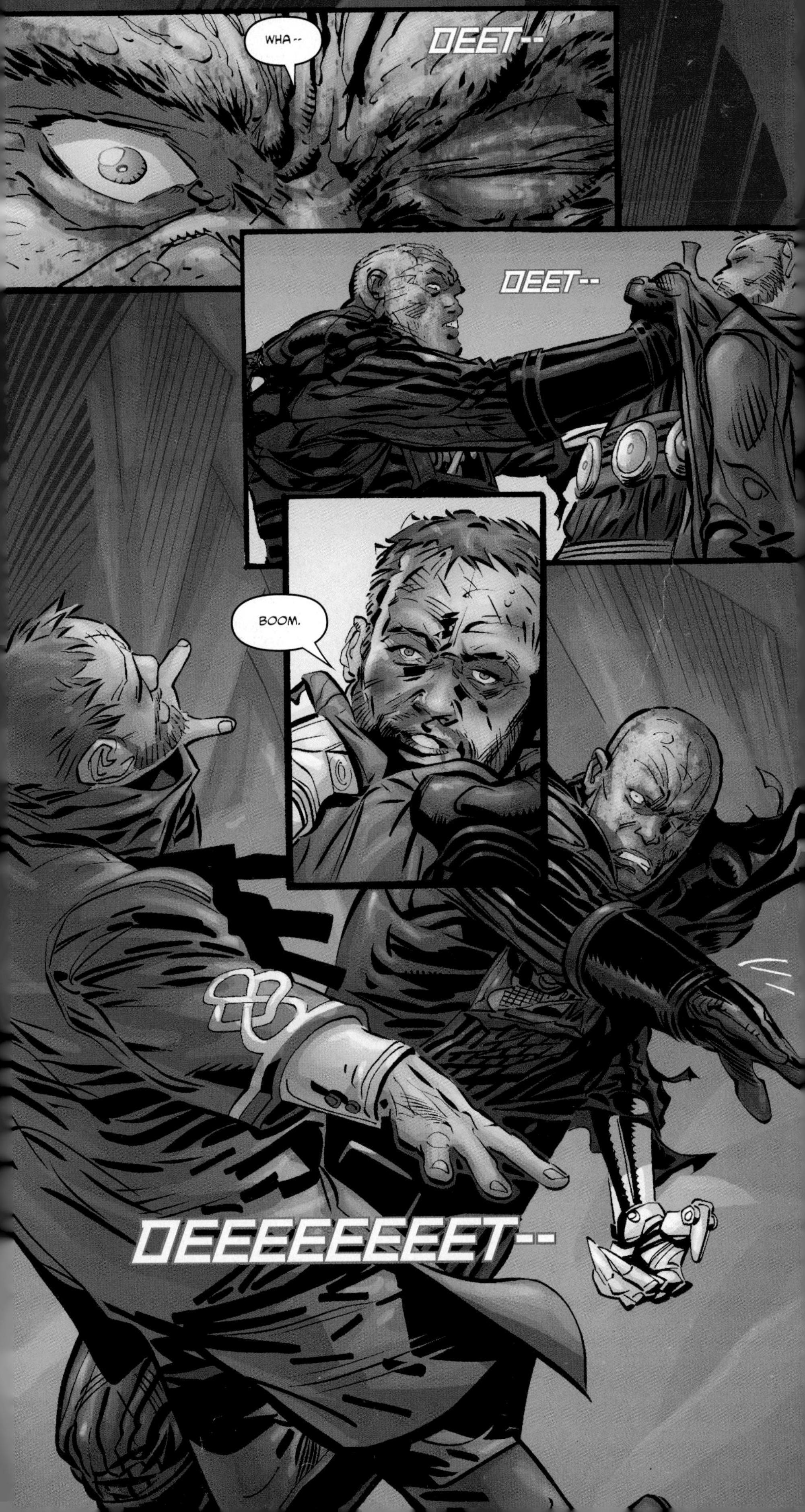
WHA--
DEET--
DEET--
BOOM.
DEEEEEEEEET--

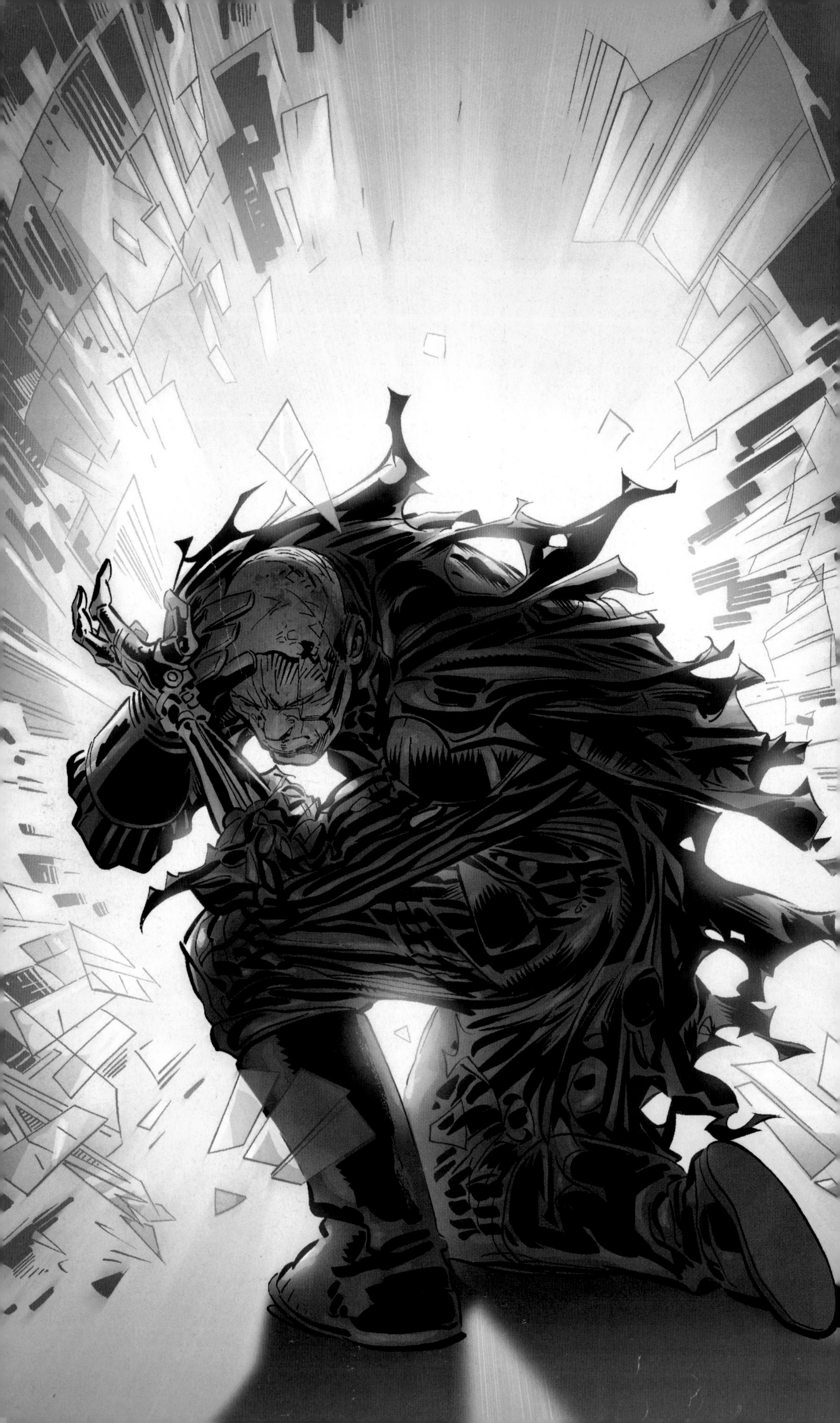

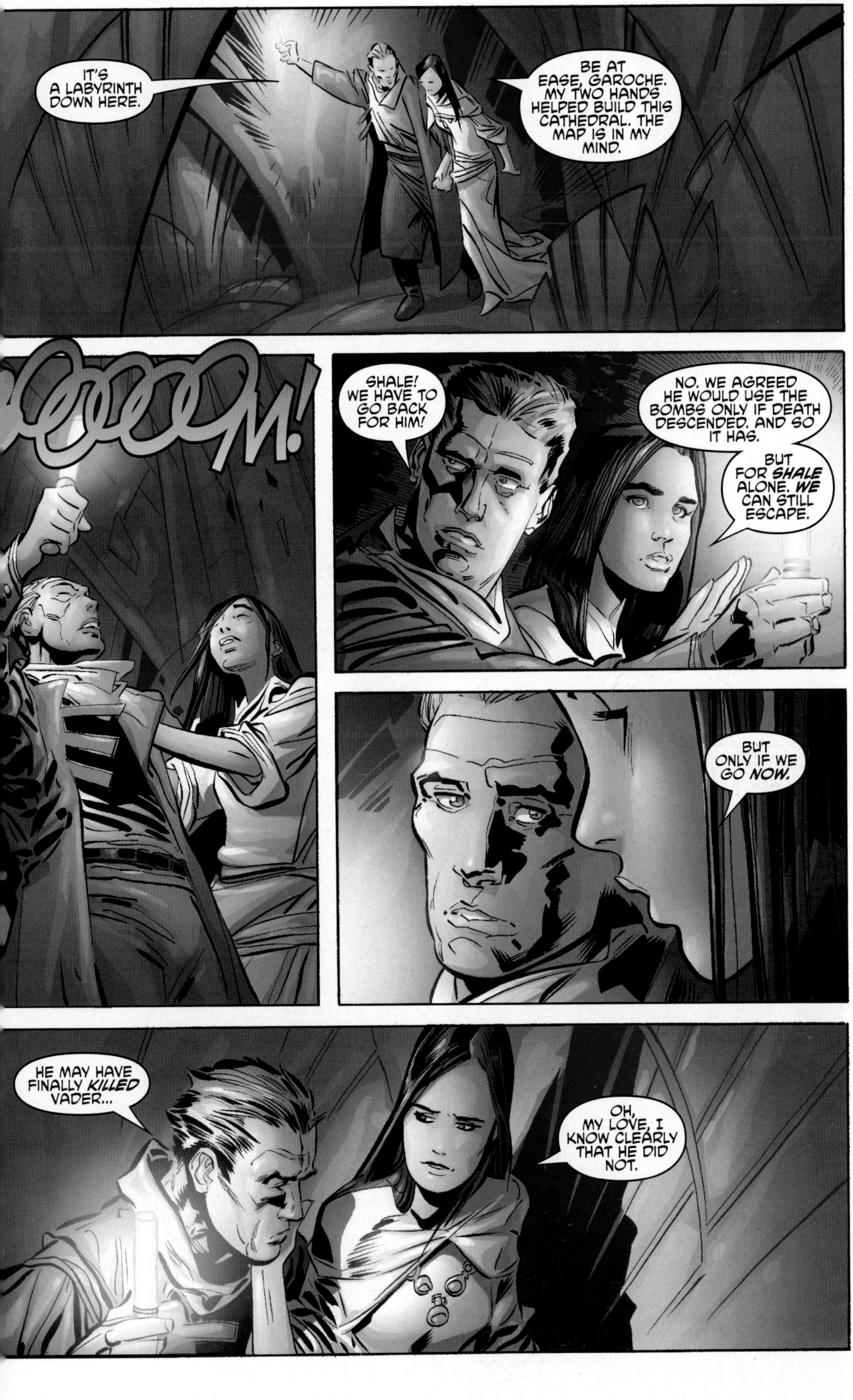
IT'S A LABYRINTH DOWN HERE.
BE AT EASE, GAROCHE. MY TWO HANDS HELPED BUILD THIS CATHEDRAL. THE MAP IS IN MY MIND.
OOOOOM!
SHALE! WE HAVE TO GO BACK FOR HIM!
NO. WE AGREED HE WOULD USE THE BOMBS ONLY IF DEATH DESCENDED. AND SO IT HAS.
BUT FOR SHALE ALONE. WE CAN STILL ESCAPE.
BUT ONLY IF WE GO NOW.
HE MAY HAVE FINALLY KILLED VADER...
OH, MY LOVE, I KNOW CLEARLY THAT HE DID NOT.

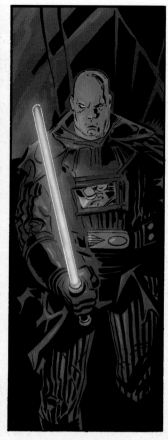

PADMÉ... YOU'VE COME BACK.

YOU KNOW THAT I HAVE *NEVER* LEFT YOU.

BUT YOU *DID* LEAVE...

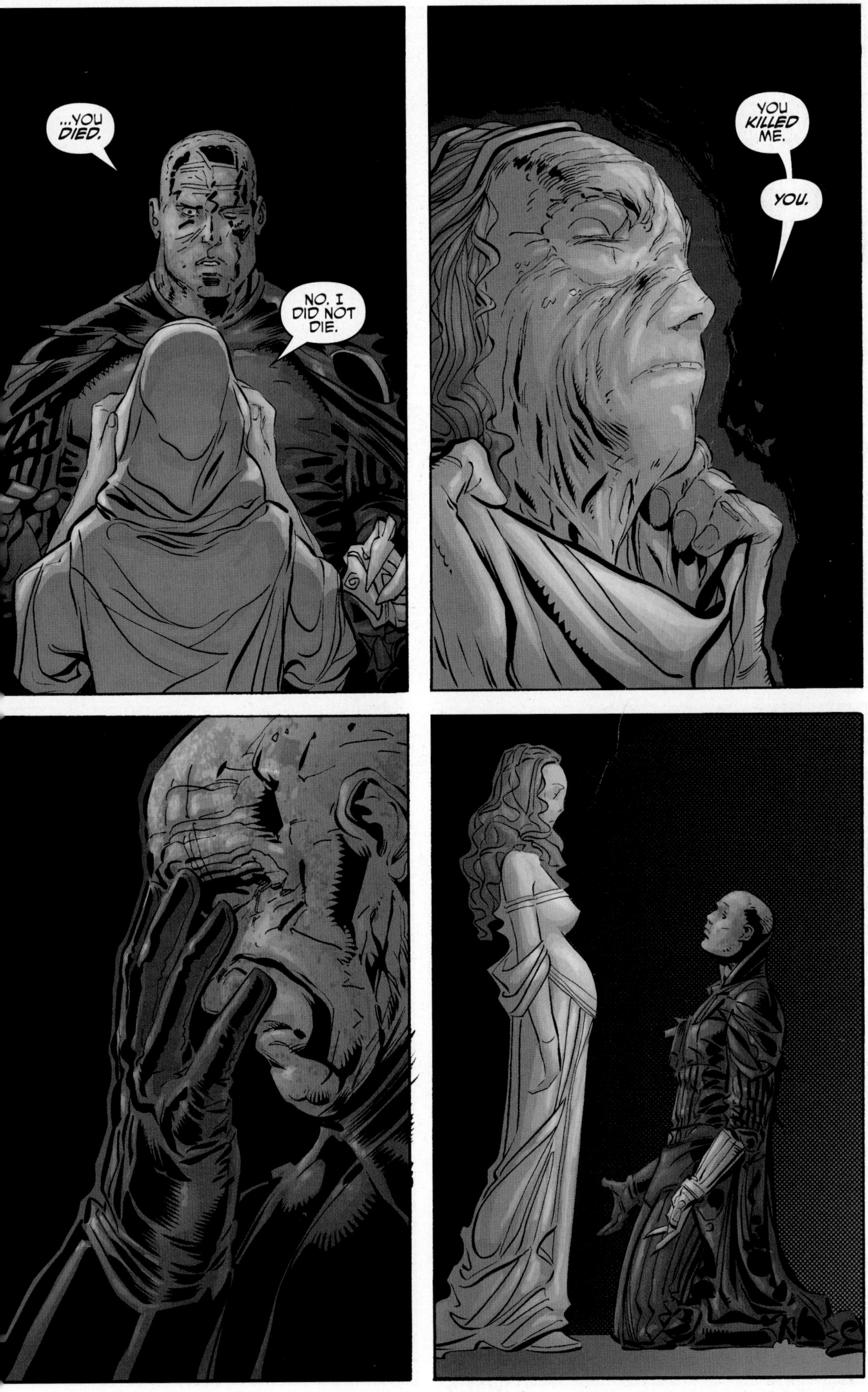
...YOU DIED.
NO. I DID NOT DIE.
YOU KILLED ME.
YOU.

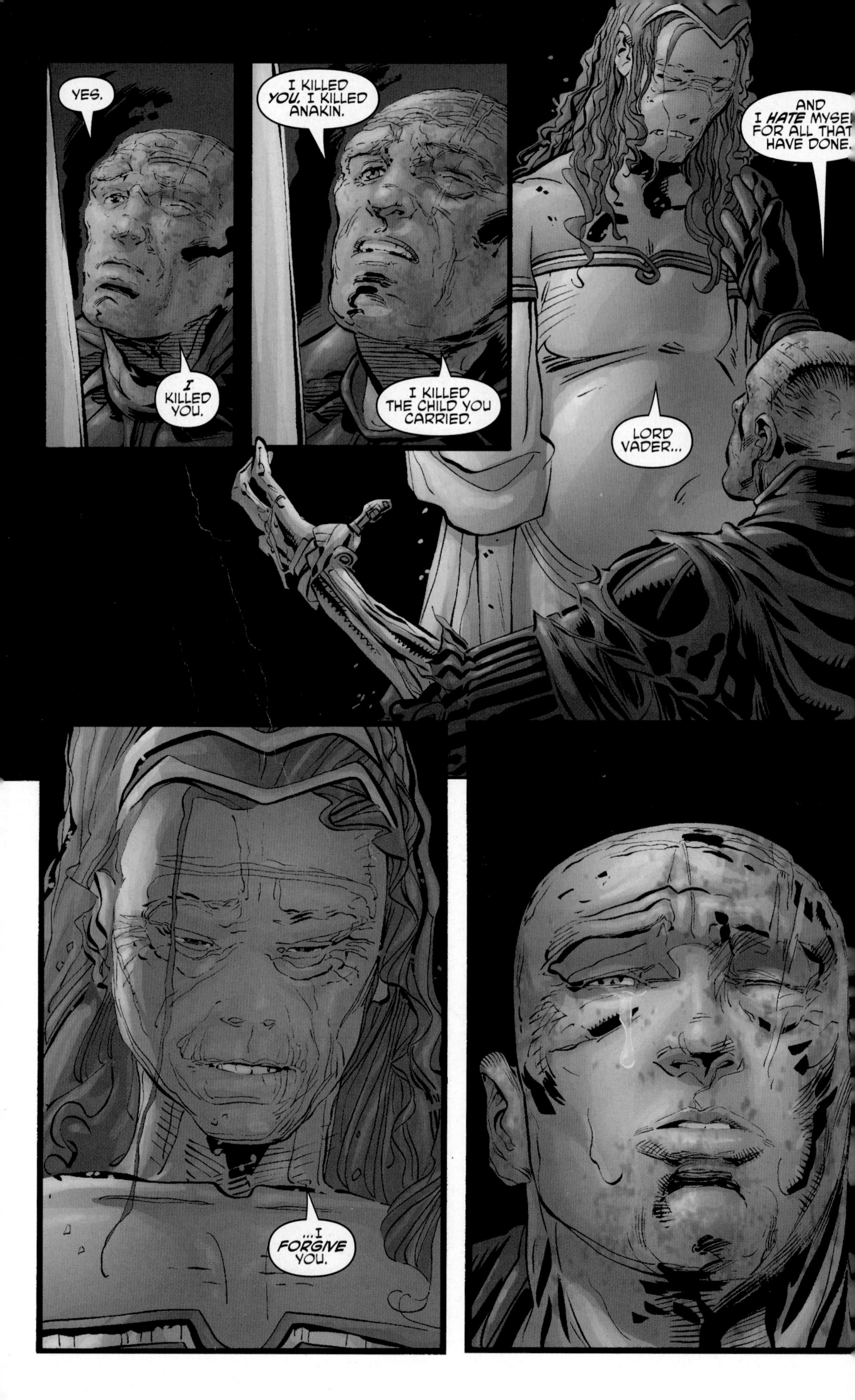
YES.
I KILLED YOU.
I KILLED YOU. I KILLED ANAKIN.
I KILLED THE CHILD YOU CARRIED.
AND I HATE MYSE
FOR ALL THAT
HAVE DONE.
LORD VADER...
...I FORGIVE YOU.

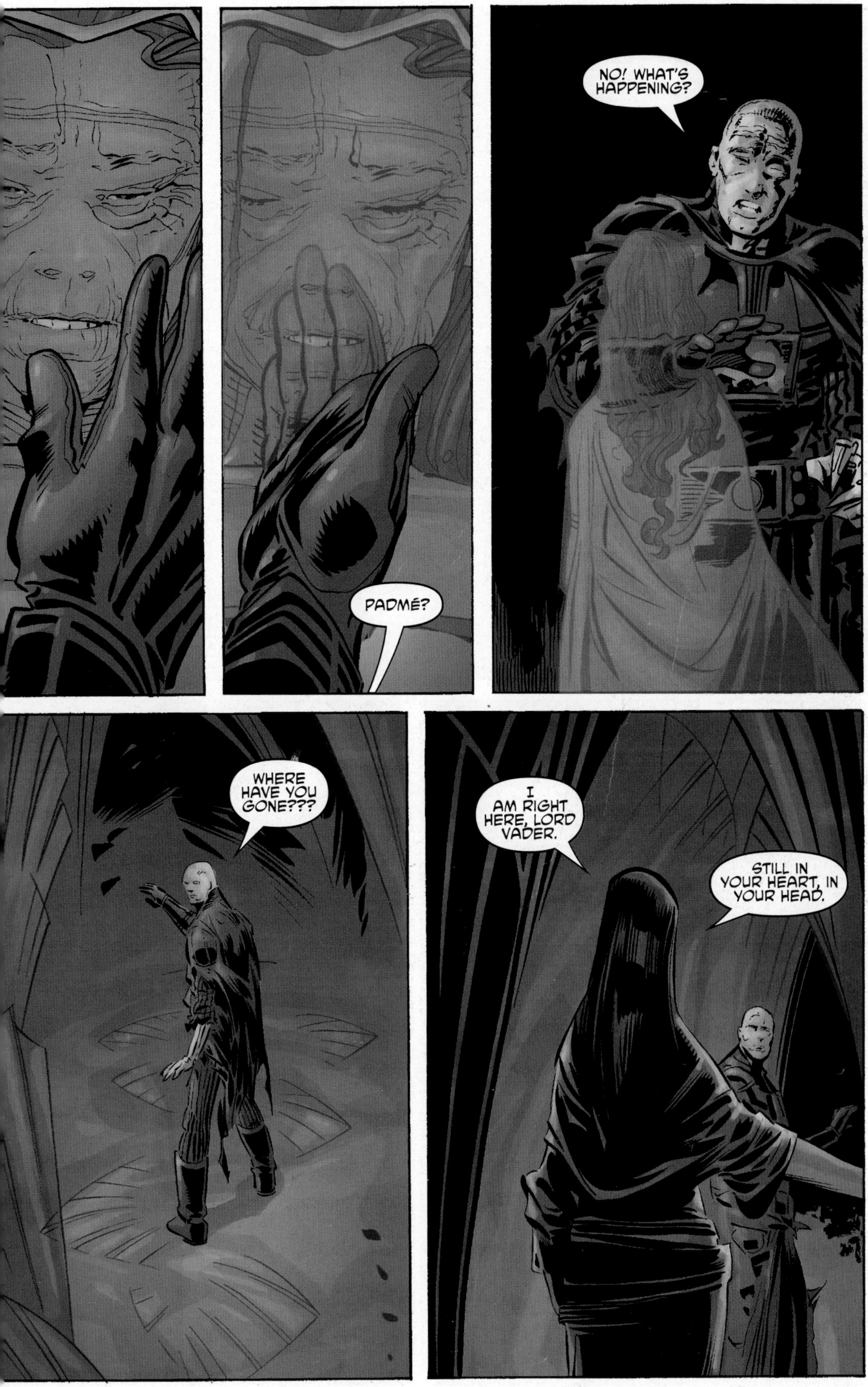
PADMÉ?
NO! WHAT'S HAPPENING?
WHERE HAVE YOU GONE???
I AM RIGHT HERE, LORD VADER.
STILL IN YOUR HEART, IN YOUR HEAD.

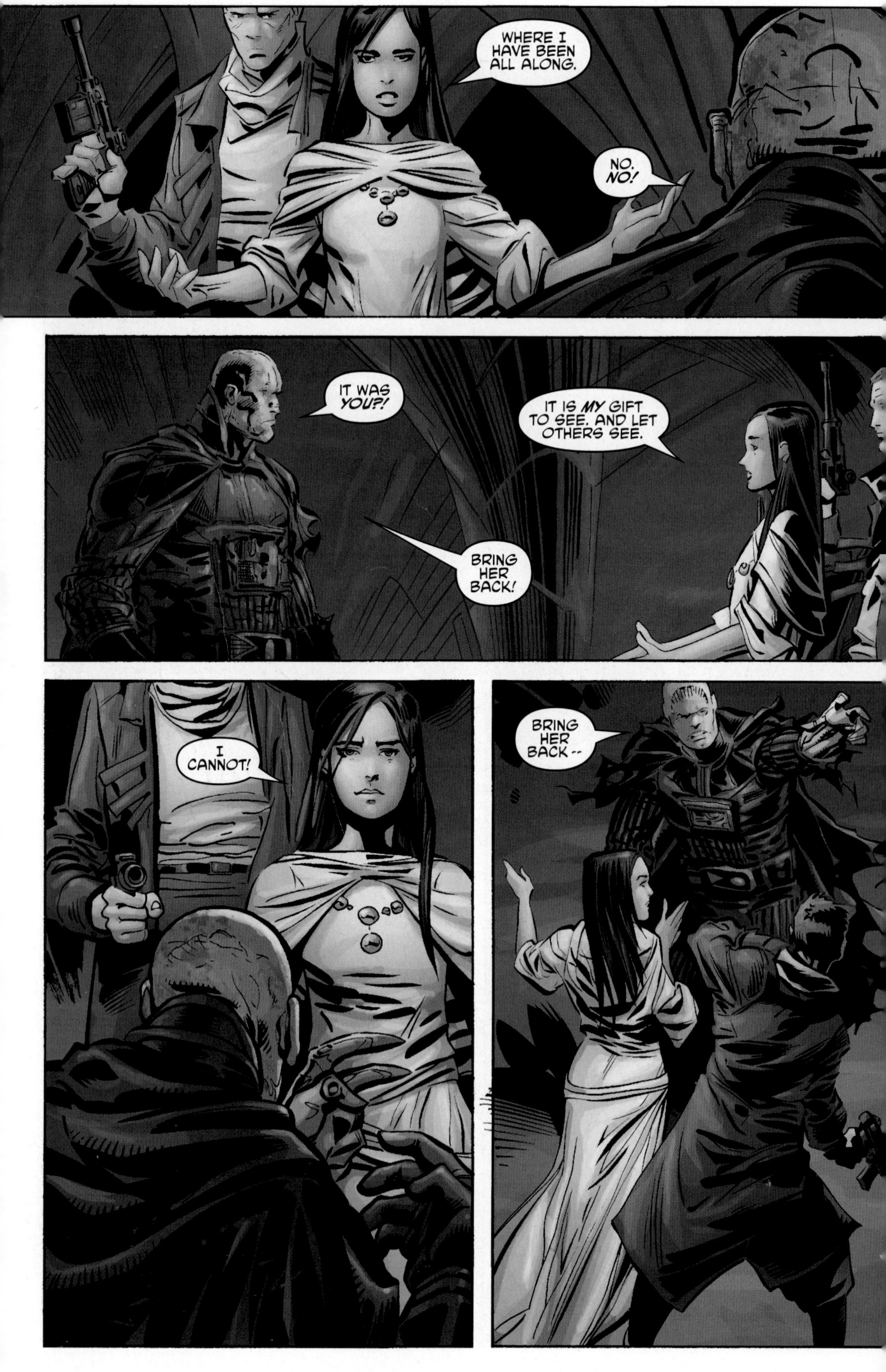
WHERE I HAVE BEEN ALL ALONG.
NO. NO!
IT WAS YOU?!
IT IS MY GIFT TO SEE. AND LET OTHERS SEE.
BRING HER BACK!
I CANNOT!
BRING HER BACK --

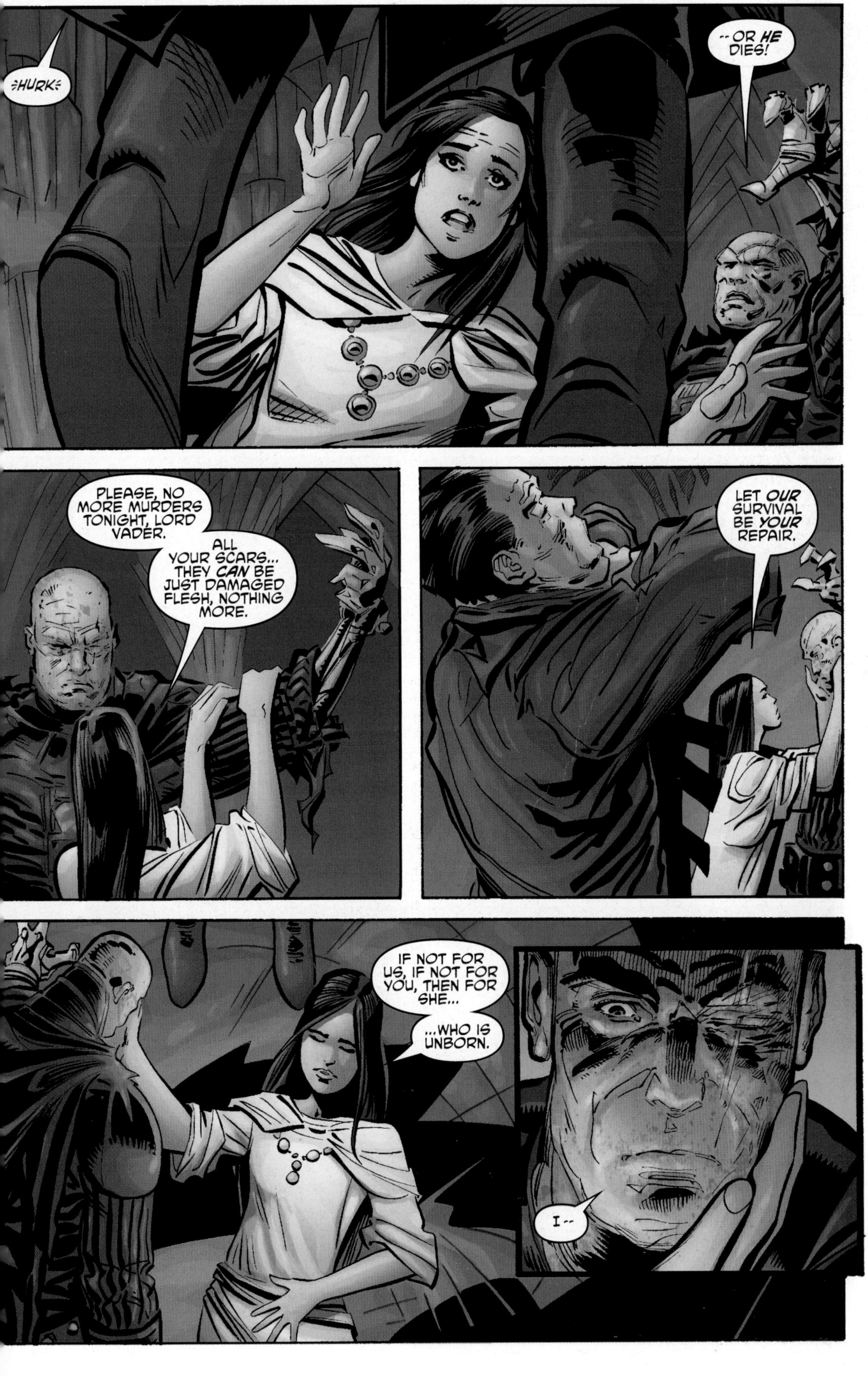

HURK
--OR HE DIES!
PLEASE, NO MORE MURDERS TONIGHT, LORD VADER.
ALL YOUR SCARS... THEY CAN BE JUST DAMAGED FLESH, NOTHING MORE.
LET OUR SURVIVAL BE YOUR REPAIR.
IF NOT FOR US, IF NOT FOR YOU, THEN FOR SHE...
...WHO IS UNBORN.
I--

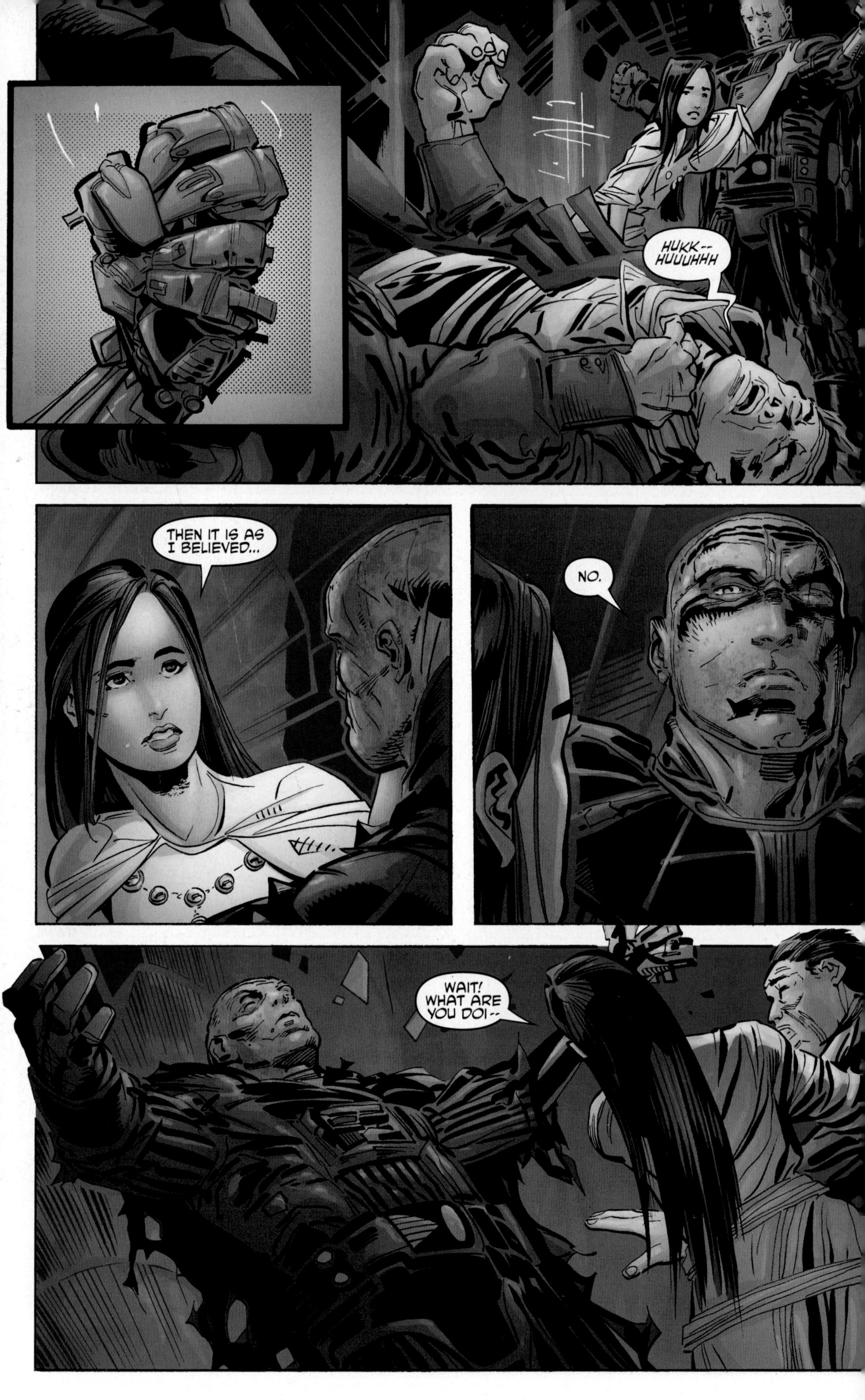
HUKK-- HUUUHHH
THEN IT IS AS I BELIEVED...
NO.
WAIT! WHAT ARE YOU DOI--

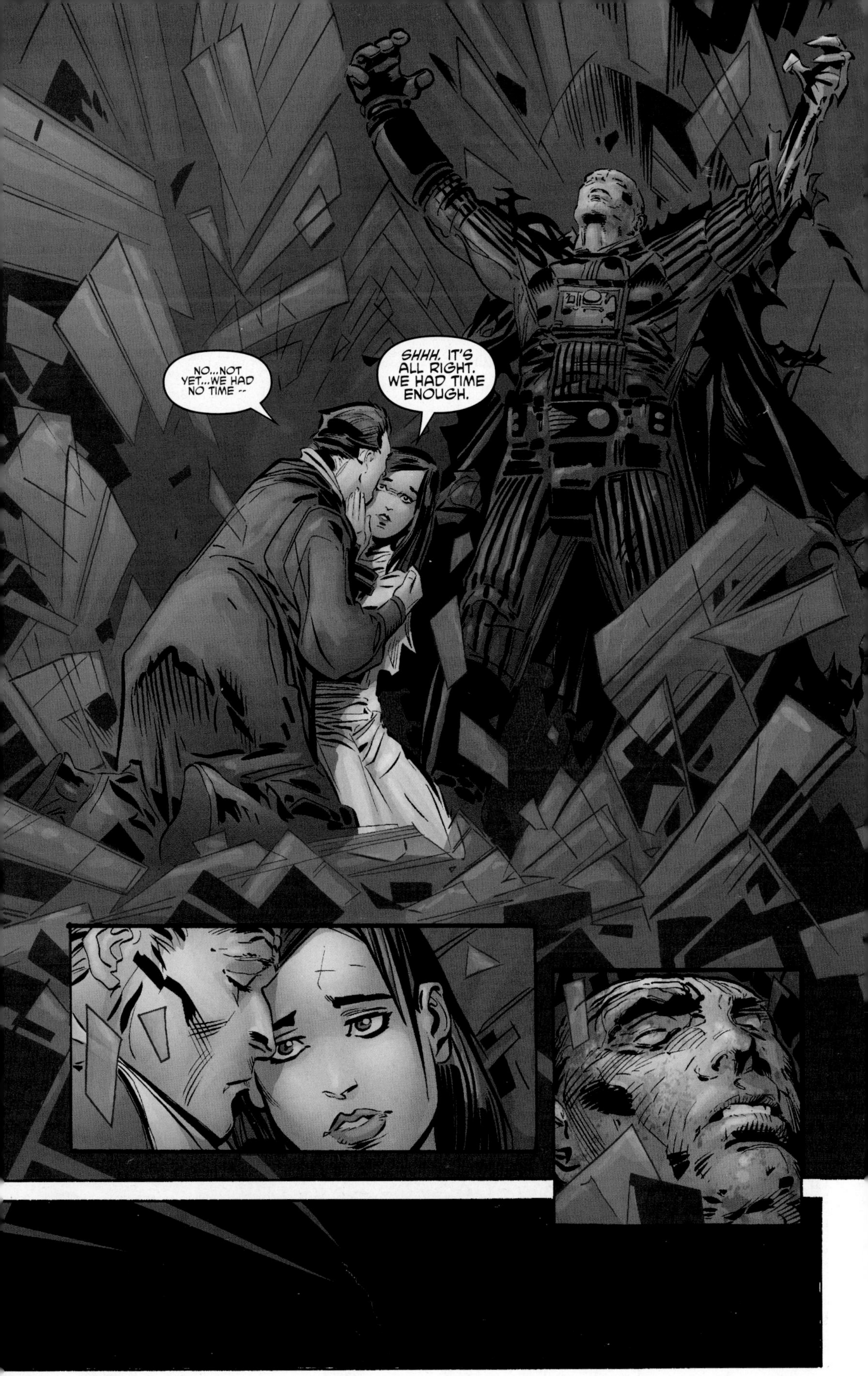
NO...NOT YET...WE HAD NO TIME --
SHHH. IT'S ALL RIGHT. WE HAD TIME ENOUGH.

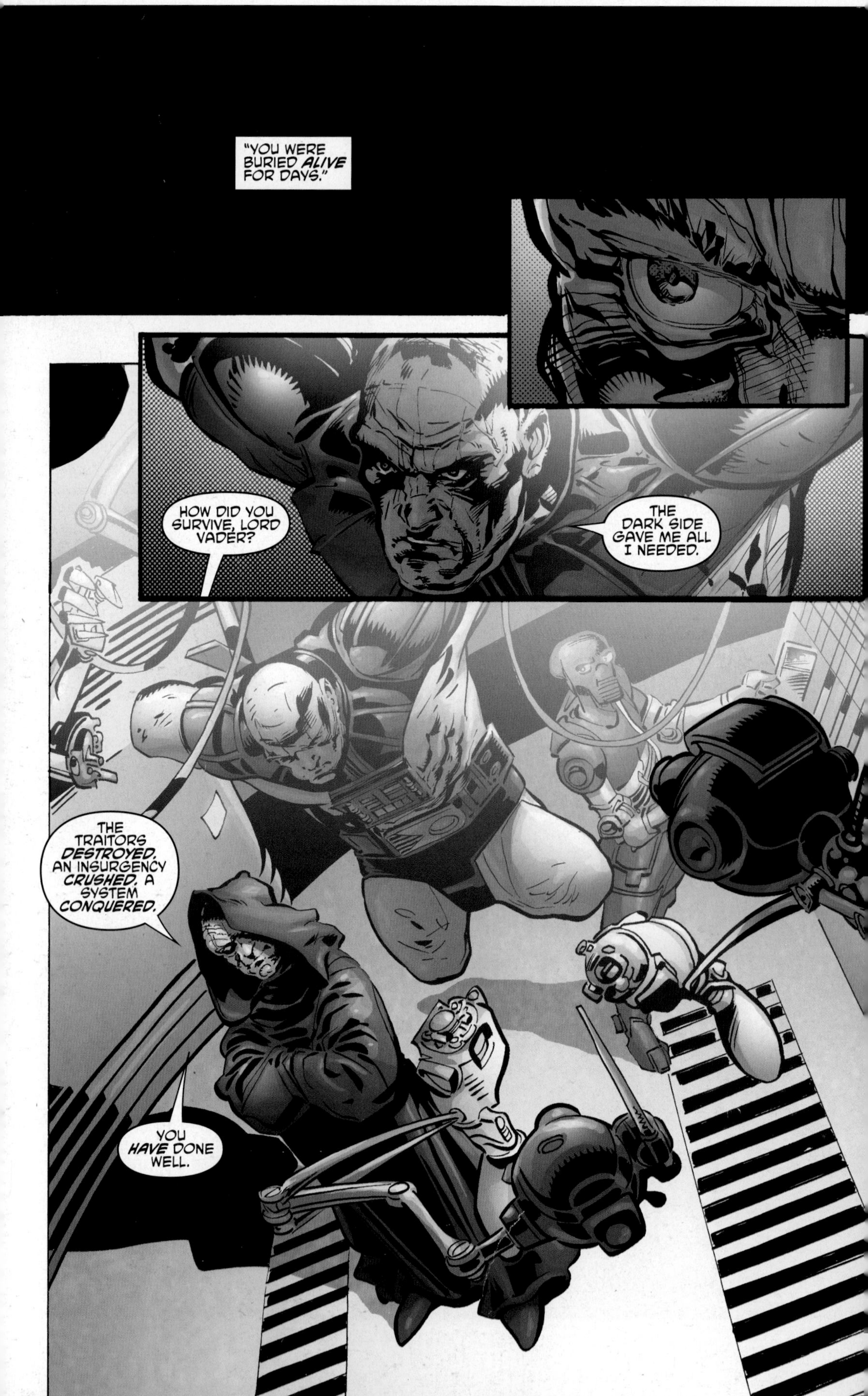
"YOU WERE BURIED *ALIVE* FOR DAYS."
HOW DID YOU SURVIVE, LORD VADER?
THE DARK SIDE GAVE ME ALL I NEEDED.
THE TRAITORS *DESTROYED*. AN INSURGENCY *CRUSHED*. A SYSTEM *CONQUERED*.
YOU *HAVE* DONE WELL.

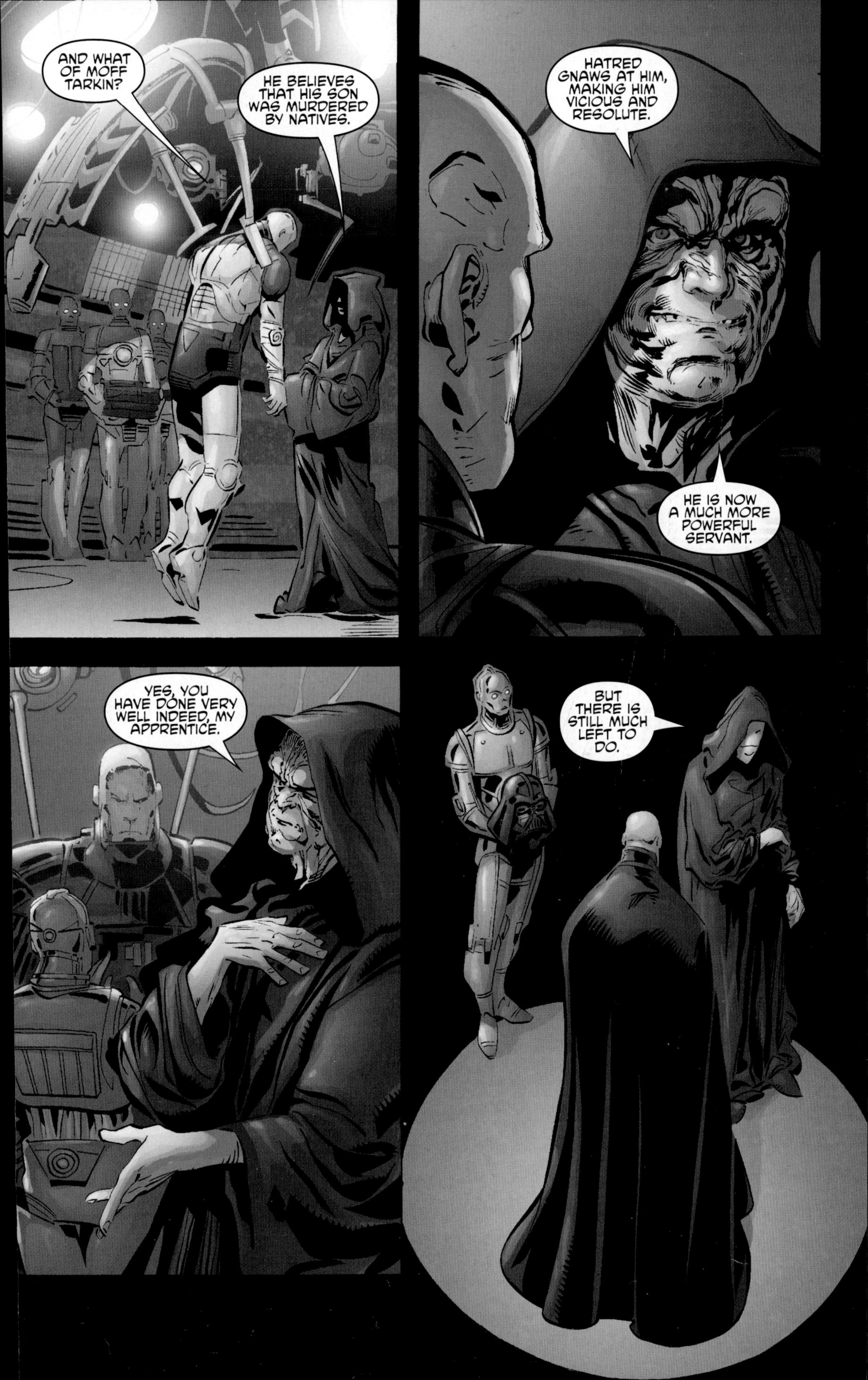
AND WHAT OF MOFF TARKIN?
HE BELIEVES THAT HIS SON WAS MURDERED BY NATIVES.
HATRED GNAWS AT HIM, MAKING HIM VICIOUS AND RESOLUTE.
HE IS NOW A MUCH MORE POWERFUL SERVANT.
YES, YOU HAVE DONE VERY WELL INDEED, MY APPRENTICE.
BUT THERE IS STILL MUCH LEFT TO DO.

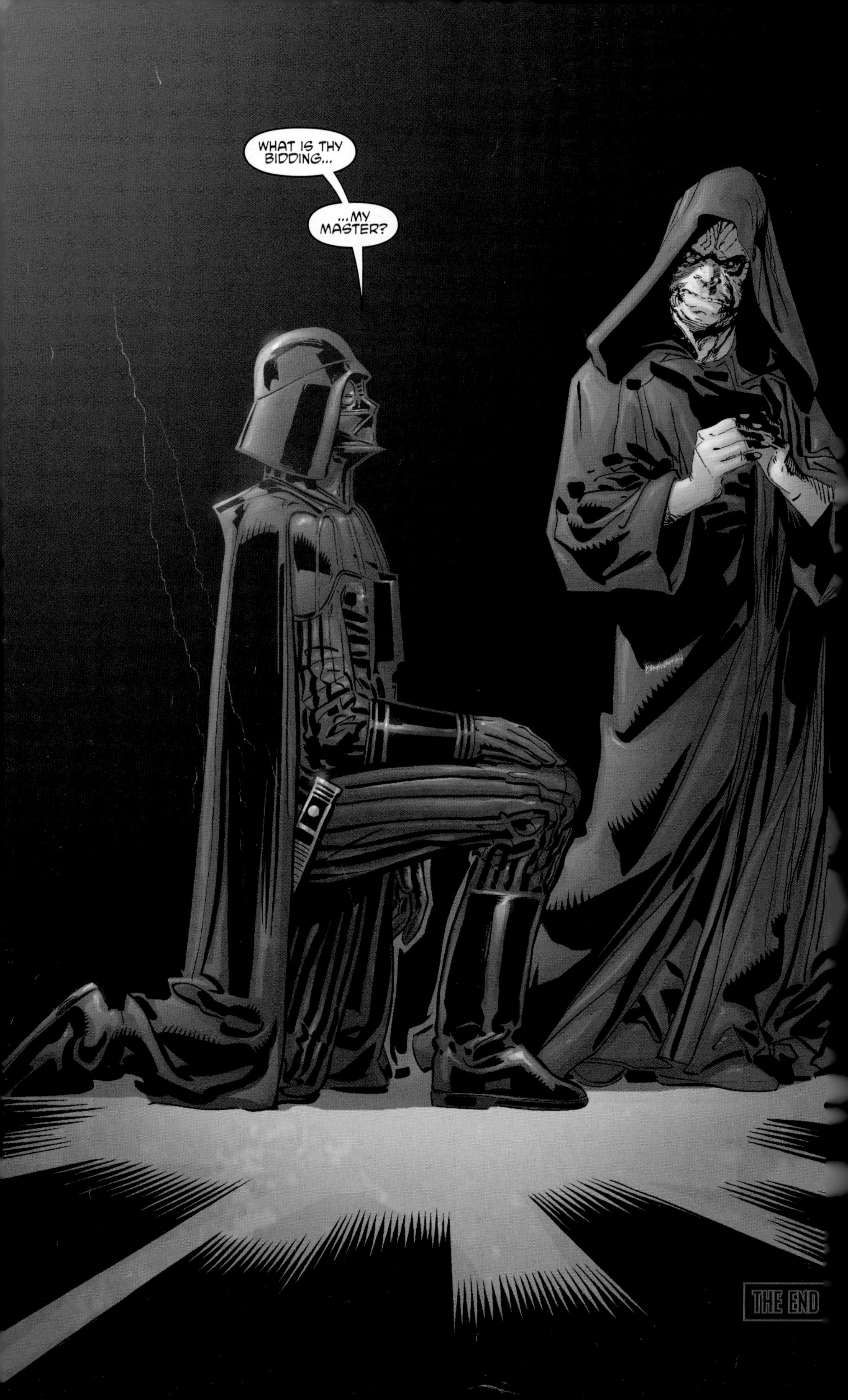
WHAT IS THY BIDDING...
...MY MASTER?
THE END

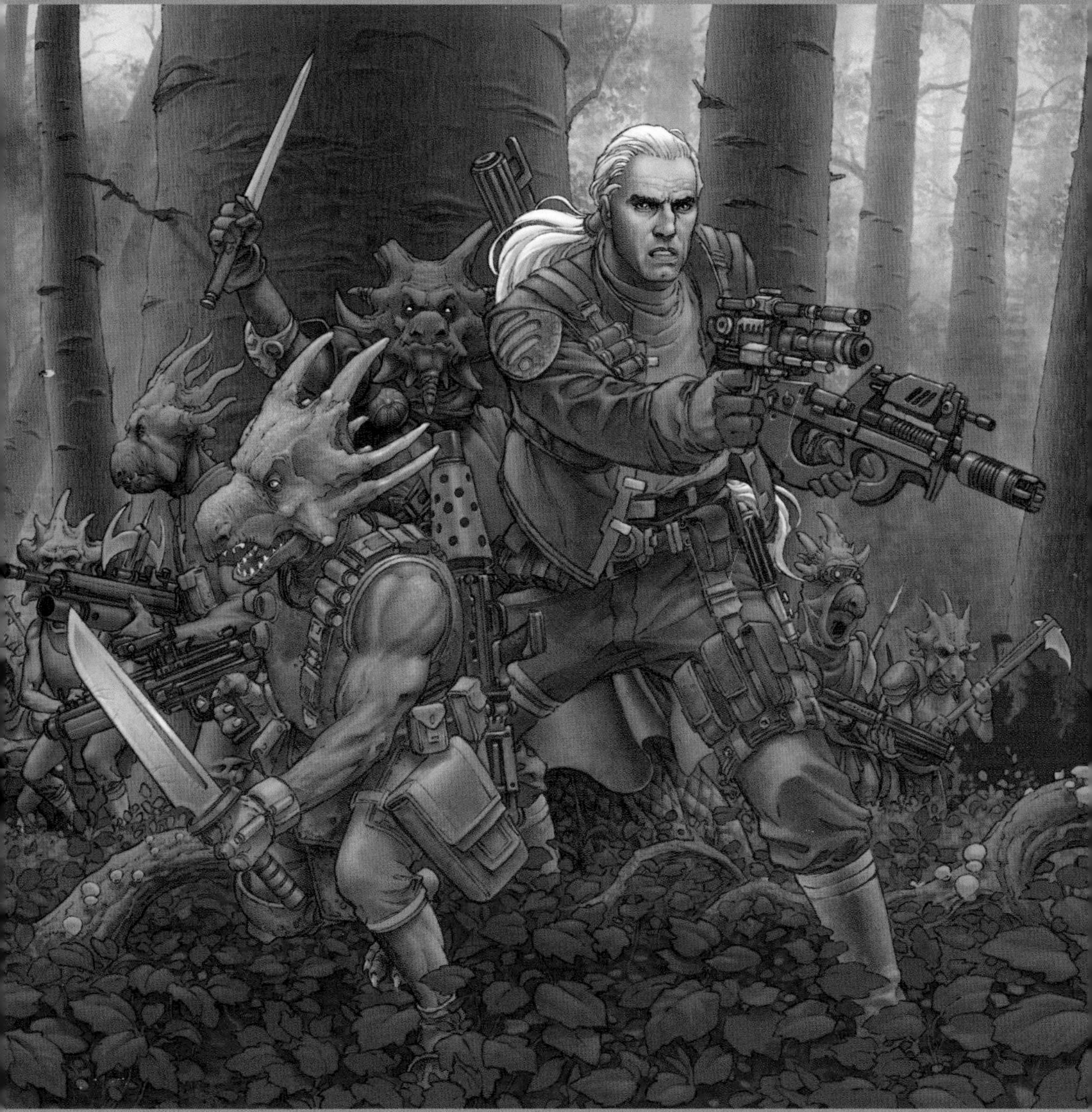

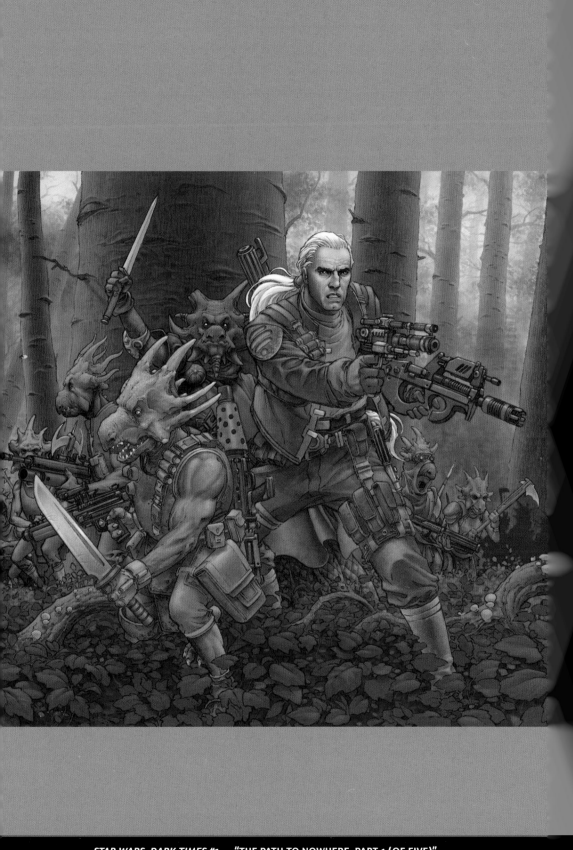

STAR WARS: DARK TIMES #1 **— "THE PATH TO NOWHERE, PART 1 (OF FIVE)"**

R: RANDY STRADLEY (AS WELLES HARTLEY & MICK HARRISON) • ARTIST: DOUGLAS WHEATLEY • COLORIST: RONDA PATTISON • LETTERER: MICHAEL DAVID THOMAS
DESIGNER: DARIN FABRICK • ASSISTANT EDITOR: DAVE MARSHALL • EDITOR: RANDY STRADLEY • COVER ARTIST: DOUGLAS WHEATLEY

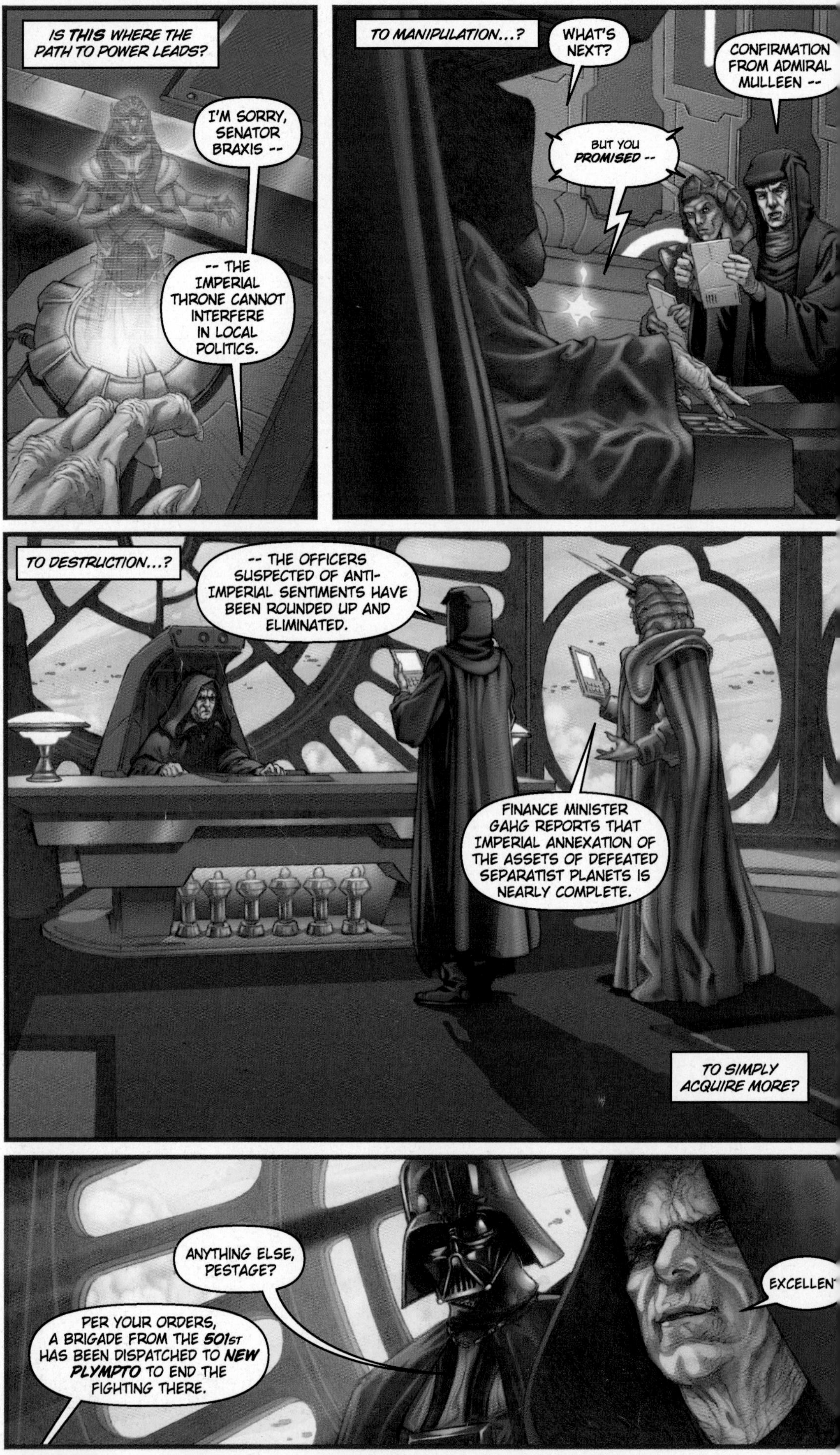
IS THIS WHERE THE PATH TO POWER LEADS?
I'M SORRY, SENATOR BRAXIS --
-- THE IMPERIAL THRONE CANNOT INTERFERE IN LOCAL POLITICS.
TO MANIPULATION...?
WHAT'S NEXT?
BUT YOU PROMISED --
CONFIRMATION FROM ADMIRAL MULLEEN --
TO DESTRUCTION...?
-- THE OFFICERS SUSPECTED OF ANTI-IMPERIAL SENTIMENTS HAVE BEEN ROUNDED UP AND ELIMINATED.
FINANCE MINISTER GAHG REPORTS THAT IMPERIAL ANNEXATION OF THE ASSETS OF DEFEATED SEPARATIST PLANETS IS NEARLY COMPLETE.
TO SIMPLY ACQUIRE MORE?
PER YOUR ORDERS, A BRIGADE FROM THE 501ST HAS BEEN DISPATCHED TO NEW PLYMPTO TO END THE FIGHTING THERE.
ANYTHING ELSE, PESTAGE?
EXCELLEN

THAT WILL BE ALL FOR NOW.

GUARDS, YOU ARE DISMISSED.

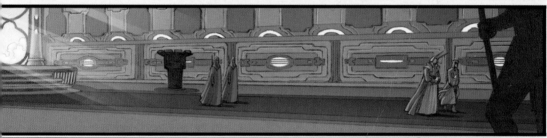

ARE THE LESSONS OF KESSEL SO SOON FORGOTTEN, APPRENTICE? GIVING IN TO YOUR EMOTIONS NEARLY LED TO YOUR DESTRUCTION.

MASTER ... I...

YOU FEEL YOU SHOULD BE DOING *SOMETHING*, DON'T YOU, LORD VADER?

WHAT WOULD YOU DO? LEAD THE 501st? *HUNT* THE JEDI? *TRACK DOWN* ANAKIN SKYWALKER'S FORMER MASTER?

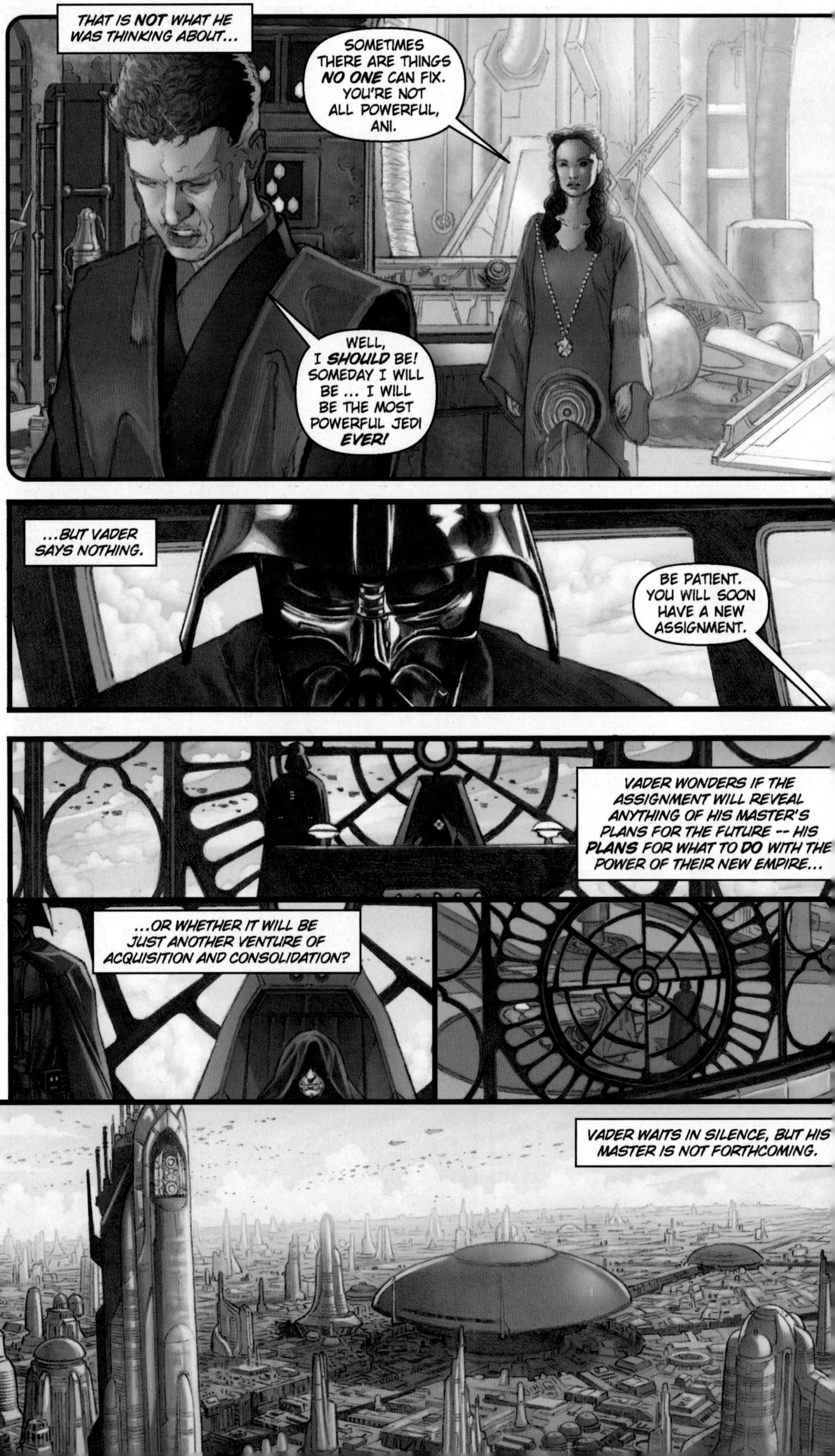
THAT IS NOT WHAT HE WAS THINKING ABOUT...
SOMETIMES THERE ARE THINGS NO ONE CAN FIX. YOU'RE NOT ALL POWERFUL, ANI.
WELL, I SHOULD BE! SOMEDAY I WILL BE ... I WILL BE THE MOST POWERFUL JEDI EVER!
...BUT VADER SAYS NOTHING.
BE PATIENT. YOU WILL SOON HAVE A NEW ASSIGNMENT.
VADER WONDERS IF THE ASSIGNMENT WILL REVEAL ANYTHING OF HIS MASTER'S PLANS FOR THE FUTURE -- HIS PLANS FOR WHAT TO DO WITH THE POWER OF THEIR NEW EMPIRE...
...OR WHETHER IT WILL BE JUST ANOTHER VENTURE OF ACQUISITION AND CONSOLIDATION?
VADER WAITS IN SILENCE, BUT HIS MASTER IS NOT FORTHCOMING.

NEW PLYMPTO, IN THE CORE WORLDS.

THIS IS THE NOSAURIANS' LAST STAND. THEIR ADOPTED GENERAL -- FORMER JEDI GENERAL **DASS JENNIR** -- KNOWS THE END IS NEAR.

AFTER ORDER 66, JENNIR WAS FORCED TO SEEK AID FROM HIS FORMER ENEMIES. THE SEPARATIST NOSAURIANS ACCEPTED HIM, AND HE JOINED THEIR CAUSE. NOW HE OVERSEES ITS DEMISE.

HIS SPIES REPORTED THE ARRIVAL OF IMPERIAL REINFORCEMENTS DURING THE NIGHT. HE KNOWS THEIR TANKS ARE APPROACHING, AND HE KNOWS HE LACKS THE STRENGTH TO STOP THEM.

THE CAUSE FOR WHICH THEY'VE FOUGHT IS LOST, BUT THERE IS STILL ONE PURPOSE THIS LITTLE ARMY CAN SERVE...

BOMO!

BOMO, CAN YOU HEAR ME? WHAT'S THE STATUS --

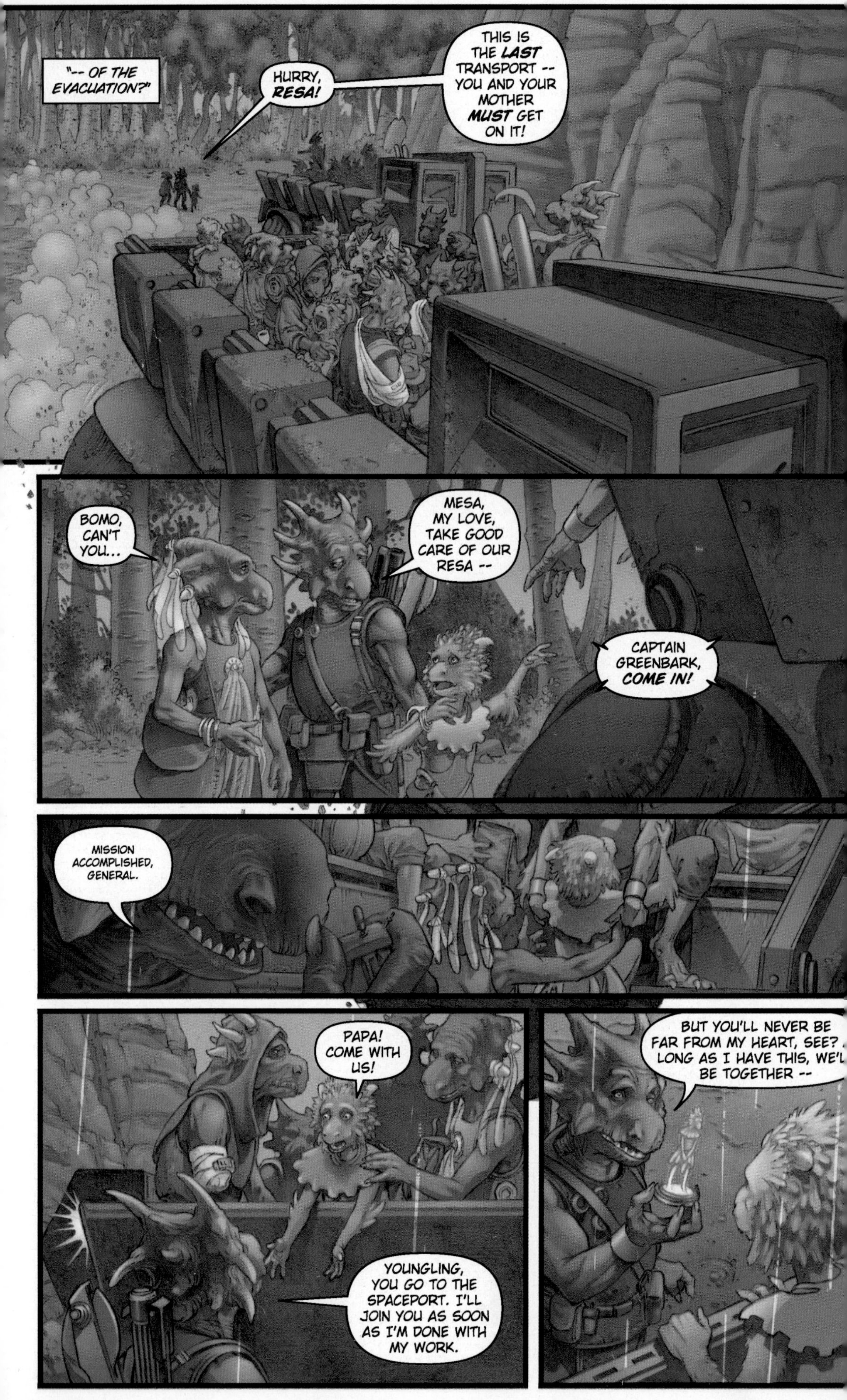
"-- OF THE EVACUATION?"
HURRY, RESA!
THIS IS THE LAST TRANSPORT -- YOU AND YOUR MOTHER MUST GET ON IT!
BOMO, CAN'T YOU...
MESA, MY LOVE, TAKE GOOD CARE OF OUR RESA --
CAPTAIN GREENBARK, COME IN!
MISSION ACCOMPLISHED, GENERAL.
PAPA! COME WITH US!
YOUNGLING, YOU GO TO THE SPACEPORT. I'LL JOIN YOU AS SOON AS I'M DONE WITH MY WORK.
BUT YOU'LL NEVER BE FAR FROM MY HEART, SEE? LONG AS I HAVE THIS, WE'L BE TOGETHER --

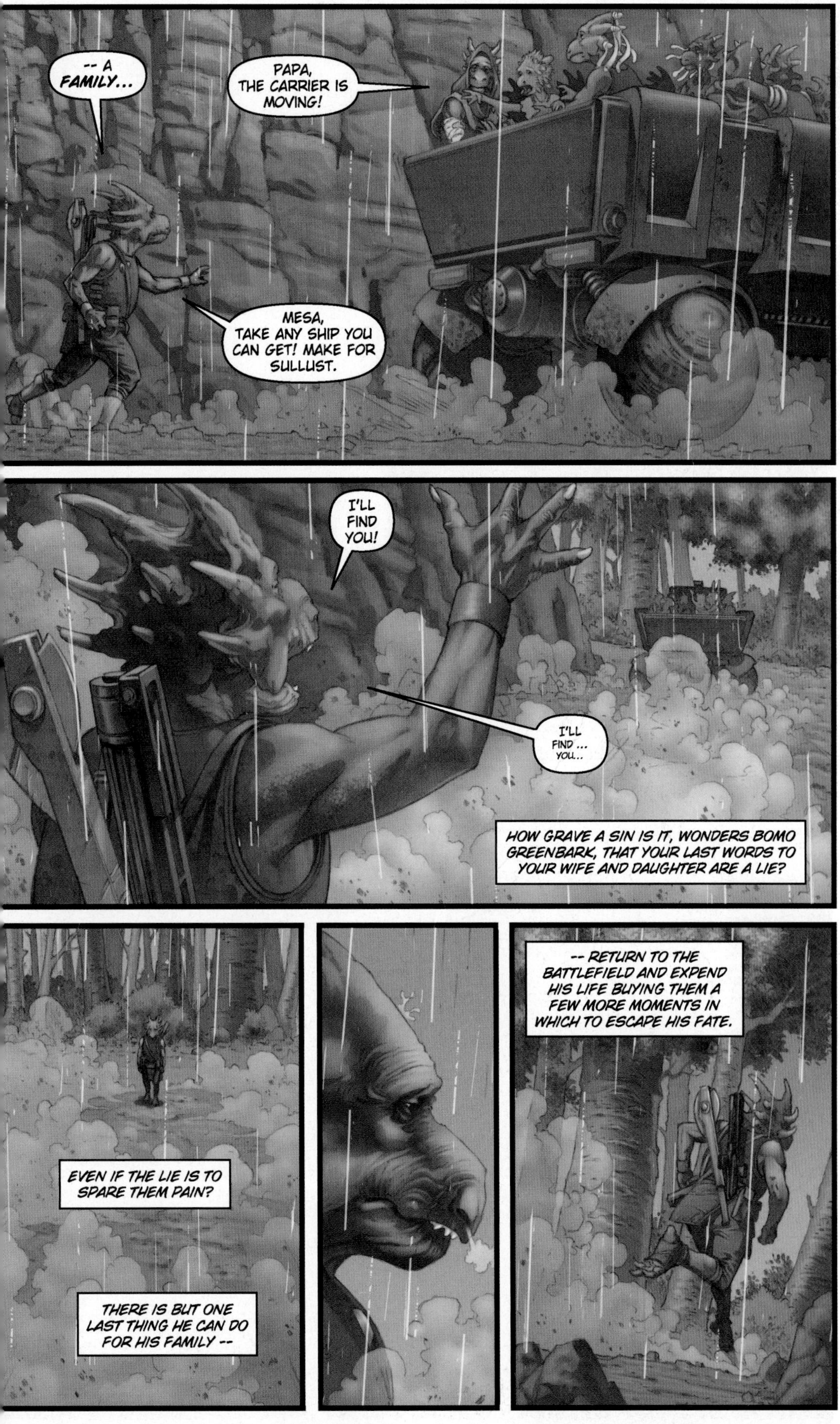
-- A FAMILY...
PAPA, THE CARRIER IS MOVING!
MESA, TAKE ANY SHIP YOU CAN GET! MAKE FOR SULLUST.
I'LL FIND YOU!
I'LL FIND ... YOU...
HOW GRAVE A SIN IS IT, WONDERS BOMO GREENBARK, THAT YOUR LAST WORDS TO YOUR WIFE AND DAUGHTER ARE A LIE?
EVEN IF THE LIE IS TO SPARE THEM PAIN?
THERE IS BUT ONE LAST THING HE CAN DO FOR HIS FAMILY --
-- RETURN TO THE BATTLEFIELD AND EXPEND HIS LIFE BUYING THEM A FEW MORE MOMENTS IN WHICH TO ESCAPE HIS FATE.

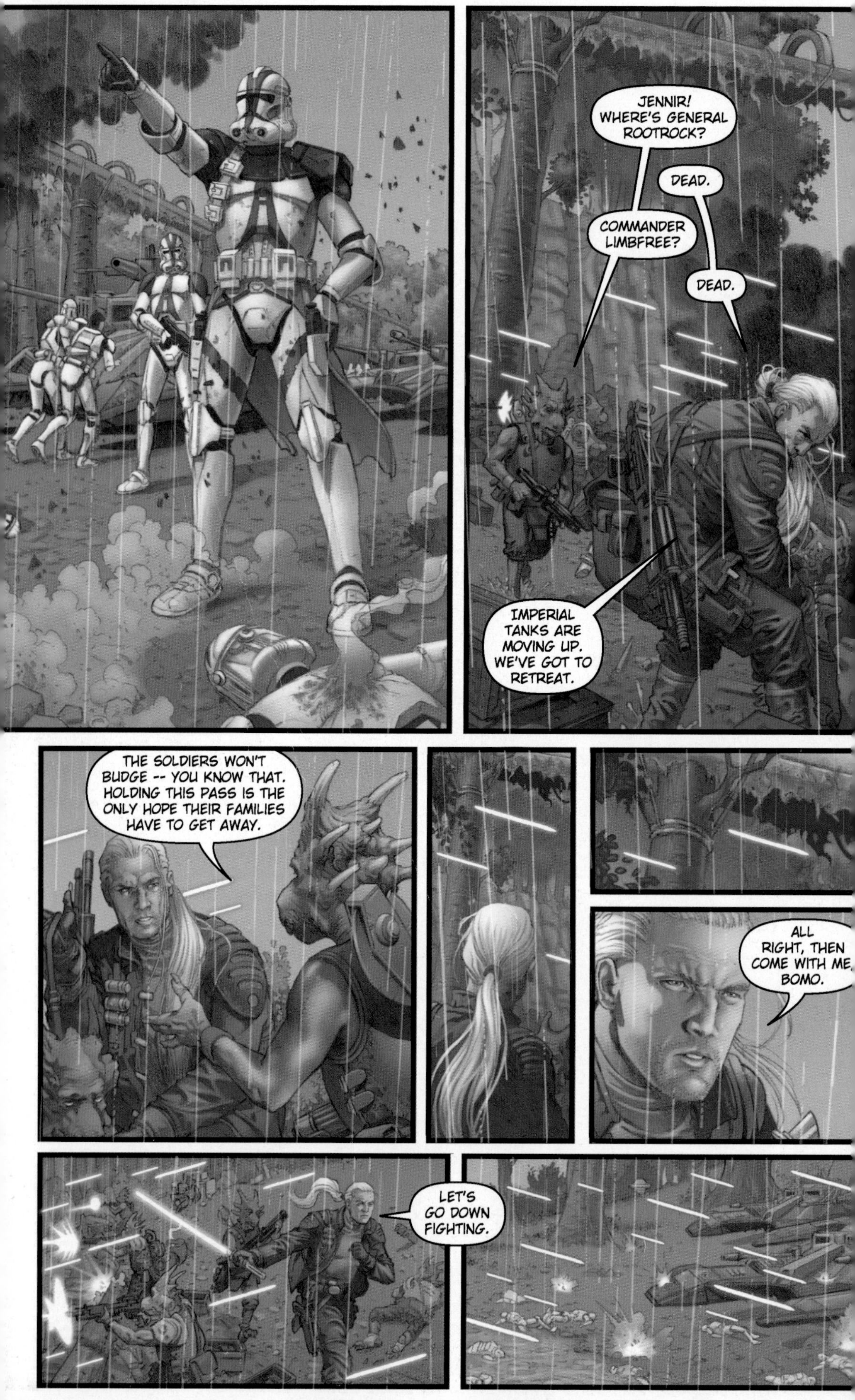
JENNIR! WHERE'S GENERAL ROOTROCK?
DEAD.
COMMANDER LIMBFREE?
DEAD.
IMPERIAL TANKS ARE MOVING UP. WE'VE GOT TO RETREAT.
THE SOLDIERS WON'T BUDGE -- YOU KNOW THAT. HOLDING THIS PASS IS THE ONLY HOPE THEIR FAMILIES HAVE TO GET AWAY.
ALL RIGHT, THEN COME WITH ME, BOMO.
LET'S GO DOWN FIGHTING.

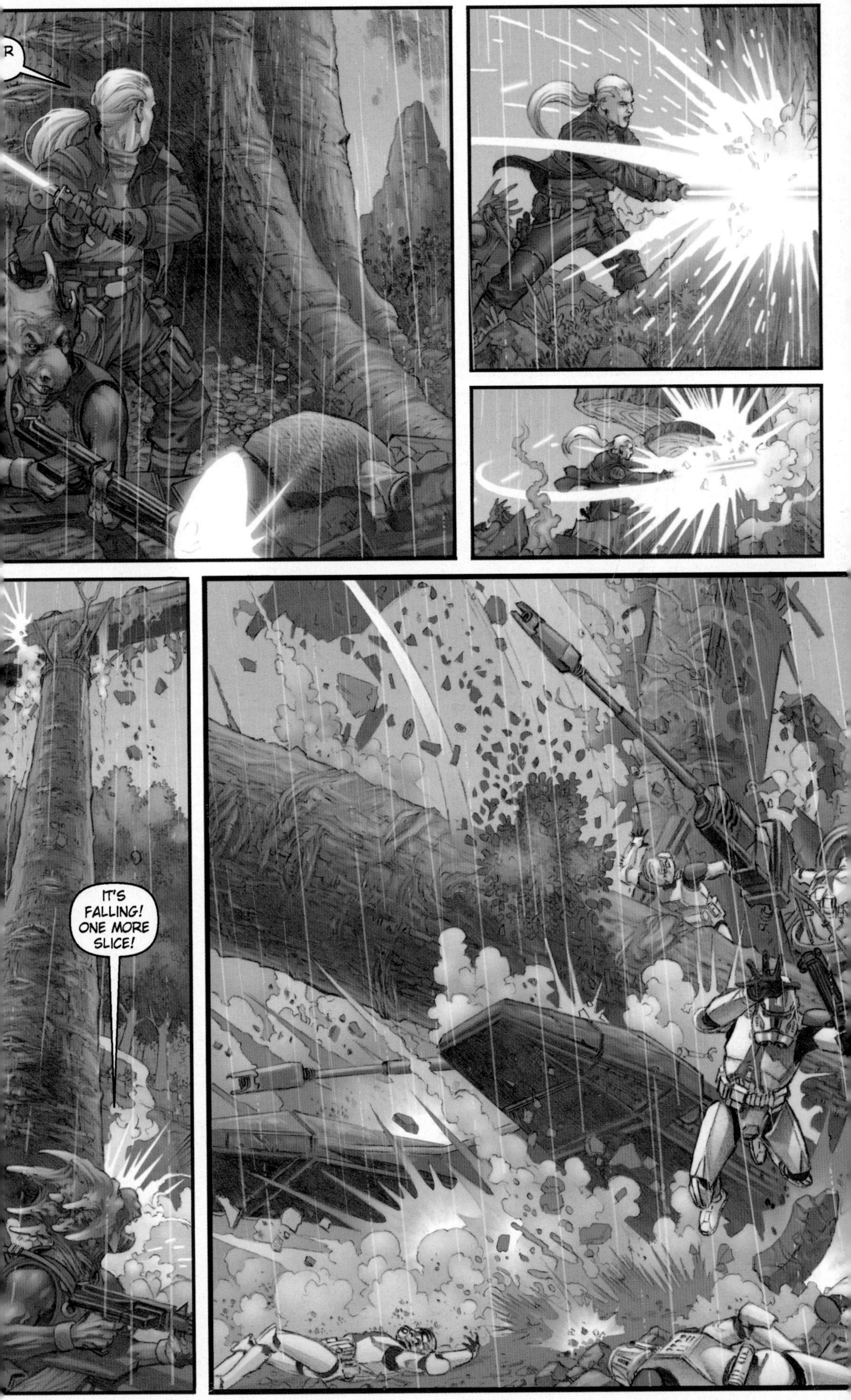
R
IT'S FALLING! ONE MORE SLICE!

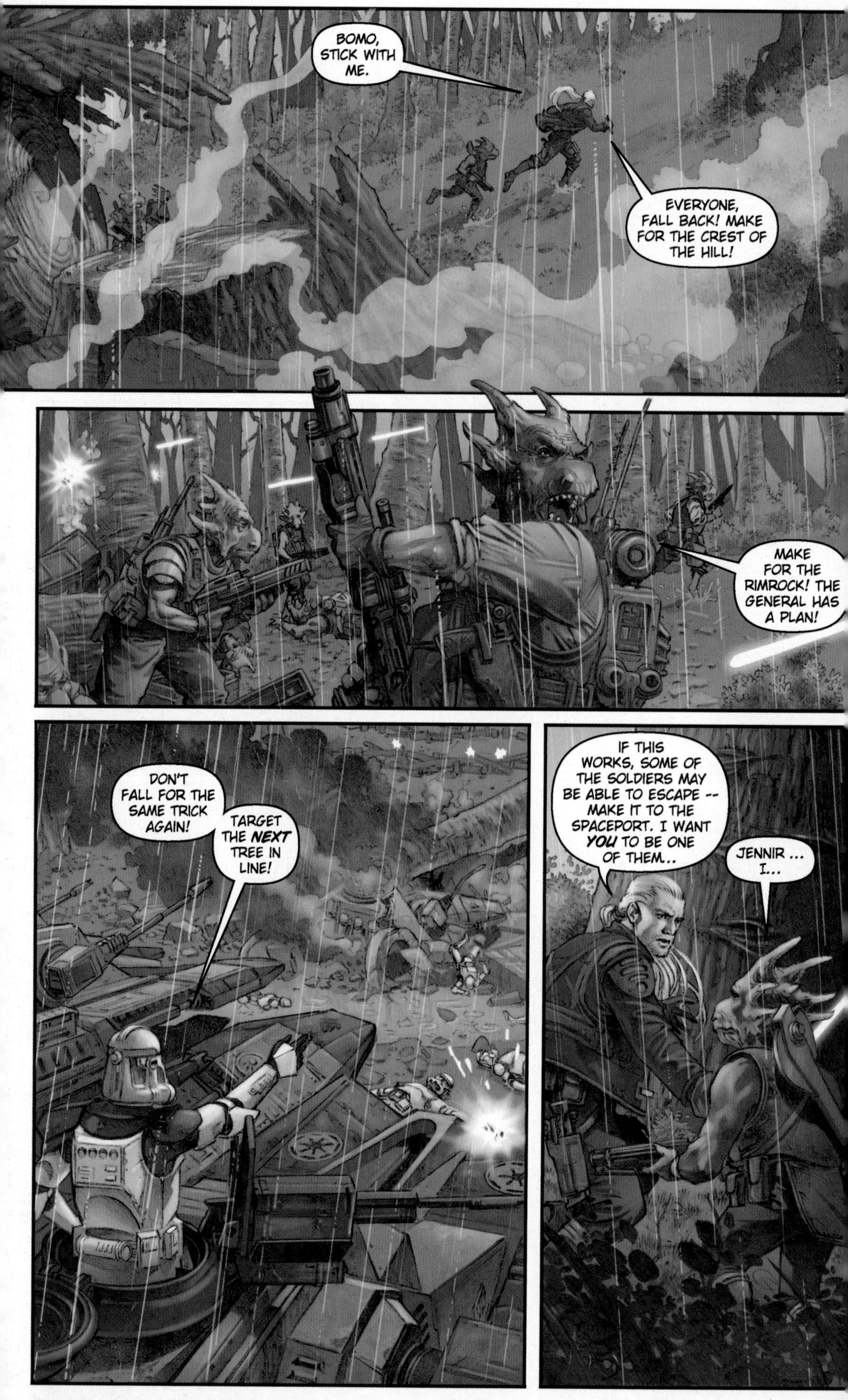
BOMO, STICK WITH ME.
EVERYONE, FALL BACK! MAKE FOR THE CREST OF THE HILL!
MAKE FOR THE RIMROCK! THE GENERAL HAS A PLAN!
DON'T FALL FOR THE SAME TRICK AGAIN!
TARGET THE *NEXT* TREE IN LINE!
IF THIS WORKS, SOME OF THE SOLDIERS MAY BE ABLE TO ESCAPE -- MAKE IT TO THE SPACEPORT. I WANT *YOU* TO BE ONE OF THEM...
JENNIR ... I...

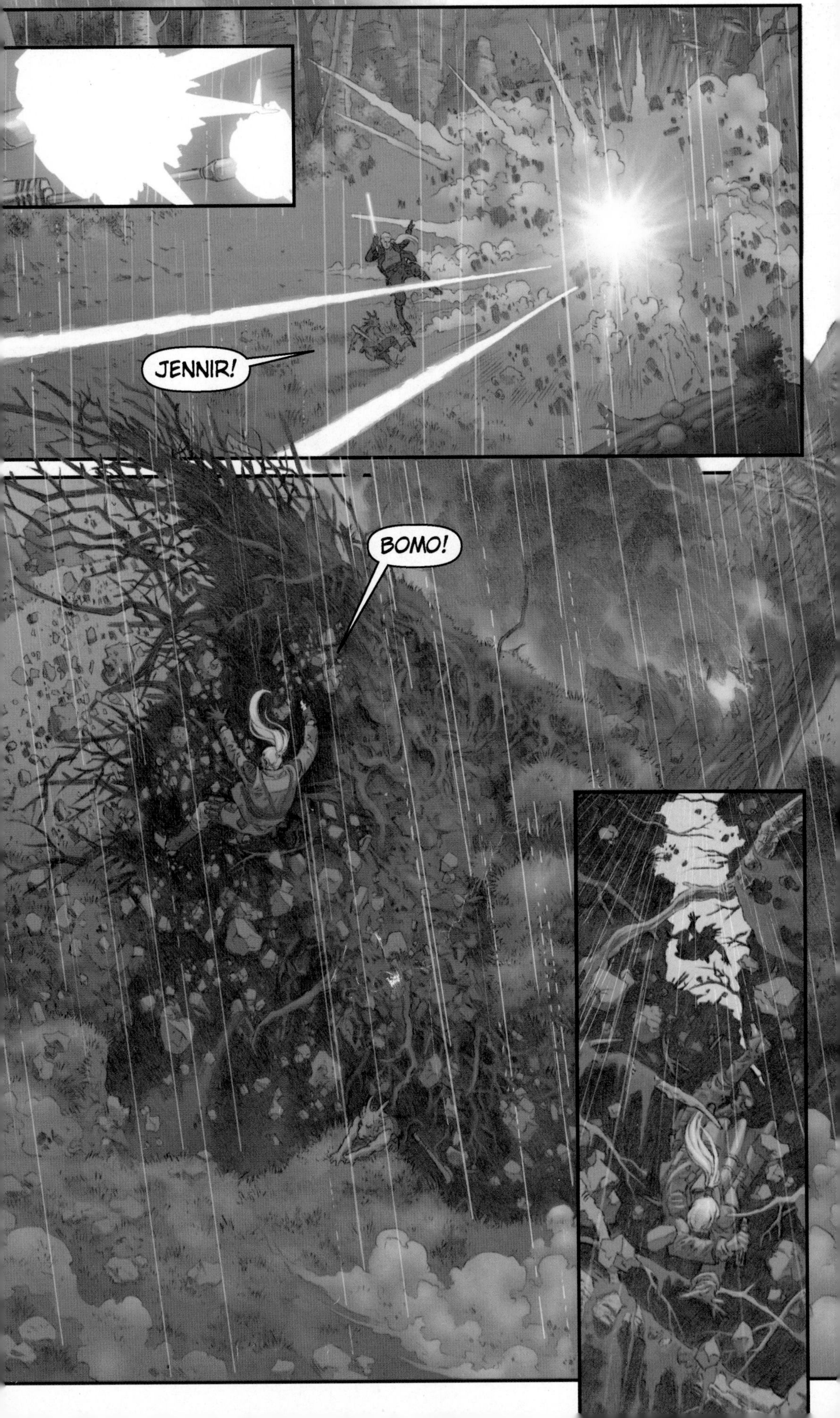
JENNIR!
BOMO!

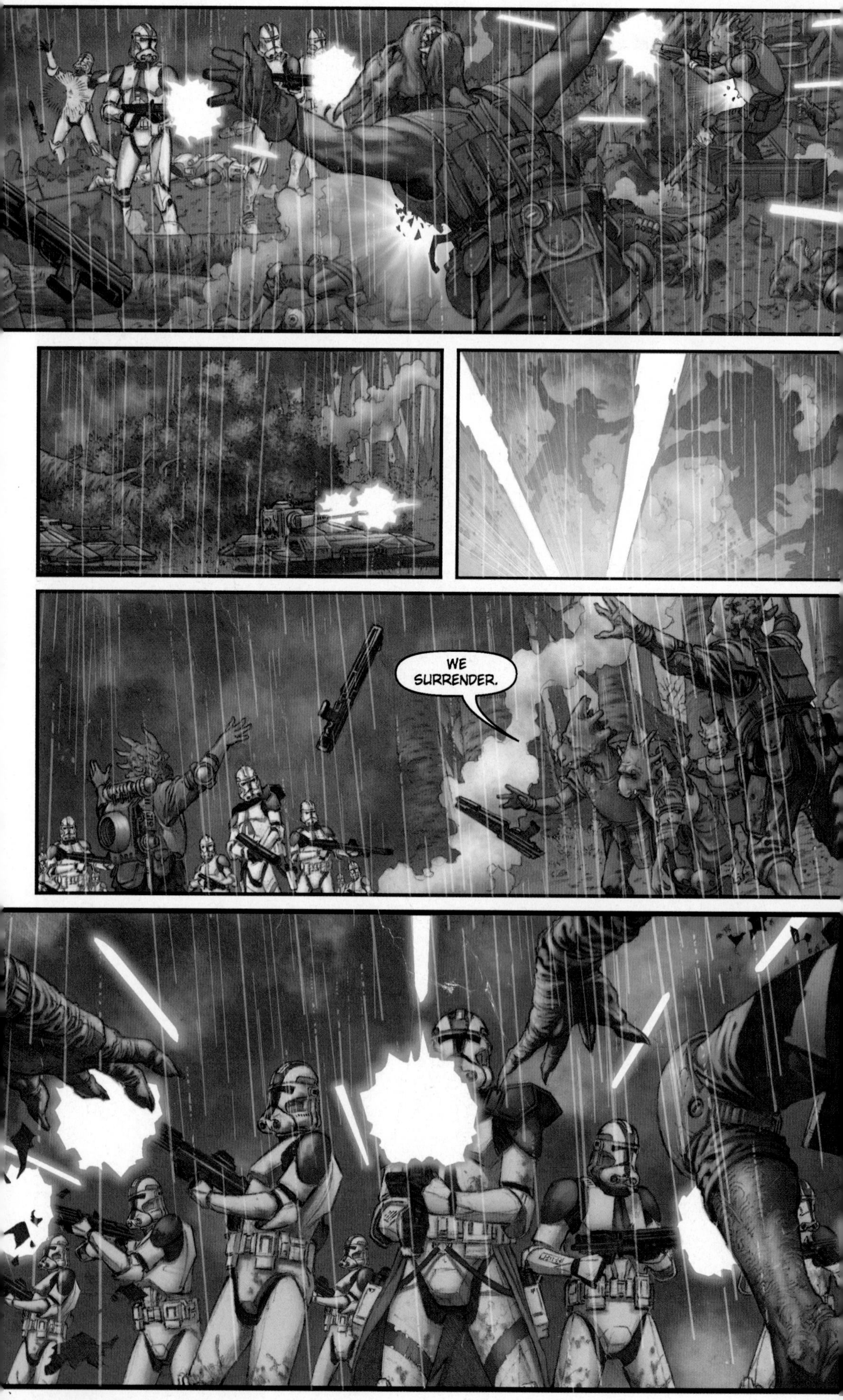
WE SURRENDER.

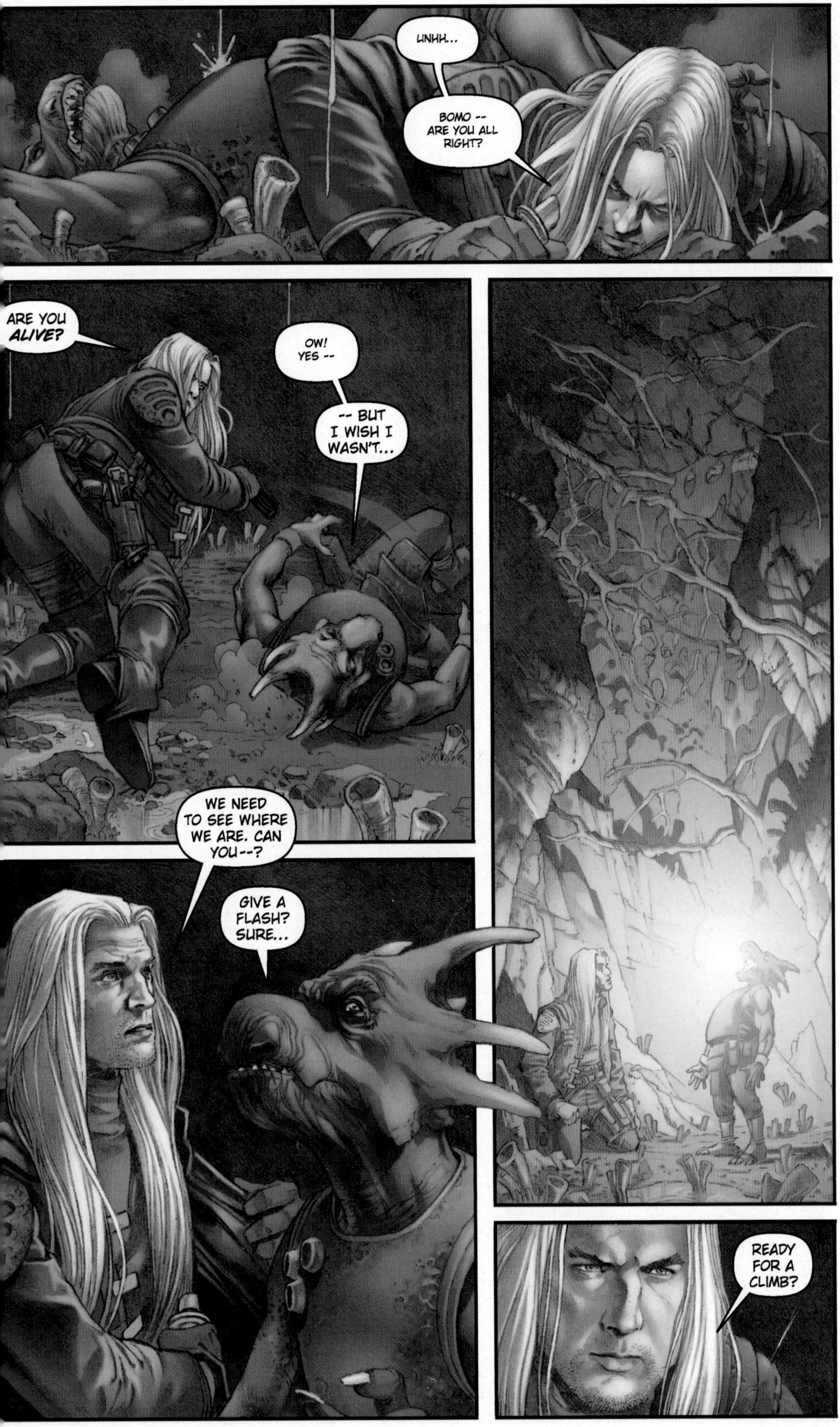

UNHH...
BOMO -- ARE YOU ALL RIGHT?
ARE YOU *ALIVE?*
OW! YES --
-- BUT I WISH I WASN'T...
WE NEED TO SEE WHERE WE ARE. CAN YOU--?
GIVE A FLASH? SURE...
READY FOR A CLIMB?

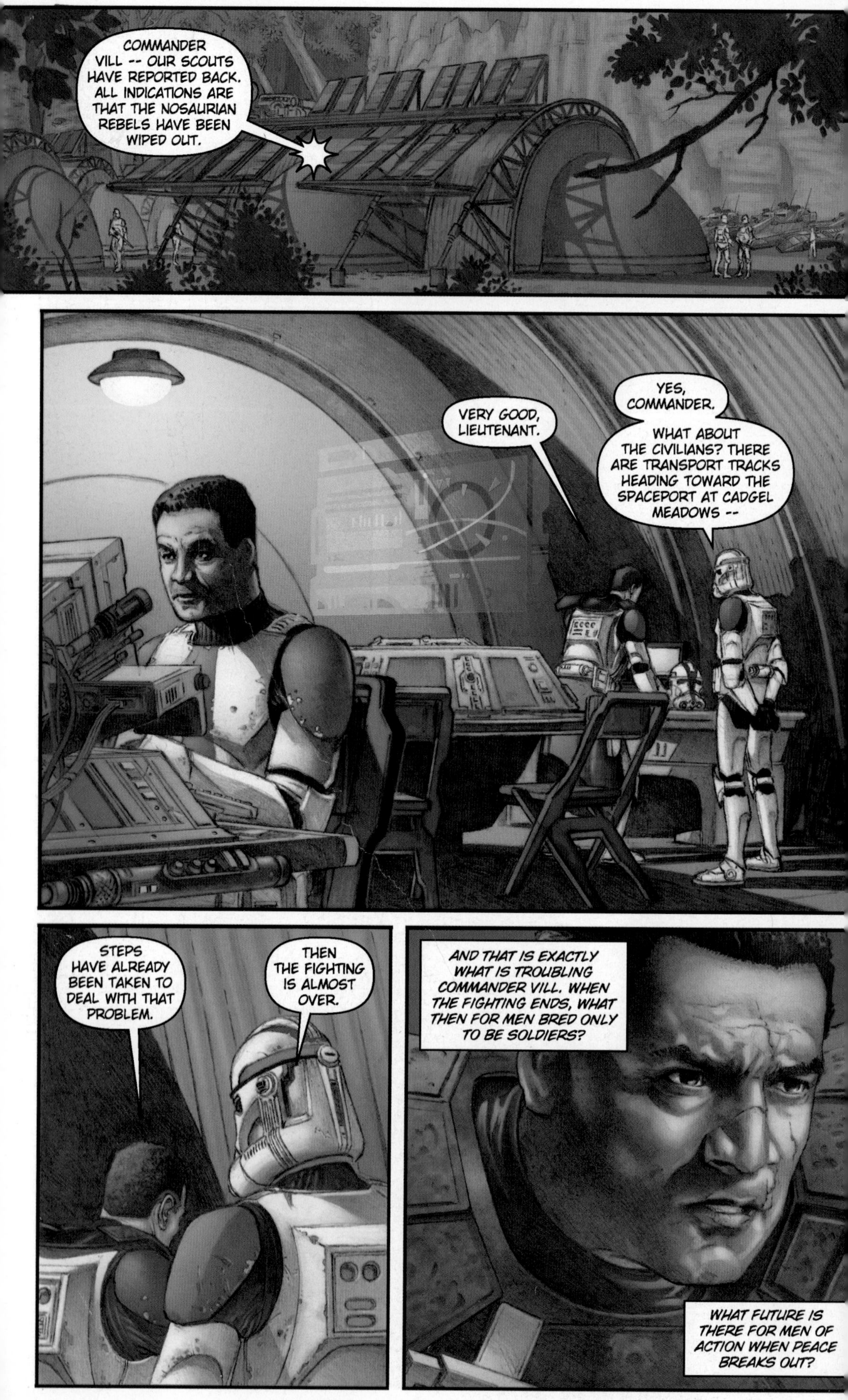
COMMANDER VILL -- OUR SCOUTS HAVE REPORTED BACK. ALL INDICATIONS ARE THAT THE NOSAURIAN REBELS HAVE BEEN WIPED OUT.
VERY GOOD, LIEUTENANT.
YES, COMMANDER.
WHAT ABOUT THE CIVILIANS? THERE ARE TRANSPORT TRACKS HEADING TOWARD THE SPACEPORT AT CADGEL MEADOWS --
STEPS HAVE ALREADY BEEN TAKEN TO DEAL WITH THAT PROBLEM.
THEN THE FIGHTING IS ALMOST OVER.
AND THAT IS EXACTLY WHAT IS TROUBLING COMMANDER VILL. WHEN THE FIGHTING ENDS, WHAT THEN FOR MEN BRED ONLY TO BE SOLDIERS?
WHAT FUTURE IS THERE FOR MEN OF ACTION WHEN PEACE BREAKS OUT?

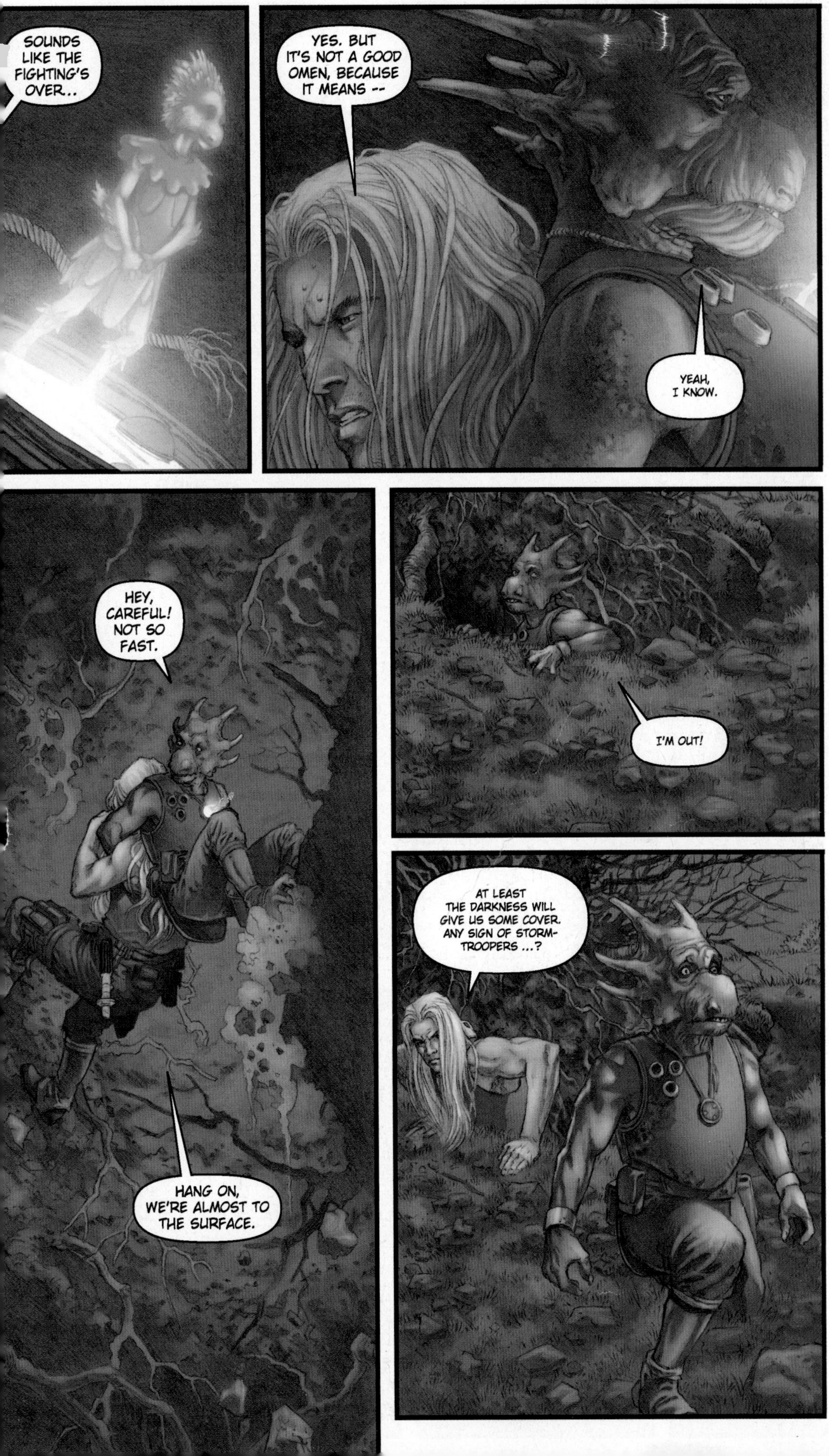
SOUNDS LIKE THE FIGHTING'S OVER...
YES. BUT IT'S NOT A GOOD OMEN, BECAUSE IT MEANS --
YEAH, I KNOW.
HEY, CAREFUL! NOT SO FAST.
HANG ON, WE'RE ALMOST TO THE SURFACE.
I'M OUT!
AT LEAST THE DARKNESS WILL GIVE US SOME COVER. ANY SIGN OF STORM-TROOPERS ...?

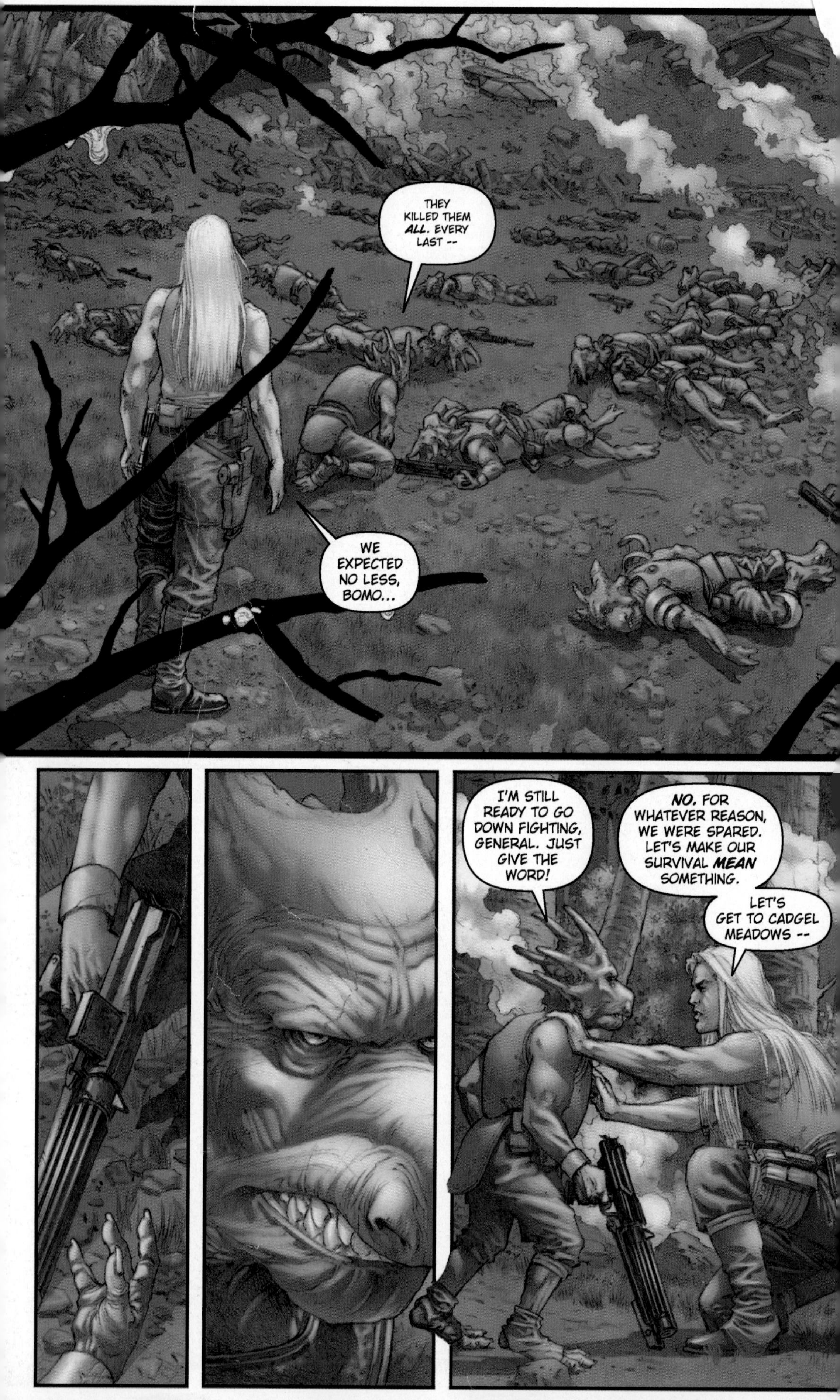
THEY KILLED THEM ALL. EVERY LAST --
WE EXPECTED NO LESS, BOMO...
I'M STILL READY TO GO DOWN FIGHTING, GENERAL. JUST GIVE THE WORD!
NO. FOR WHATEVER REASON, WE WERE SPARED. LET'S MAKE OUR SURVIVAL MEAN SOMETHING.
LET'S GET TO CADGEL MEADOWS --

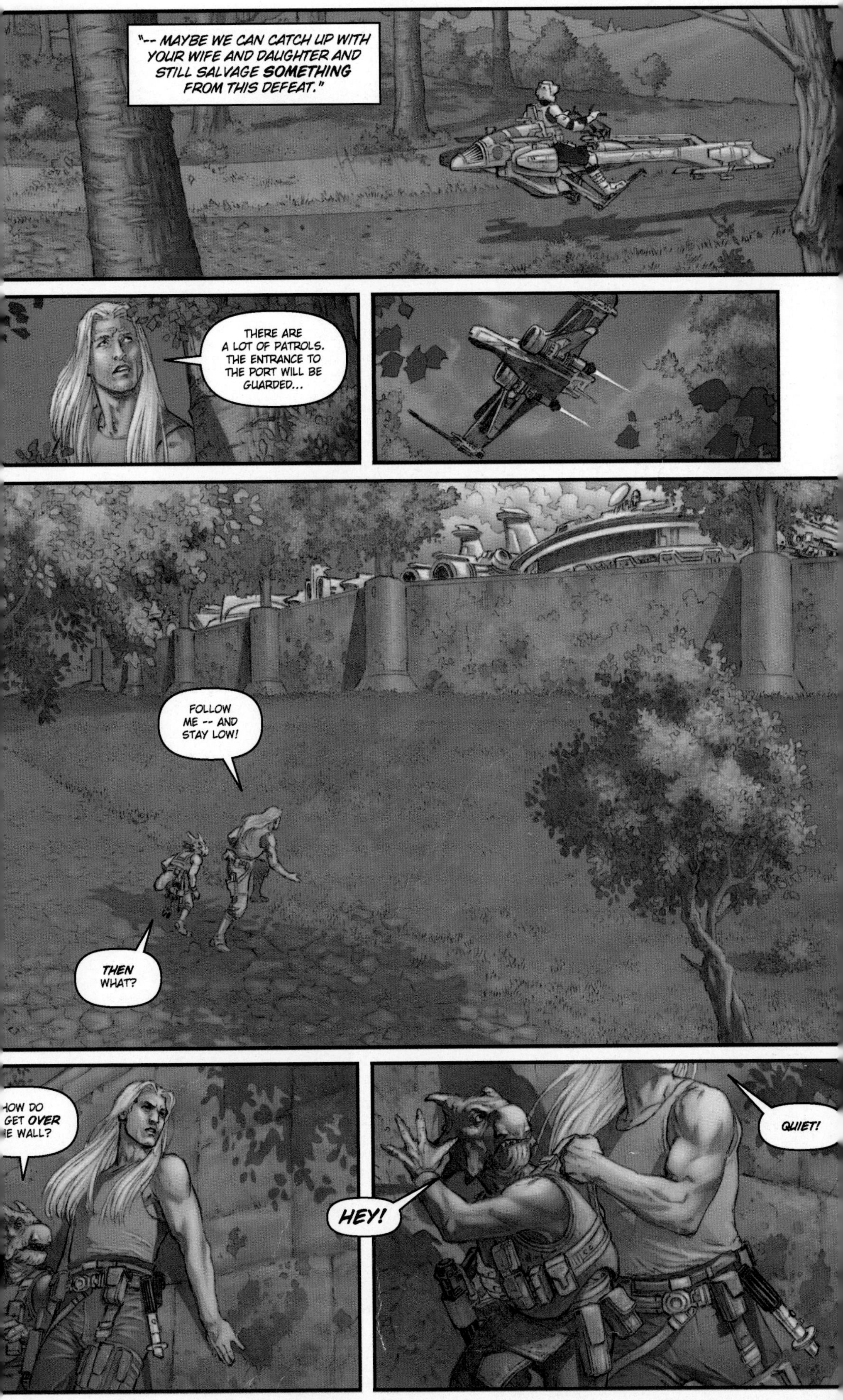
"-- MAYBE WE CAN CATCH UP WITH YOUR WIFE AND DAUGHTER AND STILL SALVAGE SOMETHING FROM THIS DEFEAT."
THERE ARE A LOT OF PATROLS. THE ENTRANCE TO THE PORT WILL BE GUARDED...
FOLLOW ME -- AND STAY LOW!
THEN WHAT?
HOW DO GET OVER E WALL?
HEY!
QUIET!

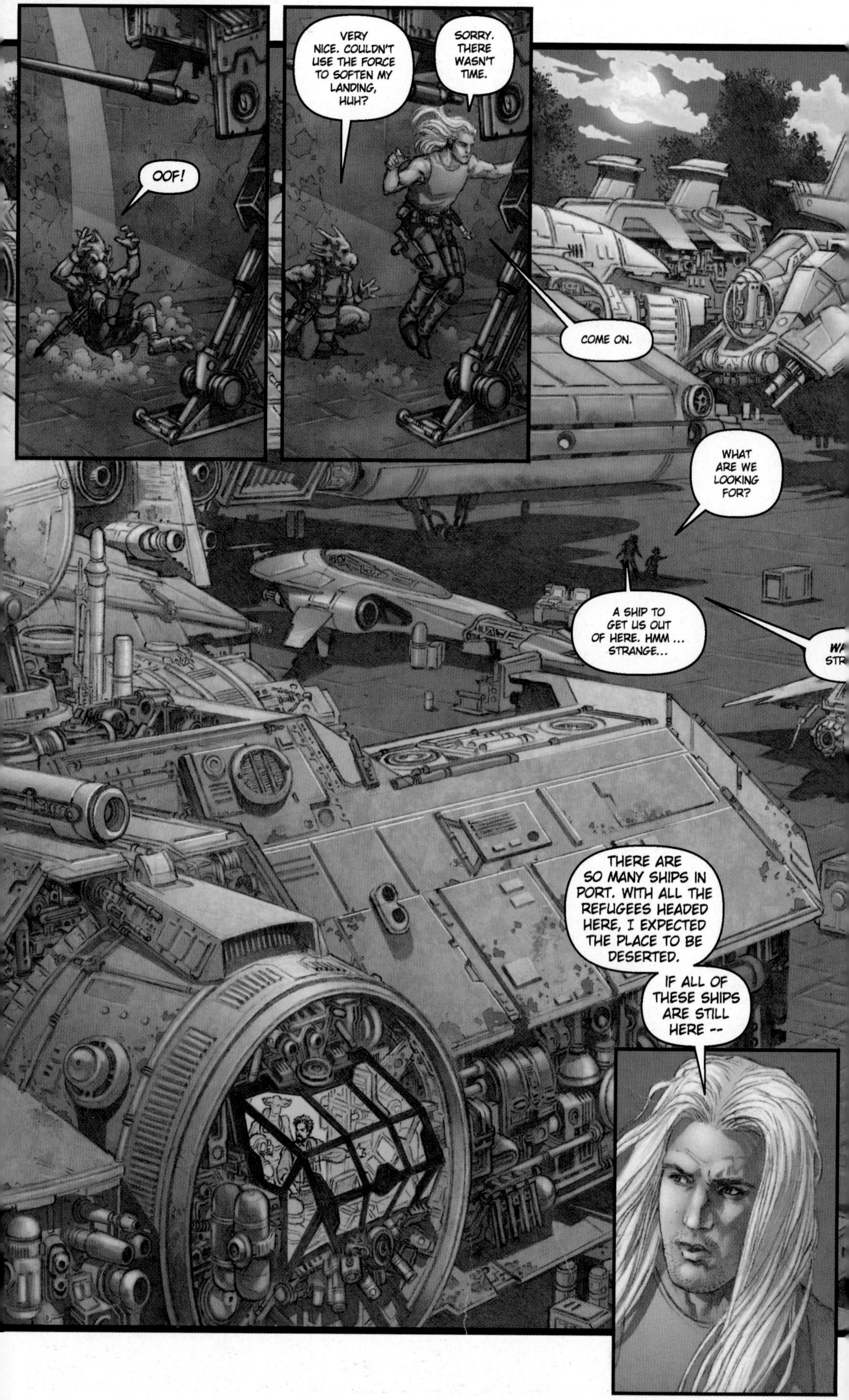
OOF!
VERY NICE. COULDN'T USE THE FORCE TO SOFTEN MY LANDING, HUH?
SORRY. THERE WASN'T TIME.
COME ON.
WHAT ARE WE LOOKING FOR?
A SHIP TO GET US OUT OF HERE. HMM ... STRANGE...
THERE ARE SO MANY SHIPS IN PORT. WITH ALL THE REFUGEES HEADED HERE, I EXPECTED THE PLACE TO BE DESERTED.
IF ALL OF THESE SHIPS ARE STILL HERE --

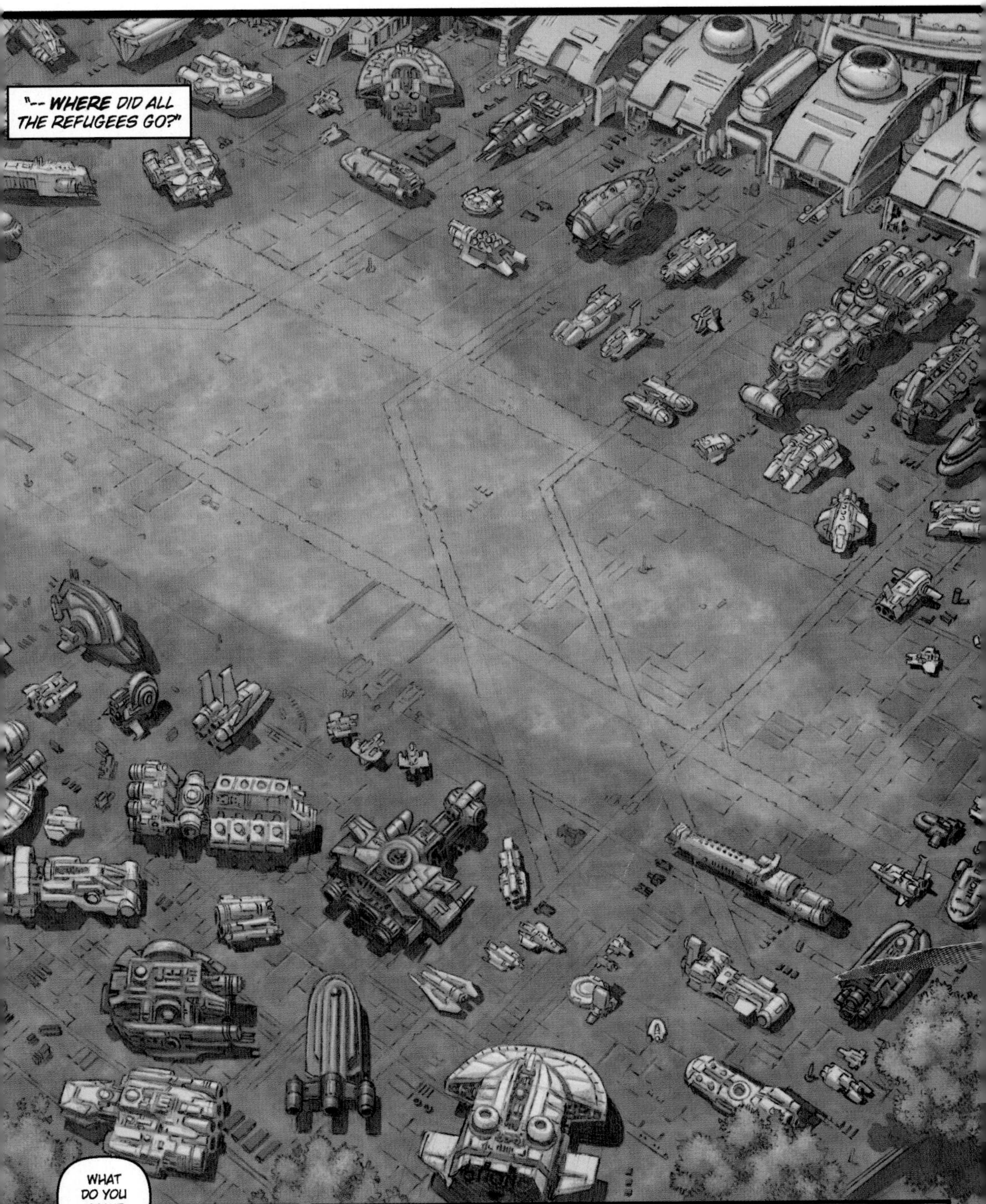
"-- WHERE DID ALL THE REFUGEES GO?"

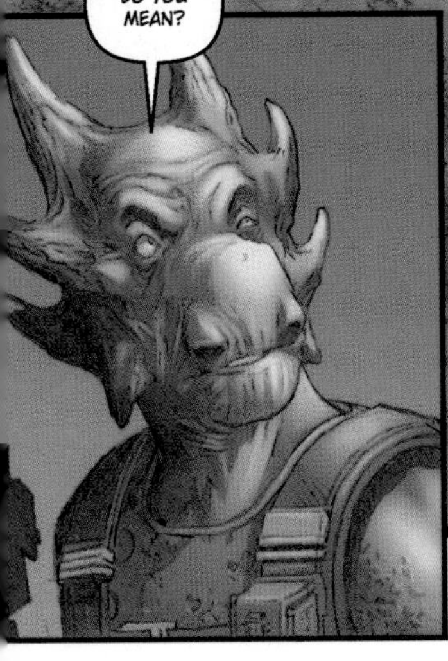
WHAT DO YOU MEAN?

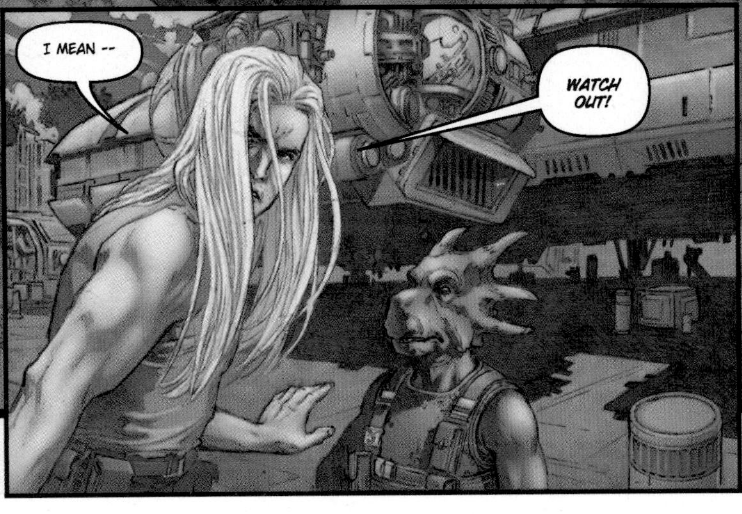
I MEAN --
WATCH OUT!

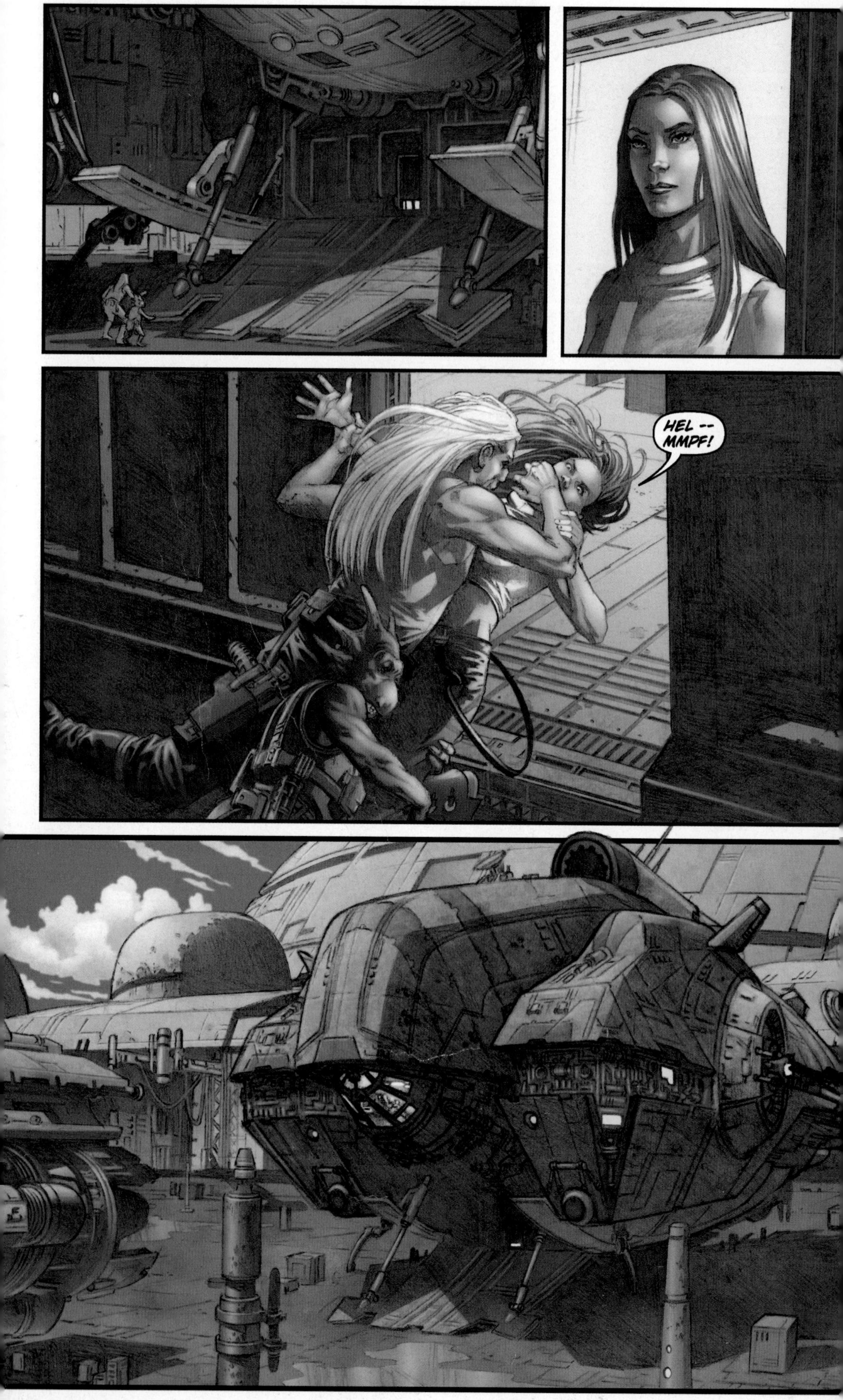
HEL -- MMPF!

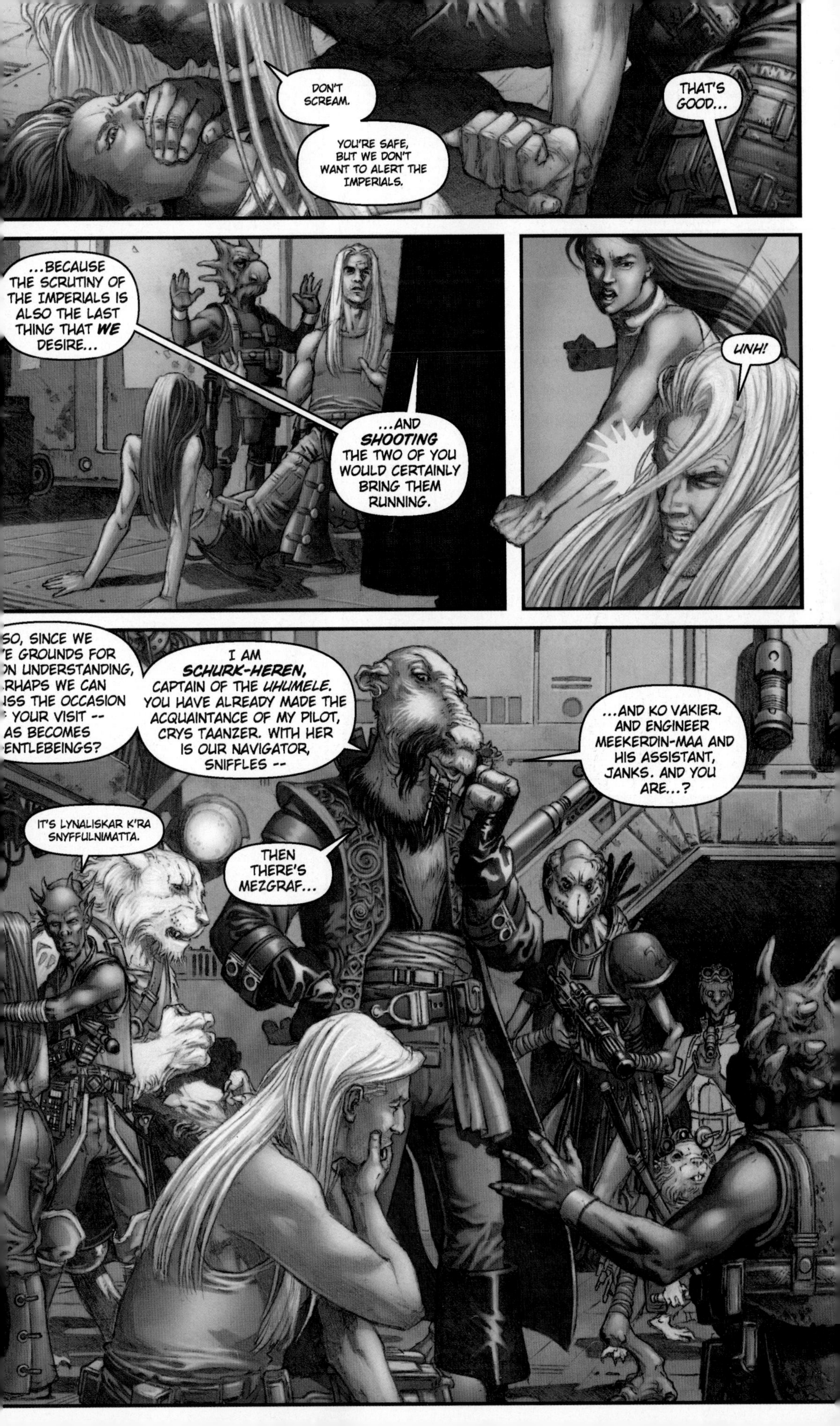
DON'T SCREAM.
YOU'RE SAFE, BUT WE DON'T WANT TO ALERT THE IMPERIALS.
THAT'S GOOD...
...BECAUSE THE SCRUTINY OF THE IMPERIALS IS ALSO THE LAST THING THAT WE DESIRE...
...AND SHOOTING THE TWO OF YOU WOULD CERTAINLY BRING THEM RUNNING.
UNH!
SO, SINCE WE 'E GROUNDS FOR ON UNDERSTANDING, RHAPS WE CAN USS THE OCCASION YOUR VISIT -- AS BECOMES ENTLEBEINGS?
I AM SCHURK-HEREN, CAPTAIN OF THE UHUMELE. YOU HAVE ALREADY MADE THE ACQUAINTANCE OF MY PILOT, CRYS TAANZER. WITH HER IS OUR NAVIGATOR, SNIFFLES --
IT'S LYNALISKAR K'RA SNYFFULNIMATTA.
THEN THERE'S MEZGRAF...
...AND KO VAKIER. AND ENGINEER MEEKERDIN-MAA AND HIS ASSISTANT, JANKS. AND YOU ARE...?

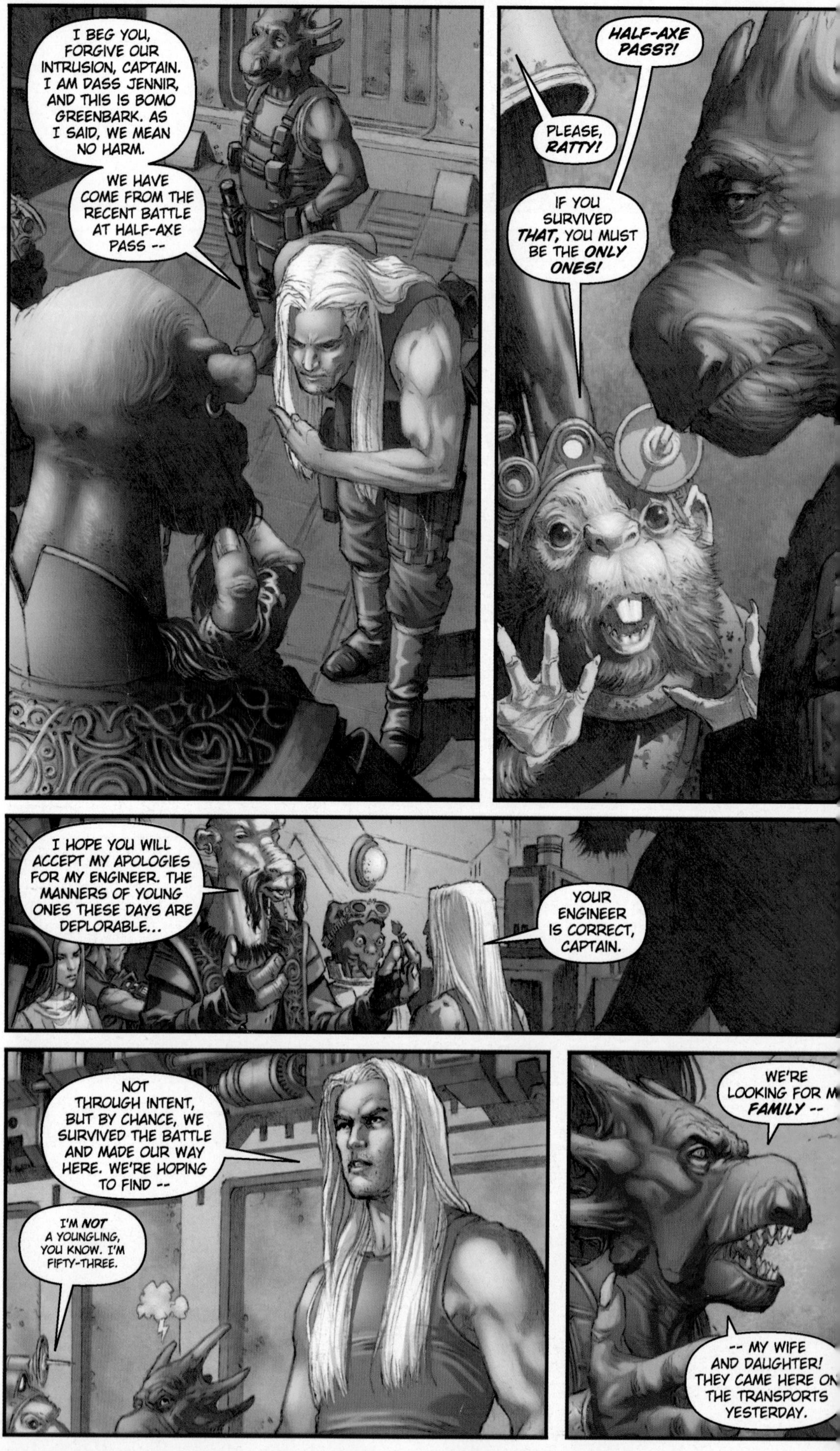
I BEG YOU, FORGIVE OUR INTRUSION, CAPTAIN. I AM DASS JENNIR, AND THIS IS BOMO GREENBARK. AS I SAID, WE MEAN NO HARM.
WE HAVE COME FROM THE RECENT BATTLE AT HALF-AXE PASS --
HALF-AXE PASS?!
PLEASE, RATTY!
IF YOU SURVIVED THAT, YOU MUST BE THE ONLY ONES!
I HOPE YOU WILL ACCEPT MY APOLOGIES FOR MY ENGINEER. THE MANNERS OF YOUNG ONES THESE DAYS ARE DEPLORABLE...
YOUR ENGINEER IS CORRECT, CAPTAIN.
NOT THROUGH INTENT, BUT BY CHANCE, WE SURVIVED THE BATTLE AND MADE OUR WAY HERE. WE'RE HOPING TO FIND --
I'M NOT A YOUNGLING, YOU KNOW. I'M FIFTY-THREE.
WE'RE LOOKING FOR M FAMILY --
-- MY WIFE AND DAUGHTER! THEY CAME HERE ON THE TRANSPORTS YESTERDAY.

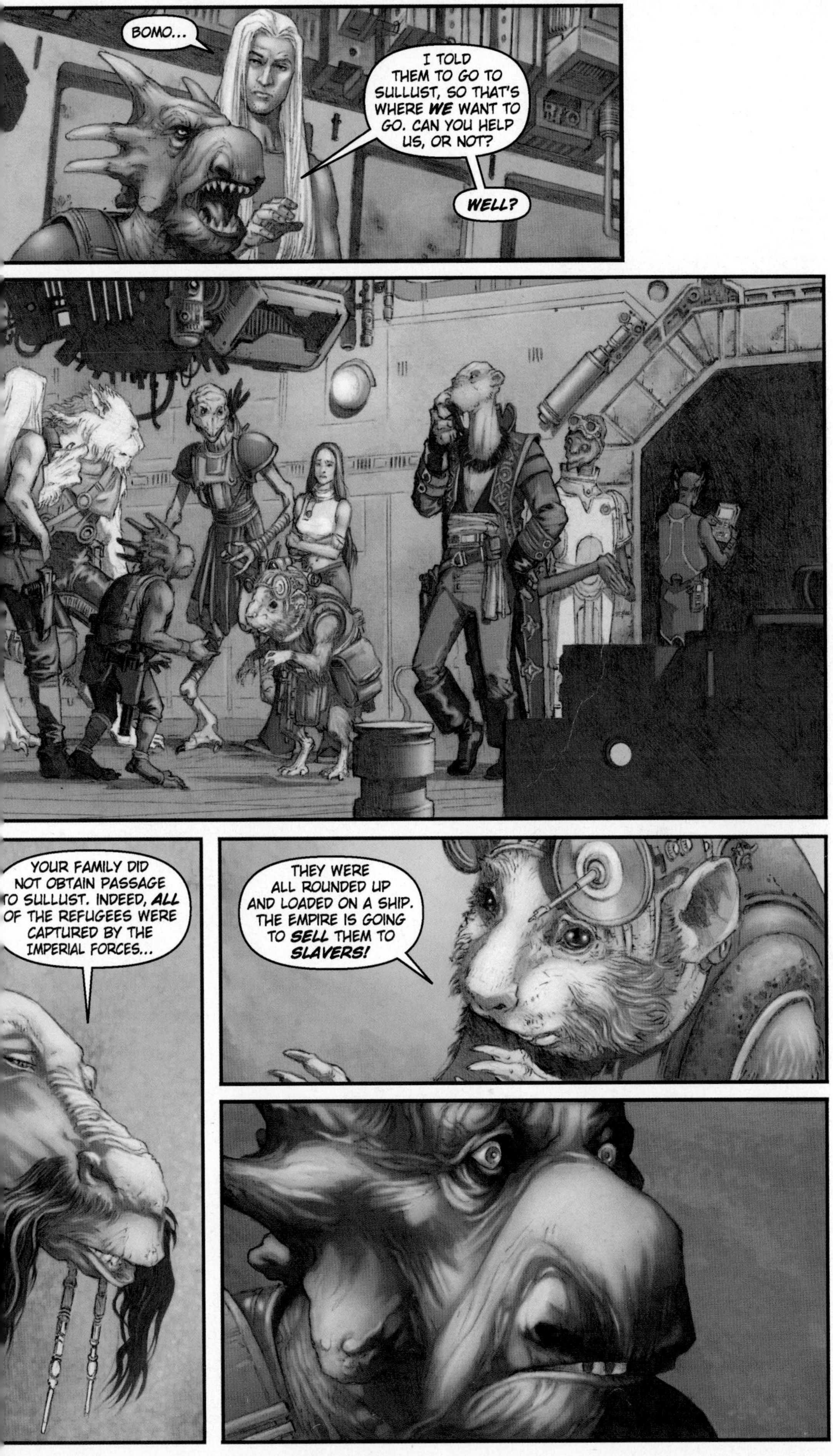
BOMO...
I TOLD THEM TO GO TO SULLUST, SO THAT'S WHERE WE WANT TO GO. CAN YOU HELP US, OR NOT?
WELL?
YOUR FAMILY DID NOT OBTAIN PASSAGE TO SULLUST. INDEED, ALL OF THE REFUGEES WERE CAPTURED BY THE IMPERIAL FORCES...
THEY WERE ALL ROUNDED UP AND LOADED ON A SHIP. THE EMPIRE IS GOING TO SELL THEM TO SLAVERS!

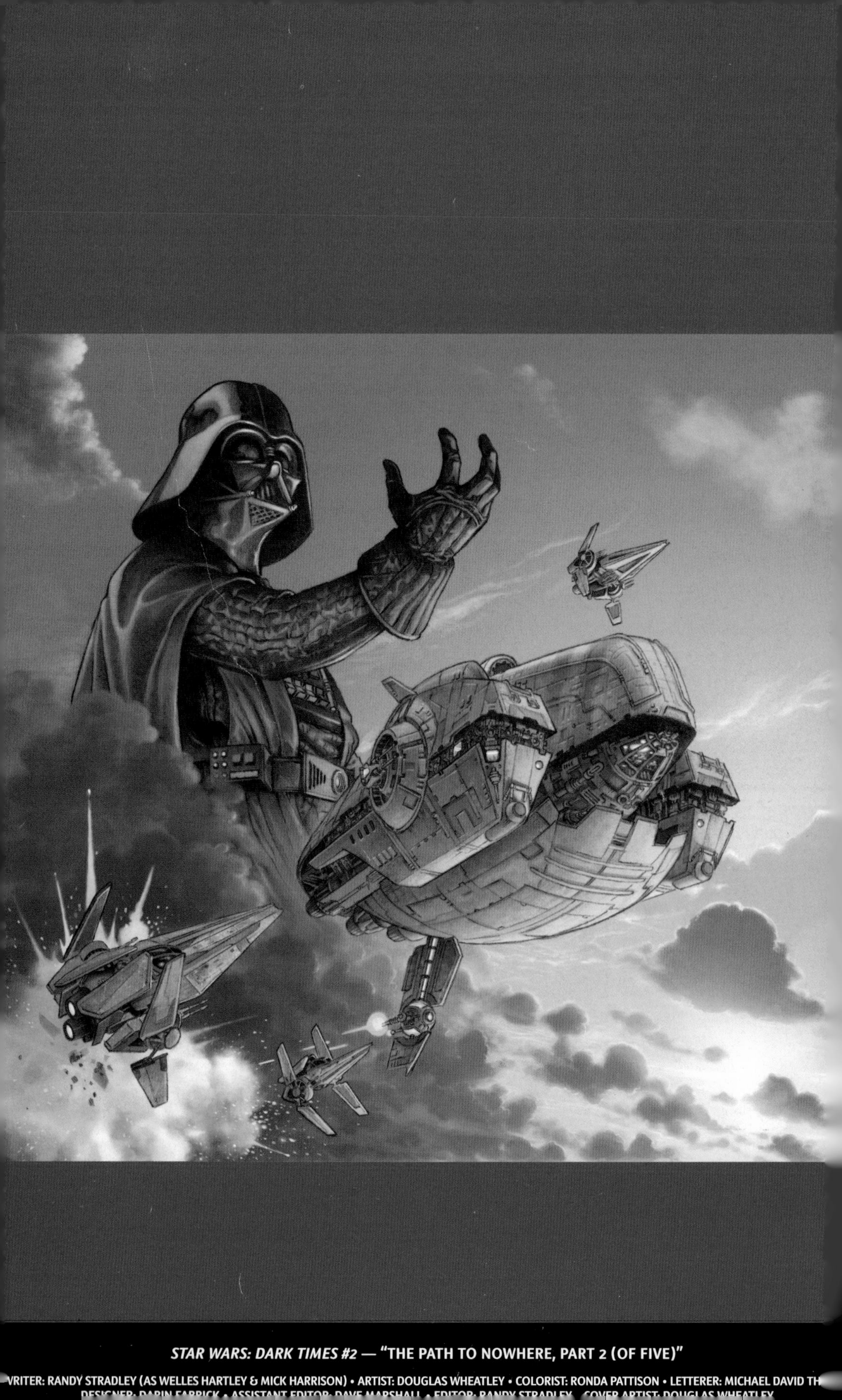

STAR WARS: DARK TIMES #2 — "THE PATH TO NOWHERE, PART 2 (OF FIVE)"

VRITER: RANDY STRADLEY (AS WELLES HARTLEY & MICK HARRISON) • ARTIST: DOUGLAS WHEATLEY • COLORIST: RONDA PATTISON • LETTERER: MICHAEL DAVID TH
DESIGNER: DARIN FABRICK • ASSISTANT EDITOR: DAVE MARSHALL • EDITOR: RANDY STRADLEY • COVER ARTIST: DOUGLAS WHEATLEY

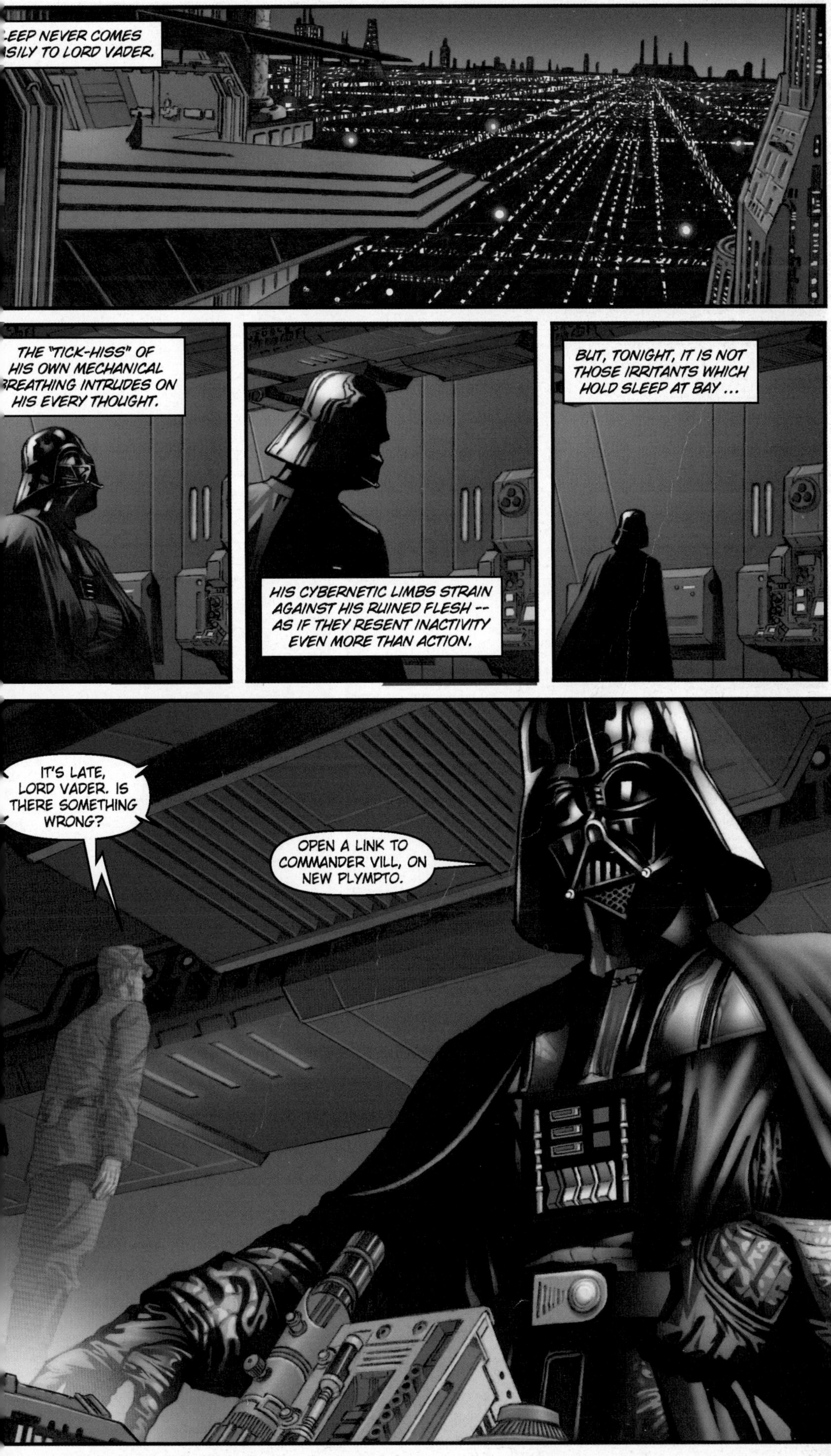

LEEP NEVER COMES
SILY TO LORD VADER.
THE "TICK-HISS" OF HIS OWN MECHANICAL BREATHING INTRUDES ON HIS EVERY THOUGHT.
HIS CYBERNETIC LIMBS STRAIN AGAINST HIS RUINED FLESH -- AS IF THEY RESENT INACTIVITY EVEN MORE THAN ACTION.
BUT, TONIGHT, IT IS NOT THOSE IRRITANTS WHICH HOLD SLEEP AT BAY ...
IT'S LATE, LORD VADER. IS THERE SOMETHING WRONG?
OPEN A LINK TO COMMANDER VILL, ON NEW PLYMPTO.

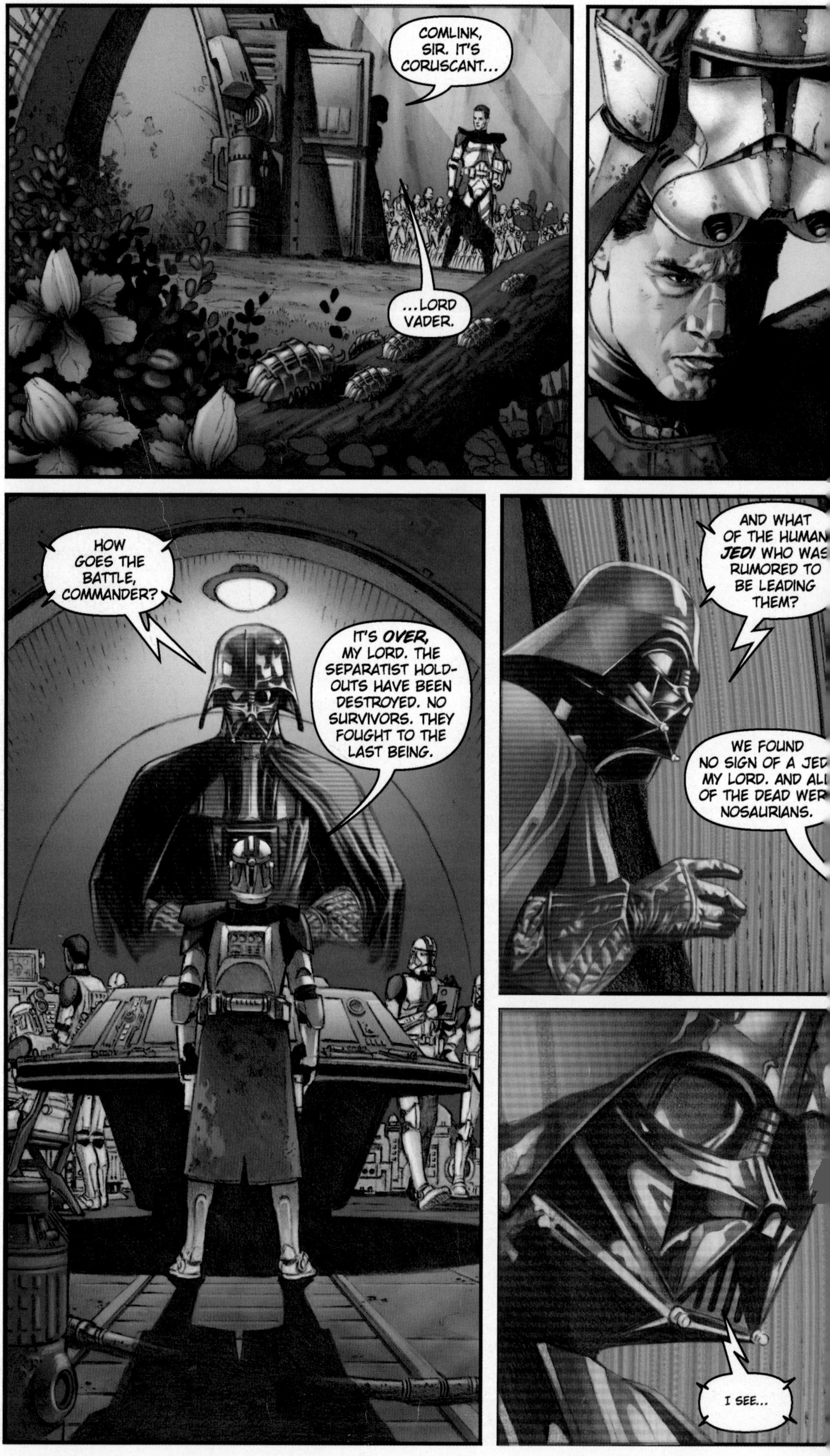
COMLINK, SIR. IT'S CORUSCANT...
...LORD VADER.
HOW GOES THE BATTLE, COMMANDER?
IT'S OVER, MY LORD. THE SEPARATIST HOLD-OUTS HAVE BEEN DESTROYED. NO SURVIVORS. THEY FOUGHT TO THE LAST BEING.
AND WHAT OF THE HUMAN JEDI WHO WAS RUMORED TO BE LEADING THEM?
WE FOUND NO SIGN OF A JEDI, MY LORD. AND ALL OF THE DEAD WERE NOSAURIANS.
I SEE...

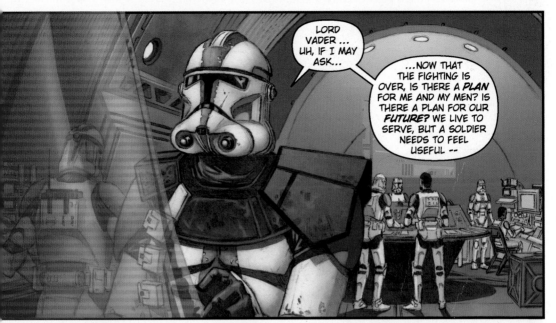

LORD VADER ... UH, IF I MAY ASK...

...NOW THAT THE FIGHTING IS OVER, IS THERE A *PLAN* FOR ME AND MY MEN? IS THERE A PLAN FOR OUR *FUTURE?* WE LIVE TO SERVE, BUT A SOLDIER NEEDS TO FEEL USEFUL --

I ... I'M *CERTAIN* THAT THE EMPEROR HAS A *PLAN*, COMMANDER. WE WILL DISCUSS IT UPON YOUR RETURN TO CORUSCANT...

YES, MY LORD. BUT I'M NOT SURE OF *WHEN* THE REGIMENT AND I WILL BE BACK -- OUR TRANSPORT WAS *RETASKED*, BY ORDER OF THE EMPEROR.

WHERE WAS IT SENT? HAS *NEW FIGHTING* BROKEN OUT SOMEWHERE?

NO, SIR. THE SHIP IS TRANSPORTING CAPTURED NOSAURIAN CIVILIANS TO THE *SLAVE MARKET* ON ORVAX FOUR.

THE PRISONERS WERE MOSTLY FEMALES AND YOUNGLINGS, SO IT WAS DECIDED THAT THEY WOULD BE SOLD FOR *PROFIT* RATHER THAN ADDED TO THE IMPERIAL WORK FORCE...

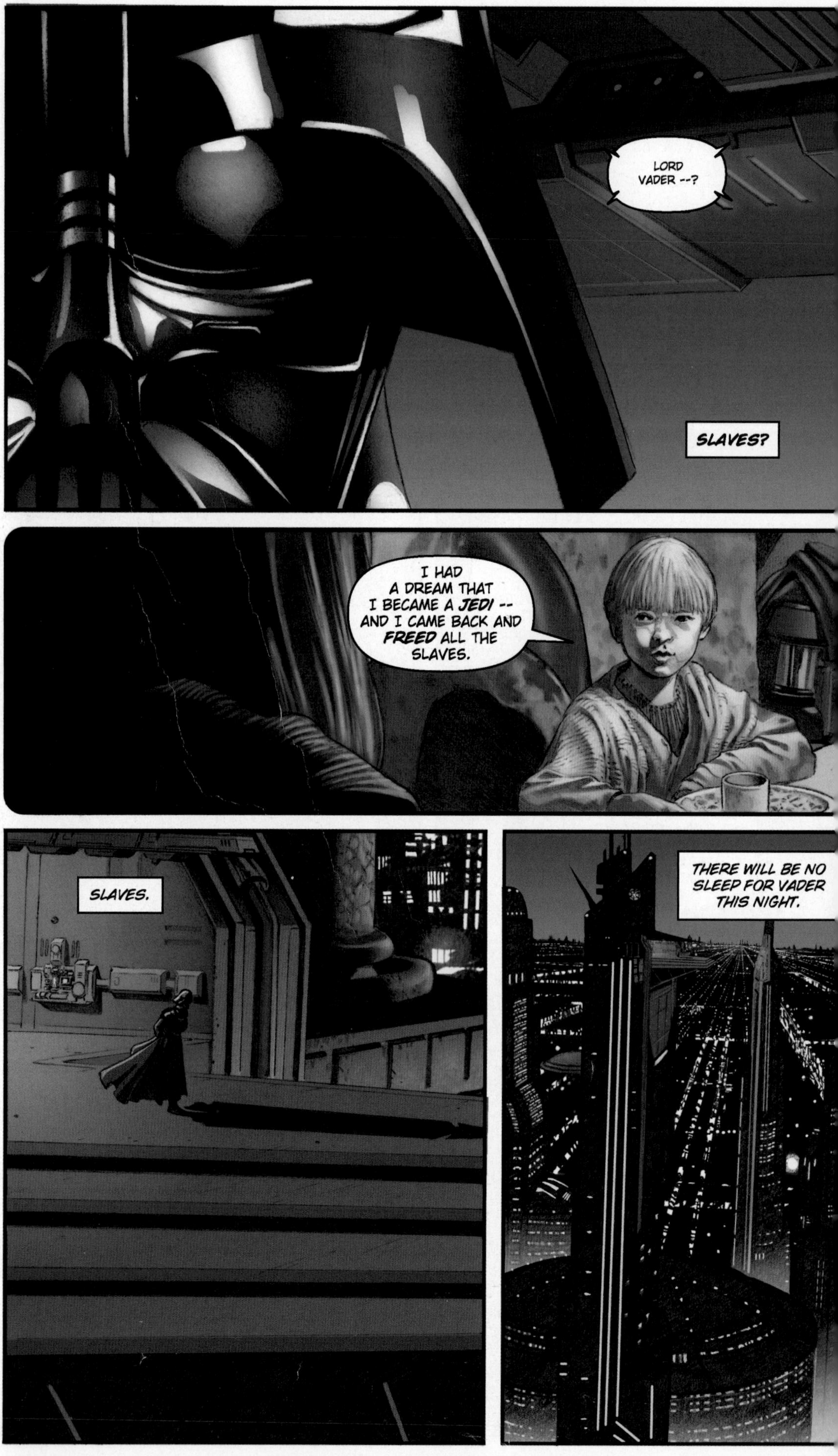
LORD VADER --?
SLAVES?
I HAD A DREAM THAT I BECAME A JEDI -- AND I CAME BACK AND FREED ALL THE SLAVES.
SLAVES.
THERE WILL BE NO SLEEP FOR VADER THIS NIGHT.

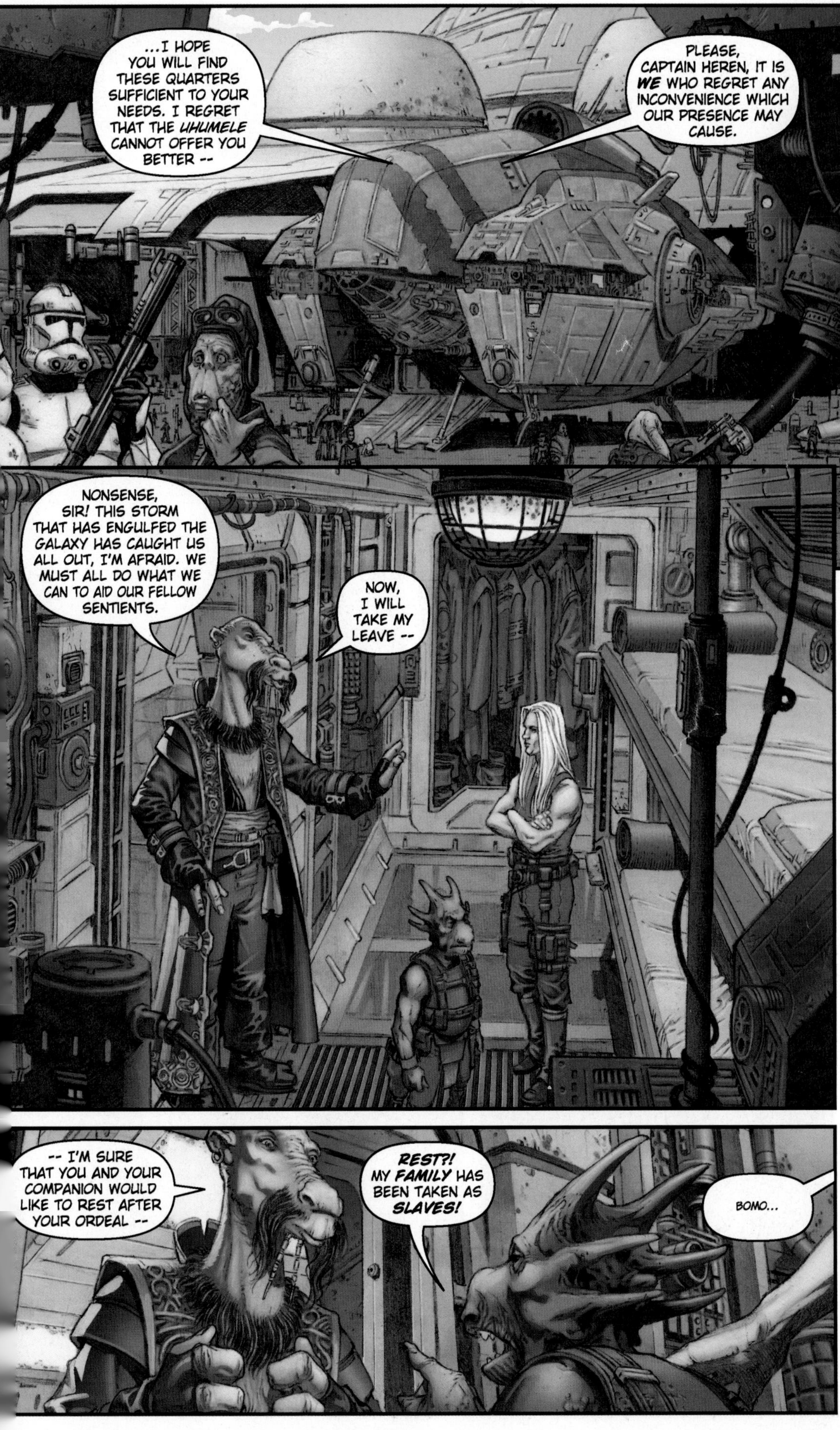
...I HOPE YOU WILL FIND THESE QUARTERS SUFFICIENT TO YOUR NEEDS. I REGRET THAT THE *UHUMELE* CANNOT OFFER YOU BETTER --
PLEASE, CAPTAIN HEREN, IT IS *WE* WHO REGRET ANY INCONVENIENCE WHICH OUR PRESENCE MAY CAUSE.
NONSENSE, SIR! THIS STORM THAT HAS ENGULFED THE GALAXY HAS CAUGHT US ALL OUT, I'M AFRAID. WE MUST ALL DO WHAT WE CAN TO AID OUR FELLOW SENTIENTS.
NOW, I WILL TAKE MY LEAVE --
-- I'M SURE THAT YOU AND YOUR COMPANION WOULD LIKE TO REST AFTER YOUR ORDEAL --
REST?! MY *FAMILY* HAS BEEN TAKEN AS *SLAVES!*
BOMO...

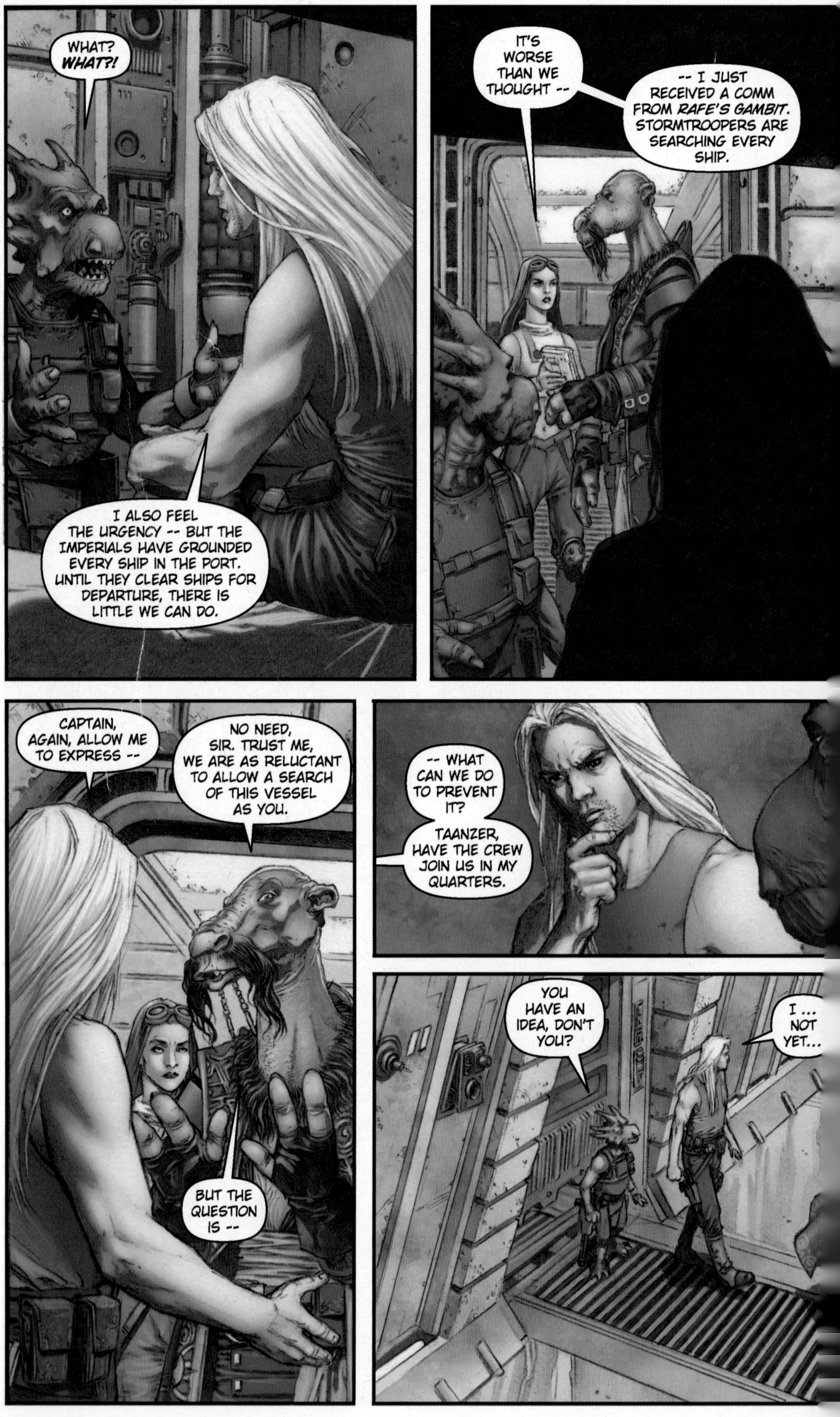
WHAT? *WHAT?!*
I ALSO FEEL THE URGENCY -- BUT THE IMPERIALS HAVE GROUNDED EVERY SHIP IN THE PORT. UNTIL THEY CLEAR SHIPS FOR DEPARTURE, THERE IS LITTLE WE CAN DO.
IT'S WORSE THAN WE THOUGHT --
-- I JUST RECEIVED A COMM FROM *RAFE'S GAMBIT*. STORMTROOPERS ARE SEARCHING EVERY SHIP.
CAPTAIN, AGAIN, ALLOW ME TO EXPRESS --
NO NEED, SIR. TRUST ME, WE ARE AS RELUCTANT TO ALLOW A SEARCH OF THIS VESSEL AS YOU.
BUT THE QUESTION IS --
-- WHAT CAN WE DO TO PREVENT IT?
TAANZER, HAVE THE CREW JOIN US IN MY QUARTERS.
YOU HAVE AN IDEA, DON'T YOU?
I ... NOT YET...

-- A DECISION WHICH WE MUST MAKE TOGETHER. SOME OF US -- KO VAKIER, MEZGRAF, AND MYSELF -- HAVE HAD OUR LIVES DISRUPTED BY THE EXCESSES OF THE REPUBLIC.

OTHERS OF YOU -- CRYS, MEEKERDIN-MAA -- OWE YOUR CURRENT STATUS TO THE IMPETUOUSNESS OF THE SEPARATIST MOVEMENT. *NONE* OF US HAS ANY REASON TO *TRUST* THIS NEW "EMPIRE"-- NOR CAN ANY GOOD COME OF ITS TROOPS *SEARCHING* THIS SHIP.

SO, I PUT IT TO YOU -- WHAT SHOULD BE OUR COURSE OF ACTION?

I VOTE WE FIGHT OUR WAY OFF PLANET -- CARVE A PATH THROUGH OUR ENEMIES.

KO VAKIER HAS A POINT. THIS SHIP IS PACKING MORE ARMAMENT THAN THE IMPERIALS SUSPECT. WE MIGHT HAVE A CHANCE.

NO. WE'D BE BLOWN OUT OF THE SKY BEFORE WE REACHED THE UPPER ATMOSPHERE. BELIEVE ME, I'VE SEEN WHAT ARC-170s AND NIMBUS FIGHTERS CAN DO.

SO WE SHOULD JUST *SIT* HERE AND WAIT TO BE BOARDED? *THAT'S* YOUR PLAN?

YOU CAN *BET* THAT'S NOT THE GENERAL'S PLAN, JANKS! MAYBE IF YOU GAVE HIM A CHANCE TO *TELL* YOU HIS IDEA -- !

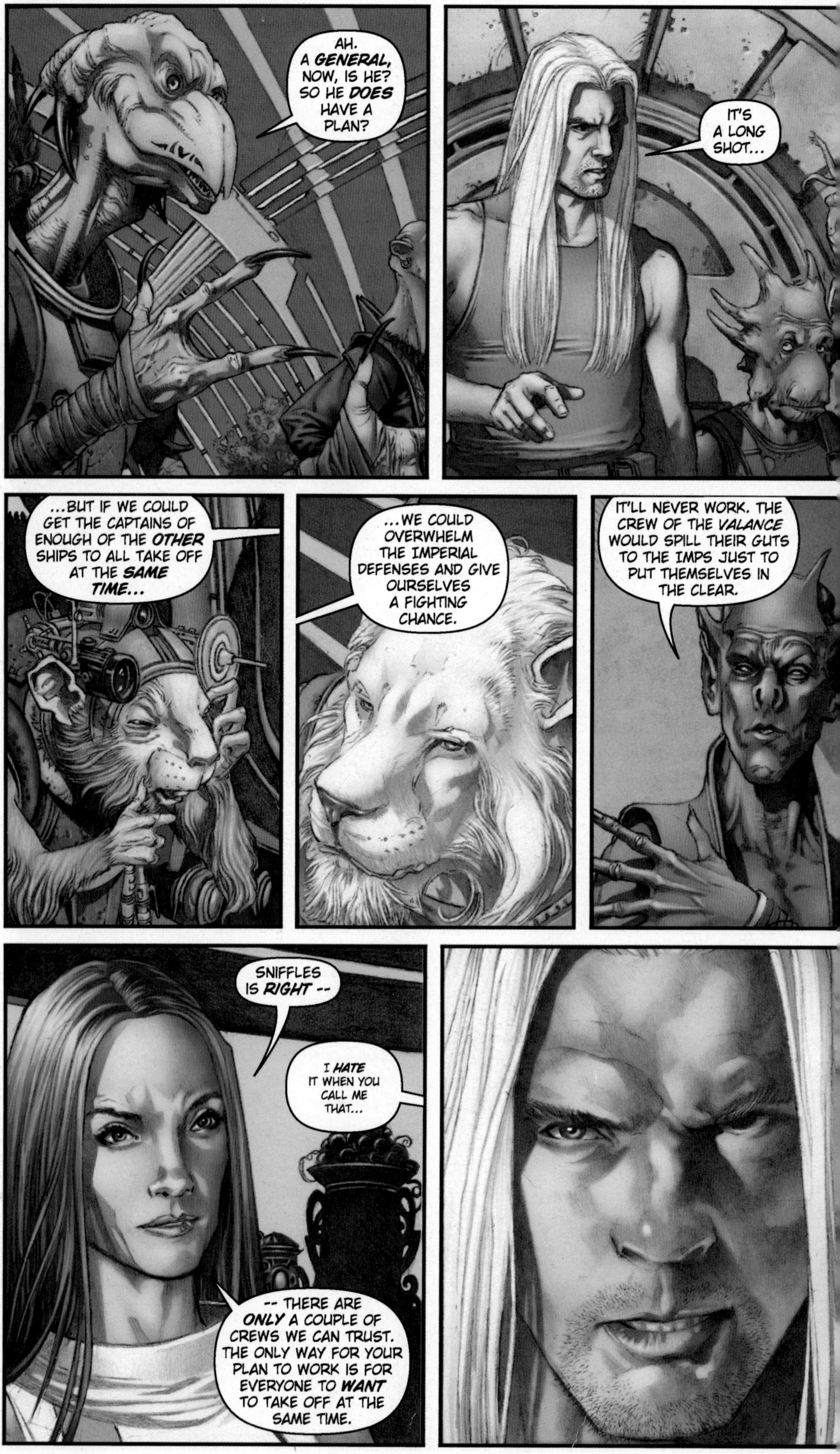
AH. A GENERAL, NOW, IS HE? SO HE DOES HAVE A PLAN?
IT'S A LONG SHOT...
...BUT IF WE COULD GET THE CAPTAINS OF ENOUGH OF THE OTHER SHIPS TO ALL TAKE OFF AT THE SAME TIME...
...WE COULD OVERWHELM THE IMPERIAL DEFENSES AND GIVE OURSELVES A FIGHTING CHANCE.
IT'LL NEVER WORK. THE CREW OF THE VALANCE WOULD SPILL THEIR GUTS TO THE IMPS JUST TO PUT THEMSELVES IN THE CLEAR.
SNIFFLES IS RIGHT --
I HATE IT WHEN YOU CALL ME THAT...
-- THERE ARE ONLY A COUPLE OF CREWS WE CAN TRUST. THE ONLY WAY FOR YOUR PLAN TO WORK IS FOR EVERYONE TO WANT TO TAKE OFF AT THE SAME TIME.

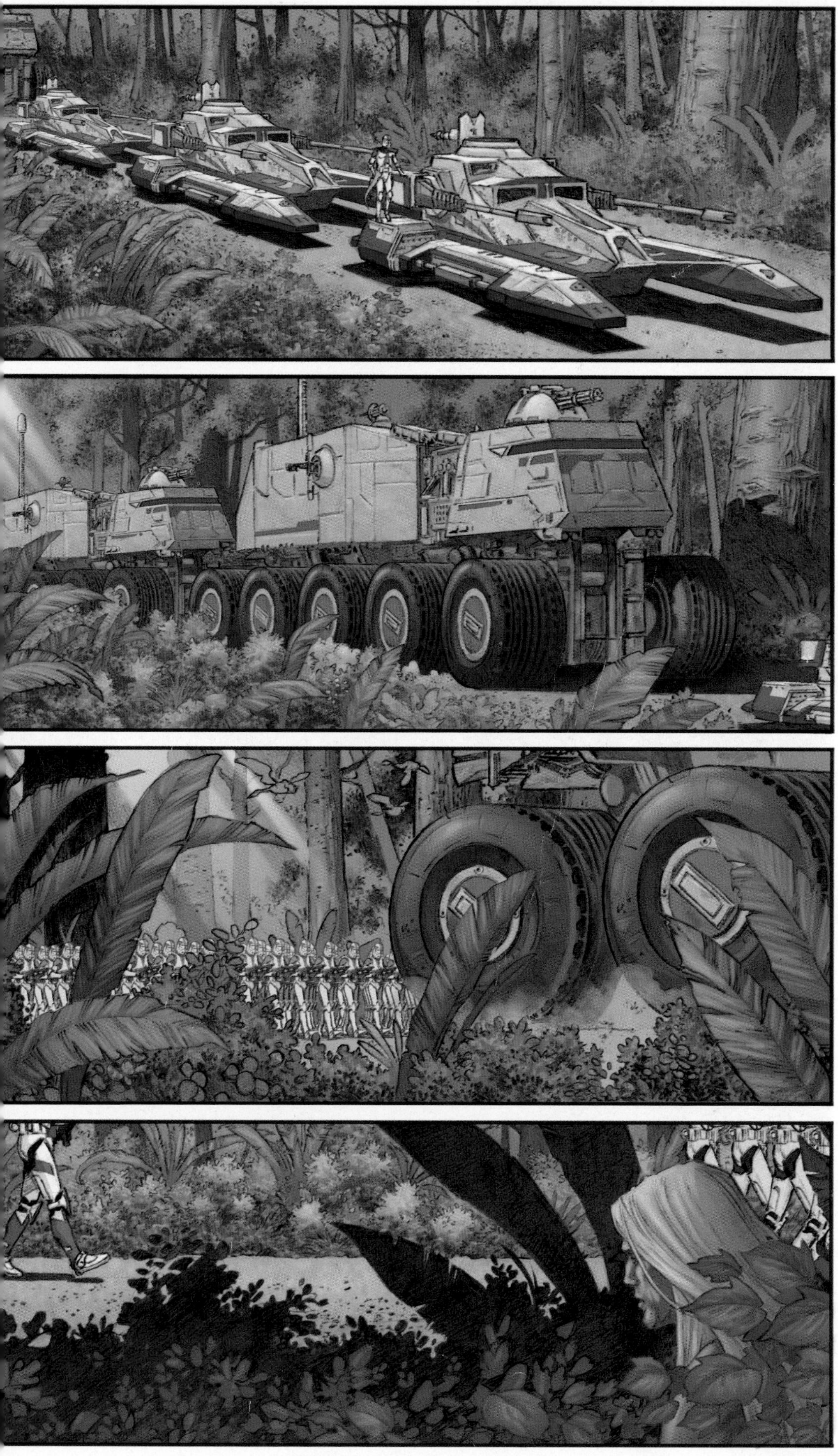

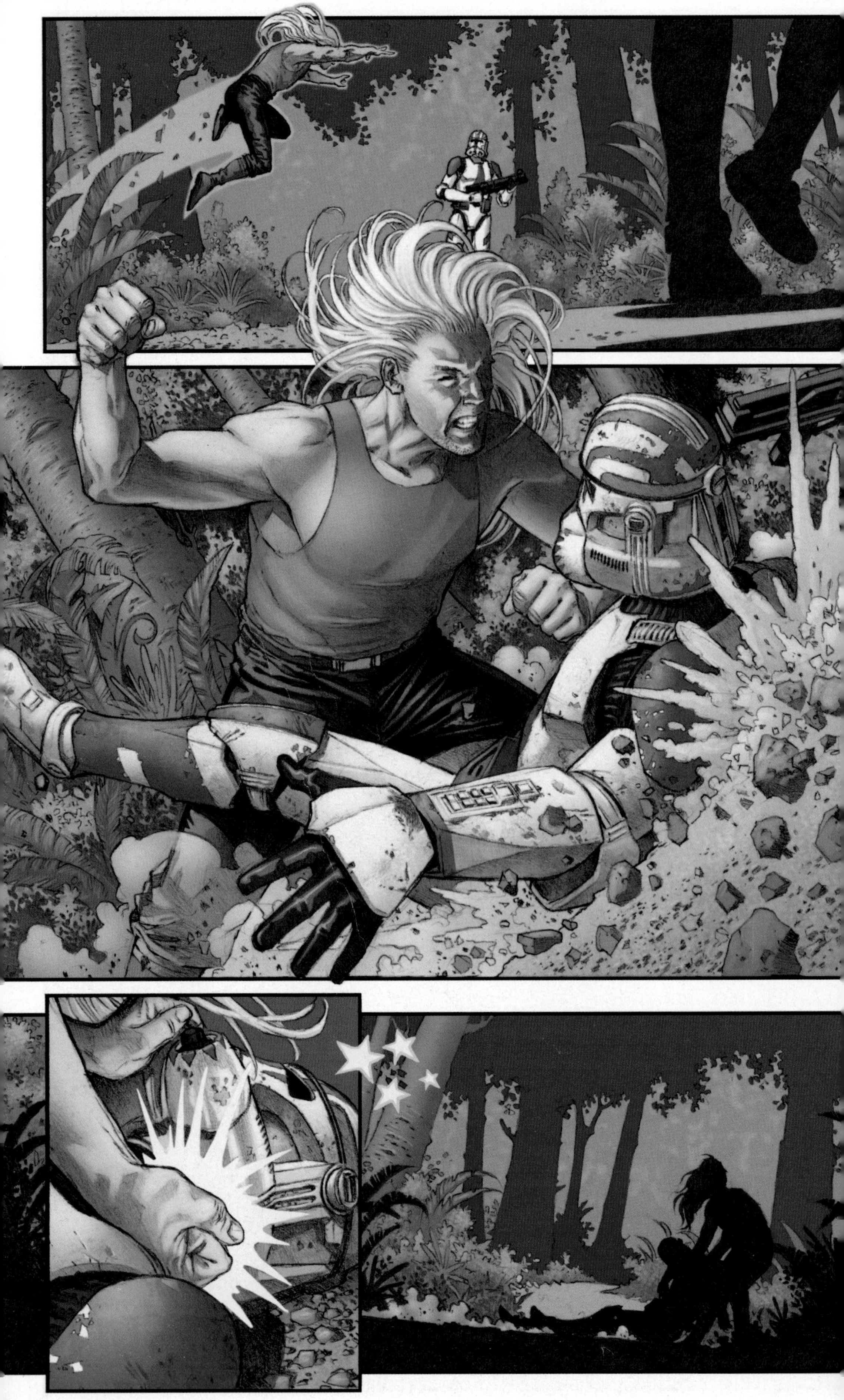

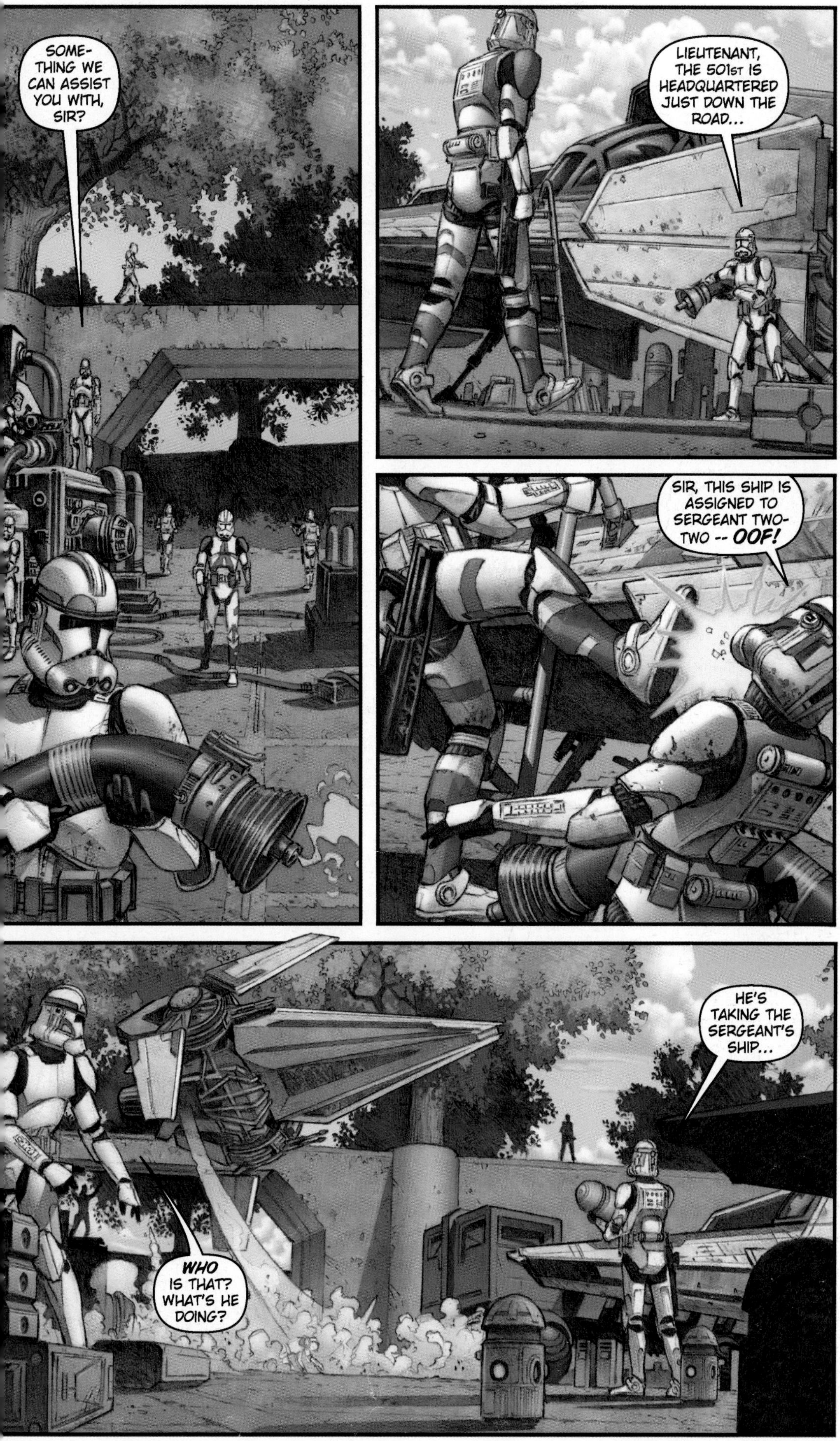
SOME-THING WE CAN ASSIST YOU WITH, SIR?
LIEUTENANT, THE 501st IS HEADQUARTERED JUST DOWN THE ROAD...
SIR, THIS SHIP IS ASSIGNED TO SERGEANT TWO-TWO -- OOF!
WHO IS THAT? WHAT'S HE DOING?
HE'S TAKING THE SERGEANT'S SHIP...

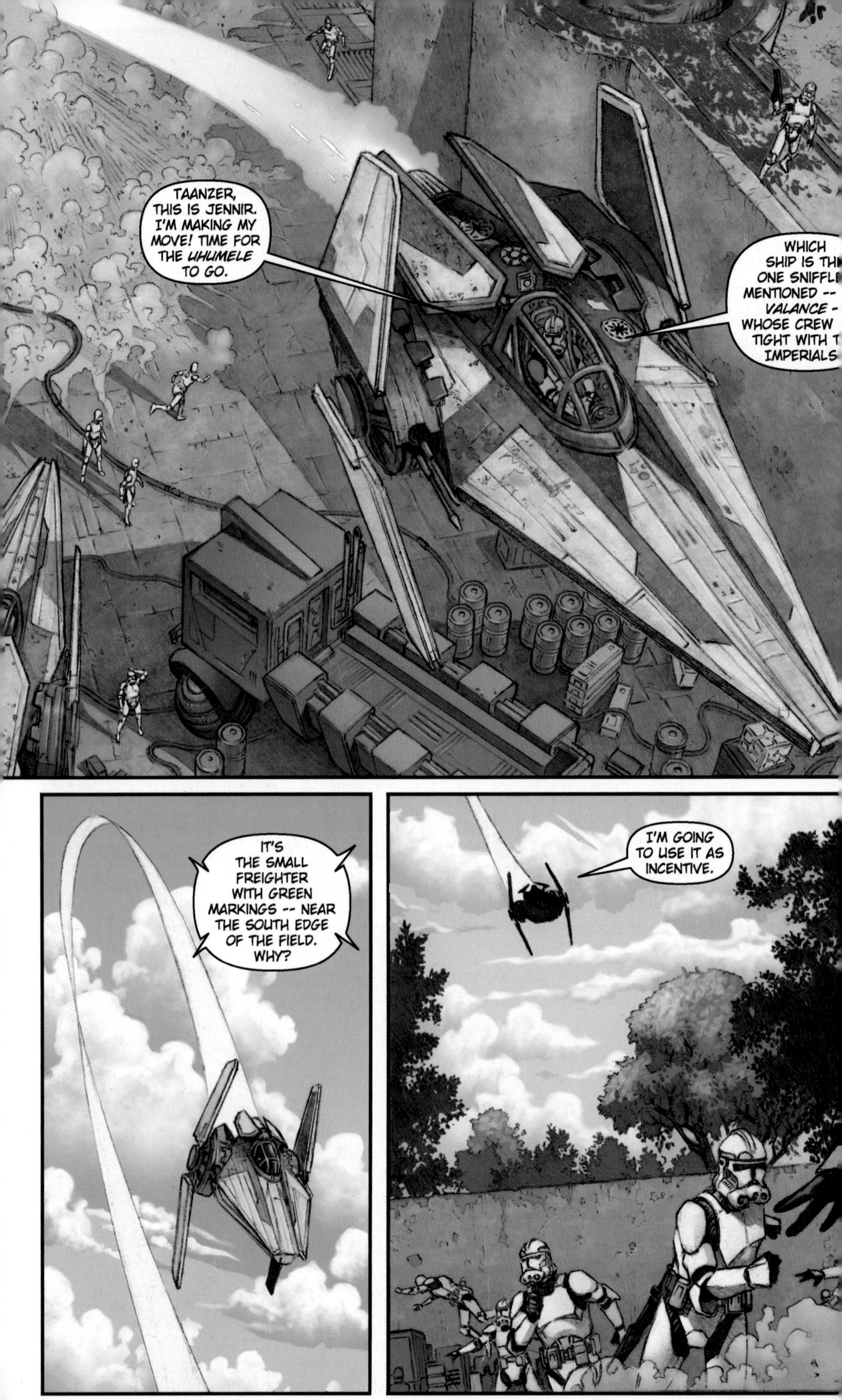

TAANZER, THIS IS JENNIR. I'M MAKING MY MOVE! TIME FOR THE *UHUMELE* TO GO.
WHICH SHIP IS TH ONE SNIFFL MENTIONED -- *VALANCE* - WHOSE CREW TIGHT WITH T IMPERIALS
IT'S THE SMALL FREIGHTER WITH GREEN MARKINGS -- NEAR THE SOUTH EDGE OF THE FIELD. WHY?
I'M GOING TO USE IT AS INCENTIVE.

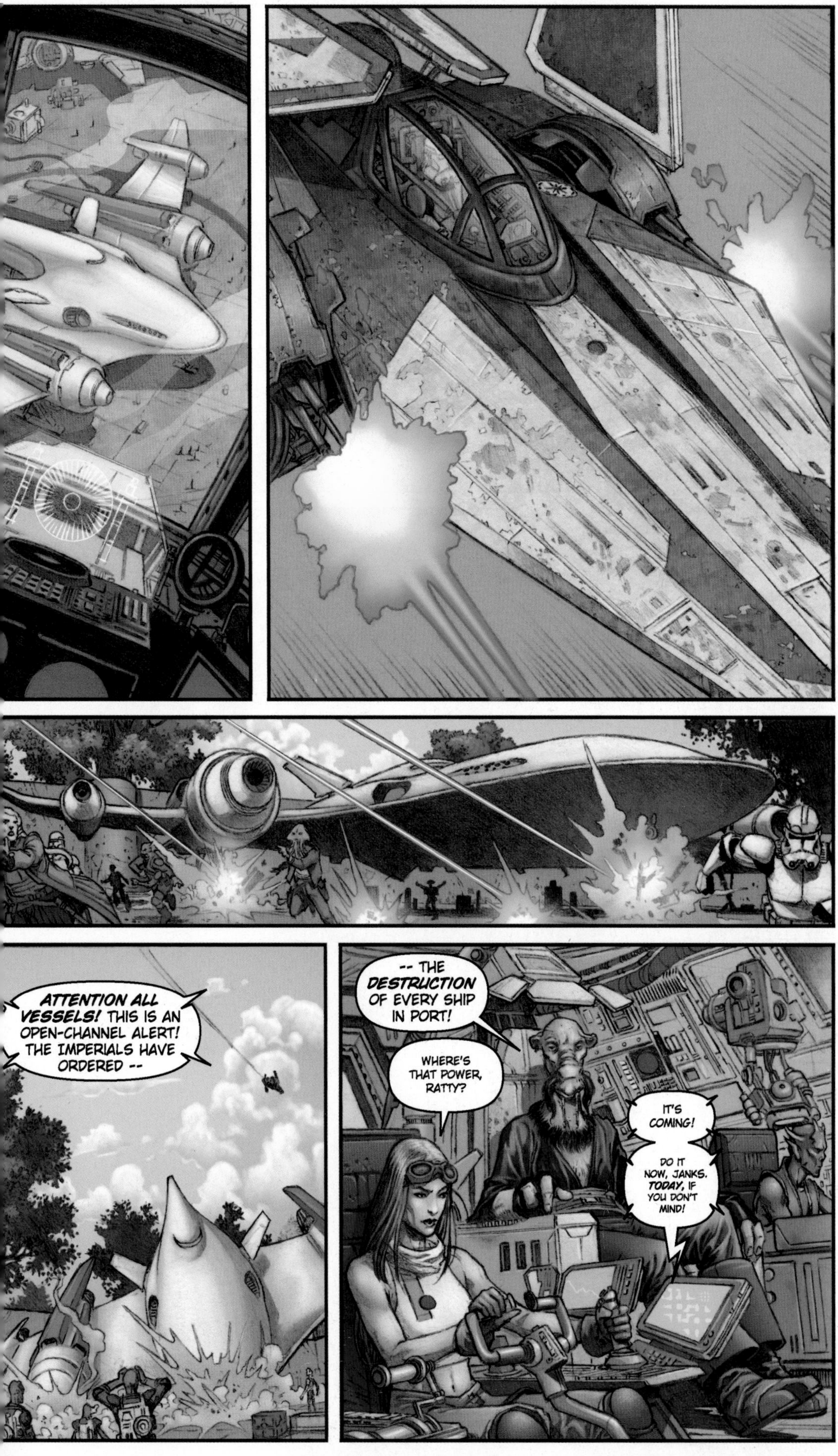
ATTENTION ALL VESSELS! THIS IS AN OPEN-CHANNEL ALERT! THE IMPERIALS HAVE ORDERED --
-- THE DESTRUCTION OF EVERY SHIP IN PORT!
WHERE'S THAT POWER, RATTY?
IT'S COMING!
DO IT NOW, JANKS. TODAY, IF YOU DON'T MIND!

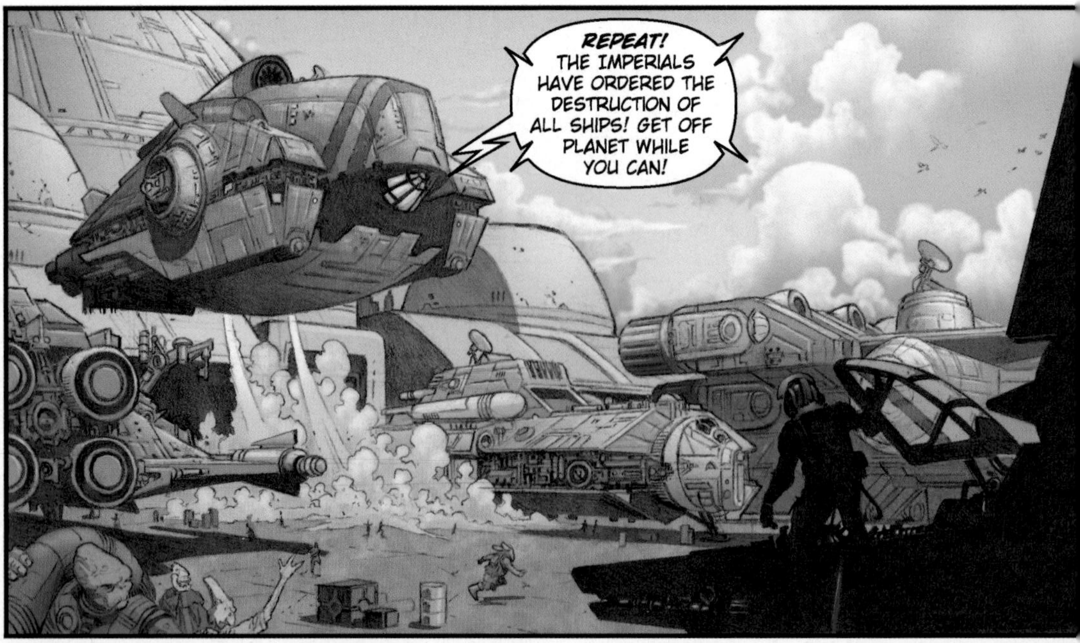
REPEAT! THE IMPERIALS HAVE ORDERED THE DESTRUCTION OF ALL SHIPS! GET OFF PLANET WHILE YOU CAN!

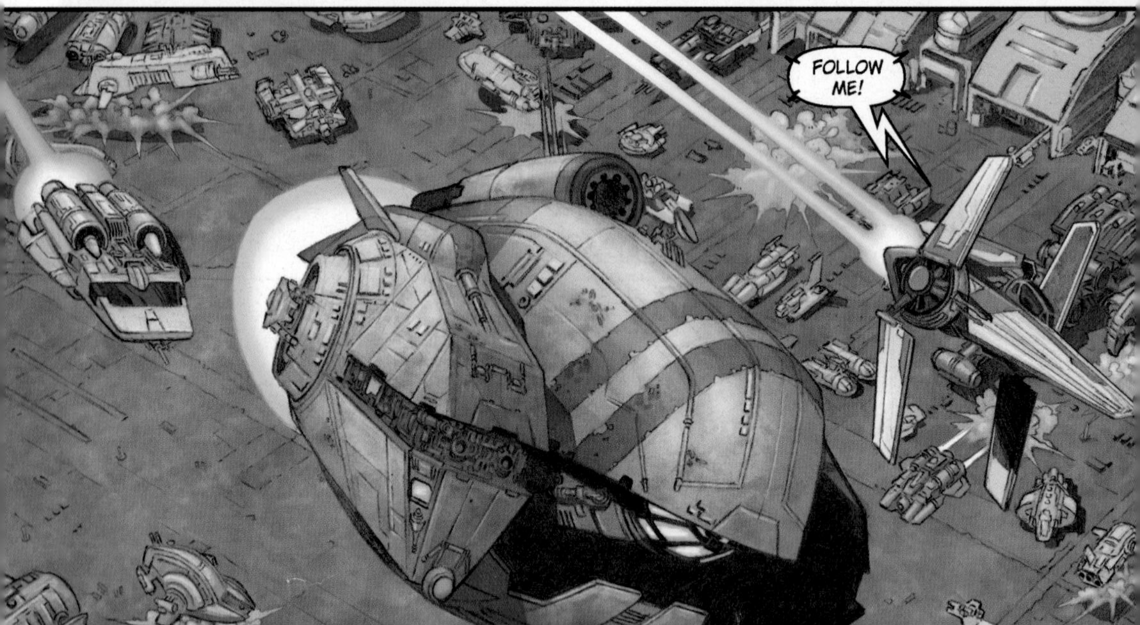
FOLLOW ME!

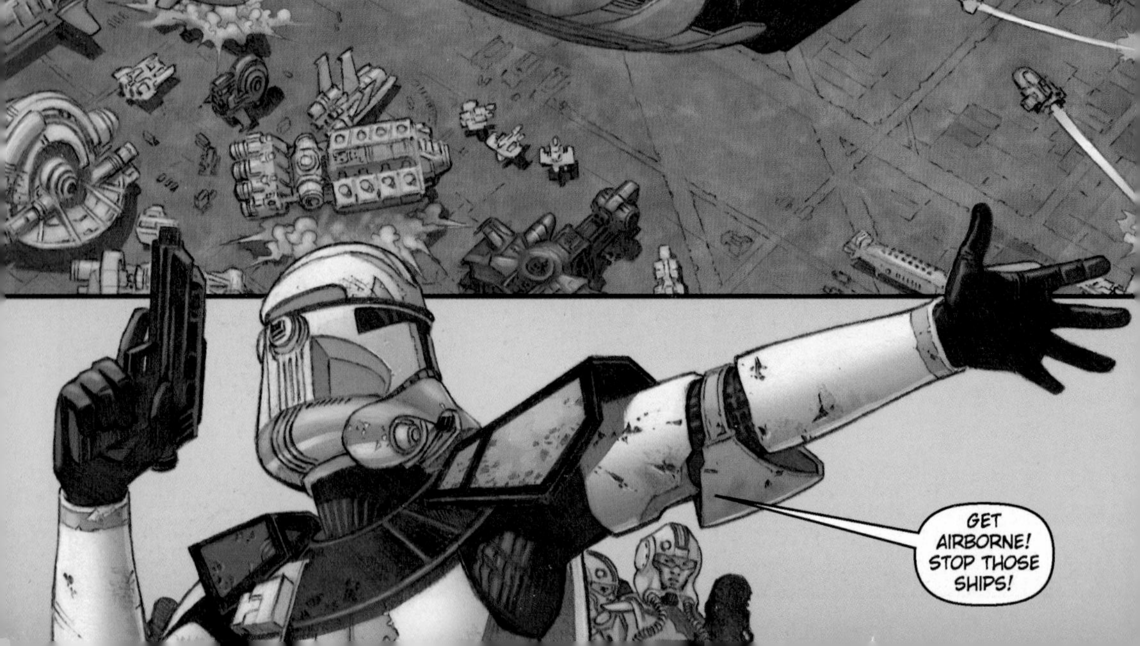
GET AIRBORNE! STOP THOSE SHIPS!

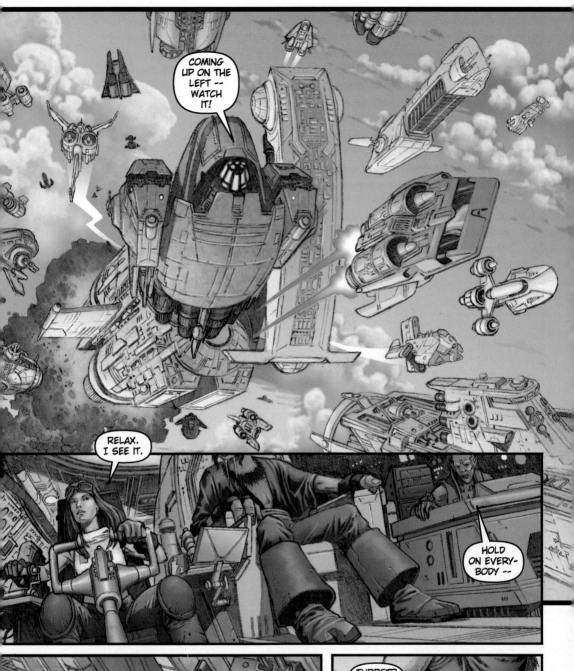

COMING UP ON THE LEFT -- WATCH IT!

RELAX. I SEE IT.

HOLD ON EVERYBODY --

-- NOT MY FAULT. *CRYS* HAS THE COM...

MEZGRAF, EXTEND THE TURRET.

RIGHT.

TURRET? *WHAT* TURRET?

"YOU'LL SEE."

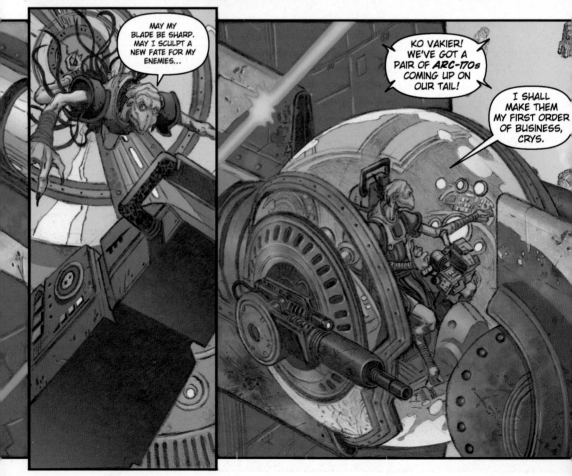

MAY MY BLADE BE SHARP. MAY I SCULPT A NEW FATE FOR MY ENEMIES...

KO VAKIER! WE'VE GOT A PAIR OF *ARC-170s* COMING UP ON OUR TAIL!

I SHALL MAKE THEM MY FIRST ORDER OF BUSINESS, CRYS.

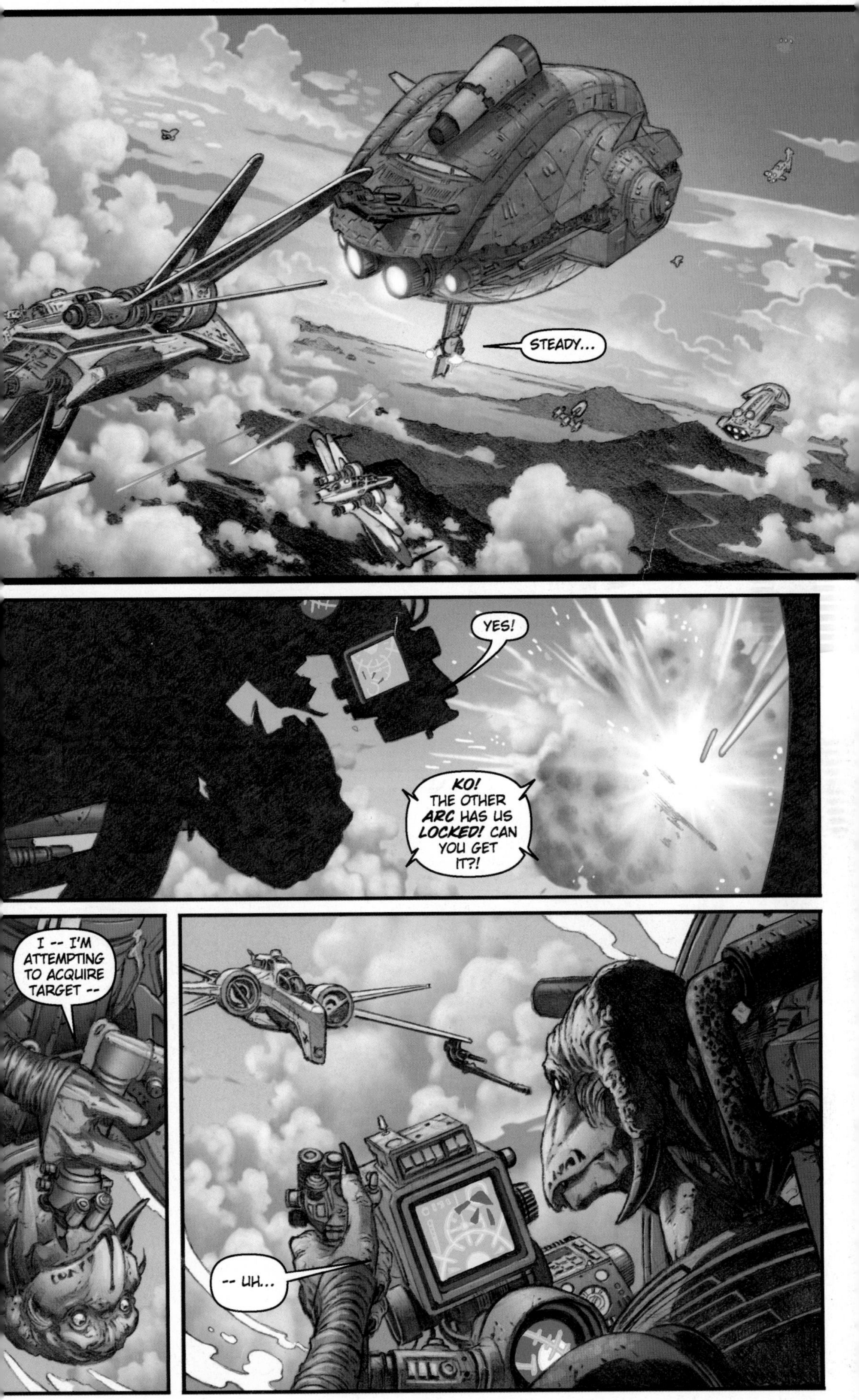
STEADY...
YES!
KO! THE OTHER ARC HAS US LOCKED! CAN YOU GET IT?!
I -- I'M ATTEMPTING TO ACQUIRE TARGET --
-- UH...

THIS IS JENNIR. I'M ON IT.

THAT WAS CUTTING IT CLOSE!

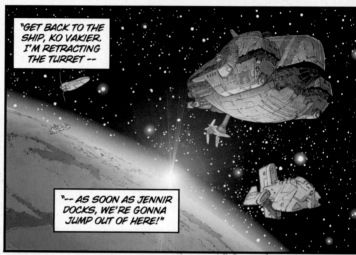

"GET BACK TO THE SHIP, KO VAKIER. I'M RETRACTING THE TURRET --

"-- AS SOON AS JENNIR DOCKS, WE'RE GONNA JUMP OUT OF HERE!"

HE'S ABOARD. MAKE THE JUMP, SNIFFLES!

IT WAS A TEAM EFFORT. WE'RE ALL EVEN.

I WISH YOU WOULD STOP CALLING ME THAT...

I OWE YOU MY LIFE, JENNIR.

GOOD WORK, GENERAL!

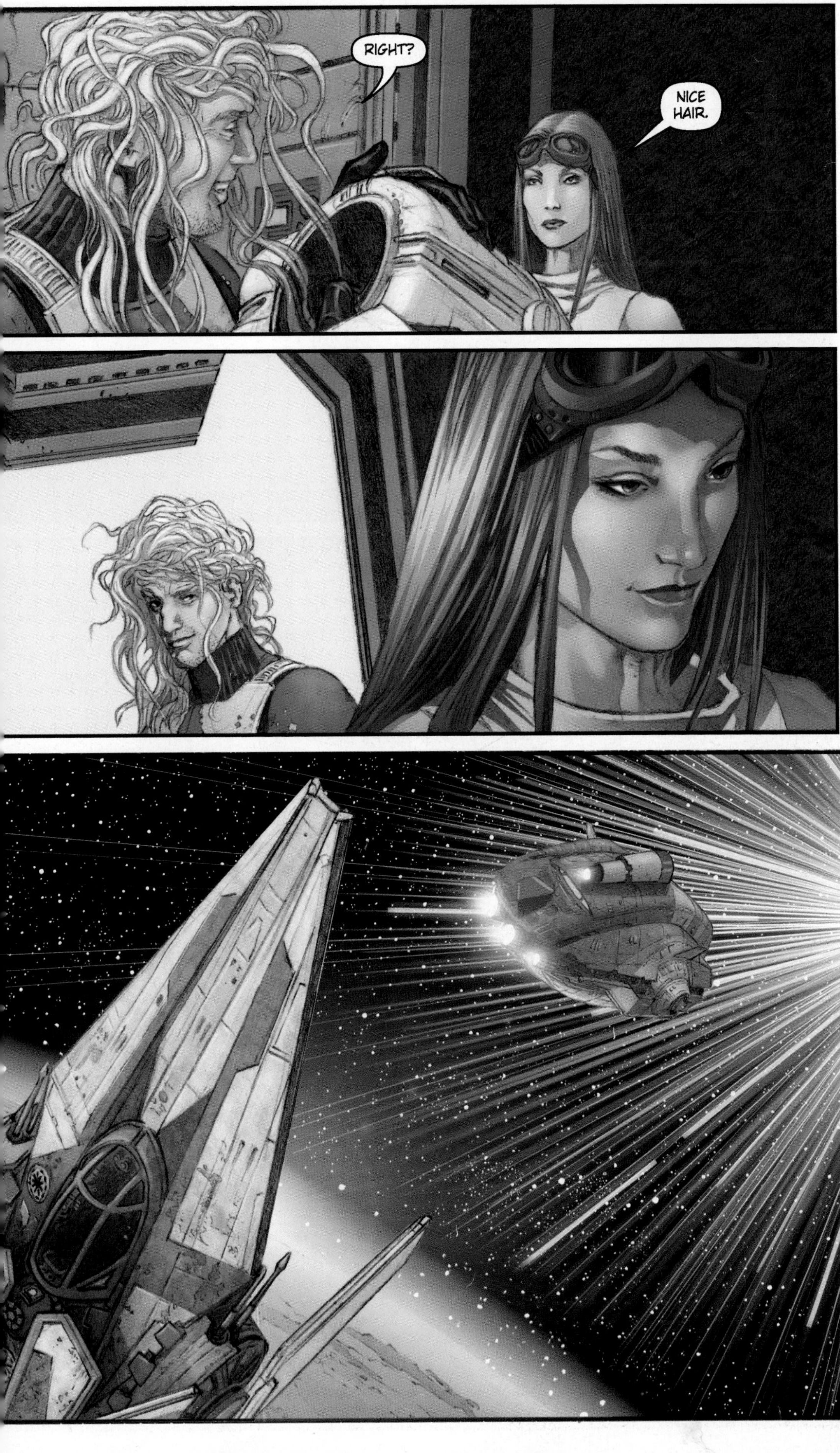
RIGHT?
NICE HAIR.

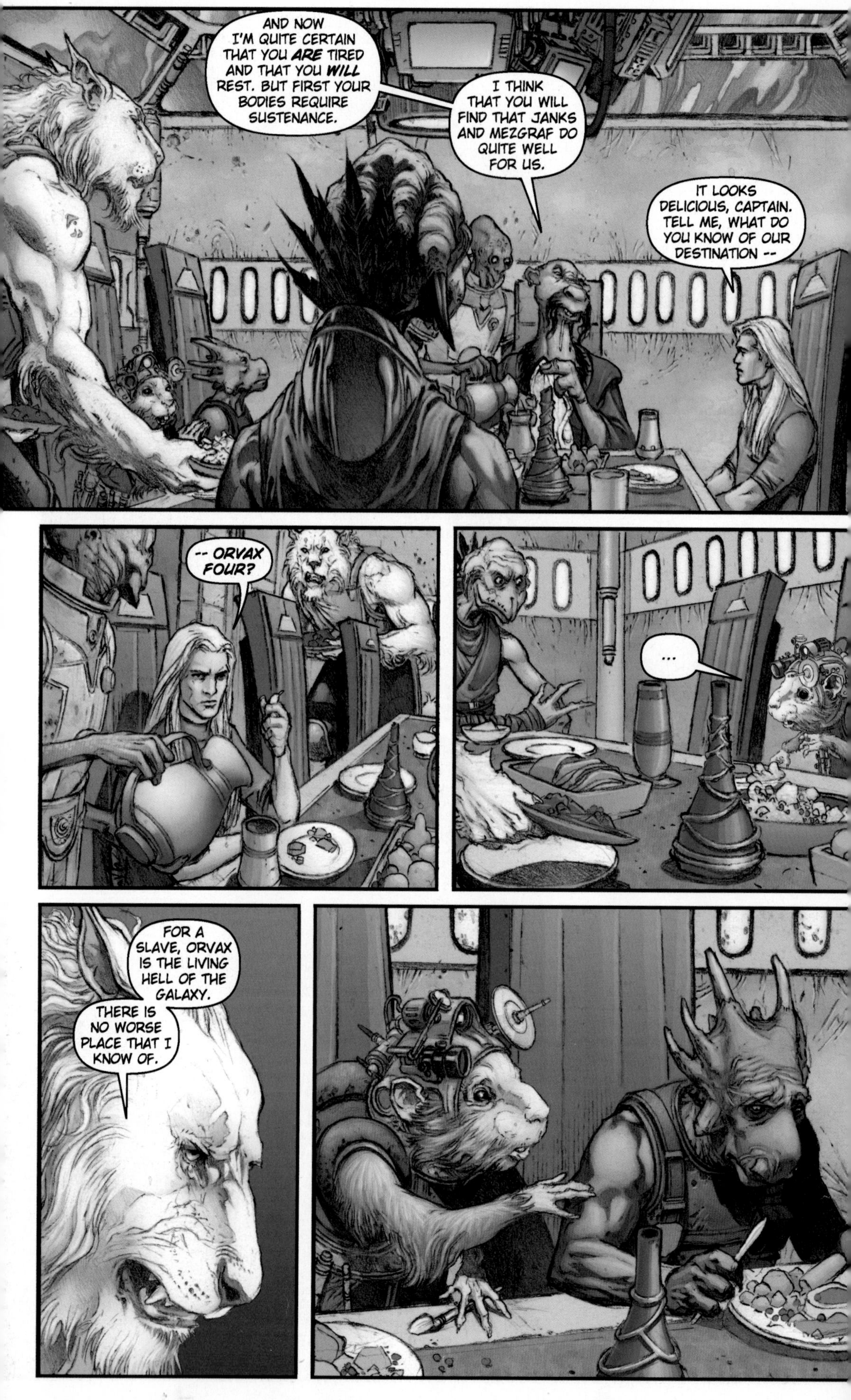
AND NOW I'M QUITE CERTAIN THAT YOU **ARE** TIRED AND THAT YOU **WILL** REST. BUT FIRST YOUR BODIES REQUIRE SUSTENANCE.
I THINK THAT YOU WILL FIND THAT JANKS AND MEZGRAF DO QUITE WELL FOR US.
IT LOOKS DELICIOUS, CAPTAIN. TELL ME, WHAT DO YOU KNOW OF OUR DESTINATION --
-- ***ORVAX FOUR?***
...
FOR A SLAVE, ORVAX IS THE LIVING HELL OF THE GALAXY.
THERE IS NO WORSE PLACE THAT I KNOW OF.

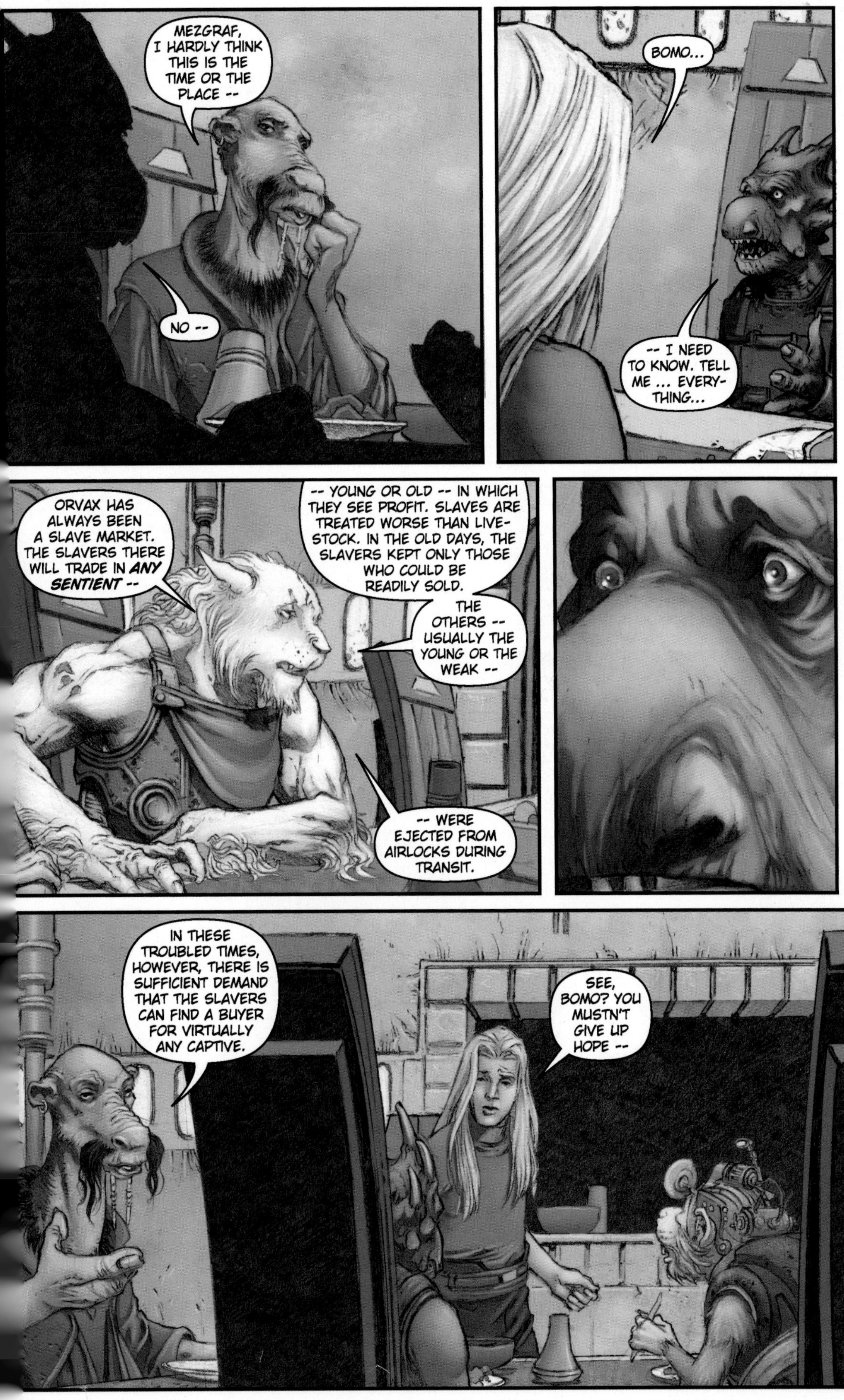
MEZGRAF, I HARDLY THINK THIS IS THE TIME OR THE PLACE --
NO --
BOMO...
-- I NEED TO KNOW. TELL ME ... EVERYTHING...
ORVAX HAS ALWAYS BEEN A SLAVE MARKET. THE SLAVERS THERE WILL TRADE IN ANY SENTIENT --
-- YOUNG OR OLD -- IN WHICH THEY SEE PROFIT. SLAVES ARE TREATED WORSE THAN LIVESTOCK. IN THE OLD DAYS, THE SLAVERS KEPT ONLY THOSE WHO COULD BE READILY SOLD.
THE OTHERS -- USUALLY THE YOUNG OR THE WEAK --
-- WERE EJECTED FROM AIRLOCKS DURING TRANSIT.
IN THESE TROUBLED TIMES, HOWEVER, THERE IS SUFFICIENT DEMAND THAT THE SLAVERS CAN FIND A BUYER FOR VIRTUALLY ANY CAPTIVE.
SEE, BOMO? YOU MUSTN'T GIVE UP HOPE --

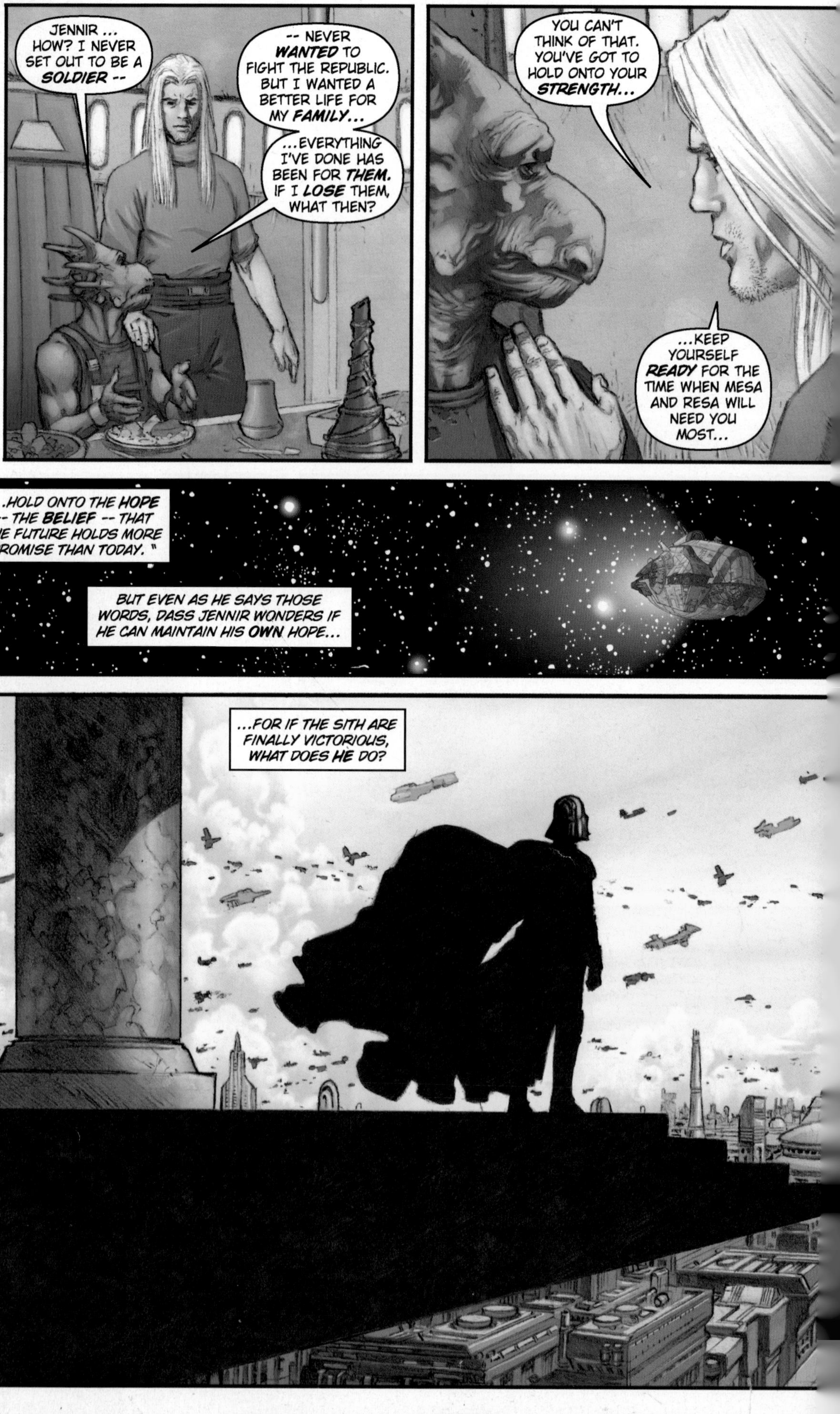
JENNIR ... HOW? I NEVER SET OUT TO BE A SOLDIER --
-- NEVER WANTED TO FIGHT THE REPUBLIC. BUT I WANTED A BETTER LIFE FOR MY FAMILY...
...EVERYTHING I'VE DONE HAS BEEN FOR THEM. IF I LOSE THEM, WHAT THEN?
YOU CAN'T THINK OF THAT. YOU'VE GOT TO HOLD ONTO YOUR STRENGTH...
...KEEP YOURSELF READY FOR THE TIME WHEN MESA AND RESA WILL NEED YOU MOST...
"...HOLD ONTO THE HOPE -- THE BELIEF -- THAT THE FUTURE HOLDS MORE PROMISE THAN TODAY."
BUT EVEN AS HE SAYS THOSE WORDS, DASS JENNIR WONDERS IF HE CAN MAINTAIN HIS OWN HOPE...
...FOR IF THE SITH ARE FINALLY VICTORIOUS, WHAT DOES HE DO?

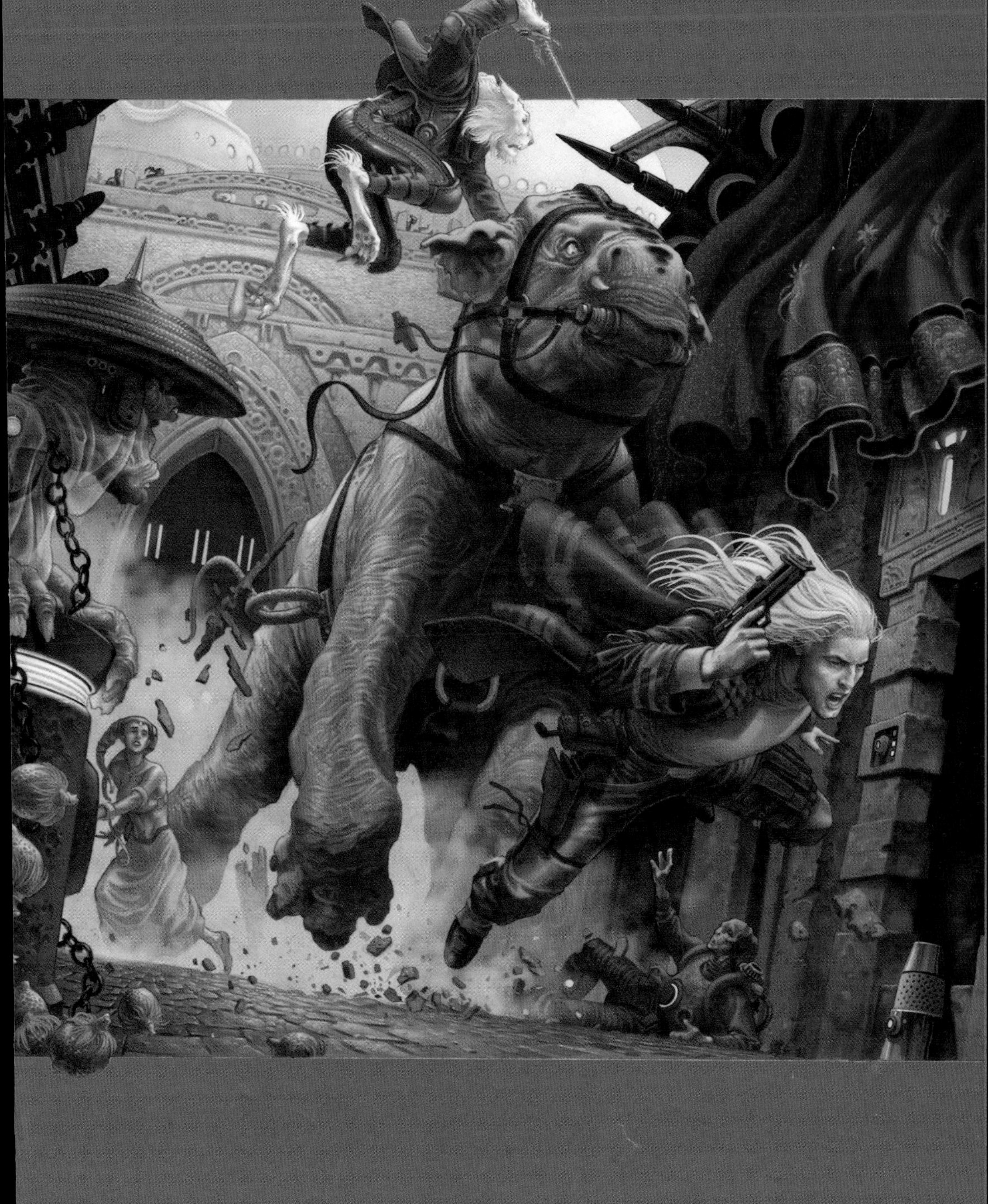

STAR WARS: DARK TIMES #3 — "THE PATH TO NOWHERE, PART 3 (OF FIVE)"

WRITER: RANDY STRADLEY (AS WELLES HARTLEY & MICK HARRISON) • ARTIST: DOUGLAS WHEATLEY • COLORIST: RONDA PATTISON
LETTERERS: MICHAEL DAVID THOMAS & DAN JACKSON • DESIGNER: DARIN FABRICK • ASSISTANT EDITOR: DAVE MARSHALL • EDITOR: RANDY STRADLEY
COVER ARTIST: DOUGLAS WHEATLEY

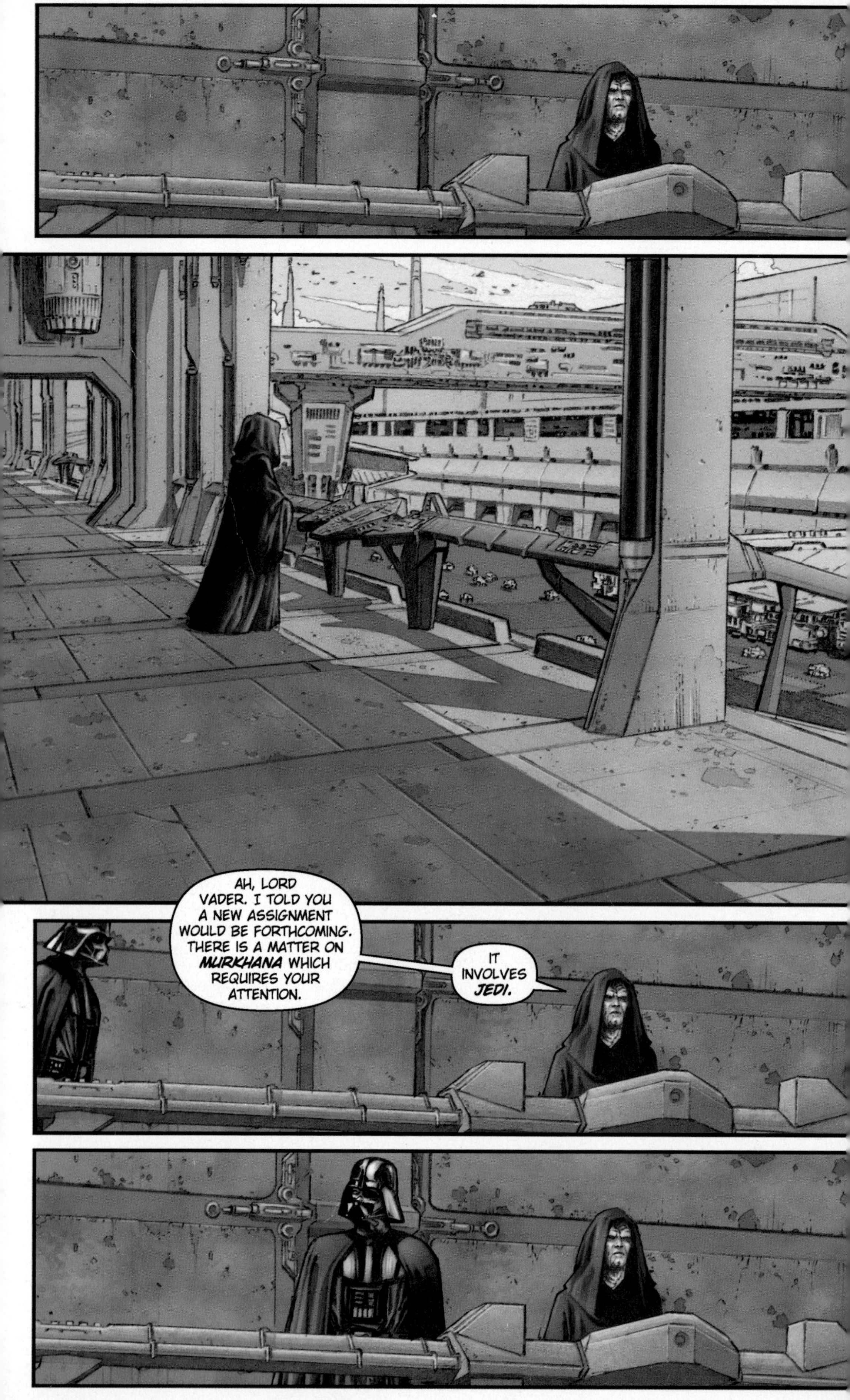

AH, LORD VADER. I TOLD YOU A NEW ASSIGNMENT WOULD BE FORTHCOMING. THERE IS A MATTER ON *MURKHANA* WHICH REQUIRES YOUR ATTENTION.
IT INVOLVES *JEDI.*

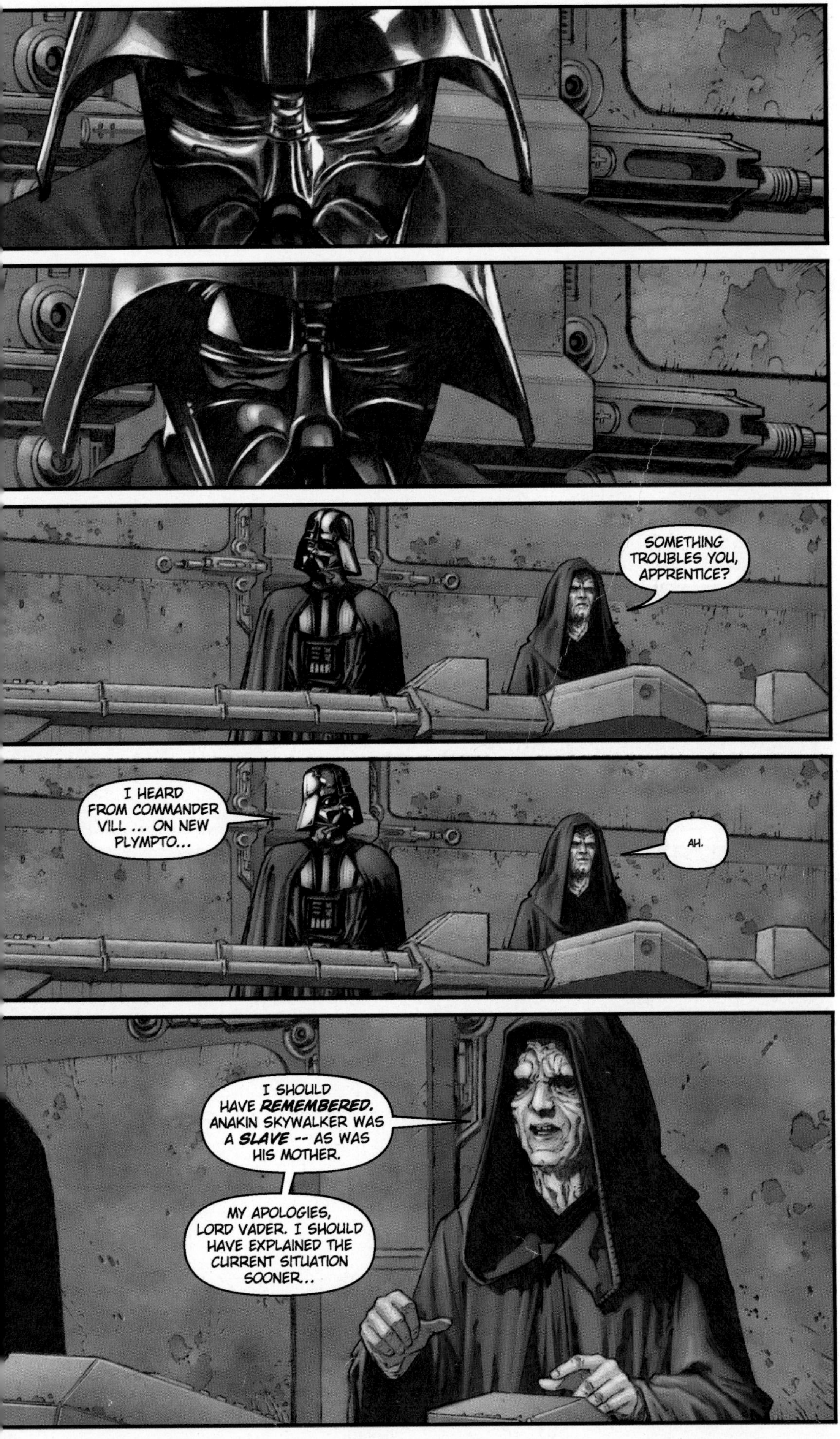
SOMETHING TROUBLES YOU, APPRENTICE?
I HEARD FROM COMMANDER VILL ... ON NEW PLYMPTO...
AH.
I SHOULD HAVE **REMEMBERED.** ANAKIN SKYWALKER WAS A **SLAVE** -- AS WAS HIS MOTHER.
MY APOLOGIES, LORD VADER. I SHOULD HAVE EXPLAINED THE CURRENT SITUATION SOONER..

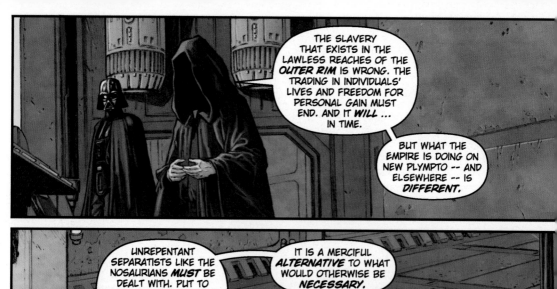

THE SLAVERY THAT EXISTS IN THE LAWLESS REACHES OF THE *OUTER RIM* IS WRONG. THE TRADING IN INDIVIDUALS' LIVES AND FREEDOM FOR PERSONAL GAIN MUST END. AND IT *WILL* ... IN TIME.

BUT WHAT THE EMPIRE IS DOING ON NEW PLYMPTO -- AND ELSEWHERE -- IS *DIFFERENT*.

UNREPENTANT SEPARATISTS LIKE THE NOSAURIANS *MUST* BE DEALT WITH. PUT TO WORK, THEY WILL MAKE A POSITIVE *CONTRIBUTION* TO THE EMPIRE, AND THEIR LIVES WILL BE *SPARED*.

IT IS A MERCIFUL *ALTERNATIVE* TO WHAT WOULD OTHERWISE BE *NECESSARY*.

I'M CERTAIN YOU UNDERSTAND.

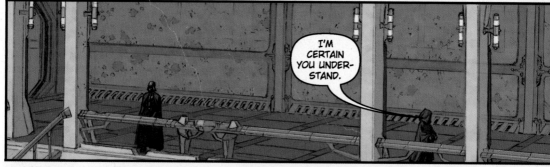

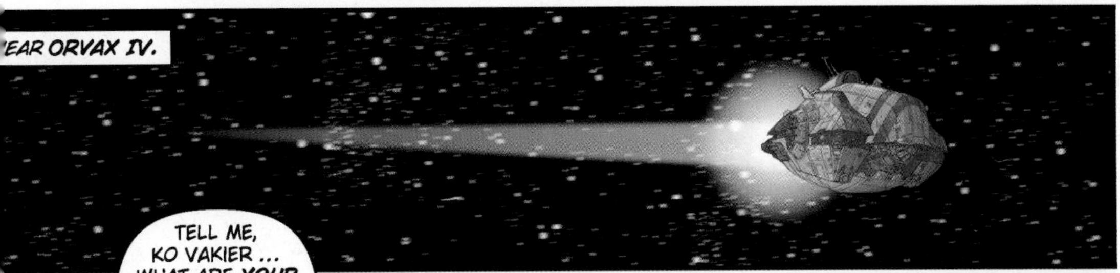
EAR ORVAX IV.

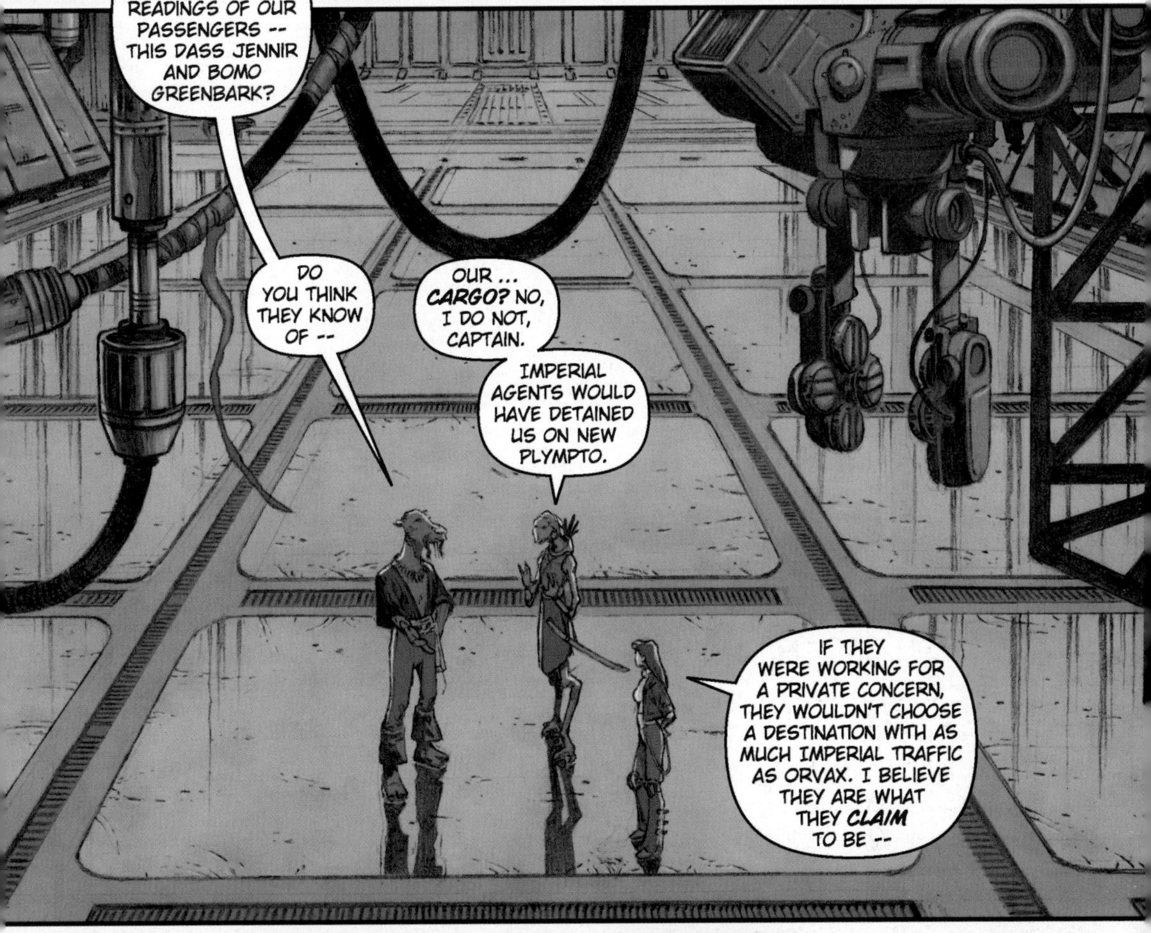
TELL ME, KO VAKIER ... WHAT ARE YOUR READINGS OF OUR PASSENGERS -- THIS DASS JENNIR AND BOMO GREENBARK?
DO YOU THINK THEY KNOW OF --
OUR ... CARGO? NO, I DO NOT, CAPTAIN.
IMPERIAL AGENTS WOULD HAVE DETAINED US ON NEW PLYMPTO.
IF THEY WERE WORKING FOR A PRIVATE CONCERN, THEY WOULDN'T CHOOSE A DESTINATION WITH AS MUCH IMPERIAL TRAFFIC AS ORVAX. I BELIEVE THEY ARE WHAT THEY CLAIM TO BE --

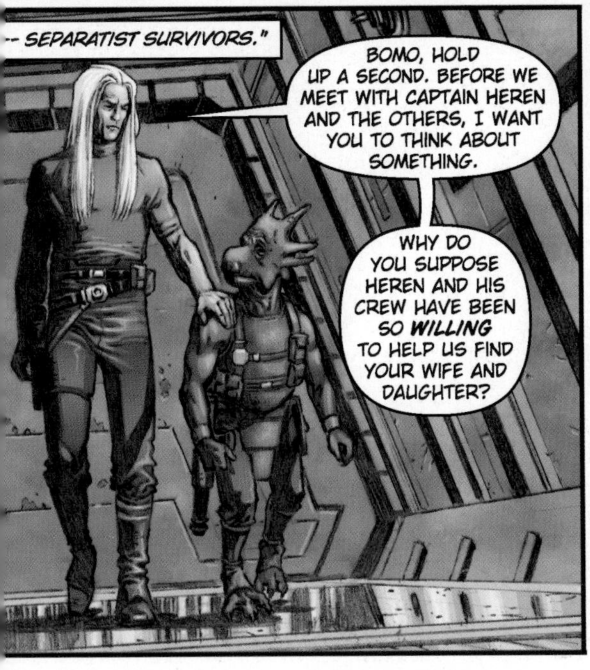
-- SEPARATIST SURVIVORS."
BOMO, HOLD UP A SECOND. BEFORE WE MEET WITH CAPTAIN HEREN AND THE OTHERS, I WANT YOU TO THINK ABOUT SOMETHING.
WHY DO YOU SUPPOSE HEREN AND HIS CREW HAVE BEEN SO WILLING TO HELP US FIND YOUR WIFE AND DAUGHTER?

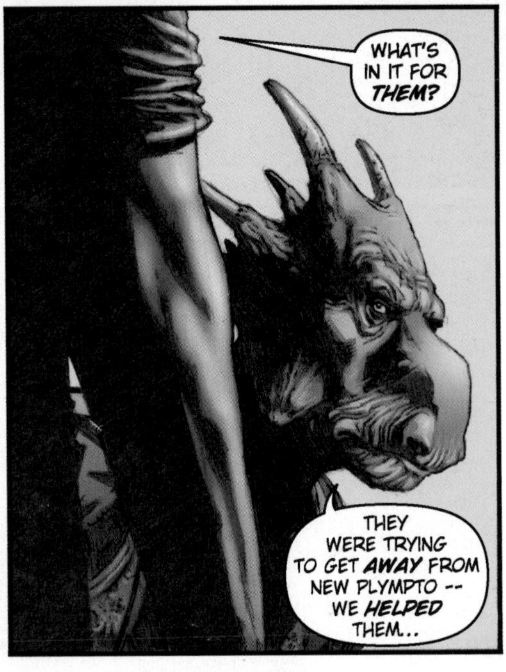
WHAT'S IN IT FOR THEM?
THEY WERE TRYING TO GET AWAY FROM NEW PLYMPTO -- WE HELPED THEM...

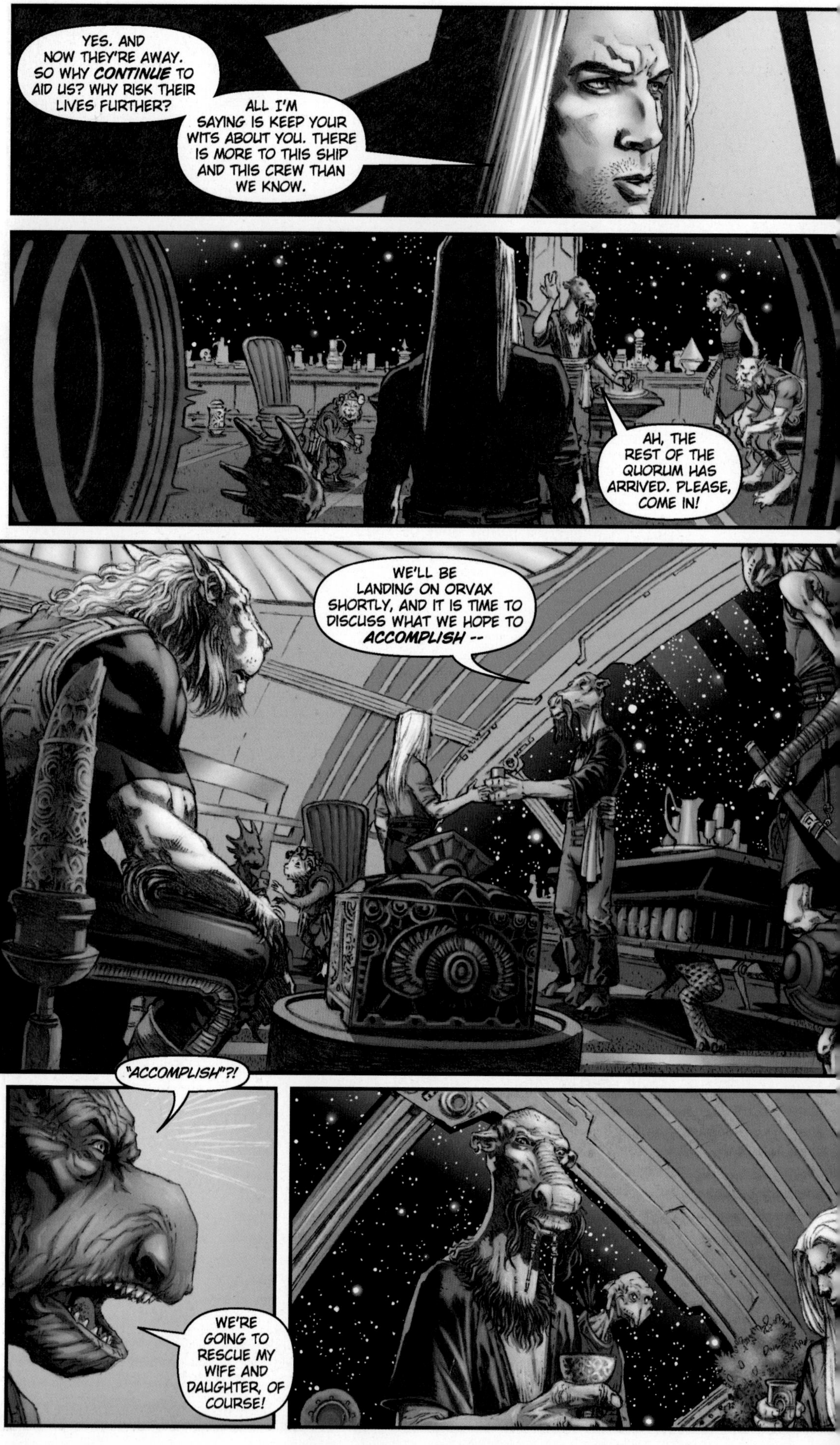
YES. AND NOW THEY'RE AWAY. SO WHY *CONTINUE* TO AID US? WHY RISK THEIR LIVES FURTHER?
ALL I'M SAYING IS KEEP YOUR WITS ABOUT YOU. THERE IS MORE TO THIS SHIP AND THIS CREW THAN WE KNOW.
AH, THE REST OF THE QUORUM HAS ARRIVED. PLEASE, COME IN!
WE'LL BE LANDING ON ORVAX SHORTLY, AND IT IS TIME TO DISCUSS WHAT WE HOPE TO *ACCOMPLISH* --
"*ACCOMPLISH*"?!
WE'RE GOING TO RESCUE MY WIFE AND DAUGHTER, OF COURSE!

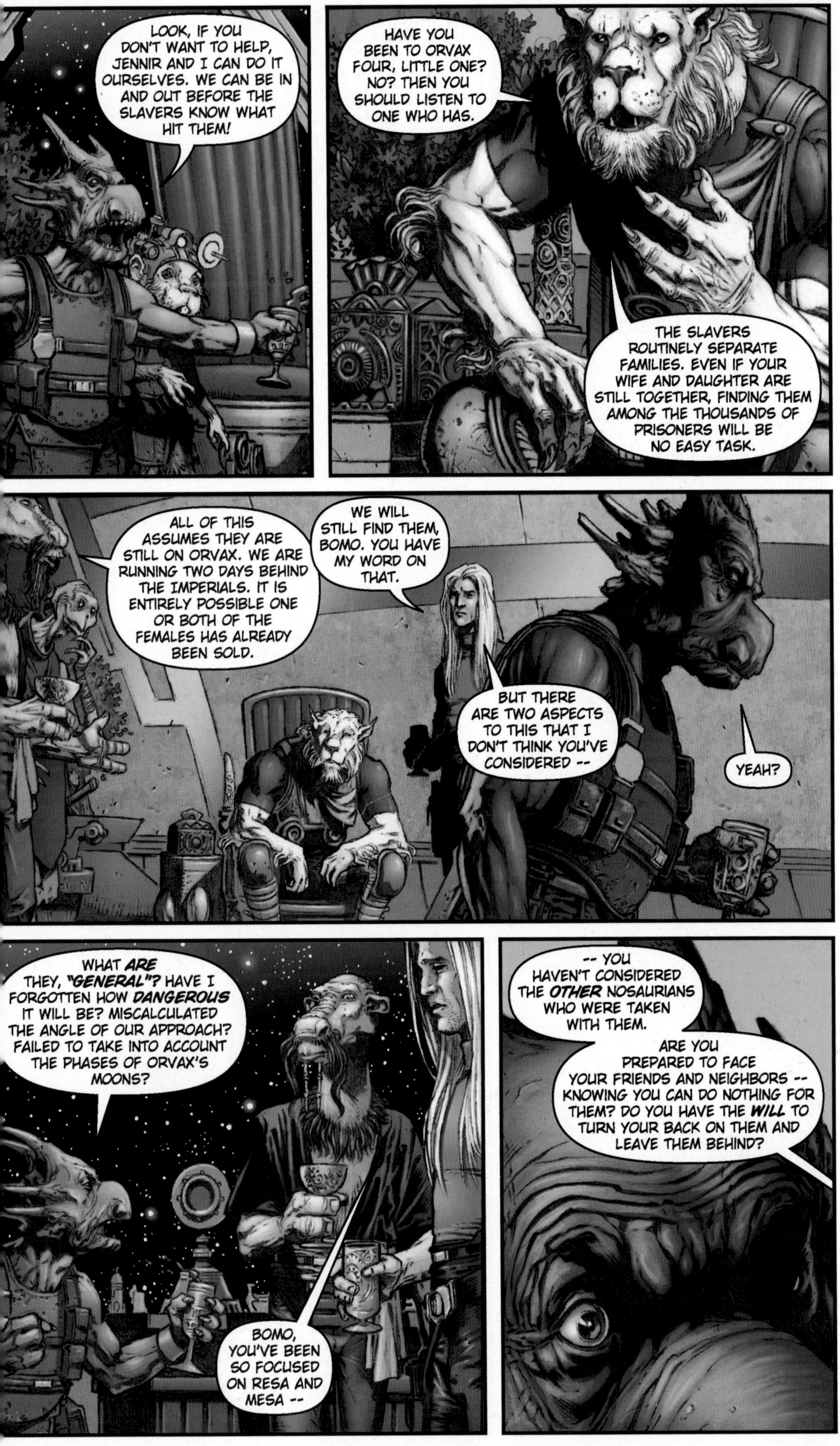
LOOK, IF YOU DON'T WANT TO HELP, JENNIR AND I CAN DO IT OURSELVES. WE CAN BE IN AND OUT BEFORE THE SLAVERS KNOW WHAT HIT THEM!
HAVE YOU BEEN TO ORVAX FOUR, LITTLE ONE? NO? THEN YOU SHOULD LISTEN TO ONE WHO HAS.
THE SLAVERS ROUTINELY SEPARATE FAMILIES. EVEN IF YOUR WIFE AND DAUGHTER ARE STILL TOGETHER, FINDING THEM AMONG THE THOUSANDS OF PRISONERS WILL BE NO EASY TASK.
ALL OF THIS ASSUMES THEY ARE STILL ON ORVAX. WE ARE RUNNING TWO DAYS BEHIND THE IMPERIALS. IT IS ENTIRELY POSSIBLE ONE OR BOTH OF THE FEMALES HAS ALREADY BEEN SOLD.
WE WILL STILL FIND THEM, BOMO. YOU HAVE MY WORD ON THAT.
BUT THERE ARE TWO ASPECTS TO THIS THAT I DON'T THINK YOU'VE CONSIDERED --
YEAH?
WHAT *ARE* THEY, *"GENERAL"*? HAVE I FORGOTTEN HOW *DANGEROUS* IT WILL BE? MISCALCULATED THE ANGLE OF OUR APPROACH? FAILED TO TAKE INTO ACCOUNT THE PHASES OF ORVAX'S MOONS?
BOMO, YOU'VE BEEN SO FOCUSED ON RESA AND MESA --
-- YOU HAVEN'T CONSIDERED THE *OTHER* NOSAURIANS WHO WERE TAKEN WITH THEM.
ARE YOU PREPARED TO FACE YOUR FRIENDS AND NEIGHBORS -- KNOWING YOU CAN DO NOTHING FOR THEM? DO YOU HAVE THE *WILL* TO TURN YOUR BACK ON THEM AND LEAVE THEM BEHIND?

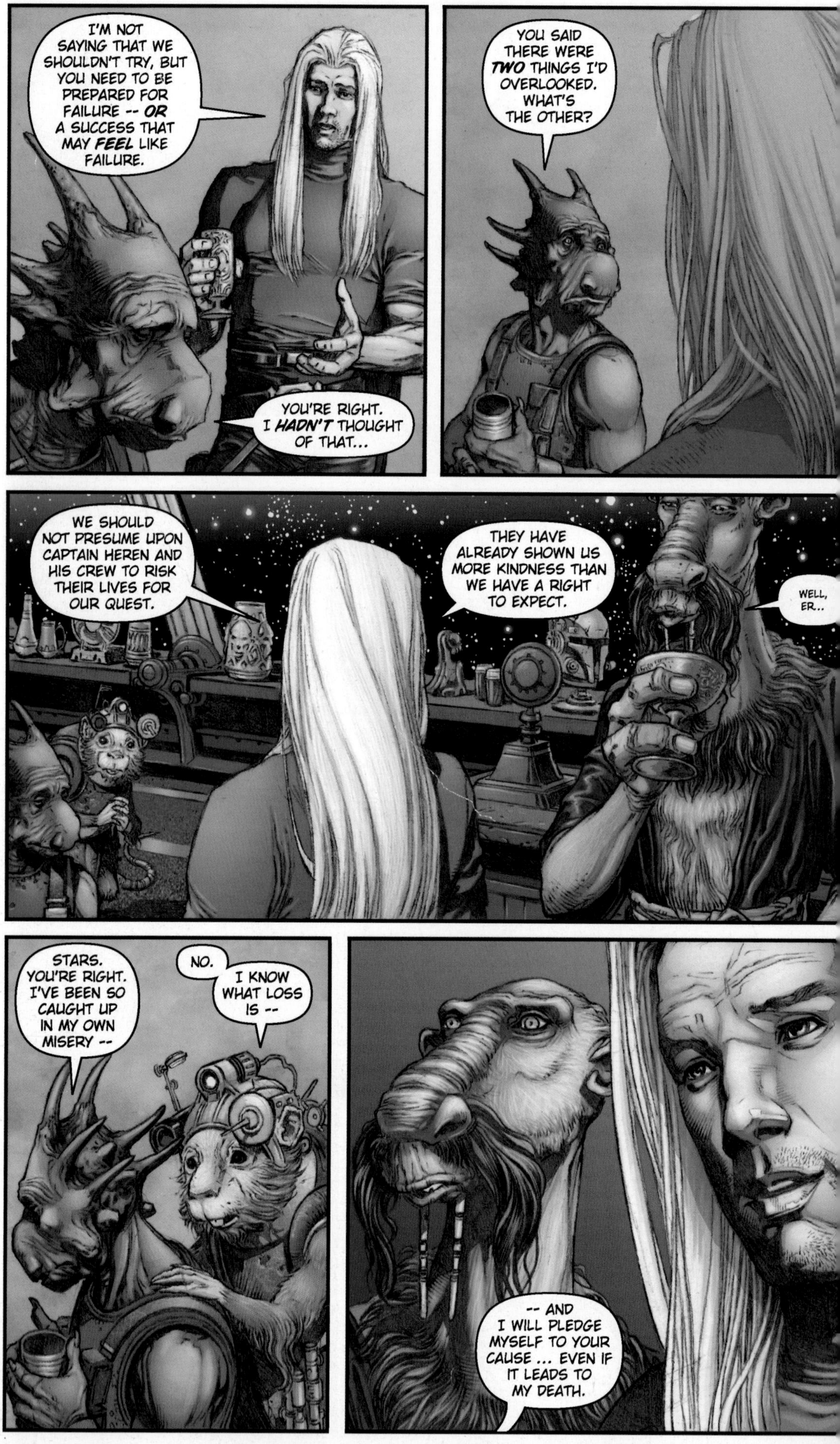
I'M NOT SAYING THAT WE SHOULDN'T TRY, BUT YOU NEED TO BE PREPARED FOR FAILURE -- OR A SUCCESS THAT MAY FEEL LIKE FAILURE.
YOU'RE RIGHT. I HADN'T THOUGHT OF THAT...
YOU SAID THERE WERE TWO THINGS I'D OVERLOOKED. WHAT'S THE OTHER?
WE SHOULD NOT PRESUME UPON CAPTAIN HEREN AND HIS CREW TO RISK THEIR LIVES FOR OUR QUEST.
THEY HAVE ALREADY SHOWN US MORE KINDNESS THAN WE HAVE A RIGHT TO EXPECT.
WELL, ER...
STARS. YOU'RE RIGHT. I'VE BEEN SO CAUGHT UP IN MY OWN MISERY --
NO.
I KNOW WHAT LOSS IS --
-- AND I WILL PLEDGE MYSELF TO YOUR CAUSE ... EVEN IF IT LEADS TO MY DEATH.

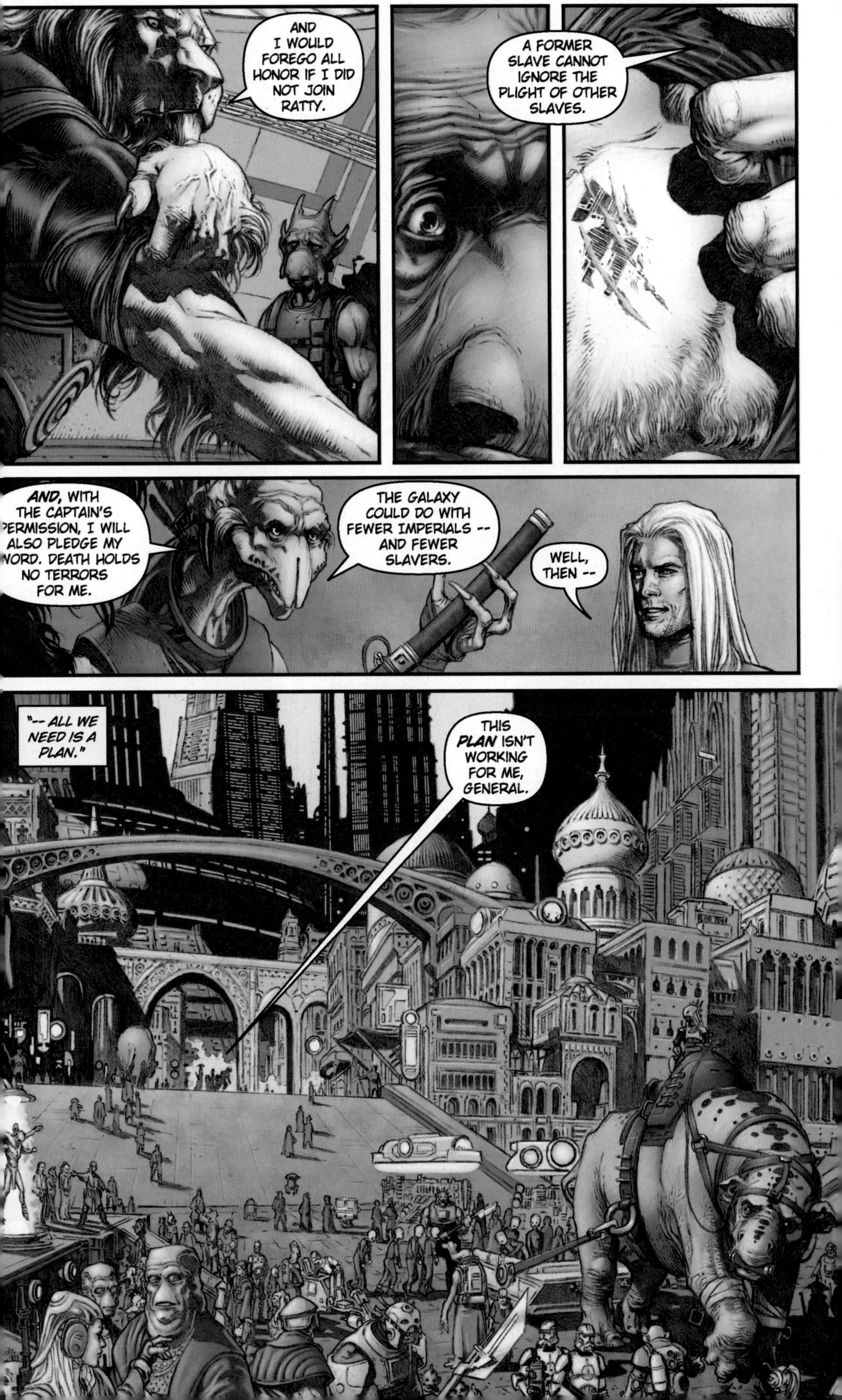
AND I WOULD FOREGO ALL HONOR IF I DID NOT JOIN RATTY.
A FORMER SLAVE CANNOT IGNORE THE PLIGHT OF OTHER SLAVES.
AND, WITH THE CAPTAIN'S PERMISSION, I WILL ALSO PLEDGE MY WORD. DEATH HOLDS NO TERRORS FOR ME.
THE GALAXY COULD DO WITH FEWER IMPERIALS -- AND FEWER SLAVERS.
WELL, THEN --
"-- ALL WE NEED IS A PLAN."
THIS PLAN ISN'T WORKING FOR ME, GENERAL.

BOMO! I TOLD YOU NOT TO SPEAK EXCEPT IN JAWAESE!

YEAH, WELL THESE LIGHTS ARE *BLINDING* ME --

-- AND I DON'T *SPEAK* JAWAESE!

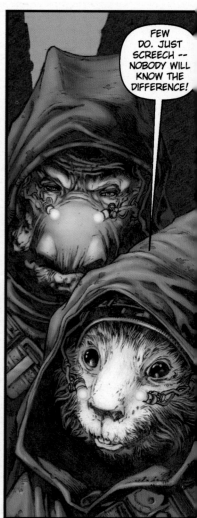

FEW DO. JUST SCREECH -- NOBODY WILL KNOW THE DIFFERENCE!

QUIET! AND LOOK FOR NOSAURIANS.

WHICH WAY, MEZGRAF?

SLAVES ARE KEPT IN THE LOWER LEVELS UNTIL THEY'RE BROUGHT UP FOR SALE.

FIND A RAMP LEADING DOWN.

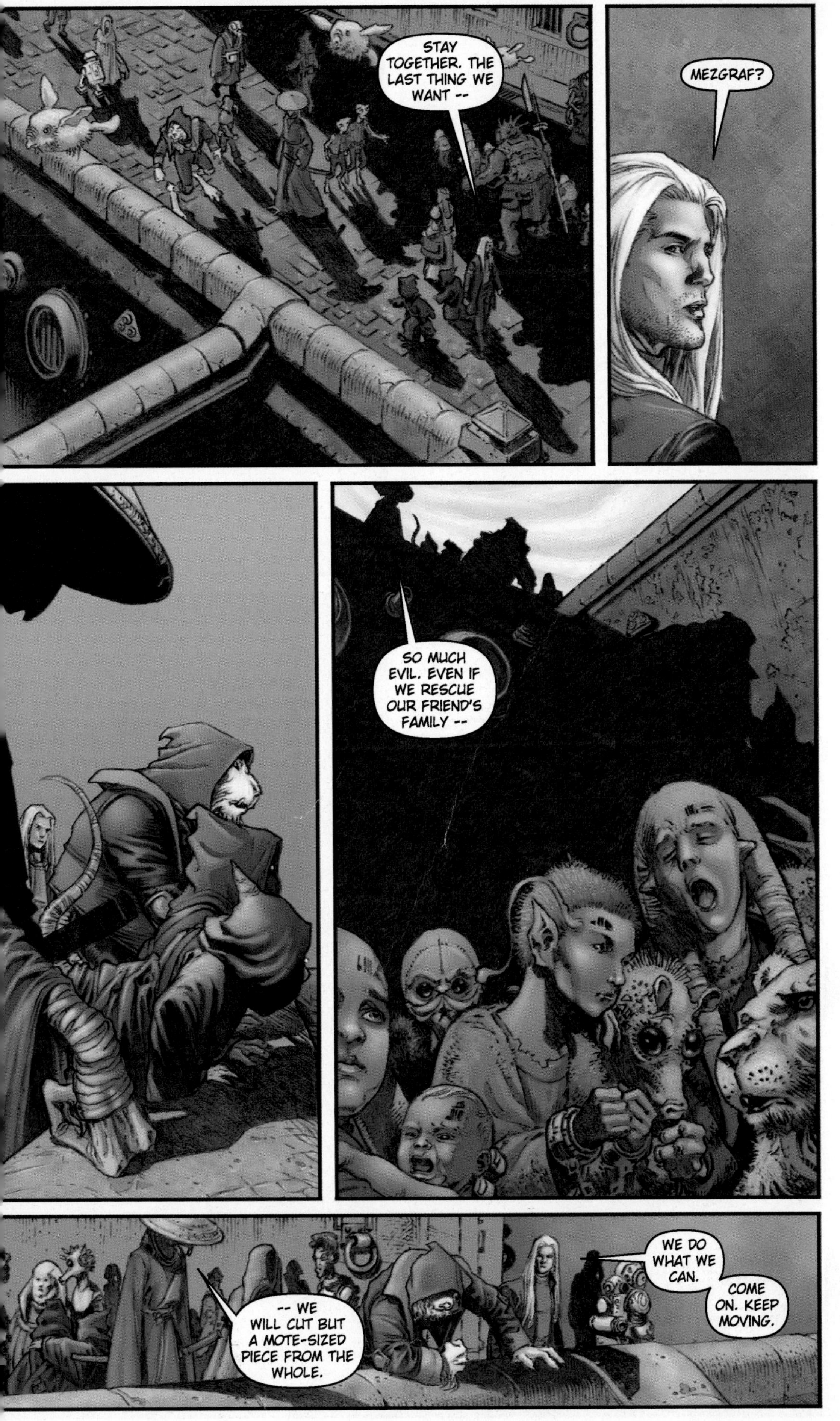
STAY TOGETHER. THE LAST THING WE WANT --
MEZGRAF?
SO MUCH EVIL. EVEN IF WE RESCUE OUR FRIEND'S FAMILY --
-- WE WILL CUT BUT A MOTE-SIZED PIECE FROM THE WHOLE.
WE DO WHAT WE CAN.
COME ON. KEEP MOVING.

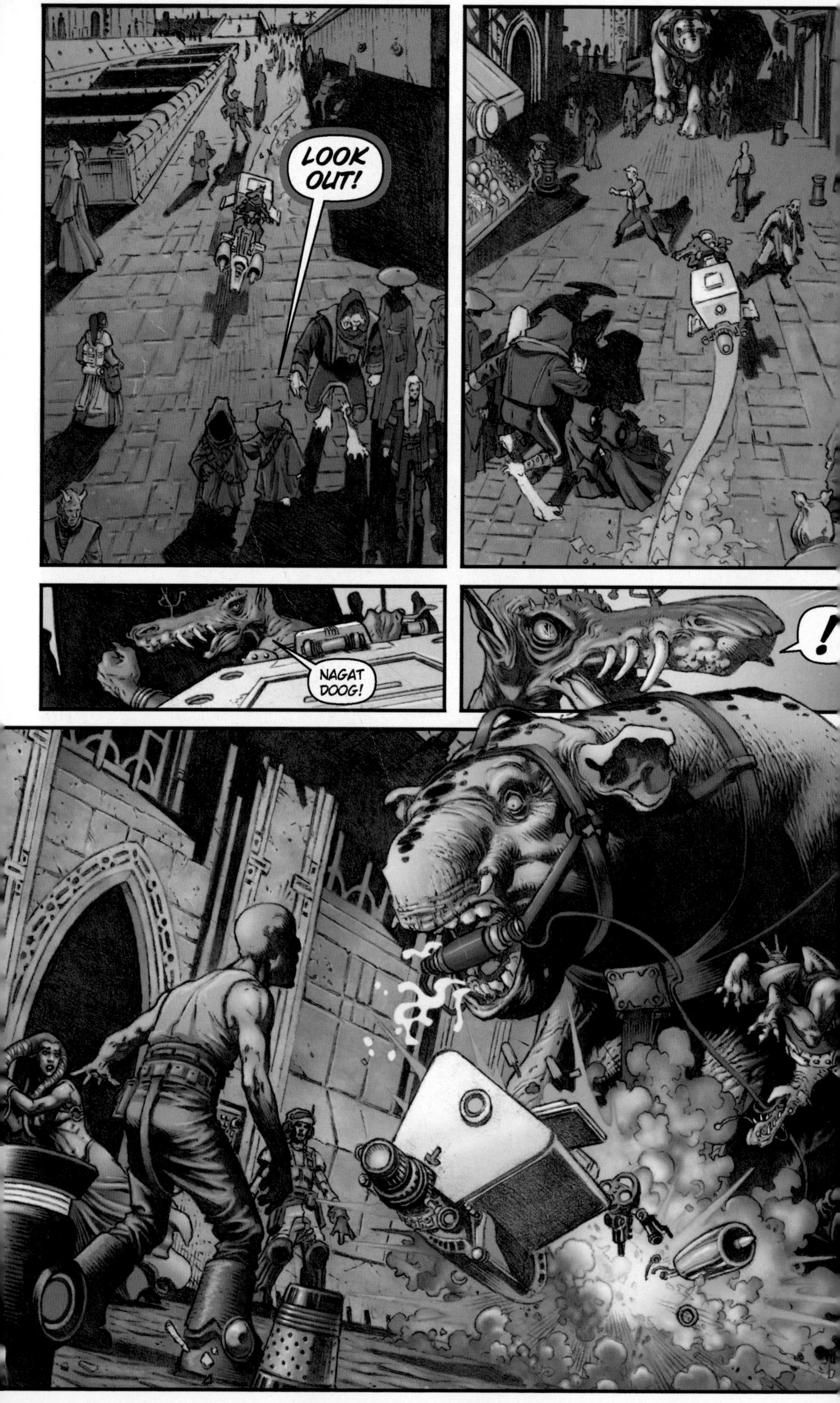
LOOK OUT!
NAGAT DOOG!
!

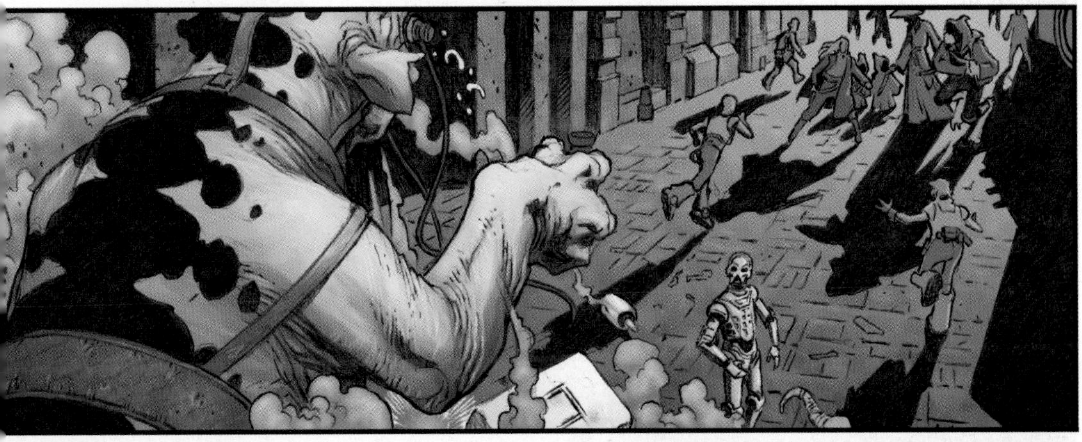

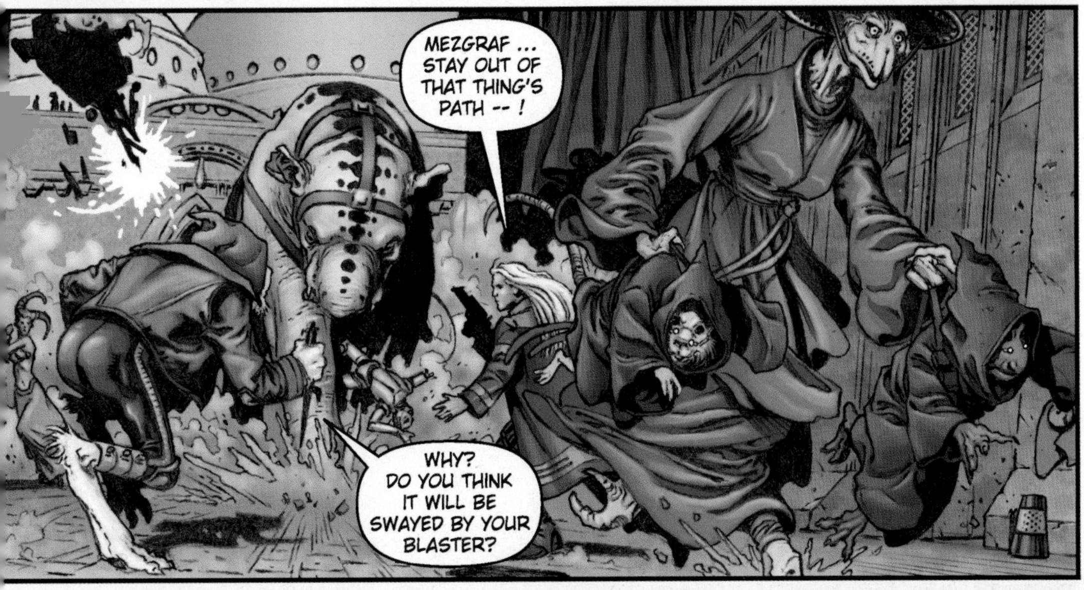

MEZGRAF ... STAY OUT OF THAT THING'S PATH -- !
WHY? DO YOU THINK IT WILL BE SWAYED BY YOUR BLASTER?

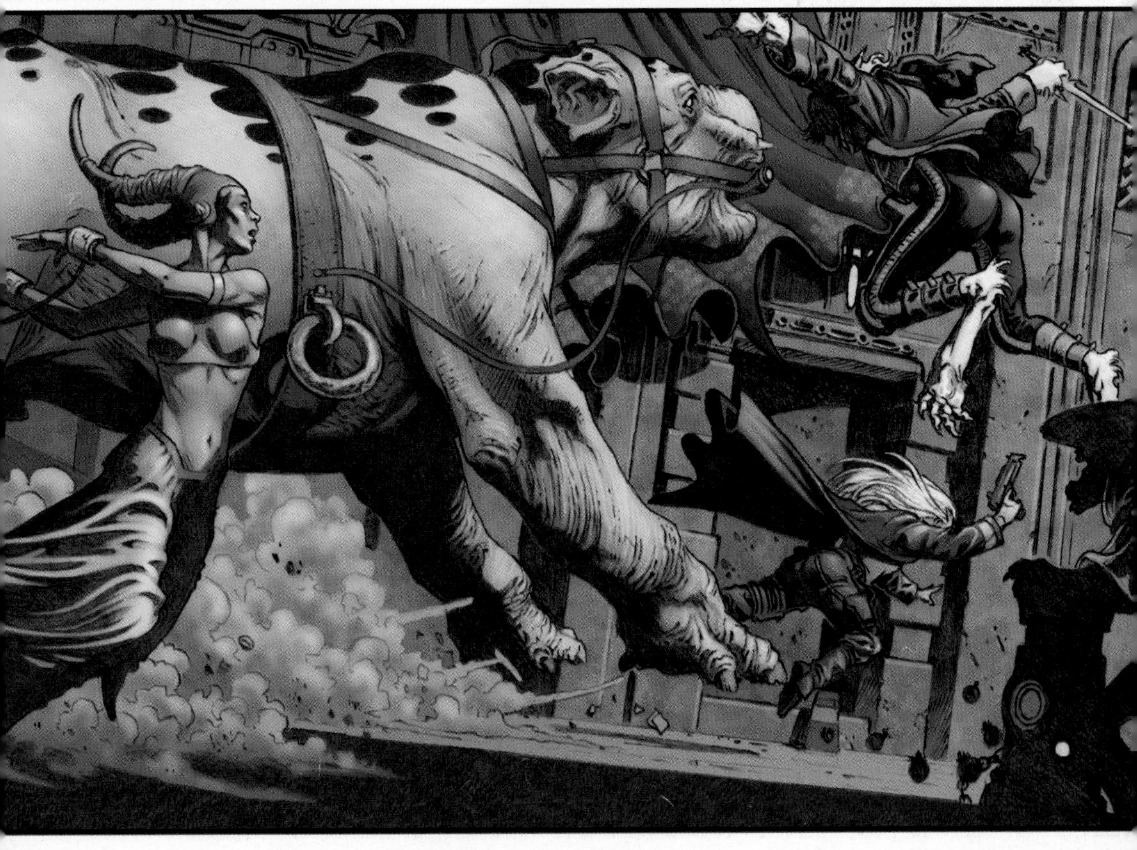

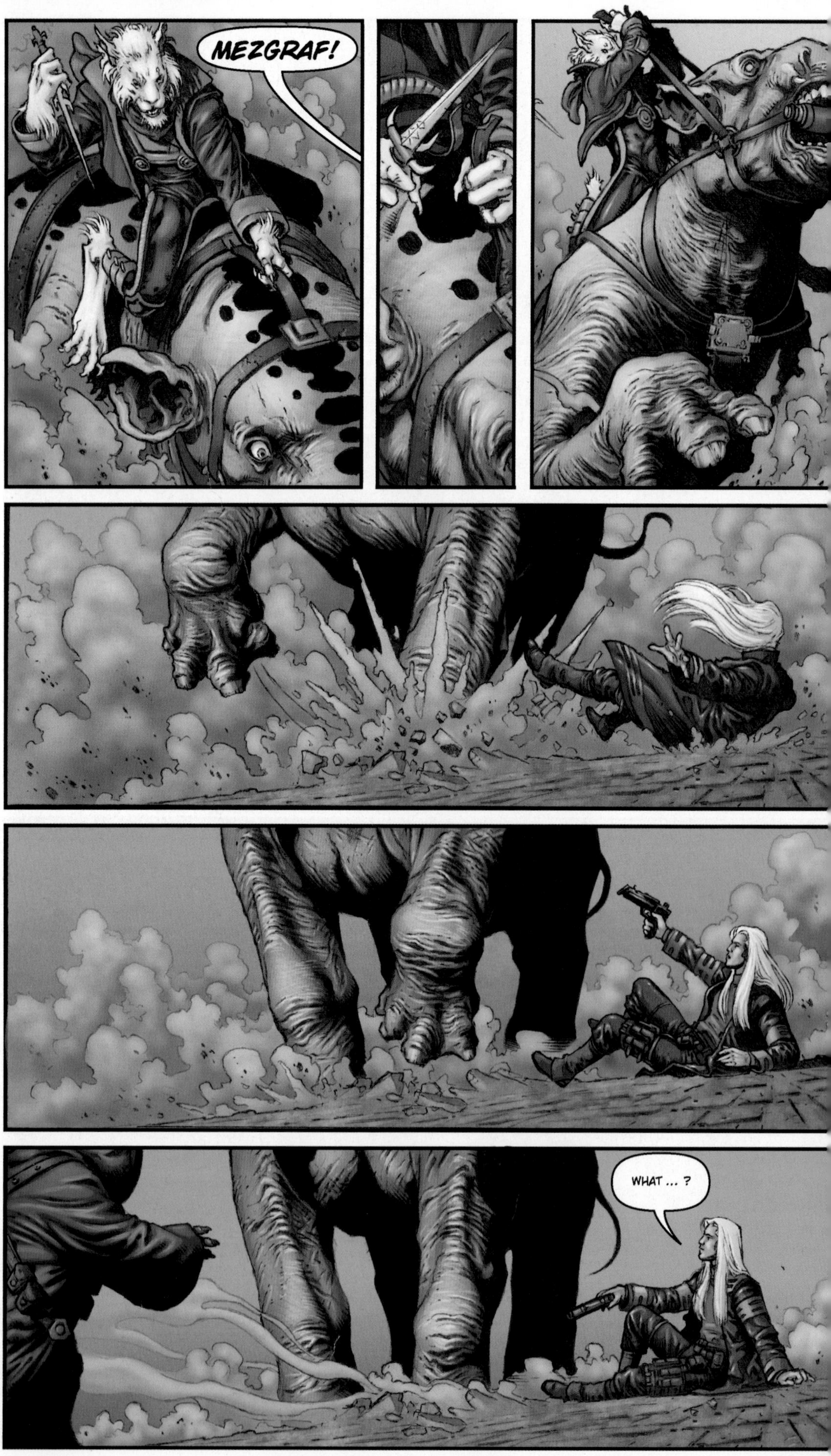
MEZGRAF!
WHAT ... ?

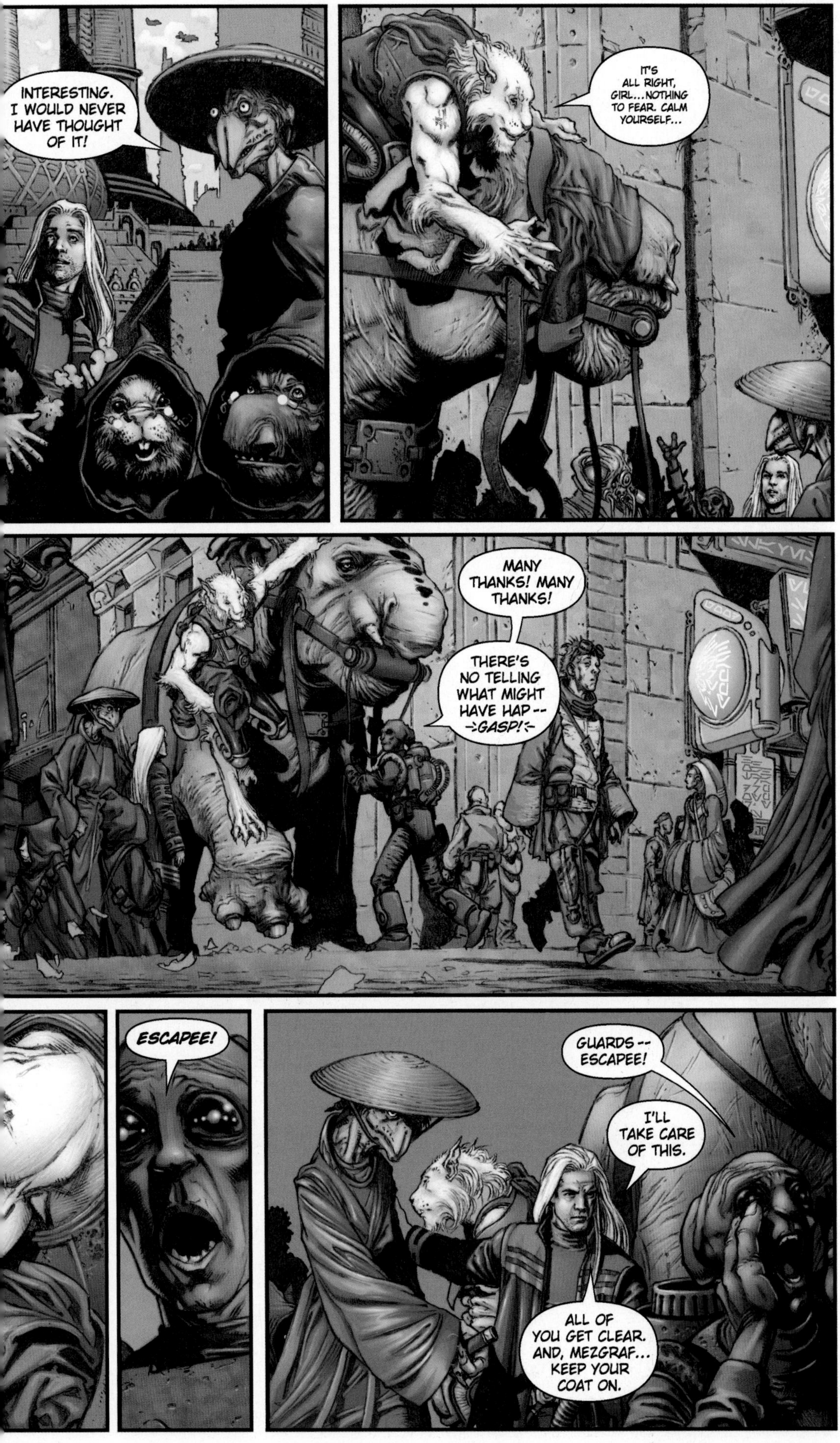
INTERESTING. I WOULD NEVER HAVE THOUGHT OF IT!
IT'S ALL RIGHT, GIRL... NOTHING TO FEAR. CALM YOURSELF...
MANY THANKS! MANY THANKS!
THERE'S NO TELLING WHAT MIGHT HAVE HAP-- -GASP!-
ESCAPEE!
GUARDS -- ESCAPEE!
I'LL TAKE CARE OF THIS.
ALL OF YOU GET CLEAR. AND, MEZGRAF... KEEP YOUR COAT ON.

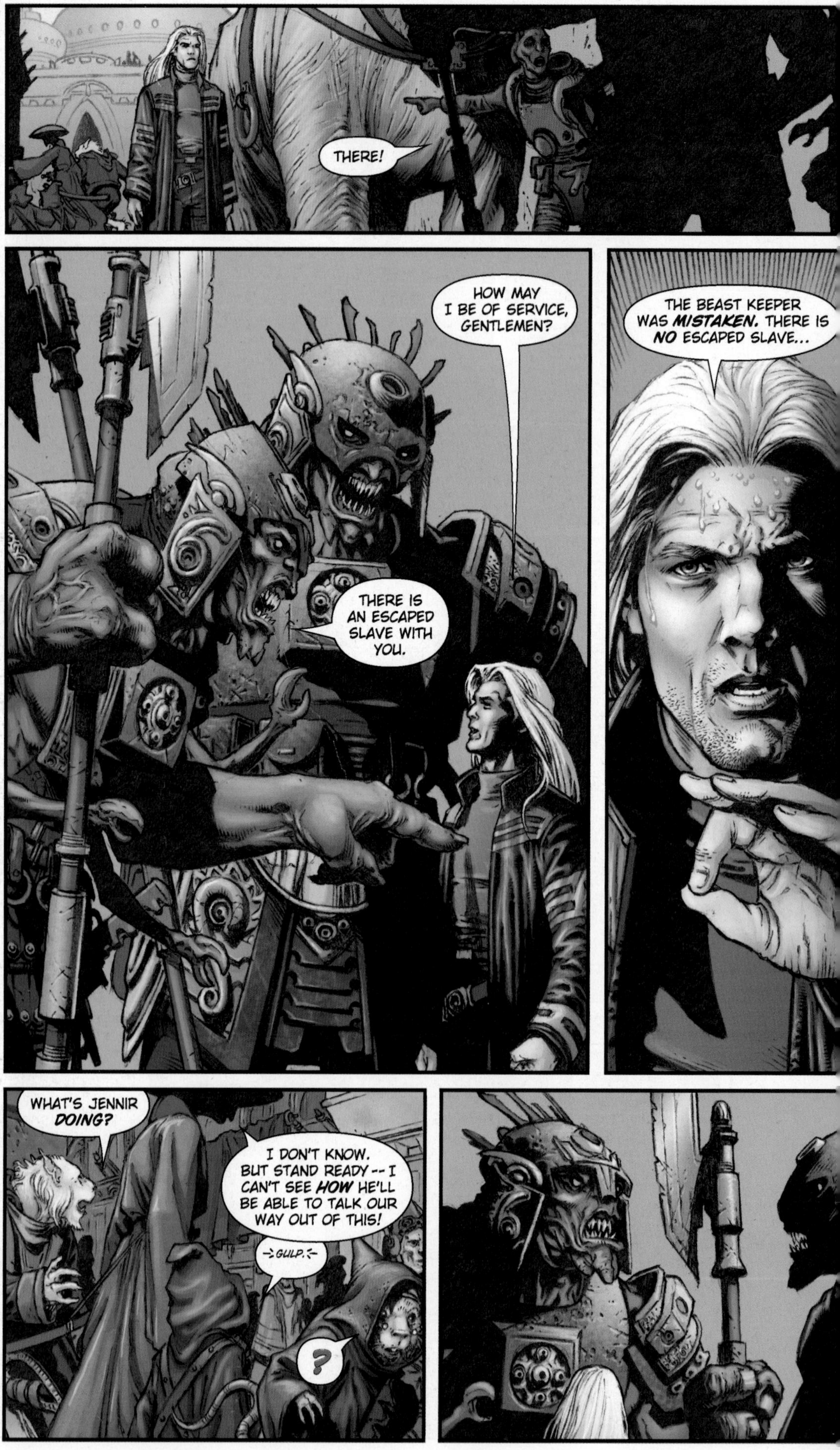
THERE!
HOW MAY I BE OF SERVICE, GENTLEMEN?
THERE IS AN ESCAPED SLAVE WITH YOU.
THE BEAST KEEPER WAS *MISTAKEN.* THERE IS *NO* ESCAPED SLAVE...
WHAT'S JENNIR *DOING?*
I DON'T KNOW. BUT STAND READY -- I CAN'T SEE *HOW* HE'LL BE ABLE TO TALK OUR WAY OUT OF THIS!
GULP.
?

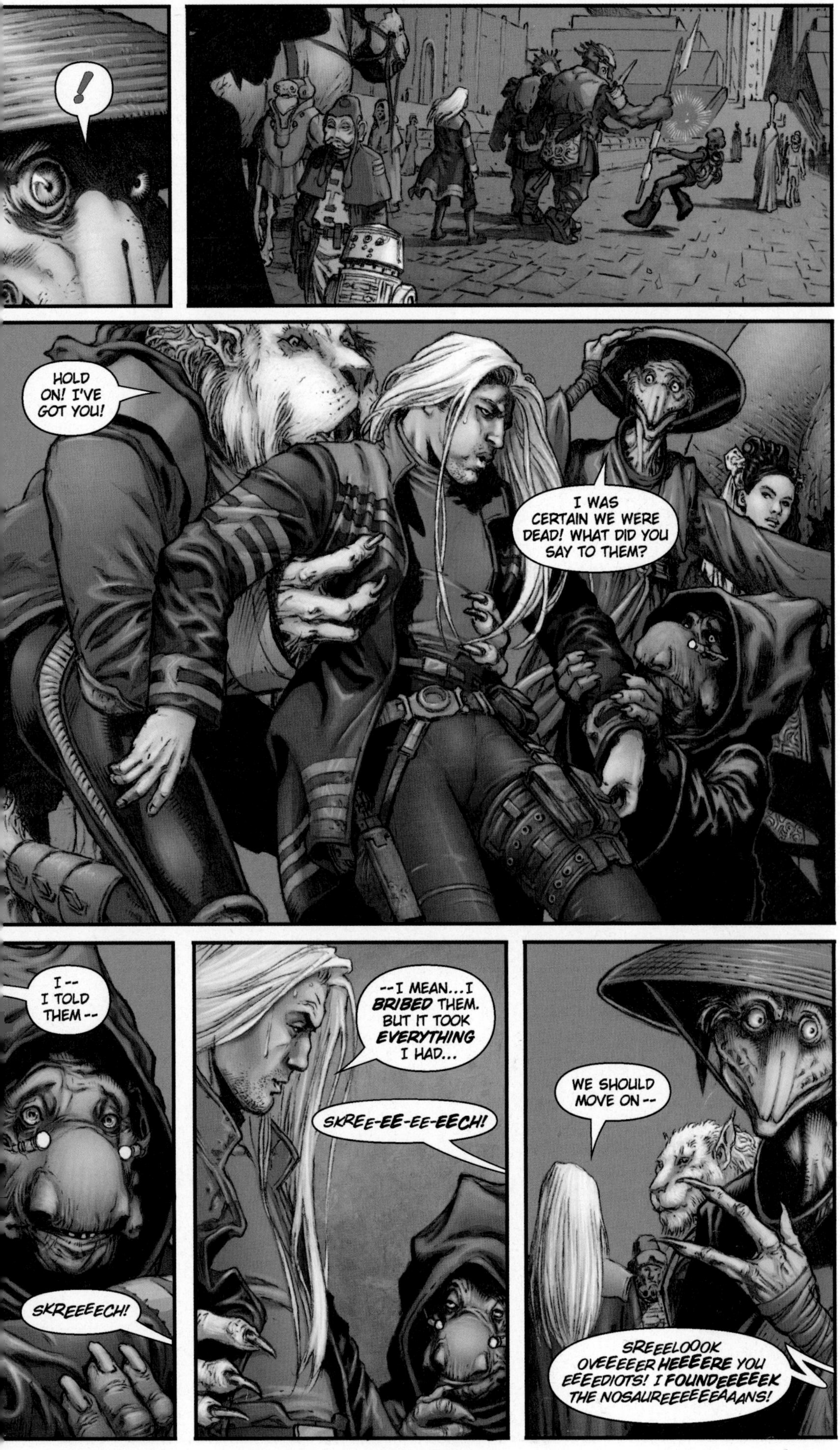
!
HOLD ON! I'VE GOT YOU!
I WAS CERTAIN WE WERE DEAD! WHAT DID YOU SAY TO THEM?
I -- I TOLD THEM --
SKREEEECH!
--I MEAN...I BRIBED THEM. BUT IT TOOK EVERYTHING I HAD...
SKREE-EE-EE-EECH!
WE SHOULD MOVE ON --
SREEELOOOK OVEEEEER HEEEERE YOU EEEEDIOTS! I FOUNDEEEEEK THE NOSAUREEEEEEAAANS!

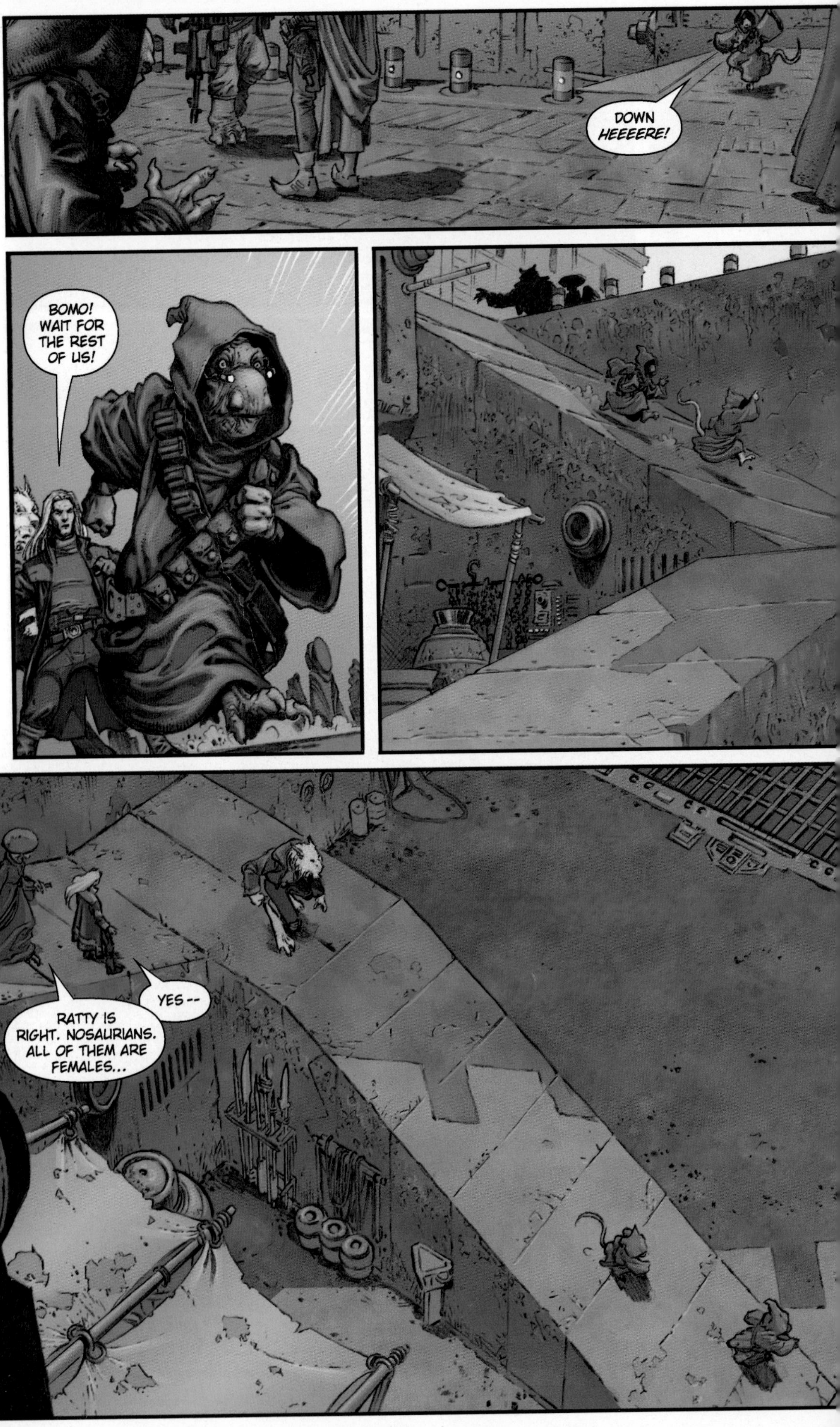
DOWN HEEEERE!
BOMO! WAIT FOR THE REST OF US!
YES --
RATTY IS RIGHT. NOSAURIANS. ALL OF THEM ARE FEMALES...

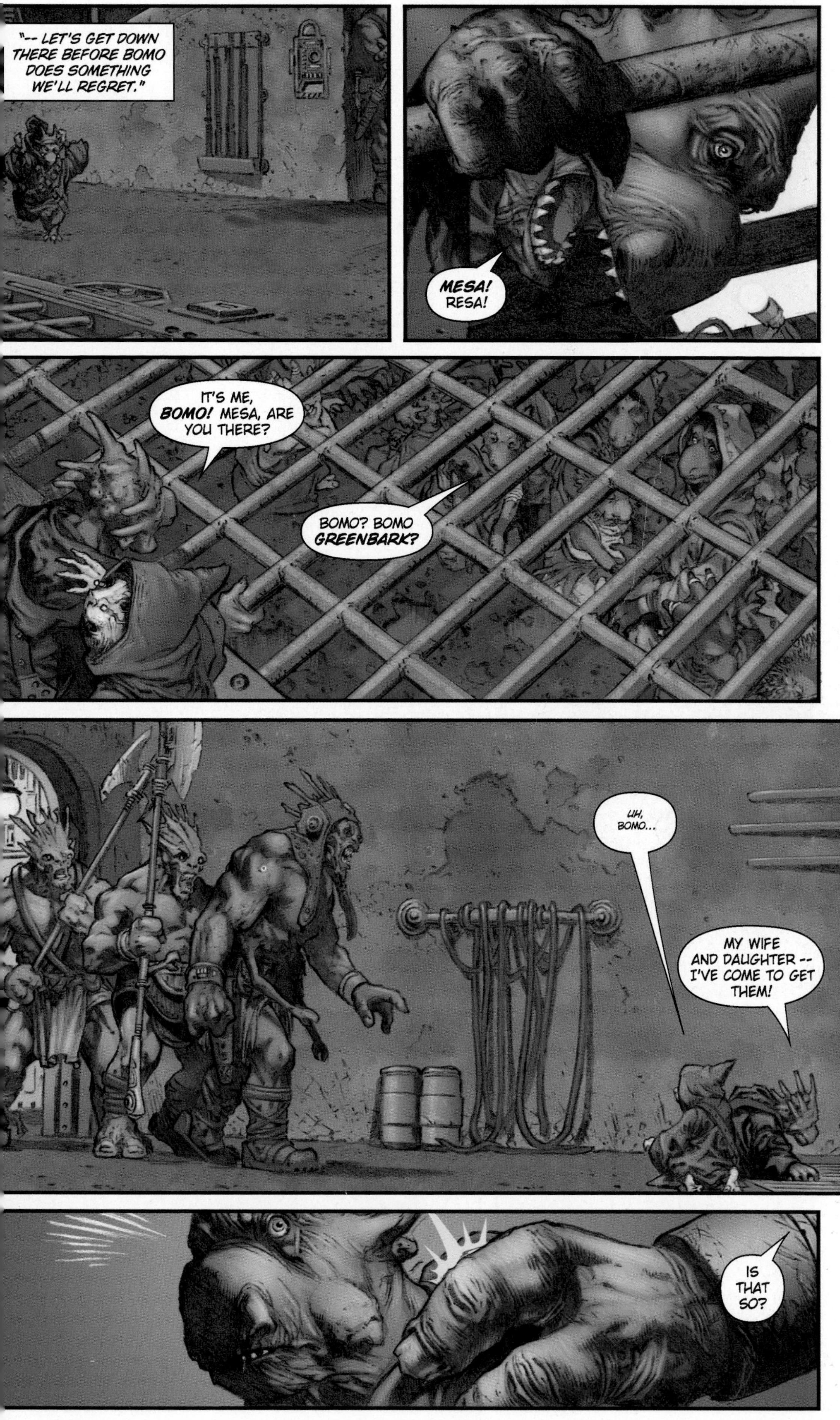
"-- LET'S GET DOWN THERE BEFORE BOMO DOES SOMETHING WE'LL REGRET."
MESA! RESA!
IT'S ME, BOMO! MESA, ARE YOU THERE?
BOMO? BOMO GREENBARK?
UH, BOMO...
MY WIFE AND DAUGHTER -- I'VE COME TO GET THEM!
IS THAT SO?

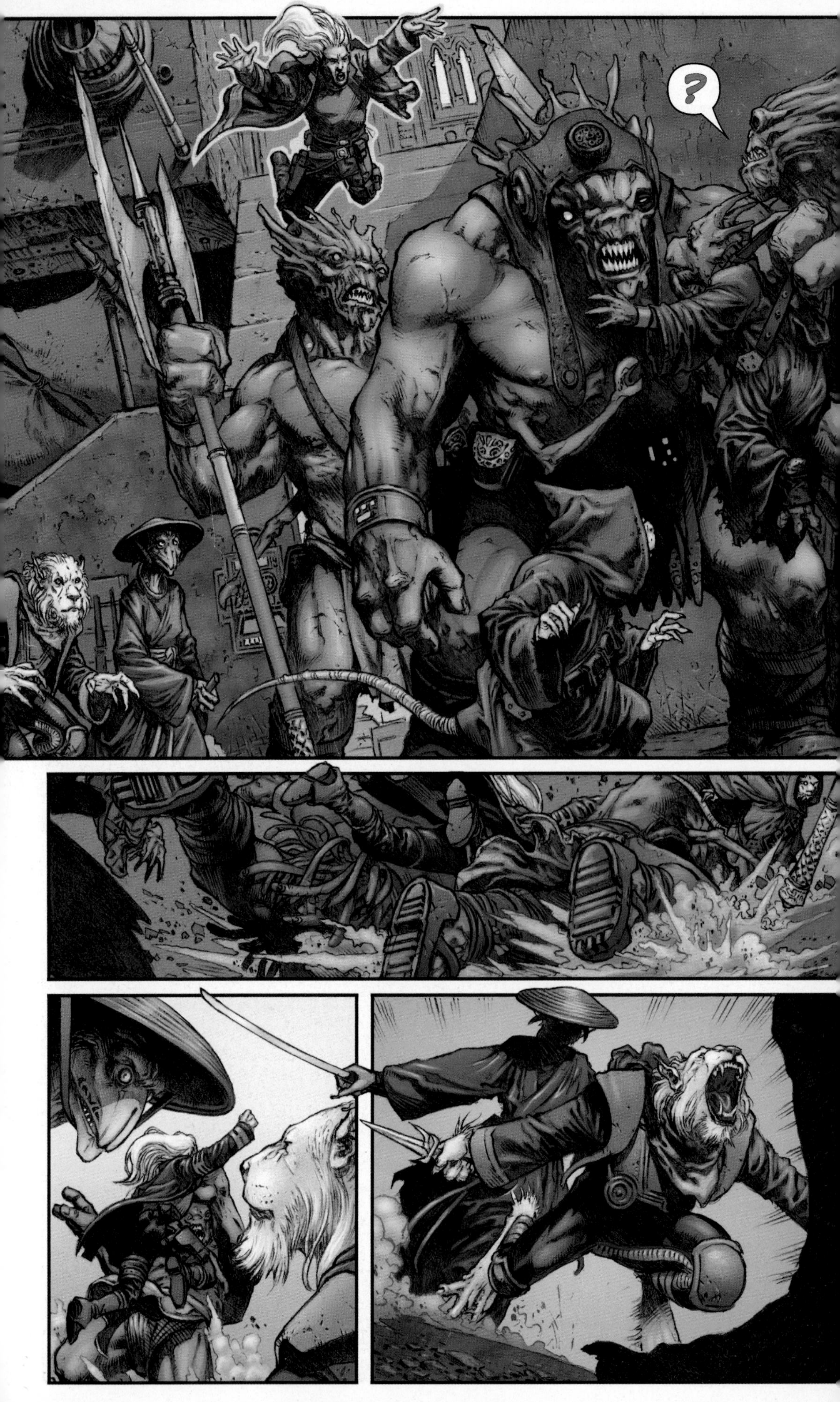
?

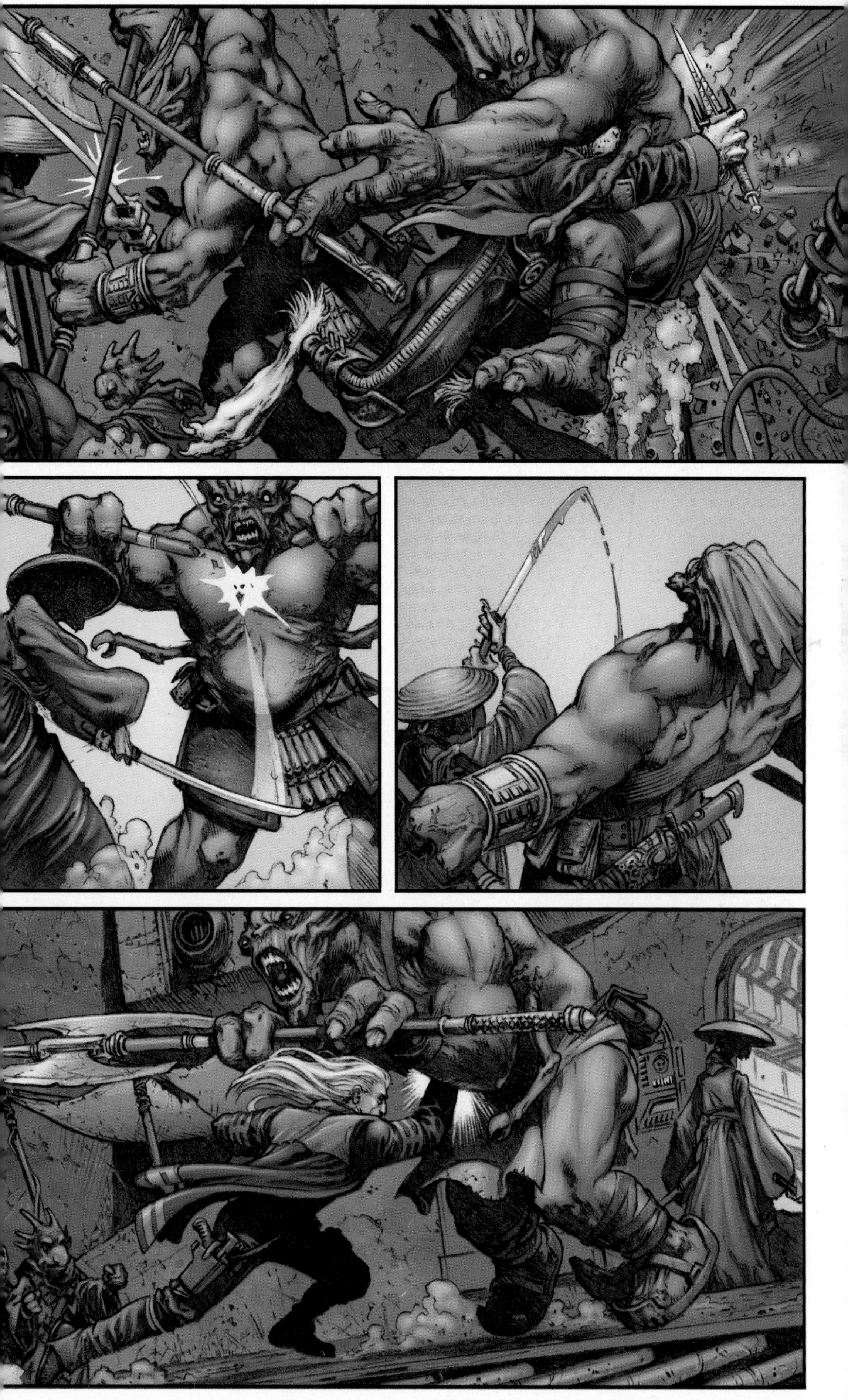

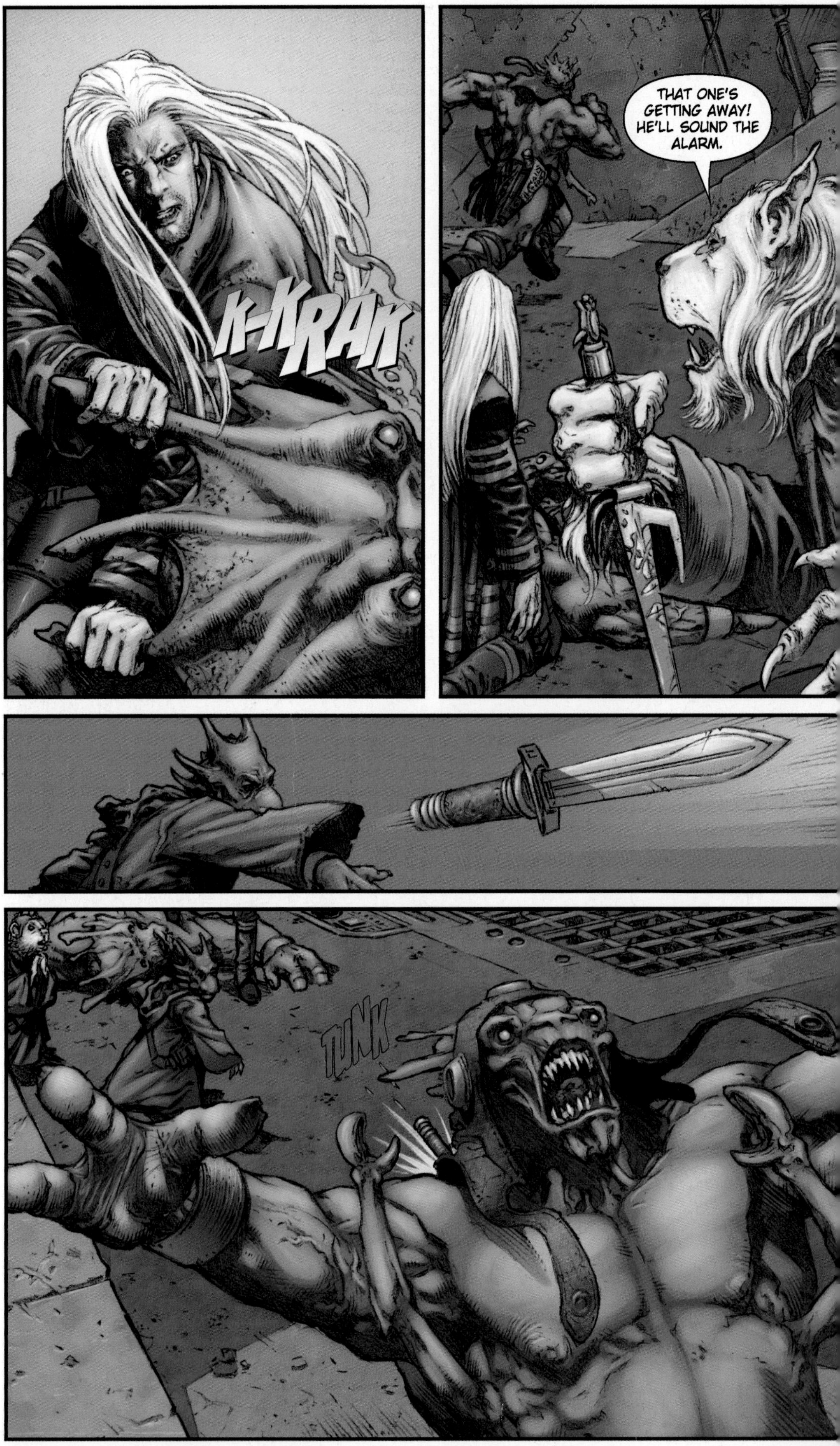
K-KRAK
THAT ONE'S GETTING AWAY! HE'LL SOUND THE ALARM.
TUNK

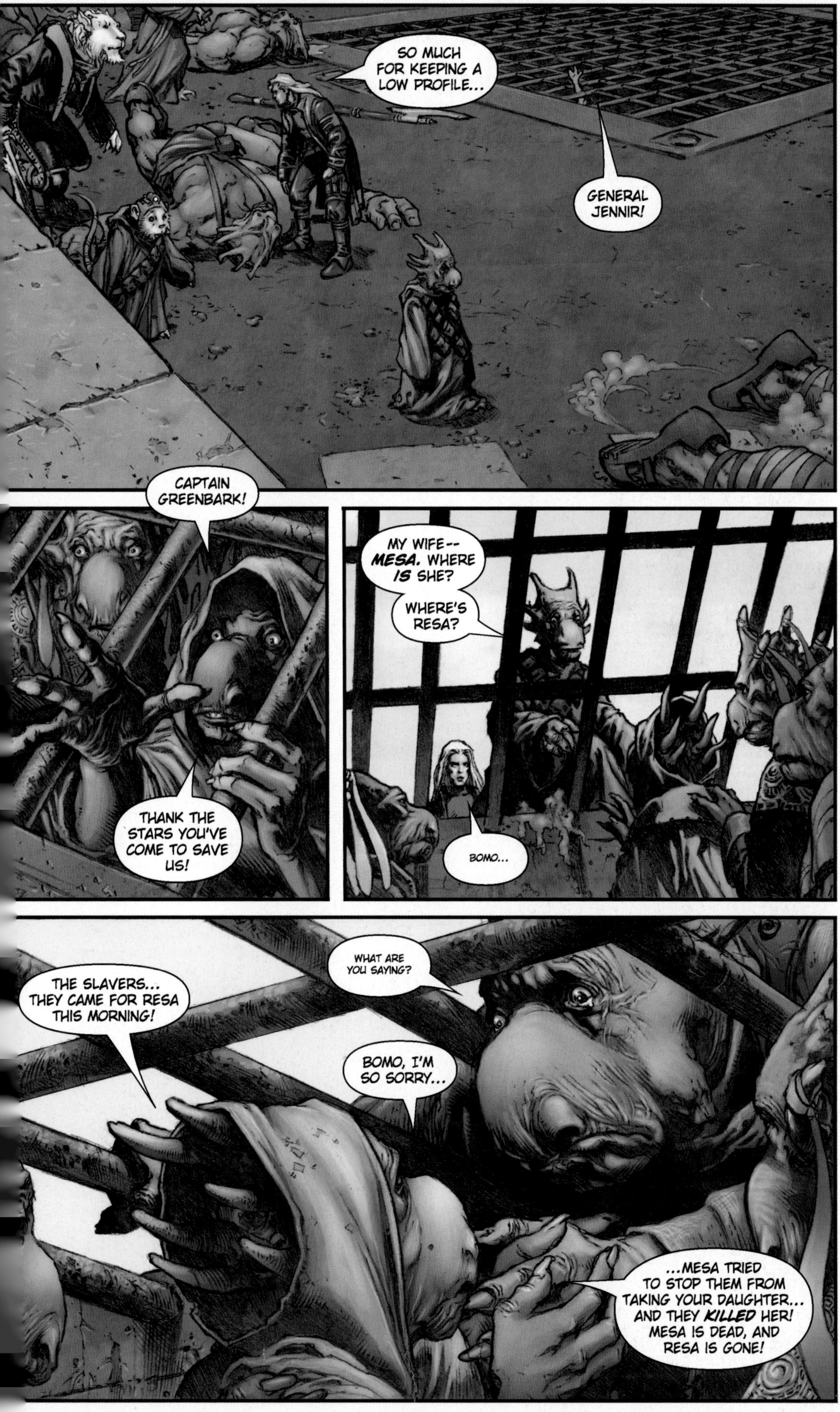
SO MUCH FOR KEEPING A LOW PROFILE...
GENERAL JENNIR!
CAPTAIN GREENBARK!
THANK THE STARS YOU'VE COME TO SAVE US!
MY WIFE-- MESA. WHERE IS SHE?
WHERE'S RESA?
BOMO...
THE SLAVERS... THEY CAME FOR RESA THIS MORNING!
WHAT ARE YOU SAYING?
BOMO, I'M SO SORRY...
...MESA TRIED TO STOP THEM FROM TAKING YOUR DAUGHTER... AND THEY KILLED HER! MESA IS DEAD, AND RESA IS GONE!

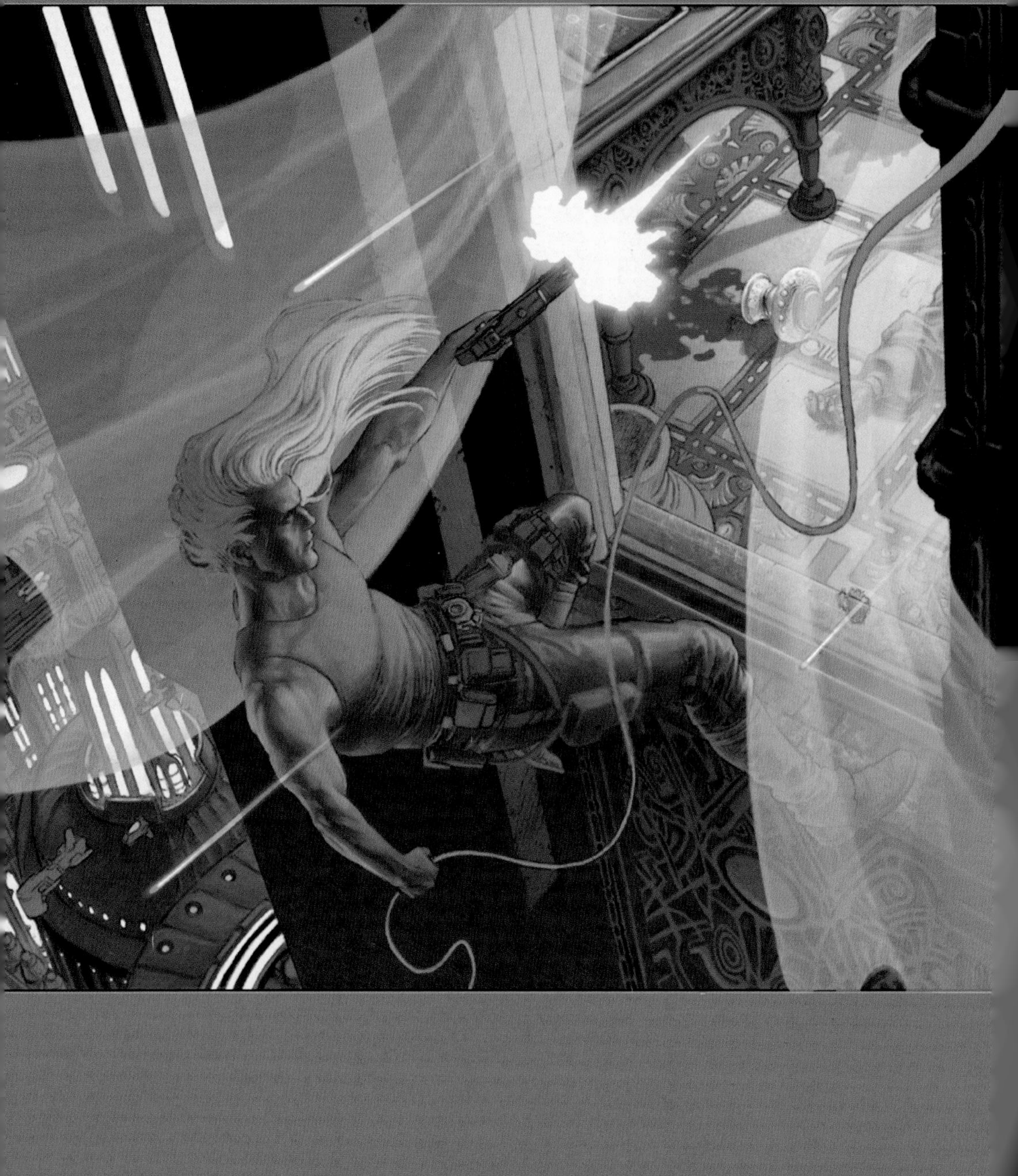

STAR WARS: DARK TIMES #4 — "THE PATH TO NOWHERE, PART 4 (OF FIVE)"

WRITER: RANDY STRADLEY (AS WELLES HARTLEY & MICK HARRISON) • ARTIST: DOUGLAS WHEATLEY • COLORIST: RONDA PATTISON • LETTERER: MICHAEL HE
DESIGNER: DARIN FABRICK • ASSISTANT EDITOR: DAVE MARSHALL • EDITOR: RANDY STRADLEY • COVER ARTIST: DOUGLAS WHEATLEY

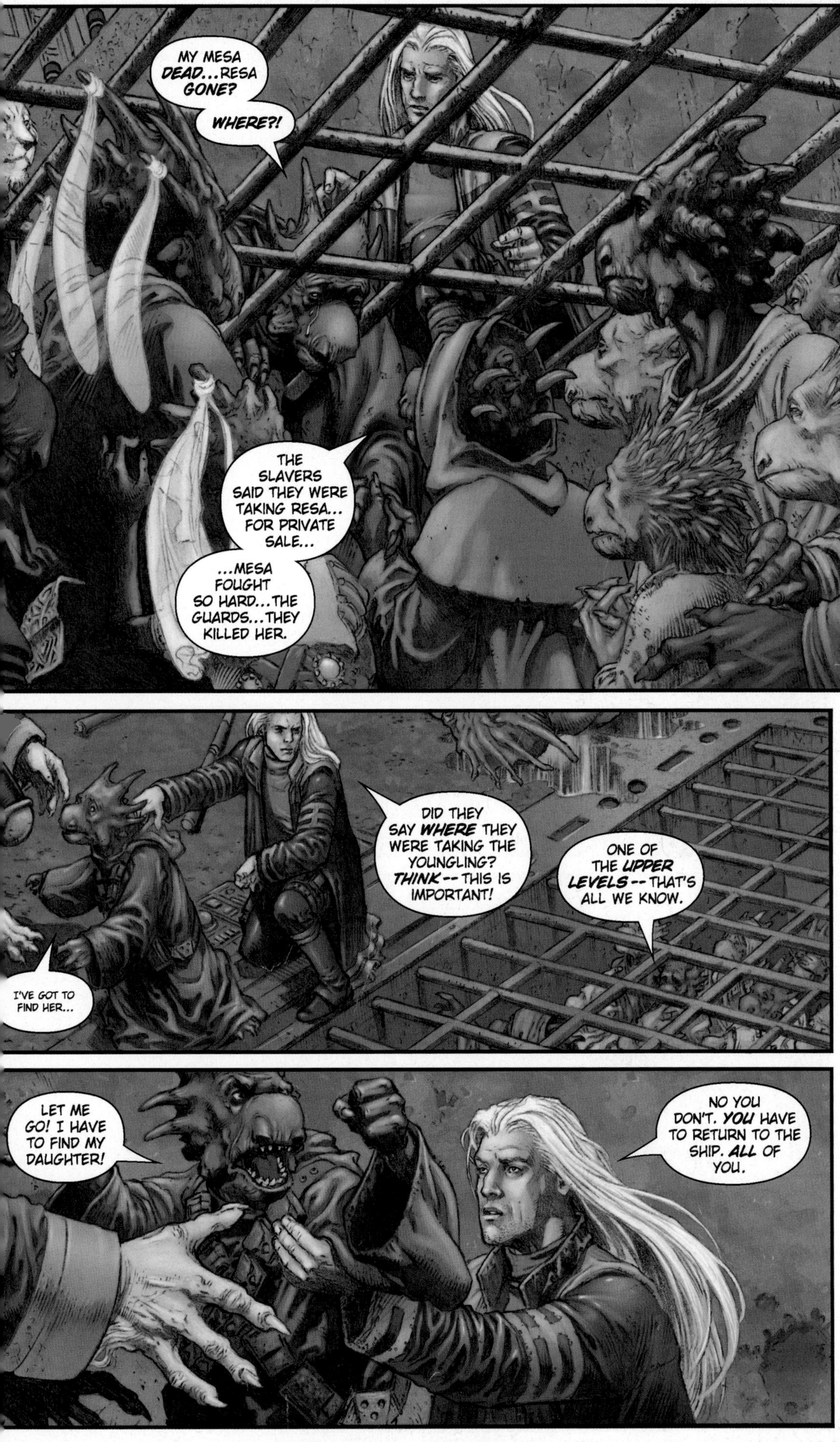
MY MESA DEAD...RESA GONE?
WHERE?!
THE SLAVERS SAID THEY WERE TAKING RESA... FOR PRIVATE SALE...
...MESA FOUGHT SO HARD...THE GUARDS...THEY KILLED HER.
DID THEY SAY WHERE THEY WERE TAKING THE YOUNGLING? THINK -- THIS IS IMPORTANT!
ONE OF THE UPPER LEVELS -- THAT'S ALL WE KNOW.
I'VE GOT TO FIND HER...
LET ME GO! I HAVE TO FIND MY DAUGHTER!
NO YOU DON'T. YOU HAVE TO RETURN TO THE SHIP. ALL OF YOU.

I'LL SEARCH FOR THE YOUNGLING. IF I'M NOT BACK BY MIDNIGHT, YOU SHOULD ASSUME I'M DEAD AND MAKE FOR WHATEVER DESTINATION SEEMS BEST TO YOU.

HAVE HEREN PREPARE FOR IMMEDIATE DEPARTURE. TELL HIM IF THERE'S TROUBLE, HE SHOULD MAKE A RUN FOR IT.

BUT--

NO. AS A GROUP WE'RE TOO CONSPICUOUS. THE DEAD GUARDS WILL BE DISCOVERED, AND WE'LL BE PULLED IN AS SUSPECTS--

-- BUT ALONE I MIGHT HAVE A CHANCE.

KEEP A CLOSE WATCH ON BOMO. DON'T LET HIM DO ANYTHING FOOLISH.

MMMPF!

WAIT.

MMMMG!

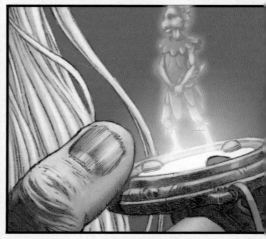

I MAY NEED THIS.

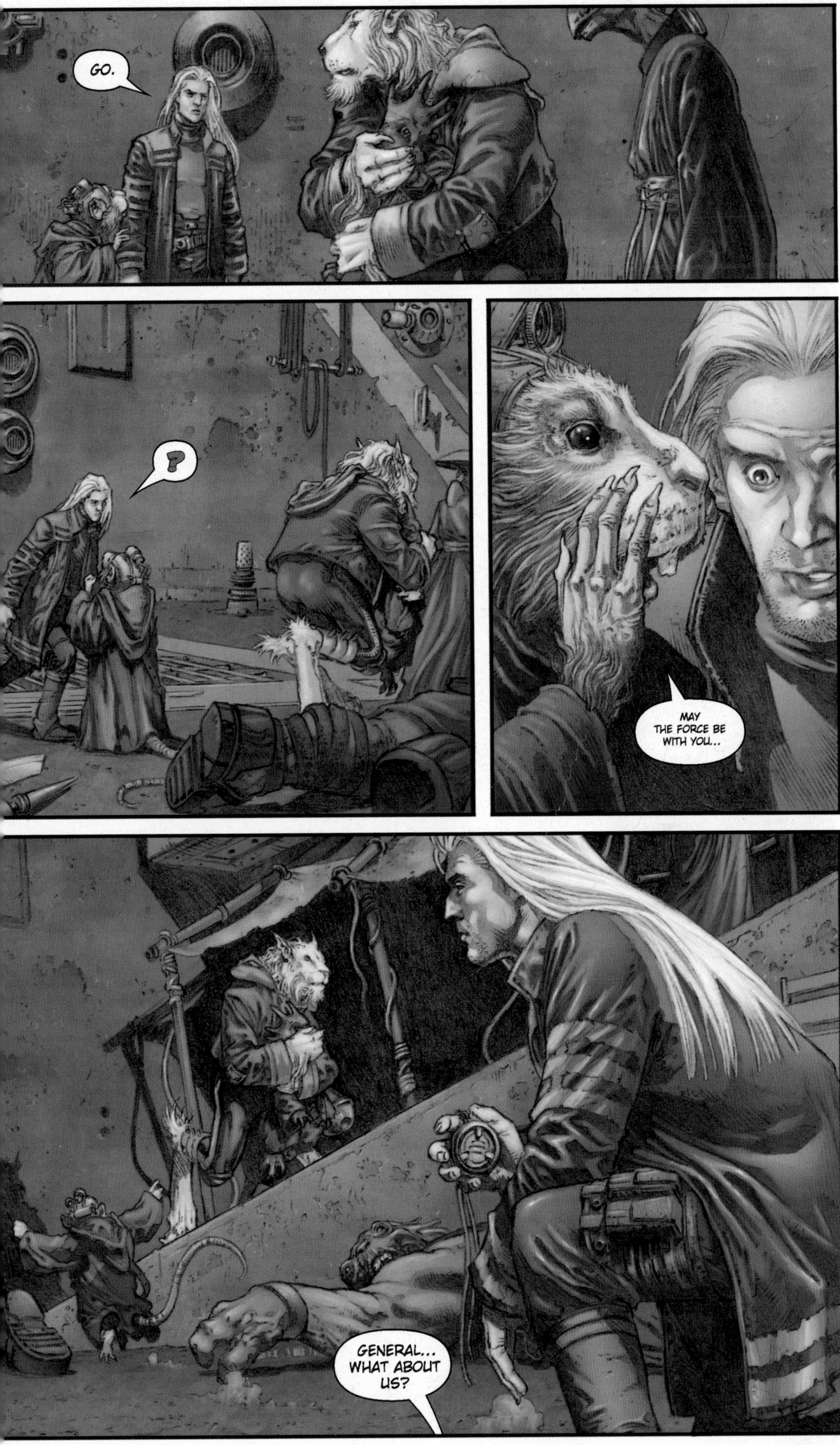
GO.
?
MAY THE FORCE BE WITH YOU...
GENERAL... WHAT ABOUT US?

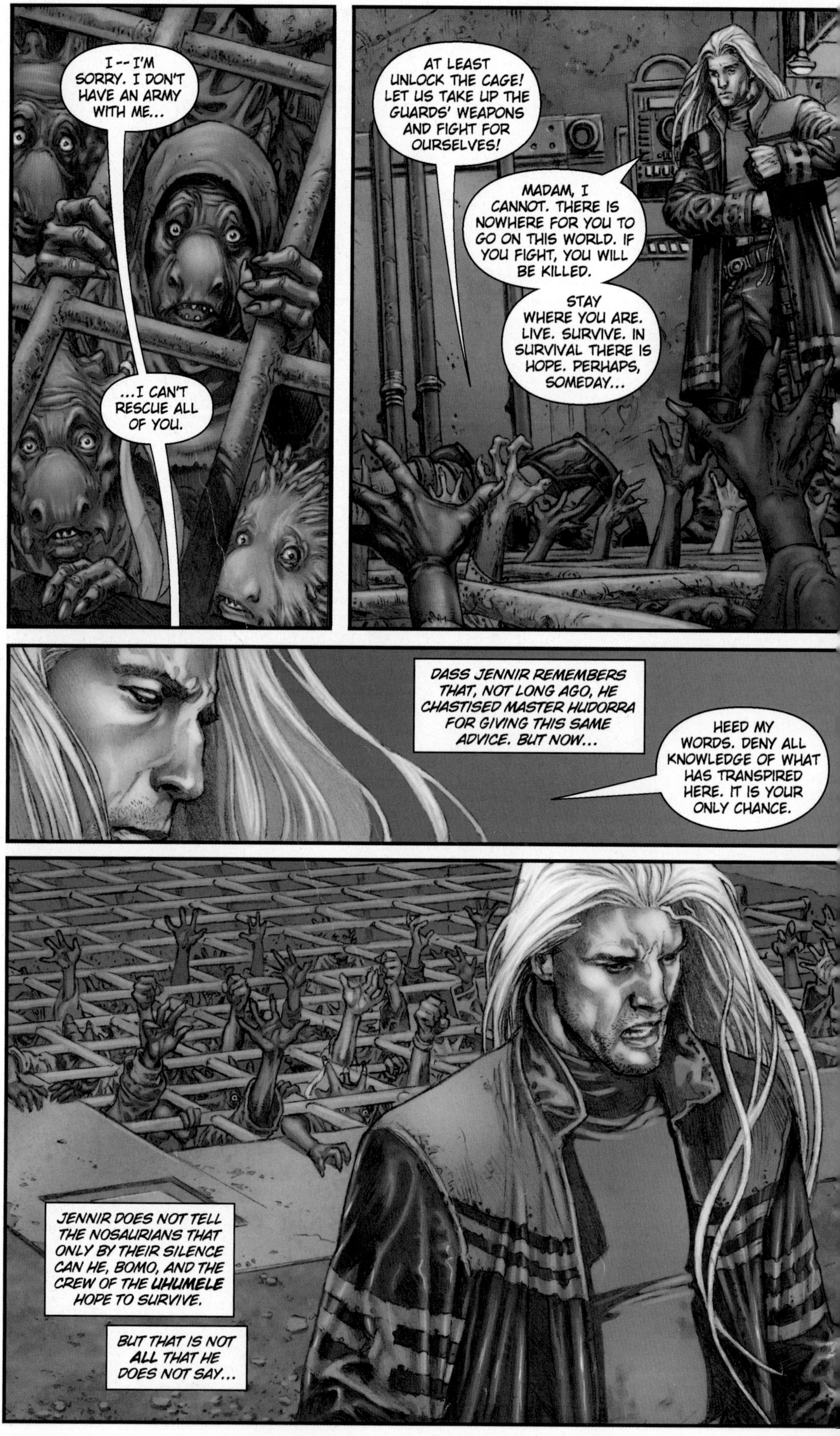
I -- I'M SORRY. I DON'T HAVE AN ARMY WITH ME...
...I CAN'T RESCUE ALL OF YOU.
AT LEAST UNLOCK THE CAGE! LET US TAKE UP THE GUARDS' WEAPONS AND FIGHT FOR OURSELVES!
MADAM, I CANNOT. THERE IS NOWHERE FOR YOU TO GO ON THIS WORLD. IF YOU FIGHT, YOU WILL BE KILLED.
STAY WHERE YOU ARE. LIVE. SURVIVE. IN SURVIVAL THERE IS HOPE. PERHAPS, SOMEDAY...
DASS JENNIR REMEMBERS THAT, NOT LONG AGO, HE CHASTISED MASTER HUDORRA FOR GIVING THIS SAME ADVICE. BUT NOW...
HEED MY WORDS. DENY ALL KNOWLEDGE OF WHAT HAS TRANSPIRED HERE. IT IS YOUR ONLY CHANCE.
JENNIR DOES NOT TELL THE NOSAURIANS THAT ONLY BY THEIR SILENCE CAN HE, BOMO, AND THE CREW OF THE UHUMELE HOPE TO SURVIVE.
BUT THAT IS NOT ALL THAT HE DOES NOT SAY...

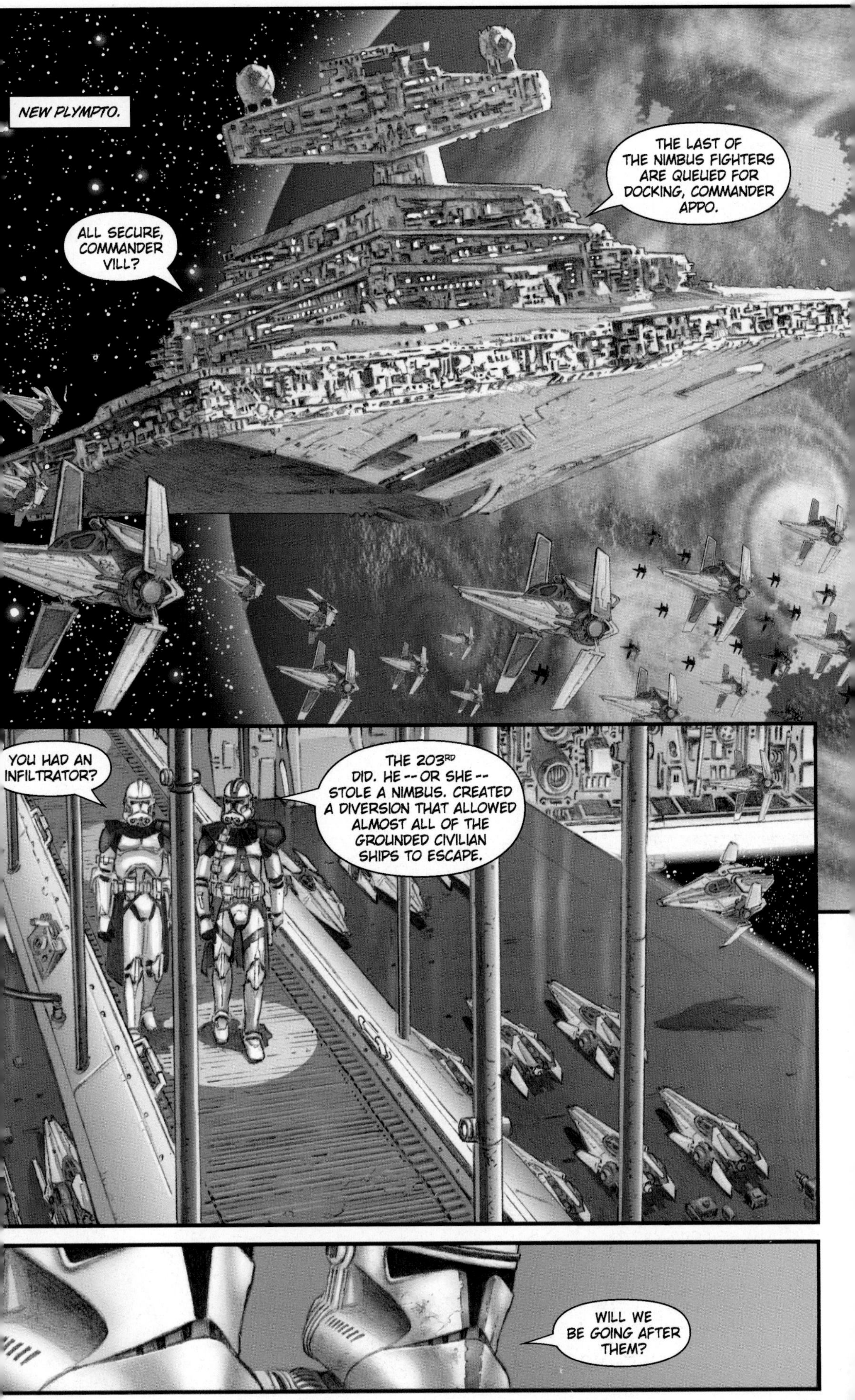
NEW PLYMPTO.
ALL SECURE, COMMANDER VILL?
THE LAST OF THE NIMBUS FIGHTERS ARE QUEUED FOR DOCKING, COMMANDER APPO.
YOU HAD AN INFILTRATOR?
THE 203RD DID. HE -- OR SHE -- STOLE A NIMBUS. CREATED A DIVERSION THAT ALLOWED ALMOST ALL OF THE GROUNDED CIVILIAN SHIPS TO ESCAPE.
WILL WE BE GOING AFTER THEM?

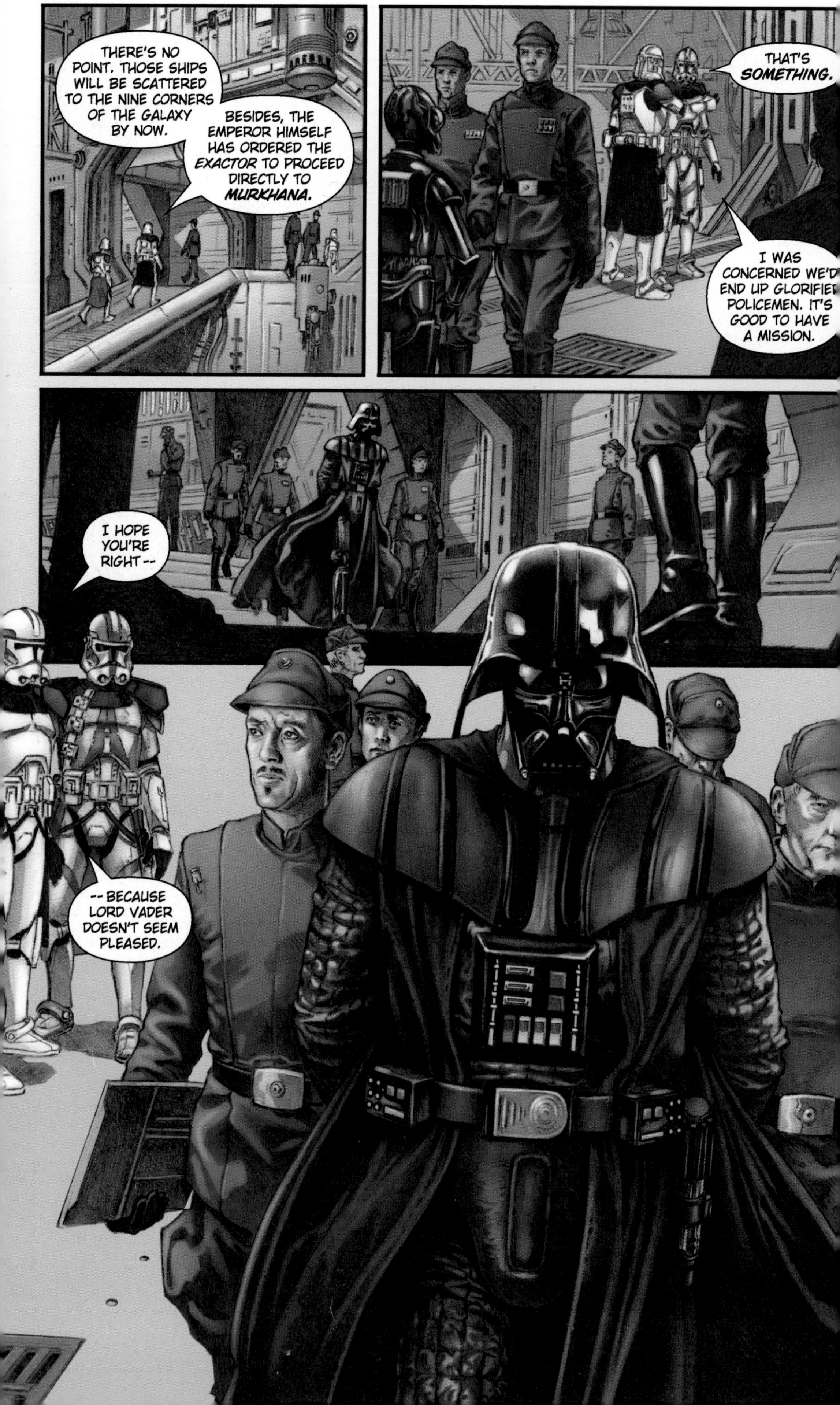
THERE'S NO POINT. THOSE SHIPS WILL BE SCATTERED TO THE NINE CORNERS OF THE GALAXY BY NOW.
BESIDES, THE EMPEROR HIMSELF HAS ORDERED THE *EXACTOR* TO PROCEED DIRECTLY TO ***MURKHANA.***
THAT'S ***SOMETHING.***
I WAS CONCERNED WE'D END UP GLORIFIED POLICEMEN. IT'S GOOD TO HAVE A MISSION.
I HOPE YOU'RE RIGHT --
-- BECAUSE LORD VADER DOESN'T SEEM PLEASED.

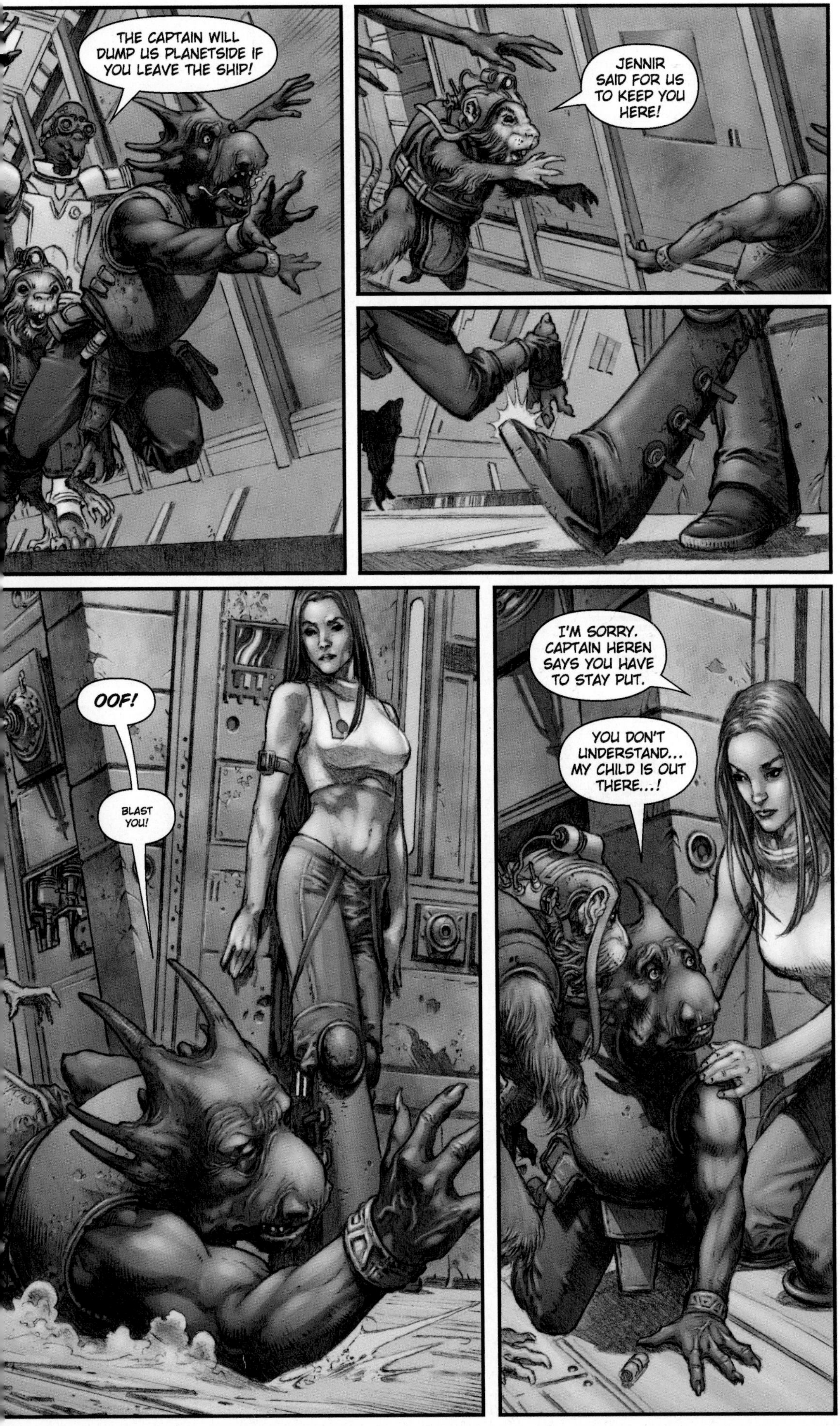
THE CAPTAIN WILL DUMP US PLANETSIDE IF YOU LEAVE THE SHIP!
JENNIR SAID FOR US TO KEEP YOU HERE!
OOF!
BLAST YOU!
I'M SORRY. CAPTAIN HEREN SAYS YOU HAVE TO STAY PUT.
YOU DON'T UNDERSTAND... MY CHILD IS OUT THERE...!

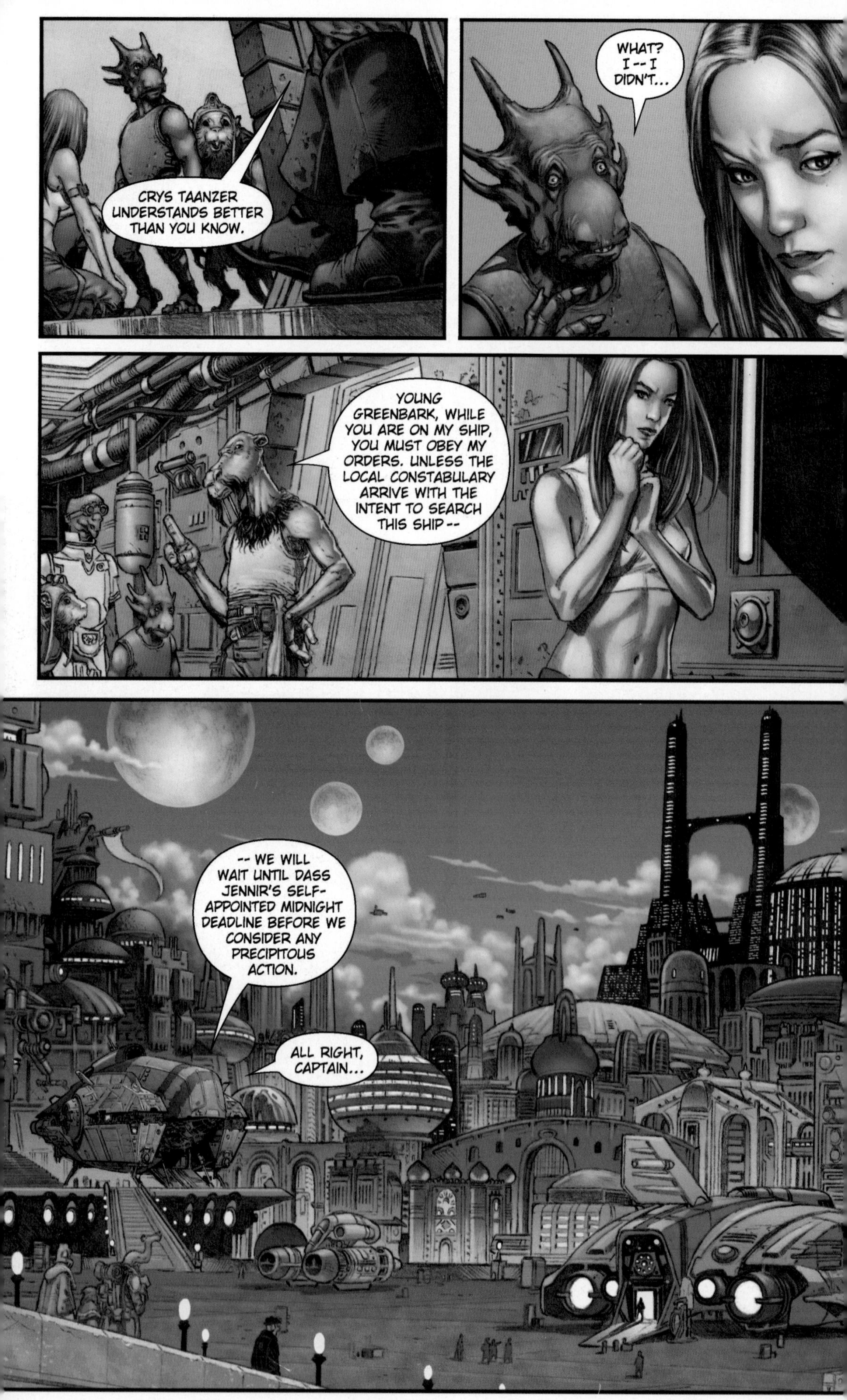
CRYS TAANZER UNDERSTANDS BETTER THAN YOU KNOW.
WHAT? I -- I DIDN'T...
YOUNG GREENBARK, WHILE YOU ARE ON MY SHIP, YOU MUST OBEY MY ORDERS. UNLESS THE LOCAL CONSTABULARY ARRIVE WITH THE INTENT TO SEARCH THIS SHIP --
-- WE WILL WAIT UNTIL DASS JENNIR'S SELF-APPOINTED MIDNIGHT DEADLINE BEFORE WE CONSIDER ANY PRECIPITOUS ACTION.
ALL RIGHT, CAPTAIN...

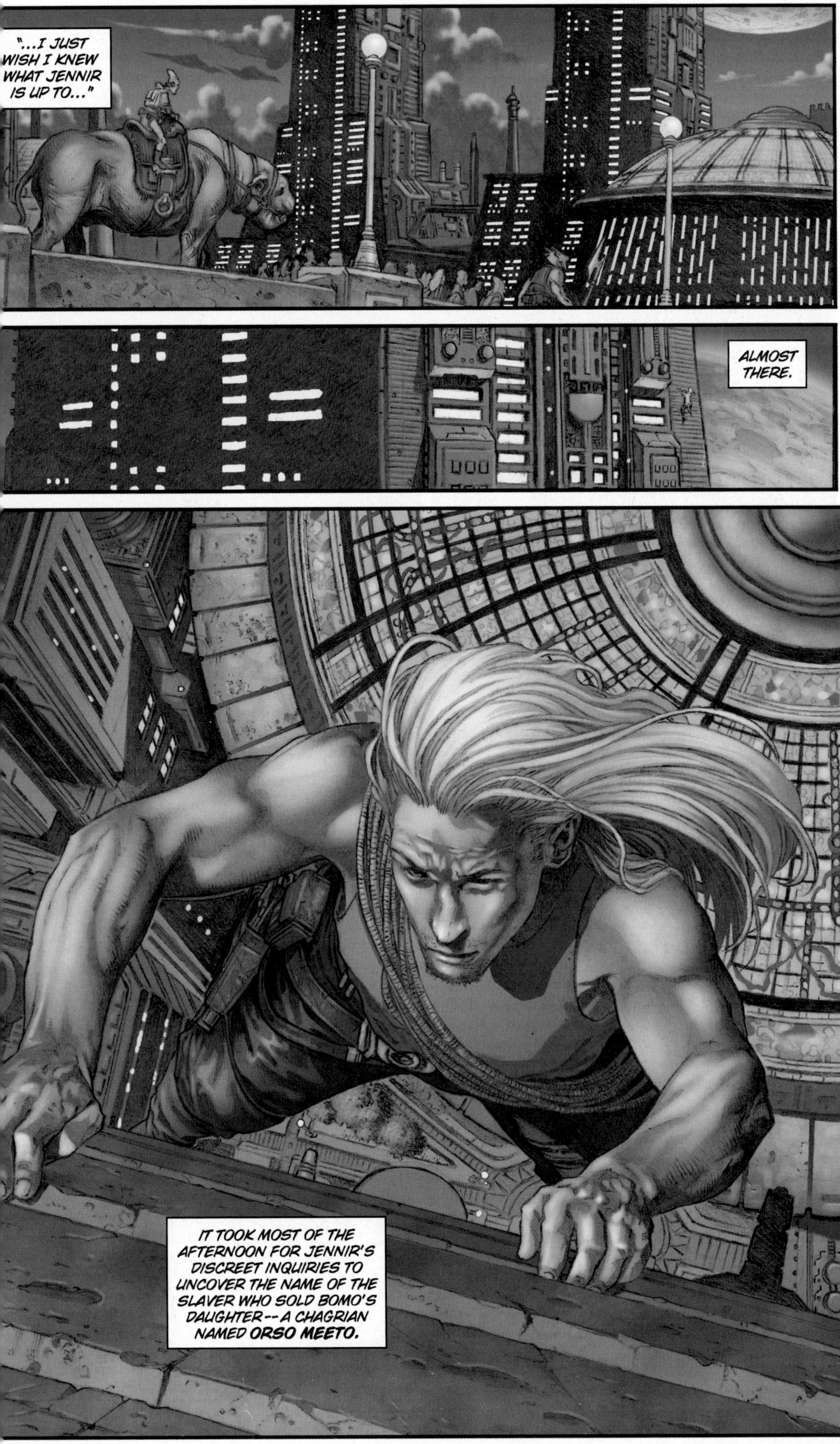
"...I JUST WISH I KNEW WHAT JENNIR IS UP TO..."
ALMOST THERE.
IT TOOK MOST OF THE AFTERNOON FOR JENNIR'S DISCREET INQUIRIES TO UNCOVER THE NAME OF THE SLAVER WHO SOLD BOMO'S DAUGHTER-- A CHAGRIAN NAMED ORSO MEETO.

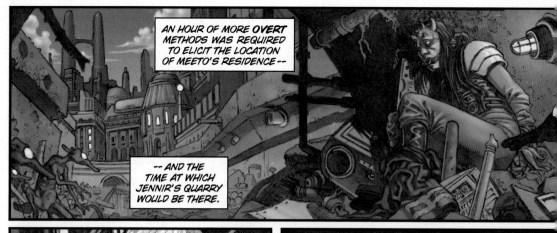

AN HOUR OF MORE **OVERT** METHODS WAS REQUIRED TO ELICIT THE LOCATION OF MEETO'S RESIDENCE --

-- AND THE TIME AT WHICH JENNIR'S QUARRY WOULD BE THERE.

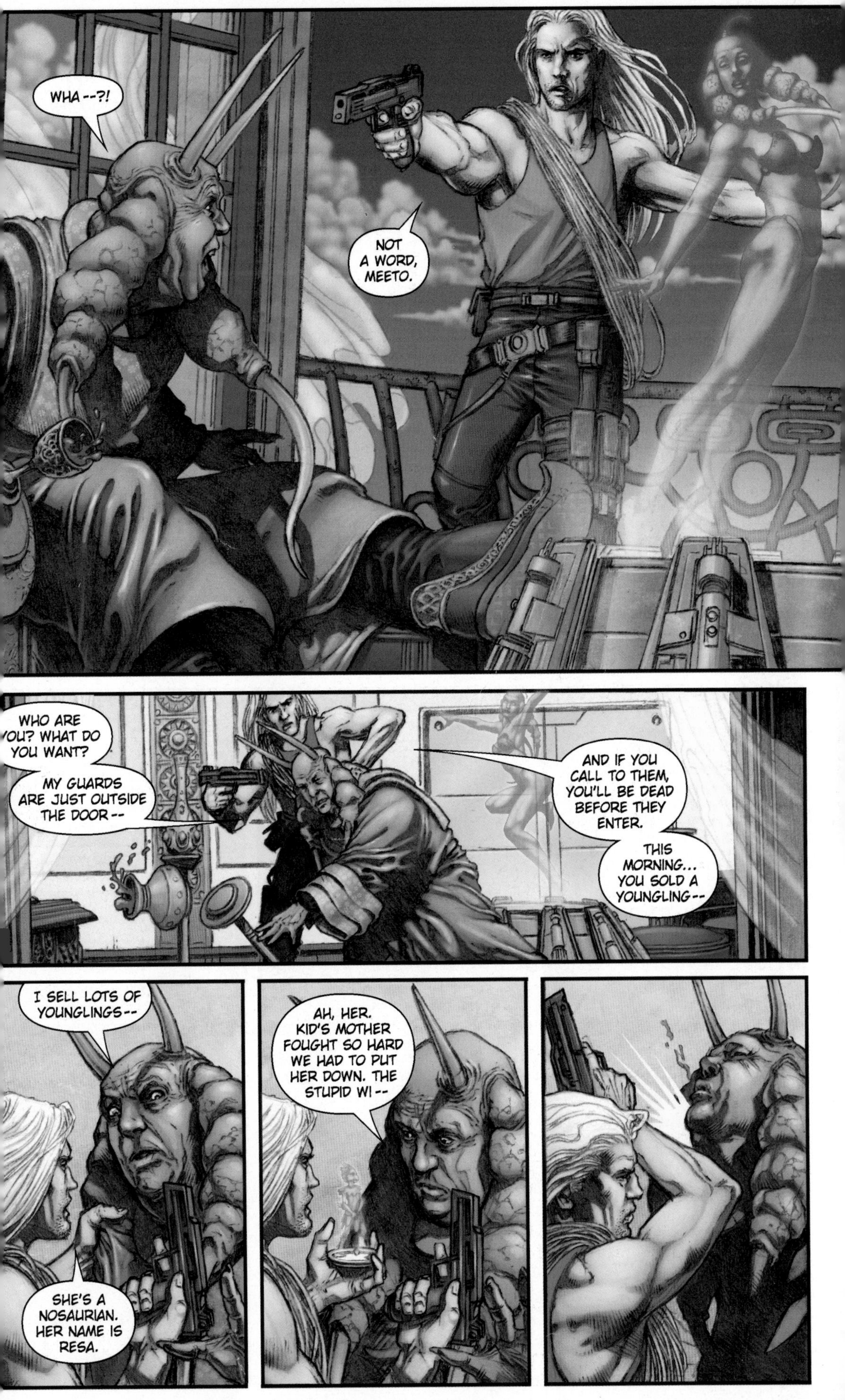
WHA--?!
NOT A WORD, MEETO.
WHO ARE YOU? WHAT DO YOU WANT?
MY GUARDS ARE JUST OUTSIDE THE DOOR--
AND IF YOU CALL TO THEM, YOU'LL BE DEAD BEFORE THEY ENTER.
THIS MORNING... YOU SOLD A YOUNGLING--
I SELL LOTS OF YOUNGLINGS--
SHE'S A NOSAURIAN. HER NAME IS RESA.
AH, HER. KID'S MOTHER FOUGHT SO HARD WE HAD TO PUT HER DOWN. THE STUPID W!--

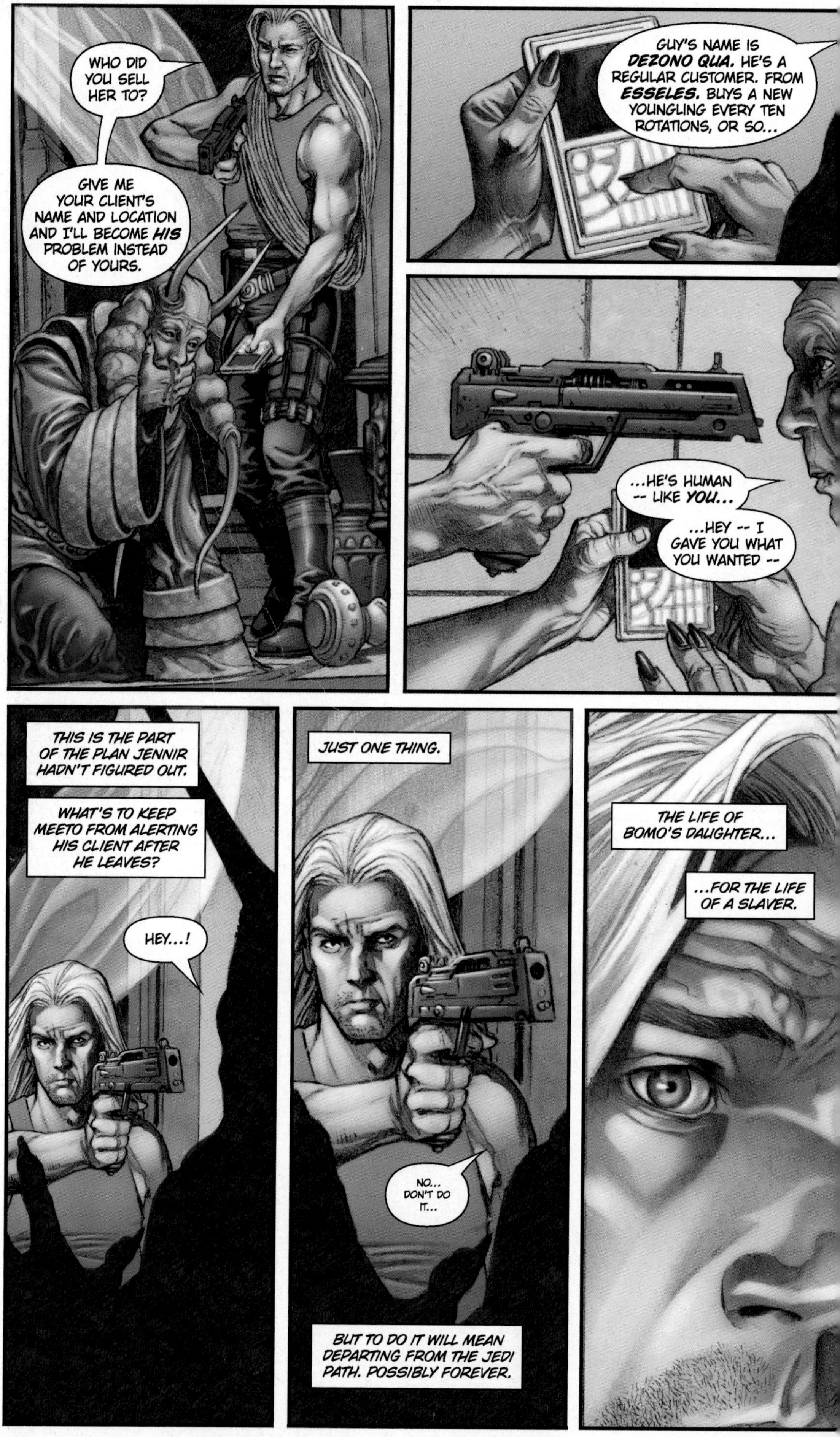
WHO DID YOU SELL HER TO?
GIVE ME YOUR CLIENT'S NAME AND LOCATION AND I'LL BECOME HIS PROBLEM INSTEAD OF YOURS.
GUY'S NAME IS DEZONO QUA. HE'S A REGULAR CUSTOMER. FROM ESSELES. BUYS A NEW YOUNGLING EVERY TEN ROTATIONS, OR SO...
...HE'S HUMAN -- LIKE YOU...
...HEY -- I GAVE YOU WHAT YOU WANTED --
THIS IS THE PART OF THE PLAN JENNIR HADN'T FIGURED OUT.
WHAT'S TO KEEP MEETO FROM ALERTING HIS CLIENT AFTER HE LEAVES?
HEY...!
JUST ONE THING.
NO... DON'T DO IT...
BUT TO DO IT WILL MEAN DEPARTING FROM THE JEDI PATH. POSSIBLY FOREVER.
THE LIFE OF BOMO'S DAUGHTER...
...FOR THE LIFE OF A SLAVER.

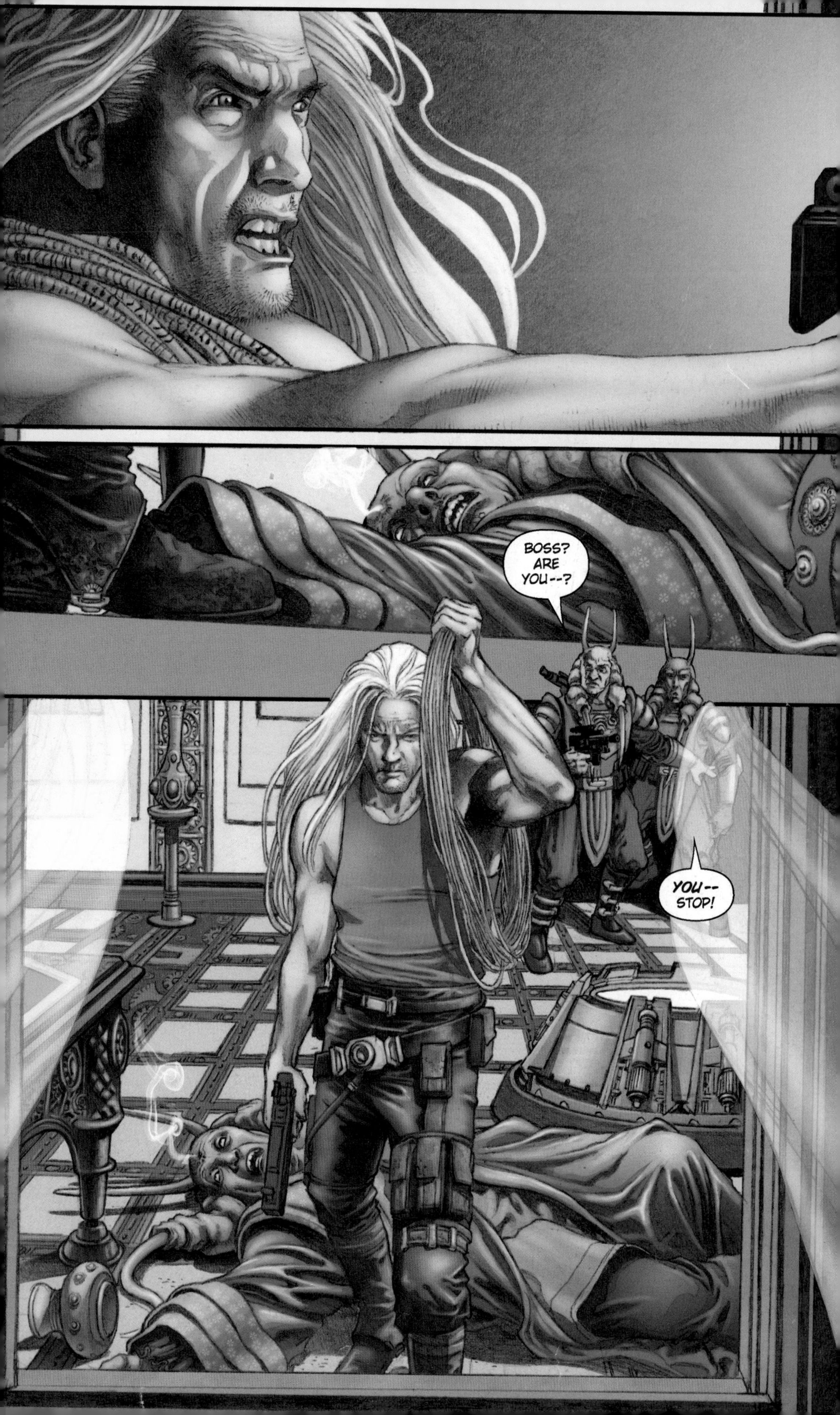
BOSS? ARE YOU--?
YOU-- STOP!

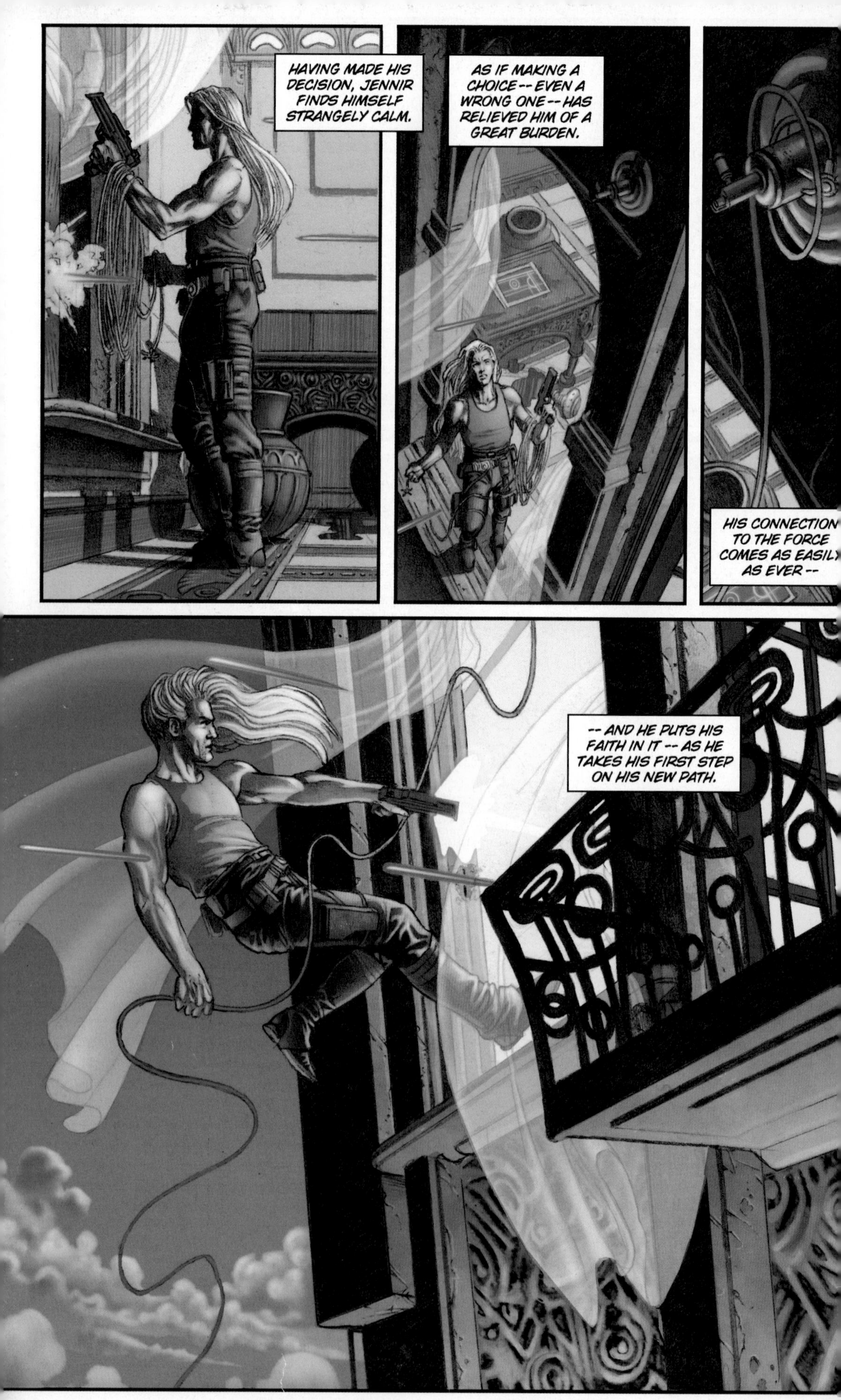
HAVING MADE HIS DECISION, JENNIR FINDS HIMSELF STRANGELY CALM.
AS IF MAKING A CHOICE -- EVEN A WRONG ONE -- HAS RELIEVED HIM OF A GREAT BURDEN.
HIS CONNECTION TO THE FORCE COMES AS EASILY AS EVER --
-- AND HE PUTS HIS FAITH IN IT -- AS HE TAKES HIS FIRST STEP ON HIS NEW PATH.

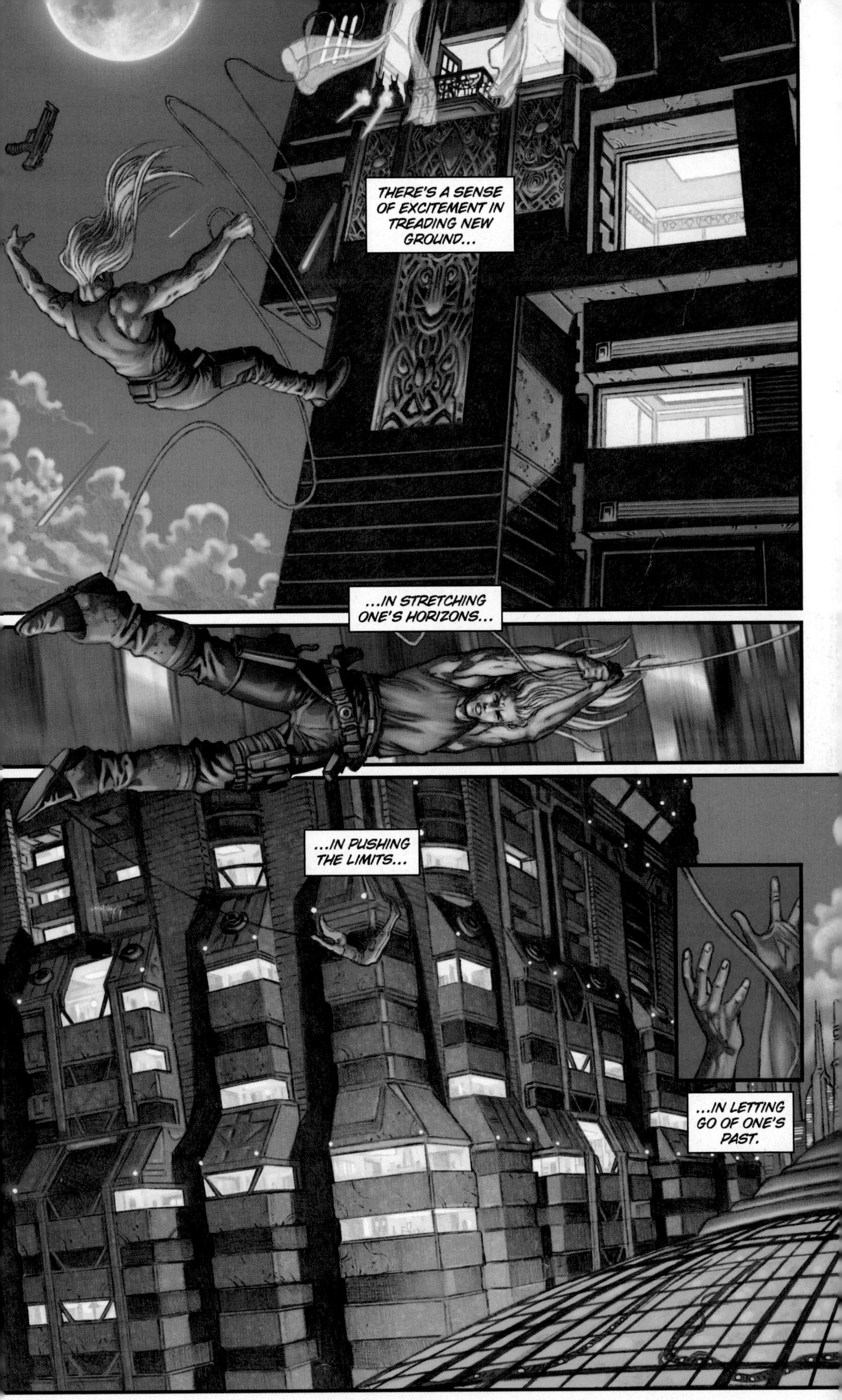

THERE'S A SENSE OF EXCITEMENT IN TREADING NEW GROUND...
...IN STRETCHING ONE'S HORIZONS...
...IN PUSHING THE LIMITS...
...IN LETTING GO OF ONE'S PAST.

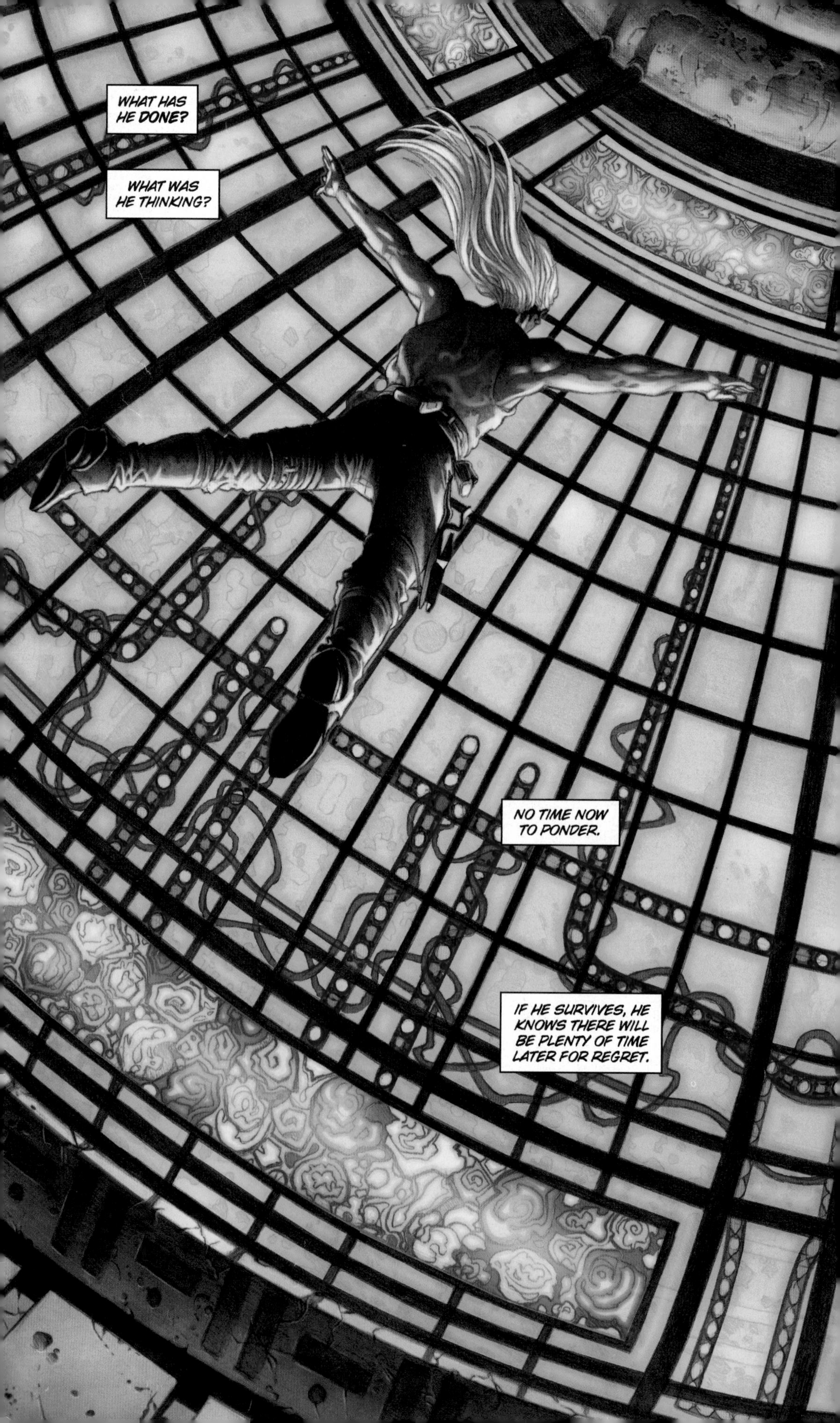
WHAT HAS HE DONE?
WHAT WAS HE THINKING?
NO TIME NOW TO PONDER.
IF HE SURVIVES, HE KNOWS THERE WILL BE PLENTY OF TIME LATER FOR REGRET.

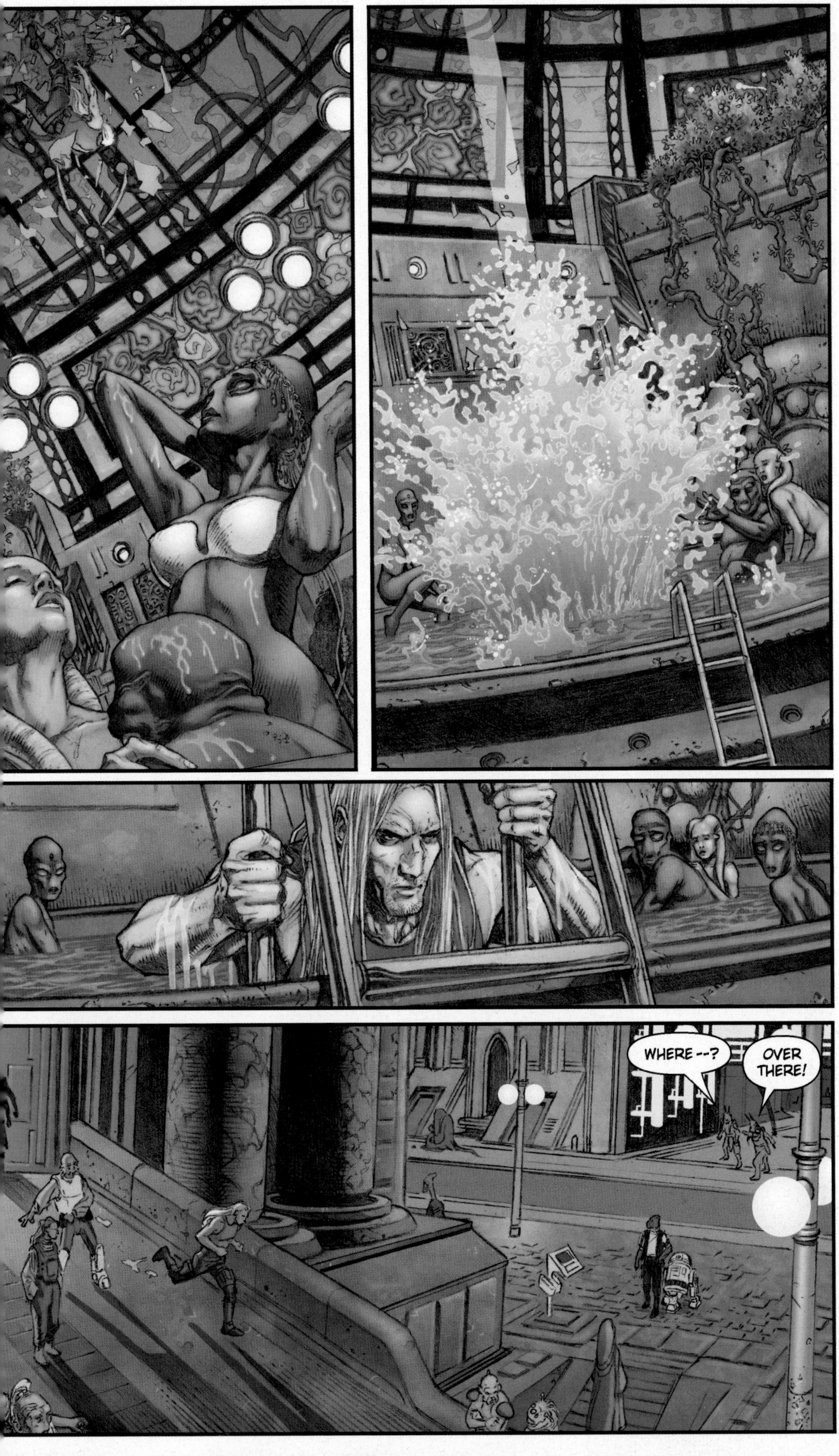
WHERE --?
OVER THERE!

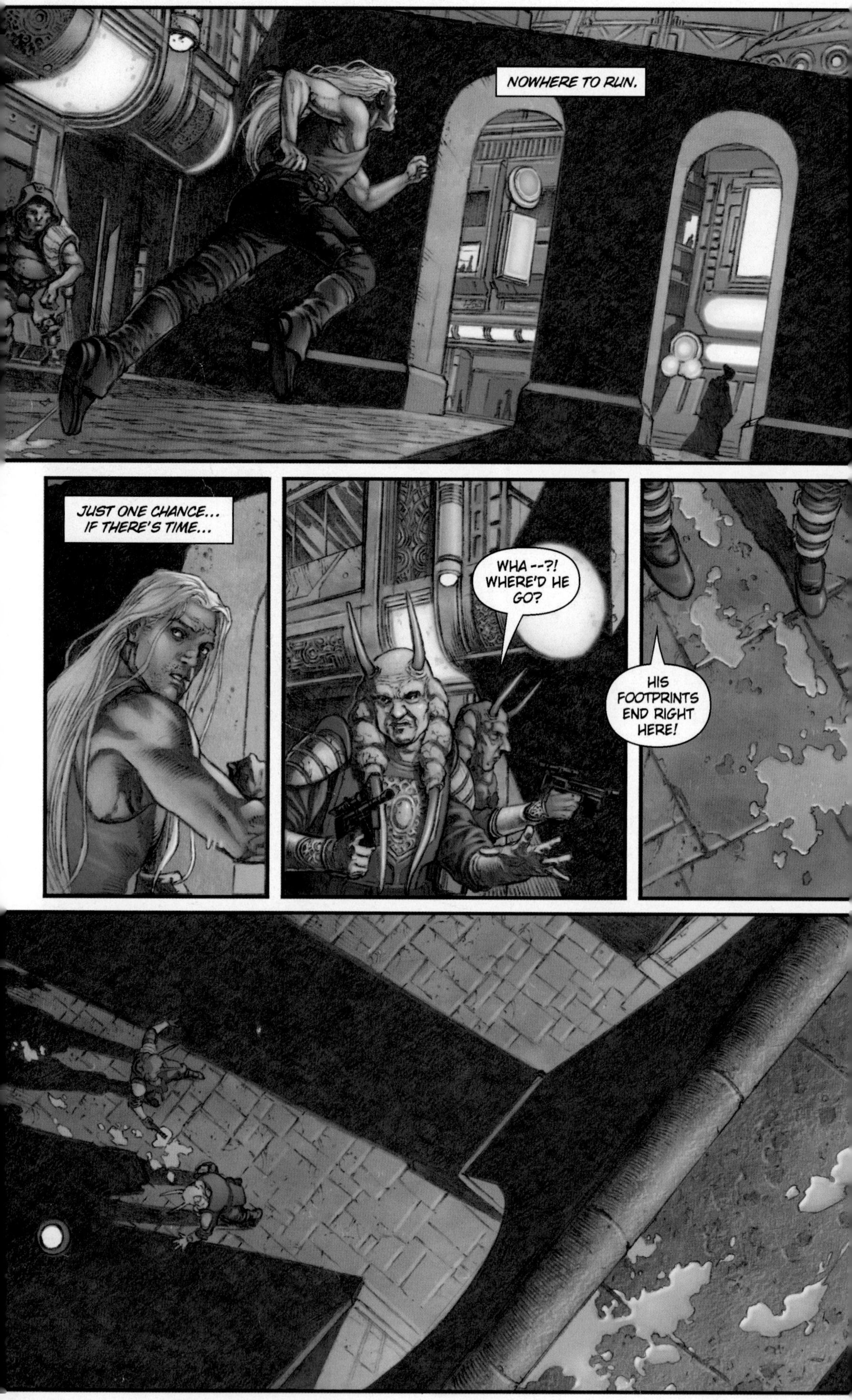
NOWHERE TO RUN.
JUST ONE CHANCE... IF THERE'S TIME...
WHA --?! WHERE'D HE GO?
HIS FOOTPRINTS END RIGHT HERE!

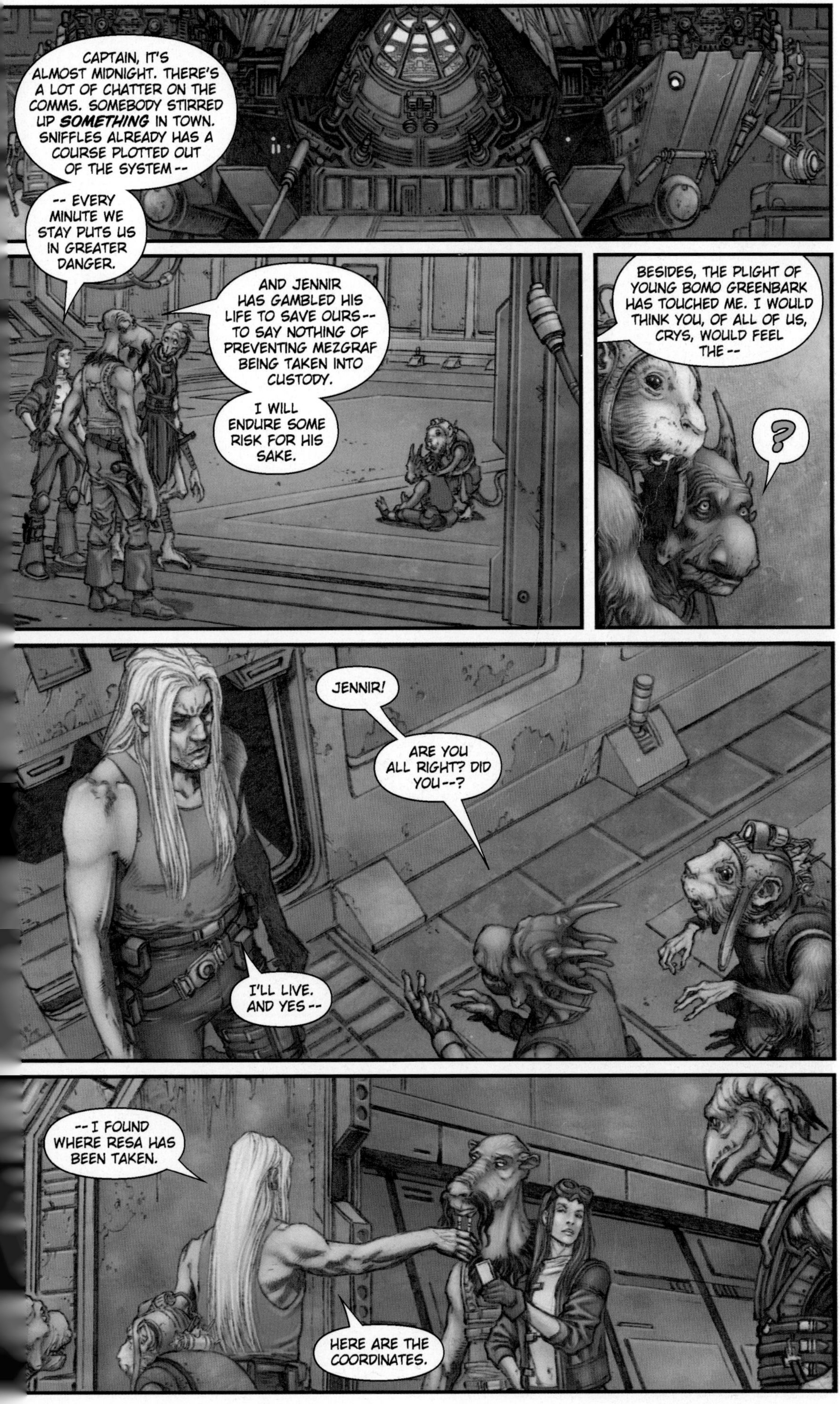
CAPTAIN, IT'S ALMOST MIDNIGHT. THERE'S A LOT OF CHATTER ON THE COMMS. SOMEBODY STIRRED UP *SOMETHING* IN TOWN. SNIFFLES ALREADY HAS A COURSE PLOTTED OUT OF THE SYSTEM --
-- EVERY MINUTE WE STAY PUTS US IN GREATER DANGER.
AND JENNIR HAS GAMBLED HIS LIFE TO SAVE OURS -- TO SAY NOTHING OF PREVENTING MEZGRAF BEING TAKEN INTO CUSTODY.
I WILL ENDURE SOME RISK FOR HIS SAKE.
BESIDES, THE PLIGHT OF YOUNG BOMO GREENBARK HAS TOUCHED ME. I WOULD THINK YOU, OF ALL OF US, CRYS, WOULD FEEL THE --
?
JENNIR!
ARE YOU ALL RIGHT? DID YOU --?
I'LL LIVE. AND YES --
-- I FOUND WHERE RESA HAS BEEN TAKEN.
HERE ARE THE COORDINATES.

SNIFFLES, NEW COURSE. ESSELES. WE'RE LEAVING.

IT'S ABOUT TIME!

IT'S A GOOD THING THAT WE'RE *USED* TO THESE SHORT-NOTICE TAKEOFFS --

-- BECAUSE IT SEEMS TO BE A REGULAR THING WITH YOU.

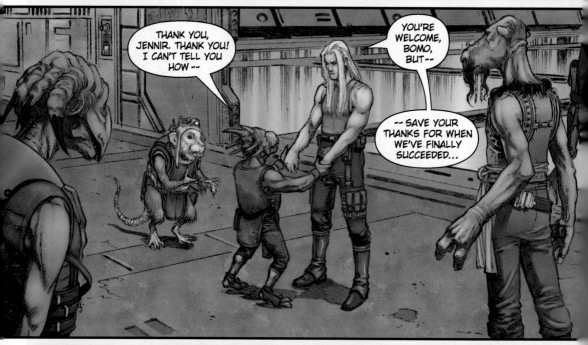

THANK YOU, JENNIR. THANK YOU! I CAN'T TELL YOU HOW --

YOU'RE WELCOME, BOMO, BUT --

-- SAVE YOUR THANKS FOR WHEN WE'VE FINALLY SUCCEEDED...

I HEAR YOU DID WELL --

-- AND THAT WE'RE GOING TO ESSELES. IT'LL BE GOOD TO GET BACK TO A PLACE THAT APPRECIATES CIVILIZATION AND CULTURE!

JANKS...

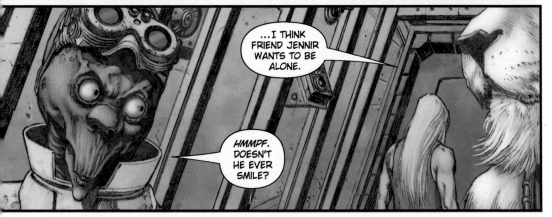

...I THINK FRIEND JENNIR WANTS TO BE ALONE.

HMMPF. DOESN'T HE EVER SMILE?

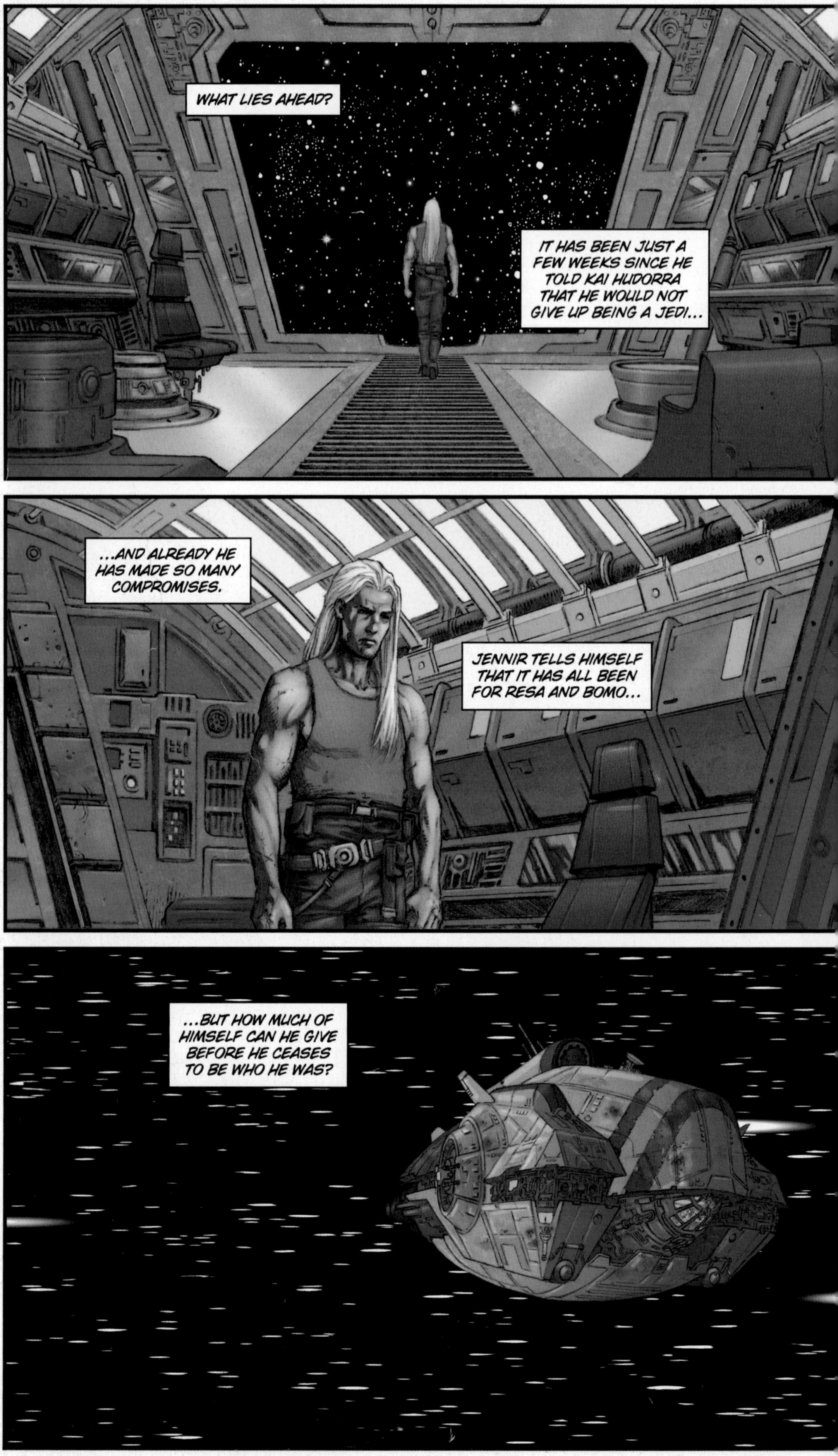
WHAT LIES AHEAD?
IT HAS BEEN JUST A FEW WEEKS SINCE HE TOLD KAI HUDORRA THAT HE WOULD NOT GIVE UP BEING A JEDI...
...AND ALREADY HE HAS MADE SO MANY COMPROMISES.
JENNIR TELLS HIMSELF THAT IT HAS ALL BEEN FOR RESA AND BOMO...
...BUT HOW MUCH OF HIMSELF CAN HE GIVE BEFORE HE CEASES TO BE WHO HE WAS?

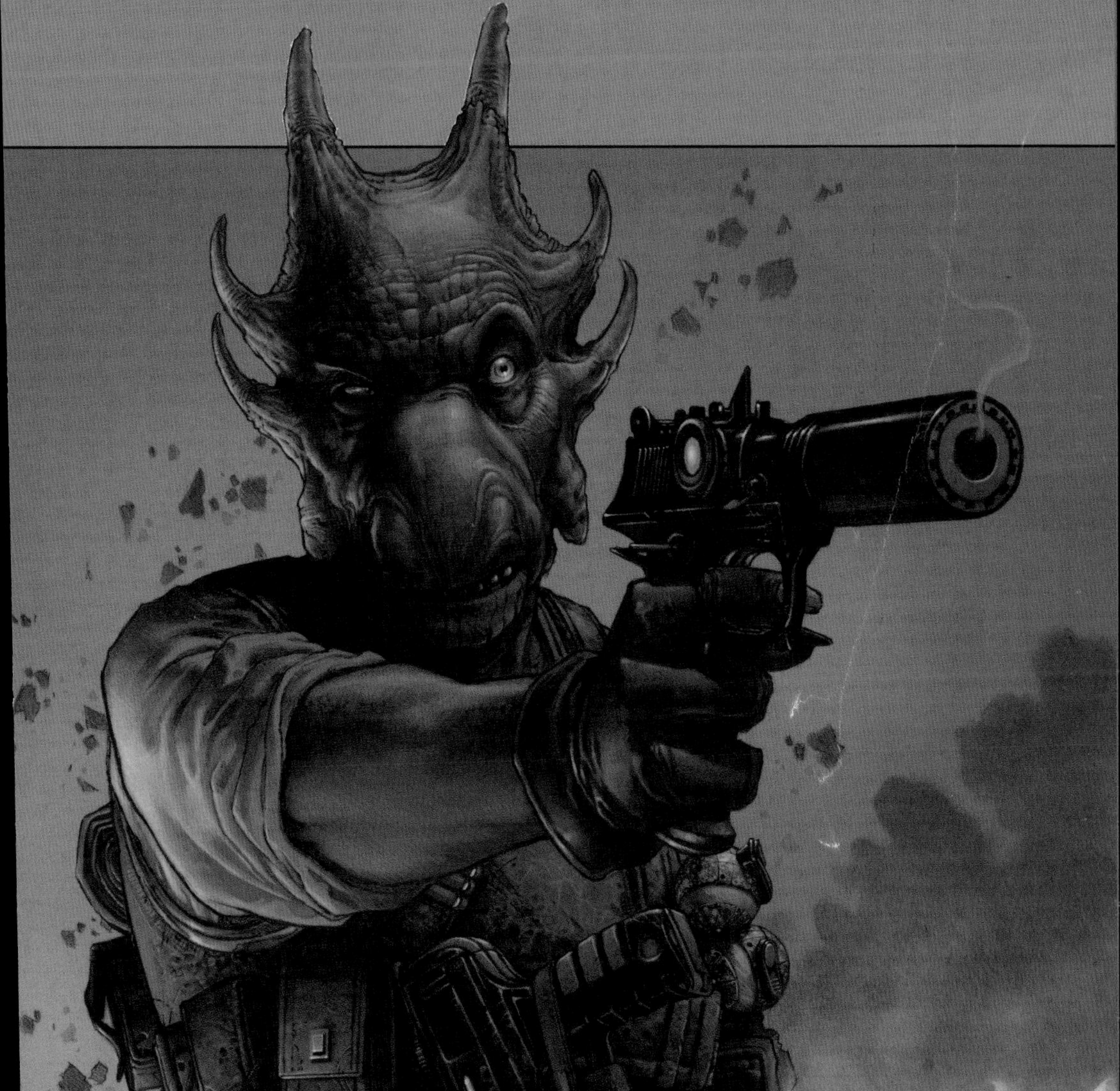

STAR WARS: DARK TIMES #5 **— "THE PATH TO NOWHERE, PART 5 (OF FIVE)"**

WRITER: RANDY STRADLEY (AS WELLES HARTLEY & MICK HARRISON), WITH ADDITIONAL DIALOGUE FROM THE NOVEL *DARK LORD*, BY JAMES LUCENO
IST: DOUGLAS WHEATLEY • COLORIST: RONDA PATTISON • LETTERER: MICHAEL HEISLER • DESIGNER: DARIN FABRICK • ASSISTANT EDITOR: DAVE MARSHALL
EDITOR: RANDY STRADLEY • COVER ARTIST: DOUGLAS WHEATLEY

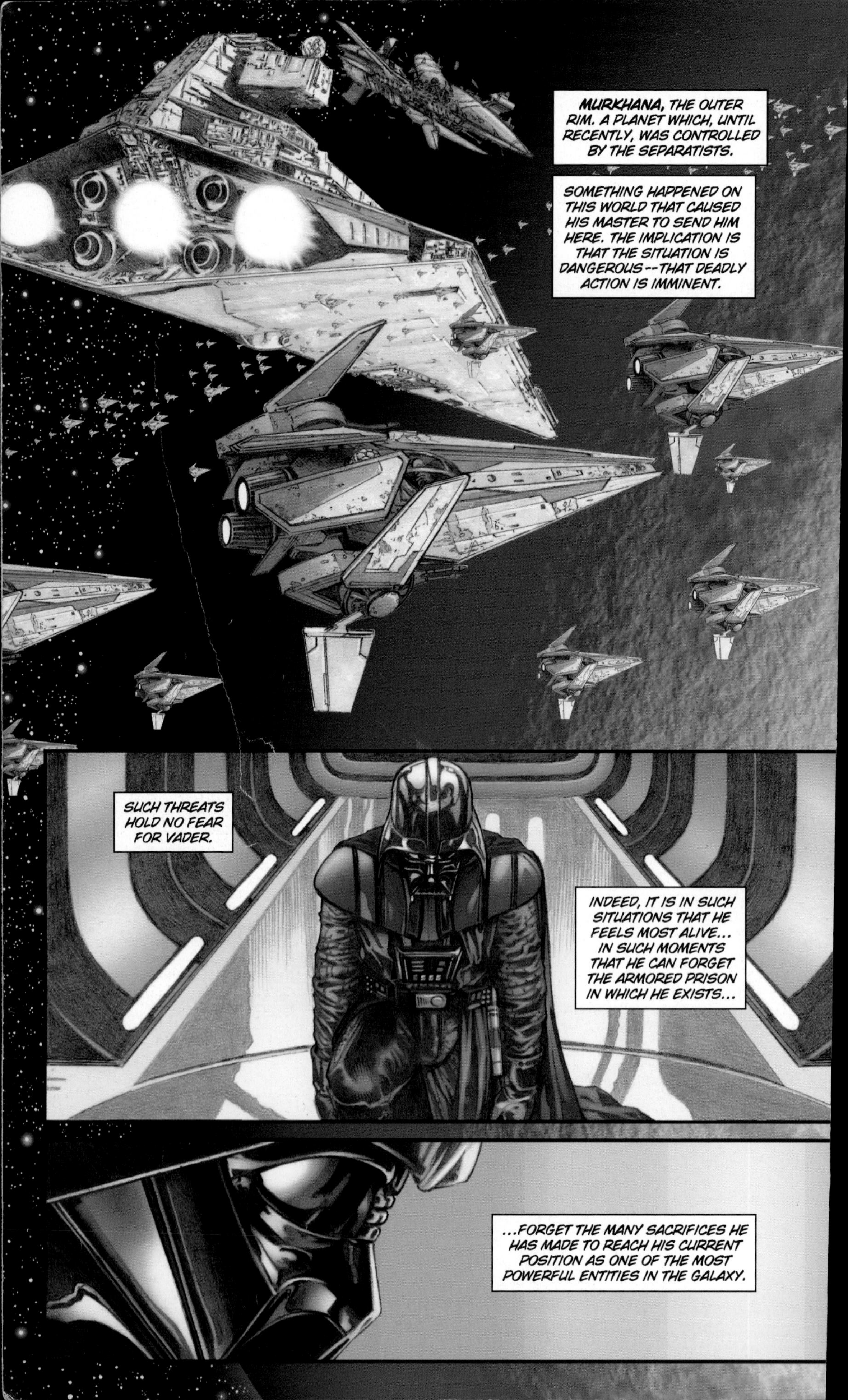
MURKHANA, THE OUTER RIM. A PLANET WHICH, UNTIL RECENTLY, WAS CONTROLLED BY THE SEPARATISTS.
SOMETHING HAPPENED ON THIS WORLD THAT CAUSED HIS MASTER TO SEND HIM HERE. THE IMPLICATION IS THAT THE SITUATION IS DANGEROUS--THAT DEADLY ACTION IS IMMINENT.
SUCH THREATS HOLD NO FEAR FOR VADER.
INDEED, IT IS IN SUCH SITUATIONS THAT HE FEELS MOST ALIVE... IN SUCH MOMENTS THAT HE CAN FORGET THE ARMORED PRISON IN WHICH HE EXISTS...
...FORGET THE MANY SACRIFICES HE HAS MADE TO REACH HIS CURRENT POSITION AS ONE OF THE MOST POWERFUL ENTITIES IN THE GALAXY.

IT IS A FACT VADER WISHES HIS MASTER WAS NOT SO KEENLY AWARE OF.

...IN DUE TIME, POWER WILL FILL THE VACUUM CREATED BY THE DECISIONS YOU MADE...THE ACTS YOU CARRIED OUT. *MARRIED* TO THE ORDER OF THE SITH --

" --YOU WILL NEED NO OTHER COMPANION THAN THE DARK SIDE OF THE FORCE."

WORD HAS REACHED ME THAT A GROUP OF CLONE TROOPERS ON MURKHANA MAY HAVE DELIBERATELY REFUSED TO COMPLY WITH *ORDER 66*...

I HAD NOT HEARD.

WHAT WAS THE CAUSE OF THE TROOPERS' INSUBORDINATION, MASTER?

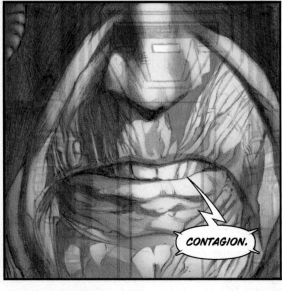

CONTAGION.

CONTAGION BROUGHT ABOUT BY FIGHTING ALONGSIDE THE *JEDI* FOR SO MANY YEARS.

CLONE OR OTHERWISE, THERE IS ONLY SO MUCH A BEING CAN BE *PROGRAMMED* TO DO. SOONER OR LATER, EVEN A LOWLY TROOPER WILL BECOME THE SUM OF HIS EXPERIENCES.

BUT YOU WILL DEMONSTRATE TO THEM THE *PERIL* OF INDEPENDENT THINKING, LORD VADER -- THE REFUSAL TO OBEY ORDERS.

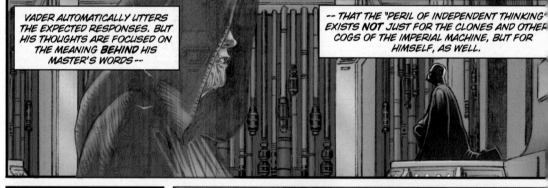

VADER AUTOMATICALLY UTTERS THE EXPECTED RESPONSES. BUT HIS THOUGHTS ARE FOCUSED ON THE MEANING *BEHIND* HIS MASTER'S WORDS --

-- THAT THE "PERIL OF INDEPENDENT THINKING" EXISTS *NOT* JUST FOR THE CLONES AND OTHER COGS OF THE IMPERIAL MACHINE, BUT FOR HIMSELF, AS WELL.

VADER'S WORLD IS NARROW AND DARK AND TIGHTLY STRUCTURED, BUT THERE IS STILL ONE DESIRE THAT STOKES HIS SMOLDERING RAGE...

IT'S POSSIBLE, THEN, THAT SOME *JEDI* MAY HAVE SURVIVED?

I AM NOT WORRIED ABOUT YOUR FORMER PATHETIC *FRIENDS,* LORD VADER. I WANT THOSE CLONE TROOPERS *PUNISHED* -- AS A REMINDER TO ALL OF THEM T[H] FOR THE REST OF THEIR ABBREVIATE[D] LIVES THEY WOULD DO WELL TO UNDERSTAND WHO THEY *TRULY SERV[E]*

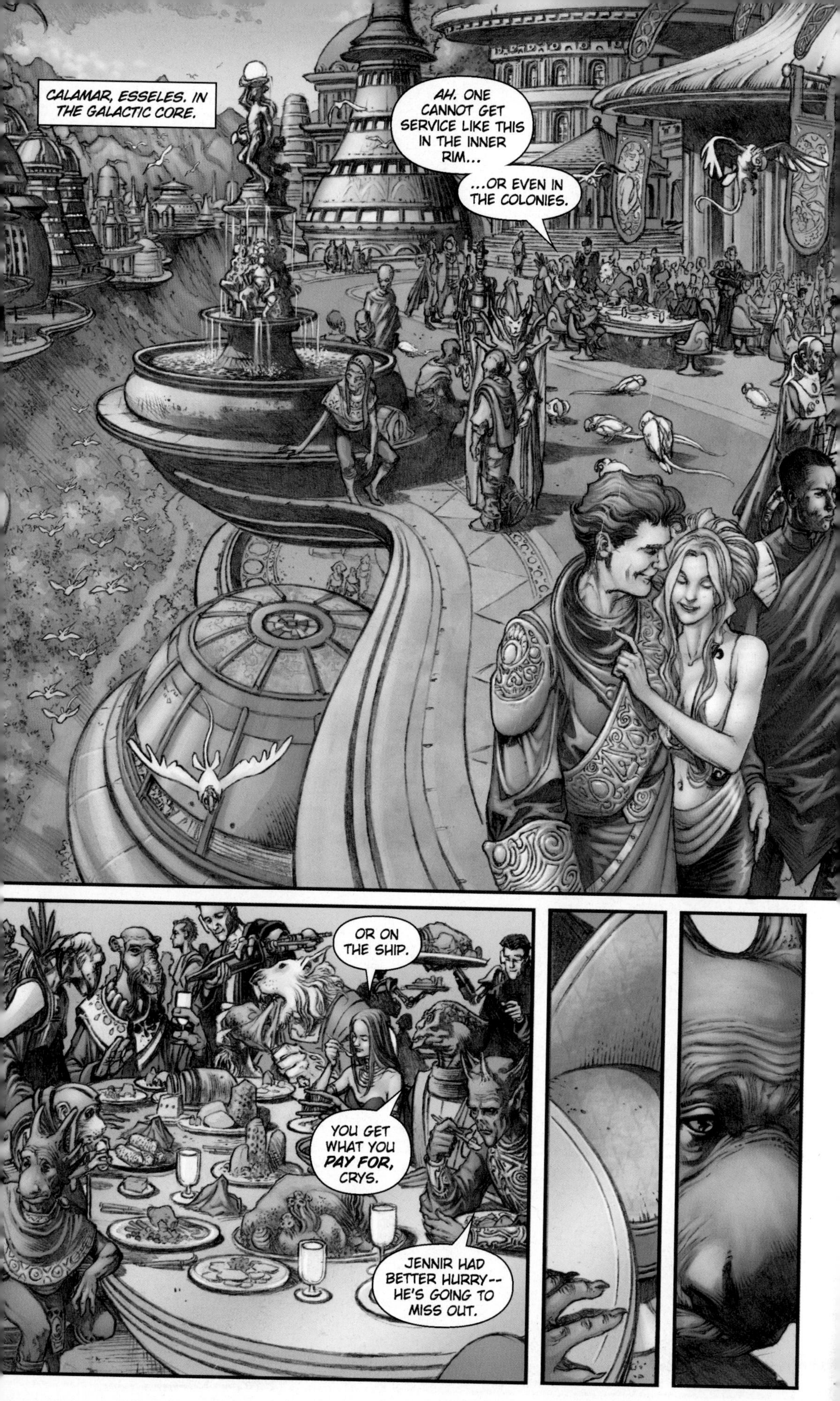
CALAMAR, ESSELES. IN THE GALACTIC CORE.
AH. ONE CANNOT GET SERVICE LIKE THIS IN THE INNER RIM...
...OR EVEN IN THE COLONIES.
OR ON THE SHIP.
YOU GET WHAT YOU PAY FOR, CRYS.
JENNIR HAD BETTER HURRY-- HE'S GOING TO MISS OUT.

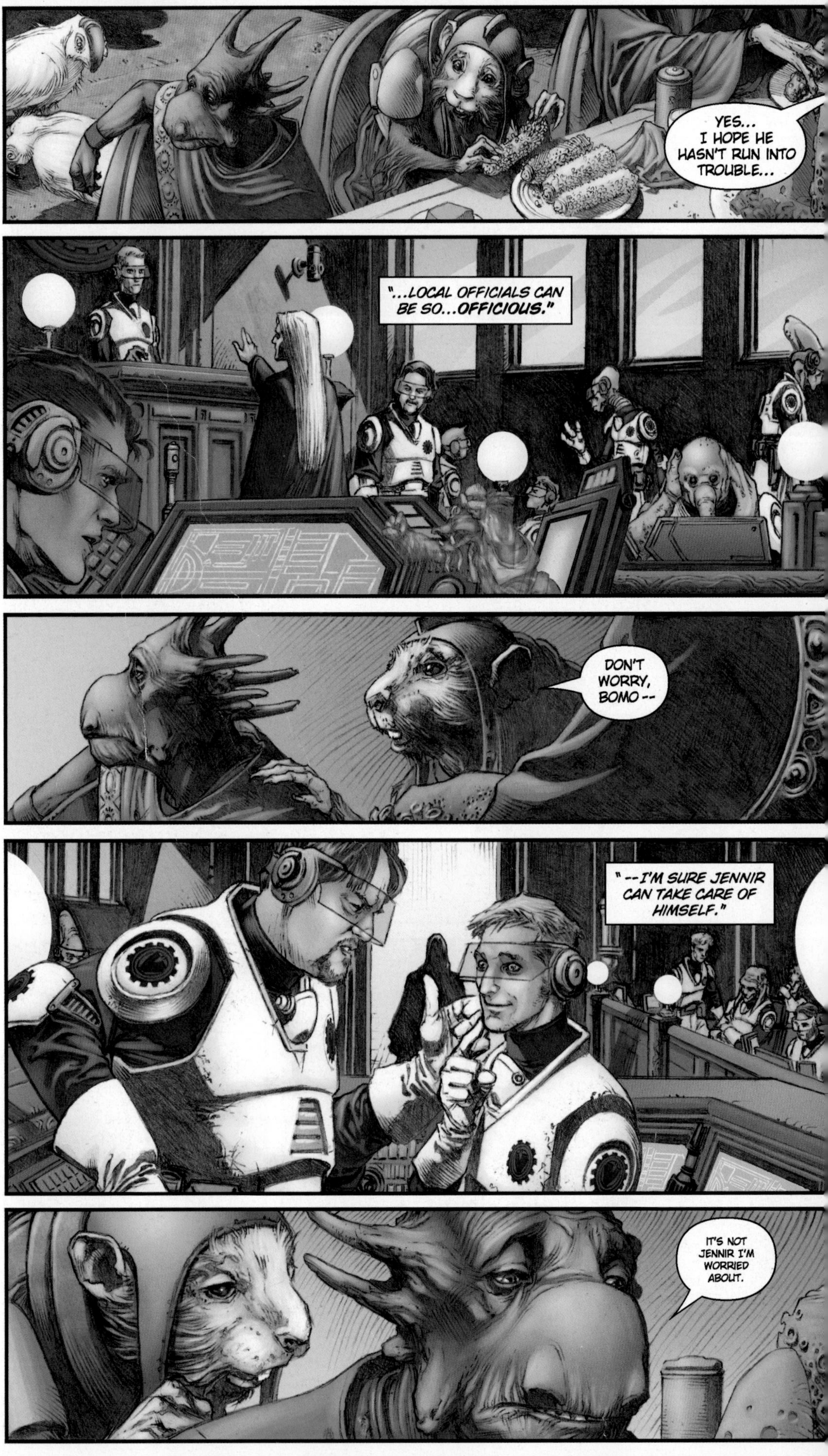
YES... I HOPE HE HASN'T RUN INTO TROUBLE...
"...LOCAL OFFICIALS CAN BE SO...OFFICIOUS."
DON'T WORRY, BOMO --
" --I'M SURE JENNIR CAN TAKE CARE OF HIMSELF."
IT'S NOT JENNIR I'M WORRIED ABOUT.

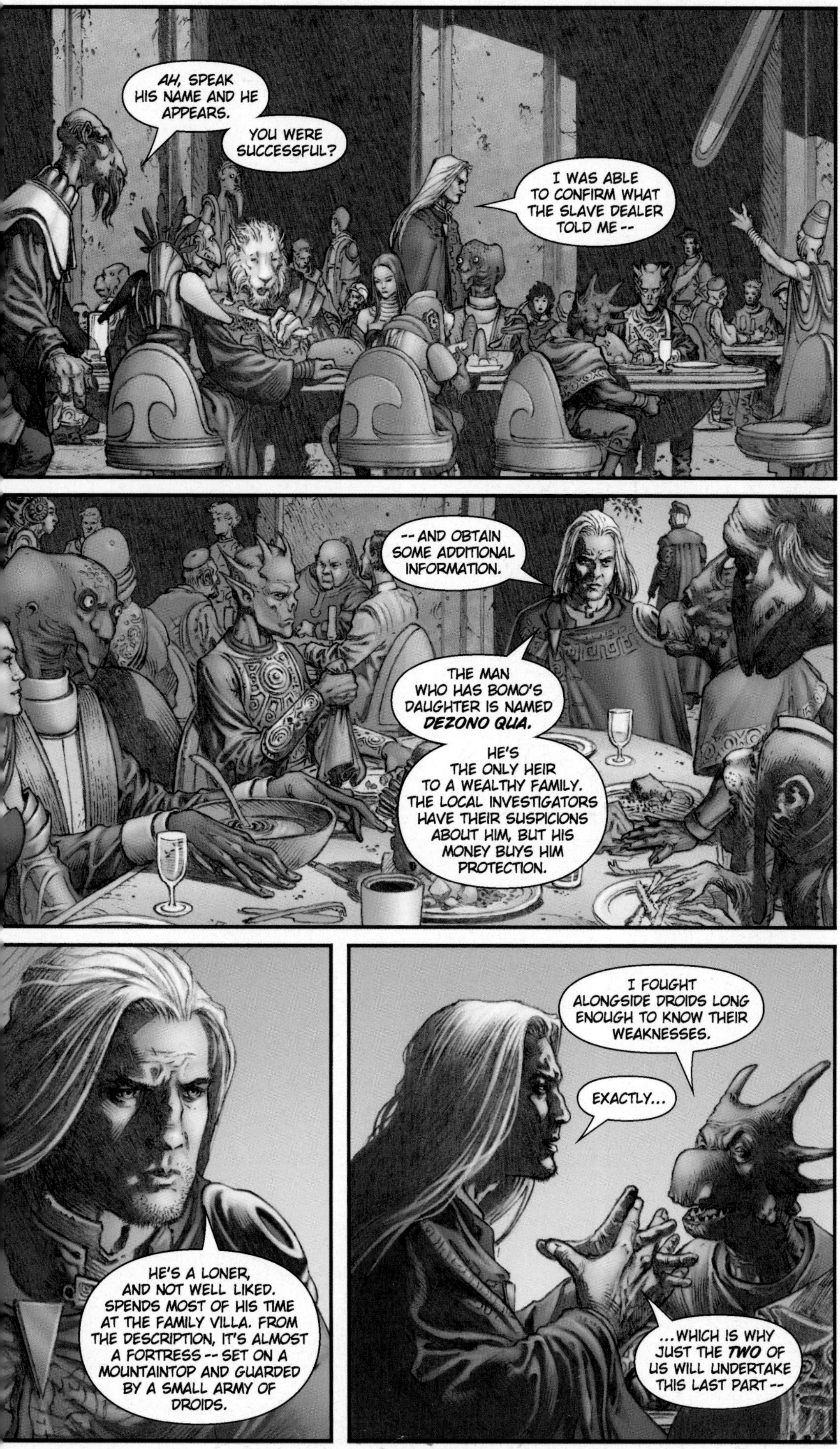

AH, SPEAK HIS NAME AND HE APPEARS.
YOU WERE SUCCESSFUL?
I WAS ABLE TO CONFIRM WHAT THE SLAVE DEALER TOLD ME --
-- AND OBTAIN SOME ADDITIONAL INFORMATION.
THE MAN WHO HAS BOMO'S DAUGHTER IS NAMED DEZONO QUA.
HE'S THE ONLY HEIR TO A WEALTHY FAMILY. THE LOCAL INVESTIGATORS HAVE THEIR SUSPICIONS ABOUT HIM, BUT HIS MONEY BUYS HIM PROTECTION.
HE'S A LONER, AND NOT WELL LIKED. SPENDS MOST OF HIS TIME AT THE FAMILY VILLA. FROM THE DESCRIPTION, IT'S ALMOST A FORTRESS -- SET ON A MOUNTAINTOP AND GUARDED BY A SMALL ARMY OF DROIDS.
I FOUGHT ALONGSIDE DROIDS LONG ENOUGH TO KNOW THEIR WEAKNESSES.
EXACTLY...
...WHICH IS WHY JUST THE TWO OF US WILL UNDERTAKE THIS LAST PART --

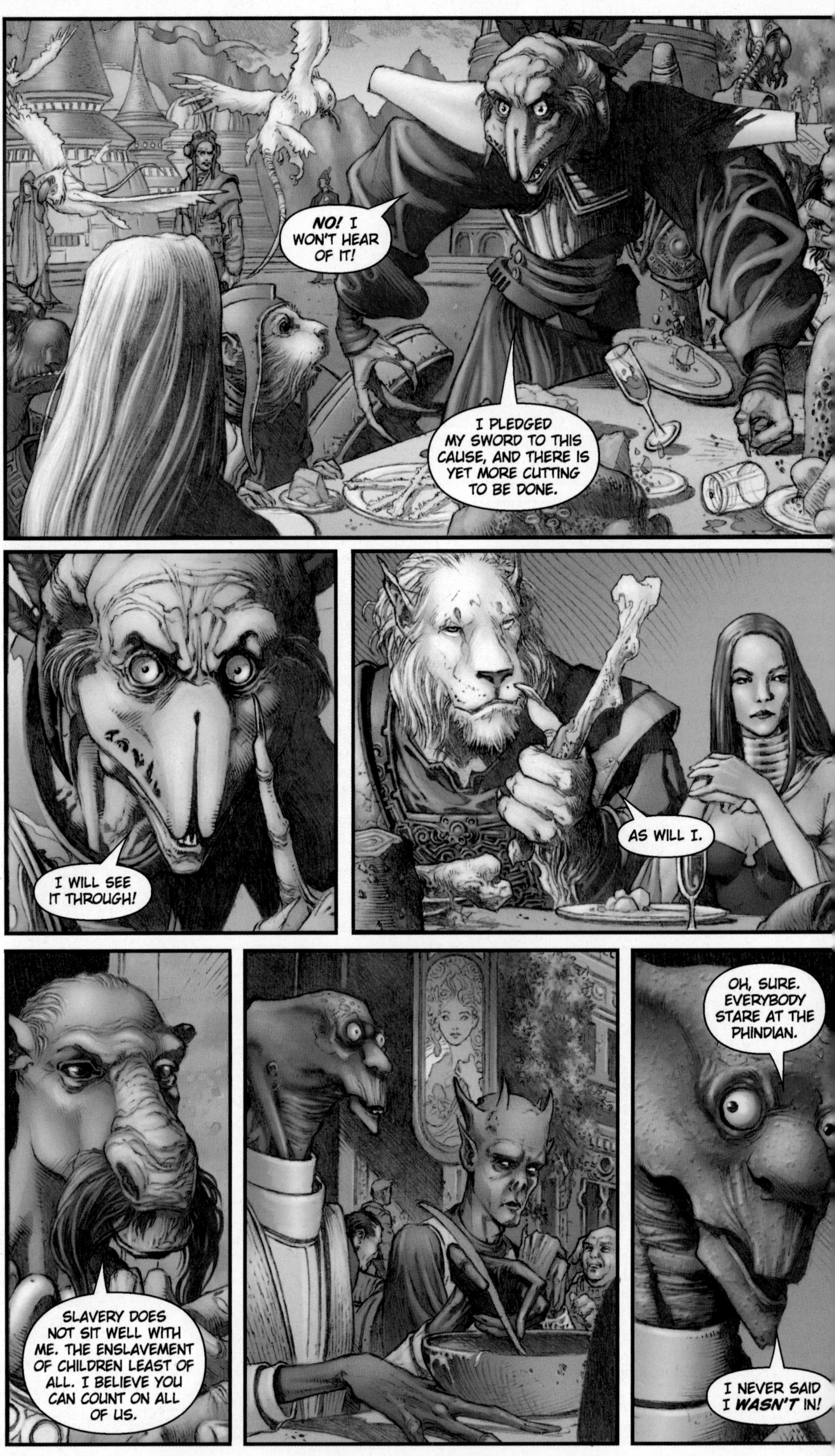
NO! I WON'T HEAR OF IT!
I PLEDGED MY SWORD TO THIS CAUSE, AND THERE IS YET MORE CUTTING TO BE DONE.
I WILL SEE IT THROUGH!
AS WILL I.
SLAVERY DOES NOT SIT WELL WITH ME. THE ENSLAVEMENT OF CHILDREN LEAST OF ALL. I BELIEVE YOU CAN COUNT ON ALL OF US.
OH, SURE. EVERYBODY STARE AT THE PHINDIAN.
I NEVER SAID I WASN'T IN!

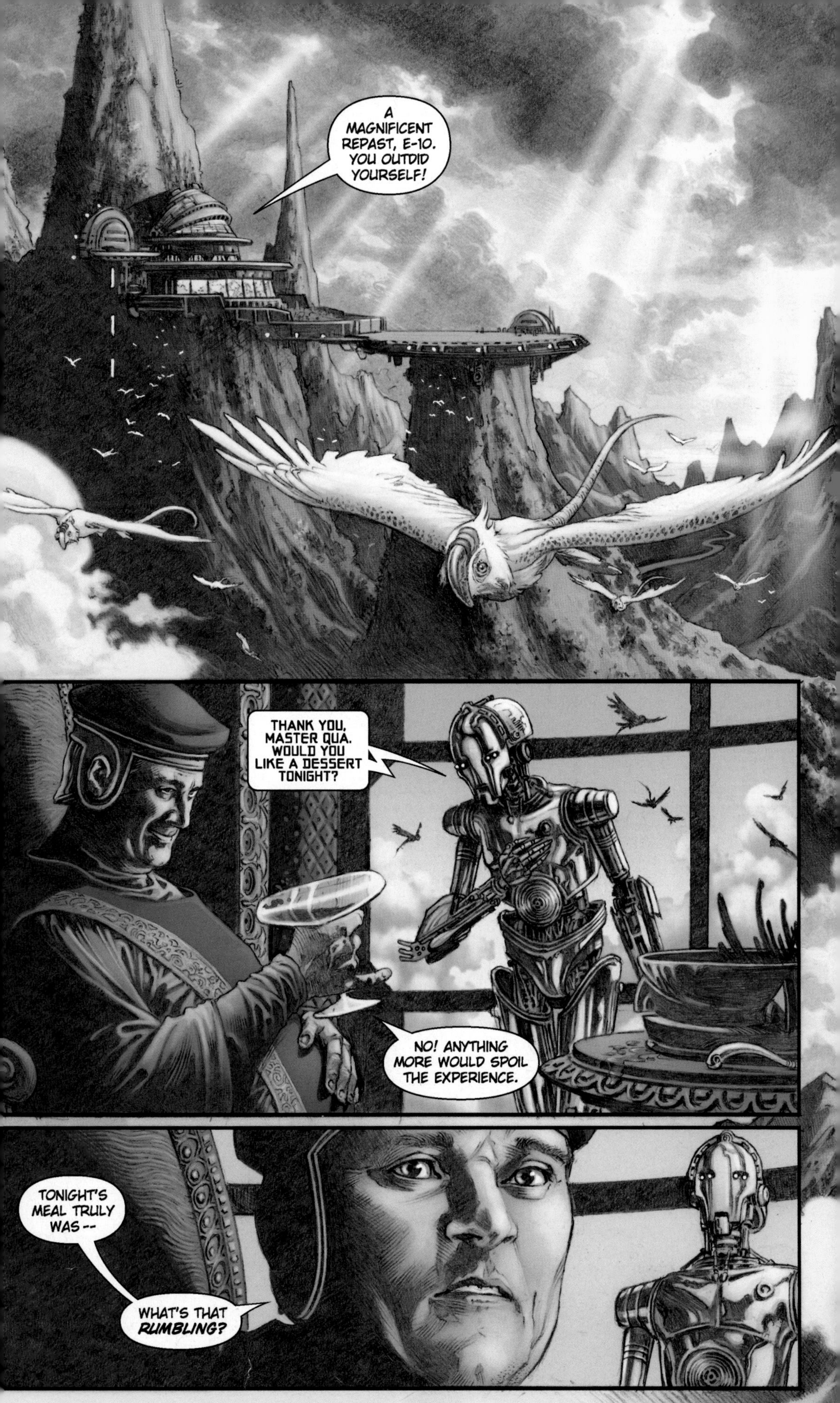
A MAGNIFICENT REPAST, E-10. YOU OUTDID YOURSELF!
THANK YOU, MASTER QUA. WOULD YOU LIKE A DESSERT TONIGHT?
NO! ANYTHING MORE WOULD SPOIL THE EXPERIENCE.
TONIGHT'S MEAL TRULY WAS --
WHAT'S THAT *RUMBLING?*

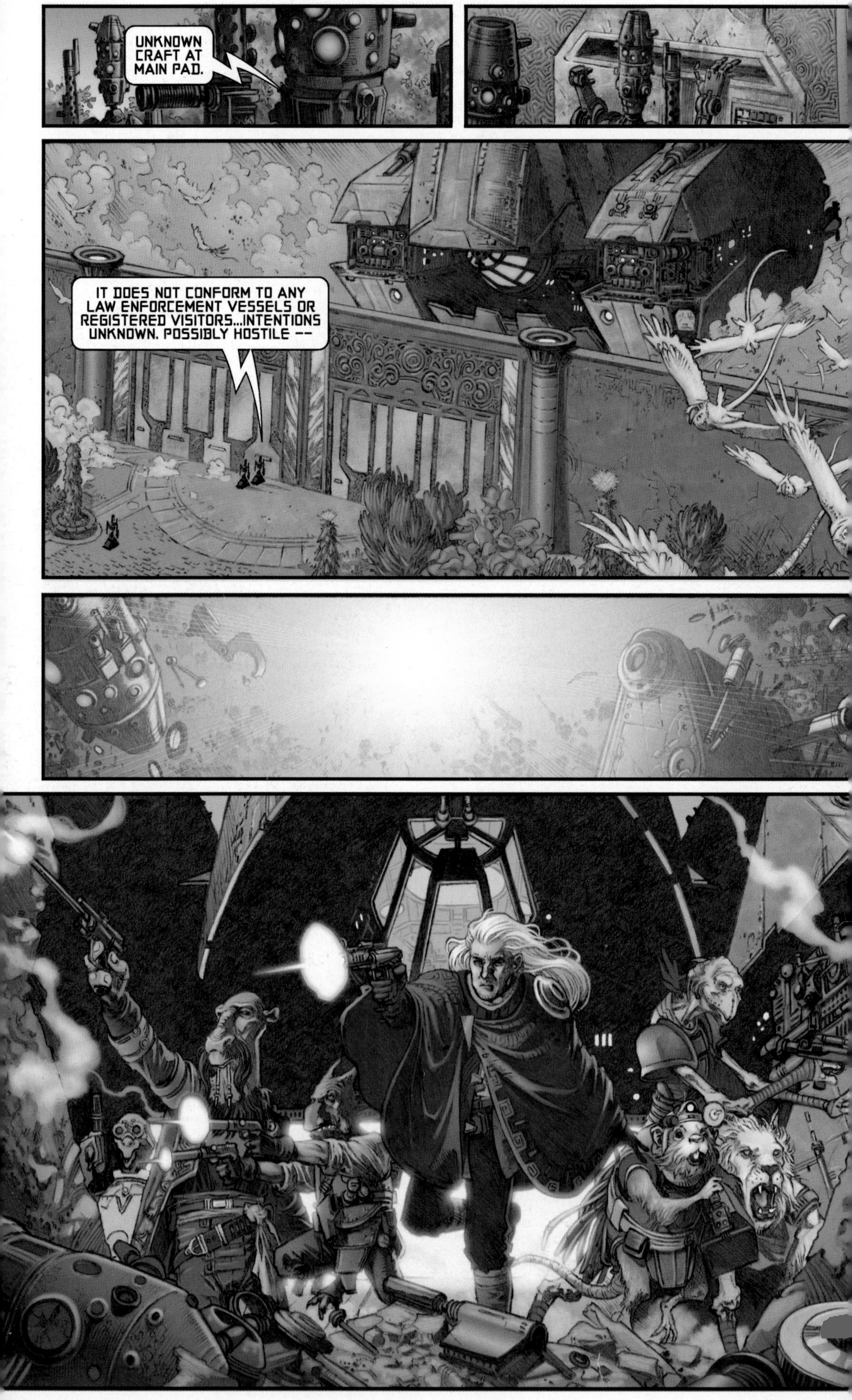
UNKNOWN CRAFT AT MAIN PAD.
IT DOES NOT CONFORM TO ANY LAW ENFORCEMENT VESSELS OR REGISTERED VISITORS...INTENTIONS UNKNOWN. POSSIBLY HOSTILE --

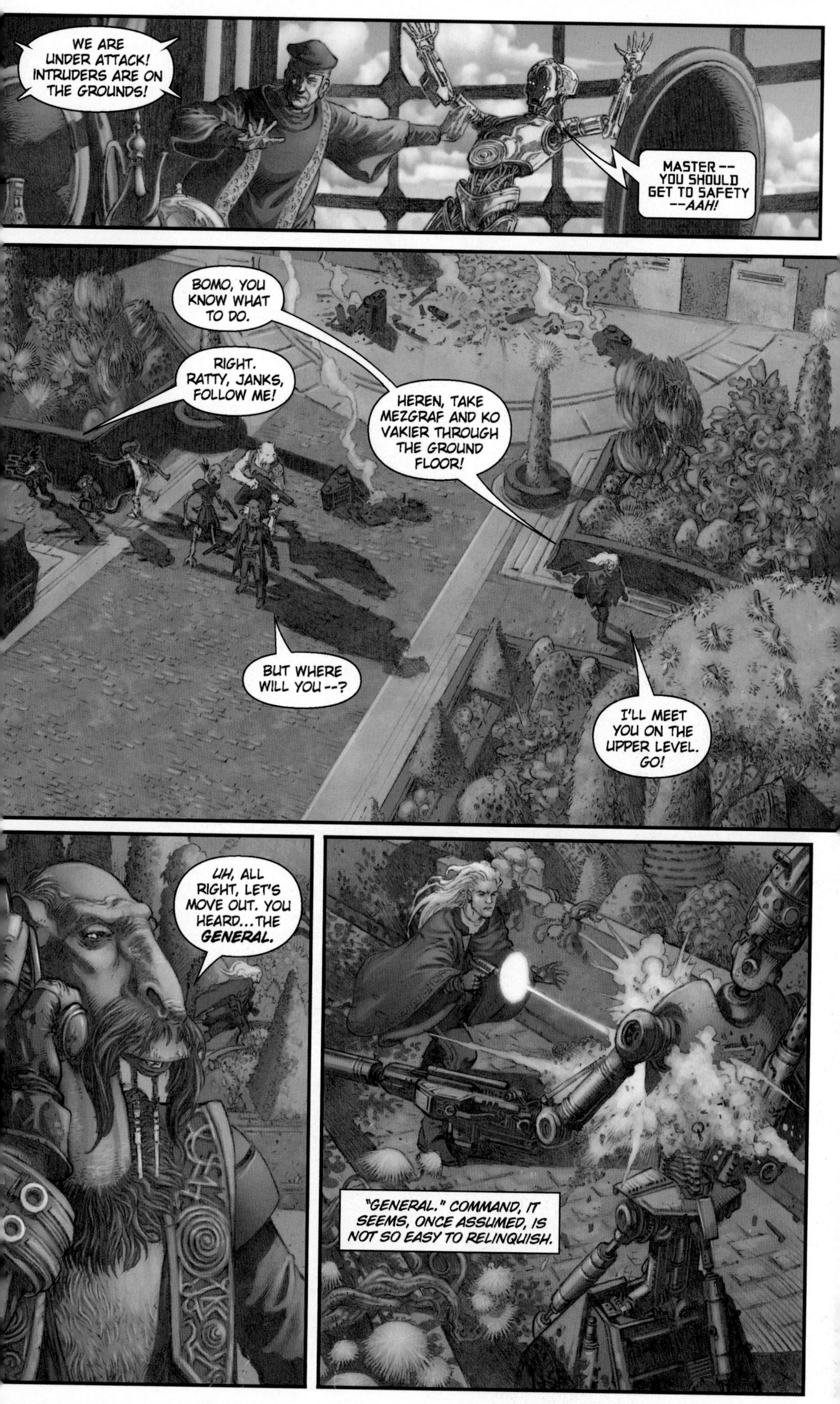
WE ARE UNDER ATTACK! INTRUDERS ARE ON THE GROUNDS!
MASTER -- YOU SHOULD GET TO SAFETY --*AAH!*
BOMO, YOU KNOW WHAT TO DO.
RIGHT. RATTY, JANKS, FOLLOW ME!
HEREN, TAKE MEZGRAF AND KO VAKIER THROUGH THE GROUND FLOOR!
BUT WHERE WILL YOU --?
I'LL MEET YOU ON THE UPPER LEVEL. GO!
UH, ALL RIGHT, LET'S MOVE OUT. YOU HEARD...THE ***GENERAL.***
"GENERAL." COMMAND, IT SEEMS, ONCE ASSUMED, IS NOT SO EASY TO RELINQUISH.

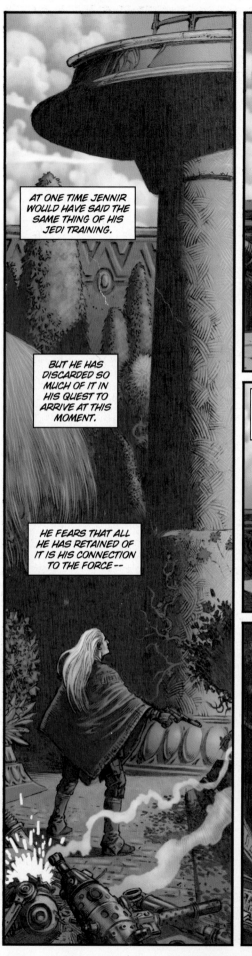

AT ONE TIME JENNIR WOULD HAVE SAID THE SAME THING OF HIS JEDI TRAINING.

BUT HE HAS DISCARDED SO MUCH OF IT IN HIS QUEST TO ARRIVE AT THIS MOMENT.

HE FEARS THAT ALL HE HAS RETAINED OF IT IS HIS CONNECTION TO THE FORCE--

--AND *THAT* ONLY FOR THE SAKE OF EXPEDIENCY.

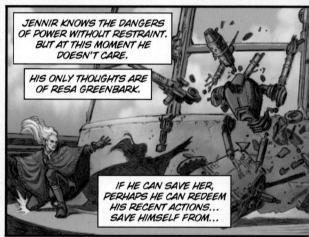

JENNIR KNOWS THE DANGERS OF POWER WITHOUT RESTRAINT. BUT AT THIS MOMENT HE DOESN'T CARE.

HIS ONLY THOUGHTS ARE OF RESA GREENBARK.

IF HE CAN SAVE HER, PERHAPS HE CAN REDEEM HIS RECENT ACTIONS... SAVE HIMSELF FROM...

...DARKNESS.

THIS IS IT -- THIS CONNECTION TIES DIRECTLY TO THE DROIDS' CONTROL CENTER.

GOOD. HOOK UP THE CHARGE!

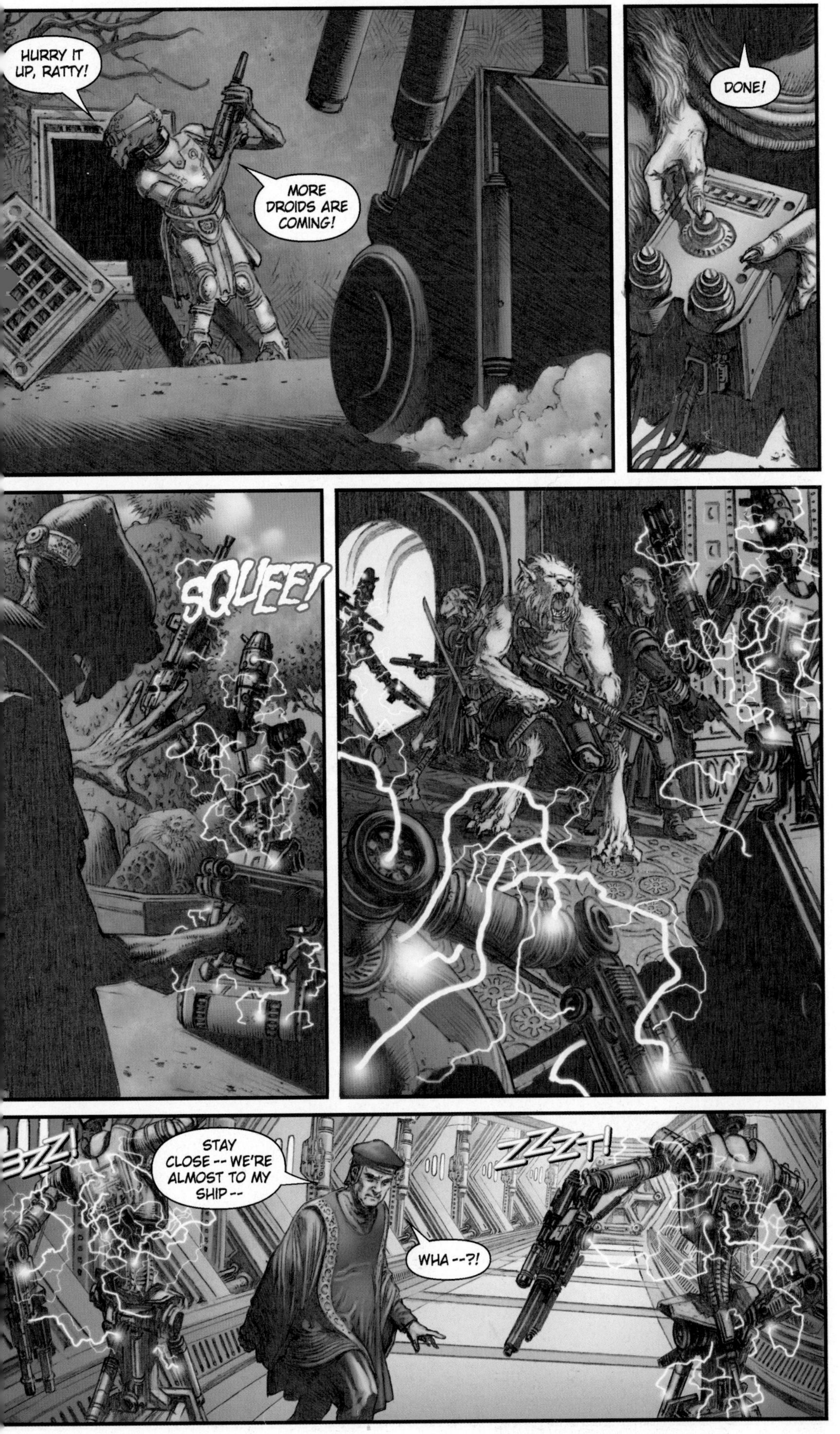
HURRY IT UP, RATTY!
MORE DROIDS ARE COMING!
DONE!
SQUEE!
ZZ!
STAY CLOSE -- WE'RE ALMOST TO MY SHIP --
ZZZT!
WHA --?!

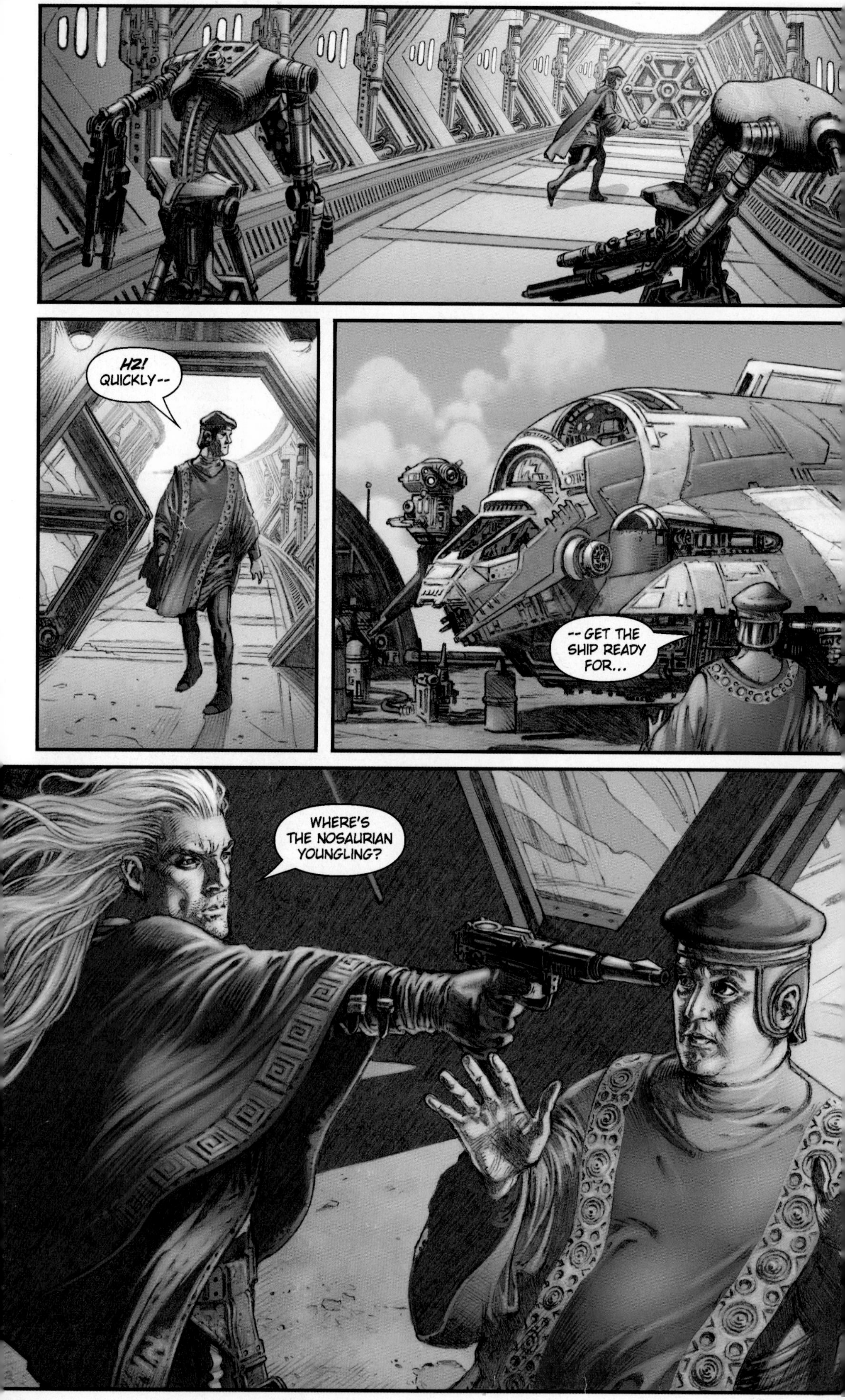
H2! QUICKLY--
-- GET THE SHIP READY FOR...
WHERE'S THE NOSAURIAN YOUNGLING?

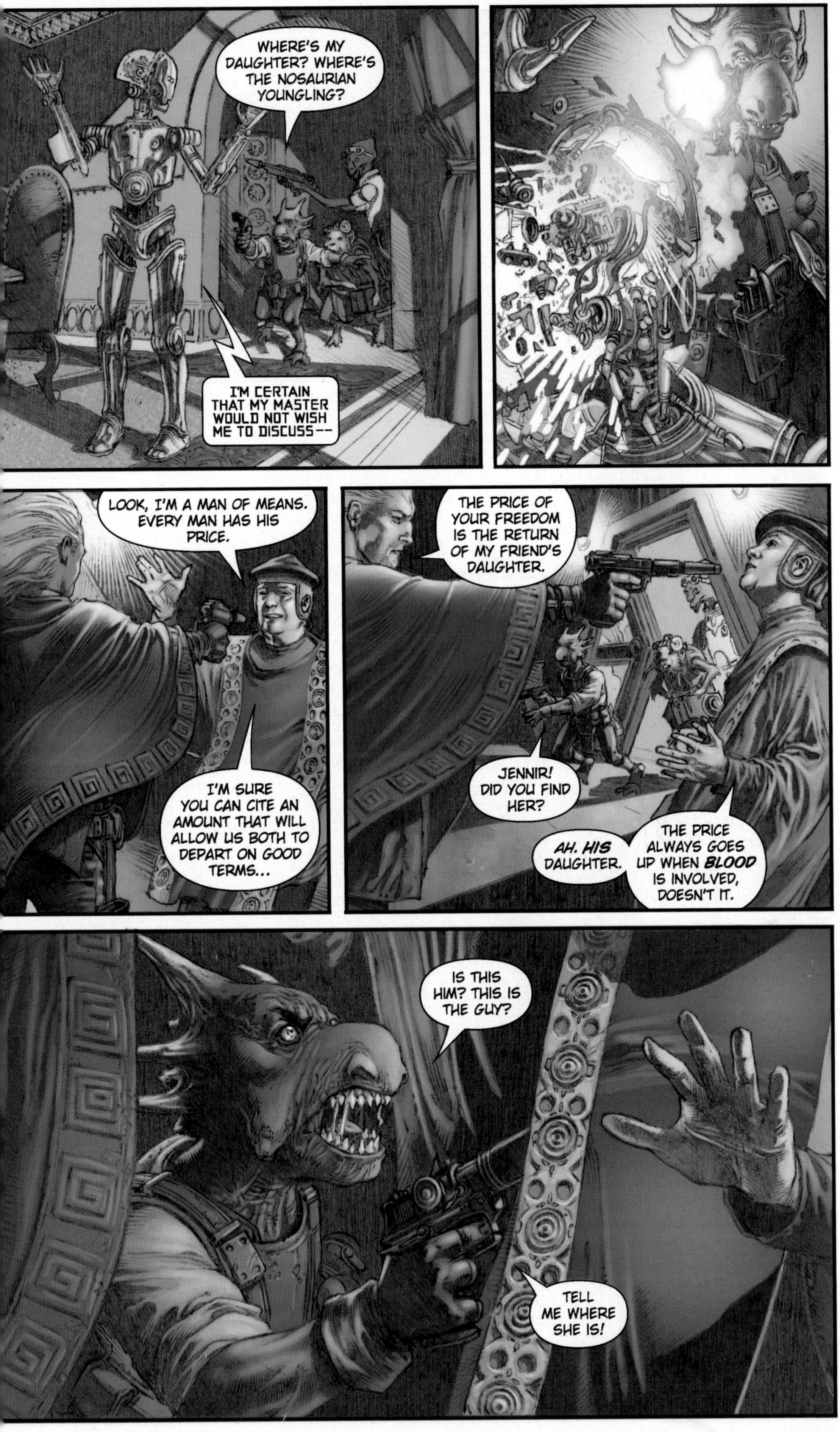
WHERE'S MY DAUGHTER? WHERE'S THE NOSAURIAN YOUNGLING?
I'M CERTAIN THAT MY MASTER WOULD NOT WISH ME TO DISCUSS--
LOOK, I'M A MAN OF MEANS. EVERY MAN HAS HIS PRICE.
I'M SURE YOU CAN CITE AN AMOUNT THAT WILL ALLOW US BOTH TO DEPART ON GOOD TERMS...
THE PRICE OF YOUR FREEDOM IS THE RETURN OF MY FRIEND'S DAUGHTER.
JENNIR! DID YOU FIND HER?
AH. HIS DAUGHTER.
THE PRICE ALWAYS GOES UP WHEN BLOOD IS INVOLVED, DOESN'T IT.
IS THIS HIM? THIS IS THE GUY?
TELL ME WHERE SHE IS!

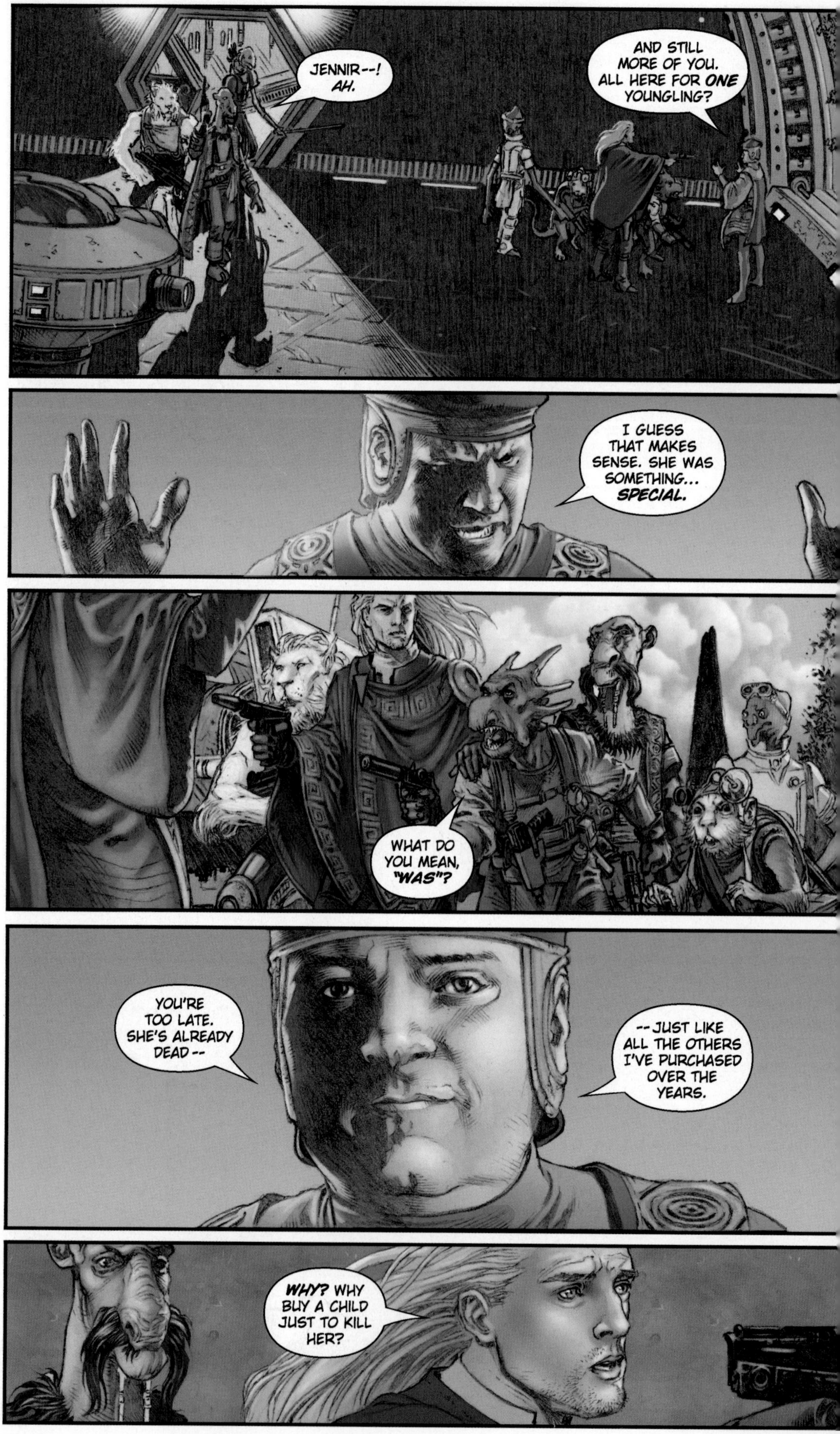

JENNIR--! AH.
AND STILL MORE OF YOU. ALL HERE FOR ONE YOUNGLING?
I GUESS THAT MAKES SENSE. SHE WAS SOMETHING... SPECIAL.
WHAT DO YOU MEAN, "WAS"?
YOU'RE TOO LATE. SHE'S ALREADY DEAD --
-- JUST LIKE ALL THE OTHERS I'VE PURCHASED OVER THE YEARS.
WHY? WHY BUY A CHILD JUST TO KILL HER?

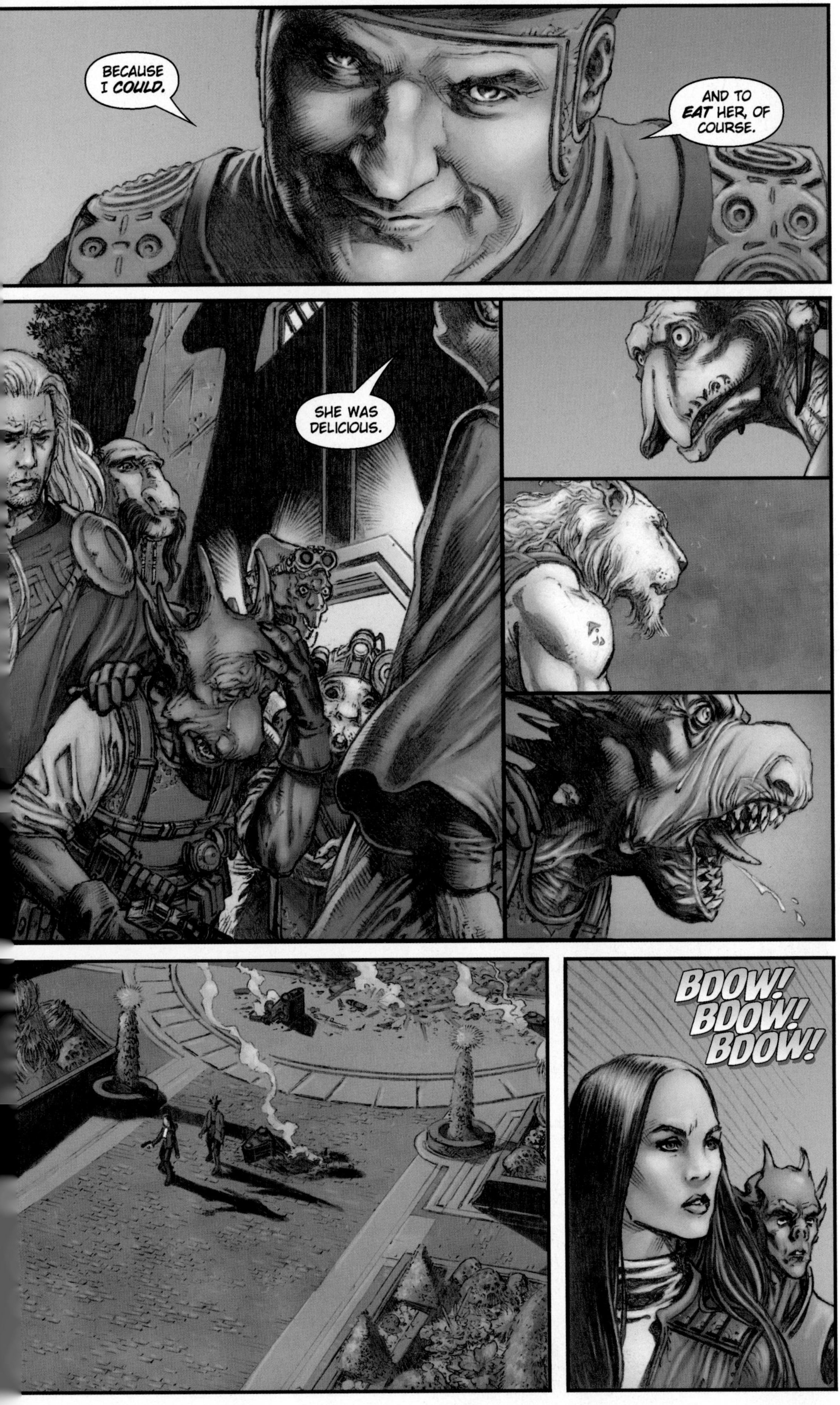
BECAUSE I COULD.
AND TO EAT HER, OF COURSE.
SHE WAS DELICIOUS.
BDOW! BDOW! BDOW!

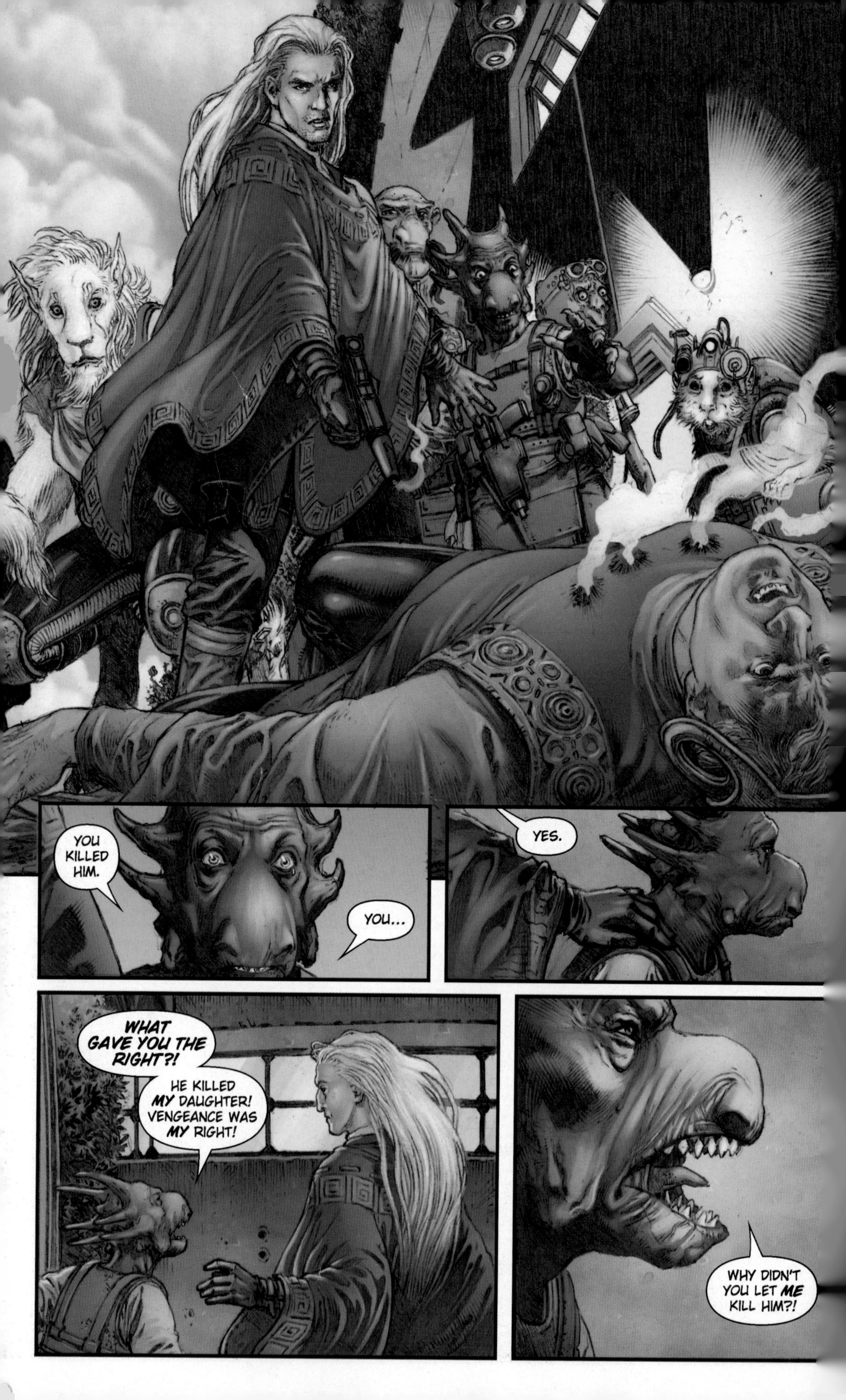

YOU KILLED HIM.
YOU...
YES.
WHAT GAVE YOU THE RIGHT?!
HE KILLED MY DAUGHTER! VENGEANCE WAS MY RIGHT!
WHY DIDN'T YOU LET ME KILL HIM?!

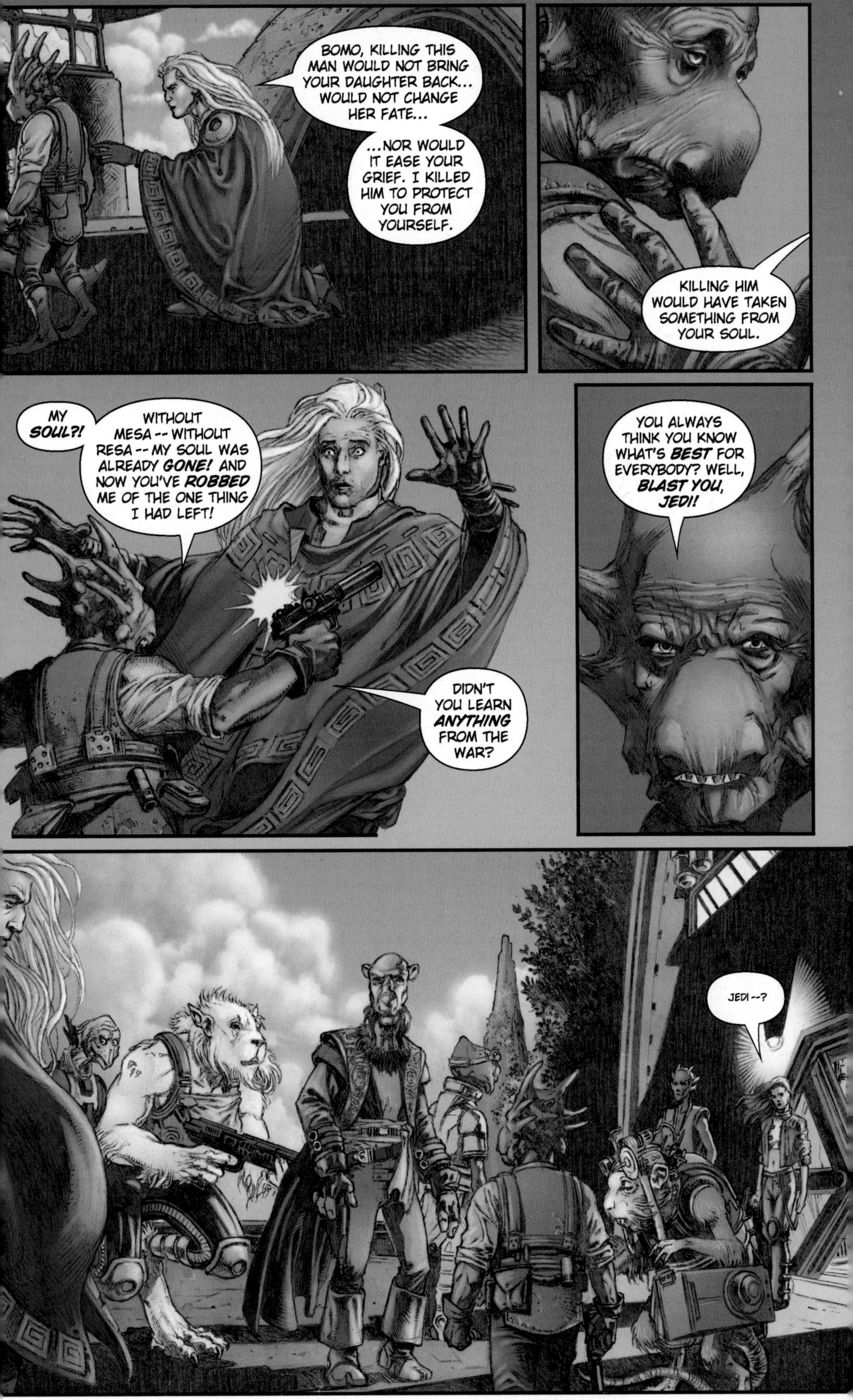
BOMO, KILLING THIS MAN WOULD NOT BRING YOUR DAUGHTER BACK... WOULD NOT CHANGE HER FATE...
...NOR WOULD IT EASE YOUR GRIEF. I KILLED HIM TO PROTECT YOU FROM YOURSELF.
KILLING HIM WOULD HAVE TAKEN SOMETHING FROM YOUR SOUL.
MY SOUL?!
WITHOUT MESA -- WITHOUT RESA -- MY SOUL WAS ALREADY GONE! AND NOW YOU'VE ROBBED ME OF THE ONE THING I HAD LEFT!
DIDN'T YOU LEARN ANYTHING FROM THE WAR?
YOU ALWAYS THINK YOU KNOW WHAT'S BEST FOR EVERYBODY? WELL, BLAST YOU, JEDI!
JEDI --?

THE JEDI USED TO SAY THAT THE FUTURE WAS ALWAYS IN MOTION, AND DIFFICULT TO READ...

...THAT ONLY THOSE WHO TURNED TO THE DARK SIDE COULD SENSE THE POSSIBILITIES OF THE FUTURE.

THE POSSIBILITIES?

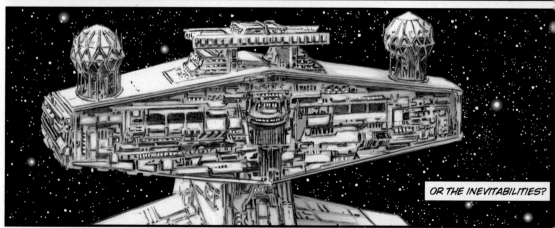

OR THE INEVITABILITIES?

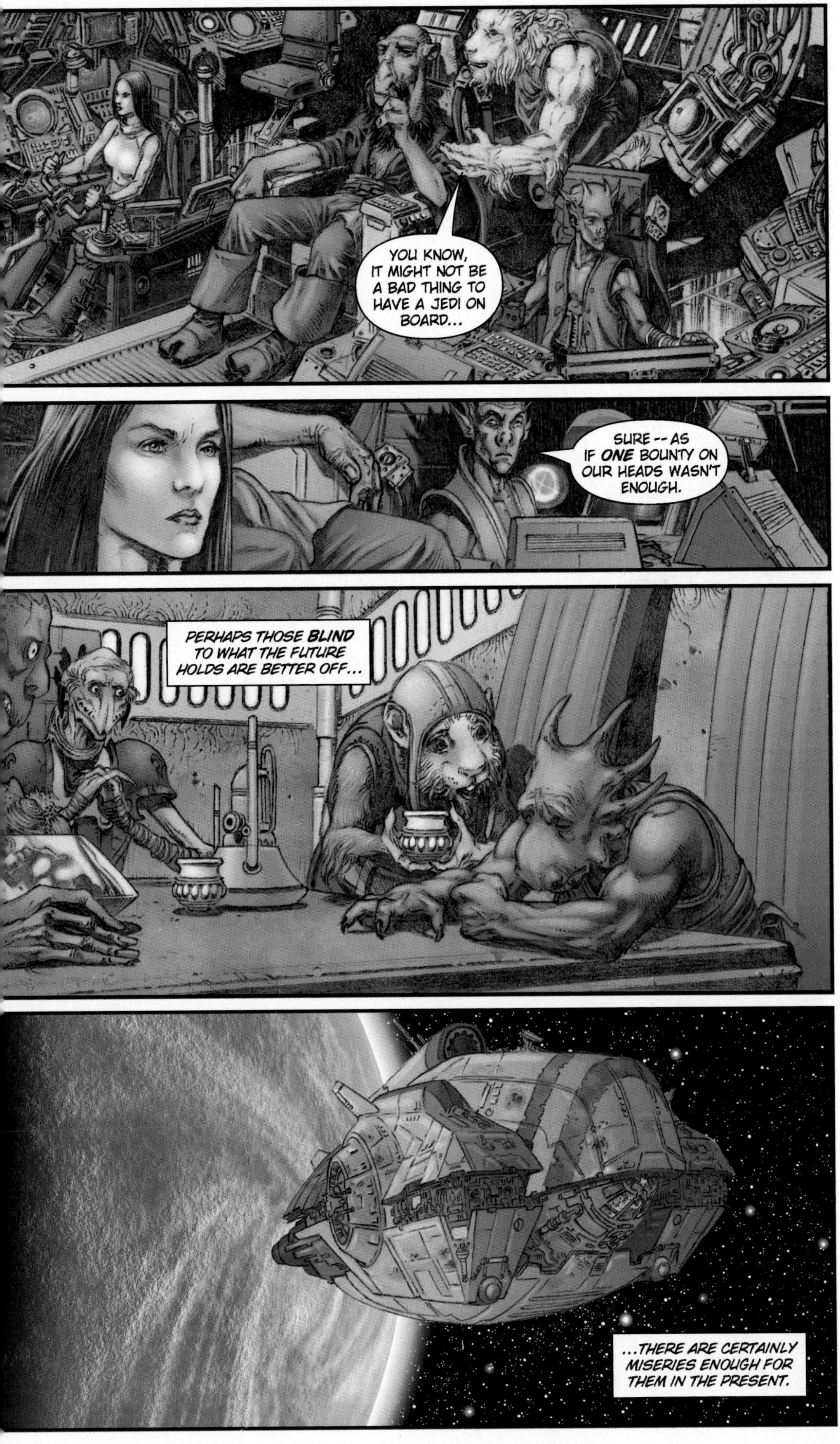
YOU KNOW, IT MIGHT NOT BE A BAD THING TO HAVE A JEDI ON BOARD...
SURE -- AS IF ONE BOUNTY ON OUR HEADS WASN'T ENOUGH.
PERHAPS THOSE BLIND TO WHAT THE FUTURE HOLDS ARE BETTER OFF...
...THERE ARE CERTAINLY MISERIES ENOUGH FOR THEM IN THE PRESENT.

LET THE FUTURE BE UNKNOWN... A MYSTERY.

BUT DASS JENNIR CANNOT RUN FROM HIS PAST.

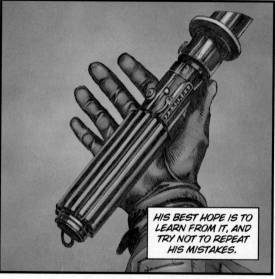

HIS BEST HOPE IS TO LEARN FROM IT, AND TRY NOT TO REPEAT HIS MISTAKES.

ALL HE HAS TO HOLD ONTO IS WHAT HIS TRAINING TELLS HIM TO BE TRUE.

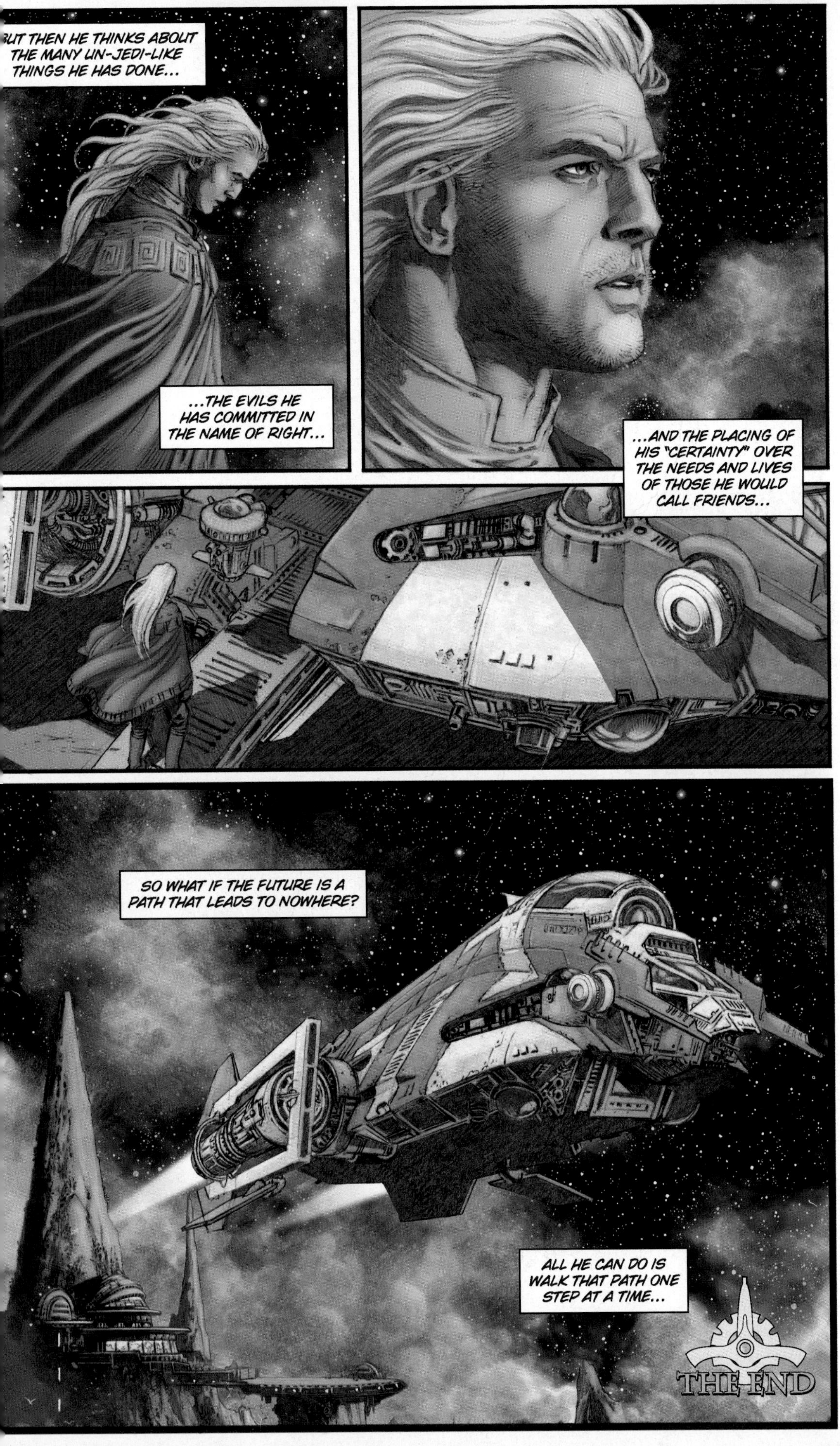
BUT THEN HE THINKS ABOUT THE MANY UN-JEDI-LIKE THINGS HE HAS DONE...
...THE EVILS HE HAS COMMITTED IN THE NAME OF RIGHT...
...AND THE PLACING OF HIS "CERTAINTY" OVER THE NEEDS AND LIVES OF THOSE HE WOULD CALL FRIENDS...
SO WHAT IF THE FUTURE IS A PATH THAT LEADS TO NOWHERE?
ALL HE CAN DO IS WALK THAT PATH ONE STEP AT A TIME...
THE END

CLONE WARS

Many Jedi have been gunned down by their own clone troops. Those lucky or skillful enough to survive Order 66 now find themselves faced with the darkest of questions. Is it too late to save the Republic they swore to defend?

ENDGAME

Some Jedi will make valiant last stands. Others will seek asylum in the shadows of the underworld, turning their backs on a galaxy that has betrayed them. Still others will try to carry on, attempting to bring freedom to the oppressed. And a resolute few will band together to topple Sith rule, setting a trap for the Emperor's new enforcer—Darth Vader!

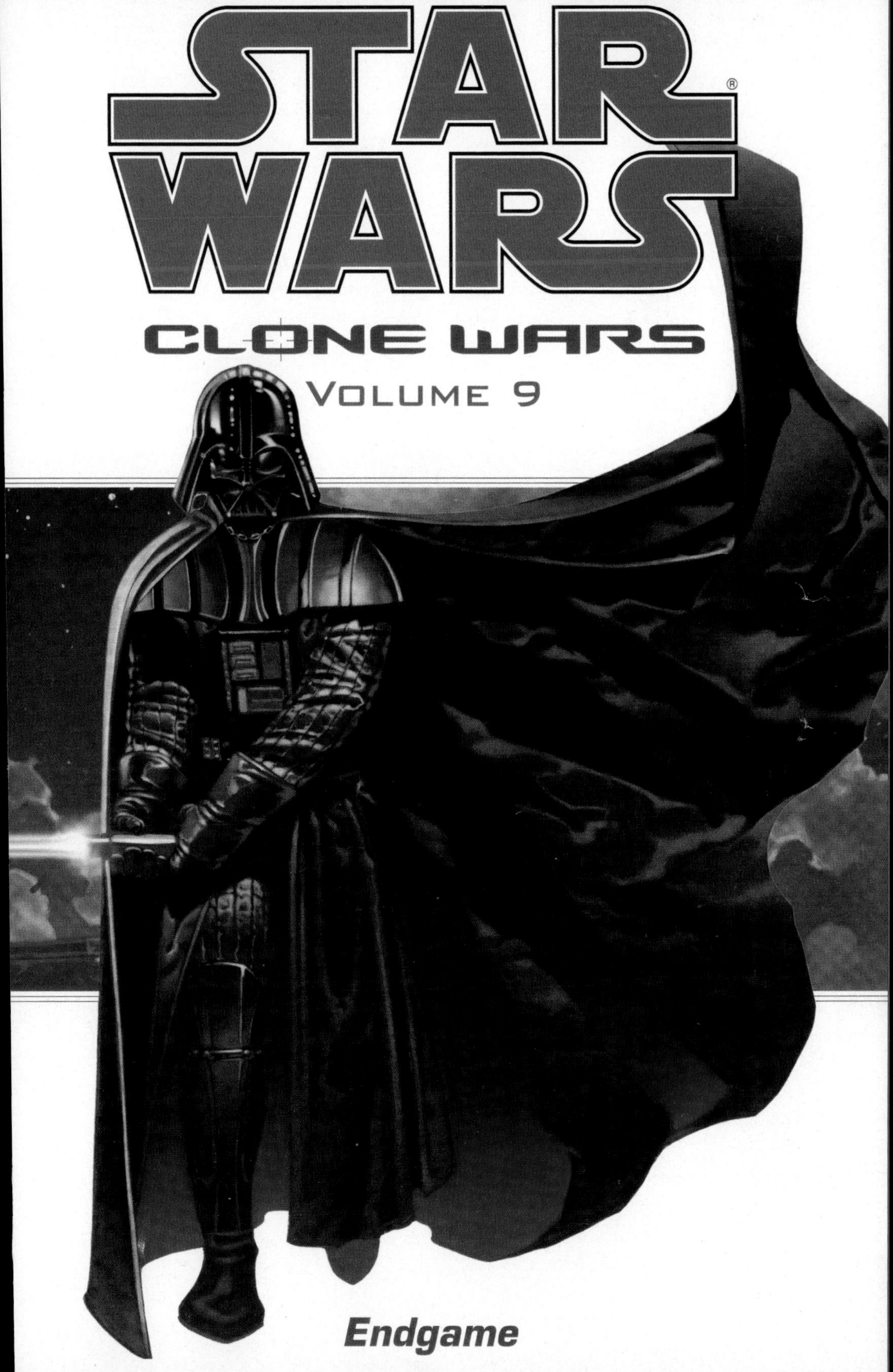
STAR WARS
CLONE WARS
VOLUME 9
Endgame

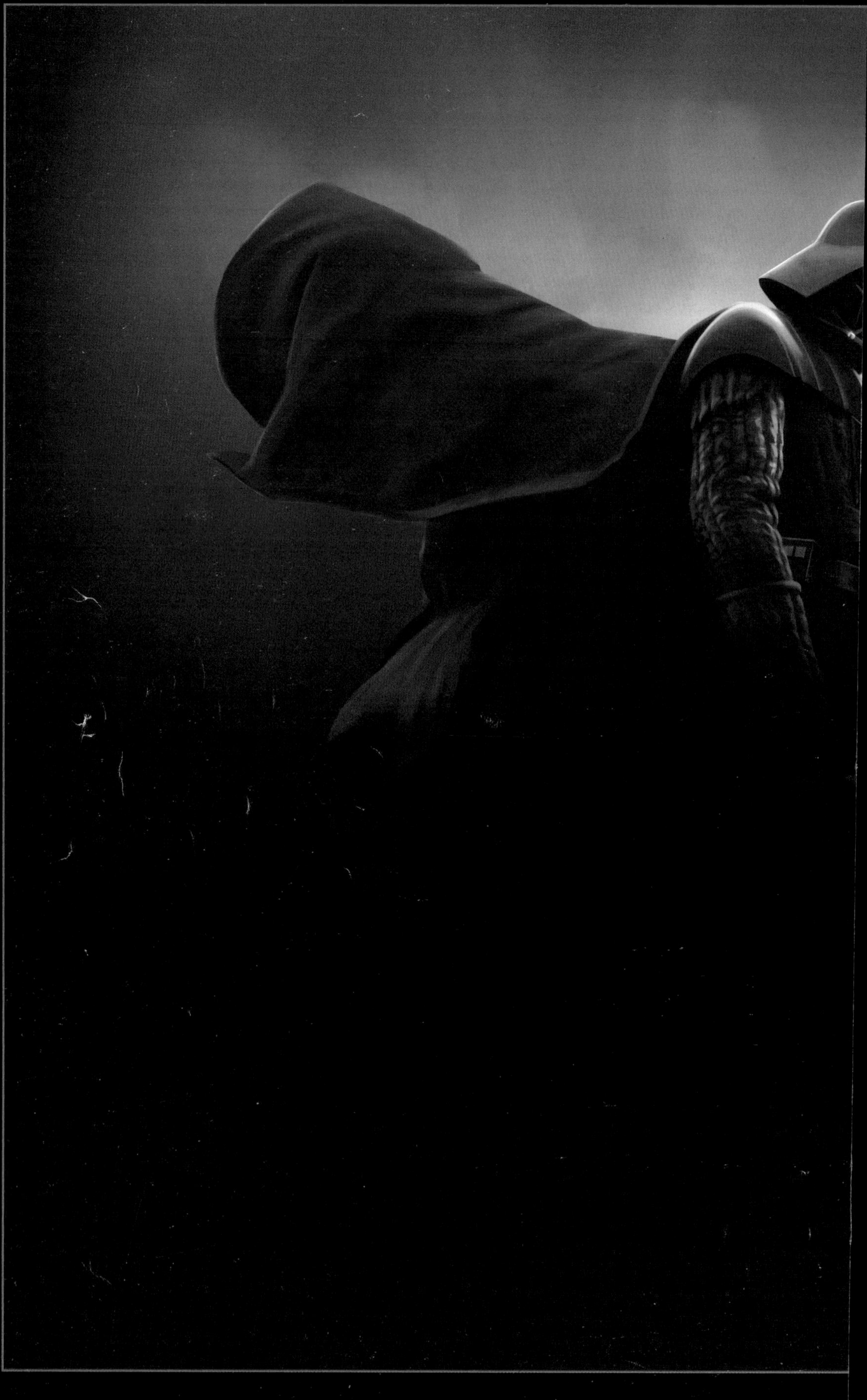

STAR WARS: DARTH VADER AND THE LOST COMMAND HC DUSTJACKET ART BY MICHAEL KUTSCHE

ALL LETTERING AND ESSENTIAL ART MUST FALL WITHIN THIS SOLID "LIVE AREA" BOX. THIS IS THE BORDER FOR A STANDARD, NON-BLEED COMIC BOOK PAGE.

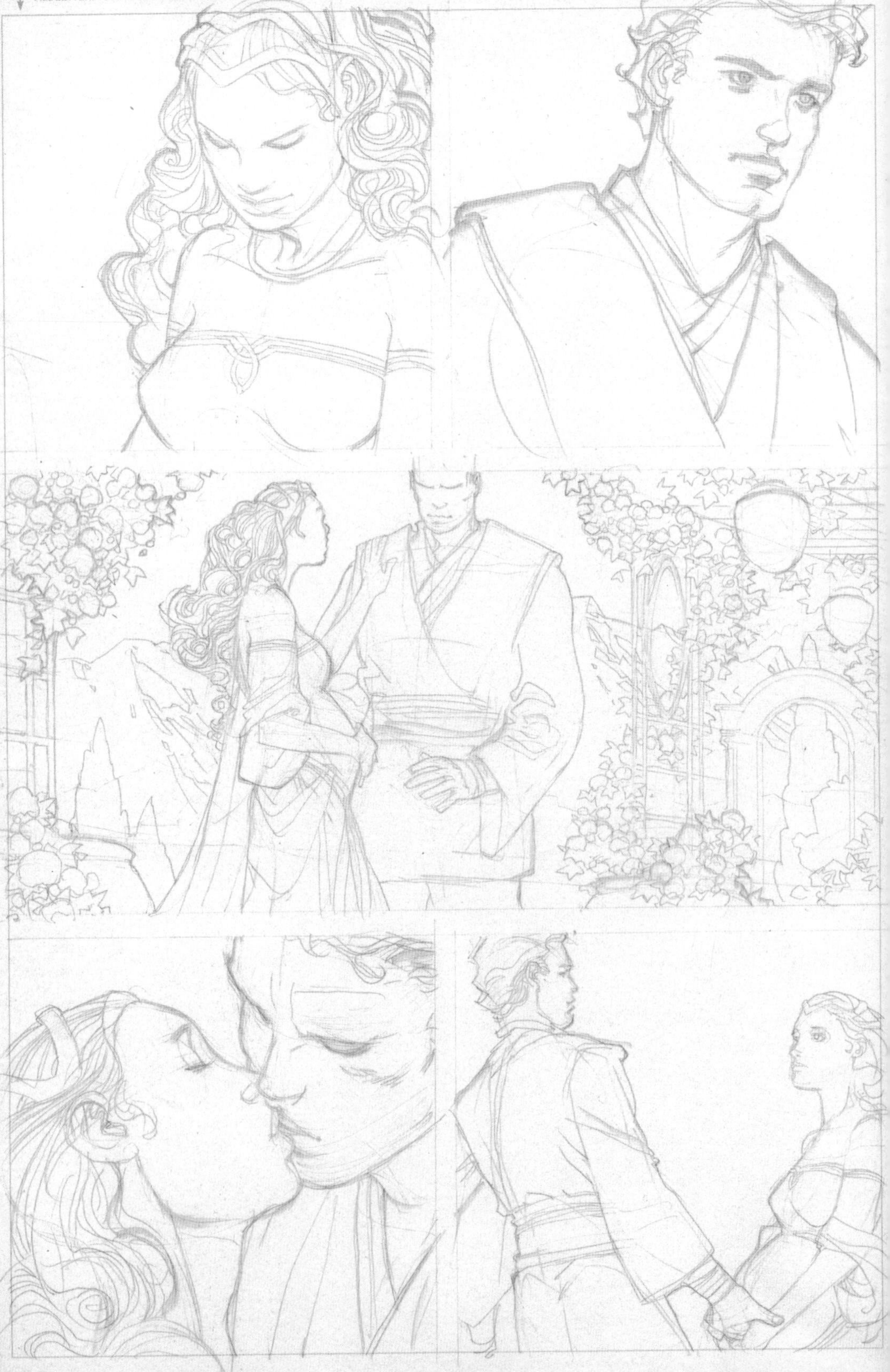

ILS BY RICK LEONARDI

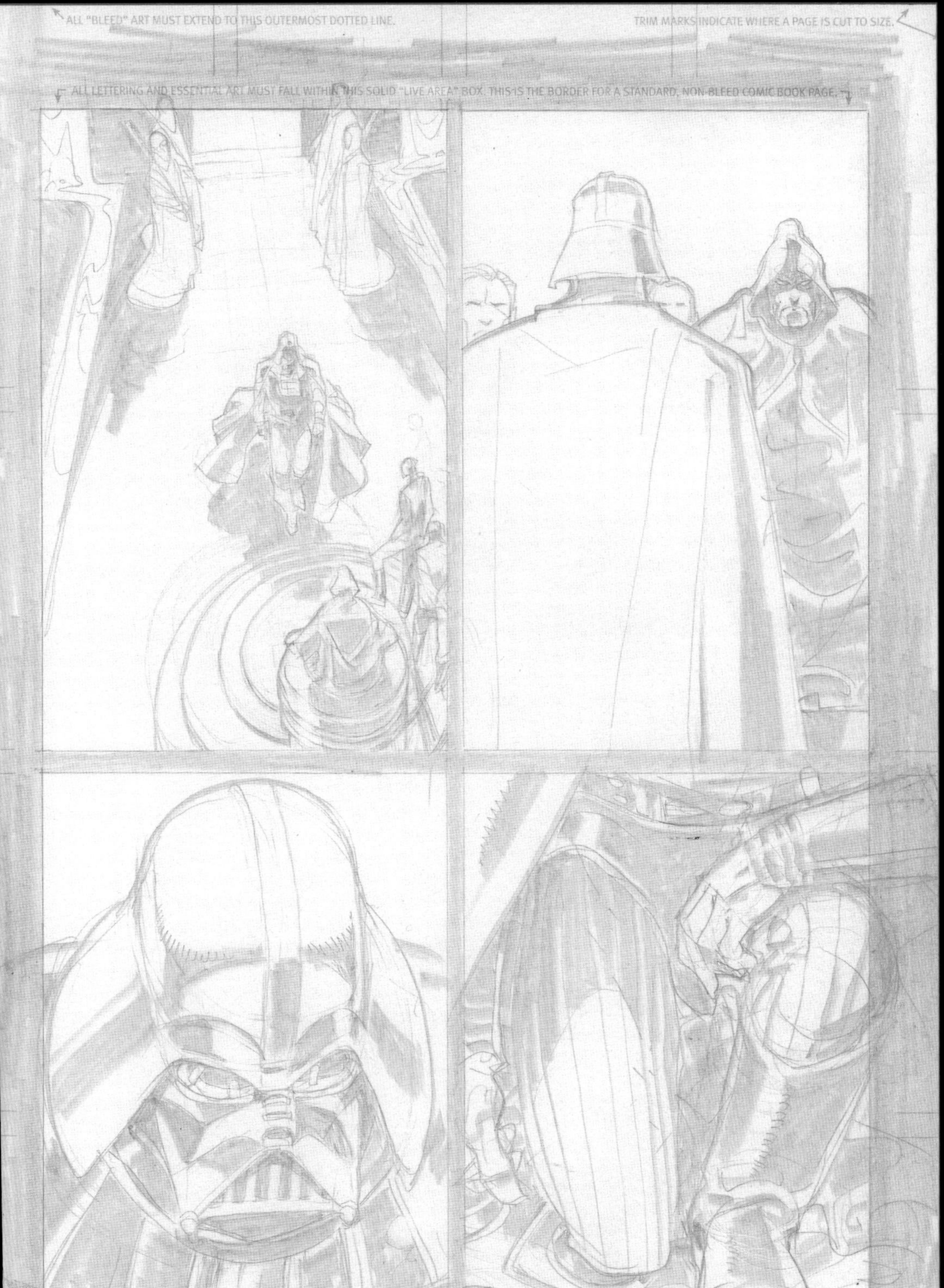
ALL "BLEED" ART MUST EXTEND TO THIS OUTERMOST DOTTED LINE.
TRIM MARKS INDICATE WHERE A PAGE IS CUT TO SIZE.
ALL LETTERING AND ESSENTIAL ART MUST FALL WITHIN THIS SOLID "LIVE AREA" BOX. THIS IS THE BORDER FOR A STANDARD, NON-BLEED COMIC BOOK PAGE.

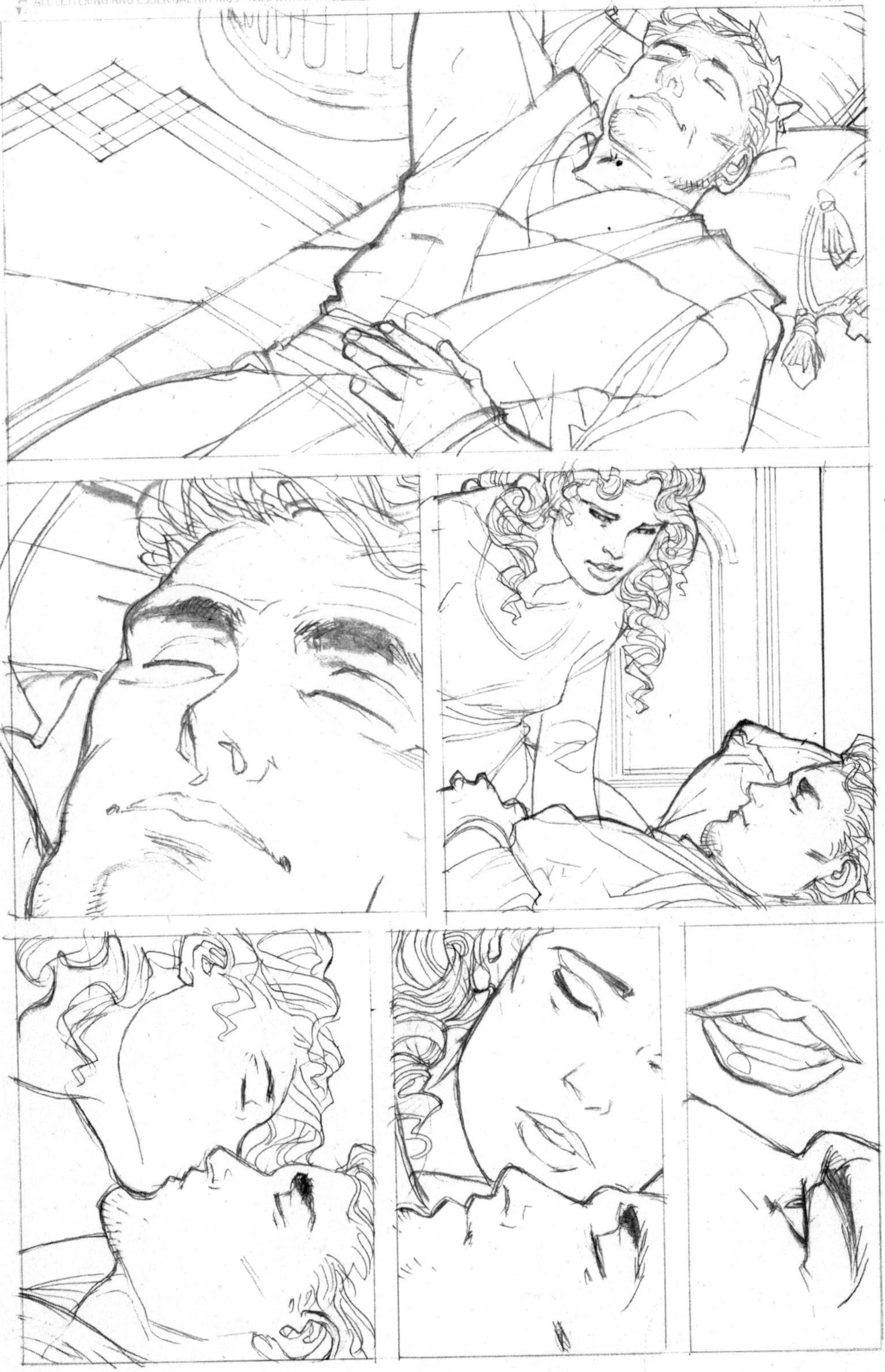

STAR WARS 30TH ANNIVERSARY COLLECTION VOL. 6: ENDGAME HC
INTRODUCTION BY DOUGLAS WHEATLEY

THE DAY THE WORLD CHANGED...

I LOOKED UP AT THE THEATER MARQUEE AND READ THE WORDS "STAR WARS" FOR THE VERY FIRST TIME. YEP, I WAS THE WHEN IT HAPPENED, WHEN THE WORLD WAS CHANGED FOREVER. I WAS EIGHT YEARS OLD.

LITTLE DID I KNOW, THIRTY YEARS LATER I WOULD BE GIVEN THE OPPORTUNITY TO CONTRIBUTE TO A VAST, FANTAST MYTHOLOGY. NOW I THINK, READ, SPEAK, AND DRAW *STAR WARS* TWELVE HOURS A DAY, SIX DAYS A WEEK. IT'S MY JOB, B ONCE IN A WHILE, WHEN I'M DEEP INTO THE NEXT ISSUE OF *STAR WARS: DARK TIMES*, FOR A SPLIT SECOND, SOMETIMES TW MY HEART WILL POUND AND I'LL FIND MYSELF TRANSPORTED TO A PLANET WITH TWO SUNS. (TWO SUNS!) AND I'M EIG YEARS OLD AGAIN.

THANK YOU, MR. LUCAS.

DOUGLAS WHEATLEY
WINNIPEG, MB
MARCH 2007

STAR WARS: DARK TIMES #1
AFTERWORD BY RANDY STRADLEY

FROM THE FIRST MOMENT THEY HEARD OLD BEN KENOBI MENTION THE "CLONE WARS" AND "THE DARK TIMES," *STAR WA* FANS HAVE BEEN BEGGING TO LEARN MORE. INFORMATION ABOUT THE CLONE WARS WAS FINALLY REVEALED, BEGINNI WITH *ATTACK OF THE CLONES*, IN 2002. THE COMICS, NOVELS, AND CARTOONS THAT FOLLOWED EXPANDED THE ACTION A SET THE STAGE FOR 2005'S CLIMACTIC *REVENGE OF THE SITH*. BUT LITTLE HAS BEEN KNOWN ABOUT THE "DARK TIMES" THOSE YEARS IMMEDIATELY FOLLOWING THE FORMATION OF THE EMPIRE — UNTIL NOW.

IN THIS NEW SERIES READERS WILL BE PLUNGED INTO THE DARKNESS OF A GALAXY STILL REELING FROM THE ONE-T PUNCH OF THE DEVASTATING EFFECTS OF THE CLONE WARS AND THE COLLAPSE OF THE REPUBLIC, A GALACTIC GOVERNME THAT HAD STOOD FOR MANY MILLENNIA. WITH EMPEROR PALPATINE'S STORMTROOPERS SPREAD THIN ACROSS THE GALA AND THE JEDI WHO LED THEM ALL BUT DESTROYED, MANY PARTS OF THE EMPIRE ARE AS WILD AND LAWLESS AS A BACKWATER WORLD IN THE OUTER RIM. IT IS A GALAXY RIPE FOR PLUNDER BY THE UNSCRUPULOUS. IT IS A HEYDAY F THIEVES, SMUGGLERS, AND SLAVERS...AND WORSE.

BUT PROVIDING A POINT OF ENTRY TO THIS NEW, UNCHARTED ERA OF *STAR WARS* HISTORY ISN'T THE ONLY REASON GET EXCITED OVER *DARK TIMES*. WITH THE PUBLICATION OF THIS ISSUE THE YEAR-LONG RETOOLING OF OUR *STAR WA* LINE, THAT BEGAN WITH THE INTRODUCTION OF THE *KNIGHTS OF THE OLD REPUBLIC* SERIES, IS COMPLETE (FOR NOW). INVITE YOU TO CHECK OUT OUR OTHER TITLES: THE AFOREMENTIONED *KOTOR* (SET APPROXIMATELY 4,000 YEARS BEFC THE EVENTS IN EPISODE IV: *A NEW HOPE*), *REBELLION* (SET IN THE MONTHS FOLLOWING *A NEW HOPE*), AND *LEGACY* (NEARLY 140 YEARS AFTER *A NEW HOPE*). WHETHER YOU'RE A CASUAL FAN WHOSE ONLY EXPERIENCE WITH THAT GALAXY F FAR AWAY HAS BEEN THE FILMS, OR WHETHER YOU'RE A HARDCORE FAN WHO KNOWS EVERY CORNER OF THE EXPANI UNIVERSE, YOU'RE SURE TO FIND SOMETHING — OR SOME *TIME* — YOU LIKE.

RANDY STRADLEY

STAR WARS: DARK TIMES CHARACTER
SKETCHES BY DOUGLAS WHEATLEY

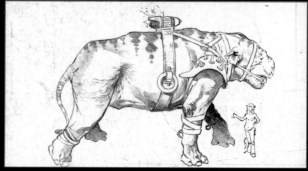

AN EARLY VERSION OF DAS JENNIR

DESIGNS FOR THE CREATURE FROM ISSUE #3

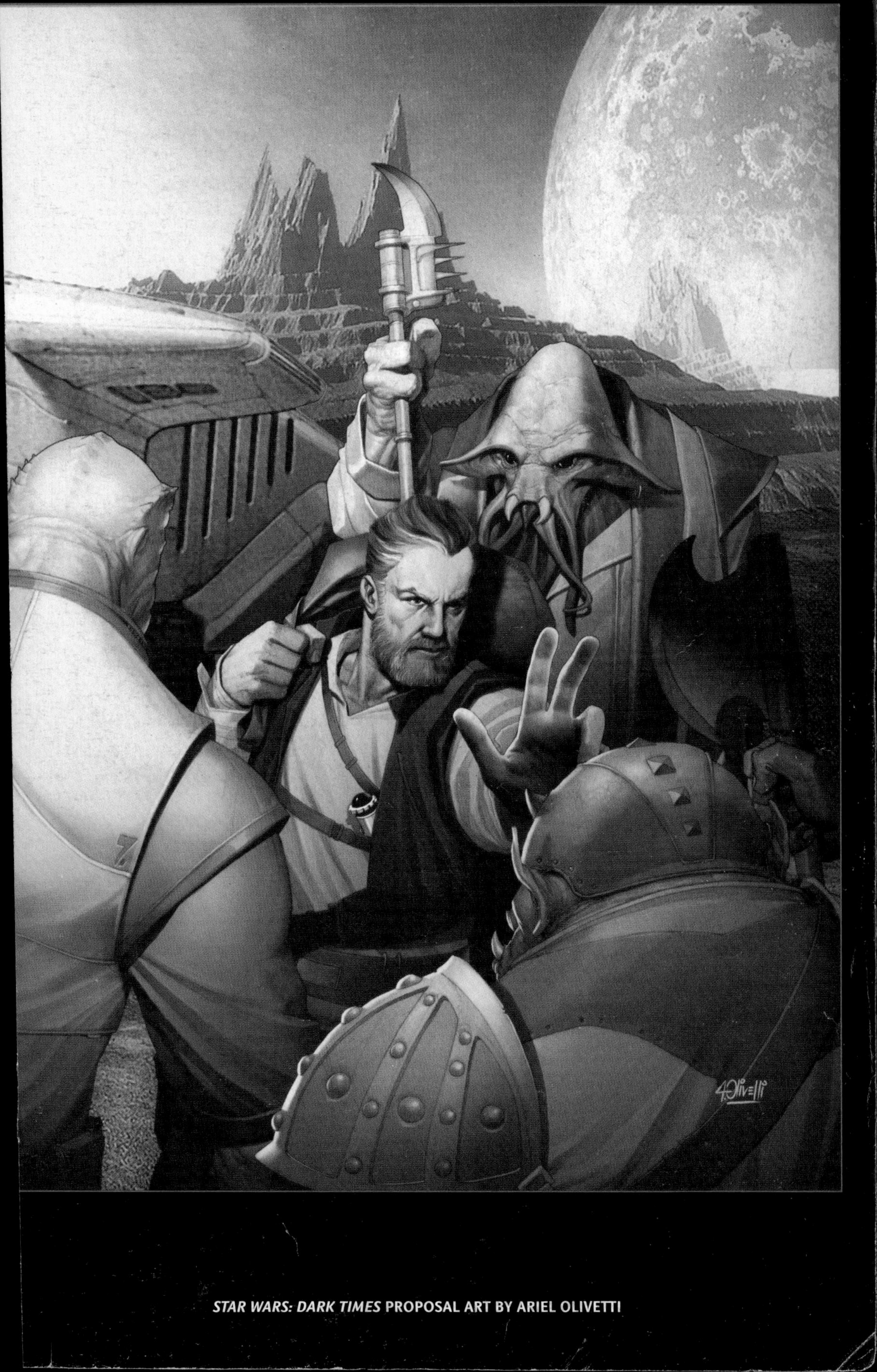

STAR WARS: DARK TIMES PROPOSAL ART BY ARIEL OLIVETTI

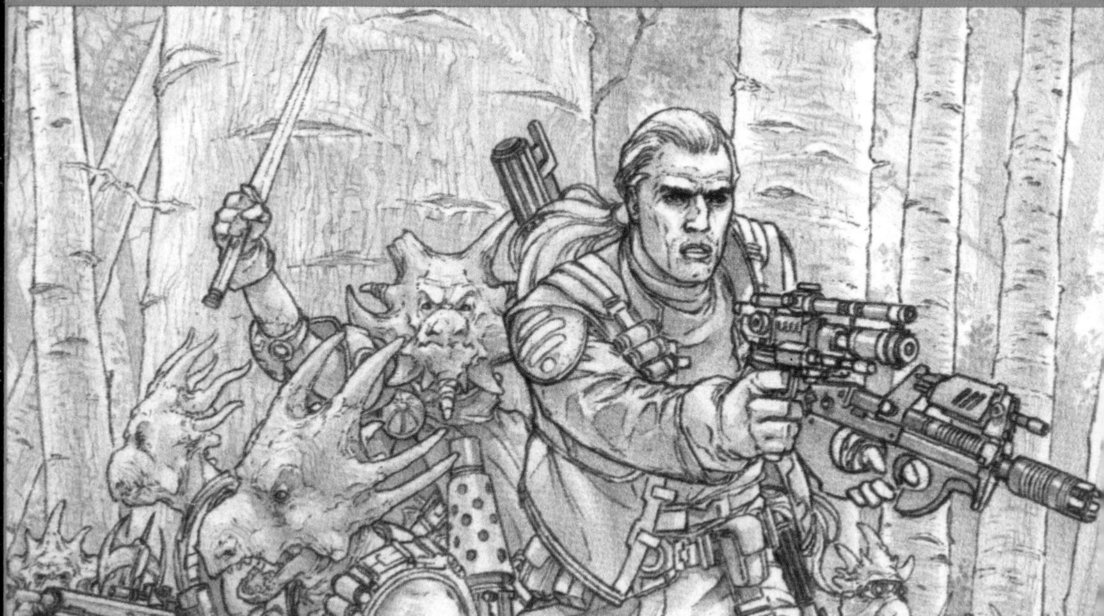

STAR WARS: DARK TIMES #1 SKETCH VARIANT COVER ART BY DOUGLAS WHEATLEY